Microsoft SharePoint 2013: Developer Reference

Paolo Pialorsi

Published with the authorization of Microsoft Corporation by:
O'Reilly Media, Inc.
1005 Gravenstein Highway North
Sebastopol, California 95472

ISBN: 978-0-7356-7071-6

1 2 3 4 5 6 7 8 9 LSI 8 7 6 5 4 3

Printed and bound in the United States of America.

Microsoft Press books are available through booksellers and distributors worldwide. If you need support related to this book, email Microsoft Press Book Support at *mspinput@microsoft.com*. Please tell us what you think of this book at *http://www.microsoft.com/learning/booksurvey*.

Acquisitions and Developmental Editor: Kenyon Brown

Production Editor: Christopher Hearse

Editorial Production: Zyg Group, LLC

Technical Reviewer: Jussi Roine

Copyeditor: Zyg Group, LLC

Indexer: Zyg Group, LLC

Cover Design: Twist Creative • Seattle

Cover Composition: Karen Montgomery

Illustrator: Rebecca Demarest

This book is dedicated to my unique and infinite love: Paola!

Contents at a Glance

Contents

PART II DEVELOPING SHAREPOINT SOLUTIONS

Introduction

Microsoft SharePoint is one of the biggest productivity frameworks released by Microsoft during the last 10 years. SharePoint 2013 is just one more step of a fabulous journey (that began in 2001) in the world of business productivity, collaboration, knowledge sharing, search technologies, enterprise social networking, and web content management.

From a developer's perspective, SharePoint is a rich set of tools, classes, libraries, and controls that are useful for building custom solutions and apps focused on making business collaboration and enterprise social networking possible.

This book is an organized reference that provides the support that you need as you develop real and concrete SharePoint solutions and apps, taking advantage of the main libraries and tools offered by the product. This book covers the key topics in the field of developing on SharePoint, targeting both junior and intermediate programmers who want to improve their knowledge of SharePoint.

Beyond the explanatory content, each chapter includes clear examples and downloadable sample projects that you can explore for yourself.

Who should read this book

This book exists to help existing Microsoft .NET developers understand the architecture and core topics of SharePoint 2013 while building Internet, intranet, and extranet sites, as well as developing custom solutions and SharePoint apps.

Although most readers likely will have no prior experience with SharePoint 2013, the book is also useful for those familiar with earlier versions of SharePoint and are interested in getting up to date on the newest features.

Assumptions

This book expects that you have at least a minimal understanding of .NET development and object-oriented programming concepts. Moreover, to develop SharePoint solutions, you need to have a solid knowledge of ASP.NET and related technologies, such as Simple Object Access Protocol (SOAP), Microsoft Windows Communication Foundation (WCF), and web services. Although you can extend and customize SharePoint with most (if not all) .NET language platforms, this book includes examples in C# only. If you are not familiar with this language, you might consider reading *Microsoft Visual C# 2012 Step by Step*, by John Sharp (Microsoft Press, 2013).

With a heavy focus on web development and server-side technologies, this book assumes that you have a basic understanding of web platforms, application servers, and scalable software architectures. Some of the topics covered in this book require a robust knowledge of .NET Framework 4.*x*, and WCF in particular.

Who should not read this book

This book does not target IT professionals who are seeking information on how to deploy, configure, and maintain a SharePoint farm. However, some discussion about deployment is given throughout the book for the sake of completeness. Similarly, this book does not cover topics concerning site branding or public-facing Internet sites.

Organization of this book

This book is divided into six parts, each of which focuses on a different aspect or technology within SharePoint 2013.

Part I, "Getting started," provides a quick overview of SharePoint 2013 and its data foundations, with a focus on using the technology as shipped, but not yet extending it with custom code.

Part II, "Developing SharePoint solutions," focuses on the core libraries for developing solutions on the server side using the SharePoint Server Object Model and the new LINQ to SharePoint provider. It also focuses on developing for the client side, using the various flavors of the SharePoint Client Object Model and SOAP services. This part of the book is full of examples and code excerpts, and you can use it as a concrete reference for everyday solutions.

Part III, "Developing SharePoint apps," covers how to develop SharePoint apps, which are some of the most interesting new features of SharePoint 2013 from a developer perspective. You will find a step-by-step guide about how to create various kinds of apps, as well as information about the new Representational State Transfer (REST) APIs introduced with SharePoint 2013 for consuming SharePoint from external apps. Moreover, you will learn how to develop remote event receivers to create apps capable of reacting to events happening in SharePoint.

Part IV, "Extending SharePoint," provides deep coverage of the various techniques and extensibility points available for customizing and extending the native SharePoint environment. Four chapters full of realistic examples will help you learn how to create Web Parts, custom pages, and web templates. You will also learn how to take advantage of Business Connectivity Services (BCS) to consume external data sources.

Part V, "Developing workflows," delves into workflow development. It starts with a brief introduction of Windows Workflow Foundation (WF) 4.0 and the new workflow architecture in SharePoint 2013, moving to workflows designed with SharePoint Designer 2013 or developed with Microsoft Visual Studio 2012. This part ends with more advanced topics, such as workflow forms, custom activities, and workflow management services.

Part VI, "Security infrastructure," examines the security infrastructure of SharePoint from an architectural viewpoint, covering topics like authentication, authorization, and the claims-based approach, and delves into identity federation and custom claims-based scenarios. You will learn how to federate SharePoint 2013 with Windows Azure Access Control Services (ACS) and with a custom self-developed identity provider.

Finding your best starting point in this book

The different sections of this book cover a wide range of technologies associated with SharePoint. Depending on your needs and your existing understanding of the SharePoint platform, you might wish to focus on specific areas of the book. Use Table 1 to determine how best to proceed.

TABLE 1 Where to start

If you are	Follow these steps
New to SharePoint development or an ASP.NET developer	Focus on Parts I, II, III, and IV, or read through the entire book in written order.
Familiar with earlier releases of SharePoint	Briefly skim Part I; Chapter 3, "Data provisioning," in Part II; and Part III if you need a refresher on the core concepts. Then read about the new app model in Chapter 8, "SharePoint apps," in Part III; and be sure to read Parts V and VI.
Interested primarily in developing workflows	Read Part II; Chapter 9, "The new SharePoint REST API," in Part III; and Part V.
Interested primarily in developing SharePoint apps	Read Part I; Chapter 3 and Chapter 4, "SharePoint features and solutions," in Part II; and Part III.

Most of the book's chapters include hands-on samples that let you try out the concepts you've learned. No matter which sections you choose to focus on, be sure to download and install the sample applications on your system.

Conventions and features in this book

This book presents information using conventions designed to make the information readable and easy to follow.

- In most cases, the book includes exercises for Microsoft Visual C# programmers.
- Boxed elements with labels such as "Note" provide additional information or alternative methods for completing a task successfully.
- Language keywords (apart from code blocks) appear in italic font.
- A vertical bar between two or more menu items (for example, File | Close) means that you should select the first menu or menu item, then the next, and so on.

System requirements

You will need the following hardware and software to complete the practice examples in this book:

- Windows 7 (x86 and x64), Windows 8 (x86 and x64), Windows Server 2008 R2 (x64), or Windows Server 2012 (x64)
- Microsoft Visual Studio 2012 (Ultimate, Premium, or Professional)
- Microsoft Office Developer Tools for Visual Studio 2012
- A valid Microsoft Office 365 developer subscription
- A computer that has a 1.6 GHz or faster processor (2 GHz recommended)
- 1 GB (32-bit) or 2 GB (64-bit) RAM (add more RAM if running SharePoint on-premises in virtual machines)
- 10 GB of available hard disk space
- 5400 RPM hard disk drive
- DirectX 9–capable video card running at a resolution of 1024×768 or higher
- DVD-ROM drive (if installing Visual Studio from DVD)
- Internet connection to download software and chapter examples

To run an on-premises SharePoint farm, you will need the following:

- Windows Server 2008 R2 Service Pack 1 (SP1) (x64) or Windows Server 2012 (x64)
- SQL Server 2008 R2 SP1 (x64) or SQL Server 2012 (x64)
- A computer that has at least a 64-bit four-core processor
- A minimum of 8 GB RAM (16GB RAM recommended)
- 80 GB of available hard disk space

Depending on your Windows configuration, you might require local administrator rights to install or configure Visual Studio 2012, SQL Server 2008/2012, and SharePoint 2013 products.

Code samples

You can download the code samples for this book from the following page:

http://aka.ms/SP2013DevRef/files

The code sample ZIP file includes a child ZIP file for each chapter, which provides sample projects. In particular, you can find the following:

- **Ch-03-Data-Provisioning.zip** Includes a single Microsoft Visual Studio 2012 project, which provisions some data structures (content types and list definitions).
- **Ch-05-Server-Object-Model.zip** Includes a single Visual Studio 2012 project illustrating how to use the SharePoint Server Object Model.
- **Ch-06-LINQ-for-SharePoint.zip** Includes a single Visual Studio 2012 project showing how to use LINQ to SharePoint.
- **Ch-07-Client-Side-Technologies.zip** Provides four Visual Studio 2012 projects, which illustrate, respectively, how to work with the .NET Client-Side Object Model (CSOM), the JavaScript Object Model (JSOM), the Microsoft Silverlight Object Model, and the REST service.
- **Ch-08-SharePoint-Apps.zip** Comprises a set of SharePoint app projects that show how to create apps providing the various hosting models (SharePoint hosted, autohosted, and provider-hosted).

- **Ch-09-New-REST-API.zip** Illustrates how to use the new REST APIs through a sample SharePoint app project.
- **Ch-10-Remote-Event-Receivers.zip** Explains how to create remote event receivers by providing a single Visual Studio 2012 project of a SharePoint app.
- **Ch-11-Developing-Web-Parts.zip** Includes a couple of Visual Studio 2012 projects, which provide samples of basic web parts, as well as of advanced web parts.
- **Ch-12-Customizing-the-UI.zip** Includes a single Visual Studio 2012 project that provides many samples about how to create custom pages, custom ribbons, custom actions, and so on.
- **Ch-13-Web-Templates.zip** Provides samples about how to create a site definition, a site template, and a web template.
- **Ch-14-Business-Connectivity-Services.zip** Includes a Visual Studio 2012 project of a SharePoint app consuming a third-party OData service, a sample project of a custom BCS model, and a WCF service available for consuming via BCS.
- **Ch-15-WF45-Intro.zip** Provides a simple Visual Studio 2012 project that illustrates the basic capabilities of WF 4.5, aside from SharePoint 2013.
- **Ch-16-SP-Workflow-Fundamentals.zip** Includes basic samples of workflows for SharePoint 2013 created by using Microsoft SharePoint Designer 2013.
- **Ch-17-Workflow-Development.zip** Provides some Visual Studio 2012 projects that illustrate how to create basic workflows, workflows in SharePoint app, custom workflow forms, and custom tasks.
- **Ch-18-Advanced-Workflows.zip** Provides three Visual Studio 2012 projects illustrating how to create advanced workflows and custom actions, and how to consume the new workflow management services.
- **Ch-20-Claims-Fed-OAuth.zip** Includes a set of Visual Studio 2012 projects that show how to create a custom identity provider, as well as a custom claims provider.

You can use these sample projects as a reference for everyday needs, and you may find it useful copy code excerpts from these samples into your real solutions.

Acknowledgments

This book has been a long and time-consuming process for me. I have worked toward the completion of this project for about one year. However, a book is the result of the work of many people. Unfortunately, only the author has his or her name on the cover. This section is only partial compensation for the other individuals who helped out.

First, I would like to thank Microsoft Press, O'Reilly, and all the publishing people who contributed to this book project. Mainly, I'd like to thank Ben Ryan and Kenyon Brown, who—once again—trusted in me and gave me the opportunity to realize an idea I have believed in for a long time. Ken supported me through this book project for more than a year; he helped me focus on the content outline, and provided suggestions and guidelines to accomplish this task. Another person deserving a really big acknowledgment is Linda Laflamme, who assisted me along the whole project timeline, keeping me on track, reviewing my chapters, and providing thorough suggestions, feedback, and tips. From the copyediting team, I would like to thank Christopher Hearse and Damon Larson for their accurate work.

I would also like to thank Jussi Roine, one of the most brilliant SharePoint Microsoft Certified Masters (MCMs) that I know, for his accurate, smart, proactive, and great technical review. Jussi, you did a really great job—thank you very much, buddy! You deserve gallons of beer!

I will never stop thanking my mentor, Giovanni Librando. As usual, Giovanni provided me a wealth of ideas, feedback, and tips to achieve this goal.

I'd like to thank my parents and my original family for their support and presence during the last year and for having trusted me during my entire professional career.

Lastly, but most importantly, I want to thank my family—my wife, Paola; my son, Andrea; and my daughter, Marta—for their support, patience, and understanding during the last year. It has been a difficult and very busy year. You have supported me greatly, and you renounced spending many hours with me because of this book. I know I've asked a huge sacrifice of you, and I want to thank you for your support, trust, and understanding!

Errata & book support

We've made every effort to ensure the accuracy of this book and its companion content. Any errors that have been reported since this book was published are listed on our Microsoft Press site at *http://www.oreilly.com*:

http://aka.ms/SP2013DevRef/errata

If you find an error that is not already listed, you can report it to us through the same page.

If you need additional support, email Microsoft Press Book Support at *mspinput@microsoft.com*.

Please note that product support for Microsoft software is not offered through the addresses above.

We want to hear from you

At Microsoft Press, your satisfaction is our top priority, and your feedback our most valuable asset. Please tell us what you think of this book at

http://www.microsoft.com/learning/booksurvey

The survey is short, and we read every one of your comments and ideas. Thanks in advance for your input!

Stay in touch

Let's keep the conversation going! We're on Twitter:

http://twitter.com/MicrosoftPress

PART I

Getting started

CHAPTER 1

Microsoft SharePoint 2013: A quick tour

This chapter explores Microsoft SharePoint 2013 and what it offers to developers who are creating real-world business solutions. To begin, you will focus on the main features and architecture of SharePoint, as well as the rich set of capabilities the platform provides. Next, you will compare the various SharePoint editions. Finally, you will explore the available developer tools. If you already know SharePoint 2013 or have worked with it, you can probably skip this chapter; however, if you haven't yet acquired SharePoint at all, or if you are working on previous versions of SharePoint, such as SharePoint 2007 or SharePoint 2010, you should continue on with the tour.

What is SharePoint?

Microsoft often defines SharePoint as a business collaboration platform that makes it easier for people to work together. As a software developer, I prefer to define it as a platform with a rich framework for developing business solutions. From a developer's perspective, SharePoint is simply a rich set of tools, classes, libraries, controls, and so on, that are useful for building business solutions focused on collaboration, content management, social networking, content searches, and more.

Many people think of SharePoint as a platform that's ready to use for building websites—usually for intranet or extranet scenarios. That's true, but it's less than half the story! Certainly, SharePoint *is* a platform for building websites, and of course, it can target intranet and extranet sites. But it is much more, as well; you can use it to build any kind of web solution, including Internet publishing sites, by taking advantage of its well-defined and ready-to-use set of tools, based on a secure, scalable, and maintainable architecture. You can think of SharePoint as a superset of Microsoft ASP.NET, with a broad set of services that can speed up the development of web-based collaborative solutions.

You should use SharePoint as a shared connection point between users, customers, and whoever else uses your websites and the applications they utilize. The basic idea of SharePoint is to share content, applications, and data to improve collaboration and provide a unique user experience.

SharePoint itself is primarily a container of content and apps. Content is organized in *lists*, and each list is made up of items. A list can consist of simple items with custom metadata properties called *fields*. Lists can also be libraries of documents, which are a particular kind of item that correspond to document files. Almost always when you develop a SharePoint solution, you manage lists and items.

In Chapter 2, "SharePoint data fundamentals," you will learn more about the architecture of data management in SharePoint 2013.

Main benefits

Microsoft grouped the features and services provided by SharePoint 2013 into five main categories of benefits: Share, Organize, Discover, Build, and Manage. Figure 1-1 shows these benefits, and the sections that follow provide a brief description of each.

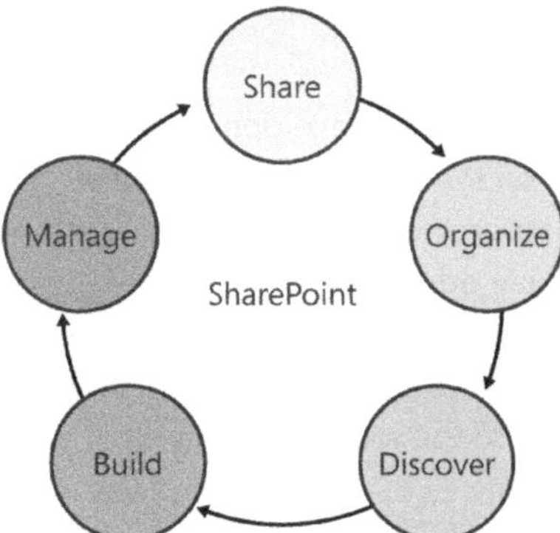

FIGURE 1-1 The native benefits of the SharePoint 2013 platform.

Share

SharePoint 2013 enables you to share ideas and content with others. For example, you can use SharePoint for storing and sharing documents, contacts, and tasks; organizing meetings; managing business processes; and more. When you share something with SharePoint, you can also put it in the social network of your colleagues, customers, partners, and contacts in general, regardless of whether they are on your corporate network, on Facebook, on Twitter, or elsewhere. Through SharePoint, people can discover what you shared, as well as share contents with you. Using the new social features of SharePoint 2013, you can keep track of what your colleagues are working on.

With SharePoint 2013 and the new Microsoft Office 2013, you can publish documents and content from any Office application, sharing them with people inside or outside your organization. You can take advantage of these capabilities from your desktop computer as well as from any Internet-capable mobile device, such as Microsoft Surface and other tablets running Microsoft Windows 8 or RT, as well as smartphones based on the Windows Phone operating system or devices based on iOS.

When you share content through SharePoint, you can update your activity feed in order to make people aware of what you are doing, keeping in touch with your colleagues wherever you are, with any kind of device.

Organize

Through SharePoint 2013, you can organize your projects and tasks, and even integrate SharePoint with Microsoft Outlook and Microsoft Project to keep your projects on track. The product will help you manage tasks, as well as their status and due dates. You will be able to keep your team connected, through specific team sites, which enable you and others to track meetings, share documents, store emails, and do whatever else is useful for your team collaboration.

The new SkyDrive Pro feature provided by SharePoint 2013, which supersedes SharePoint Workspace, allows you and your colleagues to sync all the shared files to your desktop, as well as to your tablet, with Windows 8. This way, the content will always be with you, even when you are offline, traveling, or working at home. Upon connection with the network, any files you worked on offline will be automatically synchronized with their online counterparts.

Discover

Since it was first introduced, one of stand-out features of SharePoint has been its search engine. Having a platform for storing, sharing, and organizing content would be useless without the capability to discover and retrieve it. With SharePoint 2013, you can search for content via a professional search engine, which can be customized for your needs.

With SharePoint 2010, Microsoft introduced an improved and more accurate relevance engine that was based on usage and history. Moreover, it included the FAST for SharePoint edition for supporting large-scale search scenarios, together with professional search-oriented features. Now, the FAST for SharePoint engine is no longer a separate product, and all of its main features are included in the standard SharePoint 2013 search engine. In addition, the SharePoint 2013 search engine has the ability to suggest more relevant results and provide recommendations on people and documents to follow. The search engine is now people-centric and social-centric, enabling you to find people and connect with them, based on their interests, projects they contributed to, and documents they worked on.

You can use all the content, search results, people, and insights to create reports, scorecards, dashboards, and whatever else is helpful for providing meaningful data. Microsoft Excel 2013, Excel Services, PowerPivot, and Power View for SharePoint can assist you in this task as well.

Given all these capabilities, you can consider SharePoint 2013 a solid platform for building data and content-based, search-driven applications, oriented toward social networking and collaboration.

Build

One of the most exciting new features of SharePoint 2013 is its apps-extensibility model. Thanks to this new feature, you can develop custom apps for Office 2013 and SharePoint 2013, using the power of the cloud. You can design everything from business apps for the marketplace at large to a corporate catalog targeting your employees.

Developing a custom app is as simple as combining the apps-extensibility model with such well-known technologies and protocols as JavaScript, HTML, OAuth, and the versatility of the cloud. If you prefer, of course, you can also host your custom apps on-premises, but hosting an app in the cloud provides you with a more scalable infrastructure ready to grow with your business. For an in-depth discussion of creating custom apps, see Part III, "Developing SharePoint apps."

Manage

Nowadays, a key aspect of an IT solution is management, both from a tooling perspective and from the viewpoint of budget and costs reduction. SharePoint 2013 gives you a mature, maintainable, and manageable environment, which can be hosted on-premises as well as in the cloud, using Microsoft Office 365. You can also keep some of your services and content on-premises while deploying others on Office 365, within a hybrid infrastructure.

The new capabilities of Office 365 reduce the time to market for your solutions, allowing you to concentrate your resources and time on the project, the contents, and the custom features, rather than on the infrastructure under the cover.

Many of the solutions in this book are suitable both for on-premises and cloud scenarios, thanks to the common infrastructure behind the scenes.

SharePoint basic concepts

To give you a better understanding of what SharePoint is and how to best use its features, this section takes a brief tour through the product and provides introductions to a few of its most useful features and capabilities.

SharePoint Central Administration

The target audience for this book consists of SharePoint developers, not IT professionals. Therefore, the book does not cover administrative tasks, and it does not provide instructions on how to set up SharePoint from scratch. Nevertheless, as soon as you install a SharePoint server farm, you are presented with an administrative console called SharePoint Central Administration (SPCA) with which you manage the entire farm.

More Info To learn how to deploy and administer a SharePoint farm, read *Microsoft SharePoint 2013 Administrator's Companion*, by Brian Alderman (Microsoft Press, 2013).

SPCA is a website based on the SharePoint engine; it's designed to administer and monitor a SharePoint server farm. When you deploy a new farm, by default the first server takes the role of SPCA host. Nevertheless, in a well-defined SharePoint server farm, you should deploy at least two servers hosting SPCA, for better availability and business continuity of the farm. Using SPCA, you can configure servers and servers' roles, define farm topology, and create new web applications and site collections.

Because SPCA is an actual SharePoint site, you can use everything you will learn in this book to customize this site, too. Thus, you can build solutions to extend the SharePoint administrative interface. However, keep in mind that because SPCA is an administrative site responsible for the whole farm, you should avoid using it as a development or test site.

The following list describes the main areas of SPCA:

- **Application Management** Here, you can manage existing web applications, as well as create new web applications, site collections, and content databases. You will learn more about these topics later in this chapter and in Chapter 2.
- **Monitoring** From this area, you have access to a set of tools for monitoring the farm, checking for issues, and solving problems.
- **Security** Here, you can manage administrative accounts and services' accounts of the farm, and configure all the security-related features.
- **General Application Settings** This is the area where you manage general settings, such as site directory and search engine settings, content deployment features, form services, and more.
- **System Settings** From this area, you can manage servers in the farm, the farm topology, services on servers, and farm customization features.
- **Backup and Restore** This area provides access to all the tools for managing and handling disaster recovery tasks.
- **Upgrade and Migration** Here, you can manage upgrade and patching tasks.
- **Apps** This area provides access to the app configuration and management tools. You can configure and monitor installed apps and apps licenses, as well as your corporate catalog of apps.
- **Configuration Wizards** This area provides a wizard to configure the farm from scratch.

Note You should consider using the configuration wizards very carefully, and in most cases you should avoid using them. In fact, a real SharePoint farm should never be installed using a wizard. On the contrary, you or the IT professionals you work with should carefully design the farm, assign roles to the servers, determine the services to run, and in general think about and model whatever else is needed to make your SharePoint farm work properly.

Figure 1-2 shows the SPCA home page. Note the status bar at the top of the screen, which in Figure 1-2 highlights some issues regarding the farm's current configuration that were detected by the SharePoint Health Analyzer service. The SharePoint Health Analyzer is a very useful tool that monitors the status of the farm, helping to maintain it at the optimum service level.

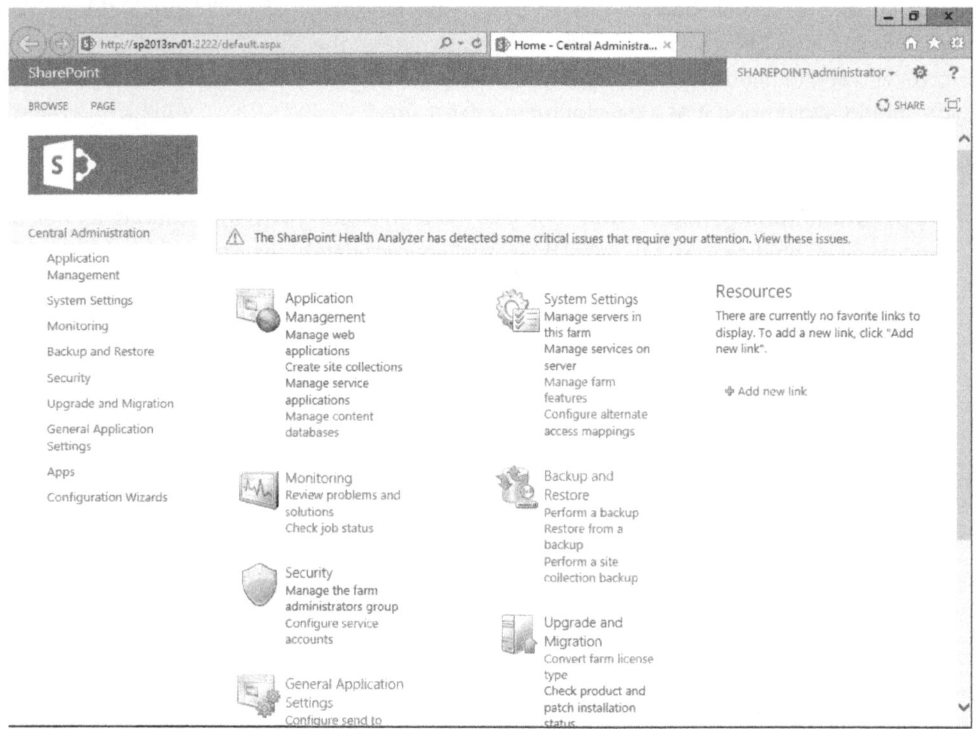

FIGURE 1-2 The SPCA home page of a SharePoint 2013 farm.

SharePoint Administration via PowerShell

As with many other server products from Microsoft, SharePoint can be managed using Windows PowerShell and scripting. SPCA is a good option for managing a SharePoint farm through a set of visual tools and a web browser. However, having a text-based scripting engine to query, manage, configure, and even install a SharePoint farm from scratch is a fundamental aid for IT professionals. In SharePoint 2013, everything you can do with SPCA can also be done using some PowerShell scripts. Moreover, PowerShell enables additional controls that are not available from SPCA.

The power of having a scripting engine for managing almost every aspect of a SharePoint farm is enormous and unpredictable. For example, you can define a PowerShell script to deploy a farm from scratch, or you can use a script to add a server to an already existing farm. You can create and configure web applications, sites, and services using a script. Moreover, you can create scripts to configure the topology of your farms. All these scripts become extremely useful and powerful whenever you need to reproduce the same tasks for multiple customers or sites.

Even if you are a developer, you can benefit from having a rich library of predefined and parameter-based PowerShell scripts. In fact, you can use those scripts to deploy development farms, as well as test environments. Moreover, using a script, you can deploy your customizations onto an on-premises farm. This book will not cover PowerShell in depth, because there are many other topics to cover that deal more specifically with SharePoint development. Nevertheless, you should consider reading a book on PowerShell for SharePoint as a companion to this book.

More Info To learn more about Windows PowerShell, consult "Windows PowerShell" on MSDN (*http://msdn.microsoft.com/en-us/library/dd835506.aspx*) or *Windows PowerShell Pocket Reference*, by Lee Holmes (O'Reilly, 2012).

Site collections and websites

One fundamental concept embodied by SharePoint is that of a site collection. A *site collection* is a logical container that holds a set of SharePoint sites hosted in a web application. Whenever you work in SharePoint and you want to publish a site, regardless of whether it's an Internet, intranet, or extranet solution, you will have at least one web application with one site collection, made of one site. Grouping sites in site collections allows those sites to share content, administrative settings, security rules, and, optionally, users and groups.

To create a new site collection, you need a web application, which you can create by selecting the Manage Web Applications menu item from the SPCA home page, or by using the corresponding PowerShell command. Avoid using the web application that hosts SPCA. After you have a web application, you can create a new site collection by selecting the Create Site Collection menu item on the SPCA home page. A dialog box will appear, asking you for a title, a description, and a URL relative to the parent web application.

Every site collection is administered by a site collection administrator, who is a user authorized to administer an entire site collection, including the websites it contains. Every site collection must have at least one site collection administrator, but it can have more than one. Thus, when creating a new site collection, you need to designate a primary site collection administrator and, optionally, a secondary one. After having created a site collection, you will be able to add as many site collection administrators as you like. A site collection administrator has the rights to create, update, or delete any site contained in a site collection. The administrator also has full rights to administer content within those sites.

When you create a site collection, you should also choose a template from which to start. If you need, you can select it from a number of predefined templates that are shipped with SharePoint. By default, the template will create a new site collection with at least one site at the root of the site collection. Templates are divided into functional groups and into two families. In fact, SharePoint 2013 comes with a new family of templates, as well as the previous template family from SharePoint 2010, for backward compatibility. Following are the five main functional groups of SharePoint 2013 templates:

- **Collaboration** These are sites whose structure has been designed to facilitate collaboration. The Collaboration group includes the following templates: Team Site, Blank Site, Document

Workspace, Blog, Group Work Site, Developer Site, Project Site, Community Site, and Visio Process Repository.

- **Meetings** This group contains templates for sites related to meetings and meeting organization. The available templates are Basic Meeting Workspace, Blank Meeting Workspace, Decision Meeting Workspace, Social Meeting Workspace, and Multipage Meeting Workspace.
- **Enterprise** These templates target enterprise-level needs in the areas of document management, policies, and so on. They include Document Center, Discover Center, Records Center, Business Intelligence Center, Enterprise Search Center, My Site Host, Community Portal, and Basic Search Center.
- **Publishing** This group corresponds to sites intended for web-publishing purposes. The available templates are Publishing Portal, Enterprise Wiki, and Product Catalog.
- **Custom** This is where you can develop your own site templates. Also in this group is a list of all the available custom templates, if any exist.

Figure 1-3 shows the home page of a site collection created by using the Team Site template of SharePoint 2013.

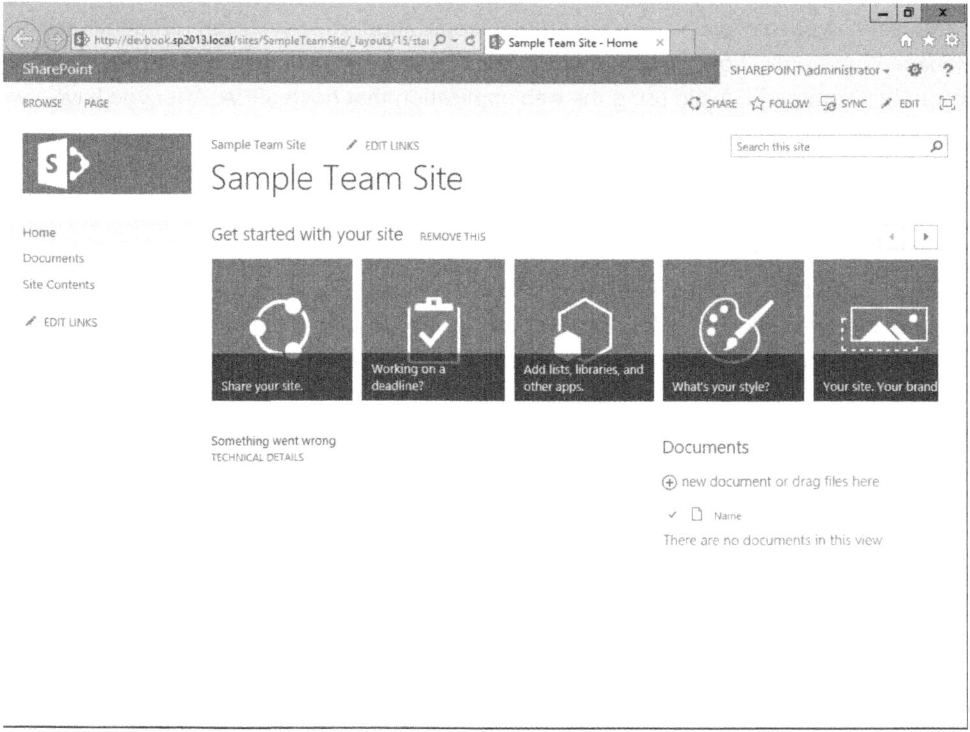

FIGURE 1-3 The home page of a Team Site template site collection.

Lists, libraries, items, documents, and other apps

Every SharePoint site is composed of lists of items. When the items are simple—that is, they don't correspond to documents or files, but are made of custom metadata properties only—they're termed *lists* and *list items*. When the items correspond to files, they're called *document libraries* or just *libraries*.

Every site template includes some predefined lists that are created when you construct a site using that template. For example, a team site provides a Documents library, a Site Assets library, a Site Pages library, and a few other predefined lists and libraries. Regardless of the site template you start from, you can always create new lists, libraries, and content, as well as activate features to customize your site.

You can browse the contents of these lists and libraries, and, if you have the proper permissions, you can create new apps, which can be lists of contents, libraries, or custom apps either taken from the public marketplace or installed from the corporate catalog. Consider that in SharePoint 2013, everything is called an app. However, a list or a library is still what it is—nothing more and nothing less. You can also add items to already existing lists or upload new files (for libraries) by simply dragging and dropping them from the file system to the webpage. Figure 1-4 shows the UI of SharePoint 2013 while browsing the contents of a document library.

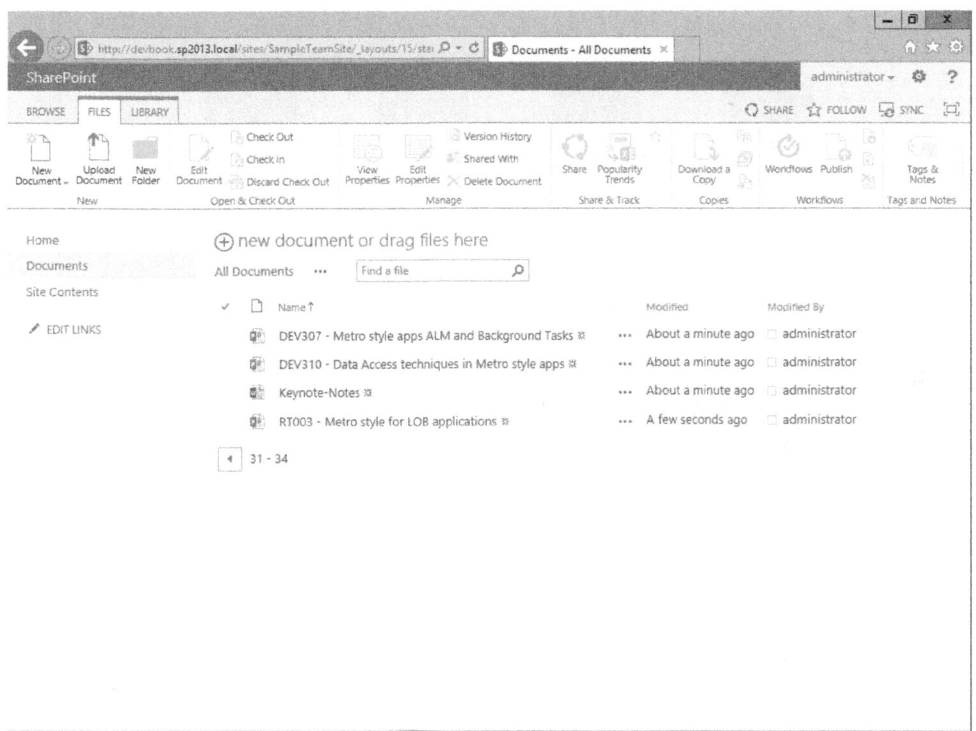

FIGURE 1-4 The default UI of SharePoint while browsing the contents of a document library.

Note also that Figure 1-4 shows the ribbon, which is a feature introduced with SharePoint 2010, to better support end users through a UI similar to the well-known Office interface.

When you want to create a new app, you simply click the gear icon, which is located in the upper-right corner of the webpage, and then select Add An App. As shown in Figure 1-5, you'll see the Apps You Can Add list, from which you can select the type of app that you would like to create.

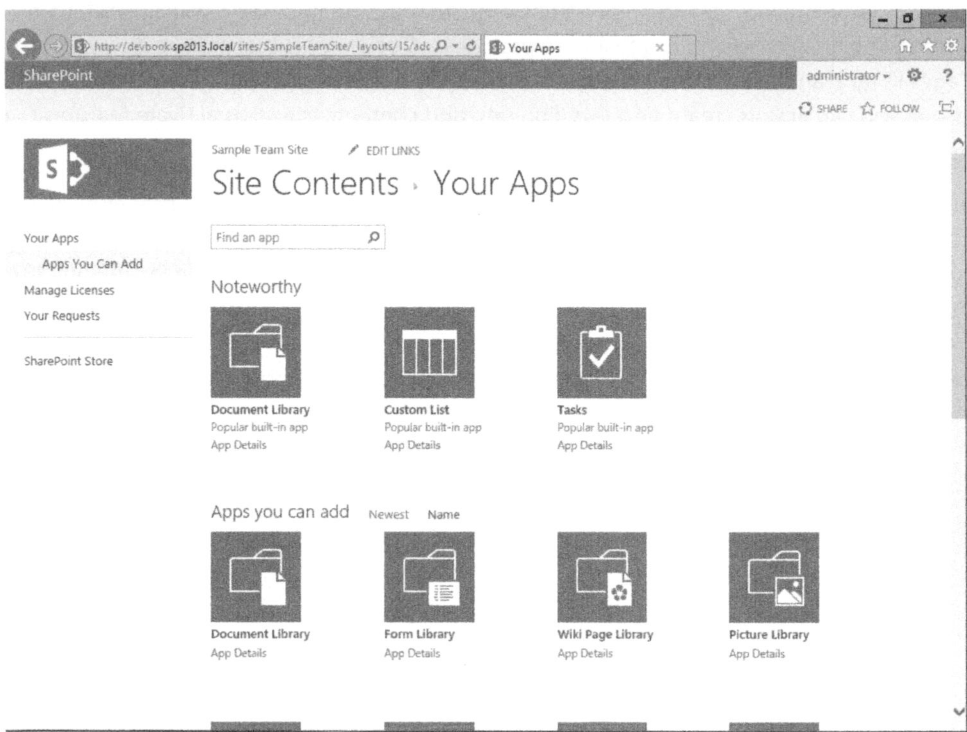

FIGURE 1-5 The UI for adding a new app to a SharePoint site.

If none of the supplied templates of lists and libraries quite fits your needs, you can try or buy an app from the marketplace, and you can install an app from a corporate catalog. Of course, in order to access these, your farm should be connected to the Internet and configured for supporting apps.

App Parts and Web Parts

App Parts are new features of SharePoint 2013, enabling you to enrich pages with external apps and content, which you can create on site or download from third-party sites or the cloud—for example, through the marketplace. An *App Part* is a block of HTML code, empowered with JavaScript and secured with OAuth, typically hosted outside the current site, and eventually integrating and/or consuming some contents within the current site. Later, in Part III of this book, you will learn how to create App Parts and how to consume them from a SharePoint site.

Web Parts have been some of the most notable features of SharePoint since its early versions. In fact, in SharePoint you can define pages made of configurable building blocks (Web Parts) that can be enabled, moved, or hidden by end users. The goal of this feature is to allow users to define their own pages, selecting content from a set of available Web Parts, with full personalization. Every page made of Web Parts is called a *Web Part page*.

With SharePoint 2013, the importance of Web Parts is declining, while the use of App Parts is becoming more prominent. You can think about App Parts as the heirs of Web Parts. A typical SharePoint 2013 solution contains some custom lists and document libraries, along with some apps presented as App Parts and configured in custom pages that show and manage the data stored in those lists and libraries, as well as outside the current site.

Architectural overview

In this section, you'll take a look at SharePoint architecture from a developer's perspective. Figure 1-6 shows some of the main components of SharePoint, from the foundation elements up to the main enterprise-level features.

Standard/Enterprise Search | Social Features | Visio Service
Work Management | Enterprise Content Management | Access Service
Excel Service | Business Intelligence | Forms
User Profiles | Web Content Management | Workflow Engine
... | ... | ...
SharePoint Server 2013

Alerts | External Data | Files/Docs | Mobile Support | Queries | Web/Site Coll.
Columns/Fields | Event Handling | Health Rules | Pages, UI & Ribbon | Solutions | Basic Search
Content Types | Features | Lists/Doc Libs | Perf. Monitoring | Web Parts | Admin/Manag.
...
SharePoint Foundation 2013

.NET Framework 4.5 and ASP.NET 4.5

Internet Information Services 7.x/8.x

Windows Server 2008 R2 SP1 (64 bit only)
Windows Server 2012 (64 bit only)

SQL Server 2012 (64 bit only)
SQL Server 2008 R2 SP1 (64 bit only)

FIGURE 1-6 The architecture of SharePoint 2013.

At the very base of SharePoint 2013 sits the operating system. Starting with SharePoint 2013, the minimum requirement for a production environment is Microsoft Windows Server 2008 R2 Service Pack (SP) 1 (Standard, Enterprise, or Datacenter) or Microsoft Windows Server 2012 (Standard or Datacenter). Although in SharePoint 2010 it was possible to install the product on a workstation machine running Microsoft Windows 7 or Microsoft Windows Vista SP1/SP2, this is no longer allowed with SharePoint 2013. Because SharePoint 2013 is available only in 64-bit versions, the minimum requirement for a deployment environment is a server-based 64-bit operating system (Windows 8 does not qualify as a host operating system for SharePoint 2013).

More Info For further details about the software and hardware requirements of SharePoint 2013, read the document "Hardware and Software Requirements for SharePoint 2013" on TechNet Online, at *http://technet.microsoft.com/en-us/library/cc262485.aspx*.

In addition to the operating system, SharePoint 2013 also requires a database server based on Microsoft SQL Server 2008 R2 SP1 or Microsoft SQL Server 2012. Regardless of which edition of SQL Server you plan to use, you must be running a 64-bit version of the product. SharePoint uses the SQL Server database to store the configuration of SharePoint server farms, as well as the contents of deployed websites and the configuration and contents of all the services under the cover of the overall farm infrastructure.

On top of the operating system and database is an application server provided by Internet Information Services (IIS) 7.5. IIS 7.5 is mandatory, both because it hosts the web applications and because it publishes endpoints for SharePoint infrastructure services, making use of the Windows Process Activation Service (WAS) feature of IIS 7. Use of IIS 8 is suggested in new scenarios that you build from scratch, allowing you to take advantage of all the new features of Windows Server 2012 and IIS 8.

More Info You can find more details about WAS on the "Hosting in Windows Process Activation Service" page on MSDN, at *http://msdn.microsoft.com/library/ms734677.aspx*.

Because SharePoint 2013 is based on Microsoft .NET Framework 4.5 and extends ASP.NET 4.5, the infrastructure requires .NET Framework 4.5. Another element at the foundation of SharePoint 2013 is the Windows Identity Foundation 1.0 framework, which provides claims-based services, extended in order to support OAuth and the new security model of SharePoint 2013. Part VI of this book, "Security infrastructure," digs deeper into these topics.

On top of this foundation sits Microsoft SharePoint Foundation 2013, which is a free platform for building basic SharePoint solutions. Although free and the most basic edition of SharePoint, SharePoint Foundation 2013 contains a great deal of functionality that developers can use to meet the needs of basic portal scenarios.

At the top of the architecture is the SharePoint Server 2013 platform, together with its high-level and enterprise-level services, such as Excel Services, Managed Metadata Services, the User Profile services, the search engine, and so forth.

From a hardware perspective, the minimum memory requirement for a SharePoint 2013 server is 8 GB for a development environment, but this hardly gives you enough room to work. A more realistic minimum, however, is 16 GB for a successful development environment. For a production environment, the suggested memory is 12 GB for a web front-end or an application server, and 24 GB for an all-in-one server. Moreover, every SharePoint 2013 server should have a 64-bit CPU with a minimum of four cores.

Logical and physical architecture

Whenever you deploy a SharePoint environment, in reality, you're deploying a logical architecture called a SharePoint farm. A *SharePoint farm* is a set of servers that have different roles and offer various services that together make up a server farm suitable for hosting a full SharePoint deployment. Here are the common server roles in a SharePoint farm:

- **Front-end web servers** These servers publish websites, often called web applications.
- **Application servers** These servers host back-end services, such as Search services, the User Profile service, Excel Services, and so forth.
- **Database servers** These servers store configuration and content data for the entire SharePoint farm.

The smallest farm you can build is based on a single server; this type is often called the single server farm deployment. However, it is highly recommended that you avoid such a scenario, except for testing or development.

In fact, for the sake of scalability and business continuity, you should deploy a minimum of two front-end web servers, two application servers, and a back-end database server capable of supporting failover (clustering, mirroring, or AlwaysOn). This topology is commonly termed the *smallest fault-tolerant farm deployment*. If you need to scale out and support a wider range of users and sites, you can deploy a more complex farm by introducing some dedicated application servers. For example, real medium-scale and large-scale farms typically have dedicated servers for the search services, as well as dedicated servers for hosting the Office Web Apps services (which is a deployment requirement).

Due to the number and size of servers required for hosting a real production SharePoint farm, SharePoint 2013 farms are usually hosted in virtualized environments, either on-premises or in the cloud. For example, you could evaluate hosting SharePoint 2013 on an Infrastructure as a Service (IaaS) environment like Microsoft Windows Azure Virtual Machines. Moreover, you could also consider directly using Microsoft Office 365.

More Info You can find further information about topologies and architectural diagrams on the "Technical diagrams for SharePoint 2013" page, on TechNet at *http://technet.microsoft.com/en-us/library/cc263199(v=office.15).aspx*.

Regardless of the deployment topology you choose, SharePoint uses a SQL Server database for storing farm configurations and content. Specifically, it creates a main and fundamental farm configuration database as soon as you deploy a new farm. Usually, this database is called *SharePoint_Config* or *SharePoint_Config_{UniqueId}*. If you use the automated setup process, this database is created for you when you deploy the farm for the first time. If you use PowerShell to deploy a new farm, which is highly suggested, you can determine the name of this database by yourself. Furthermore, the SharePoint Deployment And Configuration Wizard creates a set of satellite database files for the main services deployed. For example, it creates a database that stores the contents of the SPCA administrative site. In case you use a PowerShell script to deploy the farm, you can determine the name and location of all SharePoint databases.

From a hierarchical perspective, each SharePoint farm is composed of services, which include all the infrastructure services that make up the SharePoint environment. The most important kind of services are web application services, which correspond to the entry point for web-published solutions. Each web application is made up of at least one site collection and one content database. However, you can deploy multiple site collections within a single web application, and you can deploy multiple content databases for a single web application. A content database is a database file that stores content for one or more site collections. As it relates to SharePoint, content can include items, documents, documents versions, pages, images, and so on. Thus, the database behind a site collection can grow very fast.

Starting with SharePoint 2010 and much more with SharePoint 2013, the server roles and the configurable services have been improved to better support scale-out scenarios. In fact, you can now distribute different roles to dedicated servers, eventually with hardware redundancy.

Figure 1-7 shows a graphical representation of a SharePoint farm with a couple of front-end web servers, both of which publish the same web applications with network load balancing. The first web application (Web Application #1) is made of two site collections (Site Collections #1 and #2), both of which share a common content database (Content #1). The second web application (Web Application #2) is made up of a third site collection (Site Collection #3) and stores its contents in a dedicated content database (Content #2). All the site collections contain one or more websites.

On the back end, there are four application servers, hosting SPCA, the search services, Excel Services, and some other services.

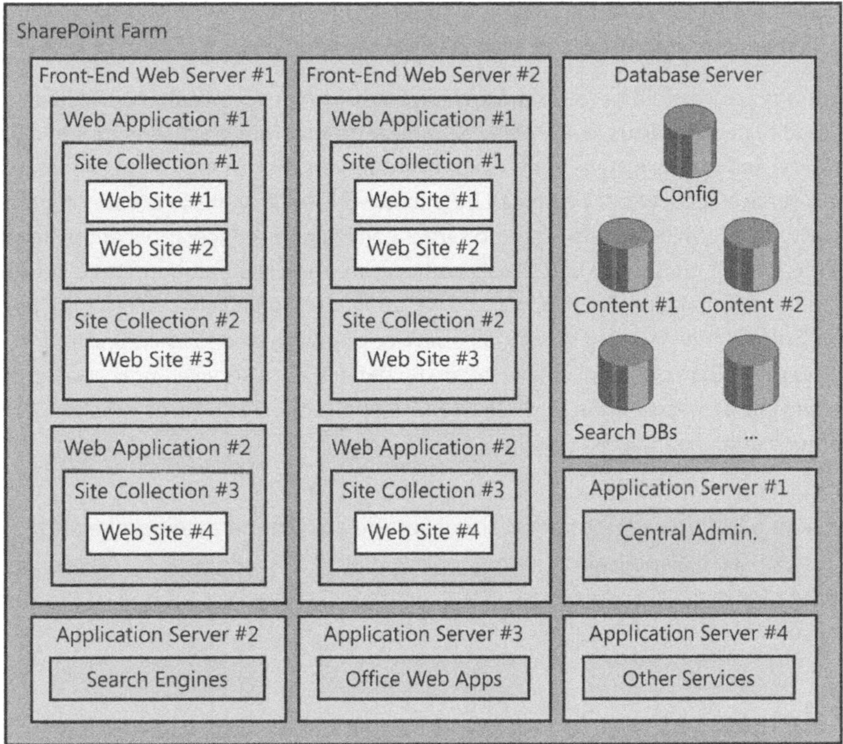

FIGURE 1-7 A simplified schema of a sample SharePoint farm with an N-tier topology.

All the data are persisted in a back-end database server that stores various database files for different purposes.

Service applications

Introduced in SharePoint Foundation 2010, service applications are software services that run in a SharePoint farm. Service applications are intended for sharing resources and capabilities across multiple sites and servers in the same farm, or even across farms. Most importantly, they are extensible and scalable, unlike the Shared Service Providers (SSPs) of Microsoft Office SharePoint 2007.

To clarify the idea of a service application, consider a couple of examples. The search engine in SharePoint 2013 is based on a service application. This means that you can share the same search engine across different servers in the same farm, which is not surprising, but you can also share the same search service across multiple farms. For example, in very large scenarios, you could deploy a search-dedicated farm, without any front-end web server, that exposes only a wide set of servers providing query, index, crawler, content -processing, and analytics components. You could then use this farm to serve many other SharePoint 2013 farms, taking advantage of that shared search service. Another example is Excel Services: if you have a farm that uses Excel Services extensively to make calculations and create reports on external data, you could decide to deploy Excel Services on two or more dedicated servers in the farm, using them from all the other servers.

These configurations are possible because the architecture of service applications has been designed with scalability in mind. Thus, every service application that runs on a server in the farm can support scalability, and can be installed on two or more servers. At the same time, a farm uses a proxy to consume a service application, which can be published locally, or in some cases can be published by a third-party farm. While a front-end web server consumes a service application, however, it ignores the real location of the service and simply concentrates on consuming it. This is possible because each SharePoint Foundation 2013 farm has a native service application, called the *Application Discovery and Load Balancer Service,* that coordinates service discovery and load balancing for services deployed on more than one application server. By default, each service application proxy communicates behind the scenes with the back-end service application via a secure channel based on Windows Communication Foundation (WCF).

More Info You can find further information about service application architecture and developing a custom service application in the book *Microsoft SharePoint 2010 Developer Reference,* by Paolo Pialorsi (Microsoft Press, 2011), which is the previous edition of this book.

The role of databases

Every SharePoint farm includes one or more back-end database servers. In fact, the back-end SQL server stores the entire configuration of the farm, as well as contents of every site collection and the data for many service applications. For example, the search service stores crawled contents, properties for crawled data, and configuration properties in multiple separate and dedicated database files. For the sake of precision, in SharePoint 2013, the Search service application allocates four databases. The Managed Metadata service has another dedicated database file, but the list of native services using one or more databases on the back end could be longer.

Important Even though you can open a SharePoint database in SQL Server Management Studio and inspect the databases of a SharePoint farm, you should avoid doing that. In addition, you should not base your software solutions on the data structure of SharePoint databases. Thus, you should avoid querying and writing the content of these databases directly. If you do need to read or write their content, take advantage of the various libraries, APIs, and object models discussed later in this book.

Now let's concentrate on pages and content. Recall that each time you create a new site collection using SPCA, you have the opportunity to choose a starting site template. The site template is a set of configuration, layout, and content files that define a site model. You can build your own site templates (you will learn how to do that later in Part IV, "Extending SharePoint"), or you can select one of the existing site templates that are packaged with SharePoint. Whichever site template you choose, under the covers, SharePoint starts from a set of files stored in the file system of all front-end web servers, and then creates some records in the content database that will host the site collection that you are creating. After the site collection has been created, when you browse to a page using a web browser, the SharePoint engine determines whether the page you have requested resides entirely on the file system, or whether it needs to retrieve some personalized content from the content database and merges that with the page model from the file system, or even whether the page content is completely stored in the content database.

Having a back-end content database available gives you the option to deploy multiple front-end web servers that can share the same content, improving horizontal scalability when necessary. At the same time, maintaining basic page models in the file system improves performance, because loading a page from the file system, unless it has been personalized, is generally faster than retrieving it from an external database server. In the section "SharePoint for developers," later in the chapter, you'll see how SharePoint differentiates between file system and database content sources.

SharePoint editions

SharePoint 2013 is offered in several editions. Even though this book is for developers (as opposed to sales or marketing personnel), it is useful to know the main differences between each edition of the product. The goal of this section is to give you the base knowledge required to choose the appropriate SharePoint edition for each of your projects.

> **More Info** For a full comparison of the SharePoint editions, see the page "SharePoint Online" at *http://technet.microsoft.com/en-us/library/jj819267.aspx*.

SharePoint Foundation

SharePoint Foundation 2013 is the most basic edition of the product. It is free—providing that you run it on a licensed copy of Microsoft Windows Server—and it offers the fundamental features for building simple document storage and collaboration solutions. By default, this edition's main capabilities are accessibility, cross-browser support, basic search features, out-of-the-box pages and Web Parts, new UI features based on dialogs and ribbons, blogs, and wikis.

The Foundation edition also supports the basic infrastructure of Business Connectivity Services, although without any client-side or Office capability. Of course, you'll also find the SPCA controls, all the farm management tools, and services such as the SharePoint Health Analyzer. In fact, if you wanted to, you could deploy a multitier farm using just SharePoint Foundation. Finally, SharePoint Foundation offers all the features supporting custom development, including the Web Parts/App Parts programming model, the Server Object Model, the Client Object Model, event receivers (local or remote), claims-based security, and so on. All these topics will be covered in detail in Part II, "Developing SharePoint solutions," and Part III, "Developing SharePoint apps."

You should use this edition of SharePoint whenever you want to develop custom solutions that do not require any high-level features, such as the document management tools, user profiles, managed metadata, and so on. When you simply need to use SharePoint as a web-based "sharing point" to store content, such as documents, contacts, tasks, and so on, this is the edition that best meets those needs. Quite often, SharePoint Foundation is the right starting point for gaining experience with SharePoint. It also serves well as a bridge: you can start installing Foundation; plus, later on, you will be able to upgrade to SharePoint Server, if the need arises.

SharePoint Server Standard

The Microsoft SharePoint Server 2013 Standard edition is built on top of SharePoint Foundation 2013, adding useful features for building business-level solutions. In particular, you will find features supporting Enterprise Content Management (ECM) and Web Content Management solutions. This edition also provides legal compliance capabilities, including records management, legal holds, and document policies. It also offers support for document sets, which give you the ability to manage related documents as if they were a single entity. It supports document IDs, which assign a unique protocol number to SharePoint site documents. Using this edition, you can target content based on *audiences*, which are profile-based groups of targets. Moreover, you have the capability to use the Managed Metadata service for managing common metadata properties, navigation elements, publishing, and product catalogs across multiple site collections and web applications.

SharePoint Server is the right choice for implementing business-level solutions. For example, SharePoint Server can help you create a content management system (CMS) solution that provides content publishing, content approval, page layouts, web standards (XHTML, WCAG 2.0, and so on) support, and so forth. This edition also supports tags and metadata-driven search refinement, people search, and the whole set of social features. As a business-level tool, it provides features for managing not only content, but also people, profiles, and personal sites. Finally, this edition of the product provides support for developing and executing workflows, hosted either on-premises or in the cloud on Windows Azure.

SharePoint Server Enterprise

Microsoft SharePoint Server 2013 Enterprise edition targets large business solutions and enterprise-level organizations. It extends the capabilities of SharePoint Server Standard by offering support for dashboards, key performance indicators (KPIs), and business intelligence features. It improves search capabilities by offering contextual search, deep search query refinement, extreme scale-out search capabilities, rich web indexing, and so on. It also provides support for Excel Services, Visio Services, Forms Services, and Access Services.

When you need to develop business analysis solutions or complex search-based solutions, you should choose the Enterprise edition.

From a developer perspective, you can install the SharePoint Server Enterprise edition if you have licensing coverage for that, and you can develop solutions for all the editions using a unique environment.

SharePoint Online

Microsoft SharePoint Online is the cloud-based SharePoint offering, based on the Software as a Service (SaaS) paradigm included in Microsoft Office 365. With this edition, you can build SharePoint solutions without building a SharePoint farm on-premises. Instead, by having your farm in the cloud, you can enjoy an external solution free of management costs. As a developer, you are freed to focus only on data, processes, ideas, the content that you want to share, and the apps you want to build. The SharePoint Online offering is available in Standard mode, as well as in Dedicated mode. The Standard offering uses an environment shared with other customers, although it is isolated according to a clear set of multitenancy rules, and you can only extend that environment with code executed in a sandbox or custom apps. On the contrary, the Dedicated offering allows you to have a dedicated server farm on which you can deploy custom solutions with full-trust execution rights, as long as your solutions passes a verification process.

SharePoint for developers

SharePoint offers developers numerous features and capabilities for building custom web solutions. This section provides an overview of those features and services so you can better understand the topics that you will be exploring in the rest of this book.

ASP.NET integration

As a developer, you might be wondering how SharePoint 2013 integrates with ASP.NET to service requests and provide its high-level features on top of the ASP.NET native infrastructure.

Since IIS 7.0, in Windows Server 2008, application pools can run in one of two modes: integrated mode or classic mode. *Classic mode* works like older versions of IIS (IIS 6), taking advantage of the Internet Server Application Programming Interface (ISAPI) filter based on the Aspnet_isapi.dll file. *Integrated mode* provides a unified request-processing pipeline for requests that target both managed (.NET) and unmanaged (non-.NET) resources. Every request is served by a module registered in the application configuration.

SharePoint 2013 provides a *Microsoft.SharePoint.ApplicationRuntime* namespace in the Microsoft.SharePoint.dll assembly. This namespace contains a set of classes that integrate and/or override the default behavior of ASP.NET while in IIS integrated mode. The primary class that handles SharePoint requests is called *SPRequestModule*. It is configured in the web.config file of every SharePoint site, in the system.webServer/modules section. This class registers a number of application events that handle requests, authentication, errors, and so on. One fundamental task of this module is to register the virtual path provider (*SPVirtualPathProvider*), which resolves requests by determining whether the requested content should be retrieved from the content database or from the file system. A *virtual path provider* is a class that provides contents to the ASP.NET pipeline by retrieving them from a virtual file system.

Server-side technologies

SharePoint offers developers a rich set of server-side tools. First, you can use the SharePoint Server Object Model, which allows you to interact with SharePoint through a large set of libraries and classes. Using these classes, you can read, manage, and administer data stored in SharePoint. More generally, you can use the Server Object Model to do almost anything that SharePoint itself can do, because SharePoint itself uses that same object model. You can use the Server Object Model on a SharePoint server only, because it has some dependencies not satisfied by other servers. You will learn more about this tool in Chapter 5, "Server Object Model."

On the server side, you can also use the LINQ (Language Integrated Query) programming model, exploiting the LINQ to SharePoint provider, by which you can query and manage SharePoint data using a fully typed programming model, much as you would when managing data stored in SQL Server using LINQ to SQL. Chapter 6, "LINQ to SharePoint," discusses this LINQ query provider in more detail.

Client-side technologies

One of the biggest news of SharePoint 2013, from a developer perspective, is the improvement of the client-side technologies for consuming SharePoint data and interacting with remote SharePoint servers. In fact, you can exploit a rich set of client-side technologies offered specifically for this purpose. For example, the SharePoint Client Object Model lets you interact with SharePoint from a client using a set of classes that are similar to the Server Object Model, but work on any client that supports .NET, Microsoft Silverlight, or JavaScript. The Client Object Model is available in three different flavors: .NET managed, Silverlight, and JavaScript. The Client Object Model versions are almost functionally identical on all three platforms. You can also use SOAP (Simple Object Access Protocol) services published by SharePoint, even though they are deprecated and available for backward compatibility only. Furthermore, you can use the REST (Representational State Transfer) API to access and manage SharePoint data by using a protocol for querying and updating data via an HTTP/XML communication channel called OData (Open Data Protocol, documented at *http://www.odata.org*). Moreover, starting with SharePoint 2013, you can take advantage of a new and rich set of APIs published via HTTP and accessible from any device; these APIs are useful for consuming data and interacting with site collections, sites, services, and whatever else you could need to create a SharePoint app or solution. From a security viewpoint, you can use the common OAuth (Open Authentication) standard to secure communication and authenticate/authorize both users and apps while consuming data and interacting with SharePoint services.

All of these client-side technologies are discussed throughout the book, and in particular in Parts II and III.

App Parts, Web Parts, and the UI

Another area of interest for developers is customizing the UI. Many SharePoint developers working on SharePoint 2010 or earlier spent their time developing Web Parts, Web Part pages, and UI customizations. SharePoint 2013 still provides a rich object model, and even backward compatibility, for building custom Web Parts and Web Part pages, as well as a set of UI customization tools that simplify working with AJAX (Asynchronous JavaScript and XML), dialog boxes, the ribbon, and so on. Now, with SharePoint 2013, you can extend and customize the UI by creating apps and App Parts. You can think about App Parts as blocks of content, consumed from a remote app, that play the same role as Web Parts did in the past. You will see how to develop App Parts in Part III of this book.

Data provisioning

As soon as you begin working with SharePoint, you will face the need to define packages for automatically deploying data structures. Working with SharePoint generally involves designing new lists and new content types, which are reusable typed definitions of metadata models. However, if you define your models using the web browser, you won't have a high-level modeling approach; everything you do must be migrated and/or executed again in the quality assurance (QA) and production environment.

Fortunately, there are tools and techniques that allow you to model a data structure—optionally based on custom contents and fields—and deploy that model to customers' sites. These tools also provide support for deploying updated versions of the solution in the future. You'll see more on this subject later in this chapter, in the section "Features, solutions deployment, and sandboxing." You will learn how to define custom data models for automated provisioning in Chapter 3, "Data provisioning."

Event receivers and workflows

With SharePoint, since version 2007, you can use local event receivers to intercept users' actions and/or events and subsequently execute some lightweight server-side code. Now, with SharePoint 2013, you also have the capability to create remote event receivers for invoking external and remote services. These receivers are capable of handling events like item insertion, updating, deletion, and so on. This is a useful feature for implementing simple process-handling solutions or business-processes coordination, activating external processes upon user actions in SharePoint. Moreover, you can use remote event receivers to make apps communicate with parent websites. Chapter 10, "Remote event receivers," dives into this subject.

Similarly, when you need to define complex and long-running business processes that respond to events from the UI and interact with end users, you can define *workflows*. With SharePoint 2013, the workflow engine has been redesigned from scratch, using the new Workflow Manager 1.0 engine, based on Workflow Foundation 4.5, together with a new application server role that can be hosted on Windows Azure or on-premises. This functionality deserves a thorough exploration, so this book discusses it in four dedicated chapters, in Part V, "Developing workflows."

Features, solutions deployment, and sandboxing

As a complete development platform, SharePoint 2010 introduced deployment services and capabilities by which you can deploy and upgrade solutions during a project's lifetime. In SharePoint 2013, all these features are still available and suitable for developing complex customizations and solutions.

Specifically, SharePoint offers the opportunity to create deployment packages, called Windows SharePoint Services Solution Packages (WSPs). You can use these packages to automate setup and maintenance tasks across an entire server farm. In addition, you can deploy these solutions in a sandboxed environment. The packages consist of features, which are atomic sets of extensions that you can develop, install, activate, and manage with a specific set of administrative tools. In Chapter 4, "SharePoint features and solutions," you will learn how to create and deploy such packages. In Part III of the book, you will learn how to create and deploy custom apps as a suitable alternative to implementing SharePoint solutions.

Security infrastructure

The SharePoint security infrastructure is another topic that affects both software development and the architecture of solutions. In fact, to develop robust and solid solutions, a developer should have a high degree of confidence in, and knowledge about, SharePoint authentication and authorization policies. The key security aspects of SharePoint 2013 are its claims-based approach and support for the OAuth protocol. Part VI of the book is fully dedicated to security matters.

Business Connectivity Services

Business Connectivity Services is another feature that is generally useful when developing solutions. This feature supports consuming external data within SharePoint, and has a design almost identical to data directly stored in SharePoint. The sources of this external data can be an RDBMS, like SQL Server or any ODBC-compliant data source; a WCF/SOAP service; a custom .NET object model; or an OData service. Chapter 14, "Business Connectivity Services," will cover this topic.

Windows PowerShell for developers

Another interesting capability is that you can administer and automate SharePoint administrative tasks using the Windows PowerShell console. Windows PowerShell is a task-based command-line shell and scripting language designed especially for system administration. It can execute commands and scripts authored by developers or system administrators, as long as they have some minimal development expertise. What makes Windows PowerShell a powerful framework for developers is its extensibility model, together with its capability to execute custom code. For example, from the Windows PowerShell console, you can not only administer a farm, but also create scripts for populating data into target lists of SharePoint. You can manage, create, and configure testing environments, and you can create custom scripts to deploy your solutions.

Developer tools

SharePoint developers can take advantage of some Microsoft-supplied tools to support their work and reduce the effort involved in developing custom solutions. This section lists these tools and identifies when they might be useful.

SharePoint Designer 2013

SharePoint Designer 2013 is a rapid application development (RAD) tool for developing SharePoint no-code solutions. You can download it for free from Microsoft's website, at *http://www.microsoft.com/download/details.aspx?id=35491*. SharePoint Designer 2013 targets advanced users, who can use it to design and compose solutions without writing any code. For example, using SharePoint Designer 2013, you can

- Personalize pages, page layouts, Web Parts, Web Part pages, layouts, and themes.
- Create and manage lists and document libraries.
- Design simple workflows or import workflows designed using Microsoft Visio 2010 or 2013.
- Manage content types and site columns to model typed lists of contents.
- Model and register external data sources using the Business Data Connectivity engine.
- Create pages with lists data bound to external data sources.
- Manage users and groups.
- Manage files and assets of the target site.

Figure 1-8 shows the main page of SharePoint Designer 2013 when connected to a SharePoint site. As you can see, it provides a user-friendly interface, consistent with the Office 2013 user experience.

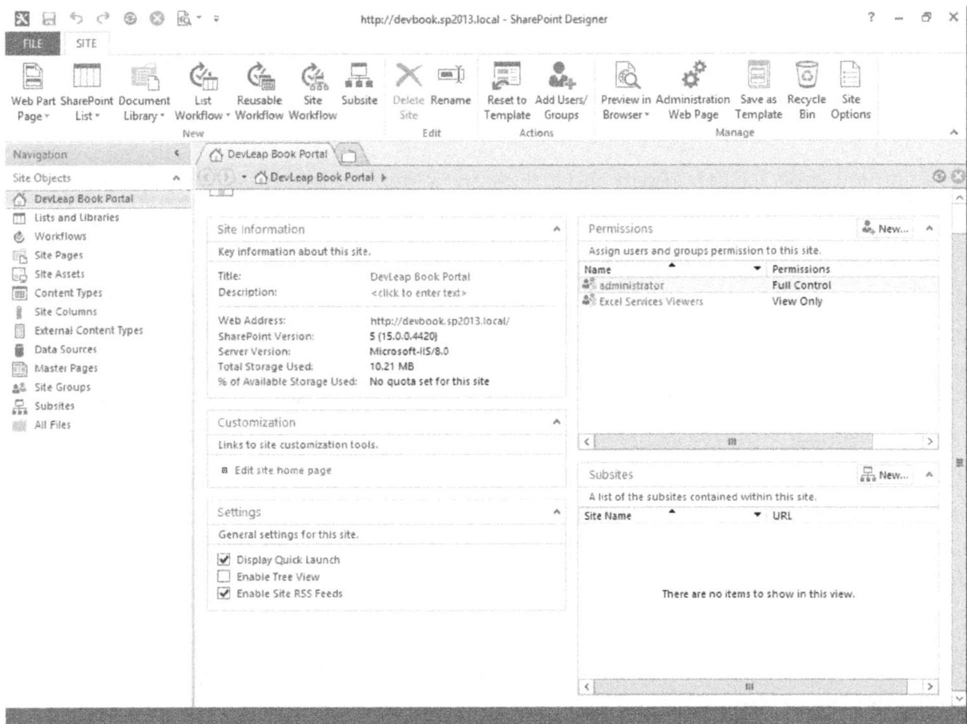

FIGURE 1-8 The SharePoint Designer 2013 main page.

As a developer, you will primarily use this tool to prototype solutions, to design Business Data Connectivity models, and to customize layouts—working with themes, master pages, XSLTs, and pages.

Note This book will not cover SharePoint Designer 2013 in depth, because it is aimed at developers who are willing to develop SharePoint solutions by writing custom code. For deep coverage of SharePoint Designer 2013, read *Microsoft SharePoint Designer 2013 Step by Step*, by Penelope Coventry (Microsoft Press, 2013).

Microsoft Visual Studio 2012

Visual Studio 2012 can be extended with a set of tools for developing SharePoint 2013 apps and solutions. These tools are named the *Microsoft Office Developer Tools for Visual Studio 2012* and can be installed through the Web Platform Installer kit or downloaded manually from MSDN. When you install Visual Studio 2012, you have also the opportunity to activate the SharePoint 2010 Developer Tools option, which installs a set of project and item templates that are ready to use in SharePoint solutions that target SharePoint 2010. Most of the code and projects you develop using the SharePoint 2010 developer tools are also supported by SharePoint 2013, for the sake of backward compatibility. Nevertheless, it is highly recommended to develop using the SharePoint 2013 tools and the new apps-oriented development model introduced in SharePoint 2013.

More Info The Microsoft Office Developer Tools for Visual Studio 2012 can be directly downloaded from the following URL: *http://msdn.microsoft.com/en-US/sharepoint/aa905690.aspx*.

The development tools for SharePoint also include some deployment tools, which are useful for packaging, releasing, and upgrading a SharePoint solution.

Note To use Visual Studio 2012 for developing SharePoint 2013 apps and solutions, you must run it under an administrative account, because you need some high-level permissions to manage the SharePoint servers while deploying solutions. In addition, you need to attach to the IIS worker process while debugging code. It is suggested to run your desktop as a standard user, but run Visual Studio 2012 with a Run As command to impersonate an administrative user. Moreover, to develop SharePoint solutions (WSPs), you need to have SharePoint installed on your development machine. On the contrary, to develop SharePoint apps, you do not need to have SharePoint on board, and you can remotely connect to an external SharePoint environment, including SharePoint Online on Office 365.

Figure 1-9 shows the Add New Project form of Visual Studio 2012, showing the project templates installed by the SharePoint extensions.

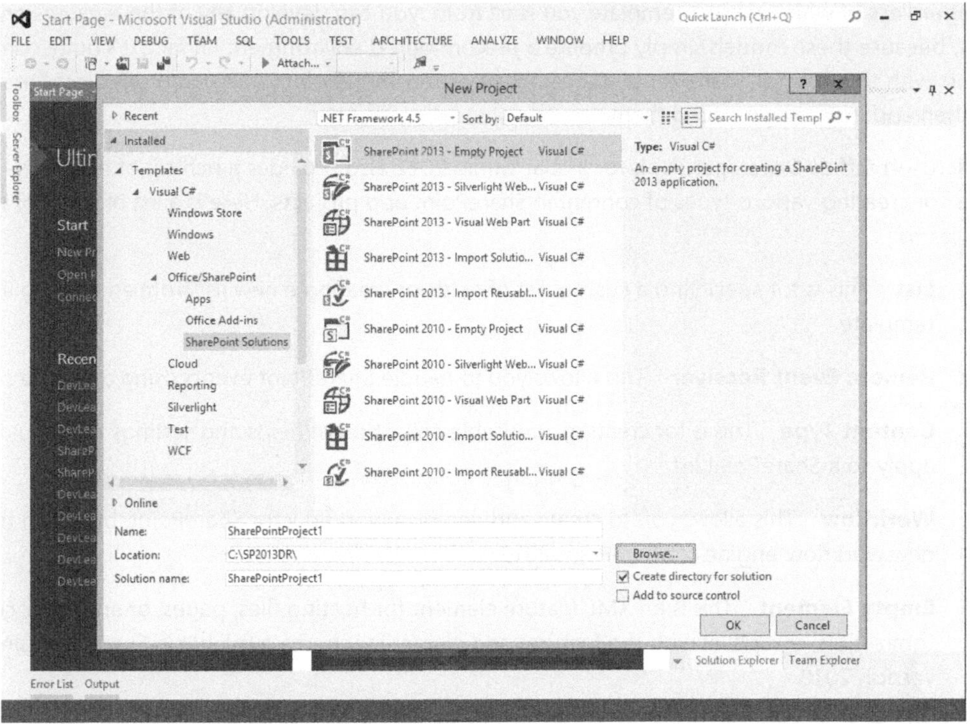

FIGURE 1-9 The Add New Project form in Visual Studio 2012.

You can create the following types of projects:

- **App for SharePoint 2013** This is the project template for creating a SharePoint 2013 app. It will be discussed in depth in Chapter 8, "SharePoint apps."
- **SharePoint 2013 Project** This is an empty project for starting a new SharePoint implementation. It provides a set of references to only the most useful libraries of SharePoint, and it provides support for automatic deployment.
- **SharePoint 2013 Silverlight Web Part** This is a project intended for developing a Web Part with a GUI based on Microsoft Silverlight.
- **SharePoint 2013 Visual Web Part** This is a project intended for developing a Web Part with a GUI based on an ASCX web control of ASP.NET.
- **Import SharePoint 2013 Solution Package** This imports an old or third-party solution package (WSP).
- **Import Reusable SharePoint 2013 Workflow** This project template is useful for importing workflows designed with SharePoint Designer 2013 that need to be extended or improved with Visual Studio 2012.

Regardless of which project template you start from, you can develop any of these extension types, because these models simply prepare a preconfigured environment. In fact, it's quite common to start with the App for SharePoint 2013 template or the SharePoint 2013 - Empty Project template, and then add items as you need them.

Microsoft Office Developer Tools for Visual Studio 2012 also provides a rich set of item templates for creating various types of content in SharePoint app projects. Here is a list of some of the main items:

- **List** This is for specifying a custom list of fields or creating a new list from an existing list template.
- **Remote Event Receiver** This allows you to handle SharePoint events using a remote service.
- **Content Type** This is for creating a reusable collection of fields and settings that you can apply to a SharePoint list.
- **Workflow** This allows you to create and deploy a workflow for SharePoint, based on the new workflow engine of SharePoint 2013.
- **Empty Element** This is an XML feature element for hosting files, pages, or any other customization, compliant with the features and elements schema available in SharePoint since version 2010.
- **Site Column** A site column item is useful for creating custom content types and list definitions.
- **Module** This is a module item for deploying files, pages, assets, and more on SharePoint.
- **Client Web Part (Host Web)** This is a client Web Part (App Part) for supporting a custom SharePoint app.
- **UI Custom Action (Host Web)** This is typically used in an app that adds a UI extension to its host site; for example, it can add an action to the ribbon or to a list menu.
- **Task Pane App** This is an app that appears in the task pane of an Office application.
- **Content App** This is an app that appears in the body of an Office document.

SharePoint Server Explorer

Another interesting feature offered by Visual Studio 2012 is SharePoint Server Explorer, an extension to Server Explorer in Visual Studio 2012 for targeting SharePoint servers. Through this extension, you can register as many SharePoint servers as you need and browse their topology and configuration using the classic tree-view approach, such as in Visual Studio Server Explorer windows.

As shown in Figure 1-10, the SharePoint Server Explorer interface lets you browse and manage the following:

- Sites and subsites
- Content types
- Features
- List templates
- Lists and document libraries
- Workflows

In addition, because SharePoint Server Explorer is based on an extensible object model, you can extend it to provide new functionalities, using Visual Studio 2012 to develop such solutions. You can already find many custom extensions that can be downloaded for free.

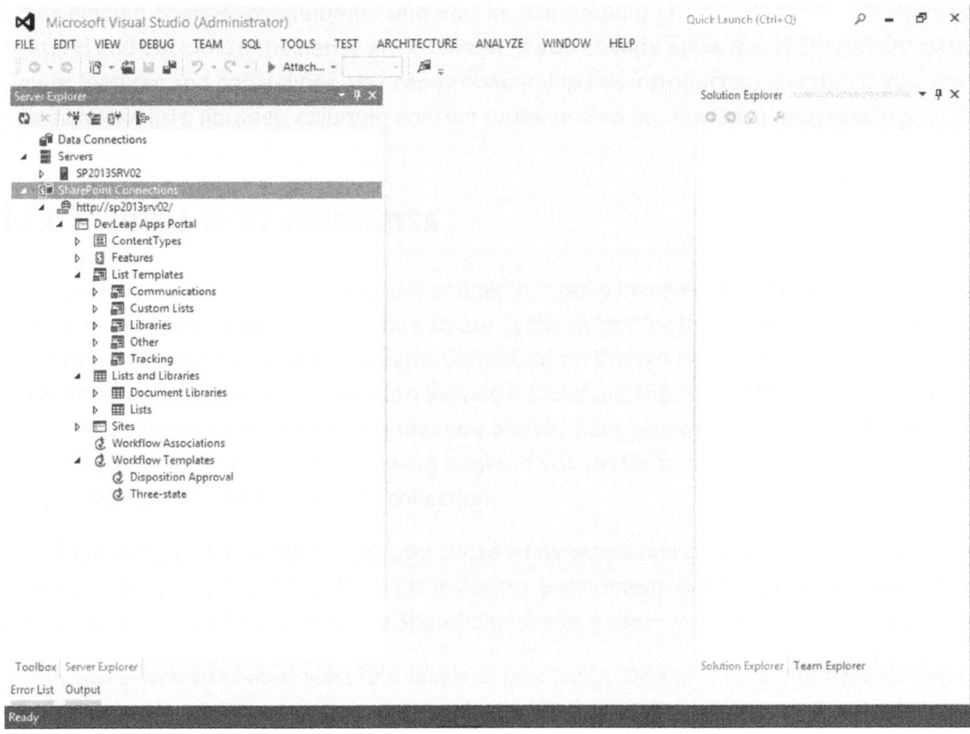

FIGURE 1-10 The SharePoint Server Explorer UI in Visual Studio 2012.

- **Site members** Users who can (by default) contribute to (add, update, delete) the contents of the site and items in the lists. Because they cannot change the overall structure of the site, however, they cannot create new list instances or change the definition of existing lists.
- **Site owners** Users who have full control of both site content and structure, allowing them to change items, create new lists, or update the definition of existing lists.

Finally, as Chapter 1 showed, a fifth group, the site collection administrators group, is responsible for administering the entire site collection. Part VI of this book, "Security infrastructure," contains an in-depth discussion of the security and permissions logic in SharePoint 2013, but for now, you simply need to understand that the permissions for the various user groups arise from the following permission levels:

- **View Only** The user can view pages, list items, and documents. Document types with server-side file handlers can be viewed in the browser but not downloaded.
- **Limited Access** The user can view specific lists, document libraries, list items, folders, or documents when given permissions. This permission cannot be assigned directly by an end user.
- **Read** The user can view pages and list items, and download documents.
- **Contribute** The user can view, add, update, and delete list items and documents.
- **Edit** The user can add, edit, and delete lists. He or she can also view, add, update, and delete list items and documents.
- **Design** The user can view, add, update, delete, approve, and customize.
- **Full Control** The user has full control.

If you are logged in to the site as a user with sufficient rights, you can create new list instances and more, as you will learn in the following sections.

Creating a new list

As discussed in Chapter 1, to create a new list, you first click the Settings control, which looks like a gear and is located in the upper-right corner of the SharePoint 2013 standard Team Site template. On the Settings menu, click Add An App, which will bring you to a page with the list of all the available content and apps available for creation. For example, to create a list of contacts, simply select the standard template for creating a contacts list, as shown in Figure 2-1.

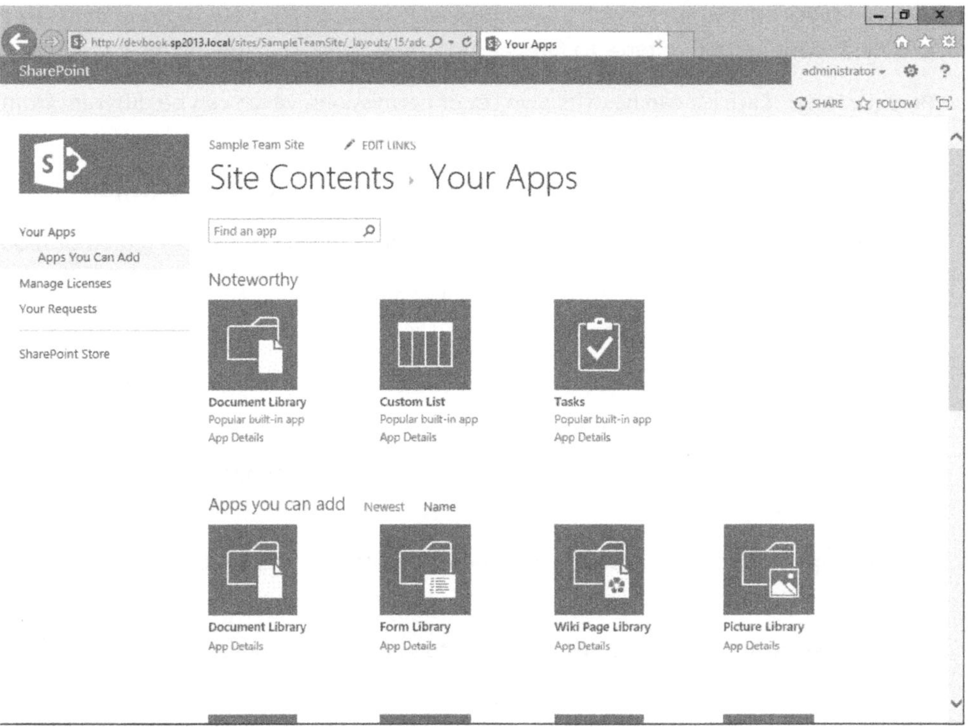

FIGURE 2-1 The web UI for adding a new app to the current site.

The result will be the creation of a new list with a set of predefined columns (metadata) for each contact item.

After you have created a list instance, you can take advantage of the full set of features and capabilities that the SharePoint 2013 data foundation provides. The following are some of the main features and capabilities of a list instance:

- **Columns** These allow you to define a set of custom columns describing the metadata of each item of the list.
- **Folders** Like file system folders, list folders can be used to partition data in subfolders. Through folders, you can also define custom permissions and partition data visibility.
- **Content types** These are models of data that can be used to store different kinds of items within a unique list instance. For example, you could have contacts of various types, such as customers, suppliers, employees, and so on. They could share some common columns, and have some specific columns, too. Chapter 3, "Data provisioning," will cover content types in detail.

- **Views** Every list can render with various views. A view can be used to group items by a specific field value or content type, to filter and/or order items, to page the results, and so forth.
- **Permissions** Each list can have its own set of permissions, which can be different from the default permissions applied to the site.
- **Versioning** This allows the list to keep track of changes and versions of items.
- **Workflows** These are business processes that execute when an item is created or modified.
- **Content approval** This is a content approval engine that you can use to enrich content provisioning, such as adding approval rules and processes.
- **Alerts** This is an alerting infrastructure that you can employ to alert people about new, updated, or deleted contents.
- **RSS feeds** This provides the capability to subscribe to and monitor a feed from any kind of feed aggregator.
- **Offline capabilities** This allows you to keep data offline by using tools such as Microsoft Outlook or SkyDrive Pro.
- **Office integration** This provides the ability to integrate list contents with Microsoft Excel, Access, and other Office applications.

In fact, you can benefit from these features without having to write any code.

Standard list templates

The richest edition of SharePoint 2013 offers nearly 30 list templates out of the box. Table 2-1 presents some of the more common list templates.

TABLE 2-1 Common list templates available in SharePoint

Template name	Description
Announcements	A list for publishing news items and information.
Asset Library	A list for sharing rich media assets, including images, audio, and video files.
Calendar	A calendar that lets users schedule meetings and events, and set deadlines. You can synchronize a Calendar list with Microsoft Outlook.
Contacts	A list of people, including their addresses. You can synchronize a Contacts list with Outlook.
Custom List	A "blank" list model, meaning that you can create whatever type of list that you like by defining custom columns and views.
Data Connection Library	A list for sharing connections to external data sources, such as databases, SOAP services, OLAP cubes, and so on.
Document Library	A list for sharing documents and files.

Template name	Description
External List	A list that supports reading and managing data from external data sources via Business Connectivity Services.
Form Library	A list for sharing XML-based business forms, such as those produced with Microsoft InfoPath.
Links	A list that stores hyperlinks to sites and resources.
Picture Library	A list for sharing pictures. This list type includes upload, preview, slideshow, and thumbnail functionalities.
Slide Library	A list to share slideshows built with Microsoft PowerPoint. It includes slide management functionality.
Survey	A list to create surveys, polls, or lists of questions. This type provides features for viewing a graphical summary of the responses.
Tasks	A list of tasks to execute. It includes deadlines, notes, and completion status.

As you can see, you can create a variety of lists. You can also customize any list so that it meets your specific needs.

Custom list templates

If none of the predefined list templates suits your needs, you can create a custom list instance and define its columns and views manually. Of course, whenever you create any list, you can define custom views and columns, but when working *with* custom list instances, which are blank lists with the minimal set of fields required by SharePoint, you always need to customize the columns to add your own fields.

By default, a custom list has only five public and visible fields:

- **Title** This is a mandatory field that defines a title for each item in the list. It is useful for rendering list items and for accessing the contextual menu that SharePoint provides for each individual item in a list.
- **Created** This is an autocalculated field that stores information about when the user created the current item.
- **Modified** This is an autocalculated field that stores information about when the last user modified the current item.
- **Created By** This is an autocalculated field that stores information about the user who created the current item.
- **Modified By** This is another autocalculated field that stores information about the user who last modified the current item.

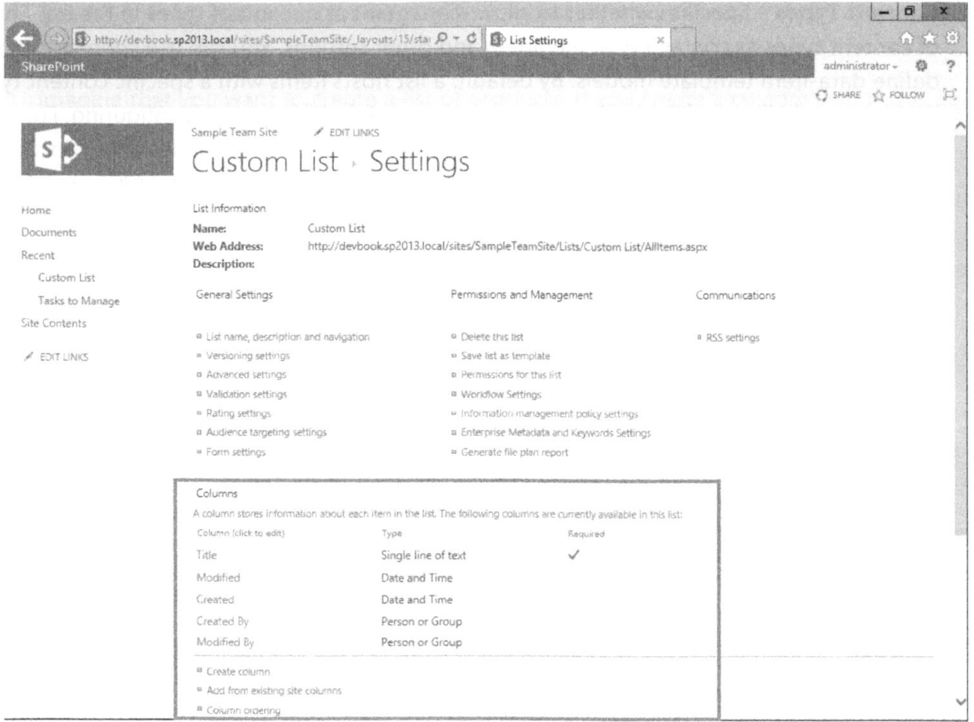

FIGURE 2-3 The List Settings page with the Columns section highlighted.

When you select Create Column, a specific SharePoint administrative page appears, requesting information about the type of column that you want to create. Figure 2-4 shows the Create Column page. Here, you can define the name of the new custom column and the field type, enter a brief description, and supply other validation rules and constraints. For example, you can define whether the new column is required or optional, whether it should have a default value, whether it should contain a value that is unique across the whole list instance, and so on.

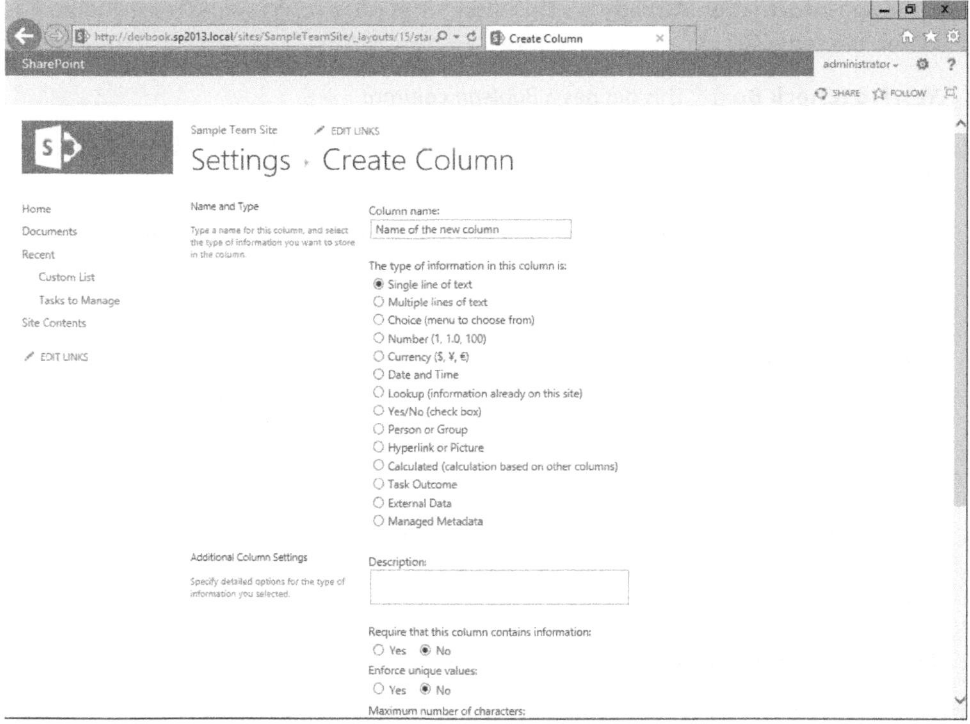

FIGURE 2-4 The Create Column page for a new list column.

As Figure 2-4 shows, you can choose from a variety of data types when creating a new column. The following are the available field types:

- **Single Line of Text** This corresponds to a single line of text.
- **Multiple Lines of Text** This corresponds to a text area with multiple columns and rows.
- **Choice (Menu to Choose From)** This has a predefined set of values. You can configure it to accept single or multiple values, and whether it should render as a drop-down menu, a radio button list, or a list of check boxes.
- **Number (1, 1.0, 100)** This defines a numeric column that can have decimals and minimum and maximum value.
- **Currency ($, ¥, €)** This corresponds to a money field, which behaves almost like a Number field type. You can select the currency format that you prefer.
- **Date and Time** This defines a Date and Time field that you can configure to handle date-only fields or date and time fields.

- **Lookup (Information Already on This Site)** This retrieves its values from another list within the same site.
- **Yes/No (Check Box)** This defines a *Boolean* column.
- **Person or Group** This is a particular type of lookup field that searches for a user or group defined in the current site.
- **Hyperlink or Picture** This column type holds an external URL, which can be either a page URL or an image URL. In the latter case, you can configure this field type to render the image available at that URL.
- **Calculated (Calculation Based on Other Columns)** This defines a formula that can be calculated based on other fields defined in the current list, and then it renders the result.
- **Task Outcome** This is a field type representing the result of a task typically related to a running workflow process or business process.
- **External Data** This is a specific field type that looks up values via Business Connectivity Services. You will find more about this topic in Chapter 16, "SharePoint workflow fundamentals."
- **Managed Metadata** This field is related to the Managed Metadata service.

If these options do not meet your needs, you can define custom field types of your own using Microsoft Visual Studio 2012 and some custom code, installing them onto the target SharePoint server farm. You're better off, however, avoiding such extensions and customization techniques. In fact, although a custom field type definition is absolutely possible and supported, it requires deploying code, XML files, and configurations on the physical file systems of the servers in the farm. Due to the invasiveness of this approach, it is a scenario that is not supported in the standard offering of Office 365. It would require you to upgrade to a dedicated farm either on-premises, or on Office 365 Dedicated.

On the contrary, if you would like to extend the available types of data, you can take advantage of the new SharePoint 2013 client-side rendering (CSR) engine. Through this new feature, you can declare custom behavior for predefined field data types by simply providing some custom JavaScript code that will be executed on the client side.

New to SharePoint 2013 is the ability to add fields and change the shape of a list or library directly from the current view of the list, just as if you were in an Excel spreadsheet. Notice the New Item and Edit This List commands at the top of the list view. Click New Item to add a new item to the list via a dedicated webpage. If you click the Edit This List command, you will switch the view to the editable and configurable grid shown in Figure 2-5. Based on some client-side HTML and JavaScript code, this grid view behaves almost like an Excel spreadsheet.

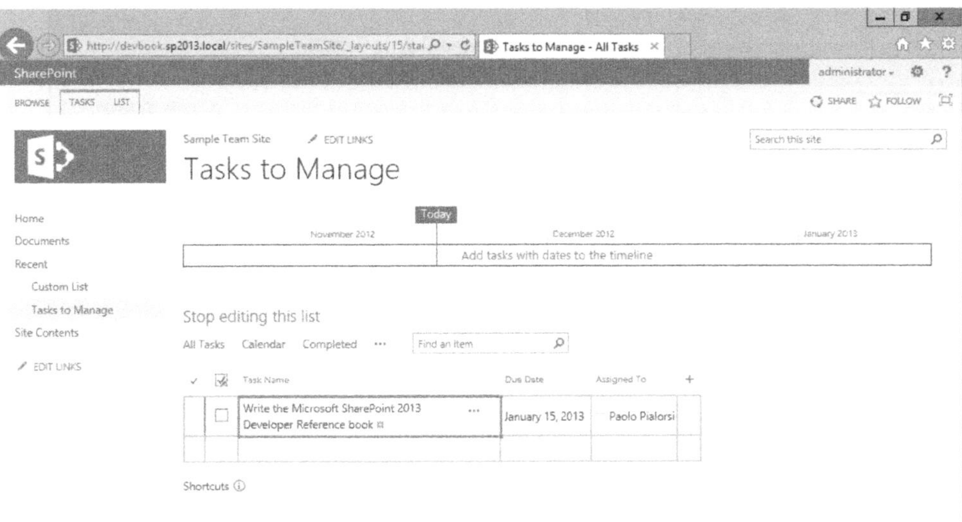

FIGURE 2-5 In this view, you can edit the data and the data structure of a list or library.

To edit the grid, click the + (plus) icon above the rightmost column. You can add new columns on the fly, choosing a proper data type and a name for the target field, as well as edit existing items and add new ones. To stop the editing session, simply click the Stop link or change to a different page.

This technique is powerful because the end user can design the shape of the data without technical skills. Nevertheless, the resulting fields and data structure will be poor from a design, planning, and taxonomy perspective. Moreover, the names of the fields created using this technique will be strange because they are a kind of hash code of four characters based on the description provided by the end user for the dynamically created field. Thus, rather than relying on these tools and facilities, the better approach for developing and designing solutions is to plan, design, and deploy fields as site columns within content types.

Views

In addition to lists and columns, you can create one or more custom views for a list. In fact, every list has at least one default view that renders the fields of each item, using predefined ordering and filtering criteria. Any user with the proper permissions can create personal views of a list, and those with sufficient permissions can create a new, shared view for the target list. For example, imagine that the Products list discussed in the preceding section is ready to use, containing custom fields such as ProductID, Description, and Price. Figure 2-6 shows the default view for this list.

- **Totals** Establish total rows selectively on each visible column.
- **Style** Select a graphical rendering style for the list view.
- **Folders** Select whether to view items by browsing through folders, or all at once with a folder flat view.
- **Item Limit** Define a limit to the amount of data to return. This is useful when working with very large lists.
- **Mobile** Configure settings to better render the view on a mobile device.

In the example list of Products, you could plan to order products based on their price, listed from least to most expensive. Figure 2-8 shows the custom view output. Custom views are useful for browsing and managing data stored in large custom lists of items, but they are not a security measure by any means. In fact, content is still visible to anyone who has at least read access to the source list, even if you hide a column from a view.

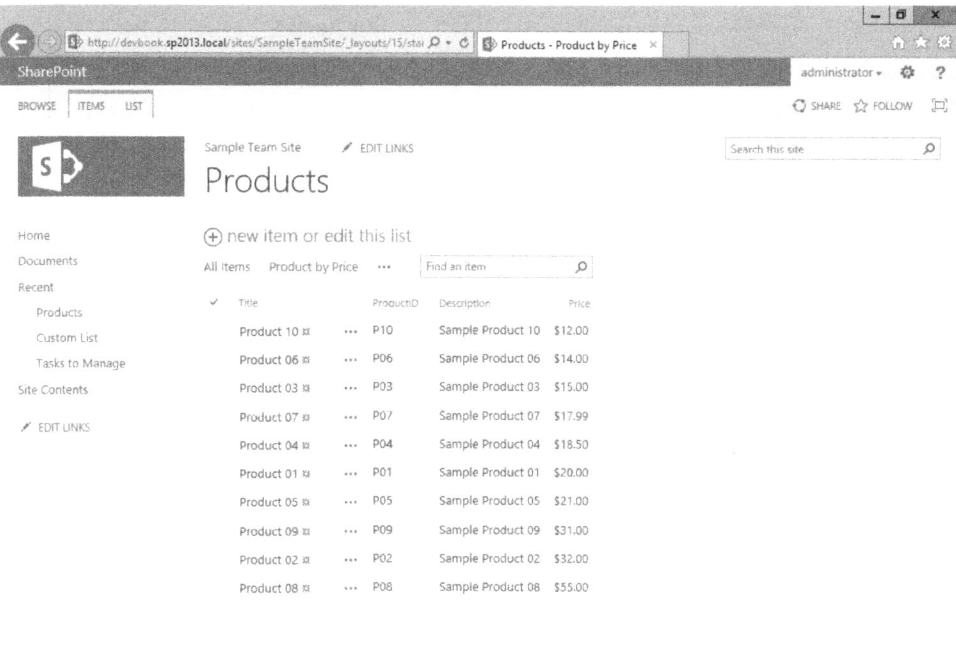

FIGURE 2-8 The output of a custom view defined for the Products list.

Creating a document library

A *document library* is a particular kind of list that is designed to host files (for instance, documents) instead of generic items. Each file corresponds to a single list item, which can also have a rich set of metadata fields to make it more meaningful. To create a document library, simply select the Document Library list template on the Add an App page, shown in Figure 2-1.

Suppose that you want to create a list of offers, which includes some custom metadata for each offer file, such as Protocol Number, Target Customer, and Offer Date Time. Begin by clicking the Settings menu, and then click the Add An App command to create the library. Lastly, select the Document Library app template.

When adding a new document library, you can choose to provide some advanced information, like a description, whether the contents of the library will be versioned using the SharePoint version control system, and a document template that can define the default template to use when creating new documents in the library.

After you create the library, you can access it through a UI that is basically the same as the one you used to manage lists of simple items. A document library, however, has some additional features and commands. For example, the Files ribbon tab (which replaces the Items tab) contains commands specifically tailored for managing files and documents. Instead of a List tab to manage the list, here you have the Library ribbon tab, shown in Figure 2-9.

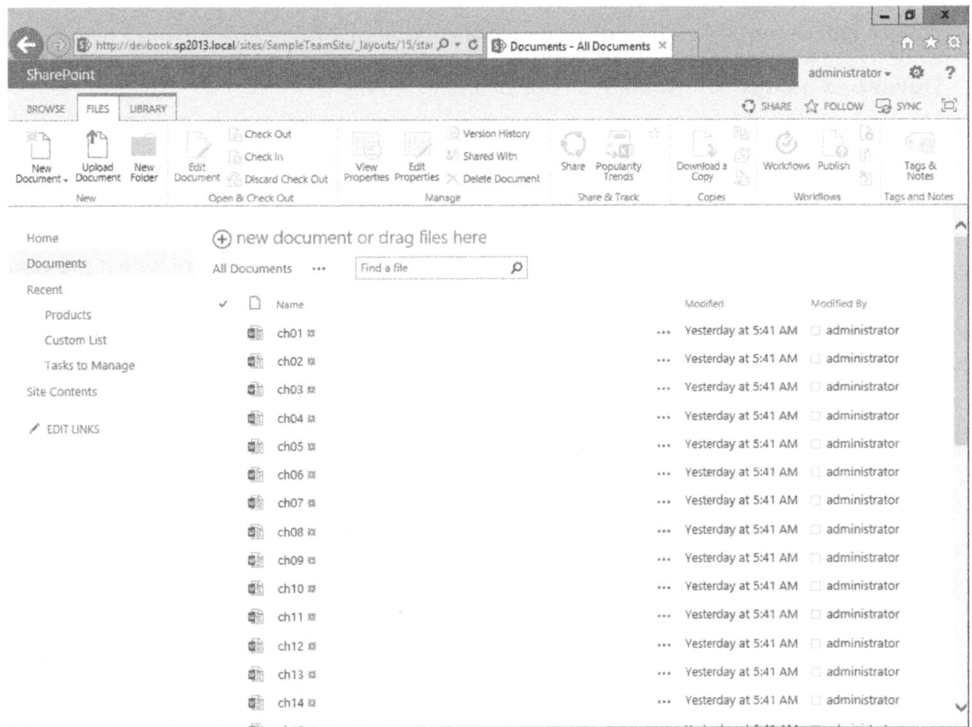

FIGURE 2-9 The Files ribbon tab of a document library.

The following are some of the most important commands available on the Files tab:

- **New Document** Creates a new document, starting from a document template.
- **Upload Document** Uploads a single document or a set of documents.
- **New Folder** Creates a new folder for organizing and navigating documents.

- **Edit Document** Opens a selected document using its corresponding editing program. For example, if you have selected a DOCX file, this command opens the file in Microsoft Word.
- **Check Out** Locks others out of the document so that you can have exclusive access to the file in read and write mode.
- **Check In** Releases the exclusive lock on the file, confirming any changes and creating a new version of the file (if file versioning is enabled).
- **Discard Check Out** Releases the exclusive lock on the file, discarding any changes.
- **View Properties** Shows the metadata properties of a selected file.
- **Edit Properties** Edits the metadata properties of a selected file.
- **Shared With** Shows the people with which you shared the current document.
- **Share** Allows you to share the current document with other people.
- **Delete Document** Deletes one or more selected files.
- **Download a Copy** Downloads a copy of a selected file.
- **Send To** Sends the selected file to a specific destination.

When working with a document library, you can configure settings and create custom columns and custom views, just as you can with a standard list. Plus, in a document library, you can configure a document template for creating any new documents. To configure this feature, select the Library Settings command on the Library ribbon tab. The Document Library Settings page appears. Select the Advanced Settings menu item to open a page on which you can configure a number of interesting parameters (see Figure 2-10). Some of these parameters are the same as the common lists; others are specific for document libraries. The following are the specific advanced settings for document libraries:

- **Document Template** This allows you to specify the relative URL of a document that will be used as the template for all new files created in the document library.
- **Opening Documents in the Browser** Here, you can define how SharePoint behaves when opening browser-enabled documents—that is, documents that can be opened within the browser. You can choose between Open In The Client Application, to open the file on the client side, within the specific client application; Open In The Browser, to open the file in the browser; and Use The Server Default, which is set by the farm administrators.
- **Custom Send to Destination** Use this to add a custom target to the Send To menu.
- **Search** This allows you to choose whether or not the contents of the current library will be available as results of queries to the search engine.
- **Site Assets Library** This determines if this library will be the default assets library for storing images, videos, and other files when users upload contents to their blogs or wiki pages.

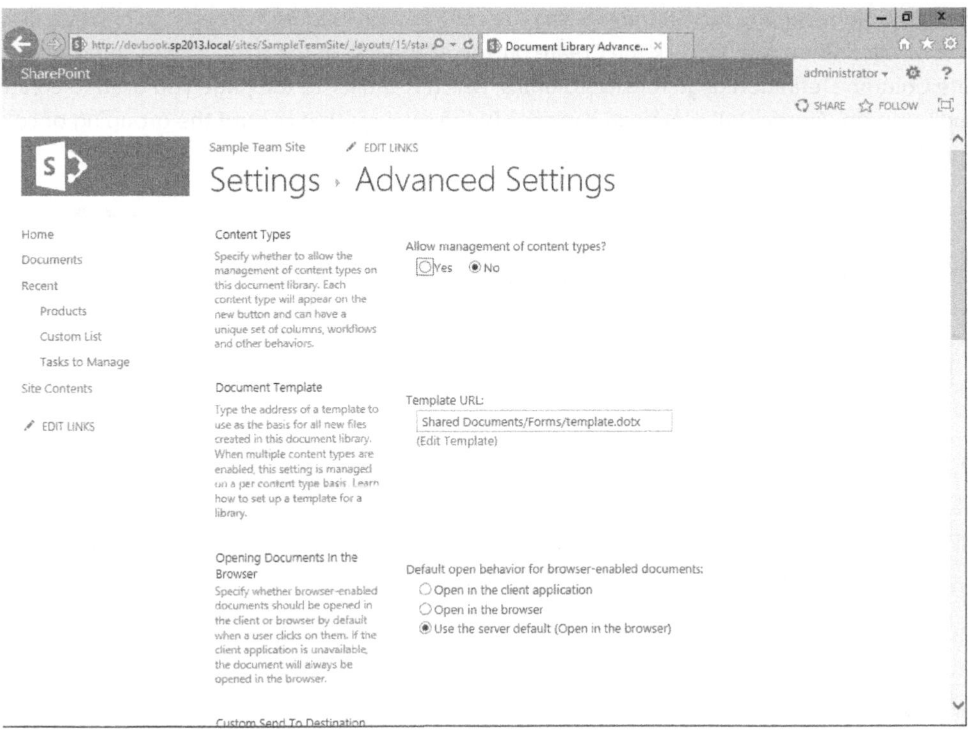

FIGURE 2-10 The Advanced Settings page for a document library.

Site columns

In the previous sections, you defined custom lists and columns by simply configuring them at the list level. In some situations, however, you need to define the same column type in multiple list instances. Wouldn't it be great to define the concept once, and then use it in many libraries? SharePoint site columns make sharing a metadata definition across multiple lists and libraries easy. A *site column* is the formal definition of a field type (a metadata type) shared at the website level. Site column definitions are hierarchical. In fact, you can define a site column in the root site of a site collection and use it in all the sites of the collection. Having a unique concept for describing metadata simplifies defining search queries and improves the quality of search results. For example, suppose you use a site column to define a protocol number that is shared across many document libraries. You could then define a query to retrieve all documents that have a protocol number field containing a value within a specified range, regardless of the library in which they are stored. A list of similar examples could be very long.

To define a new site column, browse to the Site Settings page through the Settings menu (see Figure 2-11). Under the Web Designer Galleries group, you will find a menu item named Site Columns, which brings you to the page on which you manage existing site columns or create new ones.

The Site Columns page lists all the existing site columns, divided into groups. To create a new site column definition, simply click the Create button at the top of the page. Doing so takes you to the Site Column Definition page for site columns, which is similar to the page you used to create a list-level column (Figure 2-4). Here you can specify the settings that control the grouping of columns, making it easier to retrieve them on the Gallery page.

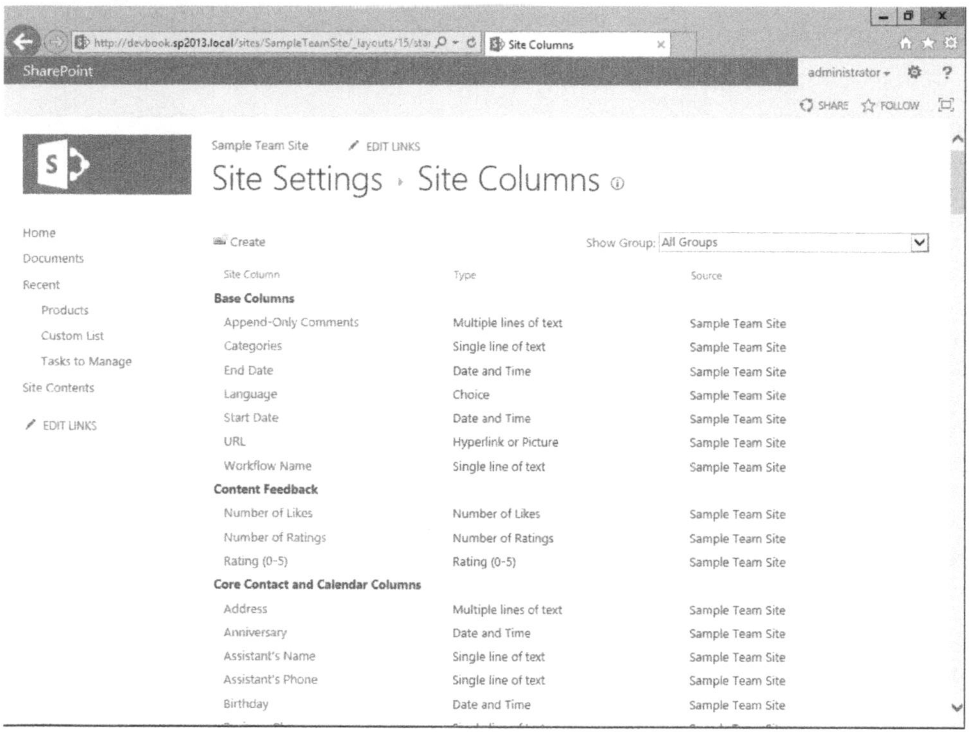

FIGURE 2-11 The Site Settings page for a site collection.

After you define a site column, you can reference it in any list or library by selecting the Add From Existing Site Columns command (Figure 2-3) on the List Settings page. You can also use a site column to define a custom content type, as you will see in the next section.

Content types

A *content type* is a formal definition of a data template or item template, a model of the data you intend to store in a particular list or document. Each time you create a new item in a list or a new document in a library, you are creating an instance of a content type. In addition, every list and library has one default content type under its cover. For example, if you create a list of type Contacts, and you add a new item, this item will be made of a set of columns that are defined in the *Contact* content type, which is a default content type provided by SharePoint. If you create a list of type document library, as you did in the previous section, by default, the library will host items with a content type of *Document*.

A content type is based on a set of site column references, together with some other optional information related to forms, rendering templates, a specific document template (for document items only), and custom XML configuration.

As you will see in more detail in Chapter 3, content types are hierarchical and exploit an inheritance pattern. At the root, there is a *System* content type, which is essentially a low-level base class for every other content type. Figure 2-12 depicts the hierarchical inheritance tree for native content types. As you can, see the *System* content type is inherited by the *Item* content type, which acts as the base class, either directly or indirectly, for every other content type. For example, the *Contact* content type you used in the list of contacts inherits from *Item*, as does the *Document* content type. The *Picture* content type, which is the default content type for a picture library, inherits from the *Document* content type.

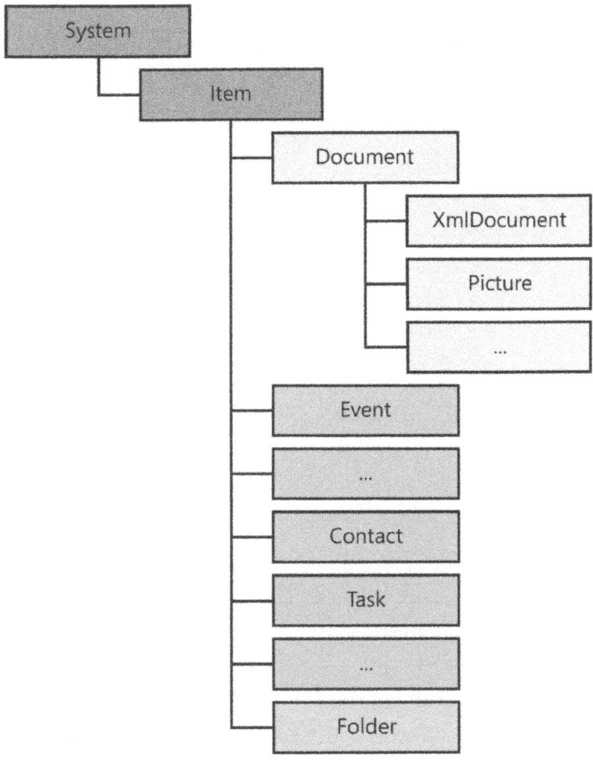

FIGURE 2-12 The inheritance hierarchy of content types in SharePoint.

Depending on the edition of SharePoint you are using and on the configuration of your farm, content types can also be shared across multiple site collections, web applications, or farms via the Content Type Hub service, which is available through the Managed Metadata service and part of the SharePoint Server 2013 Standard edition.

You can manage existing content types or define custom content types by clicking the Site Content Types command found under the Web Designer Galleries group of the Site Settings page. To create a new content type, click the Create button at the top of the page. A new page appears, asking you to supply a few settings, such as the name, description, logical group, and the parent content type of your new content type. Immediately after creating the new content type, you will be redirected to the page for content type management, shown in Figure 2-13. Here, you can configure all the content type settings, including general information about the content type, specifying a custom document template (in the event of a content type inheriting from Document), managing workflows, information management policies, and many other options. You can also configure a content type that uses a specific set of site columns. Doing this lets you share the same field types across multiple content types.

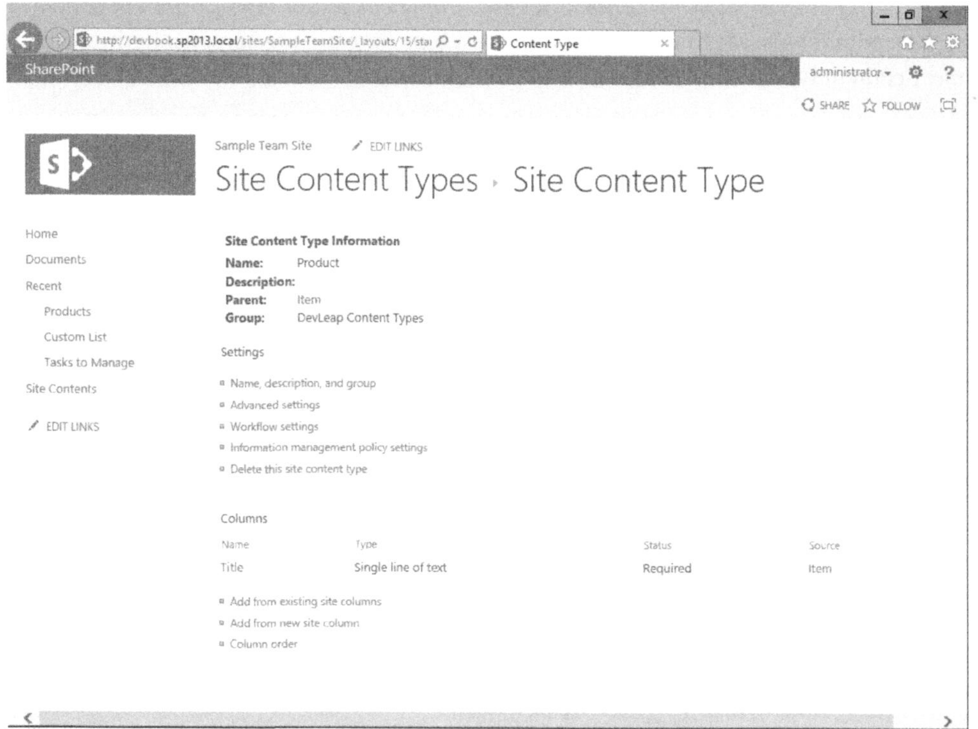

FIGURE 2-13 The page for managing a content type configuration.

After defining one or more custom content types, you can map them to lists or libraries using the list or library Advanced Settings page. Thus, the following is the process to design content in a SharePoint site:

1. Define the site columns.
2. Create the content types that will use those columns.
3. Create the lists or libraries that use the content types.

By working in this sequence, you will end up with a common set of data items (content types) that share a common set of data fields (site columns), stored in custom data repositories (lists and libraries). Be careful that you should never change or edit the out-of-the-box content types. In case of need, you should create custom content types, inheriting from ones that already exist, and customize them.

Sites

Sites are another kind of data repository that you can define. Generally, you can use a *site* as a place to hold collections of lists and libraries that are shared by the same target audience or that share the same functional meaning. For example, you could have a website for each department of your company (Sales, Human Resources, Information Technology, and so on). Sites are stored in site collections, so before you can create a new site, you first need to have a site collection.

As you may remember, each site collection contains one root site, by default. To create another site, invoke the New Subsite command on the Site Contents page. To access the Site Contents page, you can click the Settings menu, represented by a gear in the top-right corner of the webpage area, and then click the Site Contents menu item. You will be prompted to select from a wide list of site templates; the following are some of the most interesting choices:

- **Team Site** A site for a team of people who want to share documents, a calendar, announcements, and tasks.
- **Blank Site** A blank site ready for customization.
- **Blog** A site for managing a blog, which can accept comments, ratings, and so forth.
- **Project Site** A site for managing and collaborating on a project.
- **Community Site** A place where community members discuss topics of common interest.
- **Visio Process Repository** A site for teams to quickly view, share, and store Visio process diagrams.
- **Document Center** A site to centrally manage documents in an enterprise-level company.
- **Records Center** A site to manage records of documents in an enterprise-level company. It provides configurable routing tables to direct files to specific locations based on custom company rules.
- **Business Intelligence Center** A site for presenting business intelligence content in SharePoint.
- **Enterprise Search Center** A site that supports searching for documents or people in an enterprise-level company.
- **Basic Search Center** A site that delivers a basic search experience.

Although these are the most common website templates, you might see others, depending on which SharePoint edition you have installed.

Summary

This chapter discussed the fundamental parts of SharePoint data. You saw how to create lists of items, site columns, content types, and sites. By capitalizing on the information discussed in this chapter, you will be able to create simple data management solutions using SharePoint 2013 as your data repository. However, as you further read this book, you will see why you should not use SharePoint as an RDBMS surrogate; instead, SharePoint is an appropriate *companion* for a relational database. In Chapter 3, you will learn how to provision data structures using code and markup, rather than simply designing them through the web browser interface as you did in this chapter.

PART II

Developing SharePoint Solutions

CHAPTER 3

Data provisioning

The previous chapters showed you how many Microsoft SharePoint solutions rely on lists of items that contain data, such as contacts, files, and so on. When you develop a SharePoint solution, therefore, one of your main tasks is to provision data structures for these lists of items. In fact, whenever you need to develop a reusable and maintainable solution that will reside on many different site collections and has many different customers, you should formally define the data structures that you will use. Simply designing them through the SharePoint visual design interface from a web browser might seem easy (any end user can do it), but in the long run it will become a source of confusion. Formal definitions can be reused many times in multiple sites and can be versioned. Meanwhile, data structure definitions made manually through the visual design interface are difficult to reuse and can lead to duplication of definitions in multiple sites. Also, when you create SharePoint apps hosted on SharePoint, you can use the data model of lists and items provided by SharePoint for storing data and content related to your apps.

Note Within the context of this book, the term *data structure* refers to the formal definitions of custom list definitions, content types, and site columns. Such formal definitions help to ensure data consistency across lists and sites.

This chapter explores the rules for custom lists and the tools that SharePoint 2013 provides to create them. To learn how these tools behave in a real-world scenario, you will investigate how to define a custom list of contacts that can use custom forms and can be browsed through specific list views. The list in this case study will be based on two content types: *Customer* and *Supplier.*

Site columns

The first and main step in provisioning a custom data structure is to define site columns. A site column describes a reusable data type model that you can use in many different content types and list definitions, across multiple SharePoint sites. Unless you have never used SharePoint at all, you will have already defined many site columns using a web browser, within the appropriate section of the Site Settings page. To create a more flexible and reusable solution, you can also define a site column using some XML code, which in SharePoint is called a *feature element.*

More Info For further details about features and feature elements, read Chapter 11, "Developing Web Parts."

Listing 3-1 shows a very simple site column definition for a *Text* column that contains the company name of the sample contact.

LISTING 3-1 A simple site column defined in a feature element

```
<?xml version="1.0" encoding="utf-8"?>
<Elements xmlns="http://schemas.microsoft.com/sharepoint/">
  <Field
    ID="{A8F24550-55CD-4d34-A015-811954C6CE24}"
    Name="DevLeapCompanyName"
    StaticName="DevLeapCompanyName"
    DisplayName="Company Name"
    Type="Text"
    Group="DevLeap Columns" />
</Elements>
```

Aside from the *Elements* tag itself, which is simply a container element, the interesting part of the preceding column definition is the *Field* element. The most important feature of this element is the *ID* attribute, which is a globally unique identifier (GUID) that uniquely identifies the site column. You can use the *ID* attribute to reference this specific site column everywhere. Notice that you can create unique GUIDs by using the GUIDGEN tool provided with Microsoft Visual Studio 2012.

Listing 3-1 declares that the Company Name column will have an internal *Name* attribute of DevLeapCompanyName. *Name* is a required attribute, and like the *ID* attribute, it should also be unique, because it provides an alternative way to exclusively reference the column from code. In general, this example uses the developer's company name value as a prefix to better ensure the uniqueness of this name. The *Name* attribute value cannot contain spaces or any characters other than numbers (0 through 9) and letters (*a* through *z* and *A* through *Z*). Any other characters will be converted into the corresponding hexadecimal representation. For example, if you want to name a field Company Name, you must define it as *Company_x0020_Name*. If you want to name a field Revenue %, you must define it as *Revenue_x0020__x0025_*. The last thing to keep in mind is that the *Name* attribute cannot be longer than 32 characters.

The preceding site column definition also defines the optional *StaticName* attribute, which is another way of defining the internal name. The *StaticName* can be useful for referencing your field in custom code, regardless of the encoding used in the Name field. Finally, the site column definition defines the field's *DisplayName* attribute, whose value is the title that users will see in their browsers. This last attribute can take advantage of the multilanguage support provided by Microsoft .NET in general, so declaring its value as a resource string reference ("*$Resources:<Assembly_Name>,<Resource_Name>;*") instead of an explicit value will result in a multilanguage value.

Why do you need three attributes to define field name types?

At first, using three attributes to define three kinds of names for a single field may seem redundant and overly complex, but each attribute serves a purpose. Consider this: the XML schema that we use as developers is also used internally by SharePoint to represent a site column. When you define a column using the web browser interface, SharePoint automatically determines the internal name (for instance, *Name* and *StaticName*) based on the name (which becomes the *display name*) that you give it, automatically converting any nonalphanumeric characters to their corresponding hexadecimal representations, and then trimming the resulting string to 32 characters for the *Name* attribute, leaving the *StaticName* attribute value as long as needed. If a site column with the same *Name* already exists, SharePoint appends a number to the name, using a zero-based index.

If you later change the *DisplayName* of the field, SharePoint will keep both the *StaticName* and the *Name* unchanged. That scheme gives your site column three different values for the three attributes: the *DisplayName*; the *StaticName*, which is simply the original *DisplayName* with hexadecimal conversion of nonalphanumeric characters; and the *Name*, with hexadecimal conversion of nonalphanumeric characters trimmed to 32 characters.

Lastly, using the SharePoint Server Object Model (for further details, see Chapter 5, "Server Object Model"), you can change the *StaticName*, but you cannot change the internal *Name* value. Therefore, when you have to define site columns using a feature element, the best practice is to assign the same value to the *Name* and to the *StaticName* (avoiding nonalphanumeric characters) and to provide a descriptive value for the *DisplayName* attribute.

The *Type* attribute is mandatory for site column definitions. It defines the data type assigned to the field. This *Type* attribute value can be one of a predefined set of SharePoint field types, or it can be a custom field type that you have defined and deployed. Table 3-1 presents some of the main field types provided by SharePoint.

More Info For a complete list of field types, refer to the online product reference at *http://msdn.microsoft.com/en-us/library/ms437580(v=office.15).aspx.*

TABLE 3-1 Common predefined field types

Field type name	Description
Boolean	Represents a *Boolean* value (*TRUE* or *FALSE*), stored as a *bit* in Microsoft SQL Server and accessible as an *SPFieldBoolean* object through the Server Object Model.
Choice	Allows the user to select a single value from a predefined set of values. The XML schema of the *Field* element must declare the values (for further details, see Listing 3-2). It is stored as an *nvarchar* in SQL Server, and is accessible as an *SPFieldChoice* object through the Server Object Model.
MultiChoice	Allows the user to select multiple values from a predefined set of values. The XML schema of the Field element has to declare the values. It is stored as an *ntext* in SQL Server, and is accessible as an *SPFieldMultiChoice* object through the Server Object Model.
Currency	Defines a currency value. *Currency* is bound to a specific locale, using an *LCID* attribute. It can have constraints using *Min, Max,* and *Decimals* attributes. It is stored as a *float* in SQL Server and is accessible as an *SPFieldCurrency* object through the Server Object Model.
DateTime	Saves a date and time value. *DateTime* is stored as a *datetime* in SQL Server, and is accessible as an *SPFieldDateTime* object through the Server Object Model.
Lookup and *LookupMulti*	Behave almost the same as *Choice* and *MultiChoice*; however, the set of values to choose from is taken from another list of items within the same site. These field types are stored as *int types* in SQL Server, and are accessible as *SPFieldLookup* objects through the Server Object Model.
Note	Stores multiple lines of text. *Note* is stored as an *ntext* in SQL Server, and is accessible as an *SPFieldMultiLineText* object through the Server Object Model.
Number	Defines a floating-point number. *Number* can have constraints using *Decimals, Div, Max, Min, Mult,* and *Percentage*. It is stored as a *float* in SQL Server and is accessible as an *SPFieldNumber* object through the Server Object Model.
Text	Describes a single line of text of a configurable maximum length. *Text* is stored as an *nvarchar* in SQL Server, and is accessible as an *SPFieldText* object through the Server Object Model.
URL	Defines a URL with a specific *LinkType* (*Hyperlink* or *Image*). *URL* is stored as an *nvarchar* in SQL Server and is accessible as an *SPFieldUrl* object through the Server Object Model.
User and *UserMulti*	Describe a lookup for a single user or a set of users. These are stored as an *int types* in SQL Server, and are accessible as *SPFieldUser* objects through the Server Object Model.

The last attribute defined in the site column example is the *Group* attribute, which simply defines a group membership to make it easier to find custom fields through the web browser administrative interface. *Group* is an optional attribute, but it is better that you define it whenever you create a custom site column, in order to organize your columns in personalized custom groups.

Although it's not an exhaustive keyword reference, Table 3-2 shows some of the many other interesting attributes that you can use when defining custom site columns. For a complete reference of the available attributes, you can read the following page on MSDN: *http://msdn.microsoft.com/en-us/library/aa979575.aspx.*

TABLE 3-2 Interesting optional *Boolean* attributes available for the *Field* element

Field attribute	Description
Hidden	Can assume a value of *TRUE* or *FALSE*. When *TRUE*, the field will be completely hidden from the UI and will be accessible only through code, using the Object Model.
ReadOnly	Can assume a value of *TRUE* or *FALSE*. When *TRUE*, the field will not be displayed in *new* and edit forms, but can be included in read-only data views. It will remain accessible using the object model.
Required	Can assume a value of *TRUE* or *FALSE*. Its name implies its role.
RichText	Can assume a value of *TRUE* or *FALSE*. It determines whether a text field will accept rich text formatting.
ShowInDisplayForm	Can assume a value of *TRUE* or *FALSE*. When *FALSE*, the field will not be displayed in the display form of the item containing the field.
ShowInEditForm	Can assume a value of *TRUE* or *FALSE*. When *FALSE*, the field will not be displayed in the editing form of the item containing the field.
ShowInNewForm	Can assume a value of *TRUE* or *FALSE*. If it is *FALSE*, the field will not be displayed in the form to add a new item containing the field.

While Listing 3-1 introduced a basic definition, Listing 3-2 adds another level of complexity by declaring a Choice field that will be used to select the contact's country affiliation.

LISTING 3-2 A Choice site column defined in a feature element

```
<?xml version="1.0" encoding="utf-8"?>
<Elements xmlns="http://schemas.microsoft.com/sharepoint/">
  <Field
    ID="{149BF9A1-5BBB-468d-AA35-91ACEB054E3B}"
    Name="DevLeapCountry"
    StaticName="DevLeapCountry"
    DisplayName="Country"
    Type="Choice"
    Group="DevLeap Columns"
    Sortable="TRUE">
      <Default>Italy</Default>
      <CHOICES>
        <CHOICE>Italy</CHOICE>
        <CHOICE>USA</CHOICE>
        <CHOICE>Germany</CHOICE>
        <CHOICE>France</CHOICE>
      </CHOICES>
  </Field>
</Elements>
```

This example shows how you can define a set of available values for a *Choice* field. Note that the list defines a *Default* element.

Another interesting task that you can accomplish when defining a site column is to declare a custom validation rule for its content. To do that, you simply define a *Validation* element as a child of the *Field* definition. The *Validation* element can have a *Message* attribute, which defines an error message to display to end users when validation fails, and a *Script* attribute, which defines a JavaScript rule that performs the validation. Alternatively, you can define a rule using the *Formulas* syntax of SharePoint, putting the rule inside the *Validation* element.

More Info For further details on calculated fields and formulas in SharePoint, refer to the "Calculated Field Formulas" MSDN page, at http://msdn.microsoft.com/en-us/library/bb862071.aspx.

Content types

A content type schema defines a model for a specific SharePoint complex data type, and is based on a set of site column references, together with some other optional information related to forms, rendering templates, a specific document template (only in the case of document items), and custom XML configuration.

Chapter 2, "SharePoint data fundamentals," showed how SharePoint uses a hierarchical structure for defining content types, which consists of a base content type named *System* with a single child named *Item*. SharePoint then applies an inheritance paradigm (similar to object-oriented class inheritance) to define each content type descendant of *Item*. Figure 3-1 shows an excerpt of the hierarchical inheritance tree for native content types. As a consequence of this behavior, you must define inheritance information for each new content type that you declare. For more details, read the "Content type IDs" section later in the chapter.

Listing 3-3 provides an example of the *Contact* content type, defined by referencing a set of site columns.

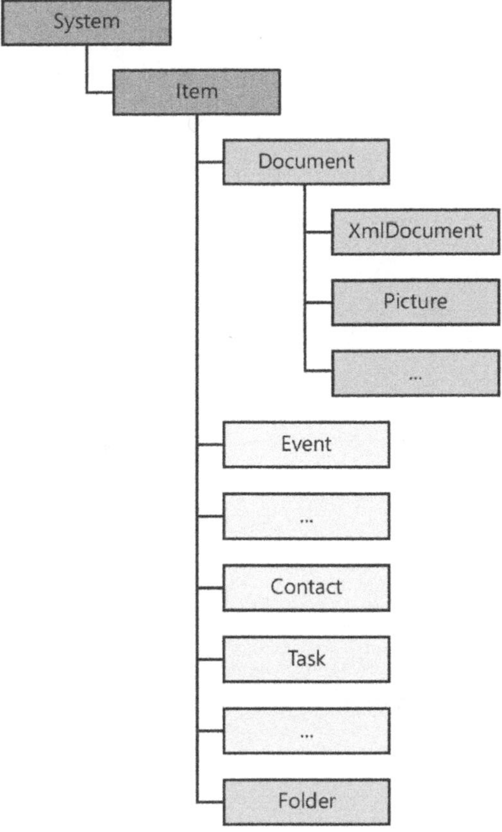

FIGURE 3-1 The content types inheritance hierarchy in SharePoint.

LISTING 3-3 A simple content type defined in a feature element, together with its site columns

```
<?xml version="1.0" encoding="utf-8"?>
<Elements xmlns="http://schemas.microsoft.com/sharepoint/">
  <!-- Site Columns used by the Content Type -->
  <Field
    ID="{C7792AD6-F2F3-4f2d-A7E5-75D5A8206FD9}"
    Name="DevLeapContactID"
    StaticName="DevLeapContactID"
    DisplayName="Contact ID"
    Type="Text"
    Group="DevLeap Columns"
    Sortable="TRUE" />
```

```xml
  <Field
    ID="{A8F24550-55CD-4d34-A015-811954C6CE24}"
    Name="DevLeapCompanyName"
    StaticName="DevLeapCompanyName"
    DisplayName="Company Name"
    Type="Text"
    Group="DevLeap Columns"
    Sortable="TRUE" />
  <Field
    ID="{149BF9A1-5BBB-468d-AA35-91ACEB054E3B}"
    Name="DevLeapCountry"
    StaticName="DevLeapCountry"
    DisplayName="Country"
    Type="Choice"
    Group="DevLeap Columns"
    Sortable="TRUE">
      <Default>Italy</Default>
      <CHOICES>
        <CHOICE>Italy</CHOICE>
        <CHOICE>USA</CHOICE>
        <CHOICE>Germany</CHOICE>
        <CHOICE>France</CHOICE>
      </CHOICES>
  </Field>
  <!-- Parent ContentType: Item (0x01) -->
  <ContentType ID="0x0100A60F69C4B1304FBDA6C4B4A25939979F"
               Name="DevLeapContact"
               Group="DevLeap Content Types"
               Description="Base Contact of DevLeap"
               Inherits="TRUE"
               Version="0">
    <FieldRefs>
      <FieldRef
        ID="{fa564e0f-0c70-4ab9-b863-0177e6ddd247}"
        Name="Title"
        DisplayName="Full name" />
      <FieldRef
        ID="{C7792AD6-F2F3-4f2d-A7E5-75D5A8206FD9}"
        Name="DevLeapContactID"
        DisplayName="Contact ID"
        Required="TRUE" />
      <FieldRef
        ID="{A8F24550-55CD-4d34-A015-811954C6CE24}"
        Name="DevLeapCompanyName"
        DisplayName="Company Name" />
      <FieldRef
        ID="{149BF9A1-5BBB-468d-AA35-91ACEB054E3B}"
        Name="DevLeapCountry"
        DisplayName="Country" />
    </FieldRefs>
  </ContentType>
</Elements>
```

This feature element example contains a *ContentType* element, which defines some descriptive information, such as the *Name*, *Group*, and *Description*. The *ContentType* element also defines a *Version* attribute, which indeed is used for managing versioning, as its name implies, but is still reserved by Microsoft for future use. Last, but most important, is the *ID* attribute, which defines the unique identifier for this content type in the site collection where it is defined. Inside the *ContentType* element is a *FieldRefs* element, which is the parent of a list of *FieldRef* or *RemoveFieldRef* elements. Each element in this list references a specific site column to be added or removed from this content type. You might notice that this example references all the site columns defined earlier in the feature element file. In fact, unless you are defining site columns for use in multiple content types, it's common to define the referenced site columns within the same feature element file—just before the content type that will use them.

Listing 3-3 also references a site column with the name Title and the ID *{fa564e0f-0c70-4ab9-b863-0177e6ddd247}*. This is the SharePoint native site column that defines the Title field for each SharePoint item. In the content type example, we changed the *DisplayName* value from *Title*, which still retains its internal name, to *Full name*, which will be the displayed name for this content type. By default, the *Title* field is also used by SharePoint to render the Edit Control Block menu, which allows you to display, edit, and manage a list item from the list UI.

Content type IDs

The *ID* attribute of a content type is not a simple GUID, as it was with the site columns definition; instead, it's a more complex value that describes the hierarchical inheritance of the type. In fact, every content type ID is composed of the *ID* of its hierarchical parent content type, followed by a hexadecimal value that's unique to the current content type. You could say that a content type ID defines its genealogy. This logic is recursive, starting with the *System* content type and extending all the way down to the current content type. Table 3-3 shows an excerpt of the base hierarchy of SharePoint content type IDs.

TABLE 3-3 An excerpt of the base hierarchy of SharePoint content type IDs

Content type	ID
System	*0x*
Item	*0x01*
Document	*0x0101*
XmlDocument	*0x010101*
Picture	*0x010102*
Event	*0x0102*
...	
Contact	*0x0106*
Task	*0x0108*
...	
Folder	*0x0120*

Table 3-3 demonstrates that the root content type is *System*, which is a special hidden content type with an *ID* value of *0x*. The *Item* content type is the only child of *System* and has an *ID* value of *0x01* (the *System ID* + *01*). The *Document* content type, which is a child of *Item*, has an *ID* value of *0x0101* (the *Item ID* + *01*), while its sibling *Event* has an *ID* of *0x0102* (the *Item ID* + *02*).

In general, the rule used to define content type IDs states that you can build an ID using either of two techniques:

- Parent content type ID + two hexadecimal values (cannot be *00*)
- Parent content type ID + *00* + hexadecimal GUID

Microsoft generally uses the first technique to define base content type IDs. Third parties, such as vendors or ISVs, typically use the latter technique to define custom content type IDs. If you want to define a hierarchy of custom content types of your own, follow these steps:

1. Identify the base content type from which you want to inherit.
2. Add 00 at the end of the base content type ID.
3. Add a hexadecimal GUID just after the 00.
4. Append two hexadecimal values to declare every specific child of your content type.

As a concrete example, suppose that you want to define a custom content type inherited from the *Document* base content type. You would start with *0x0101*, which is the *Document ID*, append *00* to it, and then append a hexadecimal GUID, making your *ID* something like *0x010100BDD3EC87EA65463AB9FAA5337907A3ED*.

If you wanted to use your custom content type as a base for some other inherited content types, you would append *01*, *02*, and so on for each child content type, as in the following:

- **Base ID** *0x010100BDD3EC87EA65463AB9FAA5337907A3ED*
- **Child 1** *0x010100BDD3EC87EA65463AB9FAA5337907A3ED01*
- **Child 2** *0x010100BDD3EC87EA65463AB9FAA5337907A3ED02*

More Info Content type IDs have a maximum length of 512 bytes. Because every two hexadecimal characters correspond to a single byte, a content type ID has a maximum length of 1,024 characters.

With that in mind, we can go back to the example custom *Contact* content type. First, you need to choose the base content type from which you want to inherit. For example purposes, assume that you decide to use the generic base *Item* as the parent content type. That means the custom content type ID will start with *0x01*, followed by *00* and then a hexadecimal GUID. The end result is the same as the ID highlighted in bold in Listing 3-3:

```
ID="0x0100A60F69C4B1304FBDA6C4B4A25939979F"
```

The goal of the case study is to define a custom list that is based on a couple of content types (*Customer* and *Supplier*) inherited from this base *Contact* content type. Listing 3-4 shows the definitions of the *Customer* and *Supplier* content types.

LISTING 3-4 *Customer* and *Supplier* content type definitions

```
<?xml version="1.0" encoding="utf-8"?>
<Elements xmlns="http://schemas.microsoft.com/sharepoint/">
  <Field
      ID="{AC689935-8E8B-485e-A45E-FF5A338DD92F}"
      Name="DevLeapCustomerLevel"
      StaticName="DevLeapCustomerLevel"
      DisplayName="Customer Level"
      Type="Choice"
      Group="DevLeap Columns">
    <Default>Level C</Default>
    <CHOICES>
      <CHOICE>Level A</CHOICE>
      <CHOICE>Level B</CHOICE>
      <CHOICE>Level C</CHOICE>
    </CHOICES>
  </Field>
  <Field
      ID="{A73DE518-B9B9-4e8d-9D94-6099B4603997}"
      Name="DevLeapSupplierAccount"
      StaticName="DevLeapSupplierAccount"
      DisplayName="Supplier Account"
      Type="User"
      Group="DevLeap Columns"
      Sortable="TRUE" />
  <ContentType ID="0x0100A60F69C4B1304FBDA6C4B4A25939979F01"
               Name="DevLeapCustomer"
               Group="DevLeap Content Types"
               Description="Customer of DevLeap"
               Version="0">
    <FieldRefs>
      <FieldRef
          ID="{AC689935-8E8B-485e-A45E-FF5A338DD92F}"
          Name="DevLeapCustomerLevel"
          Required="TRUE" />
    </FieldRefs>
  </ContentType>
  <ContentType ID="0x0100A60F69C4B1304FBDA6C4B4A25939979F02"
               Name="DevLeapSupplier"
               Group="DevLeap Content Types"
               Description="Supplier of DevLeap"
               Version="0">
    <FieldRefs>
      <FieldRef
          ID="{A73DE518-B9B9-4e8d-9D94-6099B4603997}"
          Name="DevLeapSupplierAccount"
          Required="TRUE" />
    </FieldRefs>
  </ContentType>
</Elements>
```

Both of these content types extend the base *Contact* content type; each adds a specific site column. The *Customer* content type adds a required field to define the *customer level* (*A*, *B*, or *C*) for each *Customer* instance, while the *Supplier* content type adds a field to reference a local *account*, which you can browse as a SharePoint user. You can see the inheritance hierarchy of these custom types in Figure 3-2, which shows a portion of the Site Content Type page of a site collection.

Site Content Type	Parent	Source
DevLeap Content Types		
DevLeapContact	Item	DevLeap Book Portal
DevLeapCustomer	DevLeapContact	DevLeap Book Portal
DevLeapInvoice	Document	DevLeap Book Portal
DevLeapSupplier	DevLeapContact	DevLeap Book Portal

FIGURE 3-2 The Site Content Type page of a site collection where the custom content types are provisioned.

Finally, consider that Visual Studio 2012 automatically calculates the content type IDs when you add a new content type to a SharePoint project. In fact, if you try to add a content type to a SharePoint project within Visual Studio 2012, you will be prompted with a one-step wizard, regardless of whether you are creating a Windows SharePoint Services Solution Package (WSP) or a SharePoint app. In the wizard's first and only step, you must choose the basic content type from which you would like your custom content type to inherit (Figure 3-3).

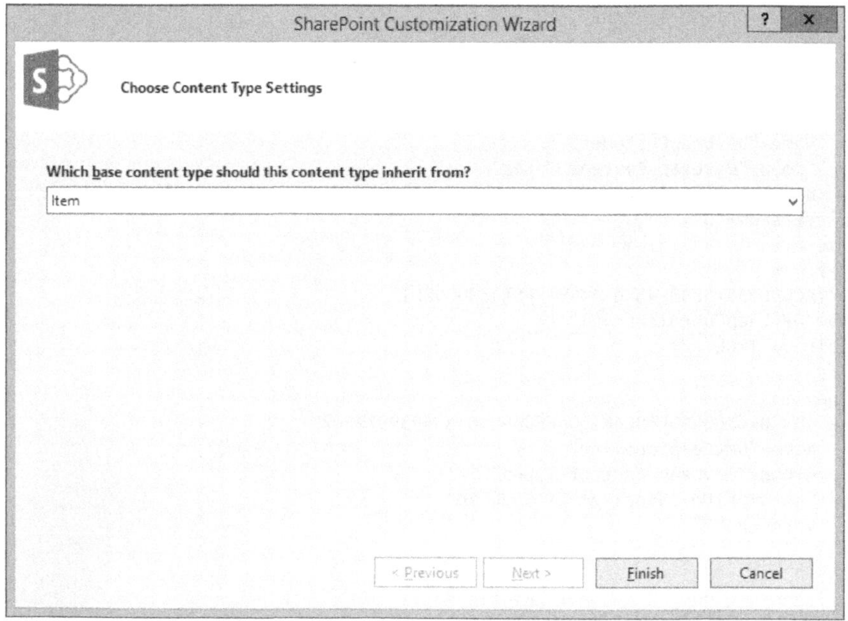

FIGURE 3-3 The wizard for creating a new content type.

After you make your choice and click finish to close the wizard, SharePoint displays a graphical designer useful to define the columns of the content type and its overall configuration. Figure 3-4 shows the two tabs available in the Content Type designer: Columns and Content Type.

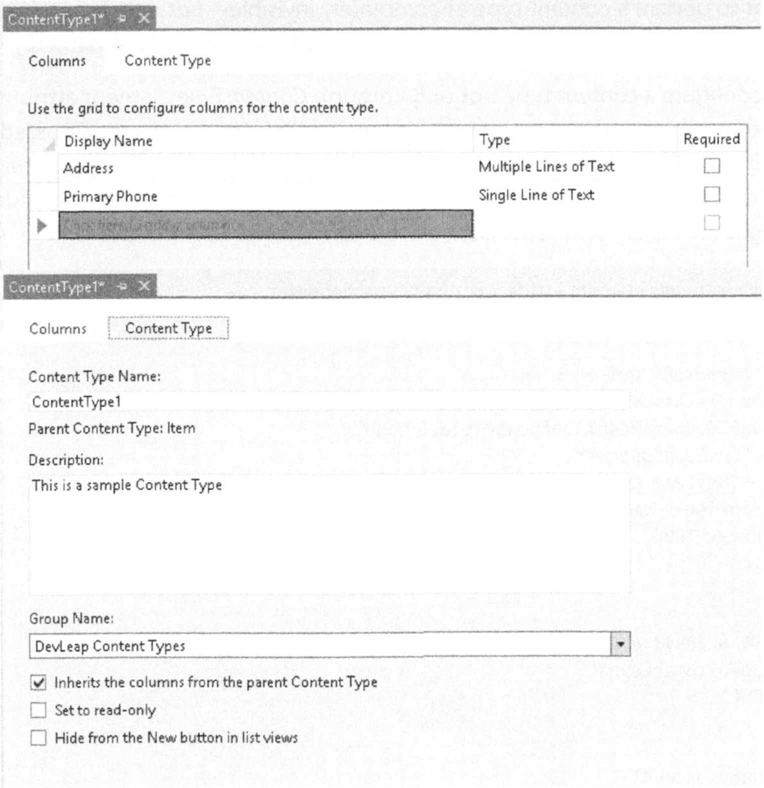

FIGURE 3-4 The two tabs available in the Content Type designer.

As you can see, the Columns tab is active. Here you can reference the site columns to use in the current content type. Note, however, that you can specify existing site columns only. The Content Type tab enables you to define the name, the description, and the group of the current content type. Lastly, through this second tab you can also determine whether the content type will inherit columns from its parent type or not, as well as if the current type will be read-only and/or hidden. Based on your settings, the designer creates an XML element manifest file that is similar to what you can code manually. Although this might seem like a worthwhile shortcut, it is somewhat limited. When you need a finer degree of flexibility in defining custom content types, manually creating or editing the XML file is a better solution.

More about content types

Sometimes you need a more restricted content type; in such cases, SharePoint offers several other interesting attributes to help you out. For example, the *ReadOnly* attribute makes the content type read-only when its value is set to *TRUE*. Likewise, when the *Sealed* attribute is set to *TRUE*, it seals a content type so that only a site collection administrator using the Server Object Model can unseal it for editing. Lastly, the *Hidden* attribute is useful for making a content type invisible so that contributors cannot create new items of this type in list views, but you will still have access to it through your custom code. If you want to declare a content type as completely invisible—not only for end users but also for site collection administrators—you can make it belong to a special group named *_Hidden*.

In addition, you can configure a content type not only through *ContentType* element attributes, but also by declaring some child elements. One of these is the *FieldRefs* child element discussed earlier in this chapter. Another useful element is *XmlDocuments*, with which you can define any kind of custom XML configuration to apply to the content type. SharePoint itself uses this element to declare custom controls and pages for the content type. Listing 3-5 shows how to use this element.

LISTING 3-5 Using the *XmlDocuments* element inside a content type definition

```
<?xml version="1.0" encoding="utf-8"?>
<Elements xmlns="http://schemas.microsoft.com/sharepoint/">
  <ContentType ID="0x0100a60f69c4b1304fbda6c4b4a25939979f01"
               Name="DevLeapCustomer"
               Group="DevLeap Content Types"
               Description="Customer of DevLeap"
               Inherits="TRUE"
               Version="0">
    <FieldRefs>
      <FieldRef
        ID="{AC689935-8E8B-485e-A45E-FF5A338DD92F}"
        Name="DevLeapCustomerLevel"
        Required="TRUE" />
    </FieldRefs>
    <XmlDocuments>
      <XmlDocument NamespaceURI=
       "http://schemas.microsoft.com/sharepoint/v3/contenttype/forms">
        <FormTemplates xmlns=
          "http://schemas.microsoft.com/sharepoint/v3/contenttype/forms">
          <Display>DevLeapCustomerDisplay</Display>
          <Edit>DevLeapCustomerEdit</Edit>
          <New>DevLeapCustomerNew</New>
        </FormTemplates>
      </XmlDocument>
    </XmlDocuments>
  </ContentType>
</Elements>
```

Listing 3-5 shows that the *XmlDocuments* element is just a container for one or more *XmlDocument* elements. Every *XmlDocument* element can have a *NamespaceURI* attribute that declares the scope of the custom configuration defined. Listing 3-5 declares a configuration that defines custom ASCX control files that are used for rendering display, edit, and add forms for instances of the current content type. The ASCX control files referenced should be deployed inside the CONTROLTEMPLATES special folder of SharePoint, through a farm-level (full-trust) solution. The content of each *XmlDocument* element derives from the referenced *NamespaceURI*. The only requirement is that the XML content must be valid against its declared XML schema.

When you consider that in a farm-level (full-trust) solution you can access any custom *XmlDocument* that you define while provisioning content types later through the Server Object Model, you can see that the model provides you with an extremely customizable environment.

Document content types

Content types inherited from the *Document* base content type (ID: *0x0101*) are a special case that you must analyze a bit more carefully than usual. In fact, every document has numerous specific configurations that it must handle. For instance, in the "Content types" section earlier in the chapter, you learned that a document can have a document template, a document information panel, or both.

Listing 3-6 shows the definition for a custom document content type that declares an *Invoice* document model.

LISTING 3-6 Defining the *Invoice* content type, inherited from the *Document* content type

```
<?xml version="1.0" encoding="utf-8"?>
<Elements xmlns="http://schemas.microsoft.com/sharepoint/">
  <!-- Parent ContentType: Document (0x0101) -->
  <ContentType ID="0x010100A5FD8267A91945DF9F3884D9EAA4F12F"
               Name="DevLeapInvoice"
               Group="DevLeap Content Types"
               Description="Invoice of DevLeap"
               Inherits="TRUE"
               Version="0">
    <FieldRefs>
      <!-- Field References here -->
    </FieldRefs>
    <DocumentTemplate TargetName="Forms/DevLeapInvoiceTemplate.dotx" />
  </ContentType>
</Elements>
```

The *Document* portion of the ID is highlighted in bold to remind you of the underlying behavior of SharePoint. The *DocumentTemplate* element (also highlighted) has a *TargetName* attribute that defines the URL (relative for the site collection) of the template item to use for every new *Invoice* instance. Listing 3-7 shows how to define a custom document information panel for a *Document* content type, assuming that you have already designed and deployed the panel.

LISTING 3-7 Defining a custom document information panel for an *Invoice* content type, inherited from the *Document* content type

```
<?xml version="1.0" encoding="utf-8"?>
<Elements xmlns="http://schemas.microsoft.com/sharepoint/">
  <!-- Parent ContentType: Document (0x0101) -->
  <ContentType ID="0x010100a5fd8267a91945df9f3884d9eaa4f12f"
               Name="DevLeapInvoice"
               Group="DevLeap Content Types"
               Description="Invoice of DevLeap"
               Inherits="TRUE"
               Version="0">
    <FieldRefs>
      <!-- Field References here -->
    </FieldRefs>
    <XmlDocuments>
      <XmlDocument NamespaceURI=
        "http://schemas.microsoft.com/office/2006/metadata/customXsn">
        <xsnLocation>http://URL/customXsn.xsn</xsnLocation>
        <cached>False</cached>
        <openByDefault>True</openByDefault>
        <xsnScope>http://URL/documentLibrary</xsnScope>
      </XmlDocument>
    </XmlDocuments>
  </ContentType>
</Elements>
```

Listing 3-7 declares the absolute URL of the document information panel by using the *xsnLocation* element. It also disables caching in the Microsoft Office client by setting the *cached* element to *FALSE*. Lastly, it defines how the document should behave relative to this new panel, through the *openByDefault* element, which is set to *TRUE*, meaning that the panel should open by default. The *xsnScope* element is required, but for now it is reserved by Microsoft for internal use only.

List definitions

Now that you have defined your content types, you are ready to use them in a real list of contacts, comprising customers and suppliers. In fact, generally, whenever you define a set of custom content types, you also define one or more list definitions that use these content types. A *list definition* is simply a formal representation, using an XML schema, of a list data model from which you are able to create one or more instances of items corresponding to that model.

In SharePoint, a list definition is a combination of two files: a Schema.xml file, which defines the data structure and configuration of the list definition model, and a feature element file that describes the *ListTemplate*, which defines the information required for provisioning and deploying the list definition model.

List schema file

The list schema file is an XML document that describes all the metadata for the list data structure. The following are the main areas of the Schema.xml file for a list definition:

- **Content Types** This section defines the content types that will be available within the list definition.
- **Fields** This section declares the list-level site columns, which correspond to the entire set of site columns referenced by all the content types associated with the list definition.
- **Views** This section defines the views that will be available to the end user for navigating among the items of list template instances.
- **Forms** This section declares the ASPX pages that will be provided to the end user to add, display, and update items of a list instance based on the current list definition.
- **Validation** This section defines the validation rules for list items.
- **Toolbar** This section declares the type of toolbar that must be provided in the browser interface.

In addition to the preceding list, the complete XML schema contains some other elements as well. Listing 3-8 shows an excerpt from a Schema.xml file that describes a list definition, together with these main sections.

LISTING 3-8 Excerpt of a list definition schema file

```
<?xml version="1.0" encoding="utf-8"?>
<List xmlns:ows="Microsoft SharePoint"
    Title="DevLeapContacts"
    FolderCreation="FALSE"
    Direction="$Resources:Direction;"
    Url="Lists/DevLeapContacts"
    BaseType="0"
    EnableContentTypes="TRUE"
    xmlns="http://schemas.microsoft.com/sharepoint/">
    <MetaData>
        <ContentTypes>
        <!-- Here are referenced the content types -->
        </ContentTypes>
        <Fields>
        <!-- Here are declared the list-level site columns -->
        </Fields>
        <Views>
        <!-- Here are defined the views -->
        </Views>
        <Forms>
        <!-- Here are declared the forms used to add, display, update items -->
        </Forms>
        <Validation>
        <!-- Here are declared the validation rules for list items -->
        </ Validation >
        <Toolbar />
        <!-- To define what kind of toolbar to use in the Web browser UI  -->
    </MetaData>
</List>
```

The *List* element

The *List* element is the root of the schema file and declares some basic attributes for the list definition. The *Title* attribute defines the name of the list definition. The *BaseType* attribute defines the base list type to use for the current list definition. The global onet.xml file of SharePoint (for further details, please read Chapter 13, "Web templates") declares the list of all the available integer values for the *BaseType* values within a *BaseTypes* element.

Note The global onet.xml file is located in the SharePoint15_Root\TEMPLATE\GLOBAL\XML folder.

The available *BaseTypes* values are

- **0** Generic/Custom List
- **1** Document Library
- **2** Not used, may be reserved for future use
- **3** Discussion Forum (deprecated, use 0 instead)
- **4** Vote or Survey
- **5** Issues List

For example, Listing 3-8 used a *BaseType* with a value of *0* because we are defining a generic/custom list definition. The *Url* attribute is optional and defines the path to the root directory containing any ASPX file specific for the list definition. The *FolderCreation* attribute is also optional, and informs SharePoint whether to show (*TRUE*) or not show (*FALSE*) the New Folder command on the list toolbar. Finally, the *Direction* attribute is optional and declares the reading direction: *RTL* (right to left) or *LTR* (left to right). In Listing 3-8, the *Direction* value is read from a resource string so that the list will be compliant with the current locale settings of the site collection. Lastly, to make the users aware of the existence of the different available content types (*Contact*, *Customer*, and *Supplier*) when they are creating new items, we need to explicitly enable content types on the list definition, setting the *EnableContentTypes* attribute to a value of *TRUE*. There are many other attributes available for the *List* definition element; Table 3-4 shows some of them.

More Info For a complete reference of all the available attributes for the List element, refer to the official product documentation on MSDN, at *http://msdn.microsoft.com/en-us/library/ms415091(v=office.15).aspx*.

TABLE 3-4 Some of the main attributes for the *List* element of a Schema.xml list definition file

Attribute	Description
DisableAttachments	Optional *Boolean* value to disable attachments on the list.
EnableMinorVersions	Optional *Boolean* value that controls versioning with major and minor version of items.
ModeratedList	Optional *Boolean* value to enable content approval on inserted items.
PrivateList	Optional *Boolean* value to specify that the list is private.
VersioningEnabled	Optional *Boolean* value to enable versioning on the list. This value can be changed when creating a list instance.

The *MetaData* element

The main child element of *List* is the *MetaData* element, which wraps all the other elements in the Schema.xml file.

One of the main child nodes of *MetaData* is the *ContentTypes* element. This element declares the entire list of content types referenced by the current list definition. Listing 3-9 declares the *ContentTypes* element for the custom Contacts list.

LISTING 3-9 The *ContentTypes* section of metadata for the sample list definition

```
<ContentTypes>
  <ContentType
    ID="0x0100A60F69C4B1304FBDA6C4B4A25939979F"
    Name="DevLeapContact"
    Group="DevLeap Content Types"
    Description="Base Contact of DevLeap"
    Inherits="TRUE" Version="0" Hidden="TRUE">
    <FieldRefs>
      <FieldRef ID="{fa564e0f-0c70-4ab9-b863-0177e6ddd247}"
                Name="Title" DisplayName="Full name" Required="TRUE" />
      <FieldRef ID="{C7792AD6-F2F3-4f2d-A7E5-75D5A8206FD9}"
                Name="DevLeapContactID" DisplayName="Contact ID"
                Required="TRUE" />
      <FieldRef ID="{A8F24550-55CD-4d34-A015-811954C6CE24}"
                Name="DevLeapCompanyName" DisplayName="Company Name" />
      <FieldRef ID="{149BF9A1-5BBB-468d-AA35-91ACEB054E3B}"
                Name="DevLeapCountry" DisplayName="Country" />
    </FieldRefs>
  </ContentType>
  <ContentType
    ID="0x0100A60F69C4B1304FBDA6C4B4A25939979F01"
    Name="DevLeapCustomer"
    Group="DevLeap Content Types"
    Description="Customer of DevLeap"
    Inherits="TRUE" Version="0">
    <FieldRefs>
      <FieldRef ID="{AC689935-8E8B-485e-A45E-FF5A338DD92F}"
                Name="DevLeapCustomerLevel" Required="TRUE" />
    </FieldRefs>
    <XmlDocuments>
      <XmlDocument NamespaceURI=
        "http://schemas.microsoft.com/sharepoint/v3/contenttype/forms">
        <FormTemplates xmlns=
          "http://schemas.microsoft.com/sharepoint/v3/contenttype/forms">
          <Display>DevLeapCustomerDisplay</Display>
          <Edit>DevLeapCustomerEdit</Edit>
          <New>DevLeapCustomerNew</New>
        </FormTemplates>
      </XmlDocument>
    </XmlDocuments>
  </ContentType>
```

```
  <ContentType
    ID="0x0100A60F69C4B1304FBDA6C4B4A25939979F02"
    Name="DevLeapSupplier"
    Group="DevLeap Content Types"
    Description="Supplier of DevLeap"
    Inherits="TRUE" Version="0">
    <FieldRefs>
      <FieldRef ID="{A73DE518-B9B9-4e8d-9D94-6099B4603997}"
                Name="DevLeapSupplierAccount" Required="TRUE" />
    </FieldRefs>
  </ContentType>
</ContentTypes>
```

Listing 3-9 defines all the content types already defined in the previous section, repeating their IDs to link these copies to the original definitions. Why repeat these declarations instead of simply referencing them in some way—such as by just linking their IDs, for example? During a content type's lifetime, its structure might change. To prevent and avoid any data loss, SharePoint copies content type definitions inside the list definitions that use them. Doing so preserves data models and data instances even if someone later changes them. Imagine what would happen if you had a simple content type reference rather than a copy; if you were to provision a *Customer* content type and use it in a custom list, then a few months later, when you have thousands of customer instances in your list, you delete a column from the *Customer* content type—or worse, you delete the entire content type! Having a complete copy of the content type definition allows SharePoint to maintain your data, even when the original content type changes or is removed.

On the other hand, whenever you want to make a change to one of your provisioned content types and you want that change applied to every instance in a site collection, you need to explicitly force the update through the browser-based content type administration page, through code using the Server Object Model, or by manually updating any references in the provisioned XML files, including the Schema.xml files for list definitions.

Listing 3-9 defines all three content types (*Contact*, *Customer*, and *Supplier*) and declares the base *Contact* as hidden, which forces users to explicitly create *Customer* or *Supplier* instances.

Another child of *MetaData* is the *Fields* element. It defines the list-level columns used to store metadata of item instances. These list-level columns are almost the same as the site columns defined in the first section of this chapter. Once again, their definitions are duplicated rather than referenced, and for the same reason: to support changes of the models without data loss during the site columns' lifetimes. The *Fields* section of the list definition contains all the columns used by any of the content types declared in the same Schema.xml file. Listing 3-10 shows the *Fields* element declared for the custom Contacts list.

LISTING 3-10 The *Fields* section of the *MetaData* element for the sample list definition

```
<Fields>
  <Field ID="{c7792ad6-f2f3-4f2d-a7e5-75d5a8206fd9}"
         Name="DevLeapContactID"
         StaticName="DevLeapContactID"
         DisplayName="Contact ID"
         Type="Text"
         Group="DevLeap Columns"
         Sortable="TRUE" />
  <Field ID="{a8f24550-55cd-4d34-a015-811954c6ce24}"
         Name="DevLeapCompanyName"
         StaticName="DevLeapCompanyName"
         DisplayName="Company Name"
         Type="Text"
         Group="DevLeap Columns"
         Sortable="TRUE" />
  <Field ID="{149bf9a1-5bbb-468d-aa35-91aceb054e3b}"
         Name="DevLeapCountry"
         StaticName="DevLeapCountry"
         DisplayName="Country"
         Type="Choice"
         Group="DevLeap Columns"
         Sortable="TRUE">
  <Default>Italy</Default>
  <CHOICES>
    <CHOICE>Italy</CHOICE>
    <CHOICE>USA</CHOICE>
    <CHOICE>Germany</CHOICE>
    <CHOICE>France</CHOICE>
  </CHOICES>
  </Field>
  <Field ID="{ac689935-8e8b-485e-a45e-ff5a338dd92f}"
         Name="DevLeapCustomerLevel"
         StaticName="DevLeapCustomerLevel"
         DisplayName="Customer Level"
         Type="Choice"
         Group="DevLeap Columns">
    <Default>Level C</Default>
    <CHOICES>
      <CHOICE>Level A</CHOICE>
      <CHOICE>Level B</CHOICE>
      <CHOICE>Level C</CHOICE>
    </CHOICES>
  </Field>
  <Field ID="{a73de518-b9b9-4e8d-9d94-6099b4603997}"
         Name="DevLeapSupplierAccount"
         StaticName="DevLeapSupplierAccount"
         DisplayName="Supplier Account"
         Type="User"
         Group="DevLeap Columns"
         Sortable="TRUE" />
</Fields>
```

Just as with the *ContentTypes* section, the *Fields* section is simply a wrapper for the copies of all the previously defined site columns. Notice that the *ID* values for the site columns are the same as those of the global site columns, serving to keep the global site columns linked to the local list-level columns.

Figure 3-5 shows how the List Settings page of a list based on the custom Contacts list definition looks in a web browser. Note that all three content types and all the list-level columns are present.

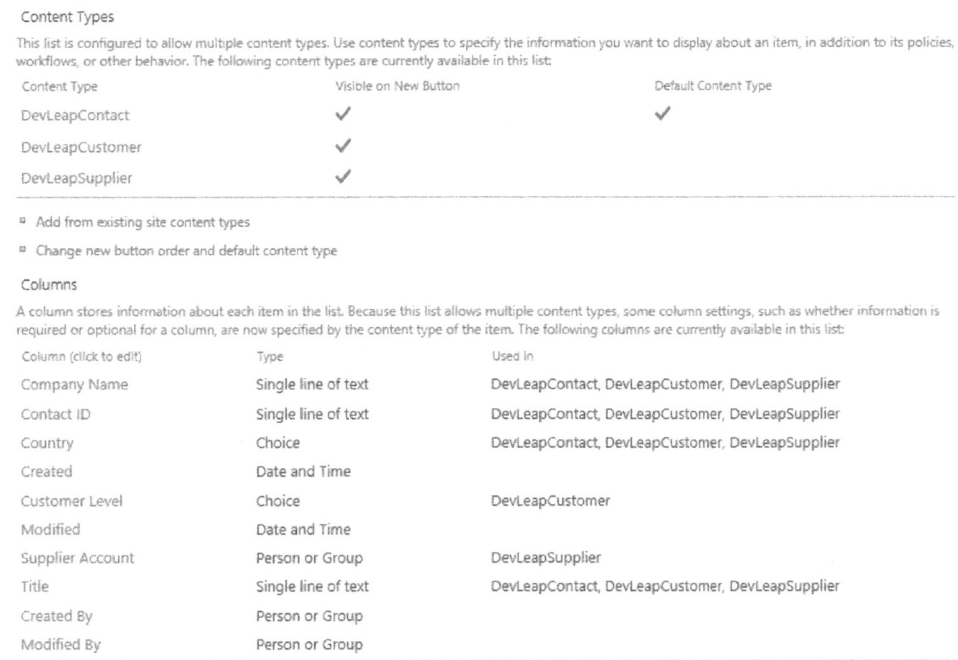

Content Types
This list is configured to allow multiple content types. Use content types to specify the information you want to display about an item, in addition to its policies, workflows, or other behavior. The following content types are currently available in this list:
Content Type
Visible on New Button
Default Content Type
DevLeapContact
DevLeapCustomer
DevLeapSupplier
Add from existing site content types
Change new button order and default content type
Columns
A column stores information about each item in the list. Because this list allows multiple content types, some column settings, such as whether information is required or optional for a column, are now specified by the content type of the item. The following columns are currently available in this list:
Column (click to edit)
Type
Used in
Company Name
Single line of text
DevLeapContact, DevLeapCustomer, DevLeapSupplier
Contact ID
Single line of text
DevLeapContact, DevLeapCustomer, DevLeapSupplier
Country
Choice
DevLeapContact, DevLeapCustomer, DevLeapSupplier
Created
Date and Time
Customer Level
Choice
DevLeapCustomer
Modified
Date and Time
Supplier Account
Person or Group
DevLeapSupplier
Title
Single line of text
DevLeapContact, DevLeapCustomer, DevLeapSupplier
Created By
Person or Group
Modified By
Person or Group

FIGURE 3-5 The List Settings page of a list instance based on the custom Contacts list definition.

Just after the *Fields* section comes the *Views* element, which is a child of *MetaData*. This section is really interesting because it is where you define the views on data that will be available to the end users in the web browser. Each *View* element, which is a child of *Views*, defines a data view declaring some configuration attributes (illustrated in Table 3-5).

More Info For a complete list of all the available *View* attributes, refer to the official documentation on MSDN, at *http://msdn.microsoft.com/en-us/library/ms438338(v=office.15).aspx*.

TABLE 3-5 Some of the main attributes for the *View* element of a Schema.xml list definition file

Attribute	Description
Type	The type of view. *Type* can be *HTML*, *Chart*, or *Pivot*.
BaseViewID	An *Integer* value that declares the ID of the view. *BaseViewID* must be unique within a Schema.xml file.
Url	The public URL to access the view from the browser.
DisplayName	The name of the view in the web browser.
DefaultView	A *Boolean* value that declares if the view is the default view for the current list.
MobileView	A *Boolean* value that specifies if the current view has to be made available to mobile devices.
MobileDefaultView	A *Boolean* value that declares if the view, enabled for mobile access, is the default view for mobile devices.
SetupPath	Defines the site-relative path to the ASPX file corresponding to the current view model. It allows provisioning a custom page for the current view.
WebPartZoneID	A string that declares the ID of the WebPartZone control where the current view will be loaded, within the ASPX Web Part page.

The *View* element also allows you to declare some other configuration details using child elements. Listing 3-11 shows the default view definition for the list of contacts.

LISTING 3-11 The default *View* definition for the sample list

```
<View BaseViewID="1" Type="HTML"
      WebPartZoneID="Main"
      DisplayName="$Resources:core,objectiv_schema_mwsidcamlidC24;"
      DefaultView="TRUE" MobileView="TRUE"
      MobileDefaultView="TRUE"
      SetupPath="pages\viewpage.aspx"
      ImageUrl="/_layouts/images/generic.png"
      Url="AllItems.aspx">
  <Toolbar Type="Standard" />
  <RowLimit Paged="TRUE">50</RowLimit>
  <ViewFields>
    <FieldRef Name="Attachments">
    </FieldRef>
    <FieldRef Name="LinkTitle">
    </FieldRef>
  </ViewFields>
  <Query>
    <OrderBy>
      <FieldRef Name="ID">
      </FieldRef>
    </OrderBy>
  </Query>
  <XslLink>main.xsl</XslLink>
  <JSLink>clienttemplates.js</JSLink>
</View>
```

Listing 3-11 declares a *BaseViewID* with a value of *1*, and specifies that this view will be the default (*DefaultView*), not only for classic web browsers, but also for mobile devices (*MobileDefaultView*). The URL to access the view will be *AllItems.aspx*, and this page will be based on the *SetupPath* file pages\viewpage.aspx filling out the *WebPartZone* control whose *ID* is *Main*.

The child elements of the *View* tag in Listing 3-11 inform SharePoint to use the *Standard* value for the toolbar. The maximum number of rows (*RowLimit*) is set to return a value of *50*, enabling paging.

Note If not specified, the default *RowLimit* is *30*.

After these configuration elements, Listing 3-11 defines some other elements that determine the data to show, declaring a *Query* element to filter and sort data, and a set of *ViewFields* elements to show, as well as some optional grouping rules. The *Query* element is simply a Collaborative Application Markup Language (CAML) query that defines the values to extract from the source list, the ordering rule, and which values will be shown in the current view. For example, Listing 3-11 queries all the items in the list, sorting them by the value of their *ID* fields.

Note CAML is an XML-based querying language that can be used to define filtering, sorting, and grouping on SharePoint data. The CAML language reference is available on MSDN, at *http://msdn.microsoft.com/en-us/library/ms467521(v=office.15).aspx*. In case you are a SharePoint 2010 developer, consider that CAML hasn't changed that much between SharePoint 2010 and SharePoint 2013.

Another important child section of the *View* element is the *ViewFields* element, which declares the fields to show in the resulting view. These fields are referenced by their internal names, using a specific *FieldRef* element.

The last child elements in the *View* are the *XslLink* and *JsLink* elements. Since SharePoint 2010, SharePoint can render views using XSLT transformations. The *XslLink* element specifies the path to the XSLT file used to render the view. This XSLT file path is relative to the folder *SharePoint15_Root\TEMPLATE\LAYOUTS\XSL*. Moreover, starting from SharePoint 2013, the *JsLink* element allows declaring a JavaScript file to include and use for rendering the view.

Note SharePoint15_Root refers to the SharePoint root folder, which is typically located at C:\Program Files\Common Files\Microsoft Shared\Web Server Extensions\15.

As an alternative to providing an explicit XSLT file path, you can use an *Xsl* element to simply declare the XSLT transformation inside the Schema.xml file. Because you may want to reuse the XSLT transformation, however, a better choice is to reference an external file. This is especially useful when you are developing a full-trust solution. The capability to define the XSLT transformation inside the

Schema.xml file is provided for those situations, such as for sandboxed solutions and SharePoint apps, when you want to avoid copying files to the file system of the target SharePoint farm.

The *Forms* element is another important configuration section for the list definition, as shown in Listing 3-12.

LISTING 3-12 The *Forms* configuration section of the custom Contacts list definition

```
<Forms>
  <Form Type="DisplayForm"
  Url="DispForm.aspx" SetupPath="pages\form.aspx" WebPartZoneID="Main" />
  <Form Type="EditForm"
  Url="EditForm.aspx" SetupPath="pages\form.aspx" WebPartZoneID="Main" />
  <Form Type="NewForm"
  Url="NewForm.aspx" SetupPath="pages\form.aspx" WebPartZoneID="Main" />
</Forms>
```

The *Forms* element contains a set of *Form* elements that declare the forms available to the end user. Each *Form* element requires a *Type* attribute that takes one of the following values:

- ***DisplayForm*** The form to display a list item
- ***EditForm*** The form to edit an existing list item
- ***NewForm*** The form to add a new list item

Every form also requires a URL where it can be accessed. Forms might include an optional *SetupPath* attribute from which to load the ASPX page model, as well as a *WebPartZoneID* attribute, which specifies the ID of the Web Part zone used to load the rendering control of the form. As an alternative to the *SetupPath* attribute, you could have a *Path* attribute, which defines a physical file system path relative to the _layouts folder for a template file, and a *Template* attribute, which specifies the name of the template to use. You can also use CAML syntax to define the template for the body, buttons, opening section, and closing section of each of these forms, using these specific child nodes of the *Form* element: *ListFormBody*, *ListFormButtons*, *ListFormClosing*, and *ListFormOpening*.

The last configuration section shown is the *Validation* element. This element, introduced with SharePoint 2010, supports defining validation rules that can apply to each item of the list. Listing 3-13 shows how to declare a custom validation rule together with a validation error message that end users will see if validation fails.

LISTING 3-13 Declaring a sample validation rule for the custom Contacts list definition items

```
<Validation Message="Please check your data, there is something wrong!">
     =Title<>"Blank"
</Validation>
```

The validation rule forces the items to have a Title field with a value not equal to *Blank*. Notice that list-level validation rules work properly only with fields shared by all the content types of the list. If you enforce a rule against a field that is not defined in all the content types of the list, then your rule will always throw an error when applied to the wrong content types. For example, if you define a rule at the list level for the DevLeapCustomerLevel field of the *Customer* content type, you will not be able to add or update any *Supplier* instances, because the *DevLeapCustomer* field is not present in the *Supplier* content type. In such cases, you should instead define the validation rule at the site column level.

Defining a custom view

When defining custom list definitions, you'll frequently want to declare some custom views that correspond to the business rules of your data model. For example, the sample model could feature one view that shows only customers and another that shows only suppliers. This section demonstrates how to define the former view; the latter's definition will be almost identical.

First, define a new *View* element under the *Views* element of the Schema.xml file. The new view will have a unique *BaseViewID*; in this example it will be *2*. The *DisplayName* will be All Customers, the *Type* will be HTML, and the *Url* will be *AllCustomers.aspx*. All the other attributes values of the *View* element are trivial. You can see the complete definition of this view in Listing 3-14.

LISTING 3-14 Defining a custom view for a custom Contacts list definition

```
<View BaseViewID="2" Type="HTML"
      WebPartZoneID="Main"
      DisplayName="All Customers"
      DefaultView="FALSE" MobileView="TRUE"
      MobileDefaultView="FALSE"
      SetupPath="pages\viewpage.aspx"
      ImageUrl="/_layouts/images/generic.png"
      Url="AllCustomers.aspx">
  <Toolbar Type="FreeForm" />
  <XslLink>Contacts_Main.xsl</XslLink>
  <RowLimit Paged="TRUE">20</RowLimit>
  <ViewFields>
    <FieldRef Name="Attachments">
    </FieldRef>
    <FieldRef Name="LinkTitle">
    </FieldRef>
    <FieldRef Name="DevLeapContactID">
    </FieldRef>
    <FieldRef Name="DevLeapCompanyName">
    </FieldRef>
    <FieldRef Name="DevLeapCountry">
    </FieldRef>
    <FieldRef Name="DevLeapCustomerLevel">
    </FieldRef>
  </ViewFields>
```

```
    <Query>
      <Where>
        <Eq>
          <FieldRef Name="ContentType" />
          <Value Type="Text">DevLeapCustomer</Value>
        </Eq>
      </Where>
      <OrderBy>
        <FieldRef Name="ID">
        </FieldRef>
      </OrderBy>
    </Query>
  </View>
```

There are some areas of interest in this view definition. First, the code defines a *Query* to filter only items with a *ContentType* value of *DevLeapCustomer* and orders the result by the item *ID*. Then it references all the fields of the *Customer* content type, defining a set of *FieldRef* elements within the *ViewFields* element. Lastly, a custom XSLT transformation is defined for rendering the custom view. SharePoint will search for this XSLT file, Contacts_Main.xsl, in the SharePoint15_Root\TEMPLATE\LAYOUTS\XSL *folde*r. The file has to be placed in that folder using the solution-provisioning tools provided by Visual Studio 2012 to create a full-trust solution. (For further details, see Chapter 4, "SharePoint features and solutions.") Otherwise, as you have already seen, you can define the XSLT code directly in the *View* schema definition, inside an *Xsl* element.

The XSLT file you reference or define in the *View* definition is a common XSLT transformation that will receive a wide range of parameters at run time from SharePoint. In the XSLT code, for example, you can access the *XmlDefinition* variable, which provides the XML definition of the current *View*. To define an XSLT for a custom view, you must provide an XSLT template that matches the *BaseViewID* of the targeted view. For the Contacts example, the following template was defined:

```
<xsl:template match="View[@BaseViewID="2"]" mode="full">
  <!-- Here is our custom XSLT transformation -->
</xsl:template>
```

The XSLT also receives a parameter named *Rows* that contains all the items to be rendered. Listing 3-15 shows an excerpt of the XML content of the *Rows* parameter. You can read it simply by using an XSLT template that copies the source content with an *<xsl:copy-of />* element.

LISTING 3-15 The content of the *Rows* parameter provided to a custom XSLT for rendering a list view

```
<Rows>
  <Row ID="1" PermMask="0x7fffffffffffffff" Attachments="0"
  Title="Customer 01" FileLeafRef="1_.000" FileLeafRef.Name="1_"
  FileLeafRef.Suffix="000" FSObjType="0"
  Created_x0020_Date="1;#2010-02-13 16:24:12" Created_x0020_Date.ifnew="1"
  FileRef="/sites/SP2010DevRef/Lists/Test/1_.000"
  FileRef.urlencode="%2Fsites%2FSP2010DevRef%2FLists%2FTest%2F1%5F%2E000"
  FileRef.urlencodeasurl="/sites/SP2010DevRef/Lists/Test/1_.000"
  File_x0020_Type=""
  HTML_x0020_File_x0020_Type.File_x0020_Type.mapall="icgen.gif||"
  HTML_x0020_File_x0020_Type.File_x0020_Type.mapcon=""
  HTML_x0020_File_x0020_Type.File_x0020_Type.mapico="icgen.gif" ContentTypeId
="0x0100A60F69C4B1304FBDA6C4B4A25939979F010044C1B948A829E64CBD49ED3F42A868C7"
DevLeapContactID="C01"DevLeapCompanyName="Company 01"
  DevLeapCountry="Italy" DevLeapCustomerLevel="Level C"
  ContentType="DevLeapCustomer"></Row>
  <!-And many other rows here, one for each list item to show -->
</Rows>
```

Listing 3-15 illustrates that the *Rows* parameter provides each row along with its data columns, specified as attributes of a *Row* element. To output the content of the rows, you simply need to retrieve the values of these attributes, placing them inside the proper HTML elements to adhere to the graphical layout that you need to render.

However, many SharePoint developers do not like writing XSLT files, because XSLT is inflexible (although very powerful) from a syntax viewpoint. Luckily, starting with SharePoint 2013, you have the option to provide a custom JavaScript file through the *JsLink* child element of the *View* element, in order to move rendering templates into client-side code. Generally speaking, this technique is known as client-side rendering (CSR). Listing 3-16 uses this new technique to define a custom view.

LISTING 3-16 A custom view definition for the custom Contacts list definition using JavaScript rendering

```
<View BaseViewID="3" Type="HTML"
      WebPartZoneID="Main"
      DisplayName="All Customers via JS"
      DefaultView="FALSE" MobileView="TRUE"
      MobileDefaultView="FALSE"
      SetupPath="pages\viewpage.aspx"
      ImageUrl="/_layouts/images/generic.png"
      Url="AllCustomersViaJS.aspx">
  <Toolbar Type="FreeForm" />
  <XslLink>main.xsl</XslLink>
  <JsLink Default="TRUE">~site/Scripts/CustomCustomersView.js</JsLink>
  <RowLimit Paged="TRUE">20</RowLimit>
```

```
  <ViewFields>
    <FieldRef Name="Attachments">
    </FieldRef>
    <FieldRef Name="LinkTitle">
    </FieldRef>
    <FieldRef Name="DevLeapContactID">
    </FieldRef>
    <FieldRef Name="DevLeapCompanyName">
    </FieldRef>
    <FieldRef Name="DevLeapCountry">
    </FieldRef>
    <FieldRef Name="DevLeapCustomerLevel">
    </FieldRef>
  </ViewFields>
  <Query>
    <Where>
      <Eq>
        <FieldRef Name="ContentType" />
        <Value Type="Text">DevLeapCustomer</Value>
      </Eq>
    </Where>
    <OrderBy>
      <FieldRef Name="ID">
      </FieldRef>
    </OrderBy>
  </Query>
</View>
```

In Listing 3-16, shows the *JsLink* element (highlighted in bold) configured as the default (*Default="TRUE"*) rendering template. SharePoint will look for the JavaScript file at a URL relative to the current site collection, because of the *~site* token at the very beginning of the URL. You can deploy the JavaScript code of the CustomCustomerView.js file to the target site simply working at the website level, using a sandboxed solution or an app deployment process. In the JavaScript code, you can reference the Client Object Model of SharePoint in order to query the current list configuration, as well as the items to render. This technique is extremely powerful. While provisioning lists for Office 365, for example, you can use this technique to move all the rendering logic to the client side, using jQuery or CSS rendering templates. With its XSLT and JavaScript support, SharePoint opens up some great business opportunities; because it gives you the capability to display fully customized rendering of list views, your solutions can support fully customized template layouts, even in extreme web content management solutions.

More Info For more information about CSR, you can read the document "How to: Customize a list view in apps for SharePoint using client-side rendering," available at *http://msdn.microsoft.com/en-us/library/jj220045.aspx*.

The *ListTemplate* definition file

ListTemplate is the feature element file that declares all the deployment properties needed to provision the list definition. It must be provisioned into a custom feature together with the Schema.xml file. Listing 3-17 shows the *ListTemplate* for the sample Contacts list definition.

LISTING 3-17 The *ListTemplate* feature element for the sample Contacts list definition

```
<?xml version="1.0" encoding="utf-8"?>
<Elements xmlns="http://schemas.microsoft.com/sharepoint/">
    <ListTemplate
        Name="DevLeapContacts"
        Type="10001"
        BaseType="0"
        OnQuickLaunch="TRUE"
        SecurityBits="11"
        Sequence="410"
        DisplayName="DevLeap Contacts"
        Description="A list of Contact for DevLeap"
        Image="/_layouts/images/dlcon.png"/>
</Elements>
```

The *Type* attribute is the most important attribute in the *ListTemplate* element. *Type* takes an integer value that should be unique at the site collection level. The code sample uses a value of *10001* to avoid overlapping with values of out-of-the-box list templates. In general, you should use a large integer value to avoid overlapping with SharePoint. Consider that values in the range between 100 and 1200 are already taken, and developers should allocate numbers greater than 10000. The uniqueness of this attribute allows you to define custom UI extensions that will target the entire set of lists with that *Type* value.

The other attributes are straightforward. The *BaseType* attribute states the base type for the current list definition. The *Name* attribute represents the internal name of the list, and the *DisplayName* is the text shown to end users, together with the *Description* and the *Image*. You can load the values of these descriptive attributes from external resource strings to provision list definitions in a multilanguage environment. The *OnQuickLaunch Boolean* attribute value controls whether SharePoint shows any instance of the list in the Quick Launch menu. You can also provision a list instance through a custom feature of type *ListInstance*, which will be explained in Chapter 4.

Finally, the *SecurityBits* attribute defines the security behavior of the list. This is a two-digit string, where the first digit controls whether users can read all items (*1*) or only their own items (*2*). The second digit defines edit access permissions. The possible values are

- **1** Users can edit any item.
- **2** Users can edit only their own items.
- **4** Users cannot edit items.

For example, a value of *22* for the *SecurityBits* attribute means that users can see and edit only their own items, while the default value of *11* means that users can see and edit all the items in the list.

More Info For a complete list of attributes for the *ListTemplate* element, refer to the official product documentation on MSDN, at *http://msdn.microsoft.com/en-us/library/ms462947(v=office.15).aspx.*

Working with lists in Visual Studio 2012

Just as you can define content types with Visual Studio 2012 and its designers, you can also define basic lists. In fact, whenever you add an item of type List to a SharePoint project, regardless of whether it is a solution or an app, you are provided with a graphical designer that allows you to design fields, content types, and views, and provide descriptive information for the list. First, you are prompted with the wizard shown in Figure 3-6. Here you can specify the name of the target list and create a customizable list definition based on a basic content type or a list instance based on an existing list definition.

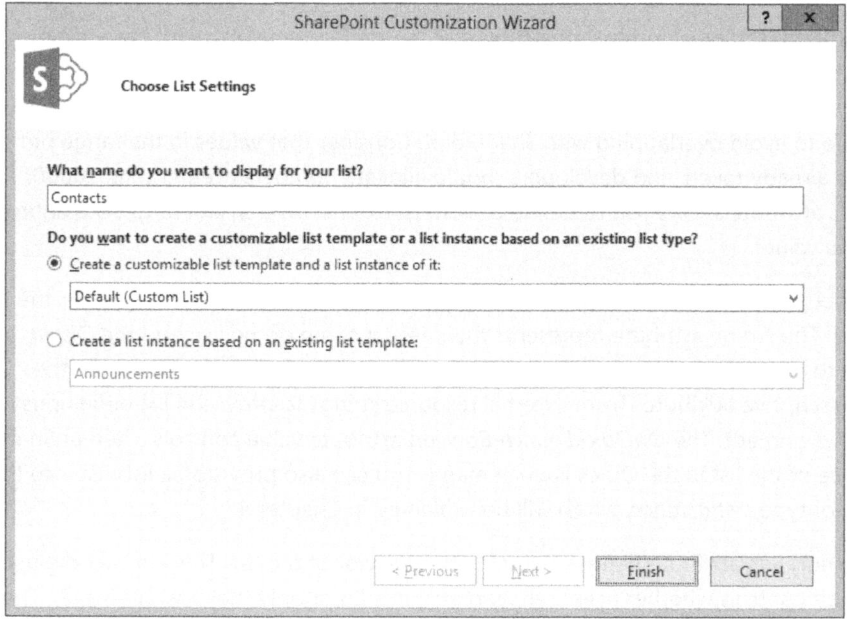

FIGURE 3-6 The wizard for creating a new list in a SharePoint solution or app.

After you complete the page and click Finish, you can configure the resulting item through a specific designer. If you created a new list definition, you will have access to a designer with three tabs, for configuring fields, content types, and views of the custom list definition. Figure 3-7 shows the designer for this chapter's example Contacts list, displaying the columns defined in the schema of the list definition.

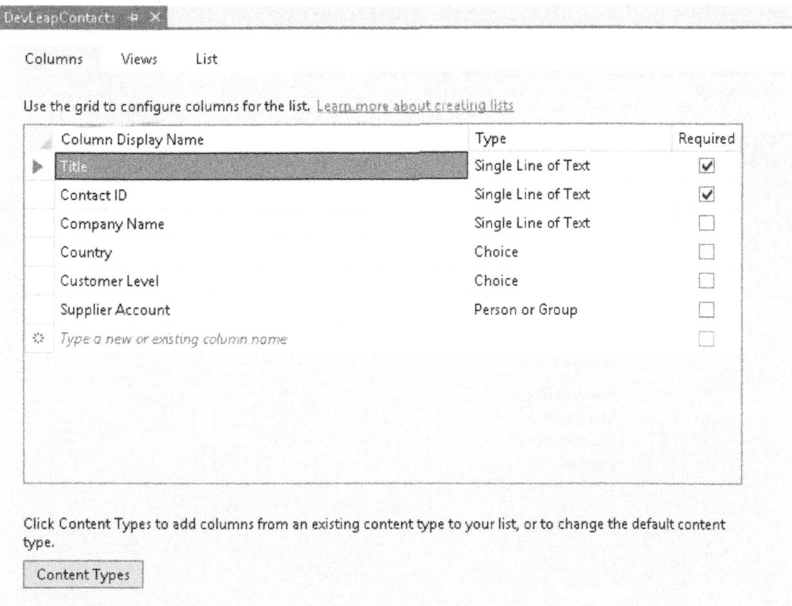

FIGURE 3-7 Configuring the fields of a custom list definition within Visual Studio 2012.

The designer also provides also a Content Types button; click it to open the dialog box shown in Figure 3-8. Here you can determine the content types associated with the current list template.

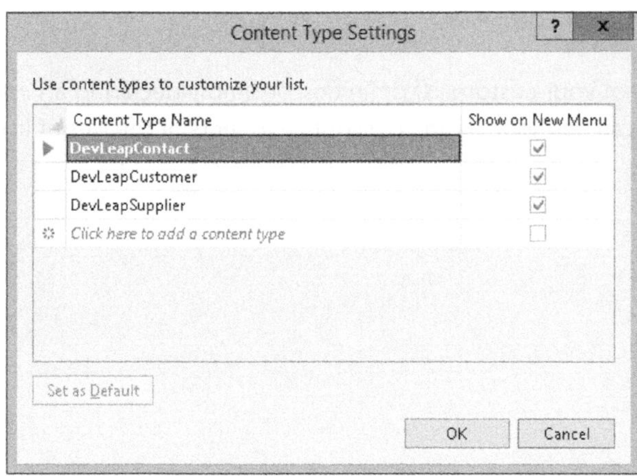

FIGURE 3-8 The dialog box for configuring the content types associated with a list definition.

Once you have defined the content types and the columns, you can determine the views for the custom list definition. Click the Views tab to access the controls shown in Figure 3-9.

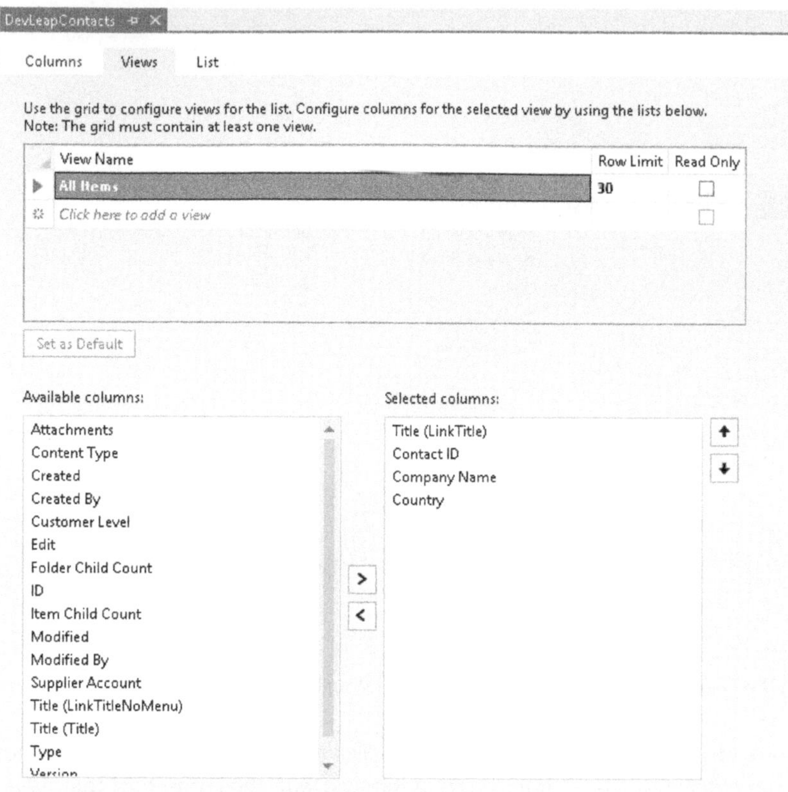

FIGURE 3-9 Determining the views for the custom list definition.

Whether you are defining an instance of your custom list definition or simply declaring an instance of an already existing list definition, you can configure some descriptive aspects of the target list using the List tab, shown in Figure 3-10.

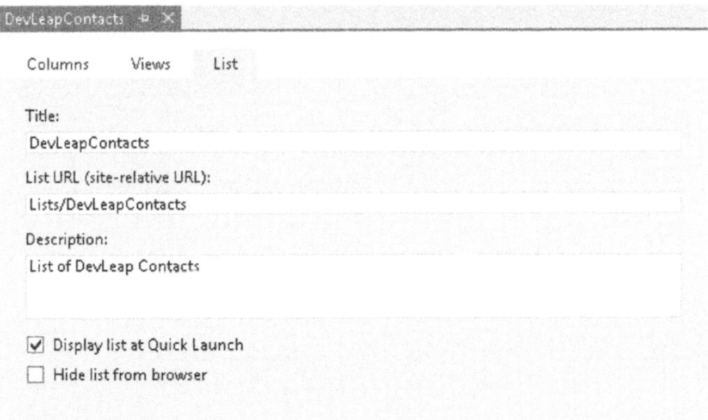

FIGURE 3-10 The List tab for configuring the list instance descriptive parameters.

By default, Visual Studio 2012 always defines a list instance together with the list definition. If you do not want to provision a list instance, you can comment the code of the *ListInstance* element created within the Elements.xml file available inside the list item in the Visual Studio project outline.

Summary

This chapter described how to define XML files to provision SharePoint data models and structures. In particular, it showed how to use feature element files to deploy site columns, content types, and list definitions. It also discussed how to do similar things using the designer provided by Microsoft Visual Studio 2012, instead of using low-level XML files. These features promise a great return on investment and a common maintenance plan.

CHAPTER 4

SharePoint features and solutions

Since its early editions, two of the most popular characteristics of Microsoft SharePoint have been its engine for managing custom features and its ability to deploy those features through the installation of solution packages. Despite the addition of the new app model in SharePoint 2013, using features and solutions is still a common way to extend on-premises environments. This chapter will walk you through the various features that you can define, as well as explain how to package SharePoint solutions to deploy those features. Because many of these features will be covered in depth in upcoming chapters, the goal here is to provide a brief overview of all features and solutions to serve as a foundation for later discussions.

Features and solutions

A *feature* is a customization or extension of the native environment that you can selectively install and activate at various scope levels to deploy solutions modularly and granularly. For example, as you learned in Chapter 3, "Data provisioning," you can use a feature to deploy custom data structures, such as site columns, content types, list definitions, and so on. You can also use a feature to deploy a custom web template (as you will learn in Chapter 13, "Web templates"), automate deployment of pages and Web Parts, and more. The upcoming "Feature element types" section contains a more complete list of the standard features that SharePoint offers.

In general, features let you develop customizations and extensions that take advantage of an out-of-the-box environment for deploying, upgrading, and managing them. The SharePoint Features engine supports automated deployment; automatic management of multiple, load-balanced, front-end web servers for reducing inconsistency issues; and automated upgrading to help avoid versioning issues. Each time you develop a feature, SharePoint creates a *feature manifest*, which is an XML file named Feature.xml that contains all the information about the feature. SharePoint stores the feature manifest on every front-end web server on the farm in a subfolder of the SharePoint15_Root\TEMPLATE\FEATURES directory.

Note SharePoint15_Root refers to the SharePoint root folder, which is typically located at C:\Program Files\Common Files\Microsoft Shared\Web Server Extensions\15.

Each feature has its own folder, named for the contained feature; thus, two features cannot share the same folder or the same name in a farm. Each feature's folder contains all the files required to implement that feature, together with the feature manifest file.

To deploy a feature, you need to install it (which means copying the feature's folder to each front-end web server), recycle the application pool, and then activate it. After you have deployed a feature, you can upgrade it for maintenance and versioning purposes. You can even deactivate and uninstall a feature.

Every feature has an activation scope that can assume one of the following values:

- ***Farm*** The feature targets the entire SharePoint farm.
- ***WebApplication*** The feature targets a single web application and all the contained site collections.
- ***Site*** The feature targets a single site collection and all of its sites.
- ***Web*** The feature targets a single site.

In addition, every feature type shares the same feature manifest file structure, which is illustrated in Listing 4-1.

LISTING 4-1 The SharePoint feature manifest file structure

```
<Feature xmlns="http://schemas.microsoft.com/sharepoint/"
    ActivateOnDefault = "TRUE" | "FALSE"
    AlwaysForceInstall = "TRUE" | "FALSE"
    AutoActivateInCentralAdmin = "TRUE" | "FALSE"
    Creator = "Text"
    DefaultResourceFile = "Text"
    Description = "Text"
    Hidden = "TRUE" | "FALSE"
    Id = "Text"
    ImageUrl = "Text"
    ImageUrlAltText = "Text"
    ReceiverAssembly = "Text"
    ReceiverClass = "Text"
    RequireResources = "TRUE" | "FALSE"
    Scope = "Text"
    SolutionId = "Text"
    Title = "Text"
    UIVersion = "Text"
    Version = "Text" >
    <ActivationDependencies>
        <ActivationDependency FeatureId = "Text" />
    </ActivationDependencies>
    <ElementManifests>
        <ElementManifest Location = "Text" />
        <ElementFile Location = "Text" />
    </ElementManifests>
```

```
    <Properties>
        <Property Key = "Text" Value = "Text" />
    </Properties>
    <UpgradeActions ReceiverAssembly = "Text" ReceiverClass = "Text">
        <AddContentTypeField />
        <ApplyElementManifests />
        <CustomUpgradeAction />
        <MapFile />
        <VersionRange />
    </UpgradeActions>
</Feature>
```

The feature element shown in Listing 4-1 belongs to the *http://schemas.microsoft.com/sharepoint/ namespace* site. It is composed of a set of attributes and accepts optional child elements. Table 4-1 lists and briefly explains each available attribute.

TABLE 4-1 Attributes supported by the *Feature* element

Attribute name	Description
ActivateOnDefault	An optional *Boolean* attribute with a default value of *True*. It applies only to *Farm*-scoped or *WebApplication*-scoped features and determines whether the feature will be activated by default during installation. For *WebApplication*-scoped features, if this attribute is set to *True*, the feature will also be activated when a new web application is created.
AlwaysForceInstall	An optional *Boolean* attribute with a default value of *False*. When set to *True*, it forces the feature to be installed—even if it is already installed.
AutoActivateInCentralAdmin	An optional *Boolean* attribute with a default value of *False*. It defines whether the feature will be activated by default in the Administrative website hosting SharePoint Central Administration (SPCA). It does not apply to *Farm*-scoped features. However, in common scenarios, it is not suggested to extend the Central Administration.
Creator	An optional description of the feature's creator.
DefaultResourceFile	Optional text that defines the name of a common resource file, usually shared with other features released by the same creator. By default, SharePoint will look for resources in a file in the path SharePoint15_Root\TEMPLATE\FEATURES\ *FeatureName*\Resources, with a filename such as *Resources.Culture.resx* (the *Culture* value can be any of the standard culture names defined by the Internet Engineering Task Force (IETF), such as *en-US*, *it-IT*, *fr-FR*, and so on). However, when you specify a name—for example, *MySharedResources*, SharePoint will use that name, searching for a file named *MySharedResources.Culture.resx* in the shared path SharePoint15_Root\Resources.
Description	Optional text that describes the feature in the UI. You can define it using a resource string in the form of *$Resources:ResourceName*. For example, if the feature description is a resource item with a key value of *FeatureDescription*, the corresponding value should be *$Resources: FeatureDescription*.
Hidden	An optional *Boolean* attribute with a default value of *False*. When set to *True*, the feature will be hidden from the UI and can be activated or deactivated only through the command-line tools or by using the object model.
Id	A required attribute of type text that must contain an ID (GUID) that uniquely identifies the feature.
ImageUrl	Optional text that defines the site-relative URL of an image used to render the feature in the UI.

Attribute name	Description
ImageUrlAltText	Optional text that defines alternate text for the image representing the feature in the UI (see *ImageUrl*). You can define this using a resource string, just like the *Description* property.
ReceiverAssembly	Optional text that defines the strong name of an assembly that SharePoint will search for in the Global Assembly Cache (GAC) and that provides a receiver class to handle the feature's events.
ReceiverClass	Optional text that defines the full class name of a receiver class to handle the feature's events. SharePoint will search for the receiver class name in the *ReceiverAssembly*.
RequireResources	An optional *Boolean* attribute with a default value of *False*. It determines whether SharePoint requires that resources exist for the language of the current website or site collection to make the feature visible in the UI. This attribute does not affect the ability to activate and manage the feature from the command line or from the object model.
Scope	A required text attribute that defines the scope within which the feature can be activated. The possible values are *Farm*, *WebApplication*, *Site*, and *Web*.
SolutionId	Optional text that defines the ID of the solution to which the features belong.
Title	Optional text that defines the title of the feature and that is visible in the UI. It is limited to a maximum length of 255 characters. You can define it using a resource string, as described in the *Description* property.
UIVersion	Optional text that declares the UI version supported by the feature. The value can be specified in multiple ways: ■ =#: The site's *UIVersion* must be equal to #. ■ <#: The site's *UIVersion* must be less than #. ■ >#: The site's *UIVersion* must be greater than #. ■ <=#: The site's *UIVersion* must be less than or equal to #. ■ >=#: The site's *UIVersion* must be greater than or equal to #. ■ #;#: The site's *UIVersion* must be in the semicolon-delimited list of numbers.
Version	Optional text that defines the version of the feature. It can be made of up to four numbers, delimited by periods. For example, it might be *1.0.0.0*, *1.0.0.1*, and so on.

A *Feature* tag of a feature manifest can also contain child elements, such as the following:

- ***ActivationDependencies*** Specifies a list of features on which activation of the current feature depends
- ***ElementManifests*** References a set of element manifests or element files, both declaring the definition of the feature
- ***Properties*** Provides a set of default values for the feature's properties, represented as a tuple of keys and values
- ***UpgradeActions*** Specifies any custom action to execute when the feature is upgraded

The most important children are those declaring one or more elements that make up the feature. These elements correspond to zero or more *ElementManifest* tags, which are defined through XML files, and zero or more *ElementFile* tags, which declare files supporting the feature. Both tags provide a *Location* attribute that references the target file as a path relative to the feature's folder. Listing 4-2 shows a feature manifest deploying a Web Part.

LISTING 4-2 A feature manifest file deploying a Web Part

```
<Feature xmlns="http://schemas.microsoft.com/sharepoint/"
  Title="DevLeap Sample Web Part"
  Description="This feature deploys a sample Web Part."
  Id="c46c270e-e722-4aa0-82ba-b66c8dd61f4e" Scope="Site"
  Version="1.0.0.0">
  <ElementManifests>
    <ElementManifest Location="SampleWebPart\Elements.xml" />
    <ElementFile Location="SampleWebPart\SampleWebPart.webpart" />
  </ElementManifests>
</Feature>
```

The example feature manifest defines only the *Scope* and the *Id* attributes for the feature, together with its *Title* and *Description* attributes; meanwhile, the Web Part is referenced by the element manifest file located in the relative folder SampleWebPart\Elements.xml. The Web Part deployment also requires a .webpart file, referenced by the *ElementFile* tag of the feature manifest.

Using the *DefaultResourceFile* and *RequireResources* attributes and the syntax illustrated in the *Description* and *Title* attributes (all shown in Table 4-1), your feature can support a multilanguage UI. Simply define a set of resource files for the feature using resource keys instead of text values. For example, Listing 4-3 replaces the explicit values of Listing 4-2 with resource strings.

LISTING 4-3 A feature manifest supporting multiple languages

```
<Feature xmlns="http://schemas.microsoft.com/sharepoint/" Version="1.0.0.0
"Title="$Resources:FeatureTitle" Description="$Resources:FeatureDescription"
Id="c46c270e-e722-4aa0-82ba-b66c8dd61f4e" Scope="Site">
  <ElementManifests>
    <ElementManifest Location="SampleWebPart\Elements.xml" />
    <ElementFile Location="SampleWebPart\SampleWebPart.webpart" />
    <ElementFile Location="Resources\Resources.resx" />
    <ElementFile Location="Resources\Resources.it-IT.resx" />
  </ElementManifests>
</Feature>
```

The feature manifest declares the *Title* and *Description* properties as resources. It also includes a couple of resource files for the default invariant culture (Resources.resx) and for the Italian culture (Resources.it-IT.resx) in the feature deployment. These files are standard .resx files that you can define manually or by using the tools in Visual Studio 2012.

Feature element types

As shown in Listings 4-2 and 4-3, the key information in every feature manifest file is the list of one or more element manifest files. Those files are based on the same XML schema as the feature manifest (*http://schemas.microsoft.com/sharepoint/*). They make use of a predefined set of tags, each of which corresponds to a specific feature type. The full schema for these XML files is defined in the wss.xsd document, available in the SharePoint15_Root\TEMPLATE\XML folder. Table 4-2 provides a brief description of the main elements available in SharePoint 2013.

TABLE 4-2 The main feature elements

Feature element name	Description
ContentTypeBinding	Provisions a content type on a list defined in a site template (see onet.xml in Chapter 13). Can be scoped to *Site*.
ContentType	Defines a content type ready to be used in lists or libraries. Content types are discussed in Chapter 3. Can be scoped to *Site*.
Control	Customizes the configuration of an existing delegate control, or declares a new delegate control to override the standard SharePoint controls. Can be scoped to *Farm*, *WebApplication*, *Site*, and *Web*.
CustomAction	Defines an extension to the standard UI. For example, you can use *CustomAction* to define a new button on a ribbon bar, a new menu item on a standard menu, or a new link on a site settings page. Custom actions are discussed in Chapter 12, "Customizing the UI." Can be scoped to *Farm*, *WebApplication*, *Site*, and *Web*.
CustomActionGroup	Groups custom actions. Can be scoped to *Farm*, *WebApplication*, *Site*, and *Web*.
DocumentConverter	Declares a document converter that can convert a document from a type X to a type Y. Requires custom development to implement the converter. Can be scoped to *WebApplication*.
FeatureSiteTemplate Association	Allows associating a feature to a specific site template definition for provisioning the feature with the site definition when you create a new site with that definition. Can be scoped to *Farm*, *WebApplication*, and *Site*.
Field	Declares a site column definition. Site columns are discussed in Chapter 3. Can be scoped to *Site*.
HideCustomAction	Hides an existing custom action defined by another custom action or implemented by default in SharePoint. Hiding custom actions are discussed in Chapter 12. Can be scoped to *Farm*, *WebApplication*, *Site*, and *Web*.
ListInstance	Provisions an instance of a list definition with a specific configuration. Can be scoped to *Site* and *Web*.
ListTemplate	Defines a list template for provisioning a custom list's definitions. List templates are described in Chapter 3. Can be scoped to *Web*.
Module	Allows provisioning custom pages or files to a site. *Module* can also be used to deploy configured Web Parts, ListView Web Parts over existing or provisioned lists, NavBar links, and custom Master Pages, as well as to configure properties of the target feature. Modules are discussed in Chapter 12 and Chapter 13. Can be scoped to *Site* and *Web*.
PropertyBag	Assigns properties and metadata to items (File, Folder, ListItem, Web) through features. Can be scoped to *Web*.
Receivers	Defines a custom event receiver. Event receivers are discussed in Chapter 10, "Remove event receivers." Can be scoped to *Web*.
WebTemplate	Allows deploying a website template, even through a sandboxed solution so that it can create site instances based on that template. Site templates are discussed in Chapter 13. Can be scoped to *Site*.
Workflow	Deploys a legacy workflow (SharePoint 2010) definition on a target site. Workflows will be covered in Part V of this book, "Developing workflows." Can be scoped to *Site*.
WorkflowActions	Defines custom workflow actions (SharePoint 2010) for SharePoint Designer 2013. Custom actions for SharePoint Designer 2013 are described in Chapter 17, "Developing workflows," and Chapter 18, "Advanced workflows." Can be scoped to *Farm*.
WorkflowAssociation	Associates a legacy workflow (SharePoint 2010) with its target. Can be scoped to *Site and Web*.

The element manifest file in Listing 4-4 declares the Web Part referenced by the feature in Listing 4-3.

LISTING 4-4 An element manifest file that defines the Web Part deployed by Listing 4-3

```
<?xml version="1.0" encoding="utf-8"?>
<Elements xmlns="http://schemas.microsoft.com/sharepoint/" >
  <Module Name="SampleWebPart" List="113" Url="_catalogs/wp">
    <File Path="SampleWebPart\SampleWebPart.webpart" Url="SampleWebPart.webpart"
      Type="GhostableInLibrary">
      <Property Name="Group" Value="DevLeap Web Parts" />
    </File>
  </Module>
</Elements>
```

Feature deployment

To deploy a feature, you need to copy the feature's folder to the SharePoint15_Root\TEMPLATE\FEATURES path of every target server for the feature. When this is complete, you can use the STSADM.exe command-line tool (found in the SharePoint15_Root\BIN folder) to install and later activate the feature. The following is the syntax to install and activate a feature via STSADM.exe:

```
STSADM.EXE -o installfeature
           {-filename <relative path to Feature.xml from system feature directory> |
            -name <feature folder>}
           [-force]
STSADM.EXE -o activatefeature
           {-filename <relative path to Feature.xml> |
            -name <feature folder> |
            -id <feature Id>}
           [-url <url>]
           [-force]
```

As an example, to forcibly install and activate the feature named *SampleWebPart*, you would use the following syntax from the command prompt:

```
STSADM.EXE -o installfeature -name SampleWebPart -force
STSADM.EXE -o activatefeature -name SampleWebPart -force -url http://server/site/subsite
```

Alternately, you can use Windows PowerShell to install and activate your feature. Specifically, you would use the *Install-SPFeature* and *Enable-SPFeature* PowerShell cmdlets, which are equivalent options to STSADM:

```
Install-SPFeature -Path <relative path to Feature.xml from system feature directory> -Force
Enable-SPFeature -Identity <identity of the target feature> -Force -Url <target URL>
```

For the *SampleWebPart* example, you would use PowerShell with the following syntax:

```
Install-SPFeature -Path SampleWebPart -Force
Enable-SPFeature -Identity "SampleWebPart" -Force -Url "http://server/site/subsite"
```

Meanwhile, to deactivate a previously activated feature, you can use the following syntax from the command prompt:

```
STSADM.EXE -o deactivatefeature
          {-filename <relative path to Feature.xml> |
           -name <feature folder> |
           -id <feature Id>}
          [-url <url>]
          [-force]
```

Here's the syntax to deactivate the *SampleWebPart* feature from the command prompt:

```
STSADM.EXE -o deactivatefeature -name SampleWebPart -force -url http://server/site/subsite
```

Within PowerShell, you can use the following cmdlet for deactivation:

```
Disable-SPFeature -Identity <identity of the target feature> -Force -Url <target URL>
```

This is the syntax to deactivate *SampleWebPart* feature:

```
Disable-SPFeature -Identity "SampleWebPart" -Force -Url "http://server/site/subsite"
```

You can also uninstall an inactive feature by using the following STSADM.exe command:

```
STSADM.EXE -o uninstallfeature
          {-filename <relative path to Feature.xml> |
           -name <feature folder> |
           -id <feature Id>}
          [-force]
```

This is the specific command for the *SampleWebPart* feature:

```
STSADM.EXE -o uninstallfeature -name SampleWebPart -force
```

Or, you can use the following PowerShell cmdlet:

```
Uninstall-SPFeature -Identity <identity of the target feature> -Force
```

From within PowerShell, you uninstall the *SampleWebPart* feature with the following:

```
Uninstall-SPFeature -Identity "SampleWebPart" -Force
```

More Info For a complete reference on all the available Windows PowerShell scripts for managing features and solutions, refer to the Microsoft TechNet page at *http://technet.microsoft.com/en-us/library/ee906565.aspx*.

All of these command prompt commands and PowerShell cmdlets offer and support a wide set of parameters; for the sake of simplicity, the examples are abridged. In real life, you should use PowerShell cmdlets because STSADM is provided only for backward compatibility. Moreover, by working with Microsoft Office 365, you will have the opportunity to use PowerShell cmdlets, but you will not be able to access the local command prompt of target servers.

To activate and deactivate a feature, you can use the web browser UI, especially if you like to manage features remotely or want to delegate feature management tasks to users who do not have access to the physical server farm. To manage features through the web browser interface, you need to go to the Site Settings page of the target site, select the Site Actions group, and then select Manage Site Features. Here, you can manage website-level features. If you need to manage site collection features, under the Site Collection Administration group, select Site Collection Features. Both of these menu items will lead you to a feature management page, from which you can activate or deactivate features.

Figure 4-1 shows the feature management page, which lists a site collection's features. If your features provide multilanguage support, this page will give you the appropriate titles and descriptions, according to the languages configured for the current site and to the current user's language.

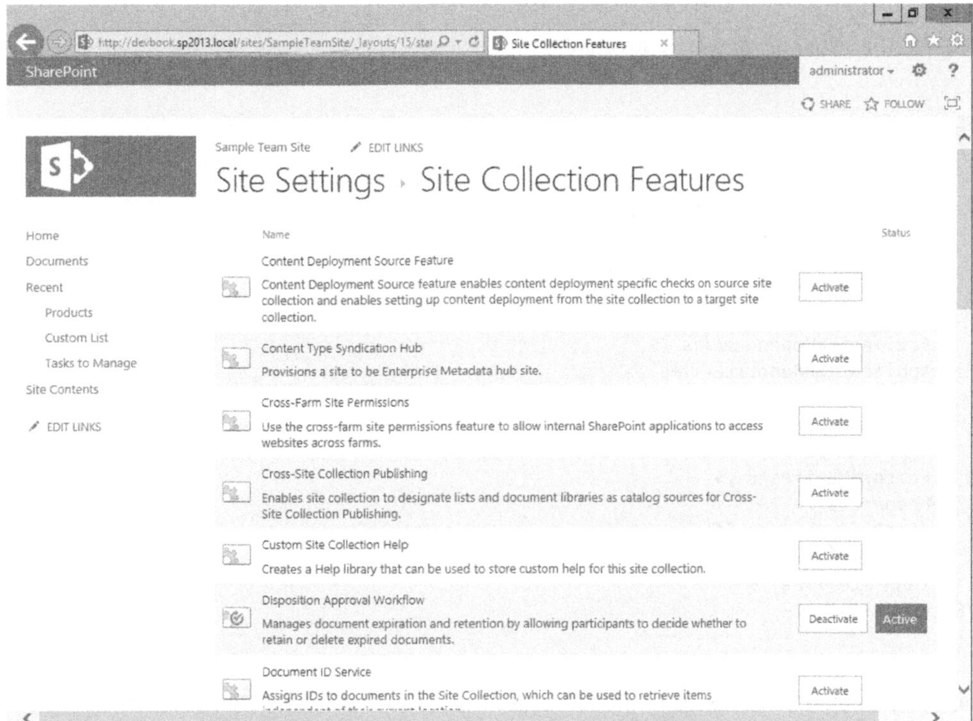

FIGURE 4-1 The Site Collection Features page.

Notice the Activate and Deactivate buttons next to the feature descriptions. You need to have the proper rights to execute these actions, regardless of whether you use the STSADM.exe tool, a PowerShell script, or the web UI. Users can activate/deactivate a feature at the website-level only if they are site owners or higher, and they should do that only with a valid reason. To manage a feature targeting a site collection, you need to have a site collection administrator account. To manage a *WebApplication*-scoped or *Farm*-scoped feature, you need to be a farm administrator.

Solution deployment

In the examples thus far, you have copied the features folders to each server by hand. Manually copying these folders is not the best practice, however, because of the high likelihood of errors. An easier and safer approach is to take advantage of a *solution package*, which is a cabinet file (a .cab compressed file) with a .wsp (Windows SharePoint Services Solution Package) extension provided to automate the process of installing features and customizations. Through a .wsp package, you can deploy a set of one or more features, automatically copying the files and folders to every front-end server from a centralized management console. A .wsp package contains a solution-specific manifest file called a *solution manifest* (yet another XML file, always with the name manifest.xml), which defines a set of information through attributes and child elements. Listing 4-5 demonstrates the structure of the solution manifest.

LISTING 4-5 The solution manifest file structure

```
<Solution
    Description = "Text"
    DeploymentServerType = "ApplicationServer" | "WebFrontEnd"
    ResetWebServer = "TRUE" | "FALSE"
    ResetWebServerModeOnUpgrade = "Recycle" | "StartStop"
    SharePointProductVersion = "Text"
    SolutionId = "Text"
    Title = "Text" >
    <ActivationDependencies />
    <ApplicationResourceFiles />
    <Assemblies />
    <CodeAccessSecurity />
    <DwpFiles />
    <FeatureManifests />
    <Resources />
    <SiteDefinitionManifests />
    <RootFiles />
    <TemplateFiles />
</Solution>
```

The *Solution* element belongs to the same namespace as the feature element (see *http://schemas.microsoft.com/sharepoint/*). Table 4-3 gives a brief description of each attribute of the *Solution* element.

TABLE 4-3 Attributes supported by the *Solution* element

Attribute name	Description
Description	Optional text that briefly describes the solution.
DeploymentServerType	Describes whether the solution targets a front-end server or an application server. It can take the values *ApplicationServer* or *WebFrontEnd*.
ResetWebServer	An optional *Boolean* attribute with a default value of *False*. If the value is *True* and the package targets a front-end server, the web server will be reset during deployment of the solution.
ResetWebServerModeOnUpgrade	Specifies the type of reset for the web server. Values are *Recycle*, for a complete recycle of the application pool, and *StartStop*, for a stop and start process. *ResetWebServerModeOnUpgrade* applies only if *ResetWebServer* has a value of *True*.
SharePointProductVersion	Defines the version of SharePoint Foundation in target for the current solution.
SolutionId	Defines the ID of the solution.
Title	Defines the title of the solution.

In addition, a *Solution* tag of a solution manifest can contain child elements, such as the following:

- ***ActivationDependencies*** Specifies a list of solutions on which the activation of the current solutions depend.
- ***ApplicationResourceFiles*** Specifies the application resource files to include in the solution, referencing local or global resource files.
- ***Assemblies*** References a set of .NET assemblies, declared with their strong name, to include in the solution deployment. The referenced assemblies will be copied to all the target servers when deploying the solution.
- ***CodeAccessSecurity*** Specifies custom code access security policies.
- ***DwpFiles*** Provides a list of Web Part deployment files (.dwp).
- ***FeatureManifests*** Provides a list of feature manifests to include in the solution deployment.
- ***Resources*** Specifies the resources to include in the solution.
- ***SiteDefinitionManifests*** Includes site definitions in the solution. To learn more about this topic, see Chapter 13.
- ***RootFiles*** Declares a list of files to include in the solution that will also be deployed on every server of the farm, in a path relative to the SharePoint15_Root folder.
- ***TemplateFiles*** Declares a list of files to include in the solution that will also be deployed on every server on the farm in a path relative to the SharePoint15_Root\TEMPLATE folder.

You can deploy a .wsp package using a PowerShell script with syntax such as this:

```
Add-SPSolution file.wsp
```

Otherwise, you can use the STSADM.exe command-line tool and the following syntax:

```
STSADM.EXE -o addsolution -filename filepath.wsp
```

After installing a solution, you need to deploy it to be able to activate and deactivate it and upgrade its features. Using PowerShell, the following is the minimal script needed to deploy a solution for all the web applications on the farm:

```
Install-SPSolution  Identity file.wsp -GACDeployment -AllWebApplications
```

While using the STSADM.exe command-line tool, you can invoke the following command:

```
STSADM.EXE -o deploysolution
           -name <Solution name>
          [-url <virtual server url>]
          [-allcontenturls]
          [-time <time to deploy at>]
          [-immediate]
          [-local]
          [-allowgacdeployment]
          [-allowcaspolicies]
          [-lcid <language>]
          [-force]
```

After you add a solution to the farm, however, with SPCA, you can also deploy it using a web browser. Go to the System Settings page, and then click Manage Farm Solutions in the Farm Management group.

Regardless of the interface that you use to deploy a solution, if your farm does not operating 24 hours a day, 7 days a week, you can schedule the deployment at night to avoid any issues or failures during peak daytime usage. If your farm does operate all day, every day, you should have a set of front-end servers configured for network load balancing so that you can deploy and upgrade solutions one server at a time without any service interruption.

Just as you can install and deploy a solution, you can also retract and remove one. To retract a solution, you can still use the SPCA interface. Alternately, you can use a PowerShell script or the STSADM.exe command-line tool. The PowerShell cmdlet takes the following form:

```
Uninstall-SPSolution -Identity <solution identity>
            [-Time <scheduled time to uninstall>]
            [-AllWebApplications]
            [-WebApplication]
```

Meanwhile, this is the STSADM.exe syntax for retracting a solution:

```
STSADM.EXE -o retractsolution
           -name <Solution name>
           [-url <virtual server url>]
           [-allcontenturls]
           [-time <time to remove at>]
           [-immediate]
           [-local]
           [-lcid <language>]
```

To completely remove an unused solution, you can use the following PowerShell cmdlet:

```
Remove-SPSolution -Identity <solution identity> [-Force]
```

If you prefer using STSADM.exe, you need the following syntax:

```
STSADM.EXE -o deletesolution
           -name <Solution name>
            [-override]
            [-lcid <language>]
```

Solutions also can help you with versioning issues. After deploying a solution, you can upgrade it through a standard and supported upgrade path, as you'll learn in the "Upgrading solutions and features" section later in this chapter. Before deploying and upgrading a solution, however, you need to package it, as the next section illustrates.

Packaging with Visual Studio 2012

Visual Studio 2012 natively provides tools that support developers in releasing SharePoint solutions. Whenever you create a SharePoint 2013 project within Visual Studio 2012, you can choose to manage the project deployment through the Packaging Explorer and the Package Designer. These tools give you the ability to graphically define the content of the package that will be compiled while building your solution. Figure 4-2 depicts the interface of the Packaging Explorer and the Package Designer for a sample Web Part project.

The interface includes a tree view on the left, in which you can explore the package structure, as well as an editing interface in the body of Visual Studio. From the editing interface, you can configure the name of the package, the features that will be put inside it (chosen from the set of features available in the current Visual Studio solution), and the order of installation of those features. At the top of the editor, there are three tabs (Design, Advanced, and Manifest) that you can use to change the display of the Package Designer editing section. Figure 4-2 shows the editing section in Design view. In Advanced view, you can provide custom .NET assemblies (DLLs) that will be deployed by the current package. In Manifest view, you can see the autogenerated XML of the manifest, and you can customize the XML template that is used to generate it to provide any custom tag or attribute that's not defined by default. You can also take full control of the XML manifest content, replacing the auto-generated code with a completely manual version.

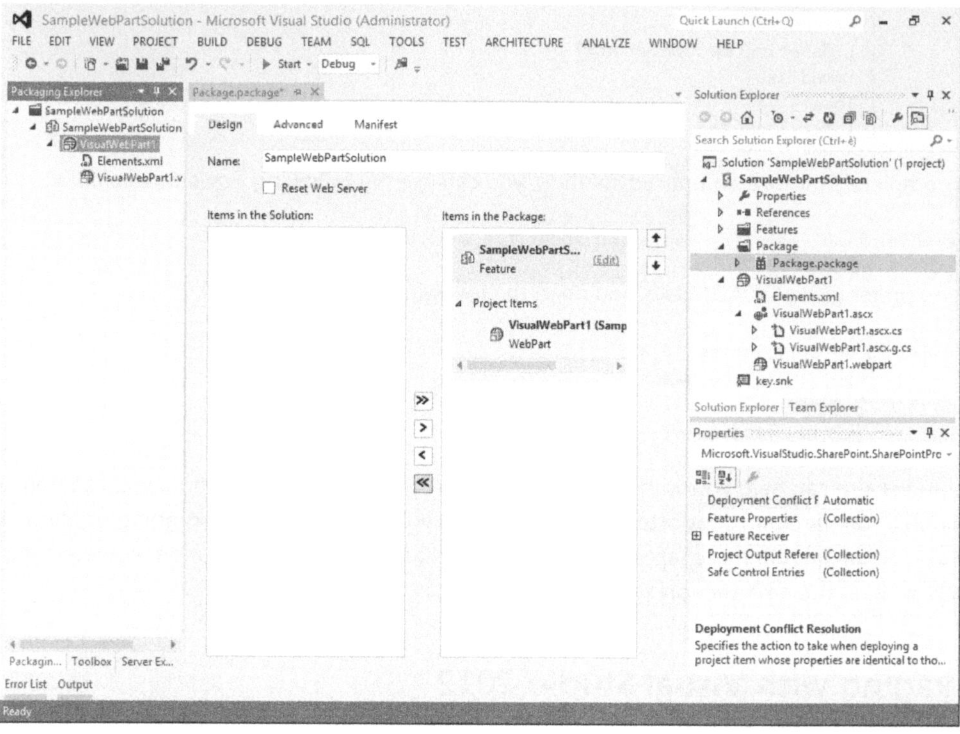

FIGURE 4-2 The Visual Studio 2010 Packaging Explorer and Package Designer interface.

In addition to using the Packaging Explorer, you have the ability to manage the configuration of each feature included in the package. To configure a feature, double-click it in the Visual Studio Solution Explorer, or click the Edit command available for each feature in the Packaging Explorer. The feature editor is the place to provide descriptive information for the feature, such as its title and description; configuration and behavioral parameters, including the target scope of the feature; the set of items that make up the feature; and any feature activation dependencies. A *feature activation dependency* gives you the ability to define a sequence of deployment for features. For example, you can create a sequence that prevents you from deploying one specific feature before another specific feature has been deployed. As with the Packaging Explorer, you can switch to Manifest view so that you can see the XML that describes the current feature. You can also customize the XML using a model or from scratch.

Note If you right-click a feature item in Solution Explorer, you can create custom resource files and add feature event receivers, which will be discussed in the upcoming "Feature receivers" section.

After you define a package, right-click the Visual Studio project that contains it, and then deploy the .wsp package by clicking Deploy. By default, Visual Studio will deploy the package on the farm that you chose when you created the project. In a development environment, you usually target the local server, which performs double-duty as the development machine and the SharePoint server for first testing your solutions. You can also simply create the package by clicking the Publish menu item, in which case you will be prompted to select the target file location. The publishing command is useful whenever you need to deploy the .wsp package into an external environment and you need to copy the .wsp file from your development environment to the target environment. Lastly, you can retract a solution from the SharePoint server where you previously deployed it by clicking the Retract menu item. If you deploy a solution on a server where you have already deployed it—for example, because you fixed some bugs and you want to repeat solution testing—the deploy process offered by Visual Studio 2012 will automatically retract the old version and release the new one, deactivating the features before retraction and activating them again during deployment. From the perspective of SharePoint, it would be better to upgrade the solutions, as you will see in the next section of this chapter. For the sake of simplicity, however, Visual Studio retracts it and deploys it again.

Upgrading solutions and features

During the course of a solution's lifetime, you may eventually need to upgrade and customize your code. SharePoint 2013 provides a rich set of capabilities to support you while upgrading solutions and features. In fact, you can upgrade a solution to update a .wsp deployment from an older version to a current one. To upgrade a solution, you can use the following PowerShell cmdlet:

```
Update-SPSolution -Identity <solution identity> -LiteralPath <path of the updated WSP>
            [-CASPolicies]
            [-FullTrustBinDeployment]
            [-GACDeployment]
            [-Force]
```

For the *SampleWebPart* deployment package, use a PowerShell script like the following:

```
Update-SPSolution -Identity file.wsp -LiteralPath c:\file_v2.wsp -GACDeployment
```

You can also use the STSADM.exe command:

```
STSADM.EXE -o upgradesolution
            -name <Solution name>
            [-filename <upgrade filename>]
            [-time <time to upgrade at>]
            [-immediate]
            [-local]
            [-allowgacdeployment]
            [-allowcaspolicies]
            [-lcid <language>]
```

Thus, for the *SampleWebPart* deployment package example, the syntax would be the following:

```
STSADM.EXE -o upgradesolution -name SampleWebPart.wsp -allowGacDeployment
```

No matter which method you use, SharePoint updates the .wsp package stored in the configuration database and synchronizes every target server in the farm with the content of the new package. For example, if your update includes new files (DLLs, ASPX pages, JS files, and so on), the upgrade process will copy them to all of the servers within the farm. At the same time, if your upgrade removes items that you will no longer use, the upgrade process will remove them from all the servers.

Important Be careful designating files for removal. If files are shared with other solutions, the SharePoint update process will still remove them, potentially breaking functionalities of other solutions. For further details about upgrading solutions, read the document "Upgrading a Farm Solution in SharePoint 2010," available on MSDN at *http://msdn.microsoft.com/en-us/library/aa543659.aspx*.

The feature's manifest schema provides elements that you can use to upgrade custom features through versioning and declarative upgrade actions. The Server Object Model provides specific types and members for this purpose. These are useful for querying at various scopes (*SPWebService*, *SPWebApplication*, *SPContentDatabase*, and *SPSite*) and retrieving the features' current versions. Listing 4-6 illustrates how to query a site collection for all the features that need to be upgraded.

LISTING 4-6 Using types to query for features that need to be upgraded

```
using(SPSite site = new SPSite("http://devbook.sp2013.local/")) {

    Boolean needsUpgrade = true;
    SPFeatureQueryResultCollection featuresToUpgrade =
        site.QueryFeatures(SPFeatureScope.Site, needsUpgrade);

    Boolean force = true;
    foreach (SPFeature feature in featuresToUpgrade) {
        feature.Upgrade(force);
    }
}
```

The *QueryFeatures* method of the *SPSite* class can search for features to upgrade while the *Upgrade* method on each *SPFeature* instance upgrades it effectively. The interesting part of the discussion is what happens during the feature upgrade process.

Every feature has a version number attribute specified in its manifest, so you can upgrade a feature by simply incrementing the version number; for example, you can use the Properties section of the Package Designer to release a new .wsp package to deploy the new version via an *upgradesolution* command. Beginning with SharePoint 2010, the feature manifest file has a section in which you can declare upgrade actions to execute during the *Upgrade* process. These upgrade actions are defined inside an *UpgradeActions* configuration element (see Listing 4-1), where you can define custom actions to execute while upgrading a feature. You can use the *AddContentTypeField* element to define a field (for instance, a site column) that will be automatically added to a content type, eventually pushing the modification to inheriting content types and lists. You can also specify element manifests to apply during an upgrade by using the *ApplyElementManifests* tag with its child elements, *ElementFile* and *ElementManifest*. Using this last element, you can create new content, like list definitions, site columns, content types, list instances, custom pages, and so forth. Using the *MapFile* element, you can specify mapping between old and new files. Lastly, if you need to execute custom code during the upgrade process, you can configure the *CustomUpgradeAction* tag, which will reference a custom upgrade action defined in a feature receiver. You will learn more about feature receivers in the next section.

Occasionally, you might need to release a version upgrade in multiple environments that require different versions of the same feature. For example, imagine having a new feature with a current version of 2.0.0.0 that you want to update on a pair of customers' farms, called Farm1 and Farm2. Farm1 is currently running version 1.0.0.0 of your feature and Farm2 is running version 1.5.0.0. In such a scenario, you should define a new package with a path to upgrade your feature from version 1.0.0.0 to version 2.0.0.0, and from version 1.5.0.0 to version 2.0.0.0, as well.

Luckily, the schema of the feature manifest supports declaration of version ranges via the *VersionRange* element—a child of the *UpgradeActions* element. Thus, you can define two different upgrade paths based on the initial version of the feature that you want to upgrade. Listing 4-7 shows an example of a feature manifest that satisfies this scenario.

LISTING 4-7 A feature manifest that supports versioning with multiple upgrade paths

```
<Feature xmlns="http://schemas.microsoft.com/sharepoint/" Version="1.0.0.0"
Title="$Resources:FeatureTitle" Description="$Resources:FeatureDescription"
Id="c46c270e-e722-4aa0-82ba-b66c8dd61f4e" Scope="Site">
  <UpgradeActions>
    <VersionRange BeginVersion="0.0.0.0" EndVersion="1.5.0.0">
      <MapFile FromPath="Oldest.aspx" ToPath="Latest.aspx" />
    </VersionRange>
    <VersionRange BeginVersion="1.5.0.0" EndVersion="2.0.0.0">
      <MapFile FromPath="Intermediary.aspx" ToPath="Latest.aspx" />
    </VersionRange>
  </UpgradeActions>
  <ElementManifests>
    <ElementManifest Location="SampleWebPart\Elements.xml" />
    <ElementFile Location="SampleWebPart\SampleWebPart.webpart" />
    <ElementFile Location="Resources\Resources.resx" />
    <ElementFile Location="Resources\Resources.it-IT.resx" />
  </ElementManifests>
</Feature>
```

The *VersionRange* element accepts two attributes: *BeginVersion* and *EndVersion*. The former is a lower inclusive limit and the latter is an upper exclusive limit. Thus, the first *VersionRange* defined in Listing 4-7 refers to features with a version greater than or equal to 0.0.0.0 and lower than 1.5.0.0, whereas the second *VersionRange* matches features with a version greater than or equal to 1.5.0.0 and lower than 2.0.0.0. In this example, the feature simply maps an old .aspx file to a newer one. Of course, during a feature's upgrade process, you can do whatever you want because you can invoke custom SharePoint code using a feature receiver.

More Info For further details, read the MSDN "Upgrading Features" page at *http://msdn.microsoft.com/en-us/library/aa544511.aspx.*

Feature receivers

A *feature receiver* is a class that executes custom code upon the occurrence of specific life cycle–related events, usually by making use of the SharePoint Server Object Model. Every feature receiver adheres to the architecture of the SharePoint event receivers, which are described in Chapter 10, "Remote event receivers." A feature receiver can trap the following events:

- **Feature activation** This occurs when a feature has been activated.
- **Feature deactivating** This occurs while a feature is deactivating.
- **Feature installation** This occurs when a feature has been installed.
- **Feature uninstalling** This occurs while a feature is uninstalling.
- **Feature upgrading** This occurs while a feature is upgrading.

To implement your own feature receivers, you need to define a new class that inherits from the base abstract class, *SPFeatureReceiver*, which is defined in the *Microsoft.SharePoint* namespace. Listing 4-8 presents the definition of the *SPFeatureReceiver* abstract class.

LISTING 4-8 The definition of the *SPFeatureReceiver* base abstract class

```
public abstract class SPFeatureReceiver {
    public SPFeatureReceiver();

    public virtual void FeatureActivated(SPFeatureReceiverProperties properties);
    public virtual void FeatureDeactivating(SPFeatureReceiverProperties
properties);
    public virtual void FeatureInstalled(SPFeatureReceiverProperties properties);
    public virtual void FeatureUninstalling(SPFeatureReceiverProperties
properties);
    public virtual void FeatureUpgrading(SPFeatureReceiverProperties properties,
  string upgradeActionName, IDictionary<string, string> parameters);
}
```

Each of the virtual methods accepts an argument of type *SPFeatureReceiverProperties*, which allows access to information about the target feature, its definition, and the current site. Listing 4-9 declares the *SPFeatureReceiverProperties* class.

LISTING 4-9 The definition of the *SPFeatureReceiverProperties* class

```
public sealed class SPFeatureReceiverProperties : IDisposable {

    public SPFeatureDefinition Definition { get; internal set; }
    public SPFeature Feature { get; }
    public SPSite UserCodeSite { get; }
}
```

Through the properties of this class, you can do practically anything that you want, writing custom code to implement everything that is not already available through standard feature elements.

Important Although the *SPFeatureReceiverProperties* class implements the *IDisposable* interface, you should not dispose of it directly; the infrastructure code of SharePoint Foundation already handles the disposal of instances of this type.

To create a feature receiver, you need to implement the receiver class, build its assembly, put it into the GAC, and declare the *ReceiverAssembly* and *ReceiverClass* attributes in a feature manifest XML file. Listing 4-10 illustrates an example of a feature manifest with a receiver declaration.

LISTING 4-10 The manifest of a feature with a custom feature receiver

```
<Feature xmlns="http://schemas.microsoft.com/sharepoint/ "Version=1.0.0.0"
Title="DevLeap Sample Web Part"
Description="This feature deploys a sample Web Part."
Id="c46c270e-e722-4aa0-82ba-b66c8dd61f4e"
ReceiverAssembly="DevLeap.SP2010.SampleFeature, Version=1.0.0.0,
Culture=neutral, PublicKeyToken=b001133e0647953d"
ReceiverClass="DevLeap.SP2010.SampleFeature.SampleWebPartEventReceiver"
Scope="Site">
  <ElementManifests>
    <ElementManifest Location="SampleWebPart\Elements.xml" />
    <ElementFile Location="SampleWebPart\SampleWebPart.webpart" />
  </ElementManifests>
</Feature>
```

Note The values of the *ReceiverAssembly* and the *ReceiverClass* attributes in Listing 4-10 need to be defined on a single of code.

Listing 4-11 shows a sample feature receiver, creating a list instance when the feature is activated and deleting the list instance while the feature is deactivating.

LISTING 4-11 A sample feature receiver that handles *FeatureActivated* and *FeatureDeactivating* events

```
public class SampleWebPartEventReceiver : SPFeatureReceiver {

    public override void FeatureActivated(SPFeatureReceiverProperties properties)
{
        // Get the parent of the feature
        // Current feature has a Site scope, thus the Parent
        // should be a Site Collection
        SPSite site = properties.Feature.Parent as SPSite;

        if (site != null) {
            SPWeb web = site.RootWeb;

            // Check to see if the list already exists
            try {
                SPList targetList = web.Lists["Sample List"];
            }
            catch (ArgumentException) {
                // The list does not exist, thus you can create it
                Guid listId = web.Lists.Add("Sample List",
                    "Sample List for SampleWebPart", SPListTemplateType.Events);
                SPList list = web.Lists[listId];
                list.OnQuickLaunch = true;
                list.Update();
            }
        }
    }

    public override void FeatureDeactivating(SPFeatureReceiverProperties
properties) {
        // Get the parent of the feature
        // Current feature has a Site scope, thus the Parent
        // should be a Site Collection
        SPSite site = properties.Feature.Parent as SPSite;

        if (site != null) {
            SPWeb web = site.RootWeb;

            // Check to see if the list already exists
            try {
                SPList list = web.Lists["Sample List"];
                list.Delete();
            }
            catch (ArgumentException) {
                // The list does not exist, thus you don't need to delete it
            }
        }
    }
}
```

Listing 4-11 illustrates that you should access the context of your feature through the *Feature.Parent* property of the current *SPFeatureReceiverProperties* argument. Depending on the scope of your feature, the *Parent* property could be the whole farm (*SPFarm*), a single web application (*SPWebApplication*), a site collection (*SPSite*), or a single website (*SPWeb*). It is up to you to know the target scope of your feature, and consequently determine the appropriate type to be hosted by the *Parent* property. In Listing 4-11, the scope of the feature is a site collection; thus, the *SPSite* type is used. If you are implementing a feature receiver that creates content during activation, it's a good habit to delete that content while deactivating. Sometimes, however, it's a good idea to leave data upon deactivation of a feature so that you don't dispose of data critical to end users. For example, if your feature created custom list instances or libraries, simply deleting them would be a bad idea. In fact, users may have used those lists and libraries to store custom data, which would be lost in a silent removal. Additionally, if your feature is activated and deactivated many times during the life cycle of your solutions, it's possible that you could activate it on a site where the contents created by the *FeatureActivated* event already exist. To prevent this, the code in Listing 4-11 checks for any previously existing list instance, prior to creating it.

Visual Studio 2012 provides a shortcut for creating feature event receivers. To access it, go to Solution Explorer and right-click a feature item within the Features folder of your SharePoint project to open the shortcut menu. There, you can select the Add Event Receiver menu item, which will create all the plumbing code for you. You will only need to write the code of the receiver's methods. Figure 4-3 shows the shortcut menu of a feature in Solution Explorer.

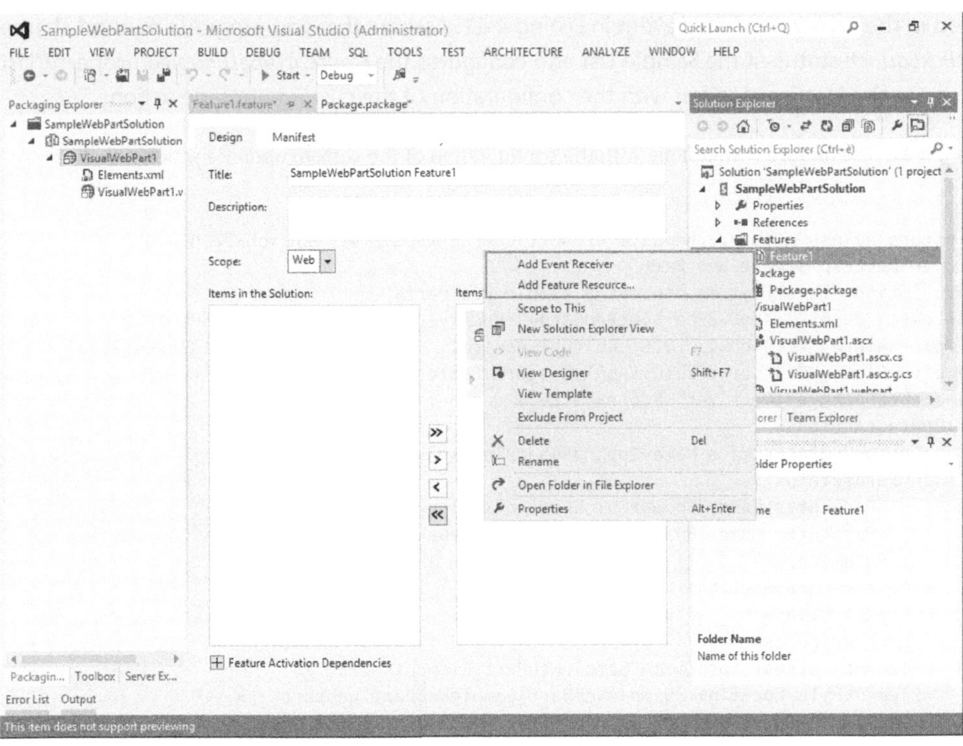

FIGURE 4-3 The Add Event Receiver menu item in a feature in Visual Studio 2012.

Important Be very careful when you define error handling code while implementing custom feature receivers. Any unhandled exception could lead to instability in your solution and block your feature deployment or removal.

Handling *FeatureUpgrading* events

One feature receiver event that deserves a dedicated section is *FeatureUpgrading*. Introduced in SharePoint 2010 for handling feature upgrades, this method targets all situations in which you need to upgrade a feature executing custom code. If you override the *FeatureUpgrading* method, you will receive an instance of the *SPFeatureReceiverProperties* type, as you do with all the other methods of the feature receivers. You will also receive an argument of type *String* with name *upgradeActionName* and an argument of type *IDictionary<String, String>* with name *parameters*. The values for these arguments can be defined in the feature manifest file, within the *UpgradeActions* section of the file schema (see Listing 4-7).

How would you use this method in practice? Suppose that you deployed the *SampleWebPart* feature version 1.0.0.0 in your environment. Later, you decide to upgrade it to version 2.0.0.0. This new version of your Web Part needs to change (by code) the configuration of the list instance that you created in the *FeatureActivated* event in Listing 4-11. Assume that your upgrade method changes the *OnQuickLaunch* status of the Sample List and configures the *ContentTypesEnabled* property. Listing 4-12 shows the feature manifest with the configuration of the custom upgrade action.

LISTING 4-12 The feature manifest file with the configuration of the custom upgrade action

```
<Feature xmlns="http://schemas.microsoft.com/sharepoint/" Version="2.0.0.0"
Title="DevLeap Sample Web Part"
Description="This feature deploys a sample Web Part."
Id="c46c270e-e722-4aa0-82ba-b66c8dd61f4e" ReceiverAssembly="DevLeap.SP2010.
SampleFeature, Version=1.0.0.0, Culture=neutral, PublicKeyToken=b001133e0647953d"
ReceiverClass="DevLeap.SP2010.SampleFeature.Features.SampleWebPart.
SampleWebPartEventReceiver" Scope="Site">
  <UpgradeActions>
    <CustomUpgradeAction Name="UpgradeSampleList">
      <Parameters>
        <Parameter Name="ShowOnQuickLaunch">False</Parameter>
        <Parameter Name="EnableContentTypes">True</Parameter>
      </Parameters>
    </CustomUpgradeAction>
  </UpgradeActions>
  <ElementManifests>
    <ElementManifest Location="SampleWebPart\Elements.xml" />
    <ElementFile Location="SampleWebPart\SampleWebPart.webpart" />
  </ElementManifests>
</Feature>
```

Note The values of the *ReceiverAssembly* and the *ReceiverClass* attributes in Listing 4-12 need to be defined on a single line of code.

The custom upgrade action is defined using a *Name* attribute and a set of *Parameter* elements. Meanwhile, Listing 4-13 demonstrates the implementation of the *FeatureUpgrading* method, which uses the custom upgrade action configuration.

LISTING 4-13 Using the *FeatureUpgrading* method implementation to handle the custom upgrade action

```
public override void FeatureUpgrading(SPFeatureReceiverProperties properties,
    string upgradeActionName,
    System.Collections.Generic.IDictionary<string, string> parameters) {

    // Get the parent of the feature
    // Current feature has a Site scope, thus the Parent
    // should be a Site Collection
    SPSite site = properties.Feature.Parent as SPSite;

    if (site != null) {
        // Check the type of upgrade action
        if (upgradeActionName == "UpgradeSampleList") {
            // Extract and convert the properties
            Boolean showOnQuickLaunch =
                Boolean.Parse(parameters["ShowOnQuickLaunch"]);
            Boolean enableContentTypes =
                Boolean.Parse(parameters["EnableContentTypes"]);

            SPWeb web = site.RootWeb;

            // Check to see if the list already exists
            try {
                SPList list = web.Lists["Sample List"];
                list.OnQuickLaunch = showOnQuickLaunch;
                list.ContentTypesEnabled = enableContentTypes;
                list.Update();
            }
            catch (ArgumentException) {
                // The list does not exist, thus you cannot upgrade it
            }
        }
    }
}
```

The method invocation receives the *Name* attribute of the *CustomUpgradeAction* element inside the *upgradeActionName* argument, as well as the set of *Parameter* elements through the parameters dictionary. Based on these arguments, the upgrade code can now do whatever is necessary to upgrade the feature.

Summary

This chapter discussed how to take advantage of features and solutions to deploy customization and custom code. Specifically, it described how to package features in .wsp packages and how to deploy them, as well as how to upgrade features using the capabilities provided with SharePoint 2013. In future chapters, especially those in Part IV, "Extending SharePoint," you will dig deeper into implementing some of the main features that are useful when developing and customizing SharePoint solutions.

CHAPTER 5

Server Object Model

As you learned in Chapter 1, "Microsoft SharePoint 2013: A quick tour," Microsoft SharePoint 2013 is based directly on Microsoft .NET and Microsoft ASP.NET. Not surprisingly, one of the main tools that you will use to develop server-side solutions interacting with the SharePoint engine is the .NET object model offered by the SharePoint infrastructure. Called the *Server Object Model*, it is a set of namespaces and classes divided into several .NET assemblies. You can reference and use it in any kind of .NET solution that will run on a SharePoint server. In fact, the Server Object Model has some dependencies that are satisfied *only* on servers in a SharePoint farm, so you cannot use it in client-side solutions, SharePoint apps, remote event receivers, or anything else that is not running on a SharePoint server.

Thus, the Server Object Model is a good choice only for code-based solutions running on a SharePoint server. These are typically deployed through a farm solution or a sandboxed solution. You cannot create farm solutions at all in Microsoft Office 365, and starting with SharePoint 2013, you should also create SharePoint apps, rather than code-based sandboxed solutions.

If you are writing a software solution that interacts with SharePoint but does not run on a SharePoint server, you can use the Client Object Model, the new REST (Representational State Transfer) API, or OData (Open Data Protocol). For more information on these, see Part II, "Developing SharePoint solutions," and Part III, "Developing SharePoint apps."

The key point of the Server Object Model is that you can use it to do in code everything (and more) that you can do with the SharePoint UI, whether through the browser, using the command-line tools, or with Windows PowerShell.

This chapter shows you how to use the major classes of the Server Object Model by examining their main members. You won't find a complete reference for the entire object model here, because it contains thousands of types—an encyclopedia would probably be insufficient.

More Info If you are looking for a complete reference of all the types in the SharePoint Server Object Model, see the ".NET server API reference for SharePoint 2013" page on MSDN, at *http://msdn.microsoft.com/en-us/library/jj193058.aspx*.

Startup environment

Before you begin working with the Server Object Model, and the examples in this chapter in particular, you need to make a few preparations. Because the UI is not a focus of this chapter, the code samples shown here mainly use a console application, which will need to execute on a SharePoint server. Consider that in real-life development, using a console application or a PowerShell script for testing code using the Server Object Model often speeds up the development by skipping the deployment phase. (Throughout the book, however, you will see the Server Object Model in action within SharePoint solutions as well.) To test the code samples in this chapter, you need to create a new Console project in Microsoft Visual Studio 2012. Next, make sure that the Target Framework setting on the Application tab of the project is set to .NET Framework 4.5. Because Microsoft SharePoint 2013 works on 64-bit machines only, specify x64 for the Platform Target setting on the Build tab of the project. Lastly, you need to reference some of the SharePoint Server Object Model assemblies, including Microsoft.SharePoint.dll, which is the main Server Object Model assembly. You can find it, along with many of the other assemblies, in the SharePoint15_Root\ISAPI folder, as well as in standard .NET references in Visual Studio.

Note SharePoint15_Root represents the SharePoint root folder, which usually is located in C:\Program Files\Common Files\Microsoft Shared\Web Server Extensions\15.

Objects hierarchy

All the main types of the Server Object Model are defined in namespaces that start with *Microsoft.SharePoint.** or *Microsoft.Office.**, and in general have a type name that begins with *SP*, which stands for SharePoint. For example, the type that represents a user is named *SPUser* and belongs to the namespace *Microsoft.SharePoint*. The type that represents a SharePoint site, also defined in that namespace, is named *SPWeb*. Figure 5-1 shows some of the main classes and their hierarchical organization in the Server Object Model.

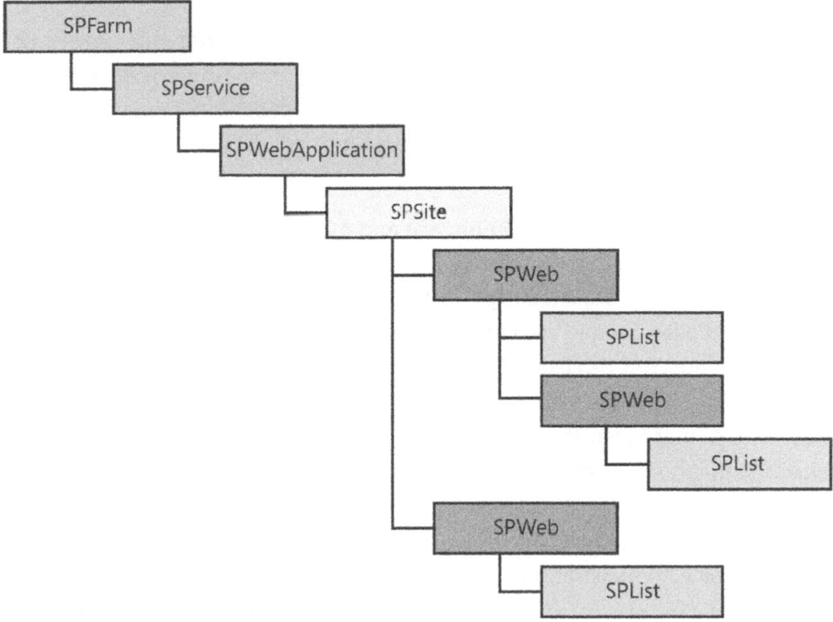

FIGURE 5-1 The hierarchy of the main types of the SharePoint Server Object Model.

The sections that follow explore the main types of the Server Object Model, briefly discussing their key members and showing some quick code samples. Later in the chapter, you will learn how to take advantage of these types in everyday solutions by working through some examples.

SPFarm, *SPServer*, *SPService*, and *SPWebApplication*

The first and main object of the Server Object Model is the *SPFarm* class, which represents a reference to an entire SharePoint server farm. This class belongs to the *Microsoft.SharePoint.Administration* namespace. You can use it to create a fresh new farm from scratch, or you can connect to an existing farm. To create a new farm, you need to invoke one of the many overloads of the public static *Create* factory method. To connect to an existing farm (the most common scenario), you provide a SQL Server connection string and the farm's secret passphrase to the public static *Open* method, which has the following signature:

```
public static SPFarm Open(SqlConnectionStringBuilder connectionString, SecureString
passphrase)
```

The connection string corresponds to the farm configuration database that is defined while configuring the farm using the SharePoint 2013 Products Configuration Wizard or PowerShell. You can also find it in the system registry at HKLM\Software\Microsoft\Shared Tools\Web Server Extensions\15.0\Secure\ConfigDB\dsn. Alternatively, you can connect directly to a local farm using the static property *SPFarm.Local*.

Important By default, the SharePoint Server Object Model impersonates the current user. Thus, whenever you create an instance of an *SP** type without providing any specific set of user credentials, your code impersonates the user running the process or the web request when you invoke the Server Object Model from a webpage.

After obtaining an instance of *SPFarm*, you can browse and manage servers and services that belong to that farm. For example, you can browse the *Servers* collection to enumerate all the physical servers that belong to the farm as objects of type *SPServer*. You can browse the *Services* property, which has the type *SPServiceCollection* and contains different kinds of services—all sharing a common base class of type *SPService*. You can examine all the Windows services, which are objects of type *SPWindowsService*, or you can access the web services, which are of type *SPWebService*. Every web service is composed of one or more web applications, each with the type *SPWebApplication*. Listing 5-1 shows a code example that browses for all these kinds of objects in the local farm. Note that you should execute this (and the following) code excerpt in a project that references the Microsoft.SharePoint.dll assembly, and you should also provide a *using* statement for Microsoft.SharePoint, as well as for Microsoft.SharePoint.Administration.

LISTING 5-1 Browsing objects in the local farm

```
SPFarm farm = SPFarm.Local;

Console.WriteLine("Here are the servers of the Farm");
foreach (SPServer server in farm.Servers) {
    Console.WriteLine("Server Name: {0}", server.Name);
    Console.WriteLine("Server Address: {0}", server.Address);
    Console.WriteLine("Server Role: {0}", server.Role);
}

foreach (SPService service in farm.Services) {

    Console.WriteLine("----------------------------------------");

    if (service is SPWindowsService) {
        Console.WriteLine("Windows Service: {0}", service.DisplayName);
        Console.WriteLine("Type: {0}", service.TypeName);
        Console.WriteLine("Instances: {0}", service.Instances.Count);
    }
    else if (service is SPWebService) {
        Console.WriteLine("Web Service: {0}", service.DisplayName);
        Console.WriteLine("Type: {0}", service.TypeName);
        Console.WriteLine("Instances: {0}", service.Instances.Count);

        SPWebService webService = service as SPWebService;
```

```
            if (webService != null) {
                foreach (SPWebApplication webApplication in
                webService.WebApplications) {
                    Console.WriteLine("Web Application: {0}",
                        webApplication.DisplayName);

                    Console.WriteLine("Content Databases");
                    foreach (SPContentDatabase db in webApplication.ContentDatabases)
                    {
                        Console.WriteLine("Content Database: {0}", db.Name);
                        Console.WriteLine("Connection String: {0}",
                           db.DatabaseConnectionString);
                    }
                }
            }
        }
        else {
            Console.WriteLine("Generic Service Name: {0}", service.DisplayName);
            Console.WriteLine("Type Name: {0}", service.TypeName);
            Console.WriteLine("Instances: {0}", service.Instances.Count);
        }
    }
```

In real life, you do not need to edit a farm's configuration on a daily basis; however, it is important to know that the Server Object Model enables you to edit it should the need arise. Moreover, sometimes it's useful to begin browsing your farm topology from the root node (*SPFarm*) so you can explore the site collections and websites in greater detail. You can also execute the same kind of code from a PowerShell script, if you prefer.

SPSite and *SPWeb*

SPSite and *SPWeb* are fundamental types in the Server Object Model. They represent a site collection and a site, respectively. From a SharePoint perspective, a website (*SPWeb*) is just a child of a collection of one or more sites (*SPSite*). As you will see later in this chapter, these classes are the basis for many typical operations in your solutions. Every time you need to access the content of a SharePoint site, you will need to reference its parent *SPSite* object (the site collection the site belongs to), and then open the corresponding *SPWeb* instance. To access an *SPSite* instance, you can create it using one of the available constructors, or you can obtain a reference to it through its parent *SPWebApplication* instance. Here are the constructors provided for building an *SPSite* instance:

```
public SPSite(Guid id);
public SPSite(string requestUrl);
public SPSite(Guid id, SPUrlZone zone);
public SPSite(Guid id, SPUserToken userToken);
public SPSite(string requestUrl, SPUserToken userToken);
public SPSite(Guid id, SPUrlZone zone, SPUserToken userToken);
```

Using the appropriate constructor, you can reference a site collection by its unique ID, which is a globally unique identifier (GUID), or with a URL that corresponds to a resource published by the site collection. Some of these six overloads of the constructor let you access the site by using a specific zone from the *SPUrlZone* enumeration, the definition of which is shown in the following:

```
public enum SPUrlZone {
    Default,
    Intranet,
    Internet,
    Custom,
    Extranet
}
```

These values correspond to the zones that you can create using the SharePoint administrative tools. Other *SPSite* constructors accept an *SPUserToken* instance. The *SPUserToken* class represents a token for a valid SharePoint user. When you create an *SPSite* instance using such a token, you can impersonate the user who owns that token rather than the current user. You can import an *SPUserToken* instance from a previously exported array of bytes, or you can create one from an object that implements the generic *System.Security.Principal.IIdentity* interface. You would, for example, take advantage of these constructor overloads to execute code on behalf of another user, probably one with elevated privileges.

More Info In the SharePoint Server Object Model, starting from *SPSite* and moving down to the *SPWeb*, *SPList*, and *SPListItem* (refer to Figure 5-1), almost every object instance has a unique and identifying *ID* property, which can be a GUID or an integer. You should become accustomed to the idea of having an ID to uniquely reference each of these types. In general, you can also use URLs or titles to reference items, but using the unique ID helps to prevent errors.

Listing 5-2 shows a code excerpt that browses all the *SPSite* and *SPWeb* instances in a set of *SPWebApplication* objects. The *webService* variable in the excerpt references an instance of an *SPWebService* object, which can be retrieved using the code illustrated in Listing 5-1.

LISTING 5-2 Browsing for *SPSite* and *SPWeb* objects of an object of type *SPWebApplication*

```
foreach (SPWebApplication webApplication in webService.WebApplications) {
    Console.WriteLine("Web Application: {0}", webApplication.DisplayName);

    foreach (SPSite site in webApplication.Sites) {
        using (site) {
            Console.WriteLine("Site Collection: {0}", site.Url);

            foreach (SPWeb web in site.AllWebs) {
                using (web) {
                    Console.WriteLine("Web Site: {0}", web.Title);
                }
            }
        }
    }
}
```

The example in Listing 5-3 shows how to obtain a reference to an *SPSite* object using its public URL.

LISTING 5-3 Getting a reference to an *SPSite* object using its public URL

```
using (SPSite site = new SPSite("http://devbook.sp2013.local/")) {
    Console.WriteLine("Current Site URL: {0}", site.Url);

    SPWeb web = site.RootWeb;
    Console.WriteLine("Current Site RootWeb Title: {0}", web.Title);
}
```

After you have a reference to an *SPSite* instance, you can browse for the sites contained in the collection, or you can change the configuration of the site collection itself. Table 5-1 lists the main members of the *SPSite* type, which you will probably use often in real projects, along with a brief description of each member.

TABLE 5-1 Some of the members of the *SPSite* type

Member name	Description
AllowUnsafeUpdates	Property to get or set whether to accept updates via HTTP *GET* or without validating data security of messages sent via HTTP *POST*. Setting this property to a value of *true* reduces the security of the website. For further details on this, read the "Common and best practices" section later in the chapter.
AllWebs	Collection property that holds references to all the websites contained in the current site collection.
CheckForPermissions	Method that checks the permissions for a given set of rights and throws an exception if the check fails.
Delete	Method (along with some overloads) that deletes the current site collection from the parent web application.

Member name	Description
DoesUserHavePermissions	Method that's almost the same as *CheckForPermissions*, but returns a *Boolean* result rather than throwing an exception when the check fails.
EventReceivers	Collection property that contains references to the event receivers configured for the current site collection. Those are the event receivers installed on the SharePoint server, not the remote event receivers that are discussed in Chapter 10, "Remote event receivers."
Features	Collection property that you can use to enumerate the features associated with the current site collection. For more information about features, refer to Chapter 4, "SharePoint features and solutions."
GetCustomListTemplates	Method that returns the list of custom list templates for a specific website in the current site collection.
GetCustomWebTemplates	Method that returns the list of custom website templates available in the current site collection, based on a specific locale ID.
GetEffectiveRightsForAcl	Method that returns the effective rights of the current user for a specified target access control list (ACL).
GetRecycleBinItems	Method that lets you query the current contents of the Recycle Bin.
GetRecycleBinStatistics	Method that lets you obtain the size and the number of items in the Recycle Bin.
ID	Read-only property that represents the ID of the current site collection.
IISAllowsAnonymous	Read-only *Boolean* property that indicates whether anonymous access is configured in Internet Information Services (IIS) for the web application containing the current site collection.
Impersonating	Read-only *Boolean* property that returns *true* when the current instance of *SPSite* has been created by impersonating a third-party identity using an *SPUserToken* object instance.
OpenWeb	Method (and its overloads) that returns an *SPWeb* instance corresponding to a specific website contained in the current site collection.
ReadLocked	Property to get or set the *ReadLocked* status of the current site collection. When **TRUE**, the site will not be accessible via the Server Object Model or remote procedure call (RPC), and will return an HTTP 403 (FORBIDDEN) status code to any web browser request. To set this value, you need global administrative rights. For example, you can use this property to suspend service for a customer with a payment overdue. In that scenario, you should set the *LockIssue* property before setting the *ReadLocked* property to *true*.
ReadOnly	Property to get or set the read-only status for the contents of the current site collection. Setting this property to *true* also sets the *WriteLocked* property to *true*.
RecycleBin	Collection property by which you can enumerate the items currently contained in the Recycle Bin of the current site collection.
RootWeb	Property that returns a reference to the root website of the current site collection.
Solutions	Collection property that supports enumerating the sandboxed solutions associated with the current site collection.
Url	Read-only property that returns the full URL to the root website of the current site collection.
WorkflowManager	Read-only property that gives you access to the object managing workflow templates and instances in the current site collection. This property relates to the legacy workflow engine provided for backward compatibility with SharePoint 2010. For further details about workflows, see Part V of this book, "Developing workflows."
WriteLocked	*Boolean* property that's similar to *ReadLocked*, but affects write access only.
Zone	Property that returns the zone used to construct the current *SPSite* instance.

An *SPSite* object is required to obtain access to an *SPWeb* instance. In fact, the *SPWeb* class does not have a public constructor. The only way to obtain a reference to a site is through its parent *SPSite* object, although you can get access to the current website using the *SPControl* and *SPContext* types, which will be discussed later, in the "*SPControl* and *SPContext*" section. The *SPSite* class provides the *OpenWeb* method (see Table 5-1) for this purpose. Listing 5-4 shows an example of accessing a specific website by using its parent site collection.

LISTING 5-4 Getting a reference to an *SPWeb* instance through its parent *SPSite* object

```
using (SPSite site = new SPSite("http://devbook.sp2013.local/")) {
    Console.WriteLine("Current Site URL: {0}", site.Url);

    using (SPWeb web = site.OpenWeb("SampleSubSite")) {
        Console.WriteLine(web.Title);
    }
}
```

Listing 5-4 uses the *SPSite.OpenWeb* method, which has the following overloads:

```
public SPWeb OpenWeb();
public SPWeb OpenWeb(Guid gWebId);
public SPWeb OpenWeb(string strUrl);

public SPWeb OpenWeb(string strUrl, bool requireExactUrl);
public SPWeb OpenWeb(string strUrl, SPSiteOpenWebOptions options);
```

The first overload opens the lowest-level website, as defined by the URL provided to the constructor of the current site collection. For example, if you created the *SPSite* instance using the root site URL, you would get a reference to the root website. In contrast, if you created the *SPSite* instance using a child website URL, you would get a reference to that website. The second overload opens the website using its unique ID. The last three overloads accept the relative URL of the website, which must be exact for the last overload if the *requireExactUrl* argument is *true*. In the last overload, you have an option of type *SPSiteOpenWebOptions*, which allows you the choice of initializing a navigation cache.

You can use an *SPWeb* reference to navigate the contents of the site or simply to read or change its configuration. You will learn how to manage site contents later in this chapter. Table 5-2 lists some of the main members of the *SPWeb* type.

TABLE 5-2 Some of the members of the *SPWeb* type

Member name	Description
AllowUnsafeUpdates	Property to get or set whether to accept updates via HTTP *GET* or without validating data security of messages sent via HTTP *POST*. Setting this property to a value of *true* reduces the security of the website. For further details on this, read the "Common and best practices" section later in the chapter.
AllUsers	Collection property that holds references to all the users who are members of the website, or who have browsed to the site as authenticated members of a domain group in the site. For further details about users and groups, see Chapter 19, "Authentication and authorization infrastructure."
AppDatabaseName	Read-only property providing the name of the app database for the current web site.
AppDatabaseServerReferenceId	Read-only property to get the ID (GUID) of the server where the app database is located.
CheckPermissions	Method that checks whether the current user has a specific set of permissions. Throws an exception in case of failure.
ContentTypes	Collection property for enumerating all the content types in the website.
Delete	Method that deletes the current website.
EventReceivers	Collection property that holds references to all the event receivers of the website. Those are the event receivers installed on the SharePoint server, not the remote event receivers that are discussed in Chapter 10.
Features	Collection property by which you can enumerate the features associated with the current website. For more information, see Chapter 4.
Fields	Collection property by which you can enumerate all the site columns of the website.
Files	Collection property that holds references to all the files in the root directory of the website.
Folders	Collection property that holds references to all the first-level folders of the website.
GetFile	Method that returns a file, based on its GUID or URL.
GetFolder	Method that returns a folder, based on its GUID or URL.
GetRecycleBinItems	Method that allows querying the current contents of the Recycle Bin.
GetSiteData	Method that queries for list items across multiple lists and multiple SPWeb instances within a site collection. It returns a object of type *System.Data.DataTable* of ADO.NET.
GetUserEffectivePermissions	Method that returns the effective permissions for a specified username.
Groups	Collection property by which you can enumerate all the groups of the website. For more information about users and groups, see Chapter 19.
ID	Read-only property that represents the ID of the current website.
Lists	Collection property by which you can enumerate all the lists of the website.
RecycleBin	Collection property by which you can enumerate the items currently in the Recycle Bin of the current website.
Site	Property for referencing the parent site collection.
SiteUsers	Collection property that holds references to all the users of the current site collection. For more information about users and groups, see Chapter 19.
Title	Property to get or set the title of the website.

Member name	Description
Update	Method that saves any changes applied to the website to the database.
Users	Collection property containing references to all the users with explicitly assigned permissions in the current website. For more information about users and groups, see Chapter 19.

One of the most interesting members of this type is the *Update* method. While working with the Server Object Model, you are reading and changing an in-memory representation of the current object. Thus, any changes you make will not be applied to the database unless you explicitly request the object to persist its state using the *Update* method. Of course, if you change an in-memory *SPWeb* instance and do not invoke the *Update* method, your changes will be lost. This behavior is common for many types in the Server Object Model, including *SPWeb*, *SPList*, and *SPListItem*. Additionally, remember that in a typical SharePoint farm, the database server runs on a separate server, which is not the web front end or the application server where your code will run. Thus, saving the state of an object and invoking the *Update* method requires crossing the wire.

Listing 5-5 shows an example that modifies the *Title* property of the current website, and then invokes the *Update* method to confirm the action.

LISTING 5-5 Modifying the title of an instance of *SPWeb*

```
using (SPSite site = new SPSite("http://devbook.sp2013.local/")) {
    Console.WriteLine("Current Site URL: {0}", site.Url);

    using (SPWeb web = site.OpenWeb("SampleSubSite")) {
        web.Title = web.Title + " - Changed by code!";
        web.Update();
    }
}
```

SPList and *SPListItem*

Quite often, you will open an *SPSite* instance and one of its child *SPWeb* instances to gain access to the contents of one or more lists. The Server Object Model offers two types that target the concept of SharePoint lists and list items: *SPList* and *SPListItem*. *SPList* corresponds to a single list instance, whether that is a list of items or a document library. *SPListItem* defines a reference to a specific item of a list. In general, you open the list to extract one or more items, and then work with those items. Listing 5-6 shows an example that obtains a reference to a list and then browses its items.

LISTING 5-6 Browsing the items contained in an *SPList* instance of an object of type *SPWeb*

```
using (SPSite site = new SPSite("http://devbook.sp2013.local/")) {
    Console.WriteLine("Current Site URL: {0}", site.Url);

    using (SPWeb web = site.OpenWeb()) {
        SPList list = web.Lists["DevLeap Customers"];

        foreach (SPListItem item in list.Items) {
            Console.WriteLine(item.Title);
        }
    }
}
```

Listing 5-6 extracts an *SPList* object by using the *Lists* indexer of the current *SPWeb* instance, which uses the list *Title* property as a key. Then it enumerates the contents of the *Items* collection property of the list instance. The *SPList* type offers a rich set of members. Table 5-3 shows some of the more important members.

TABLE 5-3 Some of the members of the *SPList* type

Member name	Description
AddItem	Method that creates a new empty item in the current list. Once it's created, you will need to compile the fields of that item according to the validation constraints of the list.
BreakRoleInheritance	Method that breaks inheritance of role assignments for the current list and eventually copies role assignments from the parent website.
CheckPermissions	Method that checks whether the current user has a specific set of permissions. Throws an exception if the call fails.
ContentTypes	Collection property containing all the content types in the list.
Delete	Method that deletes the current list.
DoesUserHavePermissions	Method that checks whether the current user has a specific permission. Returns a *Boolean* value.
EventReceivers	Collection property containing all the event receivers of the website. Those are the event receivers installed on the SharePoint server, not the remote event receivers that are discussed in Chapter 10.
Fields	Collection property containing all the fields and/or site columns in the current list.
Folders	Collection property containing all the folders, if any, in the current list.
GetItemById	Method to get an item by using its unique numeric ID.
GetItems	Method with multiple overloads, used to get a subset of items. You will see more about this in the "Lists and items" section later in the chapter.
Hidden	Property that hides or shows the current list.
ID	Read-only property that represents the ID of the current list.
ItemCount	Read-only *Int32* property that returns the number of items contained in the current list, including folders.

Member name	Description
Items	Collection property containing the items in the current list.
RootFolder	Read-only property that returns the root folder of the list.
SchemaXml	Read-only *String* property that describes the list schema in XML of the currently selected list using CAML code (see the note following this table).
Title	Property to get or set the list title.
Update	Method that saves any pending list changes to the database.

Note Collaborative Application Markup Language (CAML) is an XML-based querying language that is useful for defining filtering, sorting, and grouping on SharePoint data. The CAML querying language is the lowest-level way of accessing SharePoint data while looking for lists and items. The CAML language reference is available on MSDN, at *http://msdn.microsoft.com/en-us/library/ms462365(v=office.15).aspx.*

Just as with the *SPWeb* type, the *SPList* class provides an *Update* method that saves any changes applied in memory. Using the Server Object Model, you can browse the contents of existing lists, or you can create new lists from scratch and populate them with fresh new items. Whether you create new items or browse for existing ones, you must manage them as *SPListItem* instances. Table 5-4 shows some of the main members of the *SPListItem* type.

TABLE 5-4 Some of the members of the *SPListItem* type

Member name	Description
Attachments	Collection property containing the attachments, if any, of the current item.
BreakRoleInheritance	Method that breaks inheritance of role assignments for the current item and eventually copies role assignments from the parent list.
CheckPermissions	Method that checks whether the current user has a specific set of permissions. Throws an exception if the call fails.
ContentType	Read-only property that returns a reference to the content type associated with the current item.
ContentTypeId	Read-only property that returns the ID of the content type associated with the current item.
Copy	Static method to copy an item from one location to another within the same server. The method has a couple of overloads.
CopyFrom	Method that overwrites the current item with a source item provided as a URL from the same server.
CopyTo	Method that overwrites the target item, which is provided as a URL on the same server, with the current item.
Delete	Method that deletes the current item.
DoesUserHavePermissions	Checks whether the current user has a specific permission. Returns a *Boolean* value.
File	Read-only property that returns a reference to the file that corresponds to the current item when the item resides in a document library.

Member name	Description
Folder	Read-only property that returns a reference to the folder associated with the current item when the item is a folder item.
ID	Read-only property that represents the ID of the current item.
Recycle	Method that deletes the current item, putting it into the Recycle Bin.
SystemUpdate	Method that saves any changes applied to the current item without affecting the Modified and Modified By fields of the current item, and optionally the item version.
Title	Property to get the item title.
Update	Method that saves any pending changes applied to the current item.
UpdateOverwriteVersion	Method that saves any changes applied to the current item without creating a new version of the item.
Url	Read-only property that returns the site-relative URL of the current item.
Versions	Collection property containing the version history for the current item.
Workflows	Collection property containing the workflows running on the current item. This property relates to the legacy workflow engine provided for backward compatibility with SharePoint 2010. For further details about workflows, see Part V of this book.
Xml	Read-only property that returns the current item as an XML fragment, using an XMLDATA (*<z:row />*) format.

Later in this chapter, the "Lists and Items" section shows how you can take advantage of some of these members in realistic scenarios.

SPDocumentLibrary and *SPFile*

Whenever you use an *SPList* instance, which corresponds to a document library, you can cast that instance to an *SPDocumentLibrary* type. This type represents a document library, which is almost the same as the base *SPList* type, but has a small set of more specific members related to file handling. As an example, an *SPDocumentLibrary* object provides a collection property through which you can enumerate all the currently checked-out files. When you need to enumerate the files contained in a document library, you can browse the *SPListItem* elements of the list and access their *File* property, which is of type *SPFile*. Listing 5-7 shows some sample code that browses the files of a document library and displays their name and size in bytes.

LISTING 5-7 Browsing the files contained in an *SPDocumentLibrary* instance of an *SPWeb* object

```
using (SPSite site = new SPSite("http://devbook.sp2013.local/")) {

    Console.WriteLine("Current Site URL: {0}", site.Url);

    using (SPWeb web = site.OpenWeb()) {
        foreach (SPList list in web.Lists) {
            SPDocumentLibrary library = list as SPDocumentLibrary;

            if (library != null) {
                foreach (SPListItem item in library.Items) {
                    Console.WriteLine("{0} - {1}",
                        item.File.Name,
                        item.File.Length);
                }
            }
        }
    }
}
```

The *SPFile* class offers a rich set of members, as shown in Table 5-5.

TABLE 5-5 Some of the members of the *SPFile* type

Member name	Description
Approve	Method that approves a file submitted for content approval.
CheckedOutByUser	Read-only property that returns a reference to the *SPUser* instance for the user who checked out the file.
CheckIn	Method to check in the current file.
CheckOut	Method to check out the current file.
CheckOutType	Read-only property that returns the checkout status type for the current file. The possible values are defined in the *SPCheckOutType* enumeration: *Online, Offline*, and *None*.
CopyTo	Method that copies the current file to a specified destination URL within the same site, overwriting the target, if it exists. It has two overloads.
Delete	Method that deletes the current file.
Deny	Method to deny approval for a file submitted for content approval.
Length	Read-only property that returns the size in bytes (*long*) of the current file. When the file is a page, the property excludes the size of any Web Parts used in the page.
Lock	Method that applies a lock on the current file, preventing other users from modifying it.
LockedByUser	Read-only property that returns a reference to the *SPUser* object for the user who locked the file.
MoveTo	Method that moves the current file to a specified destination URL within the same site, overwriting the target, if it exists. It has four overloads.
Name	Read-only property that returns the file name.
OpenBinary	Method to read the file's content into a *Byte* array. It has two overloads.

Member name	Description
OpenBinaryStream	Method to read the file's content as a *Stream*. It has three overloads.
Publish	Method to submit the file for content approval.
Recycle	Method that deletes the current file, putting it into the Recycle Bin.
SaveBinary	Method to save the contents of the current file, using a *Stream* or a *Byte* array. It has seven overloads.
Title	Property to get or set the file title.
UndoCheckOut	Method to undo the current checkout process for a file.
Update	Method that saves any changes applied to the current file.
Url	Read-only property that returns the site-relative URL of the current item.
Versions	Collection property containing the version history for the current item.

In the "Document libraries and files" section later in the chapter, you will see how to use some of these members to manage files stored in SharePoint.

SPGroup, *SPUser*, and other security types

Another set of useful types for developing real solutions are the *SPGroup* and *SPUser* classes. These correspond to a group and a SharePoint user, respectively, and both inherit from *SPPrincipal*. The *SPPrincipal* type ultimately inherits from *SPMember*. From a security point of view, a set of permissions is assigned to an *SPPrincipal* object using an *SPRoleAssignment* class. Thus, you can configure permissions equivalently for a user or for a group, using the same classes and syntax. An *SPRoleAssignment* object maps an *SPPrincipal* instance to an *SPRoleDefinition* instance. *SPRoleDefinition* is the type that defines a SharePoint permission level. In Part VI of this book, "Security infrastructure," you will explore how SharePoint security works internally; for now, all you need is a high-level overview of these types. For example, Listing 5-8 shows how to enumerate role assignments and role definitions.

LISTING 5-8 Browsing role assignments and definitions for an *SPWeb* instance

```
using (SPSite site = new SPSite("http://devbook.sp2013.local/")) {
    Console.WriteLine("Current Site URL: {0}", site.Url);

    using (SPWeb web = site.OpenWeb()) {
        foreach (SPRoleAssignment ra in web.RoleAssignments) {
            Console.WriteLine("-Member Name: {0}", ra.Member.Name);

            foreach (SPRoleDefinition rd in ra.RoleDefinitionBindings) {
                Console.WriteLine("Permissions: {0}", rd.BasePermissions);
            }
        }
    }
}
```

When you target an *SPUser* object with a custom *SPRoleAssignment* instance, you will probably find the list of the main members of the *SPUser* type useful. You can see the most important members in Table 5-6.

TABLE 5-6 Some of the members of the *SPUser* type

Member name	Description
Alerts	Collection property containing any alerts configured by the user.
Email	Property that gets or sets the user's email address.
Groups	Collection property containing the groups to which the user belongs.
ID	Read-only property that returns the user member ID (inherited from *SPMember*, through *SPPrincipal*).
IsSiteAdmin	Read-only property that returns *true* if the current user is a site collection administrator.
LoginName	Read-only property that returns the login name of the user.
Name	Property to get or set the display name of the user.
RawSid	Read-only property to get the raw binary Security ID (SID) of the user, in case the user is a Windows user.
Sid	Read-only property to get the SID of the user, in case the user is a Windows user.
Update	Method to save any changes applied to the current user.
UserToken	Read-only property to get a reference to the *SPUserToken* object of the current authentication process. It can be used to create an *SPSite* instance in order to impersonate the user, as already discussed at the beginning of this chapter.
Xml	Read-only property to get the current user as an XML fragment.

If you are targeting an *SPGroup* instance, it will help to know about some of the main members explained in Table 5-7.

TABLE 5-7 Some of the members of the *SPGroup* type

Member name	Description
AddUser	Method to add an *SPUser* to the current *SPGroup*.
Description	Property to get or set the description of the group.
ID	Read-only property to get the group member ID (inherited from *SPMember* through *SPPrincipal*).
Name	Property to get or set the display name of the group.
RemoveUser	Method to remove an *SPUser* from the current *SPGroup*.
Update	Method to save any changes applied to the current group.
Users	Property that allows enumerating the users belonging to the current group.
Xml	Read-only property to get the current group as an XML fragment.

These classes can be used to make authorization checks by code, or for managing automation of users and groups. For example, you can add a user to a group inside a custom timer job written using these classes. In the "Groups and users" section later in the chapter, you will see how to write this code.

SPControl and *SPContext*

One last group of types provided by the Server Object Model of SharePoint consists of some infrastructural classes such as *SPControl* and *SPContext*. The *SPControl* type is defined in the *Microsoft.SharePoint.WebControls* namespace. It is the base class for many SharePoint server controls, and it helps when developing web controls or Web Parts. Aside from its base class role, *SPControl* provides a small set of static methods, the most useful of which let you retrieve a reference to the current *SPSite*, *SPWeb*, or *SPWebApplication* instances. Here are the signatures of these methods:

```
public static SPModule GetContextModule(HttpContext context);
public static SPSite GetContextSite(HttpContext context);
public static SPWeb GetContextWeb(HttpContext context);
public static SPWebApplication GetContextWebApplication(HttpContext context);
```

All of these methods require an *HttpContext* object instance as their sole input argument.

Another way of obtaining a reference to the current *SPSite* and *SPWeb* is to use the *SPContext* class, which provides a static property named *Current* that references the current SharePoint context. The current *SPContext* object gives you direct access to all the most useful information about the current request. Table 5-8 shows the main members offered.

TABLE 5-8 Some of the members of the *SPContext* type

Member name	Description
ContextPageInfo	Read-only property that contains information about the current list item (permissions, list ID, list item ID, and so on) for the current request.
File	Read-only property that returns a reference to the *SPFile* instance, if any, corresponding to the *SPListItem* object served by the current request.
IsDesignTime	Read-only *Boolean* property to check whether the current request is running at design time.
IsPopUI	Read-only *Boolean* property to check whether the current request is for a pop-up dialog box.
Item	Read-only property that returns a reference to either the *SPListItem* object determined by the specified list and item ID or the *SPItem* object set when the context is created.
ItemId	Read-only property to get the ID (*Int32*) of the list item associated with the current context.
List	Read-only property that returns a reference to the *SPList* object associated with the current context.
ListId	Read-only property that returns the ID (GUID) of the list associated with the current context.
ListItem	Read-only property that returns a reference to the *SPListItem* object associated with the current context.
RegionalSettings	Read-only property that returns the regional settings of the current request context.
ResetItem	Method that forces a refresh of the current item. Internally, the method reloads the in-memory cached item from the content database.
Site	Read-only property that returns a reference to the *SPSite* object corresponding to the site collection of the current request context.
Web	Read-only property that returns a reference to the *SPWeb* object corresponding to the website of the current request context.

For a complete list of all the available types and members in the Server Object Model, see the full online reference on MSDN, at *http://msdn.microsoft.com/en-us/library/ms464984.aspx*.

Common and best practices

You will use the types discussed in the previous section, together with many others, throughout this book and in your real-world SharePoint solutions. Understanding what they do is important, but knowing how to use them correctly is even more so. The goal of this section is to share some thoughts and provide some best practices so that you can profitably use the Server Object Model.

Resource disposal

The first and most important hint you need to know is how to correctly release resources while working with objects of the Server Object Model. You can either wait for the .NET Framework to do it for you or release resources manually. Which option you choose is largely determined by how critical those resources are. By default, the .NET Framework employs a *nondeterministic release* of allocated managed objects, which is based on the garbage collector and provided by the common language runtime (CLR). When an instance of a managed type that you created is no longer used, the garbage collector automatically releases the allocated memory—but at a nondeterministic (unpredictable) time. When the managed object holds references to unmanaged resources—such as window handles, files, streams, database connections, sockets, and so forth—these unmanaged resources will be released only when the garbage collector collects memory. When such unmanaged resources are scarce, are critical, happen to lock physical resources, or use a large amount of unmanaged memory, you're better off releasing them as soon as possible rather than waiting for the .NET garbage collector. To accomplish this goal, the .NET Framework infrastructure provides the *IDisposable* interface, which exposes a *Dispose* method that you should call to explicitly release these unmanaged resources. Here's the definition of the *IDisposable* interface:

```
public interface IDisposable {
    void Dispose();
}
```

There are many patterns for implementing *IDisposable*; however, it is beyond the scope of this book to give you full coverage of this topic. To learn more about resource disposal in SharePoint, consult the article "Disposing Objects" on MSDN, at *http://msdn.microsoft.com/en-us/library/ee557362.aspx*.

More Info To dig deeper into the CLR and garbage collector internals, consult Jeffrey Richter's book, *CLR via C#, Fourth Edition* (Microsoft Press, 2012), available at *http://www.oreilly.com/catalog/9780735667457/*.

For now, suffice it to know that whenever a .NET type implements the *IDisposable* interface, you should invoke the *Dispose* method as soon as you no longer need the object. Calling *Dispose* lets you release unmanaged resources in a deterministic manner.

To invoke *Dispose*, you should adopt a standard technique, such as one of the following:

- Use the *using* keyword.
- Use a *try...finally* code block.
- Explicitly invoke the *Dispose* method.

Listing 5-9 shows a code excerpt that takes advantage of the *using* keyword.

LISTING 5-9 Employing the *using* keyword while working with an *SPSite* instance to ensure timely disposal of unmanaged resources

```
using (SPSite site = new SPSite("http://devbook.sp2013.local/")) {
    // Work with the SPSite object
}
```

The compiler converts the *using* keyword into a *try...finally* code block, such as the one in Listing 5-10.

LISTING 5-10 Using the *try...finally* block while working with an *SPSite* instance to ensure timely disposal of unmanaged resources

```
SPSite site = null;
try {
    site = new SPSite("http://devbook.sp2013.local/");

    // Work with the SPSite object
}
finally {
    if (site != null)
        site.Dispose();
}
```

If you need to catch exceptions that might occur while working with disposable objects, wrap the *using* block or the *try...finally* block with an external *try...catch* block, as shown in Listing 5-11.

LISTING 5-11 Wrapping the *using* block in an external *try...catch* block while working with an *SPSite* instance so it can handle any exceptions

```
try {
    using (SPSite site = new SPSite("http://devbook.sp2013.local/")) {
        // Work with the SPSite object
    }
}
catch (SPException ex) {
    // Handle exception
}
```

Writing code this way ensures that any unmanaged resources will be released as soon as they are no longer needed. It also ensures that exceptions can be handled without overloading the environment.

You should apply this technique even when using objects from the SharePoint Server Object Model. For example, the *SPSite* and *SPWeb* types both implement the *IDisposable* interface, and both allocate unmanaged memory. If you do not correctly release *SPSite* and *SPWeb* instances, you will probably experience memory leaks, crashes, and frequent application pool recycles because of extra (and unnecessary) memory consumption.

However, you must also be careful, because you should dispose of these types only when you have explicitly created them. For example, Listing 5-12 illustrates a situation in which you *should not* dispose of an *SPSite* instance.

LISTING 5-12 Incorrect object disposal through the *using* keyword

```
try {
    using (SPSite site = SPControl.GetContextSite(HttpContext.Current)) {
        // Work with the SPSite object
    }
}
catch (SPException ex) {
    // Handle exception
}
```

In Listing 5-12, the *SPSite* instance is retrieved from the request context through the *SPControl* type. Thus, you didn't create it; the internal SharePoint Foundation code did. This means you are not responsible for disposing of it. The same logic applies to *SPSite* or *SPWeb* references retrieved from the current *SPContext* object. In contrast, Listing 5-13 shows you the correct way to write the code.

LISTING 5-13 The correct way to handle objects that do not need to be disposed of explicitly

```
try {
    SPSite site = SPControl.GetContextSite(HttpContext.Current);
    // Work with the SPSite object
}
catch (SPException ex) {
    // Handle exception
}
```

For situations in which you create both *SPSite* and *SPWeb* instances within the same code excerpt, you should employ nested *using* keywords, as you can see in many examples in this chapter (such as Listing 5-8).

Keep in mind that if you are browsing a collection of *SPWeb* items—for example, enumerating the *AllWebs* property of an *SPSite* object—you are responsible for releasing each single *SPWeb* instance, as exemplified in Listing 5-14.

LISTING 5-14 Object disposal while iterating collections

```
try {
    using (SPSite site = new SPSite("http://devbook.sp2013.local/")) {
        // Work with the SPSite object
        foreach (SPWeb web in site.AllWebs) {
            using (web) {
                // Work with the SPWeb object
            }
        }
    }
}
catch (SPException ex) {
    // Handle exception
}
```

Furthermore, there are types that internally create instances of *SPSite* or *SPWeb* that you'll need to dispose of explicitly. For example, the *SPWebPartManager* and the *SPLimitedWebPartManager* classes internally use an *SPWeb* instance that must be disposed of. These types all implement *IDisposable*, so you should handle them almost the same way as you do the *SPSite* and *SPWeb* types.

Handling exceptions

A perennially interesting area when developing software solutions is that of exception handling for intercepting code failures. The SharePoint Server Object Model provides a base class named *SPException*, which is the default exception thrown by the SharePoint Server Object Model and is also the type from which almost every specific SharePoint exception inherits. While handling exceptions, consider a few suggestions.

First, catch and handle only those exceptions that you anticipate and can manage. In other words, you should avoid simply catching all exceptions using a *catch all* block or an empty *catch* block. That way, when an exception that you don't anticipate occurs, it will bubble up to higher-level code that is able to handle it, if any exists. If the exception is unexpected through the entire stack of the current request, it's best to let the software crash. (Of course, you would inform the end user in a friendly manner and possibly automatically alert technical support.) That is exactly what SharePoint does by default for unhandled exceptions. Figure 5-2 shows the default error message that SharePoint displays when an unexpected error occurs.

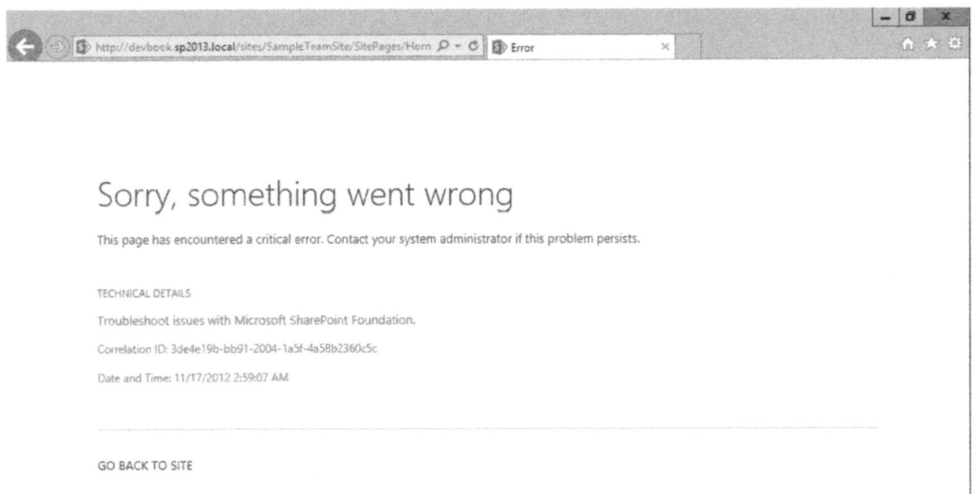

FIGURE 5-2 The default message that SharePoint 2013 displays when an unexpected error occurs.

More Info The default location for the Microsoft SharePoint 2010 Unified Logging System (ULS) logs is in the SharePoint15_Root\LOGS folder. You can search the log manually using any basic text editor. Alternatively, the log is compatible with the free ULS viewer, which you can download from *http://archive.msdn.microsoft.com/ULSViewer.*

The correlation ID (GUID) shown in the message refers to the current request context, which you can use to search for the exception in the SharePoint ULS log. Specifically, search for a row of type *Unexpected* that contains the correlation ID from the error dialog at the end of the row. That's where you can find the unhandled exception details and stack trace.

If you decide to catch unexpected exceptions with code of your own (and thereby avoid the default error message), you will probably still want to log/trace the exception by yourself. Listing 5-15 shows how to manage an unexpected exception by logging it to the ULS log.

LISTING 5-15 Logging an exception to the ULS log

```
try {
    using (SPSite site = new SPSite("http://devbook.sp2013.local/")) {
        // Work with the SPSite object
        foreach (SPWeb web in site.AllWebs) {
            using (web) {
                // Work with the SPWeb object
            }
        }
    }
}
catch (SPException ex) {
    // Log exception to ULS
    SPDiagnosticsService.Local.WriteTrace(0, new SPDiagnosticsCategory(
    "My Custom Category", TraceSeverity.Unexpected, EventSeverity.Error),
    TraceSeverity.Unexpected, ex.Message, ex.StackTrace);
}
```

Listing 5-15 illustrates that the SPDiagnosticService provides utilities for logging into the ULS log of the local server, through the WriteTrace method.

Transactions

Working within a transactional environment when manipulating data is a common application need; however, the SharePoint data engine and the SharePoint Server Object Model are not transactional. You cannot rely on them alone to build a transactional system. In fact, SharePoint is *not* an RDBMS. Data you store in SharePoint lists should not be critical and should not require a transactional environment. If you do need to store information in SharePoint using a kind of transactional behavior, you need something like a compensable system. For example, you can use a Windows Workflow Foundation 4.5 workflow that makes use of a *CompensableActivity* activity. Let's see what that means in concrete terms.

More Info For further details about Windows Workflow Foundation, read Part V of this book.

Whenever you invoke the *Update* method for a Server Object Model object (such as *SPListItem*), SharePoint updates the corresponding data in the target content database. If you change two or more items and you want to update either all or none of them, you must keep track of such changes yourself (in case you need to revert back to the original values if the process fails) because SharePoint doesn't support this. The same is true when you need to update data on SharePoint or update data using an external resource manager, such as an RDBMS. If you update the SharePoint content database first and then the RDBMS update fails, you will need to manually restore the original content values on the SharePoint side, using some custom code.

If you must have transactional support while managing data stored in SharePoint, you should probably ask yourself whether SharePoint is truly the appropriate place to store that data. Of course, the answer would be no. In such critical cases, you need a transactional RDBMS instead. You can still use SharePoint to present such data to end users, however, by taking advantage of Business Connectivity Services and external lists for this purpose.

AllowUnsafeUpdates and *FormDigest*

To avoid cross-site scripting issues, SharePoint applies a security check whenever you change data through the Server Object Model during HTTP requests. In fact, by default, SharePoint web forms use a form digest control to enforce security. The *FormDigest* is a hidden field that is sent by SharePoint web forms via HTTP *POST*, and checked by the security infrastructure on the server. When you make changes to objects by using the Server Object Model during an HTTP *GET* request, this input field will be missing, so by default SharePoint will throw an exception that looks like this excerpt:

```
Microsoft.SharePoint.SPException: The security validation for this page is invalid.
```

Similarly, if you send an HTTP *POST* request with a missing or invalid *FormDigest* value, you will receive the same error. This behavior applies only during HTTP requests. Therefore, when you reference the Server Object Model in a class library or a batch tool that runs outside of the ASP.NET pipeline, the security check will not occur. In fact, the check process looks for the *HttpContext.Current* variable; if it is *null*, the digest validation will not occur.

With that in mind, if you are developing a webpage that will respond to HTTP *GET* requests, or a custom web form page that doesn't inherit from the *WebPartPage* type and doesn't use the *FormDigest* control, you will need to instruct SharePoint to skip the digest validation; otherwise, your code will not work.

To instruct SharePoint to skip the validation, set the *Boolean AllowUnsafeUpdates* property of the current *SPSite* or *SPWeb* object to *true*. Listing 5-16 shows an example.

LISTING 5-16 Using the *AllowUnsafeUpdates* property of the *SPWeb* type to skip a security check

```
SPWeb web = SPContext.Current.Web
SPList list = web.Lists["DevLeap Customers"];

try {
    web.AllowUnsafeUpdates = true;

    list.Title = list.Title + " - Changed!";
    list.Update();
}
finally {
    web.AllowUnsafeUpdates = false;
}
```

The code in Listing 5-16 works with an *SPWeb* instance provided by the current *SPContext* instance. It sets the *AllowUnsafeUpdates* property to *true* before changing an *SPList* instance property, and then resets the property to *false* (its default value) just after invoking the *SPList.Update* method. To ensure that the *AllowUnsafeUpdates* property always reverts to its original value, the code uses a *try...finally* code block.

Conversely, when you develop a custom ASPX page and you *want* to exploit the security environment provided by SharePoint, you have a couple of choices. You can inherit from *WebPartPage*, or you can manually include a *FormDigest* control in your page. In the first case, you simply need to inherit from the *Microsoft.SharePoint.WebPartPages.WebPartPage* base class, which internally renders a *FormDigest* control. Then, in your code, you call the utility method *SPUtility.ValidateFormDigest()* to check the digest when you post the page back to the server. In the latter case, you need to include the *Microsoft.SharePoint.WebControls.FormDigest* control in your page(s), and you still need to invoke the *SPUtility.ValidateFormDigest()* method to check the digest.

Of course, in a custom ASPX page, you could also invalidate the security check by setting the *AllowUnsafeUpdates* property to *true*. However, that would be both insecure behavior and poor practice.

Real-life examples

The purpose of this section is to give you some concrete examples from real-life solutions that illustrate how to work with SharePoint Server Object Model types. The examples are divided into groups based on the target object and target goal. You should consider this section as an everyday reference for developing SharePoint solutions. Look to the following code excerpts for inspiration while developing custom controls, Web Parts, custom pages, timer jobs, or whatever else will have to run on a SharePoint server.

Creating a new site collection

This first example shows how to create a new site collection in code (see Listing 5-17).

LISTING 5-17 Creating a new site collection

```
using (SPSite rootSite = new SPSite("http://devbook.sp2013.local/")) {
    SPWebApplication webApplication = rootSite.WebApplication;

    using (SPSite newSiteCollection = webApplication.Sites.Add(
        "sites/CreatedByCode", // Site URL
        "Created by Code", // Site Collection Title
        "Sample Site Collection Created by Code", // Site Collection Description
        1033, // LCID
        15, // Compatibility level (can be 14 for 2010 or 15 for 2013)
        "STS#0", // Web Site Template for a Team Site
        "SP2013\\PaoloPi", // Owner Login
        "Paolo Pialorsi", // Owner DisplayName
        "paolo@devleap.com", // Owner EMail
        "SP2013\\MarcoR", // Secondary Contact Login
        "Marco Russo", // Secondary Contact DisplayName
        "marco@devleap.com", // Secondary Contact EMail
        "SP2013SQL", // Database Server Name for Content Database
        "WSS_Content_CreatedByCode", // Content Database Name
        null, // Database Login Name
        null // Database Login Password
        )) {
            Console.WriteLine("Created Site Collection: {0}",
                newSiteCollection.Url);
    }
}
```

Listing 5-17 uses the method of the *SPSiteCollection* type, to which you can get a reference from the *SPWebApplication.Sites* property. The method has many different overloads; the code excerpt uses one of the most complete signatures, which is as follows:

```
public SPSite Add(
    string siteUrl,
    string title,
    string description,
    uint nLCID,
    uint compatibilityLevel,
    string webTemplate,
    string ownerLogin,
    string ownerName,
    string ownerEmail,
    string secondaryContactLogin,
    string secondaryContactName,
    string secondaryContactEmail,
    string databaseServer,
    string databaseName,
    string userName,
    string password
)
```

This example shows that you can define each and every detail of the site collection configuration, including the website template name to use, and you can even assign a dedicated content database. Table 5-9 lists some of the most common website template values.

TABLE 5-9 Some of the most common website template names available in SharePoint for creating a new site collection

Site template name	Description
STS#0	Team site (15 or 14)
STS#1	Blank site (15 or 14)
STS#2	Document workspace (15 or 14)
MPS#0	Basic meeting workspace (15 or 14)
MPS#1	Blank meeting workspace (15 or 14)
MPS#2	Decision meeting workspace (15 or 14)
MPS#3	Social meeting workspace (15 or 14)
MPS#4	Multipage meeting workspace (15 or 14)
CMSPUBLISHING#0	Publishing site (15 or 14)
SPSPORTAL#0	Collaboration portal (15 or 14)
COMMUNITY#0	Community site (15 only)
COMMUNITYPORTAL#0	Community portal (15 only)

More Info To list all the available site templates names, descriptions, and compatibility levels for a specific farm, use PowerShell and the *Get-SPWebTemplate* cmdlet command.

Listing 5-17 assumes that the site collection (*http://devbook.sp2013.local/*) will allow you to create another site collection under the *sites* managed path of the parent web application. The *sites* managed path is available out of the box for any SharePoint web application. If you need to create a root site collection from scratch, however, you should retrieve a reference to the *SPWebApplication* instance through an *SPFarm* object.

Creating a new website

After you have a site collection, at some point you will probably need to create one or more websites in it. Listing 5-18 contains a code excerpt that uses the *SPWebCollection.Add* method. The method also has many overloads. The following is the overload signature used in Listing 5-18:

```
public SPWeb Add(
    string strWebUrl,
    string strTitle,
    string strDescription,
    uint nLCID,
    string strWebTemplate,
    bool useUniquePermissions,
    bool bConvertIfThere
)
```

LISTING 5-18 Creating a new website

```
using (SPSite site = new SPSite(
"http://devbook.sp2013.local/sites/CreatedByCode/")) {
    using (SPWeb newWeb = site.AllWebs.Add(
        "MyBlog", // Web Site Url
        "Blog Created By Code", // Web Site Title
        "Blogging Site Created By Code", // Web Site Description
        1033, // LCID
        "BLOG#0", // Web Site Template Name
        true,  // Use Unique Permissions
        false // Convert an existing folder
        )) {
            Console.WriteLine("New Web Site URL: {0}", newWeb.Url);
    }
}
```

While creating a website, you can specify a website template name or an object of type *SPWebTemplate*. This last type has a *CompatibilityLevel* property, which enables you to specify whether you are creating a SharePoint 2010 or SharePoint 2013 site. Some of the available values for this argument are illustrated in Table 5-10.

TABLE 5-10 Some of the website template names available in SharePoint for creating a new website

Site template name	Description
STS#0	Team site
STS#1	Blank site
WIKI#0	Wiki
BLOG#0	Blog
CMSPUBLISHING#0	Publishing site
BLANKINTERNET#0	Blank publishing site

Note the *Boolean useUniquePermissions* argument that's used in Listing 5-18. This is useful for specifying whether to inherit permissions from the parent site collection or whether the new site should have unique permissions. The *bConvertIfThere* argument is also interesting; when *true*, it instructs SharePoint to convert an existing folder into the child website; when *false*, it causes SharePoint to throw an exception if a folder already exists with the URL requested for the new website.

Of course, to be able to create a new website inside an existing site collection at all, you need to access the Server Object Model with a user account that has sufficient permissions.

Lists and items

This section includes several examples related to managing lists and list items. For example, you will learn how to create lists, as well as how to create, update, and delete items within those lists.

Creating a new list

To create a new list of items, you can use Listing 5-19 as a pattern. It demonstrates how to create a list of contacts and configure the list properties.

LISTING 5-19 Creating a new list of contacts in a website and configuring the list properties

```
using (SPSite site = new SPSite(
"http://devbook.sp2013.local/sites/CreatedByCode/")) {
    using (SPWeb web = site.OpenWeb()) {
        Guid newListId = web.Lists.Add(
            "Contacts", // List Title
            "Company's Contacts", // List Description
            SPListTemplateType.Contacts // List Template Type
            );
        SPList newList = web.Lists[newListId];
        newList.OnQuickLaunch = true;
        newList.ReadSecurity = 1; // All users have Read access to all items
        newList.WriteSecurity = 2; // Users can modify only items they've created
        newList.Update();

        Console.WriteLine("Created list: {0}", newList.Title);
    }
}
```

Listing 5-19 exploits the *SPListCollection.Add* method, using one overload that specifies the list template using an enumeration value. Here's the signature of the *Add* method used:

```
public virtual Guid Add(
    string title,
    string description,
    SPListTemplateType templateType
)
```

The *SPListTemplateType* enumeration defines about 60 templates that cover the most common list scenarios. If you wish to create a list using a custom template, you can browse the *ListTemplates* property of the current *SPWeb* instance, selecting the corresponding *SPListTemplate* instance and using the following overload of the *SPListCollection.Add* method instead:

```
public virtual Guid Add(
    string title,
    string description,
    SPListTemplate template
)
```

All the overloads of the *SPListCollection.Add* method return a *Guid* value that corresponds to the ID of the newly created list. To configure the list you just created, you need to retrieve a reference to it using that ID. Listing 5-19 uses the *SPList* object to configure the list so that it will appear on the Quick Launch menu. It configures the default item-level permissions to let all users read every item but change only items that they created. You can see the result of this item-level permissions configuration made through code in Figure 5-3.

Remember, as soon as you have finished configuring any object from the Server Object Model, you must invoke the *Update* method to confirm the changes.

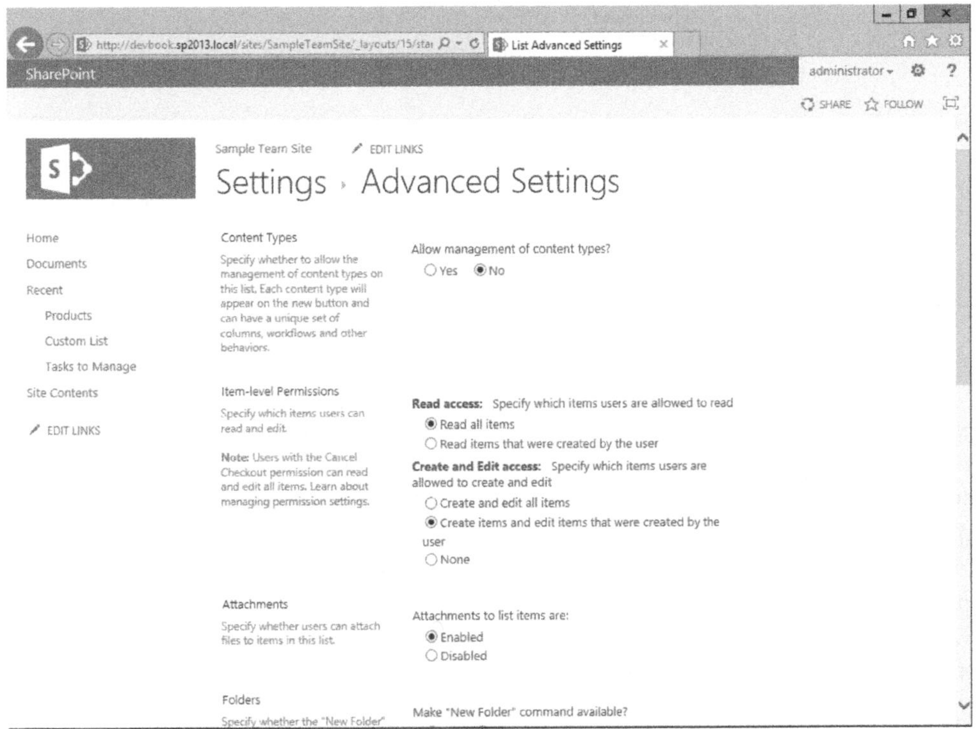

FIGURE 5-3 Item-level permissions resulting from the code in Listing 5-19.

Creating a new list item

After creating a list, you will want to populate it with new items. The code in Listing 5-20 adds a new contact item to the list created in Listing 5-19.

LISTING 5-20 Populating a list with new items

```
using (SPSite site = new SPSite(
"http://devbook.sp2013.local/sites/CreatedByCode/")) {
    using (SPWeb web = site.OpenWeb()) {
        try {
            SPList list = web.Lists["Contacts"];

            try {
                SPListItem newItem = list.Items.Add();
                newItem["Last Name"] = "Pialorsi";
                newItem["First Name"] = "Paolo";
                newItem["E-mail Address"] = "paolo@devleap.it";
                newItem.Update();
            }
            catch (ArgumentException) {
                Console.WriteLine("Invalid Field Name!");
            }
        }
        catch (ArgumentException) {
            Console.WriteLine("Invalid List Title!");
        }
    }
}
```

Again, you need to invoke an *Add* method for the corresponding collection—in this case, an *SPListItemCollection*. The method returns a new *SPListItem* instance ready to be configured and updated against the content database. To be accurate, the *Add* method simply creates a new item configured according to the target list in terms of fields, content types, and so on. However, despite its name, the *Add* method does not really add the item to the list; in fact, the new *SPListItem* instance has an ID with a value of zero (0). Only after you invoke the *Update* method of the item for the first time will it be inserted into the list and have a unique ID assigned. The code in Listing 5-20 configures three fields of the target item. The syntax you use to assign values to the fields uses each field's *DisplayName*; however, the indexer of an *SPListItem* lets you provide as arguments the *DisplayName*, the *Name*, the *StaticName* of the field, the unique ID of the field (which is useful when you are working with provisioned site columns), or the ordinal position (index) of the field within the *Fields* collection of the current item.

More Info To better understand topics such as site columns, *DisplayName*, *Name*, *StaticName*, and so on, see Chapter 2, "SharePoint data fundamentals," and Chapter 3, "Data provisioning."

For completeness, the example code catches exceptions of type *ArgumentException*, just in case you provide an invalid list title or field name. In general, you should avoid writing list titles or field names in source code; instead, you should work with provisioned contents and their corresponding IDs. Using the IDs essentially eliminates the possibility of an invalid value at run time (unless you make a typing mistake while writing the code)—but those types of issues should become apparent during testing, before the application ever reaches a production environment.

Modifying an existing list item

Another common task is modifying the metadata of an existing item. The procedure is similar to creating a new list item; the only difference is that you need to query the list to get a reference to the item that you want to update. The example in Listing 5-21 retrieves the item to update using its unique ID, via the *SPList.GetItemById* method.

LISTING 5-21 Modifying an existing item of a list

```
using (SPSite site = new SPSite(
"http://devbook.sp2013.local/sites/CreatedByCode/")) {
    using (SPWeb web = site.OpenWeb()) {
        try {
            SPList list = web.Lists["Contacts"];
            SPListItem itemToChange = list.GetItemById(1);

            itemToChange["Last Name"] += " - Changed!";
            itemToChange.Update();
        }
        catch (ArgumentException) {
            Console.WriteLine("Invalid List Title or invalid List Item ID!");
        }
    }
}
```

Note that the *SPList.GetItemById* method retrieves the full item, with all its columns of metadata. When you need to change just a few columns, it's best to retrieve only those specific columns. To do that, use the *SPList.GetItemByIdSelectedFields* method, which retrieves only the columns you specify. In this case, the line from which the example retrieves the item to change could be

```
SPListItem itemToChange = list.GetItemByIdSelectedFields(1, "Last Name");
```

But the *SPList.GetItemByIdSelectedFields* method also accepts a list of fields to retrieve from the content database as a *params* array of *String*.

When you don't know the ID of the item that you want to update, you can use the SharePoint query engine—a topic covered later in this chapter, in the "Querying for list items" section.

Concurrency conflicts

Any server-side code has the potential to serve an unpredictable number of users, so changing data in a back-end RDBMS carries the possibility of a concurrency conflict. Concurrency issues can also happen when working with data stored in SharePoint. Thus, due to the nature of SharePoint, which is a web-based product with (hopefully) a large number of concurrent users, it is highly probable that concurrency conflicts *will* arise while managing SharePoint items. Fortunately, the SharePoint team provided a standard pattern for catching concurrency conflicts. Consider the example in Listing 5-22, which changes an *SPListItem* object with two different concurrent sessions.

LISTING 5-22 Catching concurrency in *SPListItem* management

```
using (SPSite site = new SPSite(
"http://devbook.sp2013.local/sites/CreatedByCode/")) {
    using (SPWeb web = site.OpenWeb()) {
        try {
            SPList list = web.Lists["Contacts"];
            SPListItem itemToChange = list.GetItemById(1);

            itemToChange["Last Name"] += " - Changed!";

            // Before Update, simulate a concurrent change
            ChangeListItemConcurrently();

            itemToChange.Update();
        }
        catch (SPException ex) {
            Console.WriteLine(ex.Message);
        }
    }
}
```

When the code in Listing 5-22 invokes the *Update* method to save changes, a concurrency conflict exception will be raised because the *ChangeListItemConcurrently* procedure has already changed that item. The exception will be a *Microsoft.SharePoint.SPException* with this error message:

```
Save Conflict. Your changes conflict with those made concurrently by another user. If you
want your changes to be applied, click Back in your Web browser, refresh the page, and
resubmit your changes.
```

The error message is tightly tied to a web scenario (notice "click Back in your Web browser"). However, the exception itself can be caught within any kind of software solution—even running on a SharePoint server. To solve this exception, you must reload the *SPListItem* object from the content database and then apply your changes again, just as a web user would do using his or her web browser.

Deleting an existing list item

Deleting an *SPListItem* instance is a common task, similar to inserting or updating items. The program flow for deleting an item is both simple and quick, as you can see in Listing 5-23.

LISTING 5-23 Deleting an *SPListItem* instance

```
using (SPSite site = new SPSite(
"http://devbook.sp2013.local/sites/CreatedByCode/")) {
    using (SPWeb web = site.OpenWeb()) {
        SPList list = web.Lists["Contacts"];
        SPListItem itemToDelete = list.GetItemById(1);
        itemToDelete.Delete();
    }
}
```

You simply need to retrieve the *SPListItem* instance that corresponds to the item that you want to delete, and then invoke the *Delete* method (to permanently delete the item) or the *Recycle* method (to move the item into the Recycle Bin).

Querying for list items

As previously discussed, retrieving an *SPListItem* instance by ID is an uncommon task, unless you have a custom ASPX page that receives the *ListID* and the *ListItemID* values as *QueryString* parameters. More generally, you need to retrieve items from lists using a query that is based on the metadata of the items you want to extract. For example, you might need to extract all contacts whose email address contains *@devleap.com*. The Server Object Model provides a class named *SPQuery*, through which you can execute a CAML query against an *SPList* instance to retrieve items corresponding to the query. Listing 5-24 shows an example.

Note If you don't like writing CAML queries, try CAML Designer for SharePoint 2010, by Karine Bosch, which targets SharePoint 2010 and 2013. You can download this free tool from *http://karinebosch.wordpress.com/my-articles/caml-designer/*.

LISTING 5-24 Querying the items of an *SPList* instance using an *SPQuery* object

```
using (SPSite site = new SPSite(
"http://devbook.sp2013.local/sites/CreatedByCode/")) {
    using (SPWeb web = site.OpenWeb()) {
        SPList list = web.Lists["Contacts"];

        SPQuery query = new SPQuery();

        // Define columns to retrieve
        query.ViewFields = "<FieldRef Name=\"Title\" />
           <FieldRef Name=\"FirstName\" /><FieldRef Name=\"Email\" />";

        // Force retrieving only the selected columns
        query.ViewFieldsOnly = true;

        // Define the query. Remember to remove the <Query></Query> container
        // tag, in case of any
        query.Query = "<Where><Contains><FieldRef Name=\"Email\" />
           <Value Type=\"Text\">@devleap.com</Value></Contains></Where>";

        // Define the maximum number of results for each page (like a SELECT TOP)
        query.RowLimit = 10;

        // Query for items
        SPListItemCollection items = list.GetItems(query);

        foreach (SPListItem item in items) {
            Console.WriteLine("{0} {1} - {2}",
                item["First Name"],
                item["Last Name"],
                item["E-mail Address"]);
        }
    }
}
```

Listing 5-24 configures some of the properties of the *SPQuery* type, the most important of which is the *Query* argument, which contains the CAML code. However, the *SPQuery* type also has other properties that are even more fundamental for performance, such as the *ViewFields* property, which returns only specifically referenced columns, and thus avoids forcing the server to retrieve useless columns. The previous example marks the *ViewFieldsOnly* property as *true*. The *SPQuery* type also has a *RowLimit* property that supports partitioning of data results, such as for paging results. Listing 5-25 shows how to take advantage of the *RowLimit* property together with the *SPQuery.ListItemCollectionPosition* property to page results in blocks of five items for each page.

LISTING 5-25 Querying the items of an *SPList* instance using an *SPQuery* object with paging

```
using (SPSite site = new SPSite(
"http://devbook.sp2013.local/sites/CreatedByCode/")) {
    using (SPWeb web = site.OpenWeb()) {
        SPList list = web.Lists["Contacts"];

        SPQuery query = new SPQuery();

        // Define columns to retrieve
        query.ViewFields = "<FieldRef Name=\"Title\" />
           <FieldRef Name=\"FirstName\" /><FieldRef Name=\"Email\" />";

        // Force retrieving only the selected columns
        query.ViewFieldsOnly = true;

        // Define the query
        query.Query = "<Where><Contains><FieldRef Name=\"Email\" />
           <Value Type=\"Text\">@domain.com</Value></Contains></Where>";

        // Define the maximum number of results for each page (like a SELECT TOP)
        query.RowLimit = 5;

        Int32 pageIndex = 1;
        Int32 itemIndex = 1;

        do {
            Console.WriteLine("Current Page: {0}", pageIndex);

            // Query for items
            SPListItemCollection items = list.GetItems(query);

            foreach (SPListItem item in items) {
                Console.WriteLine("{0} - {1} {2} - {3}",
                    itemIndex,
                    item["First Name"],
                    item["Last Name"],
                    item["E-mail Address"]);
                itemIndex++;
            }

            // Set current position to make SPQuery able
            // to set the start item of the next page
            query.ListItemCollectionPosition =
                items.ListItemCollectionPosition;
            pageIndex++;
        } while (query.ListItemCollectionPosition != null);
    }
}
```

When you execute the code in Listing 5-25 against a list of contacts with a fictitious set of items, you will see the following console output:

```
Current Page: 1
1 - First Name 001 Last Name 001 - email_001@domain.com
2 - First Name 002 Last Name 002 - email_002@domain.com
3 - First Name 003 Last Name 003 - email_003@domain.com
4 - First Name 004 Last Name 004 - email_004@domain.com
5 - First Name 005 Last Name 005 - email_005@domain.com
Current Page: 2
6 - First Name 006 Last Name 006 - email_006@domain.com
7 - First Name 007 Last Name 007 - email_007@domain.com
[etc. ]
```

The *ListItemCollectionPosition* property is of type *SPListItemCollectionPosition*. It offers a *PagingInfo* property of type *String*, which contains the following data:

```
Paged=TRUE&p_ID=8
```

The *_ID* is the unique identifier of the last item retrieved; this allows SharePoint to know the starting position of the next page.

The *SPQuery* type offers many other properties; however, those I've described here will generally suffice for everyday tasks.

Document libraries and files

Document libraries and files are critical for many real-world SharePoint solutions. In this section, you will learn how to create document libraries, and how to upload, download, update, and manage documents. Remember that in SharePoint 2013, a document library, from a web UI perspective, is shown as an app. However, it is still a document library as it was in previous editions of SharePoint.

Creating a new document library

To create a new document library, you just need to write code using an *SPListTemplateType* value of *DocumentLibrary*, such as was shown in Listing 5-19. Although this creates a library, the library is an empty one. Because many corporations require documents to be formatted in a standardized way, quite often you may need to provide a document template to use for new documents. The code in Listing 5-26 creates a library of invoices with an Excel spreadsheet document template.

LISTING 5-26 Creating a new *SPDocumentLibrary* instance with a document template

```
using (SPSite site = new SPSite(
"http://devbook.sp2013.local/sites/CreatedByCode/")) {
    using (SPWeb web = site.OpenWeb()) {
        SPListTemplate listTemplate = web.ListTemplates["Document Library"];
        SPDocTemplate docTemplate =
            (from SPDocTemplate dt in web.DocTemplates
                where dt.Type == 122
                // 122 means "A blank Microsoft Excel document"
                select dt).FirstOrDefault();

        Guid newListId = web.Lists.Add(
            "Invoices", // List Title
            "Excel Invoices", // List Description
            listTemplate, // List Template
            docTemplate // Document Template (i.e. Excel)
            );

        SPDocumentLibrary newLibrary = web.Lists[newListId] as SPDocumentLibrary;
        newLibrary.OnQuickLaunch = true;
        newLibrary.EnableVersioning = true;
        newLibrary.Update();
    }
}
```

When run, the code in Listing 5-26 creates a new document library that you can reference as an instance of the *SPDocumentLibrary* type. Notice the LINQ to Objects query that is used to determine the *SPDocTemplate* item that corresponds to an Excel spreadsheet. Table 5-11 lists all the document templates available in a team site (STS#0) along with their *DocTemplateID* identifiers.

TABLE 5-11 The document templates available in SharePoint

DocTemplate ID	Description
100	No template used by the document library
101	A blank Microsoft Word 97–2003 document
103	A blank Microsoft Excel 97–2003 document
104	A blank Microsoft PowerPoint 97–2003 document
121	A blank Microsoft Word document
122	A blank Microsoft Excel document
123	A blank Microsoft PowerPoint document
111	A basic Microsoft OneNote 2010 Notebook
102	A blank Microsoft SharePoint Designer HTML document
105	A blank Microsoft basic page ASPX document
106	A blank Microsoft Web Part page ASPX document
1000	An empty Microsoft InfoPath form, ready for design

You can find all these IDs of the document templates for a team site in the ONET.xml files, in the folder SharePoint15_Root\TEMPLATE\SiteTemplates\sts\xml. You can also find them in the SharePoint software development kit (SDK), which is available online and as a free download.

Uploading a new document

After you create a library, uploading new content to it is simple. Recall that Table 5-3 showed that each *SPList* instance has a *RootFolder* property and a *Folders* collection property. You can reference any *SPFolder* object to browse for its contents or to upload new content using the *Add* method of the *Files* property, which is of type *SPFileCollection*. The code excerpt in Listing 5-27 uploads a dummy Excel invoice file to the root folder of the library that was created in Listing 5-26.

LISTING 5-27 Uploading a new document to an *SPDocumentLibrary* instance

```
using (SPSite site = new SPSite(
"http://devbook.sp2013.local/sites/CreatedByCode/")) {
    using (SPWeb web = site.OpenWeb()) {
        SPDocumentLibrary library = web.Lists["Invoices"] as SPDocumentLibrary;

        using (FileStream fs = new FileStream(@"..\..\DemoInvoice.xlsx",
            FileMode.Open, FileAccess.Read, FileShare.Read)) {
            SPFile fileUploaded = library.RootFolder.Files.Add(
                "DemoInvoice.xlsx", fs, true);
            Console.WriteLine("Uploaded file: {0}", fileUploaded.Url);
        }
    }
}
```

The *Add* method has 20 overloads. The preceding code used the one that accepts the destination URL of the file, an argument of type *System.IO.Stream* for the content of the file to upload, and a *Boolean* value that, when *true*, instructs SharePoint to overwrite any previously existing file. Detailed examples of all the overloads is beyond the scope of this book; however, it is interesting to group them on a functional basis. All the overloads accept the destination URL of the file as their first argument. But one group of overloads accepts the file as an object of type *System.IO.Stream*, and another group takes a *System.Byte[]* array as input. Additionally, there is a group that accepts an argument of type *HashTable*, which is a property bag for a file's metadata. This family of methods is useful whenever you need to upload a file along with its metadata in a unique transaction. Lastly, there are a couple of overloads that accept an argument of type *SPFileCollectionAddParameters*, which lets you specify some options about how to handle check-ins and check-in comments, and so on.

More Info You can find a complete overload reference online, at *http://msdn.microsoft.com/en-us/library/microsoft.sharepoint.spfilecollection.add.aspx*.

Downloading a document

For document libraries, downloading is, of course, a frequent task. Every *SPListItem* object in a document library has a *File* property of type *SPFile*. Through that property, you can access the file's content as either an object of type *System.IO.Stream* or as an array of bytes (*System.Byte[]*). Listing 5-28 presents an example that downloads the file that was uploaded in Listing 5-27.

LISTING 5-28 Downloading a document from an *SPDocumentLibrary* instance

```
using (SPSite site = new SPSite(
"http://devbook.sp2013.local/sites/CreatedByCode/")) {
    using (SPWeb web = site.OpenWeb()) {
        SPDocumentLibrary library = web.Lists["Invoices"] as SPDocumentLibrary;
        SPFile fileToDownload = web.GetFile(library.RootFolder.Url +
            "/DemoInvoice.xlsx");

        Int32 bufferLength = 4096;
        Int32 readLength = bufferLength;
        Byte[] buffer = new Byte[bufferLength];

        Stream inStream = fileToDownload.OpenBinaryStream();

        using (FileStream outStream = new FileStream(
            @"..\..\DemoInvoiceDownload.xlsx",
            FileMode.OpenOrCreate, FileAccess.Write, FileShare.None)) {
            while (readLength == buffer.Length) {
                readLength = inStream.Read(buffer, 0, bufferLength);
                outStream.Write(buffer, 0, readLength);
                if (readLength < bufferLength) break;
            }
        }
    }
}
```

The key points in Listing 5-28 are the *SPWeb.GetFile* method, which is a shortcut to retrieve an *SPFile* instance for a specified file URL, and the *OpenBinaryStream* method of the *SPFile* class. The remaining code is plumbing to manage streams and save bytes on the hard disk.

Document check-in and checkout

Another common task while managing documents is working with checkout and check-in features. As was shown in Table 5-5, the *SPFile* class provides some specific methods to handle these tasks. Listing 5-29 shows a code excerpt that checks out a file and then checks it back in again, adding a comment.

LISTING 5-29 Checking a document out and back in

```
using (SPSite site = new SPSite(
"http://devbook.sp2013.local/sites/CreatedByCode/")) {
    using (SPWeb web = site.OpenWeb()) {

        SPDocumentLibrary library = web.Lists["Invoices"] as SPDocumentLibrary;
        SPFile file = web.GetFile(library.RootFolder.Url + "/DemoInvoice.xlsx");

        if (file.CheckOutType == SPFile.SPCheckOutType.None) {
            // If the file is not already checked out ... check it out
            file.CheckOut();
        }
        else {
            // Otherwise check it in leaving a comment
            file.CheckIn("File Checked-In for demo purposes",
                SPCheckinType.MajorCheckIn);
        }
    }
}
```

When checking out a document, you should first evaluate the *CheckOutType* property, which is of type *SPFile.SPCheckOutType*—an enumeration of the following values:

- ***None*** The file is not checked out.
- ***Offline*** The file is checked out for editing on the client side.
- ***Online*** The file is checked out for editing on the server side.

When the *CheckOutType* value is *None*, you can invoke the *CheckOut* method, optionally specifying the type (*Offline* or *Online*) of checkout that you want to occur. Otherwise, you can check the file in using the *CheckIn* method, providing a comment and optionally an argument of type *SPCheckinType*, which can assume the following values:

- ***MajorCheckIn*** The check-in increments a major version of the file.
- ***MinorCheckIn*** The check-in increments a minor version of the file.
- ***OverwriteCheckIn*** The check-in overwrites the current file version.

One last option you have is the *UndoCheckOut* method, which releases a checkout without modifying the existing stored copy of the file.

Copying and moving files

Quite often in workflows and event receivers, you need to copy a file from one folder to another or move a file from one library to another.

More Info For further details about SharePoint workflows, see Part V of this book.

These actions are fully supported by the SharePoint Server Object Model. The example in Listing 5-30 copies or moves a file based on a provided argument.

LISTING 5-30 Copying and moving a document from one location to another

```
using (SPSite site = new SPSite(
"http://devbook.sp2013.local/sites/CreatedByCode/")) {
    using (SPWeb web = site.OpenWeb()) {

        SPDocumentLibrary sourceLibrary =
           web.Lists["Invoices"] as SPDocumentLibrary;

        SPDocumentLibrary destinationLibrary =
           web.Lists["Invoices History"] as SPDocumentLibrary;

        SPFile file = web.GetFile(sourceLibrary.RootFolder.Url +
           "/DemoInvoice.xlsx");

        if (move) {
            // It is a file moving action
            file.MoveTo(destinationLibrary.RootFolder.Url +
                "/DemoInvoice_Moved.xlsx", true);
        }
        else {
            // It is a file copy action
            file.CopyTo(destinationLibrary.RootFolder.Url +
               "/DemoInvoice_Copied.xlsx", true);
        }
    }
}
```

Listing 5-30 assumes that you have a library named Invoices and a library named Invoices History, and that you are copying or moving files between these two libraries. Whether you move or copy a file, both the methods receive a *Boolean* argument to force overwriting of any previously existing file in the target folder. Note that both of these methods work only within the same site.

Managing versions of documents

While working with files, you often need to manage versioning to keep track of changes during a file's life cycle and to retrieve older versions of a document. Listing 5-31 shows an example that extracts the next-to-last version of a document.

LISTING 5-31 How to manage file versions

```
using (SPSite site = new SPSite(
"http://devbook.sp2013.local/sites/CreatedByCode/")) {
    using (SPWeb web = site.OpenWeb()) {

        SPDocumentLibrary library = web.Lists["Invoices"] as SPDocumentLibrary;
        SPFile file = web.GetFile(library.RootFolder.Url + "/DemoInvoice.xlsx");

        Console.WriteLine("Available versions:");

        foreach (SPFileVersion v in file.Versions) {
            Console.WriteLine("Version: {0} - URL: {1}", v.VersionLabel, v.Url);
        }

        SPFile fileOfSecondLastVersion =
            file.Versions[file.Versions.Count - 1].File;

        Console.WriteLine(fileOfSecondLastVersion.Name);
    }
}
```

Listing 5-31 demonstrates that SharePoint makes managing file versions simple. For each available version of the document, you have access to an *SPFile* instance that you can manage exactly as you would the current version of the document.

Groups and users

The tasks discussed in this section involve the management of users and groups. You will learn how to create and manage a user, how to control users' membership against groups, and how to define custom permission levels to assign specific permissions to users or groups.

Creating a new user

As usual, the first step in the sequence of common tasks is to be able to create a new item. Remember that a user in SharePoint is an *SPUser* instance. Each *SPWeb* instance offers a set of user collections (*AllUsers*, *SiteUsers*, *Users*), which were listed in Table 5-2. Listing 5-32 shows how to add a new user, taken from Active Directory, into the list of users for a group of a site.

LISTING 5-32 Adding a new user to the *Users* collection of a group of a site

```
using (SPSite site = new SPSite("http://devbook.sp2013.local/")) {
    using (SPWeb web = site.OpenWeb()) {

        web.Groups[0].Users.Add("SP2013\\TestUser", "test@devleap.com",
           "Test User", null);
    }
}
```

The *SPUserCollection.Add* method accepts the logon name of the user, the email address, the display name, and an optional argument with textual notes about the *SPUser* Instance. When you add a previously existing user, the infrastructure ignores any duplicate insertion. However, if you simply want to get a valid *SPUser* instance that corresponds to a logon name—and you don't want to worry about whether that user exists—you can invoke the *SPWeb.EnsureUser* method. This method adds the user if that user is not already defined in the site, or uses the existing user, if there is one. Listing 5-33 shows a revised example.

LISTING 5-33 Adding a new user to a site with the *EnsureUser* method

```
using (SPSite site = new SPSite("http://devbook.sp2013.local/")) {
    using (SPWeb web = site.OpenWeb()) {

        SPUser userAdded = web.EnsureUser("SP2013\\AnotherTestUser");
        Console.WriteLine(userAdded.Xml);
    }
}
```

This time, the *EnsureUser* method directly returns the *SPUser* that you're probably expecting.

Managing group membership

Deleting a user and managing user properties are trivial tasks, so this chapter will not cover them. But it is interesting to know how to add a user to a specific SharePoint group. There are many techniques to accomplish this; however, in Listing 5-34 you will see how to do that by working with the *Groups* collection of the current *SPWeb* instance, which is the most common technique.

LISTING 5-34 Adding a user to a website group

```
using (SPSite site = new SPSite("http://devbook.sp2013.local/")) {
    using (SPWeb web = site.OpenWeb()) {
        SPUser user = web.EnsureUser("SP2013\\AnotherTestUser");
        web.Groups[web.Title + " Members"].AddUser(user);
    }
}
```

The example is clear; the last line invokes the *AddUser* method of an *SPGroup* object retrieved by group name. Using the *SPWeb.Groups* collection, you can also add, update, or delete existing SharePoint groups; however, you should be very careful when performing such actions in code, because the security model should be managed by an IT professional—and having code that creates users and groups on its own could reduce the security of the overall environment if not well defined and documented.

Managing user and group permissions

In the "*SPGroup, SPUser,* and other security types" section earlier in the chapter, you learned that both users and groups internally inherit from *SPPrincipal*, which is a fundamental type for assigning permissions. In SharePoint 2013, permissions are based on permission levels. A *permission level* consists of a set of low-level permissions, such as Browse Directory, View Pages, View Items, Add Items, and so forth. For a full and detailed list of all the available permissions and native permission levels, see Chapter 19. For now, you just need to know that you can define custom permission levels using either the browser UI or the Server Object Model. Additionally, you can assign a permission level to an *SPPrincipal* object (an instance of type *SPUser* or *SPGroup*). Listing 5-35 shows a code excerpt that creates a new permission level (composed of the following permissions: View Pages, Browse Directories, and Update Personal Web Parts) and assigns it to a specific *SPUser* instance.

LISTING 5-35 Creating a new permission level and assigning it to a user

```
using (SPSite site = new SPSite("http://devbook.sp2013.local/")) {
    using (SPWeb web = site.OpenWeb()) {

        SPUser user = web.EnsureUser("SP2013\\AnotherTestUser");

        SPRoleDefinition newRoleDefinition = new SPRoleDefinition();
        newRoleDefinition.Name = "Custom Permission Level";
        newRoleDefinition.Description = "View Pages, Browse Directories, " +
           "Update Personal Web Parts";
        newRoleDefinition.BasePermissions = SPBasePermissions.ViewPages |
           SPBasePermissions.BrowseDirectories |
           SPBasePermissions.UpdatePersonalWebParts;
        web.RoleDefinitions.Add(newRoleDefinition);

        SPPrincipal principal = user;
        SPRoleAssignment newRoleAssignment = new SPRoleAssignment(principal);
        newRoleAssignment.RoleDefinitionBindings.Add(
           web.RoleDefinitions["Custom Permission Level"]);
        web.RoleAssignments.Add(newRoleAssignment);
    }
}
```

The code in Listing 5-35 first retrieves a reference to an *SPUser* object, and then it creates a new permission level—a new instance of *SPRoleDefinition*—and assigns a set of selected permissions to it using a bit mask of permissions. Finally, it adds a binding between the *SPPrincipal* object representing the user and the permission level, using a new *SPRoleAssignment* instance.

Summary

This chapter provided an overview of the SharePoint Server Object Model, starting with the main SharePoint object hierarchy. It then provided a description of the main types. Finally, it explored basic types of everyday tasks, their problems, and solutions. It also included some suggestions and best practices for writing better and more efficient code. With this as a foundation, you're ready to take on the rest of Part II and Part III, which will expand your knowledge and use the Server Object Model to create business solutions.

CHAPTER 6

LINQ to SharePoint

When you need to develop server-side solutions, one of the most significant features of Microsoft SharePoint 2013 is its support for LINQ (Language-Integrated Query). Supported since SharePoint 2010, LINQ is a satisfying alternative to the classic object model discussed in Chapter 5, "Server Object Model." This chapter will begin with a quick overview of LINQ, just in case you're not familiar with it, and then show you how to work with it. Next, you'll learn about LINQ to SharePoint as a LINQ query provider implementation, which is useful for querying and managing items in SharePoint lists using the LINQ data access model. If you already know about LINQ, you can skip the next section and move directly to the section titled "Introducing LINQ to SharePoint."

More Info To learn more about LINQ, read Programming *Microsoft LINQ in .NET 4.0*, by Paolo Pialorsi and Marco Russo (Microsoft Press, 2010).

LINQ overview

LINQ is a programming model that introduces queries as a first-class concept into any Microsoft .NET language. Complete support for LINQ, however, requires some extensions in the language that you are using. These extensions boost developer productivity, thereby providing a shorter, more meaningful, and expressive syntax with which to manipulate data.

LINQ provides a methodology that simplifies and unifies the implementation of any kind of data access. LINQ does not force you to use a specific architecture; it facilitates the implementation of several existing architectures for accessing data, such as the following:

- RAD/prototype
- Client/server
- N-tier
- Smart client

The architecture of LINQ is based on the idea of having a set of LINQ providers, each able to target a different kind of data source. Figure 6-1 shows a schema of the main LINQ providers available in .NET Framework 4.5. Aside from SharePoint and out of the box with .NET Framework 4.5 and

Microsoft Visual Studio 2012, LINQ includes many providers suitable for accessing several different types of data sources, including the following:

- **LINQ to Objects** This is used to query in-memory data and object graphs.
- **LINQ to SQL** This was specifically designed to query and manage data stored in a Microsoft SQL Server database, using a lightweight, simplified object-relational mapper (O/RM) that maps entities to tables with a one-to-one relationship. LINQ to SQL can be considered a discontinued library. Nevertheless, you can still use it.
- **LINQ to Entities** The first-class O/RM offered by Microsoft to design solutions based on the domain model, with a real abstraction from the underlying persistence storage. LINQ to Entities is based on the Entity Framework. The .NET Framework 4.5 ships with the Entity Framework version 5.
- **LINQ to DataSet** This is a LINQ implementation targeting old-style ADO.NET *DataSet* and *DataTable* types. It is mainly offered for backward compatibility reasons.
- **LINQ to XML** This is a LINQ implementation targeting XML contents, useful to query, manage and navigate across XML nodes.

In your SharePoint solutions, you can use any of these LINQ providers, as long as you access objects, SQL Server, DBMSs, *DataSet* objects, or XML. If you need to access SharePoint data, however, you cannot use any of these providers; but read on for suggested solutions.

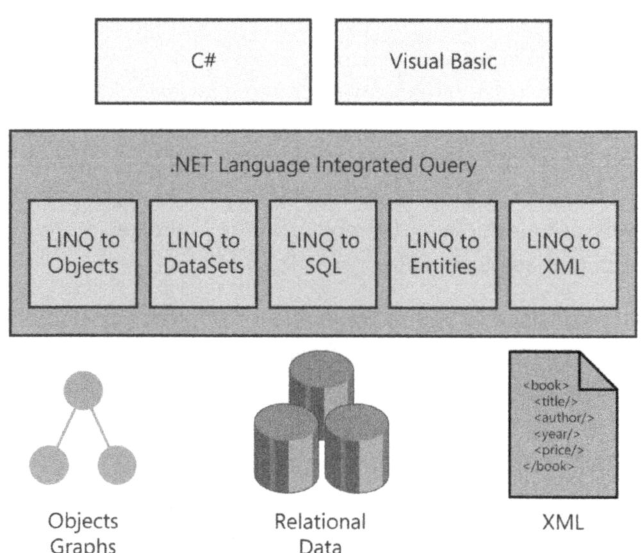

FIGURE 6-1 A graphical representation of the main LINQ providers available in .NET Framework 4.5.

The goal of LINQ

The goal of LINQ is to provide a set of tools that improve code implementation by adapting to several different architectures, rather than changing application architectures.

Today, data managed by a program can originate from many and varied data sources, such as an array, an object graph, an XML document, a database, a text file, a registry key, an e-mail message, Simple Object Access Protocol (SOAP) message content, a Microsoft Office Excel file, and so forth. The list is extensive. LINQ makes it easier to access all these various kinds of data, providing a unified programming model. In fact, each data source has its own specific data-access model. When you need to query a database, you typically use SQL. You navigate XML data by using the Document Object Model (DOM) or XPath/XQuery. You iterate an array and build algorithms to navigate an object graph. You use specific application programming interfaces (APIs) to access other data sources, such as an Excel file, an e-mail message, or the Windows registry. Put briefly, you use different programming models to access different data sources.

The unification of data access techniques into a single comprehensive model has been attempted in many ways. For example, Open Database Connectivity (ODBC) providers allow you to query an Excel file as you would a Windows Management Instrumentation (WMI) repository. With ODBC, you use an SQL-like language to access data represented through a relational model. Sometimes, however, data is represented more effectively in a hierarchical or network model instead of a relational one. Moreover, if a data model is not tied to a specific language, you probably need to manage different type systems. All these differences create an "impedance mismatch" between data and code.

LINQ addresses these issues by offering a uniform method to access and manage data without forcing the adoption of a "one size fits all" model. LINQ makes use of common capabilities in the operations in different data models instead of flattening the different structures between them. In other words, by using LINQ, you keep existing heterogeneous data structures, such as classes or tables, but you gain a uniform syntax to query all these data types, regardless of their physical representation. Think about the differences between a graph of in-memory objects and relational tables with proper relationships. With LINQ, you can use the same query syntax on both models.

Here is a simple LINQ query for a typical software solution that returns the names of customers in Italy:

```
var query =
    from   c in Customers
    where  c.Country == "Italy"
    select c.CompanyName;
```

The result of this query is a list of strings. You can enumerate these values with a *foreach* loop in C#:

```
foreach ( string name in query ) {
    Console.WriteLine( name );
}
```

Both the query definition and the *foreach* loop are regular C# statements, valid for C# 3.0 or higher, but what is *Customers*? At this point, you might be wondering what it is we are querying. Is this query a new form of Embedded SQL? Not at all. You can apply the same query (and the *foreach* loop) to the following:

- An SQL database using LINQ to SQL
- A third-party DBMS using LINQ to Entities
- A *DataSet* object using LINQ to DataSet
- An array of objects in memory using LINQ to Objects
- A remote service

In fact, you can apply the query to many other kinds of data, as well, so long as you use each kind's specific LINQ provider. For example, *Customers* could be a collection of objects:

```
Customer[] Customers;
```

Customers also could be an entity class that describes a physical table in a relational database:

```
DataContext db = new DataContext( ConnectionString );
Table<Customer> Customers = db.GetTable<Customer>();
```

Or, *Customers* could be an entity class that describes a conceptual model mapped to a relational database:

```
NorthwindModel dataModel = new NorthwindModel();
ObjectSet<Customer> Customers = dataModel.Customers;
```

And in SharePoint 2013, *Customers* could be an entity class that describes a collection of *SPListItem* types retrieved from an *SPList* of customers stored in SharePoint:

```
MySiteContext sp = new MySiteContext ( siteUri );
EntityList<Customer> Customers = sp.GetList<Customer>("Customers");
```

These examples highlight that the main goal of LINQ is to provide a unified querying and programming model—fully integrated with programming languages—that abstracts code from the underlying infrastructure.

LINQ under the hood

Now you know that a LINQ query can target any kind of data source supported by a LINQ provider. But how does LINQ work? This section gives you a tour of what's under its hood.

Suppose you write the following code that uses LINQ:

```
Customer[] Customers = GetCustomers();
var query =
```

```
    from    c in Customers
    where   c.Country == "Italy"
    select c;
```

From that query, the compiler generates this code:

```
Customer[] Customers = GetCustomers();
IEnumerable<Customer> query =
        Customers
        .Where( c => c.Country == "Italy" );
```

When the query becomes more complex, as you can see in the next example...

Note From now on, the examples will skip the *Customers* declaration for the sake of brevity.

```
var query =
    from    c in Customers
    where   c.Country == "Italy"
    orderby c.Name
    select  new { c.Name, c.City };
```

The generated code is more complex, too:

```
var query =
        Customers
        .Where( c => c.Country == "Italy" )
        .OrderBy( c => c.Name )
        .Select( c => new { c.Name, c.City } );
```

The code calls instance members on the object returned from the previous call. It calls *Where* on *Customers; OrderBy* on the object returned by *Where*; and finally, *Select* on the object returned by *OrderBy*. This behavior is regulated by what are known as *extension methods* in the host language (C# in this case). The implementation of the *Where, OrderBy,* and *Select* methods—called by the sample query—depends on the type of *Customers* and on namespaces specified in relevant *using* statements. Extension methods are a fundamental syntax feature used by LINQ so that it can maintain the same syntax across different data sources.

The basic concept behind LINQ is that queries target objects that implement either the *IEnumerable<T>* interface for in-memory data or the *IQueryable<T>* interface for data retrieved from an external store. Here's the definition of the *IEnumerable<T>* interface:

```
public interface IEnumerable<T> : IEnumerable {
    IEnumerator<T> GetEnumerator();
}
```

And here's the definition of the *IQueryable<T>* interface, together with its base interface, *IQueryable*:

```
public interface IQueryable<T> : IEnumerable<T>, IQueryable, IEnumerable {
```

```
}
public interface IQueryable : IEnumerable {
    Type ElementType { get; }
    Expression Expression { get; }
    IQueryProvider Provider { get; }
}
```

Whenever you browse for (enumerate) the results of a query—for example, by using a *foreach* statement—the compiler invokes the *GetEnumerator* method of the *IEnumerable<T>* interface, and at that point the query is effectively executed.

When the target object of your query implements only the *IEnumerable<T>* interface, the extension methods targeting that type will work against in-memory objects. For example, LINQ to Objects and LINQ to XML both work in this way.

However, when the query target object implements *IQueryable<T>*, the extension methods construct an expression tree, which describes the query from a provider-independent point of view. The expression tree is then processed by the *IQueryable* implementation of the query target object, invoking the *IQueryProvider* object published by the *IQueryable.Provider* property. The query provider visits the expression tree, using an expression visitor, and produces a query syntax that targets the concrete persistence storage.

For example, as shown in Figure 6-2, for a LINQ to SQL query engine, the query provider will generate a T-SQL query that corresponds to the LINQ query you defined in your .NET code. Similarly, when using LINQ to SharePoint, the query provider generates a CAML (Collaborative Application Markup Language) query that will be executed against the target *SPList* using the standard Server Object Model querying syntax.

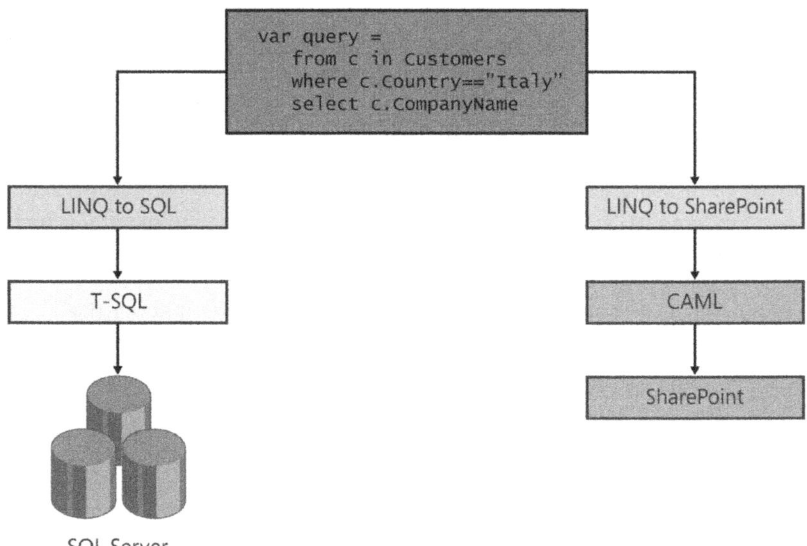

FIGURE 6-2 A graphical representation of how LINQ providers work.

Note CAML is an XML-based querying language that is useful for retrieving, manipulating, sorting, and grouping SharePoint data.

Introducing LINQ to SharePoint

With a better understanding of LINQ and generally how it works, you can dive into LINQ to SharePoint, which is just another LINQ query provider that targets SharePoint data. Figure 6-3 shows the data access model architecture of SharePoint 2013, illustrating the role of LINQ to SharePoint compared to other data access technologies available in SharePoint 2013.

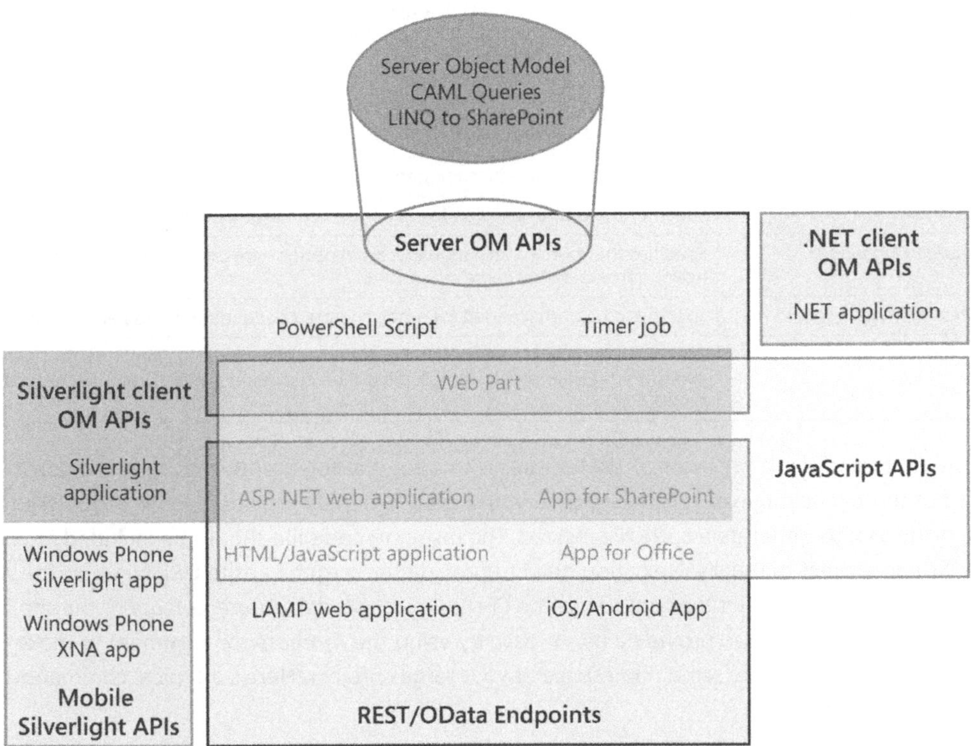

FIGURE 6-3 The SharePoint 2013 data access model architecture and the role of LINQ to SharePoint.

The key feature of LINQ to SharePoint is that it can query SharePoint data with a fully typed approach, using a common querying language (LINQ) and retrieving typed entities.

Modeling with SPMetal.exe

The first and main task when developing solutions that make use of LINQ to SharePoint is to model the typed entities. You can define these manually, but it is generally more useful to use SPMetal.exe, which can automatically generate entities for you. You can find the SPMetal.exe utility in the SharePoint15_Root\BIN folder. SPMetal.exe is a command-line tool that accepts the wide range of arguments listed in Table 6-1.

TABLE 6-1 Arguments that you can provide to SPMetal.exe

Argument	Description
/web:<url>	Specifies the absolute URL of the target website. The host address can be local, in which case, the tool uses the Server Object Model to connect to the server.
/useremoteapi	Specifies that the website URL is remote. You might not use this option if any of the lists on the website contain lookup fields. Secondary lookups are not supported by the Client Object Model.
/user:<name>	Specifies the logon username (or domain).
/password:<password>	Specifies the logon password.
/parameters:<file>	Specifies an XML file with code generation parameters.
/code:<file>	Specifies the output location for generated code (default: console).
/language:<language>	Specifies the source code language. Valid options are *csharp* and *vb* (default: inferred from source code file name extension).
/namespace:<namespace>	Specifies a namespace used for autogenerated code (default: no namespace).
/serialization:<type>	Specifies a serialization type. Valid options are *none* and *unidirectional* (default: *none*). The entities serialization topic will be discussed in the "Disconnected entities" section.

Note that the default behavior of SPMetal.exe is to output autogenerated code to the console. That's not terribly useful except for testing, so you should generally provide a */code* argument to instruct the tool to generate a code file instead. The resulting code file should be included in your Visual Studio project manually. Next, you need to provide the target website URL by using the */web* argument, and then instruct the tool to use the Client Object Model (*/useremoteapi*) if the site is remote. It's common to also provide a namespace by using the */namespace* argument to make the generated code part of the same namespace of your target project. Here's a typical command-line invocation of the tool:

```
SPMETAL.EXE /web:http://devbook.sp2013.local /code:devbook.cs /namespace:DevLeap.SP2013.Linq2SP
```

By default, SPMetal.exe creates a full model for the target site, defining a class for almost every supported content type and a list for every list instance, except for hidden lists. The tool will also create a class named *{WebSiteName}DataContext*, where *{WebSiteName}* is the name of the target website (without spaces, in case the site name has spaces in its content). This class represents the entry point for using LINQ to SharePoint, and it inherits from the *Microsoft.SharePoint.Linq.DataContext* base class.

Quite often, you do not really need to model each and every content type and list instance of the target site. Usually, you need to model only some custom data structures that you plan to query and manage with LINQ to SharePoint. The */parameters* command-line argument is provided for this purpose. In fact, by using this argument, you can provide SPMetal.exe with an XML file that instructs the tool about what to skip and what to include in the autogenerated model. Listing 6-1 shows a sample XML parameters file that excludes all the common team site default contents, but includes all other lists and content types. Notice that you cannot use both an *ExcludeList* and a *List* element targeting the same list.

LISTING 6-1 A sample XML parameters file suitable for SPMetal.exe

```
<?xml version="1.0" encoding="utf-8"?>
<Web AccessModifier="Internal"
xmlns="http://schemas.microsoft.com/SharePoint/2009/spmetal">
  <ExcludeList Name="Documents"/>
  <ExcludeList Name="Site Assets"/>
  <ExcludeList Name="Site Pages"/>
  <ExcludeList Name="Style Library"/>
</Web>
```

Listing 6-1 shows that the XML file is based on a custom XML namespace. Table 6-2 describes the supported elements that you can use to define such a file.

TABLE 6-2 The elements available for defining an XML parameters file

Element name	Description and purpose
Web	The root element of the schema. This tag defines the name of the *DataContext* generated class, configuring the *class* attribute. It also defines the access modifier used for autogenerated types. By default, SPMetal.exe uses a public access modifier.
List	Instructs SPMetal.exe to include a specified list definition. It is useful for including hidden lists. It also allows you to override the name of the list in the autogenerated code. The tag requires a *Name* attribute whose value is the list name.
ExcludeList	Excludes the generation of the specified target list from the autogenerated code. This tag requires a *Name* attribute whose value is the list name.
ExcludeOtherLists	Instructs SPMetal.exe to avoid generating any list definition except those that you explicitly define using a *List* element.
IncludeHiddenLists	Requests that SPMetal.exe generate list definitions for hidden lists. You cannot use this element together with the *ExcludeOtherLists* element.
ContentType	Forces SPMetal.exe to generate the code for a specific content type, referenced by *Name*, using a specific attribute. You can use this tag, for example, to include a hidden content type. This element can be a child of the *Web* or *List* elements.
Column	Instructs SPMetal.exe to output a property representing a field (site column) that it would not model by default. For example, you can use this element to include a hidden field. It requires a *Name* attribute, whose value is the name of the field to include.
ExcludeColumn	Excludes a field from code generation. This element requires a *Name* attribute, whose value is the name of the field to include.

ExcludeOtherColumns	Configures the tool to block code generation for columns that are not explicitly referenced by a *Column* element.
IncludeHiddenColumns	Causes SPMetal.exe to generate code for hidden column. This element cannot be used together with the *ExcludeOtherColumns* element.
ExcludeContentType	Blocks code generation for the content type specified by the value of a *Name* attribute. This element can be a child of *Web* or *List* elements.
ExcludeOtherContentTypes	Configures SPMetal.exe to block code generation for SharePoint apps not explicitly referenced by a *ContentType* element.
IncludeHiddenContentTypes	Requests that SPMetal.exe also generate code for any hidden content type. This element cannot be used together with the *ExcludeOtherContentTypes* element.

Now suppose that you have a website with a couple of custom lists: a standard document library named Invoices and a custom list of items named DevLeap Contacts in which each item can be of type *DevLeapCustomer* or *DevLeapSupplier*. Both types share a base content type called *DevLeapContact*.

Note To provision these content types and lists, see the code samples in Chapter 3, "Data provisioning."

Listing 6-2 shows another XML parameters file that includes these custom content types and lists and excludes all other content types and lists.

LISTING 6-2 Sample XML parameters file for SPMetal.exe

```
<?xml version="1.0" encoding="utf-8"?>
<Web AccessModifier="Internal" xmlns="http://schemas.microsoft.com/
SharePoint/2009/
spmetal">
  <List Name="DevLeap Contacts">
    <ContentType Name="DevLeapContact" Class="DevLeapContact" />
    <ContentType Name="DevLeapCustomer" Class="DevLeapCustomer" />
    <ContentType Name="DevLeapSupplier" Class="DevLeapSupplier" />
  </List>
  <List Name="Invoices" />
  <ExcludeOtherLists />
</Web>
```

Assume you've executed this with SPMetal.exe; now you'll examine the resulting autogenerated code. First, you have a *DevbookDataContext* class that provides entry points to access the content lists of the target site. Listing 6-3 shows the definition of this *DataContext*-inherited class.

LISTING 6-3 The *DevbookDataContext* class, autogenerated using the XML parameters file from Listing 6-2

```
internal partial class DevbookDataContext : Microsoft.SharePoint.Linq.DataContext
{

    #region Extensibility Method Definitions
    partial void OnCreated();
    #endregion

    public DevbookDataContext(string requestUrl) :
            base(requestUrl) {
        this.OnCreated();
    }
```

```
    [Microsoft.SharePoint.Linq.ListAttribute(Name="DevLeap Contacts")]
    public Microsoft.SharePoint.Linq.EntityList<DevLeapContact> DevLeapContacts {
        get {
            return this.GetList<DevLeapContact>("DevLeap Contacts");
        }
    }

    [Microsoft.SharePoint.Linq.ListAttribute(Name="Invoices")]
    public Microsoft.SharePoint.Linq.EntityList<Document> Invoices {
        get {
            return this.GetList<Document>("Invoices");
        }
    }
}
```

The class has a constructor that accepts the URL of the target website as its only argument. Internally, it invokes a partial method (*OnCreated*), which you can use to customize the context initialization. Next, there are a couple of public properties that correspond to the two modeled lists (Invoices and DevLeap Contacts). It is interesting to see that both of these properties are decorated with the *ListAttribute* attribute, stating the name of the underlying SharePoint list. Also, both of these properties are of type *EntityList<T>*, which is the type LINQ to SharePoint uses to represent a collection of typed items.

Internally, these properties invoke the *DataContext.GetList<T>* method. If you have any experience with LINQ to SQL, you will find many similarities between LINQ to SharePoint and LINQ to SQL. The *Invoices* list is made up of a set of *Document* instances, where *Document* is the typed entity autogenerated by SPMetal.exe that describes a SharePoint document from a conceptual viewpoint. The *DevLeapContacts* list is composed of items of type *DevLeapContact*, which is the typed entity corresponding to the base content type *DevLeapContact*.

One last thing to consider about the *DataContext* type is that it implements *IDisposable*, because internally it uses some types that exploit unmanaged resources such as the *SPSite* and *SPWeb* types. Therefore, you should always call *Dispose* whenever you create an instance.

More Info See the "Resource disposal" section in Chapter 5 to better understand the reasons for disposing of unmanaged resources.

Figure 6-4 shows the class diagram of the generated types.

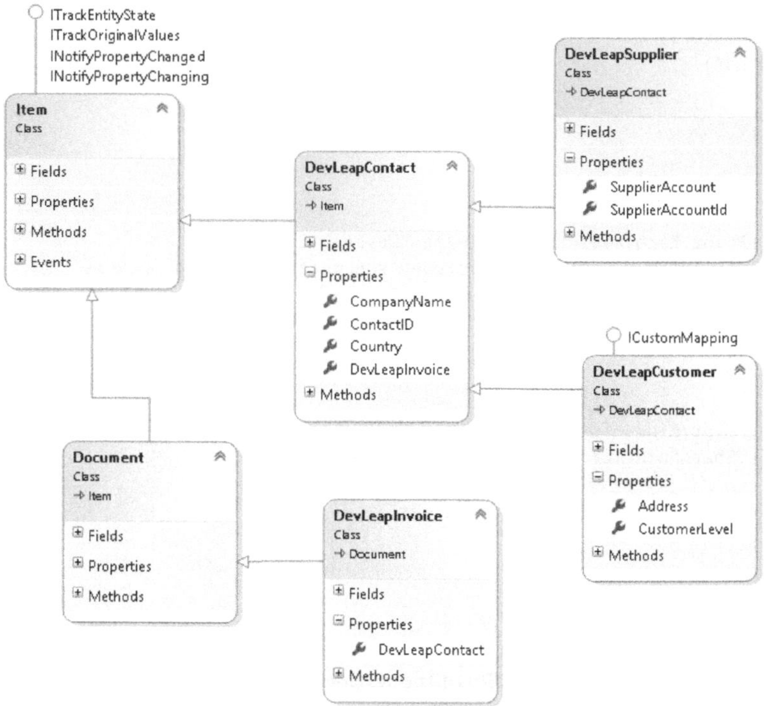

FIGURE 6-4 Class diagram of typed entities generated by SPMetal.exe.

Specifically, Figure 6-4 shows that the SPMetal.exe tool generated an *Item* base class, which internally implements some infrastructural interfaces for data management tracking (*ITrackEntityState, ITrackOriginalValues*) and for data binding (*INotifyPropertyChanged, INotifyPropertyChanging*), as well as some properties that correspond to the common data of every SharePoint list item (*Id, Path, Title,* and *Version*). The *Document* entity inherits from *Item* and adds some document-specific properties (*DocumentCreatedBy, DocumentModifiedBy,* and *Name*). The most interesting part of the model is how it defines entities that map to custom content types. In fact, SPMetal.exe modeled a *DevLeapContact* class, which inherits from *Item* and is the base class for the types *DevLeapCustomer* and *DevLeapSupplier.* This is challenging behavior; SPMetal.exe modeled the content types and lists of SharePoint, mapping them to an object-oriented model of entities, with full inheritance support.

Important Because of the need for a set of typed entities that model the content types defined in the target SharePoint site, it is good practice to use LINQ to SharePoint only against sites that have a well-defined and stable structure. To learn how to correctly provision data structures in SharePoint, see Chapter 3. Similarly, it is not as useful to use LINQ to SharePoint on sites that frequently change their structure, because you would need to refresh the typed model frequently as well. Instead, you should access and query sites with a high change frequency using the standard Server Object Model and the untyped approach, eventually using CAML at a low level.

Listing 6-4 shows a portion of the code corresponding to the base *Item* type.

LISTING 6-4 The *Item* type code autogenerated by SPMetal.exe

```
/// <summary>
/// Create a new list item.
/// </summary>
[Microsoft.SharePoint.Linq.ContentTypeAttribute(Name="Item", Id="0x01")]
[Microsoft.SharePoint.Linq.DerivedEntityClassAttribute(
Type=typeof(DevLeapContact))]
[Microsoft.SharePoint.Linq.DerivedEntityClassAttribute(Type=typeof(Document))]
internal partial class Item : Microsoft.SharePoint.Linq.ITrackEntityState,
Microsoft.SharePoint.Linq.ITrackOriginalValues,
System.ComponentModel.INotifyPropertyChanged,
System.ComponentModel.INotifyPropertyChanging {

    // Code omitted for the sake of brevity ...

    #region Extensibility Method Definition
    partial void OnLoaded();
    partial void OnValidate();
    partial void OnCreated();
    #endregion

    Microsoft.SharePoint.Linq.EntityState
    Microsoft.SharePoint.Linq.ITrackEntityState.EntityState {
            get {
                    return this._entityState;
            }
            set {
                    if ((value != this._entityState)) {
                            this._entityState = value;
                    }
            }
    }

    System.Collections.Generic.IDictionary<string, object>
    Microsoft.SharePoint.Linq.ITrackOriginalValues.OriginalValues {
            get {
                    if ((null == this._originalValues)) {
```

```
                    this._originalValues = new
                      System.Collections.Generic.Dictionary<string,
                      object>();
                }
                return this._originalValues;
        }
    }
    public Item() {
        this.OnCreated();
    }
    [Microsoft.SharePoint.Linq.ColumnAttribute(Name="ID", Storage="_id",
       ReadOnly=true, FieldType="Counter")]
    public System.Nullable<int> Id {
        get {
                return this._id;
        }
        set {
                if ((value != this._id)) {
                        this.OnPropertyChanging("Id", this._id);
                        this._id = value;
                        this.OnPropertyChanged("Id");
                }
        }
    }

    // Code omitted for the sake of brevity ...
    [Microsoft.SharePoint.Linq.ColumnAttribute(Name="Title", Storage="_title",
       Required=true, FieldType="Text")]
    public virtual string Title {
        get {
                return this._title;
        }
        set {
                if ((value != this._title)) {
                        this.OnPropertyChanging("Title", this._title);
                        this._title = value;
                        this.OnPropertyChanged("Title");
                }
        }
    }

    // Code omitted for the sake of brevity ...

}
```

It is interesting to see the class attribute decorations—which are specific for LINQ to SharePoint—that instruct the engine about the content type ID (*ID=0x01*) behind the *Item* class, as well as about the types that inherit from this base class. You can see that the base *Item* type, and thus every typed entity in the model, provides an *EntityState* property related to the *ITrackEntityState* interface implementation, and an *OriginalValues* property of type *Dictionary*, related to the *ITrackOriginalValues* interface implementation. You'll see these properties used for tracking entities' states and changes in the "Managing data" section later in the chapter. In addition, the entity offers two public properties useful for accessing the current item ID and title. These properties are marked with the *ColumnAttribute* attribute, which defines the underlying storage field and the corresponding SharePoint column. Lastly, the class provides three partial methods that you can implement to add custom behaviors to the type when loading (*OnLoaded*), validating (*OnValidate*), and creating (*OnCreated*) a type instance.

Starting from this base type, the tool arranges inheritance for all the entity types corresponding to the content types. Listing 6-5 contains an excerpt of the *DevLeapContact, DevLeapCustomer*, and *DevLeapSupplier* types.

LISTING 6-5 The autogenerated code for the custom types

```
[Microsoft.SharePoint.Linq.ContentTypeAttribute(Name="DevLeapContact",
    Id="0x010025836A76187A4B49892A35CB80CC5232")]
[Microsoft.SharePoint.Linq.DerivedEntityClassAttribute(
   Type=typeof(DevLeapCustomer))]
[Microsoft.SharePoint.Linq.DerivedEntityClassAttribute(
   Type=typeof(DevLeapSupplier))]
internal partial class DevLeapContact : Item {
    private string _contactID;
    private string _companyName;
    private System.Nullable<Country> _country;

    #region Extensibility Method Definitions
    partial void OnLoaded();
    partial void OnValidate();
    partial void OnCreated();
    #endregion

    public DevLeapContact() {
            this.OnCreated();
    }

     [Microsoft.SharePoint.Linq.ColumnAttribute(Name="DevLeapContactID",
       Storage="_contactID", Required=true, FieldType="Text")]
    public string ContactID {
       // Code omitted for the sake of brevity ...
    }

    [Microsoft.SharePoint.Linq.ColumnAttribute(Name="DevLeapCompanyName",
       Storage="_companyName", FieldType="Text")]
     public string CompanyName {
       // Code omitted for the sake of brevity ...
    }

    [Microsoft.SharePoint.Linq.ColumnAttribute(Name="DevLeapCountry",
       Storage="_country", FieldType="Choice")]
     public System.Nullable<Country> Country {
       // Code omitted for the sake of brevity ...
    }
}
```

```
[Microsoft.SharePoint.Linq.ContentTypeAttribute(Name="DevLeapCustomer",
   Id="0x010025836A76187A4B49892A35CB80CC523200D458F4EF7D494F43B84D46C30F7
BA444")]
internal partial class DevLeapCustomer : DevLeapContact {
    private System.Nullable<CustomerLevel> _customerLevel;
    #region Extensibility Method Definitions
    partial void OnLoaded();
    partial void OnValidate();
    partial void OnCreated();
    #endregion

    public DevLeapCustomer() {
            this.OnCreated();
    }

     [Microsoft.SharePoint.Linq.ColumnAttribute(Name="DevLeapCustomerLevel",
       Storage="_customerLevel", Required=true, FieldType="Choice")]
    public System.Nullable<CustomerLevel> CustomerLevel {
        // Code omitted for the sake of brevity ...
    }
}

[Microsoft.SharePoint.Linq.ContentTypeAttribute(Name="DevLeapSupplier",
   Id="0x010025836A76187A4B49892A35CB80CC523200070CB29DDC9B4566B98F94F4
1E652260")]
internal partial class DevLeapSupplier : DevLeapContact {
    // Code omitted for the sake of brevity ...
}

internal enum Country : int {
    None = 0,
    Invalid = 1,
    [Microsoft.SharePoint.Linq.ChoiceAttribute(Value="Italy")]
    Italy = 2,
    [Microsoft.SharePoint.Linq.ChoiceAttribute(Value="USA")]
    USA = 4,
    [Microsoft.SharePoint.Linq.ChoiceAttribute(Value="Germany")]
    Germany = 8,
    [Microsoft.SharePoint.Linq.ChoiceAttribute(Value="France")]
    France = 16,
}

internal enum CustomerLevel : int {
    None = 0,
    Invalid = 1,
    [Microsoft.SharePoint.Linq.ChoiceAttribute(Value="Level A")]
    LevelA = 2,
    [Microsoft.SharePoint.Linq.ChoiceAttribute(Value="Level B")]
    LevelB = 4,
    [Microsoft.SharePoint.Linq.ChoiceAttribute(Value="Level C")]
    LevelC = 8,
}
```

Listing 6-5 shows that the classes are fully connected with the original SharePoint types because each class refers to its corresponding content type using its ID, just as the *Item* base type did in Listing 6-4. Additionally, when you have a *Choice* field on the SharePoint side (for example, *DevLeapContact.Country* and *DevLeapCustomer.CustomerLevel*), the tool generates an *enum* type, giving you strongly typed access to the choice values.

Of course, you could write all this code manually and get the same results, but that's not recommended because you would be wasting your time.

Querying data

Now that you have seen how to model your data with SPMetal.exe, and what the model is, you can start querying the site for content. The key feature of this new query provider lies in its ability to query SharePoint content using LINQ queries. As an example, Listing 6-6 contains a code excerpt with a query that fetches the titles of documents in the Invoices library with the *Title* property starting with a specific word.

Note To execute the custom code illustrated in this section and in those that follow, you need to reference the Microsoft.SharePoint.Linq.dll assembly, which is available in the SharePoint15_Root\ISAPI folder of every SharePoint server. In addition, you should declare a couple of *using* statements for the namespaces *Microsoft.SharePoint.Linq* and *System.Linq* in your code.

LISTING 6-6 A code excerpt using a LINQ to SharePoint query to find documents in the Invoices list created by a specific user

```
using (DevbookDataContext spContext = new
    DevbookDataContext("http://devbook.sp2013.local/")) {
    var query = from d in spContext.Invoices
                where d.Title.StartsWith("Invoice")
                select d.Title;

    foreach (var i in query) {
            Console.WriteLine(i);
    }
}
```

Listing 6-6 creates a new instance of the *DataContext* class, passing in the URL of the target site. The target site can be the URL of any SharePoint site with a data structure that is compatible with the site from which you generated the model. Of course, in real code, the URL should not be hard coded, and you should refer to a configurable parameter. It also employs the *using* keyword to dispose of unmanaged resources expediently. Then it simply queries the *Invoices* collection provided by the current context, just as with any other LINQ query. Under the hood, the query engine creates a CAML query and sends it to the Invoices list using an *SPQuery* instance, invoking the *SPList.GetItems* method. If you want to see the autogenerated CAML query, you can set the *Log* property of the *DataContext* instance to a *TextWriter* object (for example, *Console.Out* if you are working with a *Console* application). Here's the syntax:

```
spContext.Log = Console.Out;
```

And here's the CAML code generated for the query in Listing 6-6:

```
<View>
  <Query>
    <Where>
      <And>
        <BeginsWith><FieldRef Name="ContentTypeId" />
          <Value Type="ContentTypeId">0x0101</Value>
        </BeginsWith>
        <BeginsWith>
          <FieldRef Name="Title"/><Value Type="Text">Invoice</Value>
        </BeginsWith>
      </And>
    </Where>
  </Query>
  <ViewFields>
    <FieldRef Name="Title" />
  </ViewFields>
  <RowLimit Paged="TRUE">2147483647</RowLimit>
</View>
```

The LINQ to SharePoint query engine allows you to define many kinds of queries, with partitioning (*where*), projection (*select*), and under some circumstances, relationships (*join*). Imagine that the Invoices list of documents is made of a custom content type named *DevLeapInvoice* that has a lookup field that accepts a *DevLeapContact* object from the DevLeap Contacts custom list. If you refresh the model (via SPMetal.exe) after adding such a lookup field in the Invoices list, you will see a new class that inherits from the original *Document* type, as shown in Listing 6-7.

LISTING 6-7 The definition of the *DevLeapInvoice* type

```
[Microsoft.SharePoint.Linq.ContentTypeAttribute(
   Name="DevLeapInvoice", Id="0x0101000B231F0B244C41F59EB1467059EA59E8")]
internal partial class DevLeapInvoice : Document {
    private Microsoft.SharePoint.Linq.EntityRef<DevLeapContact> _devLeapContact;

    // Code omitted for the sake of brevity ...

    public DevLeapInvoice() {
            this._devLeapContact = new
               Microsoft.SharePoint.Linq.EntityRef<DevLeapContact>();
            this.Initialize();
    }
```

```
    [Microsoft.SharePoint.Linq.AssociationAttribute(
        Name="DevLeap_x0020_Contact", Storage="_devLeapContact",
        MultivalueType=Microsoft.SharePoint.Linq.AssociationType.Single,
        List="DevLeap Contacts")]
    public DevLeapContact DevLeapContact {
            get {
                    return this._devLeapContact.GetEntity();
            }
            set {
                    this._devLeapContact.SetEntity(value);
            }
    }

    private void Initialize() {
        this._devLeapContact.OnSync += new System.EventHandler<Microsoft.
SharePoint.Linq.AssociationChangedEventArgs<DevLeapContact>>(this.
OnDevLeapContactSync);
        this._devLeapContact.OnChanged += new System.EventHandler(this.
OnDevLeapContactChanged);
        this._devLeapContact.OnChanging += new System.EventHandler(this.
OnDevLeapContactChanging);
        this.OnCreated();
    }

    private void OnDevLeapContactChanging(object sender, System.EventArgs e) {
            this.OnPropertyChanging("DevLeapContact", this._devLeapContact.
Clone());
    }

    private void OnDevLeapContactChanged(object sender, System.EventArgs e) {
            this.OnPropertyChanged("DevLeapContact");
    }

    private void OnDevLeapContactSync(object sender,
       Microsoft.SharePoint.Linq.AssociationChangedEventArgs<DevLeapContact> e) {
            if ((Microsoft.SharePoint.Linq.AssociationChangedState.Added ==
                e.State)) {
                    e.Item.InvoicesDocument.Add(this);
            }
            else {
                    e.Item.InvoicesDocument.Remove(this);
            }
    }
}
```

This new type has a property named *DevLeapContact*, of type *DevLeapContact*, which internally works with a private storage field of type *EntityRef<DevLeapContact>*. In addition, the type constructor automatically creates an instance of that field and registers some event handlers to manage the synchronization of the association between the *DevLeapInvoice* object and its corresponding *DevLeapContact* instance.

On the other side, the *DevLeapContact* type has been changed, too. In fact, now it supports a public property of type *Microsoft.SharePoint.Linq.EntitySet<DevLeapInvoice>*, which represents a reference to all the invoices for the current contact.

Now comes the nice part of the story: you can define a LINQ query that joins these entities. In addition, you can use deferred loading of entities when dynamically browsing related items. *Deferred loading* allows you to dynamically load data related to the entities you are querying, whenever you need them and without having to explicitly and manually load them. In fact, the LINQ to SharePoint provider will take care of that for you. Listing 6-8 shows a code excerpt of a sample query with a *join* syntax.

LISTING 6-8 A LINQ to SharePoint query that uses a join between contacts and invoices

```
using (DevbookDataContext spContext = new
   DevbookDataContext("http://devbook.sp2013.local/")) {

    var query = from c in spContext.DevLeapContacts
                join i in spContext.Invoices on c.Id equals i.DevLeapContact.Id
                select new { c.ContactID, c.Title, InvoiceTitle = i.Title };

    // Use the query results ...
}
```

The output of this query will be a set of new anonymous types that expose the properties *ContactID*, *Title*, and *InvoiceTitle*. The CAML query sent to the SharePoint is as follows:

```
<View>
  <Query>
    <Where>
      <And>
        <BeginsWith>
          <FieldRef Name="ContentTypeId" />
          <Value Type="ContentTypeId">0x0101000B231F0B244C41F59EB1467059EA59E8</Value>
        </BeginsWith>
        <BeginsWith>
          <FieldRef Name="DevLeap_x0020_ContactContentTypeId" />
          <Value Type="Lookup">0x010025836A76187A4B49892A35CB80CC5232</Value>
        </BeginsWith>
      </And>
    </Where>
    <OrderBy Override="TRUE" />
  </Query>
  <ViewFields>
    <FieldRef Name="DevLeap_x0020_ContactDevLeapContactID" />
    <FieldRef Name="DevLeap_x0020_ContactTitle" />
    <FieldRef Name="Title" />
  </ViewFields>
  <ProjectedFields>
    <Field Name="DevLeap_x0020_ContactDevLeapContactID" Type="Lookup"
        List="DevLeap_x0020_Contact" ShowField="DevLeapContactID" />
    <Field Name="DevLeap_x0020_ContactTitle" Type="Lookup"
```

```
    List="DevLeap_x0020_Contact" ShowField="Title" />
  <Field Name="DevLeap_x0020_ContactContentTypeId" Type="Lookup"
      List="DevLeap_x0020_Contact" ShowField="ContentTypeId" />
  </ProjectedFields>
  <Joins>
    <Join Type="INNER" ListAlias="DevLeap_x0020_Contact">
      <!--List Name: DevLeap Contacts-->
      <Eq>
        <FieldRef Name="DevLeap_x0020_Contact" RefType="ID" />
        <FieldRef List="DevLeap_x0020_Contact" Name="ID" />
      </Eq>
    </Join>
  </Joins>
  <RowLimit Paged="TRUE">2147483647</RowLimit>
</View>
```

Notice the elements *ProjectedFields* and *Joins* in the CAML code. In Listing 6-9 code excerpt illustrates deferred loading in action.

LISTING 6-9 A LINQ to SharePoint Query using deferred loading

```
using (DevbookDataContext spContext = new
   DevbookDataContext("http://devbook.sp2013.local/")) {

    var query = from c in spContext.DevLeapContacts
                select c;

    foreach (var c in query) {
        Console.WriteLine(c.Title);
        foreach (var i in c.InvoicesDocument) {
            Console.WriteLine(i.Title);
        }
    }
}
```

In Listing 6-9, the first LINQ query is converted into CAML and executed against SharePoint within the first and external *foreach* block. Then, when the inner *foreach* block browses for the *InvoicesDocument* collection of the current contact, the LINQ to SharePoint engine automatically executes a CAML query to retrieve the invoices belonging to the current contact. This is the default behavior, which you can change by setting the *DeferredLoadingEnabled* property of the *DataContext* to *false*, as shown here:

```
spContext.DeferredLoadingEnabled = false;
```

If you're familiar with LINQ, you probably use hierarchical grouped queries, making use of the *join into* (also known as *group join*) clause, which avoids the need to execute a separate query to retrieve the invoices for every single contact. However, the LINQ to SharePoint query provider has limitations due to its use of CAML queries under the covers. For example, with CAML, you cannot query more than one list at a time, so you can't use a group join. Listing 6-10 presents a code excerpt that declares an unsupported group join query.

LISTING 6-10 An unsupported LINQ to SharePoint query syntax

```
using (DevbookDataContext spContext = new
   DevbookDataContext("http://devbook.sp2013.local/")) {

    var query = from c in spContext.DevLeapContacts
                join i in spContext.Invoices on c.Id equals i.DevLeapContact.Id
                into invoices select new { c.Id, c.Title, Invoiced = invoices };
}
```

When you try to execute a query like this, the LINQ to SharePoint query provider throws an exception similar to this:

```
Unhandled Exception: System.InvalidOperationException: The query uses unsupported elements,
such as references to more than one list, or the projection of a complete entity by
usingEntityRef/EntitySet.
```

Moreover, LINQ to SharePoint does not support multifetch queries that query across multiple lists or join clauses on fields other than *Lookup* fields. For multifetch queries, you can consider using specific controls instead, such as the Content by Query Web Part or the *SPSiteDataQuery* class, which allows querying multiple lists using CAML queries. Also, you cannot define queries across multiple websites or that query different *DataContext* instances. Finally, you cannot use mathematical functions because CAML does not support them. Overall, LINQ to SharePoint does not support queries that cannot be translated into CAML syntax.

More Info For a complete list of unsupported syntax and commands, please refer to the article "Unsupported LINQ Queries and Two-stage Queries," on MSDN, at *http://msdn.microsoft.com/en-us/library/ee536585.aspx*.

Managing data

The previous section showed that LINQ to SharePoint provides a convenient syntax for executing CAML queries with a fully typed approach. Even if this is sufficient for your needs, the story becomes more interesting when you consider that LINQ to SharePoint gives you access to data using a kind of SharePoint-specific O/RM, meaning you can also manage (insert, update, delete) data using LINQ to SharePoint, and it's a fully typed approach.

Here's a quick initial example. The code in Listing 6-11 queries for a specific contact in the DevLeap Contacts list, using a LINQ to SharePoint query, and then changes the *Country* property of the retrieved item.

LISTING 6-11 Using LINQ to SharePoint to change an entity

```
using (DevbookDataContext spContext = new DevbookDataContext(
    "http://devbook.sp2013.local/")) {

    var contact = (from c in spContext.DevLeapContacts
                   where c.ContactID == "PP001"
                   select c).FirstOrDefault();

    // Let's see if we found the target contact
    if (contact != null) {
        contact.Country = Country.USA;
        spContext.SubmitChanges();
    }
}
```

As Listing 6-11 demonstrates, the process is both simple and intuitive. You just need to retrieve the object, change its properties, and then confirm the changes by invoking the *SubmitChanges* method of the *DataContext*. You should consider *SubmitChanges* the counterpart of the *Update* method in the standard Server Object Model. In fact, just as with the Server Object Model, whenever you change an instance of an entity that models an item in a SharePoint list, you are changing the in-memory copy of that data, not the SharePoint content database. Behind the scenes, the LINQ to SharePoint engine tracks this change, so you can apply it on the real content database when you invoke the *DataContext.SubmitChanges* method.

Internally, the *DataContext* base class provides an object tracker (an internal *EntityTracker* class) that tracks any changes you make to in-memory copies of typed entities. Furthermore, as you have already seen in the previous section, the base *Item* class that every LINQ to SharePoint entity inherits implements the *ITrackEntityState* interface, which provides an *EntityState* property that can assume one of the following values:

- ***Unchanged*** The entity has not been changed.
- ***ToBeInserted*** The entity is new and will be inserted into its parent list when you call *SubmitChanges*.
- ***ToBeUpdated*** The entity has been changed and will be updated in the content database when you call *SubmitChanges*.
- ***ToBeDeleted*** The entity has been deleted and will be permanently removed from the content database when you call *SubmitChanges*.
- ***ToBeRecycled*** The entity has been deleted and will be moved to the Recycle Bin when you call *SubmitChanges*.
- ***Deleted*** The entity has been deleted or recycled.

For example, if you test the *EntityState* property of the contact in Listing 6-11, you will see that the entity is in the *Unchanged* state just after retrieval. As soon as you change the *Country* property, its state becomes *ToBeUpdated*. Finally, just after you invoke the *SubmitChanges* method, the state returns to *Unchanged*, because the entity has been synchronized with the content database.

This tracking behavior is provided transparently by default whenever you create a *DataContext* instance and retrieve modeled entities. Note that tracking does not work on anonymous types, which are types that you get through LINQ queries that use custom projection. For example, the code illustrated in Listing 6-8 uses projection to extract an anonymous type made only of *ContactID*, *Title*, and *InvoiceTitle* properties. The type resulting from that query will be read-only and thus will not have tracking support.

The tracking behavior, however, has an impact on performance and resource consumption. Therefore, if you don't need to manage data (such as when you need to query and render contents in a read-only fashion), you can disable the entity tracking service by setting the *ObjectTrackingEnabled* property of the *DataContext* class to *false*:

```
spContext.ObjectTrackingEnabled = false;
```

In the next few pages, you will see how to manage data, taking advantage of the LINQ to SharePoint tracking engine through some concrete examples. You've already seen an example of updating an item in Listing 6-11, so that operation will not be repeated.

Inserting a new item

To insert a new item into a list, you first create the item instance, just as you would with any .NET object. Next, you need to configure its properties, and finally, you need to add the new item to its parent list and submit changes to the content database. The code in Listing 6-12 illustrates this process.

LISTING 6-12 Inserting a new item in a list using LINQ to SharePoint

```
using (DevbookDataContext spContext = new
   DevbookDataContext("http://devbook.sp2013.local/")) {
    DevLeapCustomer newCustomer = new DevLeapCustomer {
        Title = "Andrea Pialorsi",
        ContactID = "AP001",
        CompanyName = "DevLeap",
        Country = Country.Italy,
        CustomerLevel = CustomerLevel.LevelA,
    };
    spContext.DevLeapContacts.InsertOnSubmit(newCustomer);
    spContext.SubmitChanges();
}
```

The key point of this example, aside from the *SubmitChanges* method invocation that you have already seen, is the call to the *InsertOnSubmit* method of the *EntityList<T>* class that lies behind the *DevLeapContacts* property of the *DataContext*. The *InsertOnSubmit* method accepts an item to be inserted into the target list as soon as you invoke *SubmitChanges*. The entity passed to the method will acquire a state of *ToBeInserted*. Note that the *InsertOnSubmit* method is fully typed according to the generic type *T* of the *EntityList<T>* class. Thus, in Listing 6-12 you can invoke this method by providing a class of type *DevLeapContact* or any type inherited from *DevLeapContact*, such as *DevLeapCustomer* or *DevLeapSupplier*.

The *EntityList<T>* class also provides an *InsertAllOnSubmit* method, which lets you insert a group of entities instead of a single entity. This last method requires an argument of type *IEnumerable<T>*, representing the collection of items to insert.

Deleting or recycling an existing item

Deleting an item is much like inserting a new item. The *EntityList<T>* class provides a *DeleteOnSubmit* method, as well as a *DeleteAllOnSubmit* method, similar to the methods presented in the preceding section. The former accepts a single item to delete, whereas the latter accepts a collection of type *IEnumerable<T>*, representing the items to delete. Both of these methods permanently delete the target items from the content database when you confirm the action by invoking *SubmitChanges*. SharePoint provides a Recycle Bin feature, so the *EntityList<T>* class also provides a couple of methods specifically intended to move items into the Recycle Bin, instead of permanently deleting them. These methods are *RecycleOnSubmit* and *RecycleAllOnSubmit*. Listing 6-13 shows a code excerpt that illustrates how to delete or recycle an item.

LISTING 6-13 Deleting or recycling an item from a list using LINQ to SharePoint

```
using (DevbookDataContext spContext = new DevbookDataContext(
    "http://devbook.sp2013.local/")) {
    var contact = (from c in spContext.DevLeapContacts
                   where c.ContactID == "AP001"
                   select c).FirstOrDefault();

    // Let's see if we found the target contact
    if (contact != null) {
        if (recycle) {
            spContext.DevLeapContacts.RecycleOnSubmit(contact);
        }
        else {
            spContext.DevLeapContacts.DeleteOnSubmit(contact);
        }
        spContext.SubmitChanges();
    }
}
```

Advanced topics

In this section, you'll see some more advanced topics about using LINQ to SharePoint. These topics include managing concurrency conflicts, working with the identity management services, handling disconnected entities, supporting versioning, and extending the entity model.

Handling concurrency conflicts

Whenever you have a data management infrastructure that works when disconnected from the source repository, you will inevitably face concurrency conflicts. In fact, every single time you insert, update, or delete/recycle any data, you are working with an in-memory copy of the content; therefore, you have no guarantee that your changes will be effectively confirmed by the back-end store when you invoke *SubmitChanges*. For example, when you retrieve an item from a list to change its properties, someone else might change that same item concurrently. Moreover, your code can be executed multiple times concurrently when you are in a high-traffic solution. Thus, when you try to apply your changes to the back-end repository, it will throw a concurrency conflict exception.

Fortunately, LINQ to SharePoint has established and complete support for concurrency conflicts. In fact, the *SubmitChanges* method has three overloads:

```
public void SubmitChanges();
public void SubmitChanges(ConflictMode failureMode);
public void SubmitChanges(ConflictMode failureMode, bool systemUpdate);
```

At this point, the first overload should be familiar (you have seen it in many of the previous code listings). Both the second and the third overloads accept an argument of type *ConflictMode*, which is an *enum* defined in the following excerpt:

```
public enum ConflictMode {
    ContinueOnConflict,
    FailOnFirstConflict
}
```

The names of the available values reveal their purposes:

- ***ContinueOnConflict*** When any concurrency conflict occurs, the *DataContext* object will skip the conflicting items, but it will continue to submit changes for all nonconflicting items. When the *SubmitChanges* method completes with conflicts, it throws a *ChangeConflictException*, so you will have the opportunity to evaluate conflicts and decide what to do.
- ***FailOnFirstConflict*** This stops processing the *SubmitChanges* method as soon as any concurrency conflict occurs. This overload also throws a *ChangeConflictException* so that you can evaluate the conflict and decide what to do. Any modifications submitted before the first conflict will be persisted to the content database.

Note The third overload also accepts a *Boolean* argument with the name *systemUpdate*, which is not directly related to handling concurrency conflicts, but simply allows you to update the content database without incrementing the version number of the changed items. By default, the *SubmitChanges* overload without arguments uses a *ConflictMode* argument with a value of *FailOnFirstConflict* and a *systemUpdate* argument with a value of *false*.

When you submit changes to the content database and a change conflict occurs, you can catch a *ChangeConflictException*, which contains a description tightly bound to SharePoint's typical web scenario. As an example, here's the *Message* property for a concurrency conflict exception:

```
Database values have been updated since the client last read them.
```

To solve conflicts, you can browse the *ChangeConflicts* property of the *DataContext* class instance. This property is a collection of objects of type *ObjectChangeConflict*, which you can enumerate to inspect all conflicting items. Every *ObjectChangeConflict* instance exposes a property named *Object*, of type *System.Object*, that references the current conflicting item. You can cast that property to the real target entity instance. In addition, you can inspect the conflicting members of the current conflicting item by enumerating the *MemberConflicts* property of every *ObjectChangeConflict* instance. Finally, each element of the *MemberConflicts* collection is of type *MemberChangeConflict* and provides you with some detailed information about the member conflict. For example, you can see the member name and type, the original value of the member when you retrieved the entity from the SharePoint content database, the current value in memory, and the actual value in the content database.

With that information, to solve concurrency issues, you need to invoke the *Resolve* method, which has several overloads for both *ObjectChangeConflict* and *MemberChangeConflict* values. In essence, the *Resolve* method lets you determine which values win—those of the current user or those in the content database (the other concurrent user).

Here are the overloads for the *Resolve* method of the *ObjectChangeConflict* class:

```
public void Resolve();
public void Resolve(RefreshMode refreshMode);
public void Resolve(RefreshMode refreshMode, bool autoResolveDeletes);
```

The *RefreshMode* argument is the most interesting part of these method overloads because it determines how to resolve conflicts. *RefreshMode* is an *enum* type, defined as follows:

```
public enum RefreshMode {
    KeepChanges,
    KeepCurrentValues,
    OverwriteCurrentValues
}
```

The *ObjectChangeConflict.Resolve* method changes its behavior depending on the *RefreshMode* value you provide:

- ***KeepChanges*** Accepts the current user's changes, if any; otherwise, it reloads values from the content database. This acts like a synchronizer with the content database, without losing the user's changes.
- ***KeepCurrentValues*** Causes the current user's values to win over the current database values.
- ***OverwriteCurrentValues*** Makes all values match the latest values in the content database (the other concurrent user's values win).

The first overload of *ObjectChangeConflict.Resolve* internally assumes a value of *KeepChanges* for its *RefreshMode* argument. The third overload accepts a *Boolean* argument named *autoResolveDeletes*, which when *false*, instructs the entity tracking engine to throw an *InvalidOperationException* if a target item has been deleted.

Table 6-3 contains a matrix of possible values, which helps to explain the behavior of the *ObjectChangeConflict.Resolve* method.

TABLE 6-3 Schema of the behavior of the *ObjectChangeConflict.Resolve* method

Refresh mode	Original values	Current values	Database values	Final values
KeepChanges	Country = Italy Company = A	Country = USA Company = A	Country = Germany Company = B	Country = USA Company = B
KeepCurrentValues	Country = Italy Company = A	Country = USA Company = A	Country = Germany Company = B	Country = USA Company = A
OverwriteCurrentValues	Country = Italy Company = A	Country = USA Company = A	Country = Germany Company = B	Country = Germany Company = B

The *MemberChangeConflict.Resolve* method works almost the same as the one provided by the *ObjectChangeConflict* class. However, it affects only one member at time, instead of the whole entity. It also has a couple of overloads:

```
public void Resolve(RefreshMode refreshMode);
public void Resolve(object value);
```

The first overload works exactly the same as the *ObjectChangeConflict* method, but affects only the current member. The second overload lets you provide a custom value to force onto the content database. Thus, in this last case, you can completely change the final value of the member, providing a new value that's different from the current, original, or database values.

Lastly, there is also a *ResolveAll* method provided by the *ChangeConflictCollection* class. It is useful when you want to solve all conflicts in one shot by applying the same conflict resolution logic to all the conflicts.

Listing 6-14 shows a complete code example of managing concurrency conflicts in LINQ to SharePoint.

LISTING 6-14 Concurrency conflict management using LINQ to SharePoint

```
using (DevbookDataContext spContext = new
   DevbookDataContext("http://devbook.sp2013.local/")) {
    var contacts = from c in spContext.DevLeapContacts
                   where c.Country == Country.Italy
                   select c;

    String conflictingItemID = contacts.FirstOrDefault().ContactID;

    foreach (var item in contacts) {
        item.CompanyName += String.Format(" - Changed on {0}", DateTime.Now);
    }

    // Before submitting changes, the code simulates concurrency
    // changing one of the items from another DataContext
    using (DevbookDataContext spContextOther =
        new DevbookDataContext("http://devbook.sp2013.local/")) {
        var conflictingItem = (from c in spContextOther.DevLeapContacts
                               where c.ContactID == conflictingItemID
                               select c).FirstOrDefault();

        conflictingItem.Country = Country.USA;
        spContextOther.SubmitChanges();
    }
    try {
        spContext.SubmitChanges(ConflictMode.ContinueOnConflict)
    }    catch (ChangeConflictException ex) {
        Console.WriteLine(ex.Message);

        // Browse for conflicting items
        foreach (var conflict in spContext.ChangeConflicts) {
            // Check if the item has been deleted by
            // someone else
            if (conflict.IsDeleted) {
                Console.WriteLine("Unfortunately the item has been deleted, " +
                    "so your changes cannot be submitted!");
            }
            else {
                // Retrieve a typed reference to the conflicting item
                DevLeapContact contact = conflict.Object as DevLeapContact;

                // If the item is a DevLeapContact
                if (contact != null) {
                    Console.WriteLine("Contact with ID {0} is in conflict!",
                      contact.ContactID);
```

```
                // Browse for conflicting members
                foreach (var member in conflict.MemberConflicts) {
                    Console.WriteLine("Member {0} is in conflict.\n\t" +
                    "Current Value: {1}\n\tOriginal Value: " +
                    "{2}\n\tDatabase Value: {3}",
                        member.Member.Name,
                        member.CurrentValue,
                        member.OriginalValue,
                        member.DatabaseValue);
                }
                Console.WriteLine("Make your choice: Override Database " +
                  "Value (Y) or Skip your Current Values (N)?");
                String choice = Console.ReadLine().ToLower();

                switch (choice) {
                    case "y":
                    case "yes":
                        conflict.Resolve(RefreshMode.KeepChanges, true);
                        break;
                    case "n":
                    case "no":
                        conflict.Resolve(RefreshMode.OverwriteCurrentValues,
                           true);
                        break;
                    default:
                        break;
                }
            }
        }
    }
    spContext.SubmitChanges();
  }
}
```

Listing 6-14 uses a couple of *DataContext* instances to simulate a concurrency conflict. It asks the end user, via a console-based UI, how to solve the generated conflict. It also demonstrates that LINQ to SharePoint provides a rich set of capabilities for resolving concurrency conflicts, making it a mature technology suitable for real-world business solutions.

Identity management and refresh

At the base of every O/RM framework, there is an engine—generally called an *identity management service*—that avoids having duplicate in-memory instances of the same entity. LINQ to SharePoint also provides such a service. Consider the sample code in Listing 6-15.

LISTING 6-15 Code excerpt that illustrates identity management service behavior

```
using (DevbookDataContext spContext = new DevbookDataContext(
    "http://devbook.sp2013.local/")) {

    var contacts = from c in spContext.DevLeapContacts
                   where c.CompanyName.Contains("DevLeap")
                   select c;

    // Change the Country property of the first contact
    contacts.FirstOrDefault().Country = Country.USA;

    // Show all the retrieved contacts
    foreach (var c in contacts) {
        Console.WriteLine("Customer with ID {0} has a Country value of {1}",
            c.ContactID, c.Country);
    }

    Console.WriteLine("------------------");

    // Retrieve the same contacts with another LINQ query
    var otherContacts = from c in spContext.DevLeapContacts
                        where c.CompanyName.Contains("DevLeap")
                        select c;

    // Show all the newly retrieved contacts
    foreach (var c in otherContacts) {
        Console.WriteLine("Customer with ID {0} has a Country value of {1}",
            c.ContactID, c.Country);
    }

    // Check if the two first contacts instances are the same contact
    Console.WriteLine("Do the contacts have the same HashCode? {0}",
        contacts.FirstOrDefault().GetHashCode() ==
            otherContacts.FirstOrDefault().GetHashCode());
}
```

The code retrieves the contacts whose *CompanyName* field contains "DevLeap" from the DevLeap Contacts list, and changes the *Country* property of the first contact to *USA*. A second LINQ query retrieves the same list of contacts to check whether the result comes from the content database or from existing in-memory instances. To determine which, the code writes the *Country* value of every retrieved contact and compares the *HashCode* values of the first two instances of the retrieved contacts.

The following code is the output generated by Listing 6-15 at the console window:

```
Customer with ID PP001 has a Country value of USA
Customer with ID AP001 has a Country value of Italy
------------------
Customer with ID PP001 has a Country value of USA
Customer with ID AP001 has a Country value of Italy
Do the contacts have the same HashCode? True
```

Not surprisingly, the entities are the same; in other words, the modified contact instance takes precedence over the instance retrieved from the content database. In fact, under the covers, LINQ to SharePoint queries the content database twice, the first time executing the former query, and the second time the latter. However, because the entities requested by the second query are already in memory, the identity management service skips the data from the content database and uses the data of the existing in-memory instances instead. You might be wondering why it still executes the database query rather than using the in-memory data directly without stressing the database. The reason is that the engine *merges* the results retrieved from the database with any existing in-memory entities. If there are more items in the database than in memory, the engine will merge the new ones from the database and the rest that are already in memory. This is good behavior because it avoids duplication of data and instances.

Given this behavior, you're probably wondering how you can refresh an entity from the content database, skipping any existing in-memory instance. To do that, you can use a different *DataContext* instance, as long as you do not have to use the same *DataContext* instance. Otherwise, you can call the *DataContext* class's *Refresh* method, which has these overloads:

```
public void Refresh(RefreshMode mode, IEnumerable entities);
public void Refresh(RefreshMode mode, params object[] entities);
public void Refresh(RefreshMode mode, object entity);
```

All of these overloads accept an argument of type *RefreshMode*, which you may remember from the "Handling concurrency conflicts" section. Depending on the value you choose for the *RefreshMode* argument, the *Refresh* method will either forcibly reload data from the content database (*OverwriteCurrentValues*) or merge your changed values with those in the content database (*KeepChanges*). Generally, the value of *KeepCurrentValues* is not very useful when provided to the *Refresh* method, because it simply forces the entities to use the values already in memory.

Disconnected entities

In software solutions with a distributed architecture, you sometimes need to serialize an entity, transfer it across the wire to a remote site or consumer, and eventually get it back to update the persistent storage. When your data is stored in SharePoint, LINQ to SharePoint becomes an interesting solution for working in a disconnected manner. In fact, when you generate the entity model with SPMetal.exe and provide it with the */serialization:unidirectional* command-line argument, the tool will mark all the generated entities with the *DataContract* attribute of the .NET runtime serialization engine. Consequently, you can serialize your entities and use them, for example, as the content of a Windows Communication Foundation (WCF) message.

More Info If you would like to learn more about WCF, consider reading *Windows Communication Foundation 4 Step by Step*, by John Sharp (Microsoft Press, 2010).

Listing 6-16 shows a code excerpt that serializes a LINQ to SharePoint entity.

LISTING 6-16 Serializing a LINQ to SharePoint *DevLeapContact* entity

```
using (DevbookDataContext spContext = new DevbookDataContext(
    "http://devbook.sp2013.local/")) {
    spContext.DeferredLoadingEnabled = false;

    var contact = (from c in spContext.DevLeapContacts
                   where c.ContactID == "PP001"
                   select c).FirstOrDefault();

    // Let's see if we found the target contact
    if (contact != null) {
        // Prepare a DataContractSerializer instance
        DataContractSerializer dcs = new
            DataContractSerializer(typeof(DevLeapContact),
            new Type[] { typeof(DevLeapCustomer), typeof(DevLeapSupplier) });

        // Serialize the object graph
        using (XmlWriter xw = XmlWriter.Create(Console.Out)) {
            dcs.WriteObject(xw, contact);
            xw.Flush();
        }
    }
}
```

Note the line that disables *DeferredLoadingEnabled*. This is done to avoid circular references during entity serialization. Listing 6-17 shows the XML produced by the *DataContractSerializer* engine.

LISTING 6-17 The XML produced to serialize a *DevLeapContact* entity with *DataContractSerializer*

```
<?xml version="1.0"?>
<DevLeapContact xmlns:i="http://www.w3.org/2001/XMLSchema-instance"
  i:type="DevLeapCustomer"
  xmlns="http://schemas.datacontract.org/2004/07/DevLeap.SP2013.Linq2SP">
    <_entityState>Unchanged</_entityState>
    <_id>1</_id>
    <_originalValues xmlns:d2p1=
      "http://schemas.microsoft.com/2003/10/Serialization/Arrays" i:nil="true" />
    <_path>/Lists/DevLeap Contacts</_path>
    <_title>Paolo Pialorsi</_title>
    <_version>19</_version>
    <_companyName>DevLeap</_companyName>
    <_contactID>PP001</_contactID>
    <_country>Italy</_country>
    <_invoicesDocument xmlns:d2p1=
      "http://schemas.datacontract.org/2004/07/Microsoft.SharePoint.Linq">
        <d2p1:Loaded>true</d2p1:Loaded>
        <d2p1:entities />
    </_invoicesDocument>
    <_customerLevel>LevelB</_customerLevel>
</DevLeapContact>
```

The XML stream contains the basic private fields of the entity, its original values, and the entity state. Thus, the XML produced is not an ideal solution for an interoperable cross-platform solution, but can be used to connect WCF consumers with WCF services (from .NET to .NET).

When the consumer makes changes to the received serialized entities and sends them back to the server, you can use the *Attach* method of the *EntityList<T>* class on the service side to reattach the entity to the *DataContext* and update the content database. Here's the signature of this method:

```
public void Attach(TEntity entity);
```

This method simply accepts the entity to attach back to the *DataContext* tracking engine.

Note Even if this serialization behavior seems to be a great opportunity for defining enterprise solutions that use SharePoint as their back-end storage, it is important to understand that when you have many thousands of items corresponding to data records, it is bad practice to use SharePoint as the persistence storage. It would absolutely be better to have an external DBMS with a specific and well-designed schema, with indexes and stored procedures. Instead, when you need to render your external content as a standard SharePoint list, you can use Business Connectivity Services. In software with a distributed architecture, you should create a persistence-ignorant data access layer that ignores how, where, and what the persistence is.

Model extensions and versioning

A final topic to cover here relates to managing model extensions and entity versioning. Let's start with a couple of examples. Imagine that you have a well-defined LINQ to SharePoint model, such as the one created at the beginning of this chapter. At some point, a power user changes the data schema you provisioned, adding a custom column—such as a new Address column—to the *DevLeapCustomer* content type. To be able to see this new property, you should refresh the model via SPMetal.exe, which will then update the entity definition. However, it is not always possible to update the entity model and refresh all deployed assemblies.

Now consider a situation in which you have a content type that uses a custom field type, developed with .NET code and Visual Studio 2012, and you want to use that content type with LINQ to SharePoint. Unfortunately, SPMetal.exe does not support custom field types. Thus, you need to autonomously manage the code for reading and writing the custom field type.

To manage these situations but still use LINQ to SharePoint, you can implement the *ICustomMapping* interface for entities that you want to extend or update. This interface was specifically designed to support you when extending LINQ to SharePoint entities. Here's its definition:

```
public interface ICustomMapping {
    void MapFrom(object listItem);
    void MapTo(object listItem);
    void Resolve(RefreshMode mode, object originalListItem, object databaseListItem);
}
```

The *MapFrom* and *MapTo* methods both receive an argument of type *Object*, which internally is an *SPListItem* instance that corresponds to the native SharePoint item behind the current entity. Using the *MapFrom* method, you can read untyped values from the low-level *SPListItem* instance and use them to configure a property—or whatever you want—in the entity. The *MapTo* method writes these properties back to the underlying *SPListItem* object. The *Resolve* method is a conflict resolution method similar to the *ObjectChangeConflict* and *MemberChangeConflict* methods you've already seen; however, in this case, it is up to the project developer to define the concurrency conflict behavior. Listing 6-18 shows a custom entity type created using SPMetal.exe and extended using the *ICustomMapping* interface.

LISTING 6-18 Implementing the *ICustomMapping* interface

```
internal partial class DevLeapCustomer : ICustomMapping {

    private String _address;
    public String Address {
        get { return (this._ address); }
        set { this._ address = value; }
    }

    [CustomMapping(Columns = new String[] { "*" })]
    public void MapFrom(object listItem) {
        SPListItem item = listItem as SPListItem;
        if (item != null) {
            this.Address = item["address"].ToString();
        }
    }

    public void MapTo(object listItem) {
        SPListItem item = listItem as SPListItem;
        if (item != null) {
            item["address "] = this.Address;
        }
    }

    public void Resolve(RefreshMode mode, object originalListItem,
       object databaseListItem) {
        // Code omitted for the sake of brevity
    }
}
```

Note the *CustomMapping* attribute applied on top of the *MapFrom* method. This is an attribute that identifies new columns mapped with the *MapFrom* method. It requires an array of *InternalName* values of supported columns. In this example, the *CustomMapping* attribute accepts any kind of new column (through the use of *) in order to be useful in case of versioning.

Summary

In this chapter, you learned how to implement LINQ to SharePoint to model SharePoint data as a set of typed entities, how to query that entity model, and how to manage data retrieved from LINQ queries. You also read about some advanced topics, such as managing concurrency conflicts, identity management, serialization, and versioning of entities.

CHAPTER 7

Client-side technologies

A powerful feature of Microsoft SharePoint 2013 is the rich set of libraries and tools it offers to support development of client-side solutions. Before SharePoint 2010, the only out-of-the-box method to communicate between SharePoint and a consumer application was to use WebDAV or SharePoint ASMX web services. Both of these communication techniques were restrictive, however, and not terribly easy to use. Moreover, as of SharePoint 2013, most of the ASMX web services are deprecated and you shouldn't use them anymore. With the advent of Web 2.0 and the emerging need for a dynamic web UI, the urge to go beyond that old-style paradigm has become a necessity. In this chapter, you will see how to take advantage of the client-side technologies offered by SharePoint 2013 (as well as client-side techniques in general) to implement Web 2.0 solutions that consume SharePoint 2013 data.

Architectural overview

First of all, let's consider an architectural overview of the available technologies. Figure 7-1 shows a schema that illustrates the new data access model architecture of SharePoint 2013, which will be familiar from Chapter 6, "LINQ to SharePoint."

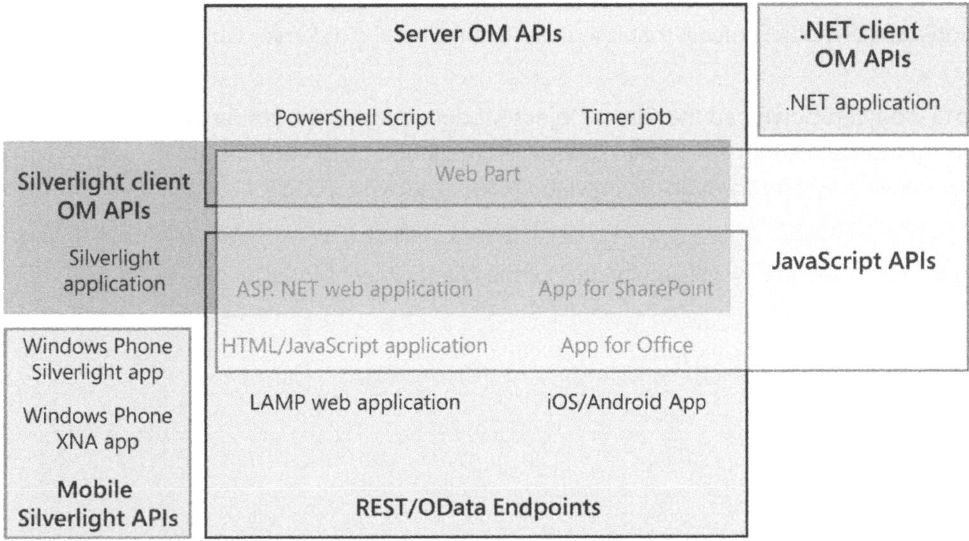

FIGURE 7-1 The SharePoint 2013 data access model architecture and the role of the Client Object Model.

From a client-side viewpoint, when you need to access SharePoint data in a strongly typed manner, you can use the REST (Representational State Transfer) API, making use of the so-called Open Data Protocol (also known as OData).

More Info To learn more about the Open Data Protocol, consult its official website at *http://www.odata.org.*

Similarly, when you simply need to access data through weakly typed entities, you can use the Client Object Model or the new *_api* endpoint introduced with SharePoint 2013, which is just a new endpoint for consuming the *_vti_bin/Client.svc* REST service. For further information about the new *_api* endpoint, please read Chapter 9, "The new SharePoint REST API." Furthermore, in case you want to develop a Windows Phone app consuming SharePoint 2013, you can use the new SDK (software development kit) project templates and libraries available for this purpose in the latest Windows Phone SDK.

More Info You can download the Windows Phone SDK from the Windows Phone Developer Center site at *http://create.msdn.com.*

Whether you prefer a strongly typed or weakly typed approach, behind the scenes you'll find the same data foundation elements that already support the Server Object Model and LINQ to SharePoint.

Client Object Model

The Client Object Model is a set of libraries and classes with which you can consume SharePoint data through a specific object model that is a subset of the SharePoint Server Object Model.

Note You can download the Client Object Model as a redistributable package that targets either x86 or x64 platforms. You'll find both versions at *http://www.microsoft.com/en-us/download/details.aspx?id=35585.*

Figure 7-2 shows the overall architecture of the Client Object Model.

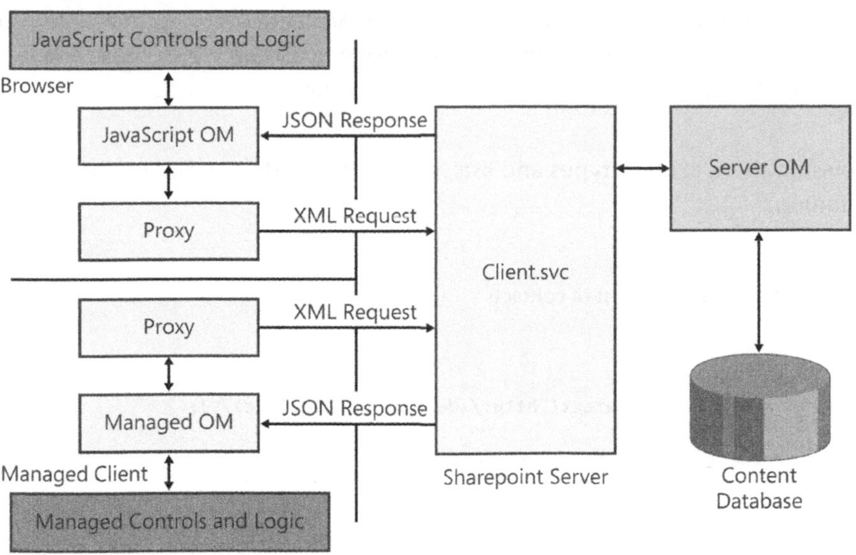

FIGURE 7-2 The architecture of the Client Object Model of SharePoint 2013.

The key advantage of Client Object Model is that it supports multiple platforms. In fact, you can use it in any solution that can run JavaScript code, via the JavaScript Client Object Model (JSOM), or in any .NET-managed application using the Client Side Object Model—even in a Silverlight solution. Behind the scenes, all these platforms consume a WCF (Windows Communication Foundation) service named *Client.svc*, which is published under the */_vti_bin/* folder of the current site. The service accepts REST requests as well as XML requests, and responds with JavaScript Object Notation (JSON) responses or XML Atom responses. In the following sections, you will see these different flavors of the Client Object Model.

.NET Client-Side Object Model

The .NET Client-Side Object Model (CSOM) is based on a set of .NET-managed assemblies, which reside in and can be referenced from the SharePoint15_Root\ISAPI folder. The most basic of these assemblies are Microsoft.SharePoint.Client.dll and Microsoft.SharePoint.Client.Runtime.dll, which any 32-bit or 64-bit .NET 3.5 (or higher) project can reference. SharePoint 2013 also offers new assemblies for consuming such SharePoint Server 2013 features as Enterprise Content Management (ECM), taxonomy, user profiles, advanced search, analytics, Business Connectivity Services (BCS), and others.

After you reference at least the two main assemblies (Microsoft.SharePoint.Client.dll and Microsoft.SharePoint.Client.Runtime.dll), you need to create an instance of the *ClientContext* class, defined in the *Microsoft.SharePoint.Client* namespace. This class represents the client context in which you are acting. It is also the proxy to the SharePoint server that you are targeting. You can think of the *ClientContext* class as the client-side version of the *SPContext* class. It has a couple of constructors based on the URL of the target site, provided as a *String* or *System.Uri* type. As soon as you have a valid reference to the *ClientContext* object, you can browse its *Site* and *Web* properties, which are references to the site collection and the site that you are targeting. Listing 7-1 shows a code excerpt that queries the contents of a list of contacts in the current website.

Note To provision these content types and lists, refer to the code samples in Chapter 3, "Data provisioning."

LISTING 7-1 Querying the contents of a list of contacts

```
// Open the current ClientContext
ClientContext ctx = new ClientContext("http://devbook.sp2013.local/");

// Prepare a reference to the current Site Collection
Site site = ctx.Site;
ctx.Load(site);

// Prepare a reference to the current Web Site
Web web = site.RootWeb;
ctx.Load(web);

// Prepare a reference to the list of "DevLeap Contacts"
List list = web.Lists.GetByTitle("DevLeap Contacts");
ctx.Load(list);

// Execute the prepared commands against the target ClientContext
ctx.ExecuteQuery();

// Show the title of the list just retrieved
Console.WriteLine(list.Title);

// Prepare a query for all items in the list
CamlQuery query = new CamlQuery();
query.ViewXml = "<View/>";
ListItemCollection allContacts = list.GetItems(query);
ctx.Load(allContacts);

// Execute the prepared command against the target ClientContext
ctx.ExecuteQuery();

// Browse the result
Console.WriteLine("\nContacts");
foreach (ListItem listItem in allContacts) {
    Console.WriteLine("Id: {0} - Fullname: {1} - Company: {2} - Country: {3}",
        listItem["DevLeapContactID"],
        listItem["Title"],
        listItem["DevLeapCompanyName"],
        listItem["DevLeapCountry"]
        );
}
```

Each time you want to access an object, you first need to add a request for that object by invoking the *Load<T>* method of the *ClientContext* instance. You can load as many objects as you like. Many of the client-side objects have a type name that is the same as that of the Server Object Model counterpart, except that on the client side, the *SP* prefix is missing. For example, *SPWeb* and *SPSite* on the server side become *Web* and *Site* on the client side. Once you are ready to effectively query SharePoint, you must invoke the *ExecuteQuery* method of the *ClientContext* instance. There is also an asynchronous version of this method, called *ExecuteQueryAsync*, for invoking the service asynchronously. Notice Listing 7-1 uses an instance of the *CamlQuery* class to query the items contained in the target list; specifically, it passes an instance of the *CamlQuery* class to the *GetItems* method of the *List* instance variable representing the list on the client.

Although the Client Object Model provides you with a subset of the classes and methods from the Server Object Model, that subset comprises a rich set of types that is too wide to be covered completely here. Instead, the chapter will focus on more practical matters and later provide some concrete examples taken from everyday life.

Note If you would like to browse the entire set of types and members available in the Client Object Model, go to the "Microsoft.SharePoint.Client namespace" MSDN page, at *http://msdn.microsoft.com/en-us/library/microsoft.sharepoint.client.aspx*.

Authenticating

One important thing to know when using any class or method is how to authenticate against a SharePoint server. By default, the CSOM uses Windows integrated authentication. Occasionally, however, you may have to work with forms-based authentication or a custom authentication mechanism. The *ClientContext* class, through its *ClientRuntimeContext* base class, provides an *AuthenticationMode* property and a *FormsAuthenticationLoginInfo* property, which are useful to configure a set of forms-based authentication credentials. The following code example shows how you should change the startup code of Listing 7-1:

```
ClientContext ctx = new ClientContext("http://devbook.sp2013.local/");
ctx.AuthenticationMode = ClientAuthenticationMode.FormsAuthentication;
FormsAuthenticationLoginInfo loginInfo = new FormsAuthenticationLoginInfo {
    LoginName = "UserLoginName",
    Password = "HereYourPassword",
};
ctx.FormsAuthenticationLoginInfo = loginInfo;
```

Note The Client Object Model behavior could change if you use it within a public website with an anonymous user session. In fact, some methods (for example, *List.GetItems*) by default cannot be called by an anonymous user. Of course, you can change default permissions to enable anonymous users to call such methods.

Data retrieval and projection

To improve performance and reduce network traffic, the data retrieval engine of the Client Object Model by default does not retrieve all of the properties of the items you load. For example, when you query the items of a list, as in Listing 7-1, and you try to access the *DisplayName* property of an item, a *PropertyOrFieldNotInitializedException* is thrown, with the following description:

```
Unhandled Exception: Microsoft.SharePoint.Client.PropertyOrFieldNotInitializedException: The
property or field 'DisplayName' has not been initialized. It has not been requested or the
request has not been executed. It may need to be explicitly requested.
```

Table 7-1 presents the list of properties that are not automatically retrieved unless you explicitly request them for the main client-side types.

Note For further details about data retrieval policies, see the "Data Retrieval Overview" MSDN page, at *http://msdn.microsoft.com/en-us/library/ee539350.aspx*.

TABLE 7-1 Properties that are not automatically retrieved through the Client Object Model

Type	Properties not available by default
Folder	ContentTypeOrder, UniqueContentTypeOrder
List	BrowserFileHandling, DataSource, EffectiveBasePermissions, HasUniqueRoleAssignments, IsSiteAssetsLibrary, OnQuickLaunch, RoleAssignments, SchemaXml, ValidationFormula, ValidationMessage
ListItem	DisplayName, EffectiveBasePermissions, HasUniqueRoleAssignments, RoleAssignments
SecurableObject	HasUniqueRoleAssignments, RoleAssignments
Site	Usage
Web	EffectiveBasePermissions, HasUniqueRoleAssignments, RoleAssignments

Listing 7-2 shows how to instruct the *ClientContext* to retrieve the *DisplayName* and the *RoleAssignments* properties for each *ListItem* instance.

LISTING 7-2 Querying the contents of a list of contacts, including some extra properties

```
// Browse the result
foreach (ListItem listItem in allContacts) {
    ctx.Load(listItem,
        item => item.DisplayName,
        item => item.RoleAssignments);

    ctx.ExecuteQuery();

    Console.WriteLine("Id: {0} - Fullname: {1} - Company: {2} - Country: {3}",
        listItem["DevLeapContactID"],
        listItem["Title"],
        listItem["DevLeapCompanyName"],
        listItem["DevLeapCountry"]
        );

    Console.WriteLine(listItem.DisplayName);
}
```

The code sample uses the *ClientContext.Load<T>* method, which accepts a parameter array of expressions of type *Expression<Func<T, Object>>*. Here is the method signature:

```
public void Load<T>(
    T clientObject,
    params Expression<Func<T, Object>>[] retrievals)
where T : ClientObject
```

The expressions define the properties to retrieve from the server. In Listing 7-2, they are defined using lambda expressions. However, the code excerpt of Listing 7-2 is a little bit stressing for the server. In fact, each item in the list of contacts queries the server for its own extra properties. It would be better to instruct the *ClientContext* to retrieve all the properties at one time. Luckily, the Client Object Model also provides an extension method called *IncludeWithDefaultProperties*. Defined in type *ClientObjectQueryableExtension*, the *IncludeWithDefaultProperties* method instructs the *ClientContext* object about the properties to retrieve by default when querying a target list of objects. Listing 7-3 shows a revised version of the code of Listing 7-2.

LISTING 7-3 Querying the contents of a list of contacts, including some extra properties, into the default list of properties

```
// Prepare a query for all items in the list
CamlQuery query = CamlQuery.CreateAllItemsQuery();
ListItemCollection allContacts = list.GetItems(query);
ctx.Load(allContacts);

// Define the extra properties to include in default properties
ctx.Load(allContacts,
    items => items.IncludeWithDefaultProperties(
        item => item.DisplayName,
        item => item.RoleAssignments));

// Execute the prepared command against the target ClientContext
ctx.ExecuteQuery();
```

If you would like to selectively define the fields to retrieve from the target list, you can use the Collaborative Application Markup Language (CAML) query definition to specify the fields to retrieve, setting the *ViewFields* property. Listing 7-4 shows the syntax.

LISTING 7-4 Querying the contents of a list of contacts and projecting fields in the output

```
// Prepare a query for all items in the list
CamlQuery query = new CamlQuery();
query.ViewXml = "<View><ViewFields><FieldRef Name='DevLeapContactID'/>"
+"<FieldRef Name='Title'/><FieldRef Name='DevLeapCountry'/></ViewFields></View>";
ListItemCollection allContacts = list.GetItems(query);
ctx.Load(allContacts);

// Execute the prepared command against the target ClientContext
ctx.ExecuteQuery();
```

Of course, if you try to access a field that is not explicitly declared in the query, you will get a *PropertyOrFieldNotInitializedException*, as with the previous examples.

Another technique to project a subset of fields for a query is to use the *Include* extension method, still defined in type *ClientObjectQueryableExtension*. Listing 7-5 presents the syntax, which produces a result equivalent to Listing 7-4, but without involving CAML.

LISTING 7-5 Querying the contents of a list of contacts and projecting fields in the output without using CAML

```
// Prepare a query for all items in the list
CamlQuery query = CamlQuery.CreateAllItemsQuery();
ListItemCollection allContacts = list.GetItems(query);

// Define the columns to include in the output
ctx.Load(allContacts,
    items => items.Include(
        item => item["DevLeapContactID"],
        item => item["Title"],
        item => item["DevLeapCountry"]
        ));

// Execute the prepared command against the target ClientContext
ctx.ExecuteQuery();
```

The signature of the *Include* method accepts an array of *Expression<Func<TSource, object>>* arguments, which define a set of inclusion rules. In Listing 7-5, these expressions are defined using some lambda expressions.

As with custom projection rules, you can also use CAML to define custom filters (for instance, data partitioning) on data to retrieve. For example, you could select only the contacts with a value of *Italy* in the *DevLeapCountry* field by using a *<Where />* CAML clause. However, one great feature of the CSOM is the support for LINQ queries. In fact, when you work with the CSOM, you can provide LINQ queries to a *LoadQuery<T>*-specific method, which will convert these queries into requests for the SharePoint server.

Important Be aware that when you define LINQ queries with the CSOM, you are using LINQ to Objects, not the custom LINQ to SharePoint query provider discussed in Chapter 6. This implies that you do not have all the infrastructural services provided by the LINQ to SharePoint query provider.

Listing 7-6 presents a code excerpt that uses LINQ to Objects and the Client Object Model to query for the Italian contacts.

LISTING 7-6 Querying the contents of a list of contacts using a LINQ query

```
// Prepare a query for all items in the list
CamlQuery query = CamlQuery.CreateAllItemsQuery();
ListItemCollection allContacts = list.GetItems(query);
var linqQuery =
    from c in allContacts
    where (String)c["DevLeapCountry"] == "Italy"
    select c;

var linqQueryResult = ctx.LoadQuery(linqQuery);

// Execute the prepared command against the target ClientContext
ctx.ExecuteQuery();
```

The key point of Listing 7-6 is the invocation of method *LoadQuery<T>*, which provides the following pair of overloads:

```
public IEnumerable<T> LoadQuery<T>(ClientObjectCollection<T> clientObjects)
    where T : ClientObject;
public IEnumerable<T> LoadQuery<T>(IQueryable<T> clientObjects)
    where T : ClientObject;
```

Similar to the *Load<T>* method, the *LoadQuery<T>* method works only with a result inheriting from *ClientObject*. As a consequence of this behavior, you cannot use the *LoadQuery<T>* method to retrieve custom anonymous types, projecting only a subset of the available fields of an item. The main difference between *Load<T>* and *LoadQuery<T>* is that the former loads data into the client objects retrieved from the SharePoint server; the latter returns an object of type *IEnumerable<T>* that represents an independent collection of items. This behavior implies that the object instances allocated by *Load<T>* will be released by the garbage collector when the *ClientContext* object goes out of scope, while object instances returned by *LoadQuery<T>* can be collected independently from the *ClientContext*.

ClientObject vs. *ClientValueObject*

The *ClientObject* type is the base abstract class defined in the .NET Client Object Model to describe any object retrieved on a remote client. The Client Object Model also provides a base abstract *ClientValueObject* class, which represents a client-side version of a server-side property value. For example, a *ListItem* type is a class inherited from *ClientObject*, while the *ContentTypeId* property of a *ListItem* is a class inherited from *ClientValueObject*. For the sake of thoroughness, a property like the *Title* property of a *List* instance is a scalar value and behaves like any classic .NET type.

The main difference between an object inherited from the *ClientObject* class and one inherited from *ClientValueObject* lies in their behavior when using them within a query or a method call. In fact, you cannot use a *ClientValueObject*-inherited object as the argument of a method or inside a query, unless you have not retrieved it from the server. However, you can reference a *ClientObject*-inherited object in another method call or query definition, even if you did not already retrieve it from the server, because it will be correctly resolved by the CSOM.

Listing 7-7 illustrates a query based on objects inherited from *ClientObject*, such as the *Web* and the *List* properties.

LISTING 7-7 Using a *ClientObject*-inherited object in a direct method call

```
// Open the current ClientContext
ClientContext ctx = new ClientContext("http://devbook.sp2013.local/");

// Prepare a reference to the target list. We can directly reference
// the property ctx.Web.Lists because both Web and Lists are of types
// inherited from ClientObject
List list = ctx.Web.Lists.GetByTitle("DevLeap Contacts");

// Retrieve the title of the list
ctx.Load(list,
    l => l.Title);

// Execute the query
ctx.ExecuteQuery();

// Show the result
Console.WriteLine(list.Title);
```

The code sample works correctly because the *ClientObject*-inherited properties will be handled by the CSOM. However, if you try to access some of the properties of the *Web* instance of the current *ClientContext* object, you will get an exception. For example, the following instruction will fail unless you explicitly do not load the *Title* property of the current website:

```
Console.WriteLine(ctx.Web.Title);
```

Listing 7-8 presents a code excerpt that illustrates the incorrect use of a *ClientValueObject*-inherited object.

LISTING 7-8 Incorrect use of a *ClientValueObject*-inherited object before loading its value

```
// Open the current ClientContext
ClientContext ctx = new ClientContext("http://devbook.sp2013.local/");

// Prepare a reference to the target list
// Here you will get a PropertyOrFieldNotInitializedException
// when accessing the Title property of the current website
List list = ctx.Web.Lists.GetByTitle(ctx.Web.Title);

// Retrieve the title of the list
ctx.Load(list,
    l => l.Title);

// Execute the query
ctx.ExecuteQuery();

// Show the result
Console.WriteLine(list.Title);
```

Here, the code fails, throwing a *PropertyOrFieldNotInitializedException*, because you need to explicitly load the *ClientValueObject*-inherited object representing the *Web* instance before using it. Listing 7-9 shows the working code example.

LISTING 7-9 Using a *ClientValueObject*-inherited object properly by loading its value before referencing it

```
// Open the current ClientContext
ClientContext ctx = new ClientContext("http://devbook.sp2013.local/");

// Retrieve the title of the website
Web web = ctx.Web;
ctx.Load(web,
    w => w.Title);

// Execute the first query
ctx.ExecuteQuery();

// Prepare a reference to the target list
List list = ctx.Web.Lists.GetByTitle(web.Title);

// Retrieve the title of the list
ctx.Load(list,
    l => l.Title);

// Execute the second query
ctx.ExecuteQuery();

// Show the result
Console.WriteLine(list.Title);
```

Listing 7-9 correctly loads the *Title* property of the current *Web* object before using it in the subsequent *GetByTitle* method call.

You can also use the method *IsPropertyAvailable*, inherited from *ClientObject*, to test the presence of a specific scalar property in a current *ClientObject* instance.

Important If the property you are looking for exists in the item schema, but it is missing on the client side, you can use the *Retrieve* method to explicitly retrieve all the scalar properties of a *ClientObject* instance, or just a set of specific scalar properties. The *Retrieve* method is documented on MSDN as "reserved for internal use only," however, so you use it at your own risk.

Silverlight Client Object Model

The Silverlight Client Object Model behaves almost the same as the .NET CSOM. You can find it in the SharePoint15_Root\TEMPLATE\LAYOUTS\ClientBin folder, and you can use it in any Silverlight 3.0 (or higher) solution by referencing the two main assemblies, Microsoft.SharePoint.Client.Silverlight.dll and Microsoft.SharePoint.Client.Silverlight.Runtime.dll. Like the CSOM, the Silverlight Client Object Model also supports development for such SharePoint Server 2013 features as ECM, user profiles, taxonomy, and so on.

Note If you would like to learn more about developing with Microsoft Silverlight, read *Microsoft Silverlight 4 Step by Step*, by Laurence Moroney (Microsoft Press, 2010).

The Silverlight Client Object Model is useful whenever you need to develop a Silverlight solution that needs to interact with data stored in a SharePoint site. For example, you can use it to build a custom data entry UI or a custom visualization of data that's ready for hosting with the Silverlight Web Part.

Imagine that you want to show the contacts contained in the sample list from the previous example by using a custom Silverlight control. First, you create a Silverlight application, and then you make a reference to the Silverlight Client Object Model assemblies. Now, assume that you want to render the contacts with a *ListBox* control, using a custom *ItemTemplate* for rendering. Listing 7-10 shows the XAML (Extensible Application Markup Language) code of the *Main* control of the sample application.

LISTING 7-10 The XAML code of the *Main* control of the sample Silverlight application

```
<UserControl x:Class="DevLeap.SilverlightClientOMDemo.MainPage"
    xmlns="http://schemas.microsoft.com/winfx/2006/xaml/presentation"
    xmlns:x="http://schemas.microsoft.com/winfx/2006/xaml"
    xmlns:d="http://schemas.microsoft.com/expression/blend/2008"
    xmlns:mc="http://schemas.openxmlformats.org/markup-compatibility/2006"
    xmlns:custom="clr-namespace:DevLeap.SP2013.SilverlightOM"
    mc:Ignorable="d"
    d:DesignHeight="300" d:DesignWidth="600">
    <UserControl.Resources>
        <custom:ListItemFieldConverter x:Key="ListItemFieldConverter" />
    </UserControl.Resources>

    <Grid x:Name="LayoutRoot" Background="LightGreen">
        <ListBox x:Name="AllContactsList">
            <ListBox.ItemTemplate>
                <DataTemplate>
                    <StackPanel Orientation="Vertical">
                        <TextBlock Text="{Binding Converter=
                          {StaticResource ListItemFieldConverter},
                          ConverterParameter='DevLeapContactID', Mode=OneWay}" />
                        <TextBlock Text="{Binding Converter=
                          {StaticResource ListItemFieldConverter},
                          ConverterParameter='Title', Mode=OneWay}" />
                        <TextBlock Text="{Binding Converter=
                          {StaticResource ListItemFieldConverter},
                          ConverterParameter='DevLeapCountry', Mode=OneWay}" />
                        <TextBlock Text="{Binding Converter=
                          {StaticResource ListItemFieldConverter},
                          ConverterParameter='DevLeapCompanyName', Mode=OneWay}"
/>
                    </StackPanel>
                </DataTemplate>
            </ListBox.ItemTemplate>
        </ListBox>
    </Grid>

</UserControl>
```

In Listing 7-10, the XAML code by itself is not particularly exciting; it just defines a *Grid* control, with a *ListBox* control inside and a *DataTemplate* control for rendering each item of the contacts list. The code behind the user control is more interesting, because it makes use of the Silverlight Client Object Model. Listing 7-11 gives you a look at the code behind the user control.

LISTING 7-11 The code behind the XAML user control of the sample Silverlight application

```
using System;
using System.Collections.Generic;
using System.Linq;
using System.Net;
using System.Windows;
using System.Windows.Controls;
using System.Windows.Documents;
using System.Windows.Input;
using System.Windows.Media;
using System.Windows.Media.Animation;
using System.Windows.Shapes;
using Microsoft.SharePoint.Client;

namespace DevLeap.SP2013.SilverlightOM {
    public partial class MainPage : UserControl {
        public MainPage() {
            InitializeComponent();
            loadDevLeapContacts();
        }

        private ListItemCollection allContacts;

        private void loadDevLeapContacts() {
            // Open the current ClientContext
            ClientContext ctx = ClientContext.Current;

            // Prepare a reference to the list of "DevLeap Contacts"
            List list = ctx.Web.Lists.GetByTitle("DevLeap Contacts");

            // Prepare a query for all items in the list
            CamlQuery query = CamlQuery.CreateAllItemsQuery();
            allContacts = list.GetItems(query);
            ctx.Load(allContacts);

            // Execute the prepared command against the target ClientContext
            ctx.ExecuteQueryAsync(onQuerySucceeded, onQueryFailed);
        }

        private void onQuerySucceeded(object sender,
            ClientRequestSucceededEventArgs args) {
            this.Dispatcher.BeginInvoke(new updateUI(refreshGrid));
        }

        private void onQueryFailed(object sender,
            ClientRequestFailedEventArgs args) {
            this.Dispatcher.BeginInvoke(new showExceptionUI(
                showException), args.Exception);
        }
```

```
        private delegate void updateUI();

        private void refreshGrid() {
            this.AllContactsList.ItemsSource = allContacts;
        }

        private delegate void showExceptionUI(Exception ex);

        private void showException(Exception ex) {
            MessageBox.Show(String.Format("Exception occurred: {0}",
                ex.Message));
        }
    }
}
```

The syntax is almost the same as that used with the CSOM. However, a small but significant difference is the way the code retrieves a reference to the *ClientContext* object. Because the Silverlight control must be hosted within a website, you could construct the Silverlight version of *ClientContext* by using the default constructor, which requires the target website as an argument of type *System.Uri*. Alternatively, you could take advantage of a shortcut to the current website context by using the *ClientContext.Current* static entry point. This is a constructive shortcut, because many times the Silverlight control will be hosted exactly in the same website that it will target. Furthermore, consider that the *ClientContext.Current* property internally uses a custom Silverlight *init* parameter with the name *MS.SP.url* and the value of the current context URL, provided to the Silverlight environment at startup. If you host your control using the Silverlight Web Part, then this *init* parameter, together with a few others, will be automatically provided to the control. However, if you directly insert the control inside a page, without using a Silverlight Web Part, then the *ClientContext.Current* property will be *null* unless you do not provide the *MS.SP.url init* parameter by yourself.

Note The *init* parameters automatically provided by the Silverlight Web Part are *MS.SP.url*, *MS.SP.formDigest*, *MS.SP.formDigestTimeoutSeconds*, *MS.SP.requestToken*, and *MS.SP.viaUrl*.

Another fundamental difference between this sample and the one based on the CSOM is the use of an asynchronous programming model. This is not a kind of virtuosity, but a real need, because in Silverlight you have to work within the confines of the asynchronous programming pattern. In fact, while working with Silverlight, if you try to execute some blocking code from the main UI thread, you will get an exception of type *InvalidOperationException* with the following message:

```
The method or property that is called may block the UI thread and is not allowed. Please use
a background thread to invoke the method or property, for example, using System.Threading.
ThreadPool.QueueUserWorkItem method to invoke the method or property.
```

The Silverlight Client Object Model also provides a synchronous pattern based on the *ExecuteQuery* method used in the CSOM. You can call this method only from threads that do not modify the UI, however.

Listing 7-11 shows that the sample directly binds the *ListItemCollection* retrieved from the server to the *ListBox* control. However, as you probably know, every *ListItem* object of SharePoint has its fields stored in a named collection, and the XAML binding syntax does not support named collections. Nevertheless, the code in Listing 7-10 binds the fields using markup. This is possible because the XAML references a custom converter registered as a resource of the user control. In XAML (for instance, Silverlight and Windows Presentation Foundation [WPF]), a converter is a type that converts one input bound to a control into another output, rendering the output of the conversion. In the XAML sample code in Listing 7-10, the converter converts the name of a field of a *ListItem* object into the corresponding field value. Listing 7-12 displays the source code of the custom converter. If you do not like to use a custom converter, you can wrap *ListItem* instances with a custom type of your own.

LISTING 7-12 A custom converter, converting from a named field to its value

```
namespace DevLeap.SP2013.SilverlightOM {
    public class ListItemFieldConverter : IValueConverter {
        public object Convert(object value, Type targetType, object parameter,
            System.Globalization.CultureInfo culture) {

            // In case the source item is NULL, just stop
            if (value == null)
                return value;

            // In case the fieldName is empty or NULL, just stop
            String fieldName = parameter as String;
            if (String.IsNullOrEmpty(fieldName))
                return null;

            // Cast the source item to ListItem
            ListItem item = value as ListItem;

            if (item != null) {
                // Return the field
                return (item[fieldName]);
            }
            else
                return (null);
        }

        public object ConvertBack(object value, Type targetType, object
        parameter,System.Globalization.CultureInfo culture) {
            // We do not support two-way conversion
            throw new NotImplementedException();
        }
    }
}
```

In a real solution, the converter could be more complete and accurate, but for the sake of simplicity, Listing 7-12 uses a concise implementation.

Aside from binding rules and asynchronous programming tasks, the Silverlight Client Object Model has the same potential, capabilities, and recommended procedures as the Client Object Model. Consider, however, that Silverlight is a discontinued technology. Thus, you should not invest too much time in developing new solutions based on it.

The JSOM

The third client object model offered by SharePoint targets the ECMAScript world. Often called the JavaScript Object Model (JSOM), it is a set of .js files built for ECMAScript-enabled (JavaScript, JScript) platforms. The main .js files that are available are

- SP.js
- SP.Core.js
- SP.Ribbon.js
- SP.Runtime.js

These files are deployed in the SharePoint15_Root\TEMPLATE\LAYOUTS directory and are automatically downloaded to the client (web browser) when a user browses to a SharePoint page. In fact, the default master pages of SharePoint define a *ScriptManager* control, which automatically includes references to these .js files. You could also reference them by yourself, however, within a custom ASPX page. Every file is also available with a debug-enabled version—these filenames end with .debug.js instead of .js. For example, the SP.js file is also available in a debug version, named SP.debug.js. The browsers supported by the scripts include Microsoft Internet Explorer 7 and higher, Firefox 3.5 and higher, and Safari 4.0 and higher.

Important For security reasons, you cannot use the JSOM in a page unless that page contains a form digest for security validation. SharePoint native pages, of course, include the *SharePoint:FormDigest* control. If you use the Client Object Model within a custom ASPX page, you will need to include the *FormDigest* control by yourself.

In everyday life, you will probably use the JSOM in a custom SharePoint page, in a custom Web Part, or in a SharePoint app that consumes a remote SharePoint web site. For a SharePoint page or a Web Part, you will need to create a new empty SharePoint project and add an item (for example, an Application Page item) to it. In order to reference the scripts, you can use the *SharePoint:ScriptLink* control, which accepts a set of arguments, including the following:

- ***LoadAfterUI*** Loads the script after the code of the UI
- ***Localizable*** Indicates if the current page can be localized
- ***Name*** Defines the relative path of the .js file to include in the page

Then you need to define a script block that uses the object model. Although the CSOM and the Silverlight Client Object Model share almost the same syntax, the JSOM does not. The data types used do not completely correspond on both platforms, and the members' names differ. For example, to access the *Title* property of an item from the JSOM, you need to invoke the *get_title()* method. In addition, some arguments are case sensitive, and there are other differences. Listing 7-13 shows an example of an application page that uses the JSOM to retrieve a *List* instance and show its *Title* property.

LISTING 7-13 A SharePoint application page using the JSOM

```
<%@ Assembly Name="$SharePoint.Project.AssemblyFullName$" %>
<%@ Import Namespace="Microsoft.SharePoint.ApplicationPages" %>
<%@ Register Tagprefix="SharePoint" Namespace="Microsoft.SharePoint.WebControls"
Assembly="Microsoft.SharePoint, Version=15.0.0.0, Culture=neutral, PublicKeyToke
n=71e9bce111e9429c" %>
<%@ Register Tagprefix="Utilities" Namespace="Microsoft.SharePoint.Utilities"
Assembly="Microsoft.SharePoint, Version=15.0.0.0, Culture=neutral, PublicKeyToke
n=71e9bce111e9429c" %>
<%@ Register Tagprefix="asp" Namespace="System.Web.UI" Assembly="System.Web.
Extensions, Version=4.0.0.0, Culture=neutral, PublicKeyToken=31bf3856ad364e35" %>
<%@ Import Namespace="Microsoft.SharePoint" %>
<%@ Assembly Name="Microsoft.Web.CommandUI, Version=15.0.0.0, Culture=neutral,
PublicKeyToken=71e9bce111e9429c" %>
<%@ Page Language="C#" AutoEventWireup="true" CodeBehind="ShowECMAScriptIn
Action.aspx.cs" Inherits="DevLeap.SP2013.JSOM.Layouts.DevLeap.SP2013.JSOM.
ShowECMAScriptInAction" DynamicMasterPageFile="~masterurl/default.master" %>

<asp:Content ID="PageHead" ContentPlaceHolderID="PlaceHolderAdditionalPageHead"
  runat="server">
<SharePoint:ScriptLink ID="SPScriptLink" runat="server" LoadAfterUI="true"
Localizable="false" Name="SP.js" />
<script language="javascript" type="text/javascript">

    var clientContext;
    var web;
    var oContactsList;

    function onQuerySucceeded(sender, args) {
        alert('Title of the List: ' + this.oContactsList.get_title());
    }

    function onQueryFailed(sender, args) {
        alert('Request failed ' + args.get_message() + '\n' +
        args.get_stackTrace());
    }
```

```
    function retrieveContacts() {
        this.clientContext = new SP.ClientContext.get_current();
        this.web = this.clientContext.get_web();
        this.oContactsList = this.web.get_lists().getByTitle("DevLeap Contacts");
        this.clientContext.load(this.oContactsList);
        this.clientContext.executeQueryAsync(
            Function.createDelegate(this, this.onQuerySucceeded),
            Function.createDelegate(this, this.onQueryFailed));
    }
</script>
</asp:Content>

<asp:Content ID="Main" ContentPlaceHolderID="PlaceHolderMain" runat="server">
<input type="button" onclick="retrieveContacts()"
  value="Click me to get the list!" />
</asp:Content>

<asp:Content ID="PageTitle" ContentPlaceHolderID="PlaceHolderPageTitle"
  runat="server">
ECMAScript Object Model Demo Page
</asp:Content>

<asp:Content ID="PageTitleInTitleArea"
  ContentPlaceHolderID="PlaceHolderPageTitleInTitleArea" runat="server" >
  ECMAScript Object Model Demo Page
</asp:Content>
```

The core of Listing 7-13 is in the method *retrieveContacts*, where the syntax is not so different from the other versions of the Client Object Model. You can get a reference to an *SP.ClientContext* instance either by using the *get_current()* method from Listing 7-13 or by using a constructor that accepts the server-relative URL of the target site. The latter syntax is useful when you need to work with data from a target site that differs from the site at your location (for example, when your code is in a remote SharePoint app). The only fundamental difference is syntactical and involves using the *get_* and *set_* prefixes for every property accessor, as well as using the asynchronous pattern when executing the query against the SharePoint server. For a more interesting and powerful example of this, consider Listing 7-14, which combines jQuery with the JSOM.

LISTING 7-14 A SharePoint application page using jQuery together with the JSOM

```
<%@ Assembly Name="$SharePoint.Project.AssemblyFullName$" %>
<%@ Import Namespace="Microsoft.SharePoint.ApplicationPages" %>
<%@ Register Tagprefix="SharePoint" Namespace="Microsoft.SharePoint.WebControls"
Assembly="Microsoft.SharePoint, Version=15.0.0.0, Culture=neutral, PublicKeyToke
n=71e9bce111e9429c" %>
<%@ Register Tagprefix="Utilities" Namespace="Microsoft.SharePoint.Utilities"
Assembly="Microsoft.SharePoint, Version=15.0.0.0, Culture=neutral, PublicKeyToke
n=71e9bce111e9429c" %>
```

```
<%@ Register Tagprefix="asp" Namespace="System.Web.UI" Assembly="System.Web.
Extensions, Version=4.0.0.0, Culture=neutral, PublicKeyToken=31bf3856ad364e35" %>
<%@ Import Namespace="Microsoft.SharePoint" %>
<%@ Assembly Name="Microsoft.Web.CommandUI, Version=15.0.0.0, Culture=neutral,
PublicKeyToken=71e9bce111e9429c" %>
<%@ Page Language="C#" AutoEventWireup="true" CodeBehind="UseJQueryWithECMA
Script.aspx.cs" Inherits="DevLeap.SP2013.JSOM.Layouts.DevLeap.SP2013.JSOM.
UseJQueryWithECMAScript" DynamicMasterPageFile="~masterurl/default.master" %>

<asp:Content ID="PageHead" ContentPlaceHolderID="PlaceHolderAdditionalPageHead"
runat="server">
    <SharePoint:ScriptLink ID="SPScriptLink" runat="server" LoadAfterUI="true"
Localizable="false" Name="SP.js" />
    <script type="text/javascript"
src="http://ajax.aspnetcdn.com/ajax/4.0/1/MicrosoftAjax.js"></script>
    <script type="text/javascript"
src="http://ajax.aspnetcdn.com/ajax/jQuery/jquery-1.8.3.min.js"></script>
    <script type="text/javascript"
src="http://code.jquery.com/ui/1.9.2/jquery-ui.min.js"></script>
    <link href="http://code.jquery.com/ui/1.9.2/themes/redmond/jquery-ui.css"
rel="Stylesheet" type="text/css" />

<style type="text/css">
        #listOfContacts .ui-selecting {
            background: #FECA40;
        }
        #listOfContacts .ui-selected {
            background: #F39814;
            color: white;
        }
        #listOfContacts {
            list-style-type: none;
            margin: 0;
            padding: 0;
            width: 60%;
        }
        #listOfContacts li {
            margin: 3px;
            padding: 0.4em;
            font-size: 1em;
            height: 15px;
            width: 600px;
        }
    </style>
    <script language="javascript" type="text/javascript">

        var clientContext;
        var web;
        var oContactsList;
        var listItems;

        _spBodyOnLoadFunctionNames.push("InitData");
```

```
    function onQuerySucceeded(sender, args) {
        dataBindList();
    }

    function onQueryFailed(sender, args) {
        alert('Request failed ' + args.get_message() + '\n' +
           args.get_stackTrace());
    }

    function InitData() {
        this.clientContext = new SP.ClientContext.get_current();
        this.web = this.clientContext.get_web();
        this.oContactsList = this.web.get_lists()
        .getByTitle("DevLeap Contacts");

        var camlQuery = new SP.CamlQuery();
        var q = '<View><RowLimit>100</RowLimit></View>';
        camlQuery.set_viewXml(q);
        this.listItems = this.oContactsList.getItems(camlQuery);
        this.clientContext.load(this.listItems);

        this.clientContext.executeQueryAsync(
            Function.createDelegate(this, this.onQuerySucceeded),
            Function.createDelegate(this, this.onQueryFailed));
    }

    function dataBindList() {
        var listItemsEnumerator = this.listItems.getEnumerator();

        // iterate though all of the items
        while (listItemsEnumerator.moveNext()) {
            var item = listItemsEnumerator.get_current();
            var id = item.get_id();
            var title = item.get_item("Title");
            var contactId = item.get_item("DevLeapContactID");
            var companyName = item.get_item("DevLeapCompanyName");
            var country = item.get_item("DevLeapCountry");

            $("#listOfContacts").append('<li class="ui-widget-content"
              id="item_' + id + '">Title: ' + title + ' - Contact ID: ' +
              contactId + ' - Company Name: ' +
              companyName + ' - Country: ' + country + '</li>');
        }

        $("#listOfContacts").selectable();
    }
  </script>
</asp:Content>
<asp:Content ID="Main" ContentPlaceHolderID="PlaceHolderMain" runat="server">
    <div id="listOfContactsContainer">
        <ol id="listOfContacts"></ol>
    </div>
```

```
</asp:Content>
<asp:Content ID="PageTitle" ContentPlaceHolderID="PlaceHolderPageTitle"
  runat="server">
    jQuery and ECMAScript Object Model Demo Page
</asp:Content>


<asp:Content ID="PageTitleInTitleArea"
  ContentPlaceHolderID="PlaceHolderPageTitleInTitleArea" runat="server">
    jQuery and ECMAScript Object Model Demo Page
</asp:Content>
```

Listing 7-14 uses jQuery version 1.8.3, which is the most current version at the time of this writing. It also uses a custom jQuery UI theme (named Redmond). For the sake of simplicity, the sample project loads the .js file of the jQuery world, the CSS (Cascading Style Sheets) code, and images of the UI theme from publicly available content delivery networks (CDNs). Additionally, the sample page of Listing 7-14 loads the well-known list of contacts and renders them using a custom selectable order list. The core methods are *InitData*, to configure and start downloading data, and *dataBindList*, which renders the items retrieved. The first thing you should notice is the invocation of a method to execute the *InitData* function as soon as the page loads; the method uses this syntax:

```
_spBodyOnLoadFunctionNames.push("InitData");
```

This method is provided by the JavaScript infrastructure of SharePoint and can be implemented in any page. The *InitData* function prepares and loads the queries, executing them asynchronously to keep the UI fluent, even when downloading data. The syntax used here is not substantially different from before. As soon as data is available, the *dataBindList* method does the real job: using jQuery to enumerate the list items and bind them to dynamic HTML content. Figure 7-3 depicts the output of the application page implemented with jQuery and the JSOM.

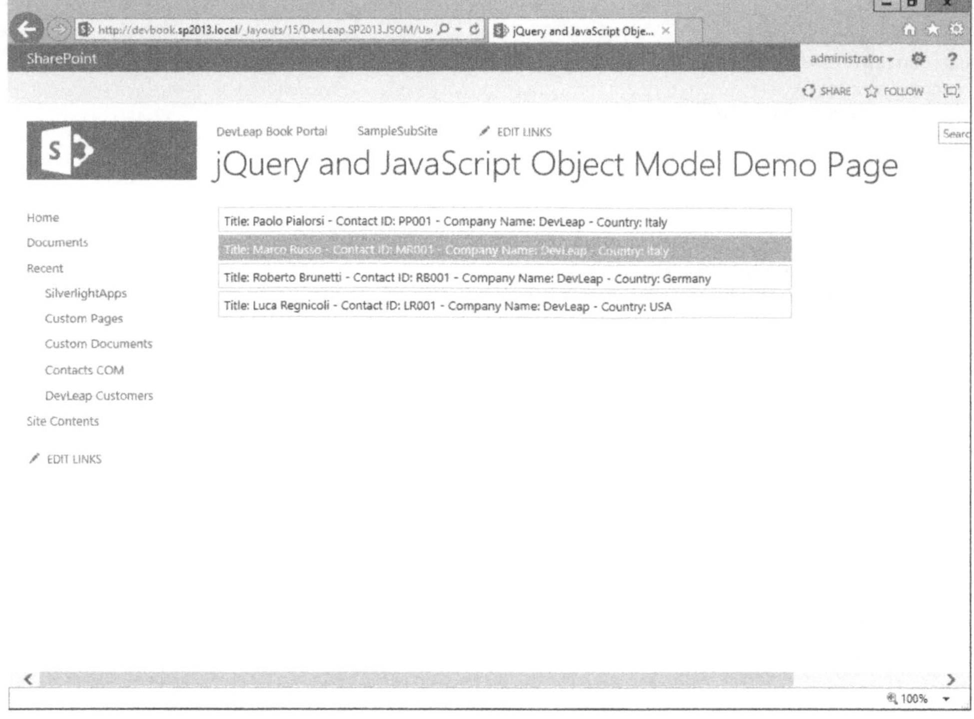

FIGURE 7-3 A sample SharePoint page that uses jQuery and the JSOM.

More generally, you can consider using the JSOM whenever you need to dynamically load or even change SharePoint data from a JavaScript-enabled environment; you can use it in conjunction with jQuery or while developing custom ribbons. You will learn about this in Chapter 12, "Customizing the UI." Another scenario in which you will surely use the JSOM is when developing custom SharePoint apps, as you will discover in Part III, "Developing SharePoint apps."

Client Object Model examples

This section provides examples of common operations that use the CSOM within a .NET-managed client or a Silverlight control. The operations fall into two basic categories:

- Working with lists and items
- Managing document libraries and files

More Info For further examples about these topics, you can also have a look at the "Apps for Office and SharePoint Samples" page on MSDN, at *http://code.msdn.microsoft.com/officeapps*.

Creating a new list

Creating new contents using the CSOM involves using some types specifically provided for the purpose. In fact, from the client viewpoint, the creation of a new *List*—or new *ListItem*, or whatever else—implies the need to request that the server execute the necessary action. Thus, for creating a new list, there is a class named *ListCreationInformation*, which describes the request to create a new list instance. The code excerpt in Listing 7-15 uses this type to create a new list of contacts.

LISTING 7-15 Creating a new *List* instance using the CSOM

```
ClientContext ctx = new ClientContext("http://devbook.sp2013.local/");

ListCreationInformation lci = new ListCreationInformation();
lci.Title = "Contacts CSOM";
lci.Description = "Contacts Created by Client Side Object Model";
lci.TemplateType = (Int32)ListTemplateType.Contacts;
lci.QuickLaunchOption = QuickLaunchOptions.On;

List newList = ctx.Web.Lists.Add(lci);
ctx.ExecuteQuery();
```

Listing 7-15 demonstrates how the *ListCreationInformation* instance defines the main properties of the list to be created, such as *Title, Description*, and *QuickLaunchOption*. The object also defines the *TemplateType* property, which defines the base model to use for creating the list instance. If you want to create a new list instance based on a custom list definition, you can use the property *ListCreationInformation.TemplateFeatureId* to reference the GUID (globally unique identifier) of the feature provisioning the list definition.

More Info For further details about data provisioning, refer to Chapter 3.

If you try to create a list that already exists with the *Title* provided by your code, you will get an exception of type *Microsoft.SharePoint.Client.ServerException*, with the following error message:

```
Unhandled Exception: Microsoft.SharePoint.Client.ServerException: A list, survey, discussion
board, or document library with the specified title already exists in this Web site. Please
choose another title.
```

One last thing to consider is that just after *ExecuteQuery* method invocation, the *List* instance you get back from the *Add* method of the *Lists* property is a fully functional instance that you can use to add items, configure properties, and so on.

Creating and updating a list item

When you create a list instance, you need to add new items to the list. Listing 7-16 demonstrates how to add a contact to the newly created list of contacts.

LISTING 7-16 Creating a new list item using the CSOM

```
ClientContext ctx = new ClientContext("http://devbook.sp2013.local/");

List contactsList = ctx.Web.Lists.GetByTitle("Contacts CSOM");

ListItem item = contactsList.AddItem(new ListItemCreationInformation());
item["Title"] = "Paolo Pialorsi";
item["Email"] = "paolo@devleap.com";
item["Company"] = "DevLeap";
item.Update();

ctx.ExecuteQuery();
```

Listing 7-16 adds the *ListItem* object to the *List* instance using a *ListItemCreationInformation* type, which simply defines a creation task for a new *ListItem*. The result of the *AddItem* method is a *ListItem* instance that can be used to configure fields of the item, and then finally allows the *Update* method to be invoked to confirm the values of the fields. As usual with the CSOM, however, you need to inform the server about what you want to do. Thus, you need to call the *ExecuteQuery* method on the *ClientContext* instance.

Updating a *ListItem* instance is similar to creating a new item. The only difference is that you need to retrieve the item from the store. You can do this by enumerating the items returned from a *CamlQuery* object, as shown in Listing 7-14, or you can retrieve a specific item by ID using the *GetItemById* method of the *List* type. Listing 7-17 presents an example of updating the item created in Listing 7-16.

LISTING 7-17 Updating a list item by using the CSOM

```
ClientContext ctx = new ClientContext("http://devbook.sp2013.local/");

List contactsList = ctx.Web.Lists.GetByTitle("Contacts CSOM");
ListItem itemToUpdate = contactsList.GetItemById(1);

itemToUpdate["Company"] = "DevLeap - Changed!";
itemToUpdate.Update();

ctx.ExecuteQuery();
```

Exception handling with lists

While working with lists and items, you occasionally may look for one that does not exist. Due to the architecture of the Client Object Model, you must query the server to determine if the desired item exists. Suppose you use a *try...catch* code block to trap the exception related to the missing item. In this case, the exception would be a *ServerException*, with the following error message:

```
Unhandled Exception: Microsoft.SharePoint.Client.ServerException: Item does not exist. It
may have been deleted by another user.
```

You could then follow a backup path to avoid issues on the client side, create the missing item from scratch, or try to retrieve another item. If you look for a list that does not exist, you'll receive the following exception:

```
Unhandled Exception: Microsoft.SharePoint.Client.ServerException: List 'Contacts CSOM' does
not exist at site with URL 'http://devbook.sp2013.local'.
```

This time, you will probably need to query the server for new data or create the missing list. Listing 7-18 illustrates one possible scenario.

LISTING 7-18 Code excerpt showing how to retrieve or create a list in the event that it is missing, and then add an item to it

```
ClientContext ctx = new ClientContext("http://devbook.sp2013.local/");
List contactsList = null;

try {
    contactsList = ctx.Web.Lists.GetByTitle("Contacts CSOM");
    ctx.Load(contactsList);
    ctx.ExecuteQuery();
}
catch (ServerException) {
    ListCreationInformation lci = new ListCreationInformation();
    lci.Title = "Contacts CSOM";
    lci.Description = "Contacts Created by Client Side Object Model";
    lci.TemplateType = (Int32)ListTemplateType.Contacts;
    lci.QuickLaunchOption = QuickLaunchOptions.On;

    contactsList = ctx.Web.Lists.Add(lci);
    ctx.ExecuteQuery();
}
finally {
    ListItem item = contactsList.AddItem(new ListItemCreationInformation());
    item["Title"] = "Paolo Pialorsi";
    item["Email"] = "paolo@devleap.com";
    item["Company"] = "DevLeap";
    item.Update();
    ctx.ExecuteQuery();
}
```

The boldface code in Listing 7-18 shows the three calls to the *ExecuteQuery* method. In the worst situation, this code could execute all the *try...catch...finally* blocks, invoking the server via *ExecuteQuery* three times. This could lead to performance degradation and also put a great deal of stress on the server side. Luckily, the CSOM provides a class named *ExceptionHandlingScope* that is specifically defined to support such situations and avoid executing multiple queries against the server.

Listing 7-19 displays the prototype of using the *ExceptionHandlingScope* type.

LISTING 7-19 The prototype for using *ExceptionHandlingScope*

```
ClientContext ctx = new ClientContext("http://devbook.sp2013.local/");

ExceptionHandlingScope scope = new ExceptionHandlingScope(ctx);

using (scope.StartScope()) {
    using (scope.StartTry()) {
        // Try to do something on the server side
    }
    using (scope.StartCatch()) {
        // Do something else in case of failure on the server side
    }
    using (scope.StartFinally()) {
        // Execute this code, whatever is the result of previous code blocks
    }
}

// Now invoke the server, just one time
ctx.ExecuteQuery();
```

Behind the scenes, the *ExceptionHandlingScope* instance collects activities (internally called *ClientActions*) to execute on the server side for all the three situations (*try*, *catch*, and *finally*). The server will begin executing the code inside the *StartTry* block, and then in case of failure, it will execute the code in the *StartCatch* block. Regardless of whether exceptions occur in the *StartTry* block, the server will finally execute the code in the *StartFinally* block. However, the request sent to the server defining all the previously described code blocks is just one, as well as the response. Listing 7-20 presents a complete example.

LISTING 7-20 The complete code to retrieve or create a list in the event that it is missing, and then add an item to it

```
ClientContext ctx = new ClientContext("http://devbook.sp2013.local/");
ExceptionHandlingScope scope = new ExceptionHandlingScope(ctx);
List contactsList;

using (scope.StartScope()) {
    using (scope.StartTry()) {
        // Try to reference the target list
        contactsList = ctx.Web.Lists.GetByTitle("Contacts CSOM");
    }
    using (scope.StartCatch()) {
        // Create the list, in case it doesn't exist
        ListCreationInformation lci = new ListCreationInformation();
        lci.Title = "Contacts CSOM";
        lci.Description = "Contacts Created by Client Side Object Model";
        lci.TemplateType = (Int32)ListTemplateType.Contacts;
        lci.QuickLaunchOption = QuickLaunchOptions.On;

        contactsList = ctx.Web.Lists.Add(lci);
    }
    using (scope.StartFinally()) {
        // Add the ListItem, whether the list has just been created
        // or was already existing
        contactsList = ctx.Web.Lists.GetByTitle("Contacts CSOM");

        ListItem item = contactsList.AddItem(new ListItemCreationInformation());
        item["Title"] = "Paolo Pialorsi";
        item["Email"] = "paolo@devleap.com";
        item["Company"] = "DevLeap";
        item.Update();
    }
}

// Now invoke the server, just one time
ctx.ExecuteQuery();
```

Deleting an existing list item

Another common scenario is deleting an item from a list. Listing 7-21 illustrates how to do this.

LISTING 7-21 Deleting a *ListItem* instance

```
ClientContext ctx = new ClientContext("http://devbook.sp2013.local/");

List contactsList = ctx.Web.Lists.GetByTitle("Contacts CSOM");

// This will work only in case an item with ID = 1 exists.
// Otherwise you should change the ID or search for a specific item to delete.
ListItem itemToDelete = contactsList.GetItemById(1);

itemToDelete.DeleteObject();

ctx.ExecuteQuery();
```

This is very similar to the syntax used to update an item. The only difference is the invocation of the *DeleteObject* method.

Paging queries of list items

Already in this chapter you've seen many ways of querying items in a list. Real-life applications, however, can contain thousands of items. Thus, it is not realistic to query these items with a unique query batch as shown in these smaller-scale examples. For such situations, take advantage of the paging capabilities of the SharePoint querying engine. Listing 7-22 shows a code excerpt that demonstrates how to efficiently paginate query results.

LISTING 7-22 How to efficiently paginate query results using the CSOM

```
ClientContext ctx = new ClientContext("http://devbook.sp2013.local/");

List contactsList = ctx.Web.Lists.GetByTitle("Contacts CSOM");
ListItemCollectionPosition itemPosition = null;
Int32 currentPage = 0;

do {
    CamlQuery query = new CamlQuery();
    query.ListItemCollectionPosition = itemPosition;
    query.ViewXml = "<View><RowLimit>10</RowLimit></View>";
    ListItemCollection pageOfContacts = contactsList.GetItems(query);
    ctx.Load(pageOfContacts);
    ctx.ExecuteQuery();
```

```
    itemPosition = pageOfContacts.ListItemCollectionPosition;
    currentPage++;
    Console.WriteLine("Page #: {0}", currentPage);

    foreach (ListItem item in pageOfContacts) {
        Console.WriteLine("Contact: {0}", item["Title"]);
    }
    Console.WriteLine();
} while (itemPosition != null);
```

First, to paginate data, you need to instruct the CAML query about the page size by using a *<RowLimit/>* element. In this example, the page size is 10 items per page. Next, declare a variable of type *ListItemCollectionPosition to* define a paging context for the running *CamlQuery* object. Each time you execute the query, which invokes the *GetItems* method of the *List* instance, set the property *ListItemCollectionPosition* of the query in order to instruct SharePoint about the page that you want to retrieve. You can retrieve the value to provide for each page from the *ListItemCollectionPosition* property of the class *ListItemCollection*. When retrieving the last page, the *ListItemCollectionPosition* property will have a *null* value, and you will know that you've consumed the whole set of data.

Creating a new document library

In addition to creating a standard list, at times you will need to create a custom document library. Listing 7-23 demonstrates the code to do the job.

LISTING 7-23 Creating a custom document library

```
ClientContext ctx = new ClientContext("http://devbook.sp2013.local/");

ListCreationInformation lci = new ListCreationInformation();
lci.Title = "Custom Documents";
lci.Description = "Custom Documents Created by Client Side Object Model";
lci.TemplateType = (Int32)ListTemplateType.DocumentLibrary;
lci.QuickLaunchOption = QuickLaunchOptions.On;
List newList = ctx.Web.Lists.Add(lci);

ctx.ExecuteQuery();
```

The only difference between Listing 7-23 and Listing 7-15 is the value of *ListTemplateType*. For a document library, you could also define a *DocumentTemplateType* property to specify a custom document template.

Uploading and downloading documents

Uploading files to and downloading files from a document library is simple. To upload, use code similar to that shown in Listing 7-24.

LISTING 7-24 Uploading a file to a document library using the CSOM

```
ClientContext ctx = new ClientContext("http://devbook.sp2013.local/");

List targetList= ctx.Web.Lists.GetByTitle("Custom Documents");

FileCreationInformation fci = new FileCreationInformation();
fci.Content = System.IO.File.ReadAllBytes("SampleFile.txt");
fci.Url = "SampleFile.txt";
fci.Overwrite = true;

File fileToUpload = newList.RootFolder.Files.Add(fci);
ctx.Load(fileToUpload);

ctx.ExecuteQuery();
```

The key point of Listing 7-24 is the creation of an instance of *FileCreationInformation* type. The *FileCreationInformation* instance accepts a relative value for the *Url* property of the file to upload, and then collects the file in the right folder, based on the folder where the *FileCreationInformation* instance will be added. To upload a file, you can use the *SaveBinaryDirect* static method provided by the *File* class.

To avoid problems while uploading files, be careful to check the maximum upload file size. If necessary, you have the option to increase the maximum upload file size.

Listing 7-25 illustrates downloading a file.

LISTING 7-25 Downloading a file from a document library using the CSOM

```
ClientContext ctx = new ClientContext("http://devbook.sp2013.local/");

List targetList = ctx.Web.Lists.GetByTitle("Custom Documents");
ctx.Load(targetList, lst => lst.RootFolder);
ctx.ExecuteQuery();

String fileToDownload = (targetList.RootFolder.ServerRelativeUrl +
"/SampleFile.txt");
FileInformation fileInfo = File.OpenBinaryDirect(ctx, fileToDownload);

using (System.IO.StreamReader sr = new System.IO.StreamReader(fileInfo.Stream)) {
    String content = sr.ReadToEnd();
    Console.WriteLine(content);
}
```

Notice that the listing retrieves a *Stream* object from the *FileInformation* object to manage the file at a low level. Additionally, the *FileInformation* instance can be retrieved by invoking the *OpenBinaryDirect* static method of the *File* class.

Checking documents in and out

As with downloading and uploading a file, to check a document in and out, you need to use the corresponding methods *File.CheckIn* and *File.CheckOut*. It's a good habit to check the *CheckOutType* property of the current *File* instance to determine if the file has to be checked in or checked out. Listing 7-26 provides an example.

LISTING 7-26 Check-in and checkout of a file in a document library using the CSOM

```
ClientContext ctx = new ClientContext("http://devbook.sp2013.local/");

List targetList = ctx.Web.Lists.GetByTitle("Custom Documents");
ctx.Load(targetList, lst => lst.RootFolder);
ctx.ExecuteQuery();

String fileToRetrieve = (targetList.RootFolder.ServerRelativeUrl +
"/SampleFile.txt");
File file = ctx.Web.GetFileByServerRelativeUrl(fileToRetrieve);
ctx.Load(file);
ctx.ExecuteQuery();

if (file.CheckOutType == CheckOutType.None) {
    file.CheckOut();
}
else {
    file.CheckIn("Finished check-out!", CheckinType.MajorCheckIn);
}

ctx.ExecuteQuery();
```

Just as on the Server Object Model, the *CheckIn* method allows you specify the revision (minor, major, or overwrite) of the document that you want to check in.

Copying and moving files

To copy and move a file from a document library, you first need to retrieve a reference to the target *File* instance, as you did in the previous examples. Once you have the reference, you can invoke the *MoveTo* method or the *CopyTo* method, depending on whether you want to move the file or copy it. Listing 7-27 demonstrates how.

LISTING 7-27 Copying or moving a file between document libraries

```
ClientContext ctx = new ClientContext("http://devbook.sp2013.local/");

List targetList = ctx.Web.Lists.GetByTitle("Custom Documents");
ctx.Load(targetList, lst => lst.RootFolder);
ctx.ExecuteQuery();

String fileToRetrieve = (targetList.RootFolder.ServerRelativeUrl +
"/SampleFile.txt");
File file = ctx.Web.GetFileByServerRelativeUrl(fileToRetrieve);

file.CopyTo("Shared Documents/SampleFileCopy.txt", true);
file.MoveTo("Shared Documents/SampleFileMoved.txt", MoveOperations.Overwrite);

ctx.ExecuteQuery();
```

Both of these methods accept some parameters beyond the destination file relative URL. The *CopyTo* method accepts a *Boolean* argument that determines if the file should overwrite any existing destination item, and the *MoveTo* method uses an enumeration for almost the same purpose. Note that both methods copy or move not only the binary content of the file, but also its field values (metadata).

The REST API

The last client-side API that I'll discuss in this chapter is the REST API, a feature introduced with SharePoint 2010 that has been greatly improved in SharePoint 2013.

Note REST (Representational State Transfer) embodies the idea of accessing data across the Internet network, referencing resources using a clear and unique syntax. For example, when you open a browser and navigate to the URL *http://www.microsoft.com*, you identify Microsoft's website using its identifying URL, and a web server at Microsoft returns the content you requested. When you browse to *http://www.w3.org*, you use a different URL that identifies a different resource. A REST API is an API that represents commands and instructions using a similar paradigm.

As you will see in this section, you will have the opportunity to reference a resource published by a SharePoint website by using a unique URL, which is a representation of that item. For further details about REST, refer to the document that first introduced the concept of REST in 2000, which is available at *http://www.ics.uci.edu/~fielding/pubs/dissertation/rest_arch_style.htm.*

SharePoint 2013 publishes a WCF service endpoint that can provide data using a REST protocol. This service listens at the virtual URL */_vti_bin/ListData.svc* of every SharePoint website and can be used by any third party willing to read and eventually change data stored in SharePoint.

If you open your browser and navigate to the URL of the REST service, you will get back an XML list of all the available contents of the target SharePoint website. Figure 7-4 shows an example of what the browser returns when you query the REST service for this book's sample site (*http://devbook.sp2013.local/_vti_bin/ListData.svc*).

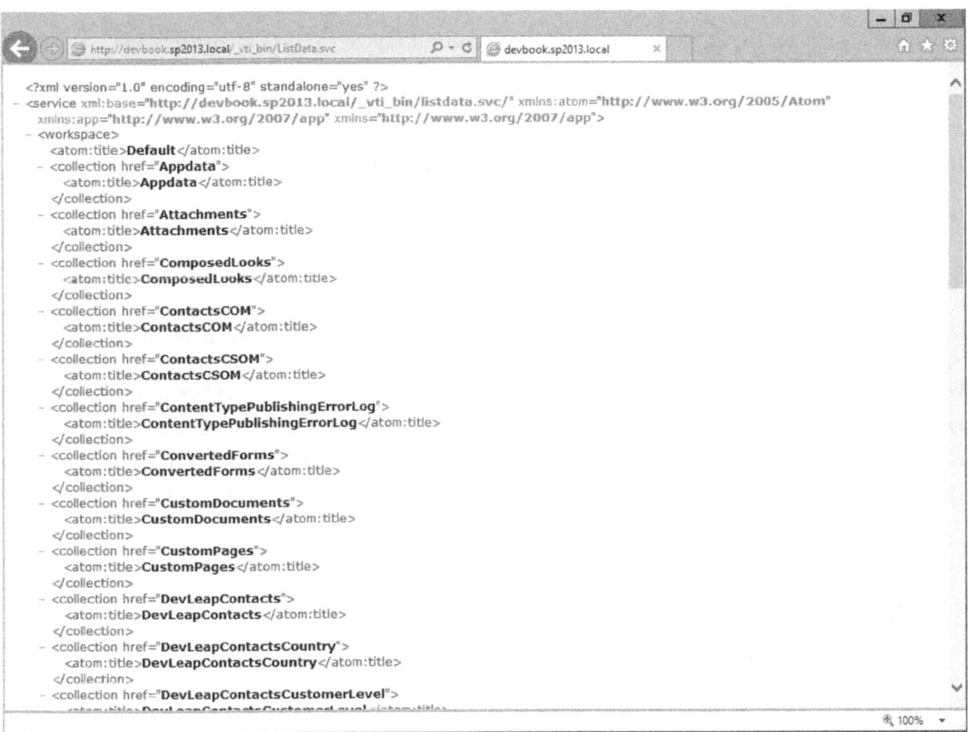

FIGURE 7-4 The result of requesting the *ListData.svc* endpoint on this book's sample site.

> **Note** To read the representation of the list's contents as XML in Internet Explorer, you first need to turn off the "Feed reading view" feature. To do so, go to Tools | Internet Options | Content | Feeds And Web Slices | Settings, and then clear the check box adjacent to Turn On Feed Reading View.

As Figure 7-4 illustrates, the result is a collection of items, each with its own relative URL (*href* attribute) corresponding to the lists contained in the current site. If you try to access the REST service URL, appending one of these relative URLs to the service URL, you will gain access to the content of the corresponding list. For example, suppose you request the following URL:

```
http://devbook.sp2013.local/_vti_bin/ListData.svc/DevLeapContacts
```

By default, the browser will show you a list of items in the form of a syndication feed, because the output XML is built using the Atom Syndication format (see *http://www.w3.org/2005/Atom*). If you request a URL such as the following, then the REST service will return the XML representation of the contact with an ID value of 1.

```
http://devbook.sp2013.local/_vti_bin/ListData.svc/DevLeapContacts(1)
```

If you need to retrieve the value of the field *CompanyName* of the item with an ID value of 1, you can request the following URL:

```
http://devbook.sp2013.local/_vti_bin/ListData.svc/DevLeapContacts(1)/CompanyName
```

Still, the result of this last query will be wrapped in an XML element. However, if you are interested in retrieving only the bare value, you can append to the URL the command */$value*, and the REST service will return only the text value of the *CompanyName* field.

```
http://devbook.sp2013.local/_vti_bin/ListData.svc/DevLeapContacts(1)/CompanyName/$value
```

In general, the URI mapping access rule is like the following:

```
http://siteurl/_vti_bin/ListData.svc/{EntityName}[({Identifier})]/[{Property}]/[{$command}]
```

This is a very useful interface for querying data by using a URL-based syntax that can be consumed by any device able to access HTTP and to read XML (which today means almost any device at all). You can use the same URL syntax to write queries to partition (filter) data, to order data, to query paged data, and so on. The following list presents the main keywords available as query string parameters:

- ***$filter={predicate}*** Filter the data.
- ***$expand={Entity}*** Include related objects.
- ***$orderby={property}*** Order results.
- ***$skip=n*** Skip the first *n* results (useful for paging).
- ***$top=n*** Retrieve the first *n* results (also useful for paging).
- ***$metadata*** Get metadata describing the published entities.

The syntax that is being used is based on an open standard called OData, as proposed by Microsoft under the Microsoft Open Specification Promise.

More Info For further details about the Microsoft Open Specification Promise, see *http://www.microsoft.com/openspecifications/en/us/programs/osp/default.aspx*. To find out more about OData, see *http://www.odata.org*.

Querying for data with .NET and LINQ

The previous section showed you how to consume the SharePoint REST API using an HTTP client, such as the *WebClient* class of *System.Net*. However, it wouldn't be very pleasant to manually compose all the URLs corresponding to every kind of query, and then manually parse the responses in XML (Atom) format. Fortunately, Microsoft Visual Studio and .NET provide established support for services compliant with the OData specification. In fact, if you add a service reference to the *ListData.svc* service within a Visual Studio 2012 .NET project, the environment will recognize the service as an OData service and will provide you with a high-level interface to access the published resources.

Every OData service can provide a set of metadata, which is available by invoking the URL *$metadata*, and the Add Service Reference tool can read this metadata to create a set of typed classes representing each published resource. Figure 7-5 shows the Add Service Reference dialog box while a reference to an OData-compliant service is being added. Remember that you must refresh the reference each time you change or update the schema of your data in SharePoint.

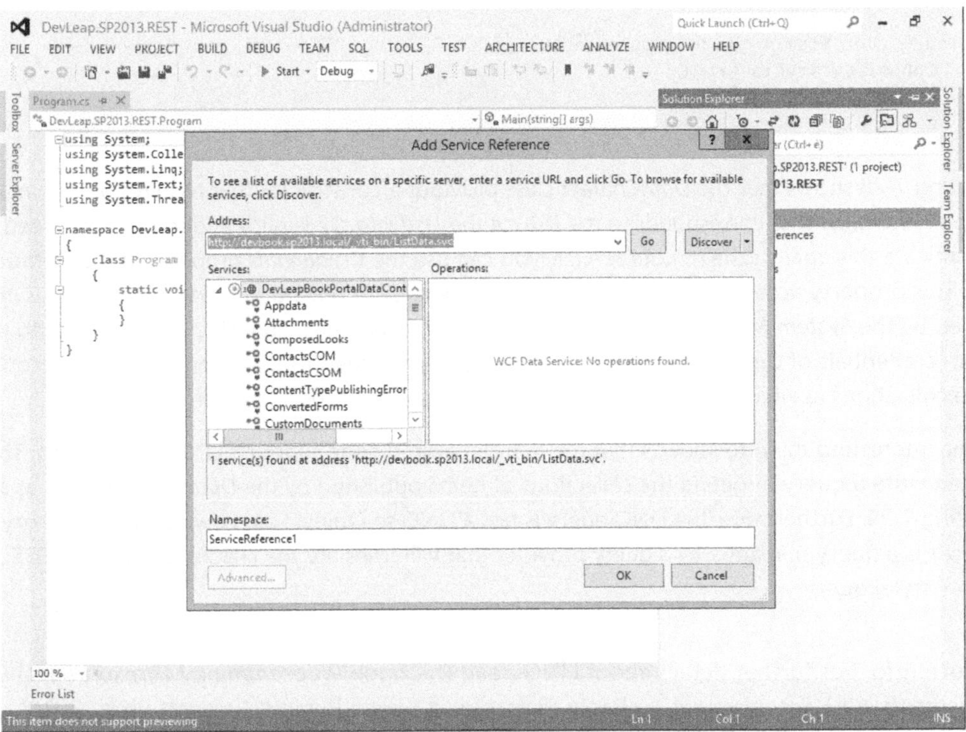

FIGURE 7-5 The Add Service Reference dialog box, shown while adding a reference to an OData-compliant service.

After you create a service reference to an OData service, you will be able to create an instance of an object called *{ServiceName}DataContext* that represents the proxy to the service and inherits from *System.Data.Services.Client.DataServiceContext*. If you're using a SharePoint REST service, the proxy class will have a name like *{SiteTitle}DataContext*, where *SiteTitle* represents the title of the target site, without spaces. In the book's example, the site title is DevLeap Book Portal, so the class will have a long but clear and self-explanatory name: *DevLeapBookPortalDataContext*.

Through instances of this class, you will be able to access and query the list items of the site as if they were collections of typed entities. In fact, every list corresponds to a collection property of the proxy class. Every content type corresponds to an entity type. For instance, for the book's sample site, the DevLeap Contacts list of SharePoint will correspond to a *DevLeapContacts* collection property of the proxy class. This collection will host typed instances of contact items. Listing 7-28 displays an example of querying the contacts using the REST proxy.

LISTING 7-28 Querying contacts using the REST proxy

```
DevLeapBookPortalDataContext dc = new DevLeapBookPortalDataContext(
        new Uri("http://devbook.sp2013.local/_vti_bin/ListData.svc"));

dc.Credentials = System.Net.CredentialCache.DefaultCredentials;

foreach (var item in dc.DevLeapContacts) {
    Console.WriteLine(item);
}
```

Listing 7-28 shows that the *DataContext* class provides a constructor that requires an argument of type *System.Uri* that corresponds to the URL of the *ListData.svc* service endpoint. If you need to authenticate this against the remote service, you can use the *Credentials* property of the *DataContext* class. This property accepts a type implementing *System.Net.ICredential*, which for example is implemented by the *System.Net.CredentialCache.DefaultCredentials* class, and which corresponds to the system credentials of the current application. Then you only need to query (enumerate) the content of the collections in which you are interested to access the corresponding items.

One interesting thing to know is that the autogenerated code supports LINQ queries, too. Thus, you can write a query targeting the collections of items published by the *DataContext* class, as shown in Listing 7-29. Furthermore, the LINQ query is not a LINQ to Objects query working in memory; rather, it is a query managed by a query provider that will translate the LINQ query into a REST (OData-style) query.

More Info For further details about LINQ, read the book *Programming Microsoft LINQ in Microsoft .NET Framework 4*, by Paolo Pialorsi and Marco Russo (Microsoft Press, 2010).

LISTING 7-29 Querying contacts by using a LINQ query

```
DevLeapBookPortalDataContext dc = new DevLeapBookPortalDataContext (
        new Uri("http://devbook.sp2013.local/_vti_bin/ListData.svc"));
dc.Credentials = System.Net.CredentialCache.DefaultCredentials;

var query = from c in dc.DevLeapContacts
            where c.ContentType == "DevLeapCustomer"
            select new {
                c.ContactID,
                c.Title,
                c.CompanyName,
                c.CustomerLevelValue
            };

foreach (var item in query) {
    Console.WriteLine(item);
}
```

Notice that the *DevLeapContacts* property of the *DataContext* class is of type *System.Data.Services.Client.DataServiceQuery<DevLeapContactsItem>*. The *DataServiceQuery<T>* class implements the *IQueryable<T>* interface of the LINQ infrastructure and represents the proxy to the OData LINQ query provider, also known as WCF Data Services Client Library.

More Info If you would like to go deeper into WCF Data Services, see the "WCF Data Services" page on MSDN, at *http://msdn.microsoft.com/en-us/library/cc668792.aspx.*

If you step into the code and add a watch on the *query* variable, you will see that the variable internally represents the query as a REST request, as with the following:

```
http://devbook.sp2013.local/_vti_bin/ListData.svc/DevLeapContacts()?$filter=ContentType
  eq 'DevLeapCustomer'&$select=ContactID,Title,CompanyName,CustomerLevelValue
```

If you try to copy this URL and paste it into the browser address bar, you will get back exactly the results of the query, represented in XML format.

If you like to query data of a SharePoint site while ignoring that it is a SharePoint site, then the REST way is your way, because you have a typed collection of items—even queryable with LINQ—that abstracts from the underlying repository. Of course there are some limitations with this approach. For instance, you cannot write just any kind of query, and there are some keywords and operators (*join, average, First, FirstOrDefault*, and so on) that by now are not supported by the WCF Data Services Client Library. If you try to invoke an unsupported query command, you will get back an exception like the following one:

```
Unhandled Exception: System.NotSupportedException: The method 'Join' is not supported.
```

Note The full list of unsupported keywords and methods can be found on MSDN, at *http://msdn.microsoft.com/library/ee622463.aspx.*

Listing 7-30 displays a code excerpt of an unsupported query syntax.

LISTING 7-30 An unsupported query syntax

```
// This query does not work, because join is not supported
var query = from c in dc.DevLeapContacts
            where c.ContentType == "DevLeapCustomer"
            join i in dc.Invoices on c.Id equals i.InvoiceCustomerLookupId
            select new { c.ContactID, c.Title, c.CompanyName, i.Name };
```

However, there are already a lot of useful commands and keywords that are supported. For example, you can do paging by using *Skip* and *Take*, and you can do ordering and more. Listing 7-31 demonstrates how to implement paging across a list of items.

LISTING 7-31 Paging in a LINQ query

```
// Get the second page, with a page size of 10
var query = (from c in dc.ContactsCOM
            select c).Skip(10).Take(10);
```

The URL request corresponding to the query in Listing 7-31 is the following:

```
http://devbook.sp2013.local/_vti_bin/ListData.svc/ContactsCOM()?$skip=10&$top=10
```

You can see the *$skip* and *$top* parameters illustrated in the previous section, which apply the paging rules defined in the code of Listing 7-31.

Managing data

The ability to query SharePoint data using the REST API is very interesting and by itself is probably sufficient to boost the enthusiasm level for this API. However, this is just half of the story. With the REST API, from the perspective of the OData specification, you can also manage (insert, update, or delete) data using a fully typed approach, even if you are working on the client side.

The *DataContext* class provides an identity management service, which allows working with retrieved entities as though they were entities of a typical object-relational mapper (O/RM), such as LINQ to SQL, LINQ to Entities, or LINQ to SharePoint.

Whenever you retrieve an entity—not a custom anonymous type based on a custom projection—you can manage its properties and inform the source SharePoint server about your changes, applying them with a batch job. Listing 7-32 shows a code excerpt that updates the property of an existing item.

LISTING 7-32 Updating a previously existing item via REST

```
DevLeapBookPortalDataContext dc = new DevLeapBookPortalDataContext(
        new Uri("http://devbook.sp2013.local/_vti_bin/ListData.svc"));
dc.Credentials = System.Net.CredentialCache.DefaultCredentials;

DevLeapContactsItem item = (from c in dc.DevLeapContacts
                            where c.ID == 1
                            select c).First();
item.CompanyName += " - Changed!";
dc.UpdateObject(item);

dc.SaveChanges();
```

As the code sample shows, immediately after updating the entity, you need to manually invoke the *UpdateObject* method of the *DataContext* class to instruct it about the change you made. This is a requirement because internally the *DataContext* proxy class does not automatically track changes to objects. You can change many entities at the same time, and when you have finished, you simply need to invoke the *SaveChanges* method of the *DataContext* object in order to send your changes back to the server.

If you need to add a new item to a target list, you can use the general-purpose *AddObject* method provided by the *DataContext* class. In the following snippet, you can see the signature of this method:

```
public void AddObject(string entitySetName, object entity);
```

You can also use a fully typed method called *AddTo{ListName}*, which is a wrapper around the *AddObject* untyped method, and is automatically generated by the tools that generate the service reference. For the sake of clarity, the following shows the definition of the method *AddToDevLeapContacts*:

```
public void AddToDevLeapContacts(DevLeapContactsItem devLeapContactsItem) {
    base.AddObject("DevLeapContacts", devLeapContactsItem);
}
```

Listing 7-33 presents a code excerpt that adds an item to the sample list of contacts.

LISTING 7-33 Adding a new item to a list

```
DevLeapBookPortalDataContext dc = new DevLeapBookPortalDataContext(
        new Uri("http://devbook.sp2013.local/_vti_bin/ListData.svc"));
dc.Credentials = System.Net.CredentialCache.DefaultCredentials;

DevLeapContactsItem item = new DevLeapContactsItem {
    Title = "Sample Customer",
    ContactID = "CC001",
    ContentType = "DevLeapCustomer",
    CompanyName = "Sample Company",
    CountryValue = "Germany",
    CustomerLevelValue = "Level A"
};
dc.AddToDevLeapContacts(item);

dc.SaveChanges();
```

The sample code creates a new instance of an object with a type compliant with the target list. Then it sets the properties of the item (for instance, the fields) and adds it to the target list using the *AddTo{ListName}* method. Lastly, it invokes the *SaveChanges* method of the *DataContext* object to confirm the changes on the server side. Notice that the target list accepts two kinds of content types, so the sample also configures the *ContentType* property of the item in order to instruct SharePoint about the right content type to use on the server side.

The last common task in managing data is deleting entities. The *DataContext* class offers a *DeleteObject* method, which accepts an entity that will be marked to be deleted at the next *SaveChanges* invocation. Thus, to delete an item, you simply need to invoke *SaveChanges*, as Listing 7-34 demonstrates.

LISTING 7-34 Deleting an item from a list

```
DevLeapBookPortalDataContext dc = new DevLeapBookPortalDataContext(
        new Uri("http://devbook.sp2013.local/_vti_bin/ListData.svc"));
dc.Credentials = System.Net.CredentialCache.DefaultCredentials;

DevLeapContactsItem item = (from c in dc.DevLeapContacts
                            where c.ContactID == "CC001"
                            select c).First();
dc.DeleteObject(item);

dc.SaveChanges();
```

The OData client library available in Visual Studio 2012 also provides full support for handling concurrency issues while managing data. However, it is beyond the scope of this chapter (and this book) to give you the proper coverage of the WCF Data Services Client Library. The key is understand the potential of this API while managing SharePoint data and external data in general whenever you have an OData provider available.

Summary

This chapter covered the client-side technologies offered by SharePoint 2013 with which you can query and manage data from a remote consumer. In particular, it discussed how to use the Client Object Model, together with its different flavors, such as the CSOM, the Silverlight Client Object Model, and the JSOM. It also covered how to use the REST service to query data—even with LINQ queries—and how to manage data. Now you are ready to develop SharePoint solutions and apps, armed with a solid understanding of the available tools and technologies.

PART III

Developing SharePoint apps

CHAPTER 8

SharePoint apps

Without doubt, the biggest news of Microsoft SharePoint 2013 is the new app model, with which you can create apps and publish them in a public marketplace or corporate app catalog. You can use the app model on Microsoft Office 365 and SharePoint Online or in on-premises solutions. For example, you can create a custom app that addresses a common need and sell it worldwide to millions of users through the Microsoft Office Store. The main goal of this new app model is to enable developers to customize and extend SharePoint sites without full-trust access to the target farm. This goal adheres perfectly to the cloud-computing offering model and philosophy. In this chapter, you will tour the app model architecture, as well as learn about app development and deployment.

Introducing apps

When developing a new SharePoint app, you can choose between three configurations:

- **Full-page** Based on one or more web pages, these apps include a dedicated UI. You should provide a back button for returning to the parent site, where the app is launched from—but your app will have a UI of its own.
- **App Parts** Also called Client Parts, these render some app content in an IFrame inside pages of the parent site. Usually, App Parts are used to provide users with a small piece of information or functions that can directly interact with the SharePoint user interface.
- **UI command extension** Used to extend the UI of the parent site, these apps may include a ribbon button or an ECB (Edit Control Block) command to lead the user to a page or function provided by an external app.

SharePoint apps can use three hosting models, as well:

- **SharePoint-hosted** This model relies on a subweb of the parent site (also called an *app web*) and enables you to use all the common SharePoint artifacts for implementing the UI and the behavior of the SharePoint app. You can take advantage of all the features of SharePoint, such as lists, Web Parts, pages, workflows, and so on.
- **Autohosted** Apps following this model are hosted on Microsoft Windows Azure, which can access a Microsoft SQL Azure database for managing data, too. The apps are automatically deployed on Windows Azure on your behalf and can communicate with SharePoint through

events and the Client Object Model. Secure communication with SharePoint is enforced using OAuth.

- **Provider-hosted** From a functional perspective, apps that follow this model are almost the same as autohosted apps. The only difference is that a provider-hosted app has to be deployed on your own hosting environment and does not necessarily use the Windows Azure environment.

Regardless of the hosting model and configuration, every SharePoint app is mainly a web application that interacts with SharePoint using the Client Object Model and the new REST API introduced with SharePoint 2013 (which is covered in Chapter 9, "The new SharePoint REST API"). One key feature of SharePoint apps is that they can be developed with any programming language or technology, as long as you host them outside SharePoint (that is, using an autohosted or provider-hosted model). In fact, you can create a SharePoint app using PHP, Java, or any other technology capable of communicating with SharePoint via the new REST API and the OAuth protocol.

Development environment

You have two choices for your environment to develop and test a custom SharePoint app. Your first option is a SharePoint 2013 site based on the Developer Site site template and hosted on a properly configured, on-premises SharePoint farm. (For more information about configuring an on-premises farm for deployment of apps, read the "App management configuration and deployment" section later in the chapter.) Otherwise, you can sign up for an Office 365 Developer Site subscription, which is freely available, as long as you have a valid license of Microsoft Visual Studio Premium or Ultimate with MSDN Subscription, and enables you to develop and test apps using SharePoint 2013 Online. (To create a subscription, go to *http://msdn.microsoft.com/en-us/library/fp179924.aspx*.)

Moreover, if you want to develop the app using Microsoft .NET and Microsoft Visual Studio 2012, you will need the Office Developer Tools for Visual Studio 2012, which can be downloaded and installed through the Web Platform Installer 4.0 tool. You also will need to install the following tools and libraries:

- SharePoint client components
- Windows Identity Foundation SDK
- Workflow Tools SDK and Workflow Client SDK
- Windows Identity Foundation SDK and Windows Identity Foundation extensions

If you are working on a server with SharePoint 2013 installed, you need to add only Visual Studio 2012 and the Office Developer Tools for Visual Studio 2012. All the other libraries and tools are already part of the installation set of any SharePoint 2013 environment.

Your first app

The best way to learn about SharePoint apps is to develop one. Throughout the chapter, you will complete a sample introductory app, evaluating possible scenarios along the way. Imagine that you want to create an app for managing contacts. In this section, you will start hosting the app on SharePoint. First, you'll create a new project. To do so, start Visual Studio 2012 and open the New Project dialog box (File | New Project). Select the Office/SharePoint | Apps group of projects and choose App For SharePoint 2013. Figure 8-1 shows the project type highlighted in the New Project window of Visual Studio 2012.

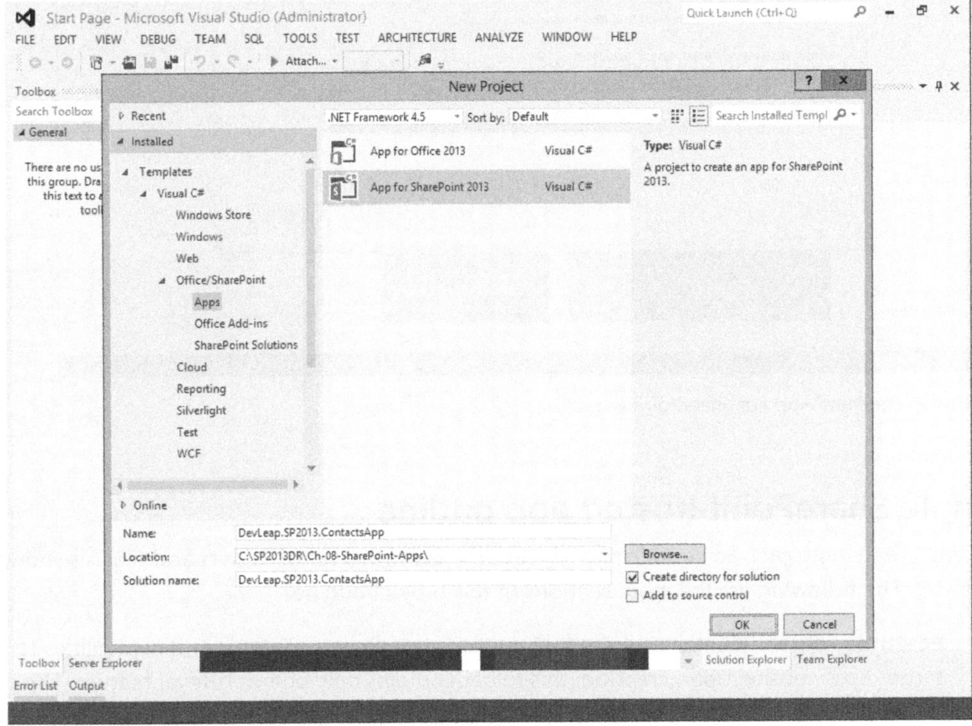

FIGURE 8-1 The New Project window of Visual Studio 2012 with the App for SharePoint 2013 project highlighted.

As soon as you choose to add a new SharePoint app, Visual Studio prompts you with a wizard for configuring the target developer site URL, as well as the hosting model you would like to use. Figure 8-2 shows the first step of the wizard. For this first exercise, you should choose a SharePoint-hosted app, in order to make it simpler to develop and host the app.

If you choose to host your SharePoint app on an Office 365 developer site, click the Validate button, which is located just beside the target site URL. Depending on your configuration, you may be prompted with an Office 365 logon screen.

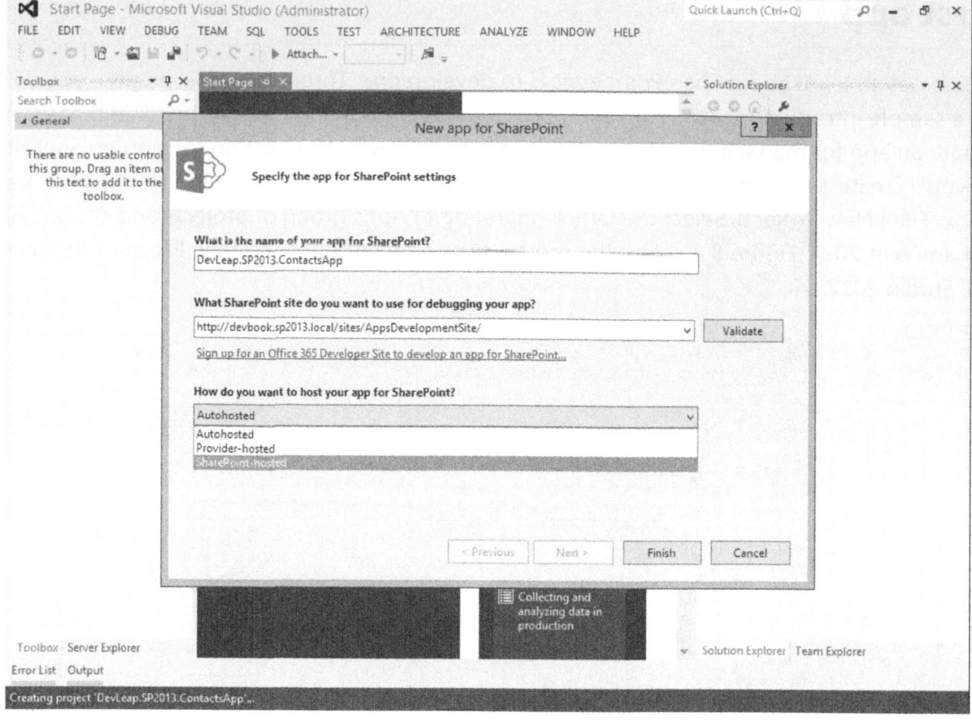

FIGURE 8-2 The New App For SharePoint wizard.

Sample SharePoint-hosted app outline

After you create a project, Solution Explorer presents you with a set of folders and files, as shown in Figure 8-3. The following are the main sections of this project outline:

- **Features folder** Contains all the features for provisioning contents and capabilities to the target app website. Upon creation, this folder contains only one web-level feature. The goal of this feature is to provision all the other contents to the target app website.
- **Package folder** Contains the package for deploying the app on the target site.
- **Content folder** Deploys custom CSS styles related to the app and is a *Module* feature.
- **Images folder** Deploys all the images related to the app and is a *Module* feature. Upon creation, the folder contains only the AppIcon.png file, which represents the icon of your app. To customize the look of your app, replace the default AppIcon.png file with a customized 96×96-pixel PNG image.
- **Pages folder** Holds a *Module* feature for deploying all the pages of the target app website. By default, the project template creates a Default.aspx page, but you can create more pages by yourself.

- **Scripts folder** Represents a *Module* feature that is composed of JavaScript files for deploying jQuery scripts, some JavaScript references, and the App.js file, which is the JavaScript Client Object Model entry point of the app.
- **AppManifest.xml file** Contains all the configuration and deployment information related to the app. It's the fundamental file of every app, and it will be discussed in detail in the "Inside AppManifest.xml" section later in the chapter.
- **packages.config file** Relates to the jQuery package automatically configured in the current project. In general, this file holds the information about the packages referenced by the Visual Studio project.

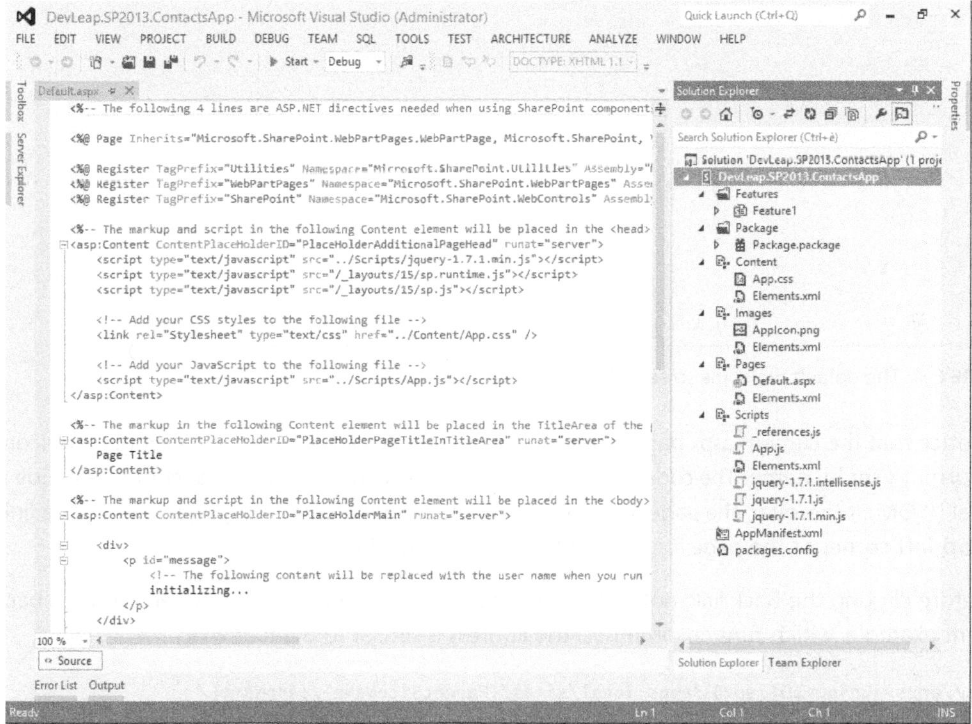

FIGURE 8-3 The outline of an app for SharePoint 2013 project.

To begin playing with the current app project, just press F5 to start debugging it on the target site. First, you will notice that Visual Studio 2012 starts compiling, packaging, deploying, and installing the solution. Then your default web browser will start, showing the Default.aspx page of the current app. Figure 8-4 shows the output.

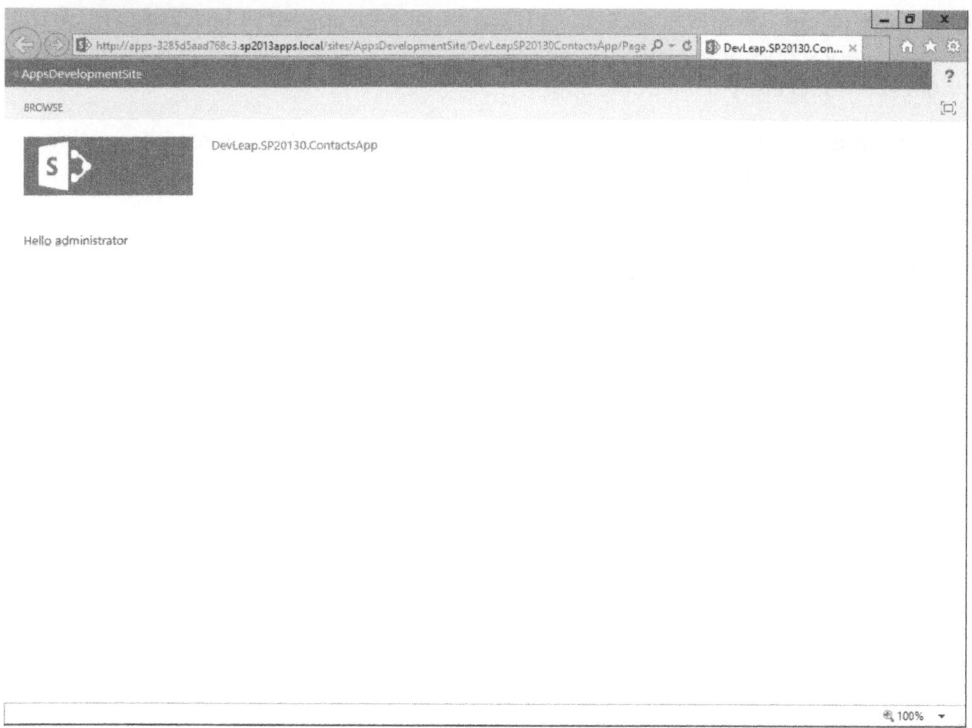

FIGURE 8-4 The default welcome screen of a SharePoint-hosted app.

Notice that the Default.aspx page, after a quick initialization message ("initializing..."), welcomes the current user by name. The code for retrieving the user name uses the JavaScript Client-Side Object Model (JSOM). Moreover, the page looks like every other SharePoint 2013 page, and it has a link at the top-left corner of the page for coming back to the host site.

Before clicking the Back link, notice the URL of the current page in the browser's address bar. In the current example, which runs on-premises, the address is similar to the following:

```
http://apps-{UniqueID}.sp2013apps.local/sites/{ParentSiteName}/{AppName}/
```

Later, in the section "App management configuration and deployment," you will learn how to configure a SharePoint web application or tenant for hosting such a URL. If you are targeting an Office 365 developer site, the URL of the app will be something like this:

```
https://{TenancyName}-{UniqueID}.sharepoint.com/sites/{ParentSiteName}/{AppName}/
```

Eventually, you will be prompted with the Office 365 logon screen to access the target host site and the app. Lastly, whether you are on-premises or in the cloud, the app URL will be enriched with a long list of query string parameters. (You'll learn more about these later in this chapter.)

The app website

When you install your app onto the target development site, the site lists it on the Site Contents page in the Lists, Libraries, and other Apps category. As shown in Figure 8-5, the example app's listing has a custom AppIcon.png file with the company's logo.

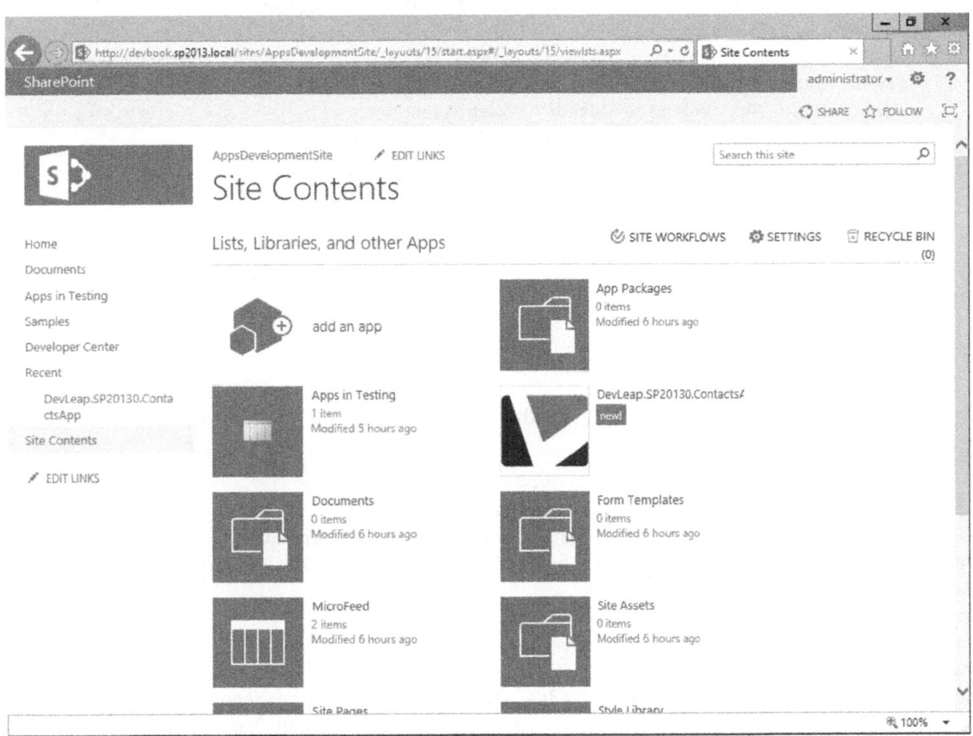

FIGURE 8-5 The Site Contents page of a developer site with a custom app installed.

Remember, the SharePoint-hosted app uses an app website, which is a subweb of the current site collection, dedicated for hosting the app. You cannot access the app website with SharePoint Designer 2013, because support for it is disabled for this kind of website. Nevertheless, you can access it through PowerShell; simply use the Client-Side Object Model (CSOM) or any third-party tool to browse the site structure. Listing 8-1 demonstrates how to access the app website through PowerShell, by iterating through the child websites of the current site collection.

LISTING 8-1 A sample PowerShell script to retrieve information about the current app website

```
Add-PSSnapin Microsoft.SharePoint.PowerShell -erroraction SilentlyContinue

$site = Get-SPSite "http://devbook.sp2013.local/sites/AppsDevelopmentSite/"
Write-Host "Here are the sub-webs of the current site collection root web"
foreach ($web in $site.AllWebs) {
    Write-Host "ID: " $web.ID " - Title: " $web.Title
    if ($web.IsAppWeb -eq $true) {
        Write-Host "App Web Site Author: "$web.Author
        Write-Host "App Web Site Is App Web?" $web.IsAppWeb
        Write-Host "App Web Site Is Root Web?" $web.IsRootWeb
        Write-Host "App Web Site Is Provisioned?" $web.Provisioned
        Write-Host "App Web Site URL?" $web.Site.Url
        Write-Host "App Web Site parent Web Application:"
        $web.Site.WebApplication
    }
}
```

When you execute a PowerShell script like the one in Listing 8-1, the host console will display output similar to the following:

```
Here are the sub-webs of the current site collection root web
ID:  75f26332-940d-4f08-838d-cda4b6e11c62  - Title:  AppsDevelopmentSite
ID:  43d8c941-d442-490c-8ed5-4408a41d5516  - Title:  DevLeap.SP20130.ContactsApp
App Web Site Author:  SHAREPOINT\system
App Web Site Is App Web? True
App Web Site Is Root Web? False
App Web Site Is Provisioned? True
App Web Site URL? http://apps-3285d5aad768c4.sp2013apps.local/sites/AppsDevelopmentSite
App Web Site parent Web Application: SPWebApplication Name=DevLeap Book Portal
```

The most interesting information you can glean from the script output is

- The app website is automatically provisioned by the Local System account.
- The app website has an explicit flag stating that it is the site hosting an app.
- The parent site collection and web application of the app website are the site collection and web application of the extended site.
- The app website is a subweb of the current site collection.

Provisioning content

Now that you understand the basics of a SharePoint-hosted app, you're ready to provision some content into the app web of your first sample app. Imagine that you want to add a list of contacts based on a custom content type. In Chapter 3, "Data provisioning," you already learned how to provision list definitions based on custom content types. Thus, this section will skip all the details, and the goal will be to create a list of contacts made of the following fields: Title, Description, Telephone, Email, and Photo.

To present the custom Contacts list to the end user, you could add a direct link to the default view of the list into the home page (Default.aspx file) of the app, but there's an even better way. You can use the app's Default.aspx page, which is a common SharePoint page. Open the Default.aspx file, and put some ASPX code inside the content region named *PlaceHolderMain*, as shown in Listing 8-2. The list-relative URL used is *Lists/AppContacts*.

LISTING 8-2 The Default.aspx page source ASPX code changed to show the custom list of contacts

```
<%-- The following 4 lines are ASP.NET directives needed when using SharePoint
components --%>
<%@ Page Inherits="Microsoft.SharePoint.WebPartPages.WebPartPage, Microsoft.
SharePoint, Version=15.0.0.0, Culture=neutral, PublicKeyToken=71e9bce111e9429c"
MasterPageFile="~masterurl/default.master" Language="C#" %>
<%@ Register TagPrefix="Utilities" Namespace="Microsoft.SharePoint.Utilities"
Assembly="Microsoft.SharePoint, Version=15.0.0.0, Culture=neutral, PublicKeyToke
n=71e9bce111e9429c" %>
<%@ Register TagPrefix="WebPartPages" Namespace="Microsoft.SharePoint.
WebPartPages" Assembly="Microsoft.SharePoint, Version=15.0.0.0, Culture=neutral,
PublicKeyToken=71e9bce111e9429c" %>
<%@ Register TagPrefix="SharePoint" Namespace="Microsoft.SharePoint.WebControls"
Assembly="Microsoft.SharePoint, Version=15.0.0.0, Culture=neutral, PublicKeyToke
n=71e9bce111e9429c" %>

<%-- The markup and script in the following Content element will be placed in the
<head> of the page --%>
<asp:Content ContentPlaceHolderID="PlaceHolderAdditionalPageHead" runat="server">
    <script type="text/javascript" src="../Scripts/jquery-1.7.1.min.js"></script>
    <script type="text/javascript" src="/_layouts/15/sp.runtime.debug.js">
</script>
    <script type="text/javascript" src="/_layouts/15/sp.debug.js"></script>

    <!-- Add your CSS styles to the following file -->
    <link rel="Stylesheet" type="text/css" href="../Content/App.css" />

    <!-- Add your JavaScript to the following file -->
    <script type="text/javascript" src="../Scripts/App.js"></script>
</asp:Content>

<%-- The markup and script in the following Content element will be placed in the
<body> of the page --%>
<asp:Content ContentPlaceHolderID="PlaceHolderMain" runat="server">

    <div>
        <p id="message">
            <!-- The following content will be replaced with the user name when
you run the app - see App.js -->
            initializing...
        </p>
    </div>
```

```
        <WebPartPages:WebPartZone ID="spWebPartZone" runat="server">
            <WebPartPages:XsltListViewWebPart runat="server"
                ListUrl="Lists/AppContacts"
                IsIncluded="True"
                JsLink="clientTemplate.js"
                NoDefaultStyle="TRUE"
                PageType="PAGE_NORMALVIEW"
                Default="False"
                ViewContentTypeId="0x">
            </WebPartPages:XsltListViewWebPart>
        </WebPartPages:WebPartZone>

    </asp:Content>
```

As you can see, the *WebPartZone* control (highlighted in bolded text) wraps a classic SharePoint *XsltListViewWebPart* control, which shows the items of the custom Contacts list. Figure 8-6 illustrates the resulting output in the browser after some sample contacts have been added. As you can see, the layout and the behavior of the page are the same of any other SharePoint page, because the app website is yet another SharePoint site.

Important Remember that an app website is provisioned and unprovisioned together with its app. Thus, you create an app that stores content inside its app web. If your end users remove or uninstall the app, however, not only will the app web be decommissioned, but your data will be lost as well. In order to intercept such events, you can handle app-related events. For example, you can use the *AppUninstalling* event (discussed in Chapter 10, "Remote event receivers") together with other remote events.

Moreover, the Default.aspx page, as well as any other custom page you add to the app, is based on server controls or client-side code only. For example, you cannot add an application page (see Chapter 12, "Customizing the UI," for further details) based on server-side code, because this would require a full-trust deployment of your page, which is not allowed for SharePoint-hosted apps. In case you need to create an app that uses server-side code, you should create an autohosted or a provider-hosted app.

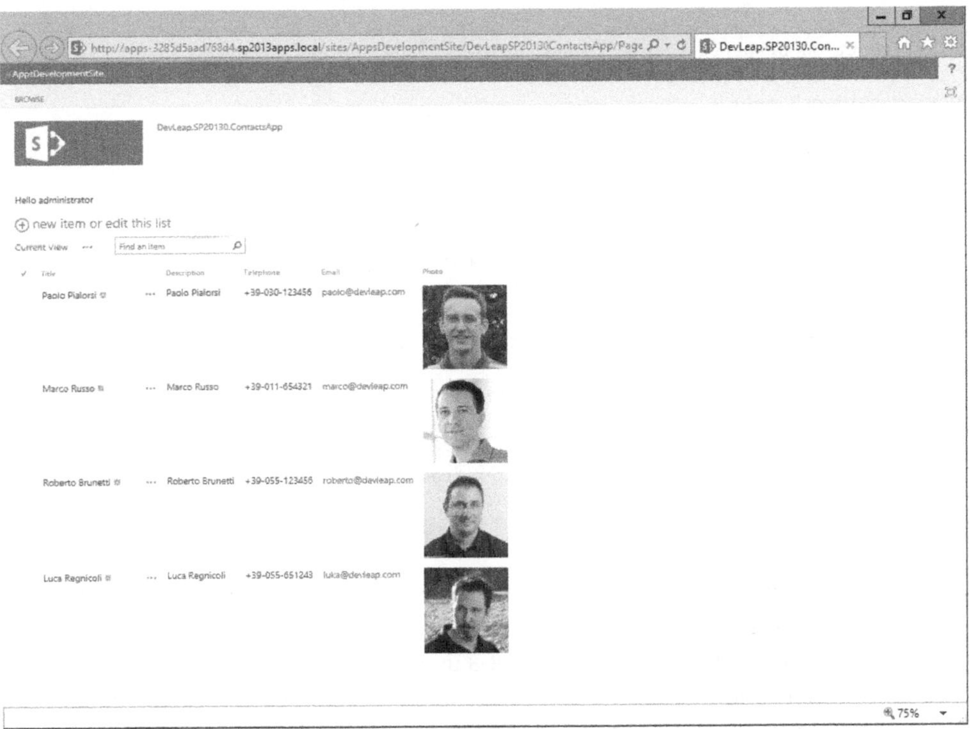

FIGURE 8-6 The output of the Default.aspx page after adding an *XsltListViewWebPart* control for showing the custom Contacts list.

Using the Client-Side Object Model

For the sake of completeness, have a look at how the JSOM interacts with your app website. Open the App.js file provided in the Scripts folder of the project. In Listing 8-3, you can see the default content of that file.

LISTING 8-3 The JavaScript code provided by default within the App.js file inside the Scripts folder of a SharePoint-hosted app project

```
var context;
var web;
var user;

// This code runs when the DOM is ready and creates a context object, which
// is needed to use the SharePoint object model
$(document).ready(function () {
    context = SP.ClientContext.get_current();
    web = context.get_web();
    getUserName();
});
```

```
// This function prepares, loads, and then executes a SharePoint query
// to get the current user's information
function getUserName() {
    user = web.get_currentUser();
    context.load(user);
    context.executeQueryAsync(onGetUserNameSuccess, onGetUserNameFail);
}

// This function is executed if the above OM call is successful
// It replaces the contents of the 'helloString' element with the user name
function onGetUserNameSuccess() {
    $('#message').text('Hello ' + user.get_title());
}

// This function is executed if the above call fails
function onGetUserNameFail(sender, args) {
    alert('Failed to get user name. Error:' + args.get_message());
}
```

As discussed in Chapter 7, "Client-side technologies," you can use the JavaScript Client Object Model (JSOM) to interact with the current site or site collection, as well with remote sites (as long as you have a set of authorized credentials). Listing 8-3 uses a jQuery directive to register for the DOM document *ready* event. There it retrieves a reference to the current website in order to get the current user name. Because the JSOM natively provides asynchronous behavior, the code queries for the current user by invoking the *executeQueryAsync* method of the current context and, when successful, shows the *title* property of the current user in the paragraph (that is, the HTML element *<p>*) with an ID value of *message*, which is defined in the Default.aspx page. You can see that paragraph element in Listing 8-2, just before the code highlighted in bold.

If you want to enrich your custom app with client-side code and the JSOM, you can simply add your custom code to this App.js file. Then you should invoke your custom functions from within the Default.aspx page or from any other custom page you will provision together with your SharePoint app. Everything you have already learned about the JSOM is valid in this context, too.

Inside AppManifest.xml

The main content of every SharePoint app project, regardless of its hosting model, is in the AppManifest.xml file. This file contains information about the app in general, the permissions required by the app, the prerequisites for running the app, the supported languages/locales, and any remote endpoint. By double-clicking the AppManifest.xml file, you can open the specific designer provided by Visual Studio 2012 and edit all these configurations. For example, Figure 8-7 shows the AppManifest.xml designer, which is made of a set of tabs for managing the various configuration properties, grouped by category. In the next section, you will learn all the details about these properties.

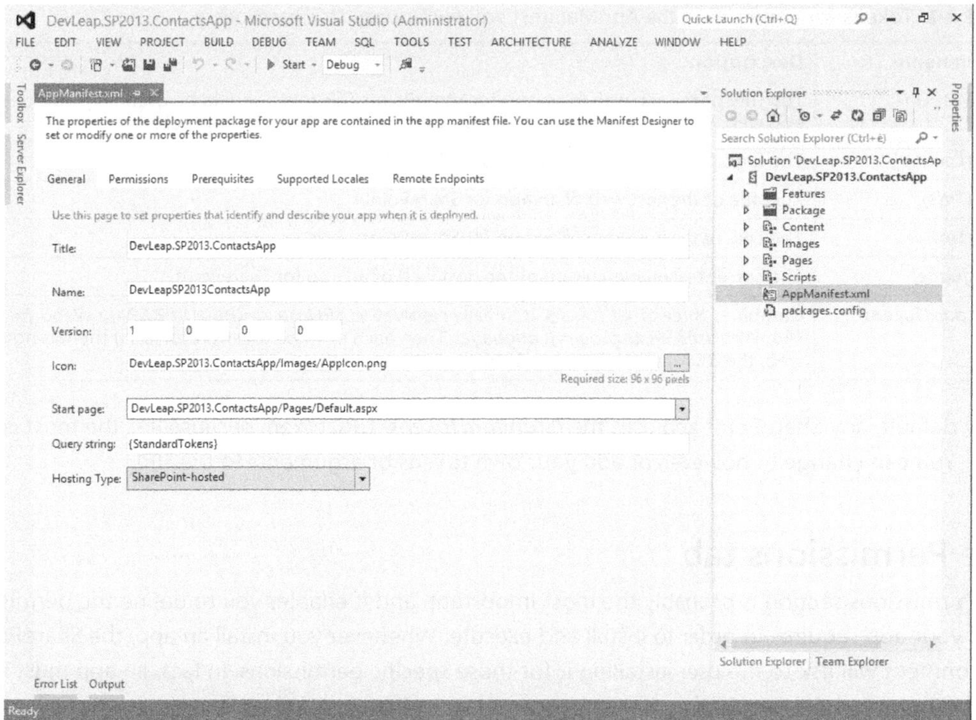

FIGURE 8-7 The designer for AppManifest.xml provided by Visual Studio 2012.

More Info Under the hood, the AppManifest.xml file is just an XML file based on the XML schema with a namespace URI value of http://schemas.microsoft.com/sharepoint/2012/app/manifest. You can find further details about the AppManifest.xml schema at *http://msdn.microsoft.com/en-us/library/jj583347.aspx.*

The General tab

The first and main configuration tab, General, holds general information about the app, such as the title, name, and version, as well as the icon to show in the SharePoint UI. You can also choose the start page of the app, which will become the default page of the app website provisioned while installing the app. Finally, yet importantly, you can configure the query string behavior of the app. As shown in the previous section, when your app is activated, it receives a rich and long set of query string arguments. If you configure the query string property of you app, you can determine the list of arguments that the app will receive. In this property, you can use the tokens illustrated in Table 8-1. All these tokens will be resolved and appended to the URL of the default page of your app during activation.

TABLE 8-1 Tokens for configuring the AppManifest.xml file's query string property

Token name	Description
{AppWebUrl}	The URL of the app web in an app for SharePoint. This token should be used only outside an app web. Within the app web itself, use *{Site}* for the URL of the app web.
{HostLogoUrl}	The logo for the host web of an app for SharePoint.
{HostTitle}	The title of the host web of an app for SharePoint.
{HostUrl}	The URL of the host web of an app for SharePoint.
{Language}	The current language/culture of the host web of an app for SharePoint.
{StandardTokens}	Combines three other tokens. It initially resolves to *SPHostUrl={HostUrl}&SPAppWebUrl={AppWebUrl}&SPLanguage={Language}*. Then each of these tokens resolves. If there is no app web, the *&SPAppWebUrl={AppWebUrl}* portion is not present.

By default, any SharePoint app uses the *{StandardTokens}* URL token, because it is the most complete. You can change it, however, or add your own tokens or arguments to the URL.

The Permissions tab

The Permissions section is probably the most important, and it enables you to define the permissions your app requires in order to install and execute. Whenever you install an app, the SharePoint environment will ask to the user installing it for those specific permissions. In fact, an app must be explicitly granted the required permissions in order to be installed. When installing an app, users can grant only permissions that they have, and they can grant or deny permissions with an all-or-nothing approach only. Users cannot grant a subset of the required permissions. If a user tries to install an app that requires permissions the user does not have, the SharePoint environment will raise an exception, showing a message that states the user does not have sufficient permissions to complete the action.

Every app has an identity of its own, which is associated with a security principal called the *app principal*. The app principal of an app has full control rights against the app web hosting the app itself. Thus, you do not need to request permissions for accessing the app web from your app. On the contrary, if your app needs to access the parent site or any external location outside the app web, you will need to request specific permissions for that.

The available permissions are defined by scope, and scopes are represented as URIs in the AppManifest.xml file. In the UI for configuring the permission, however, you see only literal names, for the sake of simplicity. Table 8-2 lists the available scopes.

TABLE 8-2 Available scopes and permissions for an app

Scope	Available permissions	Description
BCS	Read	Corresponds to the URI *http://sharepoint/bcs/connection* and allows defining the permission to access Business Connectivity Services (BCS) data.
Enterprise Resources	Read, Write	Allows accessing enterprise-level resources of Microsoft Project Server 2013. It is defined by the URI *http://sharepoint/projectserver/enterpriseresources*.

Scope	Available permissions	Description
List	Read, Write, Manage, FullControl	Allows defining permissions for accessing lists. It corresponds to the URI *http://sharepoint/content/sitecollection/web/list* and supports extended properties for defining a specific target BaseTemplateId number, in case you would like to define permissions only for lists based on a particular BaseTemplateId.
Micro Feed	Read, Write, Manage, FullControl	Corresponds to the URI *http://sharepoint/social/microfeed* and relates to the Social Features group of scopes. It allows defining permissions for accessing the social microfeed.
Multiple Projects	Read, Write	Allows defining permissions for accessing multiple projects of Project Server 2013. It corresponds to the URI *http://sharepoint/projectserver/projects*.
Project Server	Manage	Corresponds to the URI *http://sharepoint/projectserver* and defines the permission to manage Project Server 2013.
Reporting	Read	Allows defining the permission to read reporting information from Project Server 2013 and corresponds to the URI *http://sharepoint/projectserver/reporting*.
Search	QueryAsUserIgnoreAppPrincipal	Defines permission to search contents via the app as the user principal, instead of using the app principal. It corresponds to the URI *http://sharepoint/search*.
Single Project	Read, Write	Allows defining permissions for accessing a single project of Project Server 2013. It corresponds to the URI *http://sharepoint/projectserver/projects/project*.
Site Collection	Read, Write, Manage, FullControl	Corresponds to the URI *http://sharepoint/content/sitecollection* and defines the permissions related to a site collection.
Social Core	Read, Write, Manage, FullControl	Provides permissions for accessing core information of the social features. It corresponds to the URI *http://sharepoint/social/core*.
Statusing	SubmitStatus	Allows defining the permission to submit status to Project Server 2013. It corresponds to the URI *http://sharepoint/projectserver/statusing*.
Taxonomy	Read, Write	Provides permission configuration for accessing the taxonomy engine and corresponds to the URI *http://sharepoint/taxonomy*.
Tenant	Read, Write, Manage, FullControl	Corresponds to the URI *http://sharepoint/content/tenant* and defines permissions for accessing the content at the tenant level.
User Profile	Read, Write, Manage, FullControl	Corresponds to the URI *http://sharepoint/social/tenant* and defines permissions for accessing the users' social features at the tenant level.
Web	Read, Write, Manage, FullControl	Defines permissions for accessing a specific website within a site collection and corresponds to the URI *http://sharepoint/content/sitecollection/web*.
Workflow	Elevate	Allows defining the permission to elevate privileges in workflows of Project Server 2013. It corresponds to the URI *http://sharepoint/projectserver/workflow*.

Where available, the FullControl permission cannot be requested for apps that you want to publish to the Office Store. Moreover, the permission scopes related to Project Server 2013 are available only in environments where Project Server 2013 is installed.

App permissions are inherited hierarchically, and a permission applied to a parent object is implicitly applied to all of its children. For example, if you grant a Write permission at the *Site Collection* scope, the app will have that same permission for all of the sites within the target site collection.

Figure 8-8 shows how the Permissions tab behaves in the AppManifest.xml designer. For the sake of clarity, the AppManifest.xml file illustrated requires all the available permissions.

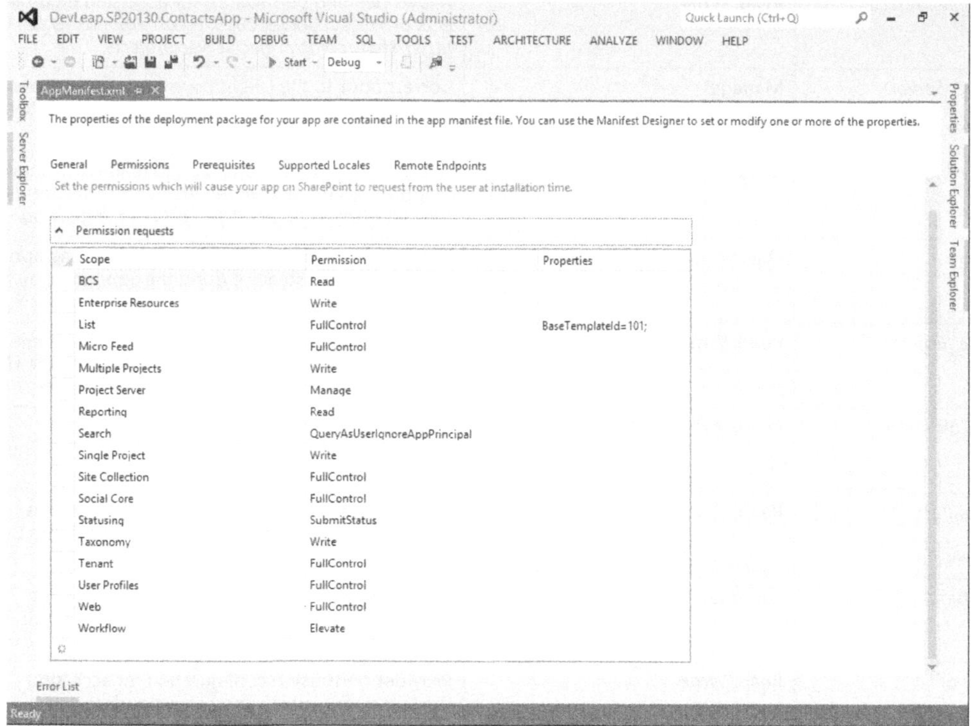

FIGURE 8-8 The Permissions tab in the designer for AppManifest.xml.

Listing 8-4 provides the XML source of an AppManifest.xml file configured as illustrated in Figure 8-8.

LISTING 8-4 The XML source of an AppManifest.xml file with all the available permission scopes defined

```
<?xml version="1.0" encoding="utf-8" ?>
<!--Created:cb85b80c-f585-40ff-8bfc-12ff4d0e34a9-->
<App xmlns="http://schemas.microsoft.com/sharepoint/2012/app/manifest"
     Name="DevLeapSP20130ContactsApp"
     ProductID="{abe98779-6d6c-490c-83d4-8bf9acd4820c}"
     Version="1.0.0.0"
     SharePointMinVersion="15.0.0.0">
  <Properties>
    <Title>DevLeap.SP20130.ContactsApp</Title>
    <StartPage>~appWebUrl/Pages/Default.aspx?{StandardTokens}</StartPage>
  </Properties>

  <AppPrincipal>
    <Internal />
  </AppPrincipal>

  <AppPermissionRequests>
    <AppPermissionRequest Scope="http://sharepoint/bcs/connection" Right="Read"
/>
    <AppPermissionRequest Scope="http://sharepoint/projectserver/
enterpriseresources" Right="Write" />
    <AppPermissionRequest
Scope="http://sharepoint/content/sitecollection/web/list" Right="FullControl" >
      <Property Name="BaseTemplateId" Value="101" />
    </AppPermissionRequest>
    <AppPermissionRequest Scope="http://sharepoint/social/microfeed"
Right="FullControl" />
    <AppPermissionRequest Scope="http://sharepoint/projectserver/projects"
Right="Write" />
    <AppPermissionRequest Scope="http://sharepoint/projectserver" Right="Manage"
/>
    <AppPermissionRequest Scope="http://sharepoint/projectserver/reporting"
Right="Read" />
    <AppPermissionRequest Scope="http://sharepoint/search"
Right="QueryAsUserIgnoreAppPrincipal" />
    <AppPermissionRequest
Scope="http://sharepoint/projectserver/projects/project" Right="Write" />
    <AppPermissionRequest Scope="http://sharepoint/content/sitecollection"
Right="FullControl" />
    <AppPermissionRequest Scope="http://sharepoint/social/core"
Right="FullControl" />
    <AppPermissionRequest Scope="http://sharepoint/projectserver/statusing"
Right="SubmitStatus" />
    <AppPermissionRequest Scope="http://sharepoint/taxonomy" Right="Write" />
    <AppPermissionRequest Scope="http://sharepoint/content/tenant"
Right="FullControl" />
    <AppPermissionRequest Scope="http://sharepoint/social/tenant"
Right="FullControl" />
    <AppPermissionRequest Scope="http://sharepoint/content/sitecollection/web"
Right="FullControl" />
    <AppPermissionRequest Scope="http://sharepoint/projectserver/workflow"
Right="Elevate" />
  </AppPermissionRequests>
</App>
```

Notice the *List* permission, highlighted in bold, with the optional property *BaseTemplateId* configured to a value of *101* (for "document library"). When you install an app with some custom permissions requests, the SharePoint environment will ask you to trust it. Figure 8-9 illustrates how the request to trust the app is prompted to an end user. As you can see, the form asks the end user to choose the library to which you would like the app to have access. If you trust the app and give it the requested permissions, then you will be able to use it.

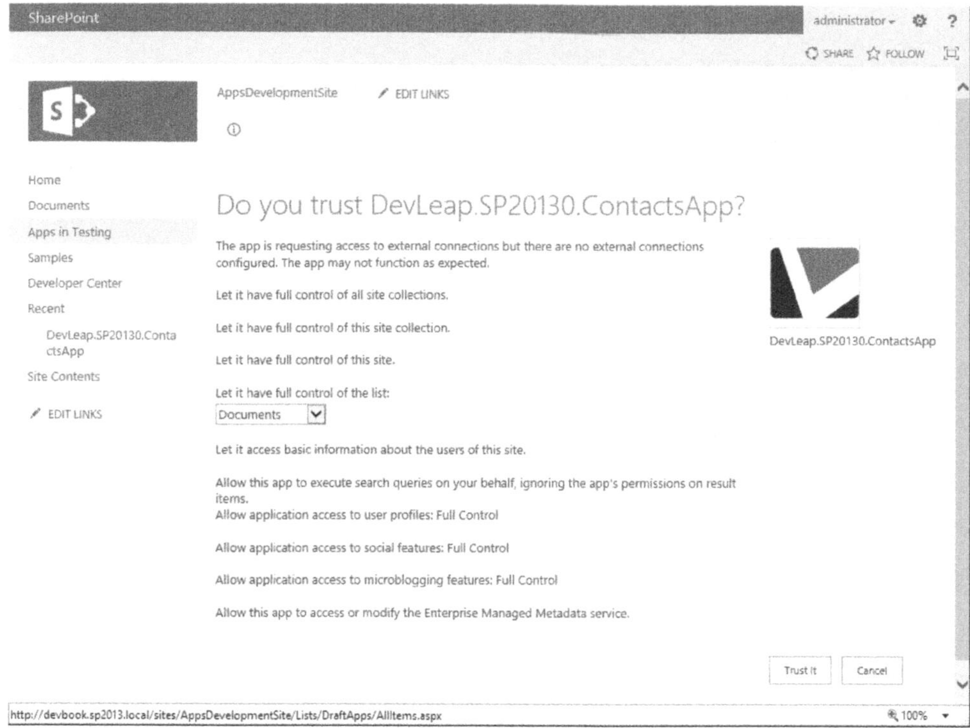

FIGURE 8-9 The page for trusting an app during installation.

In case you later decide to change or retract permissions from an app, you can remove the whole app, or you can go to the permissions-management page specific for that app. To view that page, go to the Site Contents page, click the ellipsis just behind the app icon, and select the Permissions link on the ECB menu. This link will lead you to the permissions-management page that is illustrated in Figure 8-10.

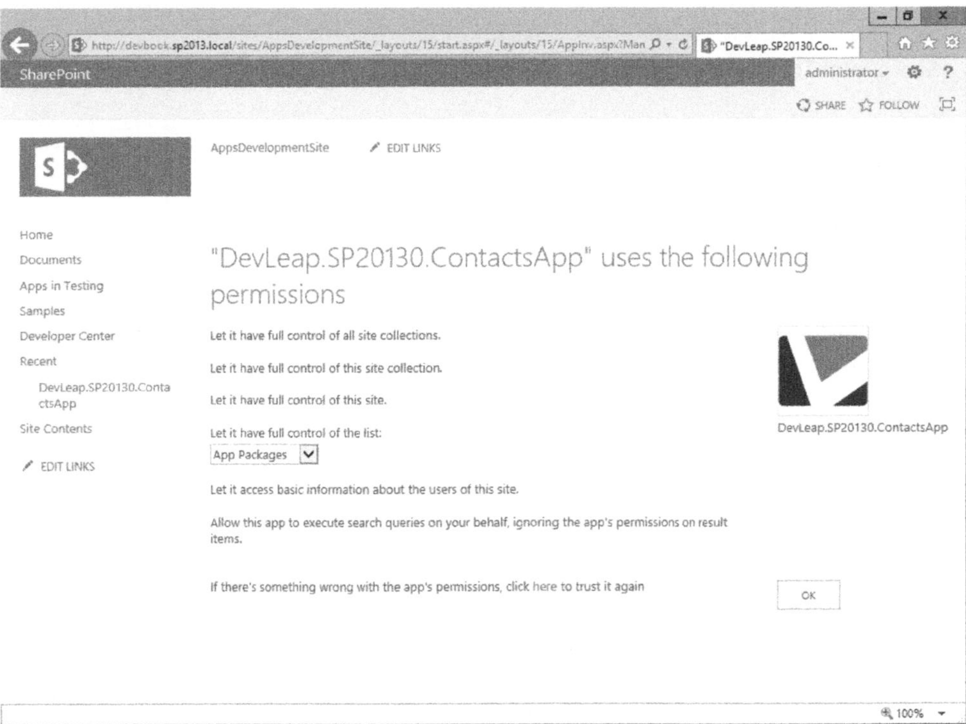

FIGURE 8-10 The permissions-management page for an app.

The Prerequisites tab

The third configuration tab of the AppManifest.xml file, Prerequisites, provides a grid for configuring the list of the prerequisites that must be installed on the SharePoint site in order for the app to be installed. If necessary, you can configure the following prerequisites:

- Access V14 (aka Access 2010)
- Access V15
- Duet Enterprise Services
- Education Services
- Managed Metadata Web Service
- PowerPoint Services
- Search Services

- Secure Store Services
- SharePoint Translation Services
- SharePoint Workflow Services
- User Profile Service
- Visio Services
- Work Management Service

Each prerequisite feature or service can also specify a minimum version requirement. Figure 8-11 shows the outline of this configuration tab, with all of the out-of-the-box prerequisites configured.

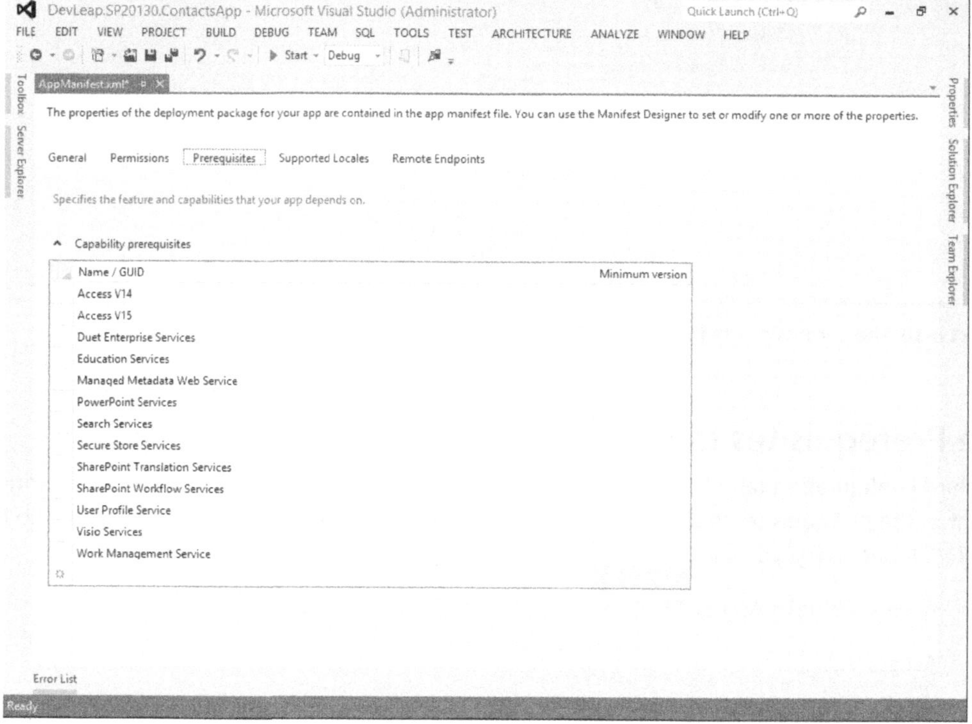

FIGURE 8-11 The outline of the tab for configuring app prerequisites.

The resulting configuration defines an *AppPrerequisites* element in the AppManifest.xml file, filled with a set of elements with name *AppPrerequisite*. Each *AppPrerequisite* element is configured with a *Type* attribute, an *ID* attribute, and an optional *MinimumVersion* attribute. Here is the XML definition of the *AppPrerequisite* element for the Visio Services capability:

```
<AppPrerequisite Type="Capability" ID="778D6B91-D46F-40E6-B7A4-1C666B800D03"
MinimumVersion="15.0.0.0" />
```

As you can see, the prerequisite is referenced by *ID*, which in general is a globally unique identifier (GUID). The *Type* attribute can assume values of *Feature*, *Capability*, or *AutoProvisioning*. The first two values are self-explanatory; the *AutoProvisioning* value is suitable only for autohosted apps. In fact, for autohosted apps, you can automatically provision components that the app needs while provisioning the app itself. In this case, the *ID* attribute can assume literal values (instead of GUIDs) corresponding to *RemoteWebHost* and *Database*, for provisioning a Windows Azure website and a SQL Azure database, respectively. The *MinimumVersion* attribute is in the form of a product version: *{number} ({major version}.{minor version}.{build number}.{revision})*.

For services such as Excel, Access, or Visio Services, the infrastructure will verify that the service is installed and licensed. For features at the *Farm*, *WebApplication*, or *Site* scope, the infrastructure will verify that they are deployed and activated. For features that can be activated at the *Web* scope on the target app web, the environment will automatically activate them during app installation.

The Supported Locales tab

Through the Supported Locales tab, you can configure the locales supported by your app, together with the resource files corresponding to each locale. Every SharePoint app can support one or more locales, providing dedicated resources and resource files. On this tab, you simply need to configure a locale ID (using the culture name) and the name and content of the corresponding resource file. Each time you configure a supported locale, Visual Studio 2012 creates the corresponding .resx file for you. Figure 8-12 shows the tab configured for supporting the Italian locale and the French locale. It also shows the SharePoint app project outline, with the .resx files corresponding to these supported locales.

Important By default, apps have no locales configured. If you want to publish your app on the Office Store, however, you must declare at least one supported locale, and you should support the English locale (1033).

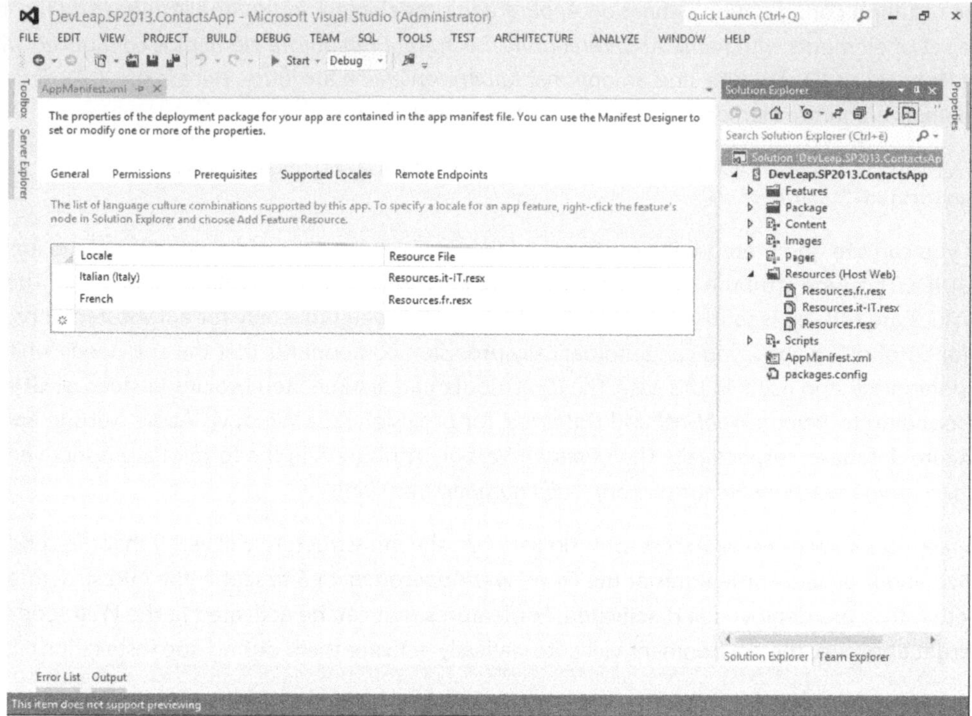

FIGURE 8-12 The tab for configuring the supported locales for an app.

The Remote Endpoints tab

The last tab of the AppManifest.xml configuration panel is Remote Endpoints. A *remote endpoint* is a URL that your app will use for accessing data or services from external domains. Nowadays, there are cross-site scripting (XSS) policies denying access to external domains via JavaScript code. When you are developing an HTML-and-JavaScript-based SharePoint app, use this tab to configure the list of allowed remote endpoints. SharePoint will then provide a JavaScript-based API (*SP.RequestExecutor*) that will call the configured remote endpoints for you, and pass back the data it receives. Figure 8-13 shows how the configuration for remote endpoints behaves in Visual Studio 2012.

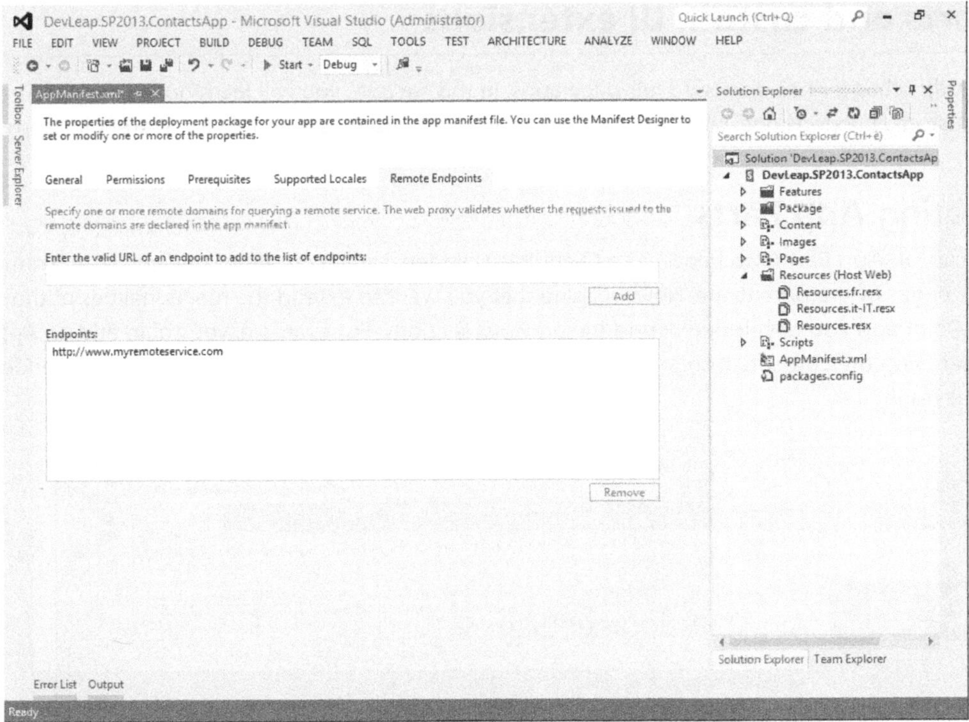

FIGURE 8-13 The tab for configuring the remote endpoints for an app.

Configuring the remote endpoints on this tab results in the creation of an XML section within the AppManifest.xml file, such as the following:

```
<RemoteEndpoints>
  <RemoteEndpoint Url="http://www.myremoteservice.com" />
</RemoteEndpoints>
```

In Chapter 9, you will learn how the *SP.RequestExecutor* API works and how to take advantage of it in your apps.

App Parts and custom UI extensions

So far, this chapter has discussed full-page apps. In this section, you will learn how to create App Parts and custom UI extensions, which are the two other configurations available for SharePoint apps.

Creating App Parts

To recap, an App Part (also known as a Client Part) renders some content of the app in an IFrame inside pages of the parent site. Now, imagine that you want to extend the functionalities of the SharePoint app you developed during the previous sections. For example, you could add an App Part for searching the contacts from within the parent SharePoint site. Figure 8-14 shows the intended output result.

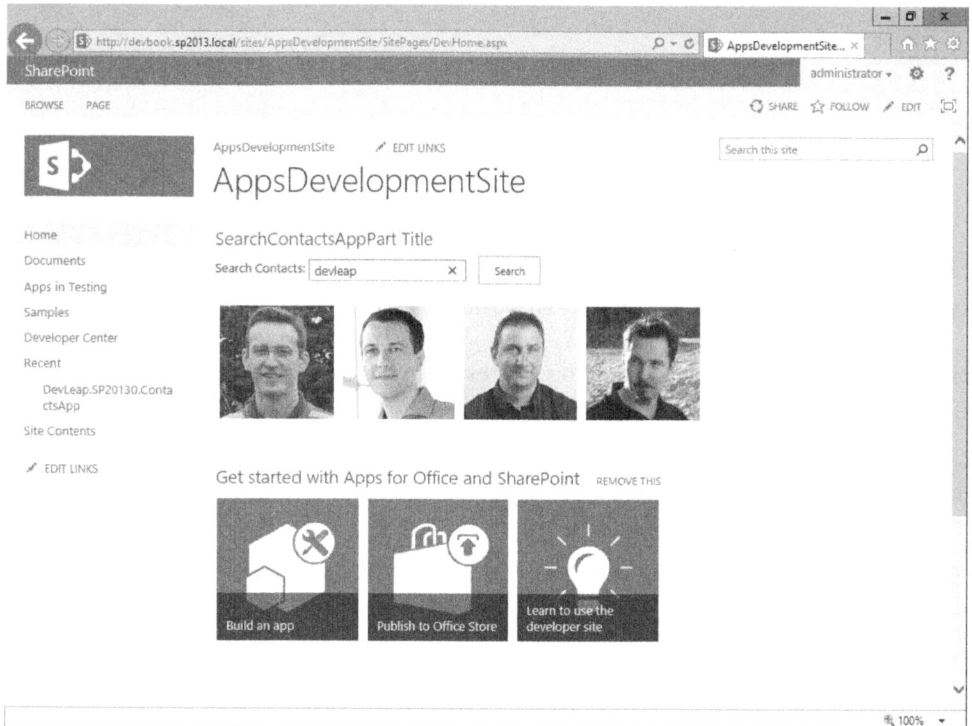

FIGURE 8-14 The sample App Part in action while searching app contacts.

To add a new App Part, simply right-click the app project while in Visual Studio and select Add | New Item | Client Web Part (Host Web) from the list of available item templates. Then provide a name for the target App Part. For this example, call it *SearchContactsAppPart*. When you add an App Part to a project, a wizard will prompt you to enter some information about the App Part, as shown in

Figure 8-15. In this wizard, you can choose between creating a new App Part and using an already existing ASPX page, which will be loaded inside the IFrame that will host the App Part. Click the Finish button to create an ASPX page file and a new feature element for provisioning your App Part.

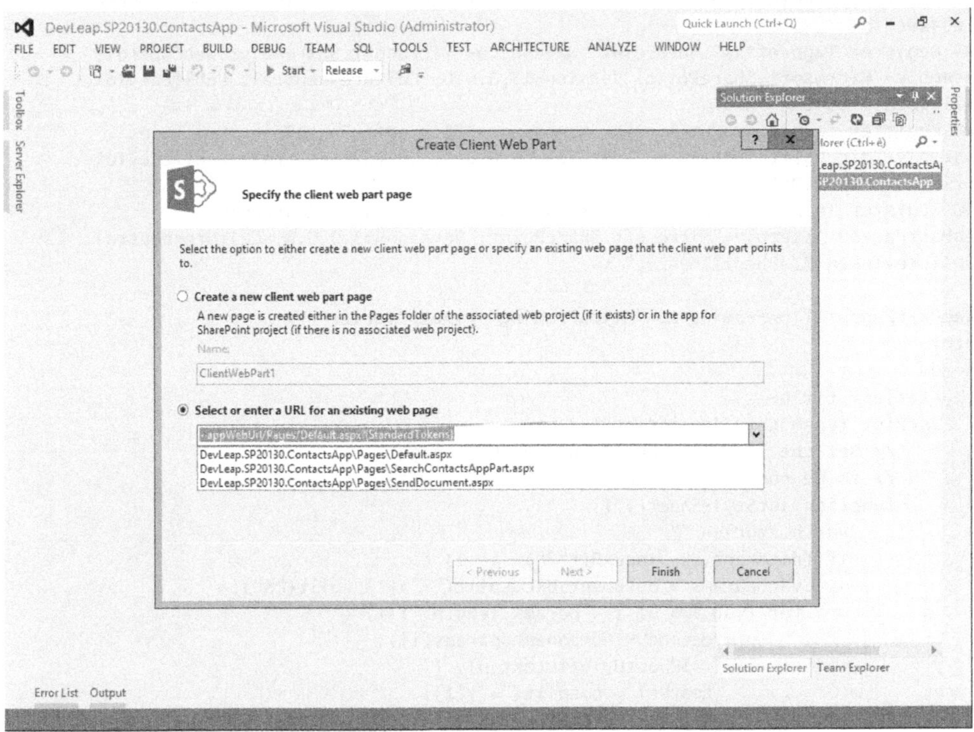

FIGURE 8-15 The UI for adding an App Part to a target project.

The ASPX page file is just another web page that will be hosted in your app web, and that will have the same capabilities of the Default.aspx page or any other custom ASPX page. Here you can use the JSOM to interact with SharePoint and with your app web. Listing 8-5 shows the default content of the SearchContactsAppPart.aspx file created by Visual Studio 2012 upon creation of the App Part.

LISTING 8-5 The default content of the SearchContactsAppPart.aspx page behind the custom App Part

```
<%@ Page language="C#" Inherits="Microsoft.SharePoint.WebPartPages.WebPartPage,
Microsoft.SharePoint, Version=15.0.0.0, Culture=neutral, PublicKeyToken=71e9bce1
11e9429c" %>
<%@ Register Tagprefix="SharePoint" Namespace="Microsoft.SharePoint.WebControls"
Assembly="Microsoft.SharePoint, Version=15.0.0.0, Culture=neutral, PublicKeyToke
n=71e9bce111e9429c" %>
<%@ Register Tagprefix="Utilities" Namespace="Microsoft.SharePoint.Utilities"
Assembly="Microsoft.SharePoint, Version=15.0.0.0, Culture=neutral, PublicKeyToke
n=71e9bce111e9429c" %>
<%@ Register Tagprefix="WebPartPages" Namespace="Microsoft.SharePoint.
WebPartPages" Assembly="Microsoft.SharePoint, Version=15.0.0.0, Culture=neutral,
PublicKeyToken=71e9bce111e9429c" %>

<WebPartPages:AllowFraming ID="AllowFraming" runat="server" />
<html>
<head>
    <title></title>
    <script type="text/javascript">
        // Set the style of the client web part page
        // to be consistent with the host web.
        function setStyleSheet() {
            var hostUrl = ""
            if (document.URL.indexOf("?") != -1) {
                var params = document.URL.split("?")[1].split("&");
                for (var i = 0; i < params.length; i++) {
                    p = decodeURIComponent(params[i]);
                    if (/^SPHostUrl=/i.test(p)) {
                        hostUrl = p.split("=")[1];
                        document.write("<link rel=\"stylesheet\" href=\"" +
                        hostUrl + "/_layouts/15/defaultcss.ashx\" />");
                        break;
                    }
                }
            }
            if (hostUrl == "") {
                document.write("<link
rel=\"stylesheet\" href=\"/_layouts/15/1033/styles/themable/corev15.css\" />");
            }
        }
        setStyleSheet();
    </script>
</head>
<body>
</body>
</html>
```

As you can see, the page references the classic SharePoint server-side libraries and controls, and inherits its behavior from the *Microsoft.SharePoint.WebPartPages.WebPartPage* base class, without defining any master page file. Moreover, the server-side control called *AllowFraming* enables your page to be rendered inside an IFrame.

Just after the server control for allowing the frame support is HTML and JavaScript code for rendering the basic elements of the page, together with default theming consistent with the host SharePoint website. By default, the page will try to locate the *SPHostUrl* parameter in the query string and will download the CSS style (if it exists) from the URL *_layouts/15/defaultcss.ashx* relative to the *SPHostUrl*. If the *SPHostUrl* argument is missing, the App Part will be rendered using the *CoreV15.css* style of the current app website.

To implement the App Part, you will have to add some HTML and JavaScript code to the page. For the current sample, you will reuse some ideas and code already shown in Chapter 7. For example, you'll add a text box and a button for searching contacts. Inside the *body* element of the page, add the following markup:

```
Search Contacts: <input type="text" name="textToSearch" id="textToSearch" />
  <input type="button" value="Search" onclick="javascript:searchContacts();" />
  <br /> <br />
  <div id="searchOutput" style="overflow:auto; height: 130px;"></div>
```

Then, just before the closing tag of the *head* element of the page, add the following references to scripts:

```
<script type="text/javascript"
  src="http://ajax.aspnetcdn.com/ajax/4.0/1/MicrosoftAjax.js"></script>
  <script type="text/javascript"
  src="http://ajax.aspnetcdn.com/ajax/jQuery/jquery-1.8.3.min.js"></script>
  <script type="text/javascript"
  src="http://code.jquery.com/ui/1.9.2/jquery-ui.min.js"></script>
  <script type="text/javascript"
  src="/_layouts/15/sp.runtime.debug.js"></script>
  <script type="text/javascript" src="/_layouts/15/sp.debug.js"></script>
  <script type="text/javascript"
  src="../Scripts/SearchContacts.js"></script>
```

Now you will need to add a new JavaScript file in the Scripts folder of the project. For example, give it a name of SearchContacts.js. Listing 8-6 shows how the code should look.

LISTING 8-6 The JavaScript code behind the App Part defined in the SearchContactsAppPart.aspx page

```
var clientContext;
var web;
var contactsList;
var listItems;

// This code runs when the DOM is ready and creates a context object which is
// needed to use the SharePoint object model
$(document).ready(function () {
    clientContext = SP.ClientContext.get_current();
    web = clientContext.get_web();
});
```

```
// This function prepares, loads, and then executes a SharePoint
// query to get the search query for app contacts results
function searchContacts() {
    contactsList = web.get_lists().getByTitle("App Contacts");

    var textToSearch = $("#textToSearch").val();
    var camlQuery = new SP.CamlQuery();
    var q = '<View><Query><Where><Contains><FieldRef ' +
      'Name="DevLeapAppContactDescription" /><Value Type="Text">' +
      textToSearch + '</Value></Contains></Where></Query></View>';
    camlQuery.set_viewXml(q);
    listItems = contactsList.getItems(camlQuery);

    clientContext.load(listItems);
    clientContext.executeQueryAsync(onSearchQuerySucceeded, onSearchQueryFailed);
}

// Output the result
function onSearchQuerySucceeded(sender, args) {
    $("#searchOutput").empty();

    if (listItems.get_count() > 0) {
        var listItemsEnumerator = listItems.getEnumerator();

        // Iterate though all of the items
        while (listItemsEnumerator.moveNext()) {
            var item = listItemsEnumerator.get_current();

            var id = item.get_id();
            var contactDescription = item.get_item(
            "DevLeapAppContactDescription");
            var contactTelephone = item.get_item("DevLeapAppContactTelephone");
            var contactEmail = item.get_item("DevLeapAppContactEmail");
            var contactPhoto = item.get_item("DevLeapAppContactPhoto").get_url();

            $("#searchOutput").append('<a href="mailto:' + contactEmail + '">' +
                '<img style="float: left; margin: 5px;" src="' +
                contactPhoto + '" align="left" alt="' + contactDescription +
                '"/></a>');
        }
    }
    else {
        $("#searchOutput").append('<div>No results matching the query. ' +
          'Try again ...</div>');
    }
}

function onSearchQueryFailed(sender, args) {
    alert('Request failed ' + args.get_message() + '\n' + args.get_stackTrace());
}
```

As you can see, the code is made of standard JSOM directives for searching the target list of contacts using Collaborative Application Markup Language (CAML).

The last piece of code to evaluate is the feature element for provisioning the App Part. In fact, when you add an App Part to a SharePoint app project, Visual Studio 2012 adds also a feature element to the project. In Listing 8-7 shows the one related to the sample App Part illustrated in this section.

LISTING 8-7 The feature element file for provisioning the sample SearchContactsAppPart

```
<?xml version="1.0" encoding="utf-8"?>
<Elements xmlns="http://schemas.microsoft.com/sharepoint/">
  <ClientWebPart Name="SearchContactsAppPart" Title="SearchContactsAppPart Title"
                 Description="SearchContactsAppPart Description"
                 DefaultWidth="600"
                 DefaultHeight="200">

<!-- Content element identifies the location of the page that will render inside
the client web part

Properties are referenced on the query string using the pattern _propertyName_
Example: Src="~appWebUrl/Pages/ClientWebPart1.aspx?Property1=_property1_" -->

    <Content Type="html" Src="~appWebUrl/Pages/SearchContactsAppPart.aspx" />
    <!-- Define properties in the Properties element.
         Remember to put Property Name on the Src attribute of the
         Content element above. -->
    <Properties>
    </Properties>
  </ClientWebPart>
</Elements>
```

The *ClientWebPart* element provisions an App Part, providing descriptive information like *Name*, *Title*, *Description*, *DefaultWidth*, and *DefaultHeight*. If you are creating a multilingual app, you should at least provide a resource-based value for both the *Title* and *Description* attributes, using the classic *$Resources:ResourceName;* syntax and providing a value for the key *ResourceName* in every RESX file.

In addition, you can include a list of custom properties, defined through a set of *Property* elements (children of the *Properties* element). Every *Property* element can assume the structure illustrated in Listing 8-8 and define a property that will be configurable through the SharePoint UI while managing the page hosting the App Part. You can also define properties that are not configurable by the end users, but that are still needed by the App Part internal logic.

LISTING 8-8 *Property* element structure

```
<Property xmlns="http://schemas.microsoft.com/sharepoint/"
    Name="Text"
    DefaultValue="Text"
    Multilingual= "true" | "false"
    PersonalizationScope="user" | "shared"
    PersonalizableIsSensitive= "true" | "false"
    Type= "string" | "int" | "boolean" | "enum"
    RequiresDesignerPermission= "true" | "false"
    WebBrowsable= "true" | "false"
    WebCategory="Text"
    WebDescription="Text"
    WebDisplayName="Text"
    ManagedLinkConvertServerLinksToRelative= "true" | "false"
    ManagedLinkFixup= "true" | "false" >
    <EnumItems>
        <EnumItem
            Value="Text"
            WebDisplayName="Text" />
    </EnumItems>
</Property>
```

The most interesting things to notice are the available data types, which are *string*, *int*, *Boolean*, and *enum* (shown in Figure 8-15). In case of the *enum* type, you will have to provide the admitted values using the *EnumItems* child element. Some other interesting attributes are *PersonalizationScope*, for defining whether the property can be personalized by each user or will assume a shared value; and *RequiresDesignerPermission*, for determining whether the user has to have designer permissions to edit the property value. Moreover, you can define attributes to configure the appearance of every single property in the UI, including *WebBrowsable*, *WebCategory*, *WebDescription*, and *WebDisplayName*. These last attributes have names and meanings that correspond to similar properties of SharePoint Web Parts, which will be discussed in Chapter 11, "Developing Web Parts." Listing 8-9 demonstrates how to define an *enum* property for defining the orientation (horizontal or vertical) of results for the sample App Part for searching contacts.

LISTING 8-9 A sample *Property* element defining a property of type *enum*, defined for the sample App Part for searching contacts

```
<Property Name="FlowDirection"
          DefaultValue="Horizontal"
          Multilingual="true"
          PersonalizationScope="shared"
          PersonalizableIsSensitive="true"
          Type="enum"
          RequiresDesignerPermission="true"
          WebBrowsable="true"
          WebCategory="Custom Properties"
          WebDescription="Flow Direction"
          WebDisplayName="Flow Direction"
          ManagedLinkConvertServerLinksToRelative="true"
          ManagedLinkFixup="true">
  <EnumItems>
    <EnumItem Value="Horizontal" WebDisplayName="Horizontal"/>
    <EnumItem Value="Vertical" WebDisplayName="Vertical"/>
  </EnumItems>
</Property>
```

The selected values of configurable properties can be passed via query string to the ASPX page behind the App Part. The syntax for passing the properties is to append them to the *Src* attribute value at the end of the App Part page URL. The name for the query string arguments can be anything you like, while the value has to be represented as *_{PropertyName}_*. For example, to get the value of a property with the name *FlowDirection* into an argument with the name *Direction*, you should write the *Src* attribute value as follows:

```
Src="~appWebUrl/Pages/ClientWebPart1.aspx?Direction=_FlowDirection_"
```

Remember that the feature element is an XML file, so any special characters, such as *&* or *%*, should be represented in URL-encoded format. To access the provided values while executing the App Part, use jQuery extensions or custom JavaScript code, just as you would with any other HTML or JavaScript application.

Figure 8-16 shows how the various types of properties are rendered in the SharePoint UI. To display the tool pane, click the Edit Web Part menu, which is available while the page is in Edit mode, as it is for any other classic Web Part in SharePoint.

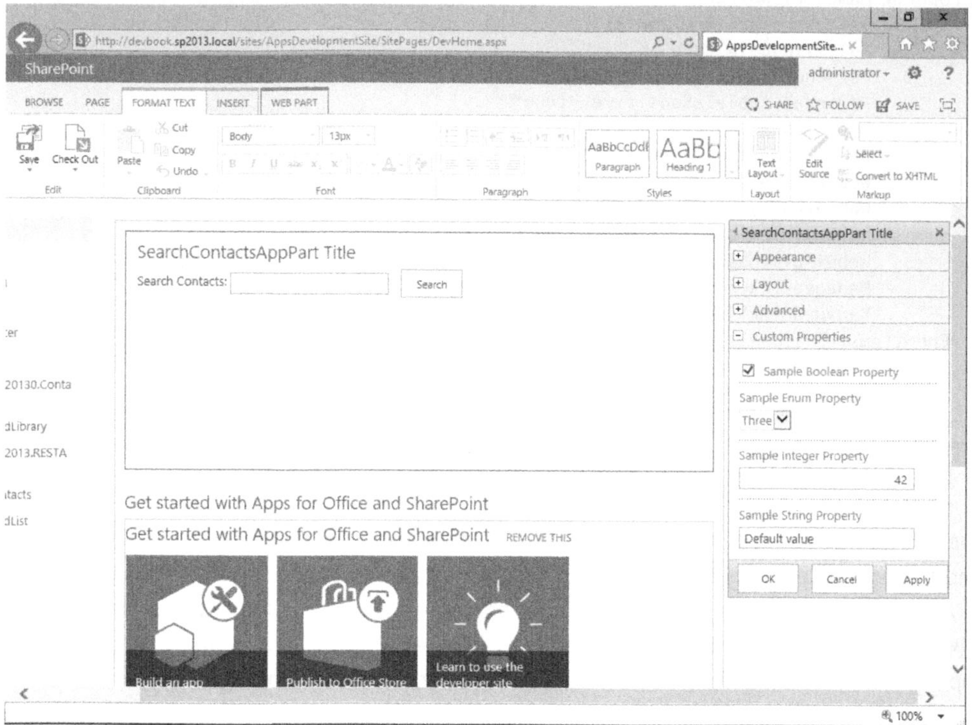

FIGURE 8-16 The UI for configuring the properties of an App Part.

After you install your app, you can add the App Part to a target page. You simply need to edit the page, and on the ribbon's Insert tab, click the App Part button. You will be prompted with the list of all the available App Parts, including *SearchContactsAppPart*. Figure 8-17 illustrates the UI for inserting the sample App Part in a target page.

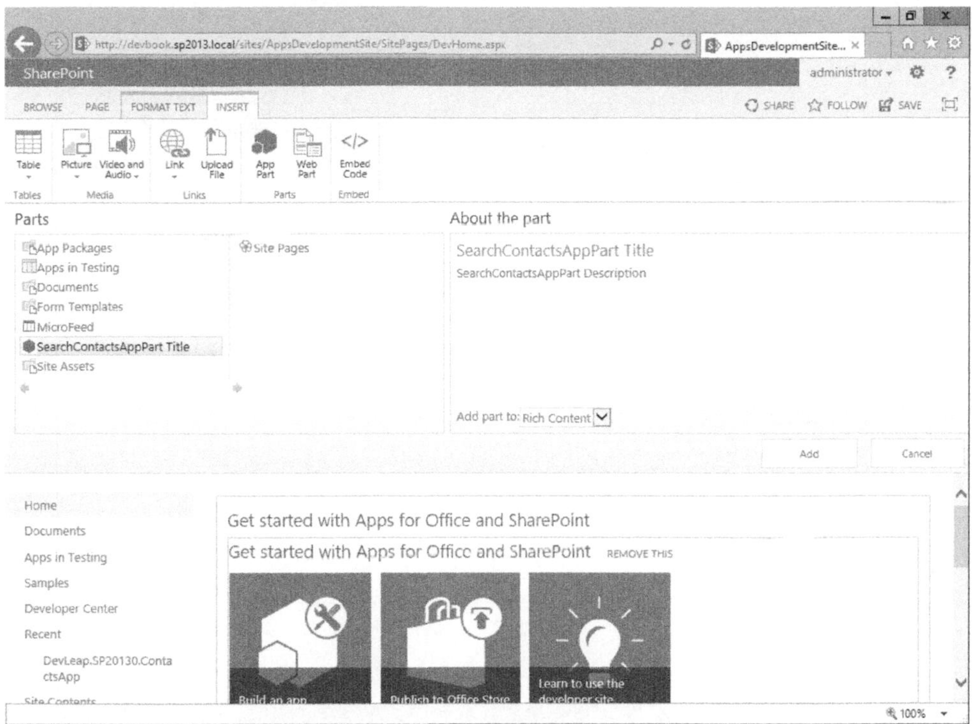

FIGURE 8-17 The UI for adding an App Part to a target page.

Notice that, although you are still in edit mode, your App Part is fully functional already. In fact, the code behind the App Part is based on JavaScript and runs both in edit and design mode.

Creating custom UI extensions

Custom UI extensions allow your SharePoint apps to interact with the end user through the standard UI of SharePoint. You can add custom menu items in the ECB, and custom ribbon commands and tabs to the ribbons of standard SharePoint pages, while using exactly the same tools and techniques you would for any other UI customization (see Chapter 12). In addition, while working in SharePoint apps, you also have the support of a few dedicated tools and wizards.

To create a custom UI extension, you simply need to add a new item to an already existing SharePoint app project. To add a new menu item, right-click the project in Visual Studio 2012 Solution Explorer, select Add from the menu, and then choose New Item and finally Menu Item Custom Action. In the wizard that appears, provide the appropriate answers to create the new menu item. Figure 8-18 depicts the first step of this wizard.

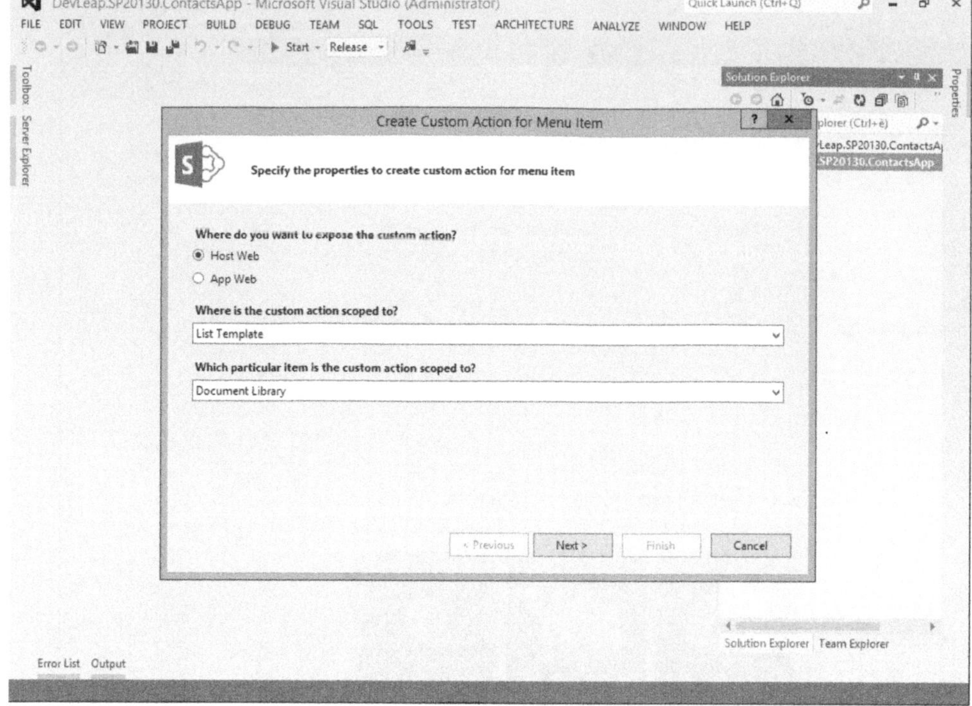

FIGURE 8-18 The first step of the wizard for creating a new menu item extension.

First, you can choose whether the menu item will be created within the app web or the host web. Then you can choose where the menu item will be scoped. The available options are

- **List Template** The new menu item will be scoped to every list based on a specified template.
- **List Instance** The new menu item will be scoped to a specific list instance.
- **Content Type** The new menu item will be scoped to a specific content type, regardless of the list template or list instance where it will be used.
- **File Extension** The new menu item will be scoped to a particular file extension of items in libraries.

The wizard will adapt to the selection you make. For example, if you choose List Instance, then you will have to choose the specific target instance; when choosing Content Type, you will have to select the target content type; and so on.

In the second step of the wizard (Figure 8-19), you define the caption of the menu item, as well as the target URL to drive the user to when the menu item is selected.

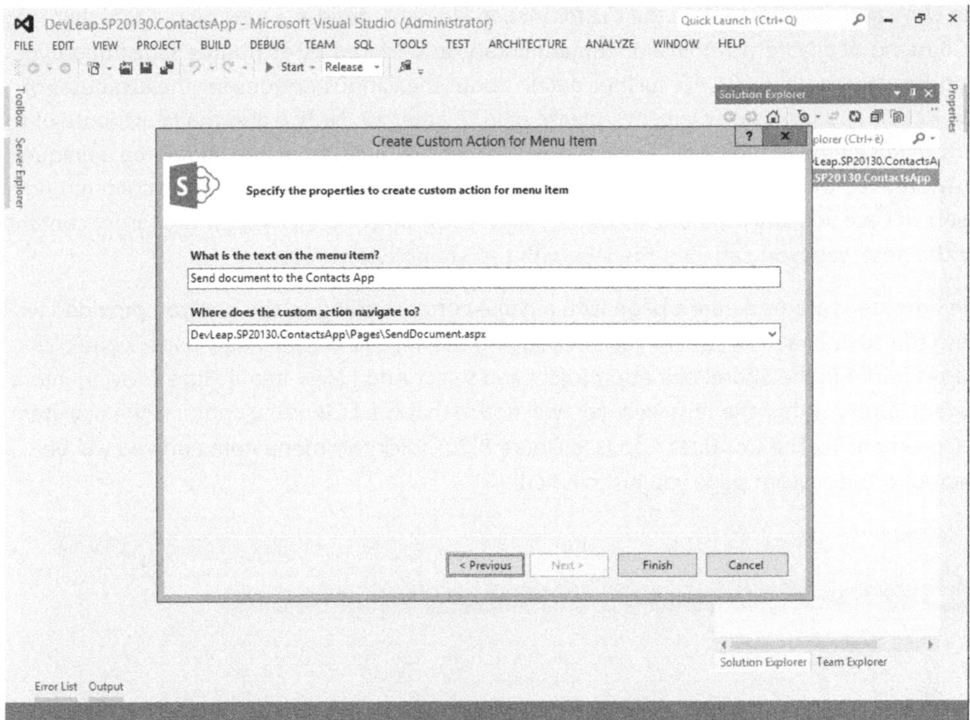

FIGURE 8-19 The second step of the wizard for creating a new menu item extension.

After you complete the wizard, Visual Studio will prompt you with a new feature element that defines the custom action. Listing 8-10 shows sample content for such a file.

LISTING 8-10 A sample feature element for provisioning a menu item extension

```
<?xml version="1.0" encoding="utf-8"?>
<Elements xmlns="http://schemas.microsoft.com/sharepoint/">
  <CustomAction Id="db823841-8f6c-4b9a-912d-2b839eeddb43.SendDocumentToContact"
                RegistrationType="List"
                RegistrationId="101"
                Location="EditControlBlock"
                Sequence="10001"
                Title="Send document to the Contacts App">
    <!--
    Update the Url below to the page you want the custom action to use.
    Start the URL with the token ~remoteAppUrl if the page is in the
    associated web project, use ~appWebUrl if page is in the app project.
    -->
    <UrlAction Url="~appWebUrl/Pages/SendDocument.aspx" />
  </CustomAction>
</Elements>
```

The *UrlAction* element, within the *CustomAction* element, defines a new menu item that targets the ECB menu of any item within a document library, as declared by attributes *RegistrationType = List* and *RegistrationId = 101*. For further details about the various options for the attributes of *CustomAction* and *UrlAction* elements, please read Chapter 12. Notice also the *Id* attribute of the *CustomAction* element, which defines the unique ID of the menu item and should be a unique literal value. Moreover, the *Url* attribute defined in the *UrlAction* element can reference content under the app web, in case you start the URL with the *~appWebUrl* token. Otherwise, if the target content is under the host web, you can start the URL with the *~remoteAppUrl* token.

The next steps are to create a page with a name corresponding to the one you provided while defining the custom action, and to start debugging the app. To create a new page, right-click the Pages folder in the SharePoint app project and select Add | New Item | Page. Moving into a document library within the host web, you will notice that the ECB menu contains the new item Send Document To The Contacts App (see Figure 8-20). Click this menu item and you will be redirected to the custom page you just created.

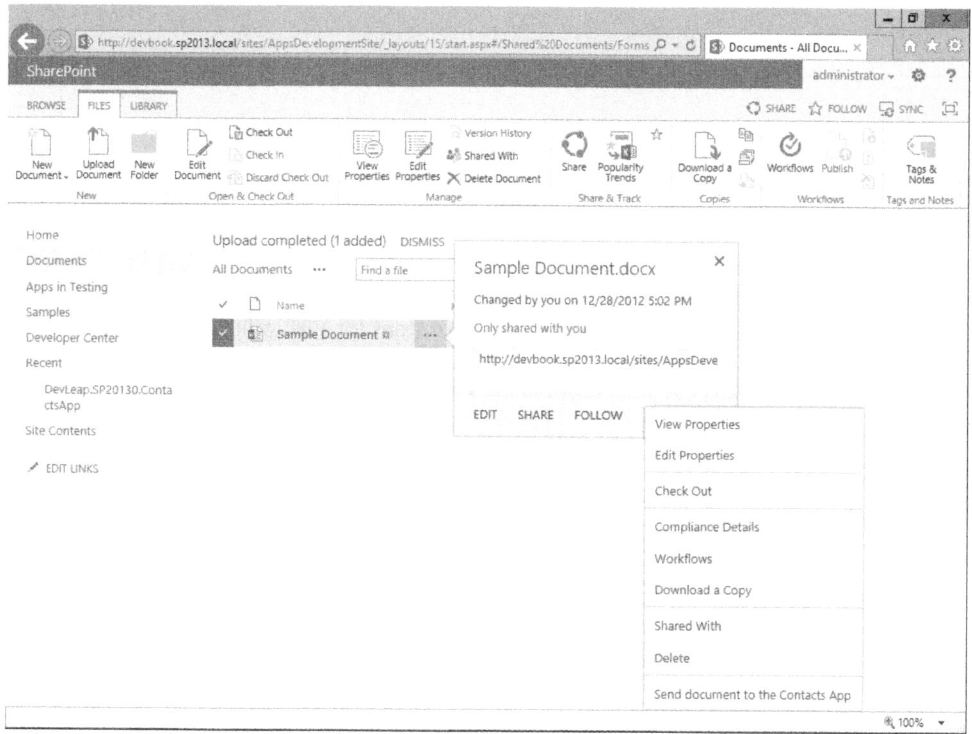

FIGURE 8-20 The custom menu item extension in action.

Behind the scenes, the SharePoint environment invokes a *GET* method to redirect the browser to a URL such as the following:

```
_layouts/15/appredirect.aspx?client_id={clientId}&redirect_uri=%7EappWebUrl%2FPages%2FSendDocum
ent%2Easpx
```

where the *{clientId}* argument is a token describing the current context. If you want to provide some arguments to the target URL—for example, the ID of the source document or the *ListId* of the source library—you can modify the *Url* attribute of the *UrlAction* element, including some predefined tokens. Here is a sample *Url* value for this purpose:

```
<UrlAction Url="~appWebUrl/Pages/SendDocument.aspx?ItemId={ItemId}&amp;ListId={ListId}" />
```

All the available URL tokens will be discussed in the "Custom actions" section of Chapter 12.

Many menu item customizations apply to custom ribbons, as well. To add a custom ribbon, for example, right-click the SharePoint app project and select Add | New Item | Ribbon Custom Action. A wizard will ask you questions very similar to those for creating a new menu item. This time, however, you can choose from only three scope values: *List Template*, *List Instance*, and *None*. While the first two scopes are the same as before, while creating custom menu items, the *None* option creates a ribbon command independent from any target scope.

The second step of the wizard (Figure 8-21) is specific for ribbons and asks you to provide information about the location of the ribbon command, the caption, and the target URL. The location of the ribbon can be one of the predefined locations (see Chapter 12) or a custom location.

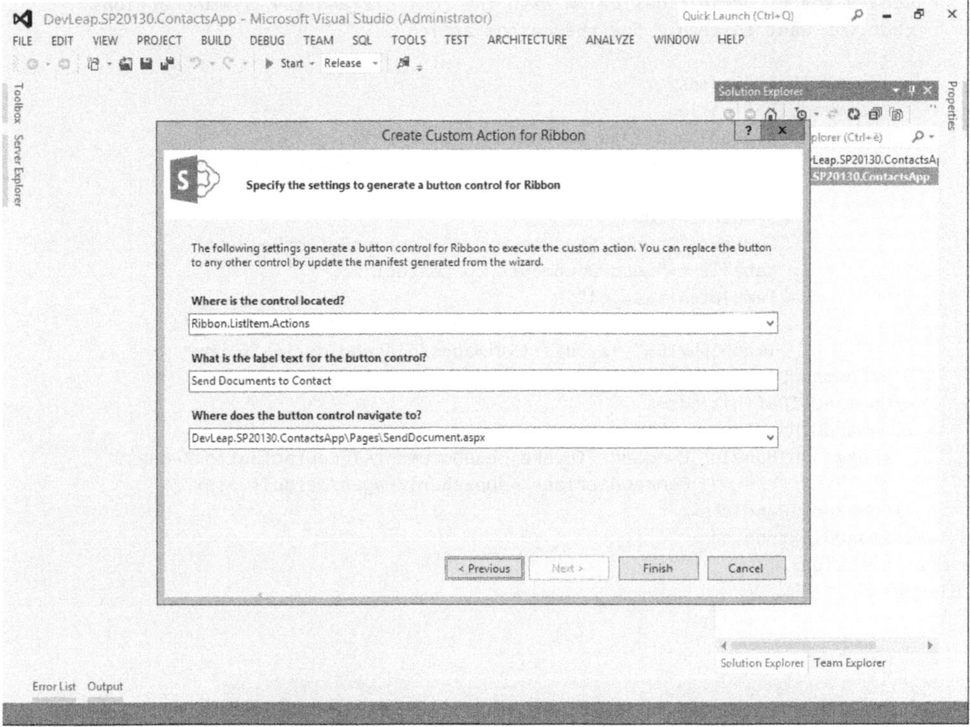

FIGURE 8-21 The second step of the wizard for creating a new ribbon command extension.

Once again, the result of the wizard will be an XML file defining a feature element of type *CustomAction*. This time, the *CustomAction* will use the syntax to define a ribbon command. (For more details about defining ribbon commands, ribbon tabs, and groups, read Chapter 12.) An interesting thing to notice is that with a ribbon command, you can either define a target URL to redirect the end user to, or you can provide a JavaScript set of instructions to execute directly in the context of the current page. Listing 8-11 shows the resulting XML feature element, while Figure 8-22 illustrates the resulting ribbon command.

LISTING 8-11 A sample feature element for provisioning a menu item extension

```
<?xml version="1.0" encoding="utf-8"?>
<Elements xmlns="http://schemas.microsoft.com/sharepoint/">
  <CustomAction Id="56116170-9f53-4000-ba3e-5eafe9c43ec3.SendDocumentsToContact"
                RegistrationType="List"
                RegistrationId="101"
                Location="CommandUI.Ribbon"
                Sequence="10001"
                Title="Invoke &apos;SendDocumentsToContact&apos; action">
    <CommandUIExtension>
      <!--
      Update the UI definitions below with the controls and the command actions
      that you want to enable for the custom action.
      -->
      <CommandUIDefinitions>
        <CommandUIDefinition
        Location="Ribbon.Documents.Manage.Controls._children">
          <Button Id="Ribbon.Documents.Manage.SendDocumentsToContactButton"
                  Alt="Send Documents to Contact"
                  Sequence="100"
                  Command="Invoke_SendDocumentsToContactButtonRequest"
                  LabelText="Send Documents to Contact"
                  TemplateAlias="o1"
                  Image32by32="_layouts/15/images/placeholder32x32.png"
                  Image16by16="_layouts/15/images/placeholder16x16.png" />
        </CommandUIDefinition>
      </CommandUIDefinitions>
      <CommandUIHandlers>
        <CommandUIHandler Command="Invoke_SendDocumentsToContactButtonRequest"
                          CommandAction="~appWebUrl/Pages/Default.aspx"/>
      </CommandUIHandlers>
    </CommandUIExtension >
  </CustomAction>
</Elements>
```

FIGURE 8-22 The custom ribbon command extension created in the sample.

Autohosted apps

This section will move on from the SharePoint-hosted scenario to discuss the autohosted hosting model. The autohosted model uses a site that is automatically provisioned for you on Windows Azure websites. Thus, you can take advantage of the out-of-the-box capabilities of Windows Azure websites, including multitenancy, load balancing, high availability, and support for the SQL Azure data repository.

Creating an autohosted app

From a practical viewpoint, an autohosted app can do almost everything a SharePoint-hosted app can do. However, by default, an autohosted app does not have an app web for storing data and information; instead, it uses a persistence infrastructure of its own, which can be based on SQL Azure. The autohosted model works only for SharePoint sites hosted on Office 365 or SharePoint Online. At the time of this writing, Microsoft has not yet announced the pricing model for hosting apps on Windows Azure websites. In fact, so far, apps hosted on Windows Azure cannot be published to the Office Store.

To create an autohosted app, you can start Visual Studio 2012 and create a new SharePoint app. In the first step of the resulting wizard, provide the URL of an Office 365–hosted site and choose the autohosted hosting model. The procedure may be similar, but the solution outline (see Figure 8-23) is slightly different compared to a SharePoint-hosted app.

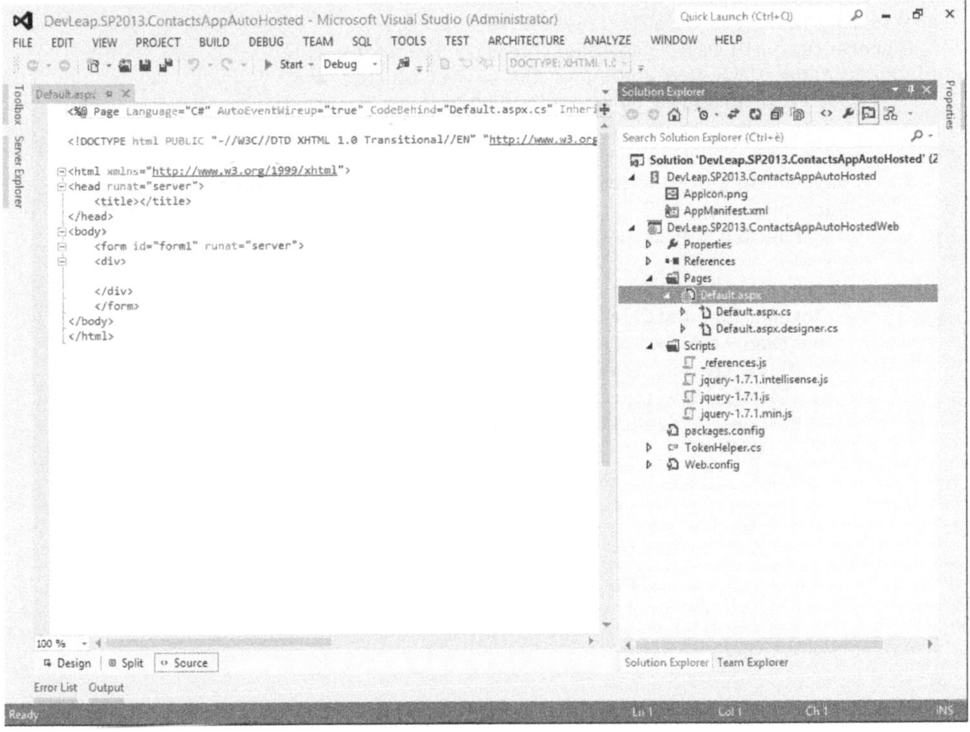

FIGURE 8-23 The solution outline for an autohosted app for SharePoint.

The outline includes a classic ASP.NET web application, which can be any kind of ASP.NET web application, as well as a SharePoint app project, which contains only the AppIcon.png and AppManifest.xml files. These two files are the same as those of a SharePoint-hosted app. You could add to the SharePoint app project feature elements for provisioning content types, pages, lists, and so on; however, these elements would require an app website. On the contrary, because you are developing an autohosted app, you will probably prefer to benefit from the Windows Azure environment instead of using SharePoint for storing data and content of your app.

The ASP.NET web application is made of a Pages folder with a Default.aspx page, a Scripts folder with some useful JavaScript files, the classic web.config file, and a TokenHelper.cs file, which supports the application in managing and handling the secure communication with SharePoint. The Default.aspx file, unlike the SharePoint-hosted app page, will have some .NET code behind it. If you open the Default.aspx.cs file, you will find code similar to Listing 8-12.

LISTING 8-12 The .NET code behind the Default.aspx page of an autohosted app

```
using System;
using System.Collections.Generic;
using System.Linq;
using System.Web;
using System.Web.UI;
using System.Web.UI.WebControls;

namespace DevLeap.SP2013.ContactsAppAutoHostedWeb.Pages {
    public partial class Default : System.Web.UI.Page {
        protected void Page_Load(object sender, EventArgs e) {
            // The following code gets the client context and
            // Title property by using TokenHelper.
            // To access other properties, you may need to request
            // permissions on the host web.
            var contextToken = TokenHelper.GetContextTokenFromRequest(
            Page.Request);
            var hostWeb = Page.Request["SPHostUrl"];

            using (var clientContext =
              TokenHelper.GetClientContextWithContextToken(
              hostWeb, contextToken, Request.Url.Authority)) {
                clientContext.Load(clientContext.Web, web => web.Title);
                clientContext.ExecuteQuery();
                Response.Write(clientContext.Web.Title);
            }
        }
    }
}
```

The main part of the code is the *Page_Load* method, where the page retrieves the *Title* property of the host web and writes it back to the HTTP response. Because the autohosted app site is hosted outside SharePoint, the code needs to retrieve a security context token with proper authorizations to access the host web and its properties. The following line does the magic:

```
var contextToken = TokenHelper.GetContextTokenFromRequest(Page.Request);
```

It uses the *TokenHelper* class, which is automatically generated by the project template, and that class reads a few arguments from the query string to create a secured communication session against the host web. The code of the *TokenHelper* class is open, you can read it and eventually change it. Of course, just because you can it does not mean you should change it. Probably the best thing to do is to read through the *TokenHelper* class—without changing it—to better understand how it works with the CSOM. You can see that the page uses the CSOM to retrieve the *Title* of the host web and creates a *ClientContext* object instance based on the *contextToken* gained through the page request. You can replace this code with anything else, and if you like to interact with the host web, you can simply use the CSOM to provide an authenticated and authorized context token to the *ClientContext*. (For more thorough detail on the CSOM, see Chapter 7.)

If you start debugging the app, you will have to provide credentials to access the Office 365 environment before you are presented with the page for trusting the app. Because an autohosted app works outside the context of SharePoint, you will always have to trust it during installation. Next, you will be redirected to the site hosting the app. Notice that while debugging in your development environment, the autohosted app site will run locally on Internet Information Services (IIS) Express so that you can debug it on your local machine. In the next section, you will learn how to publish the app, once you have finished development and testing.

As you can see from the output of the app in the web browser, you can control all the UI and UX details for an autohosted app. Thus, the layout of the output is up to you and your code.

Converting a site to a SharePoint app

Starting from scratch is one way to create your SharePoint App, but luckily for ASP.NET developers, there is another way: you can convert a classic ASP.NET project into a SharePoint autohosted app, meaning you can take advantage of the new and more productive MVC4 (Model-View-Controller 4.0) pattern available in ASP.NET 4.x. To try this option, create a new solution made of an ASP.NET 4.0 site based on MVC4, or use an already existing site you want to convert to a SharePoint app. Right-click the web project node in Solution Explorer and select the Add App For SharePoint Project menu item (Figure 8-24). Of course, you can use this functionality against any kind of ASP.NET project, not only with MVC4 sites.

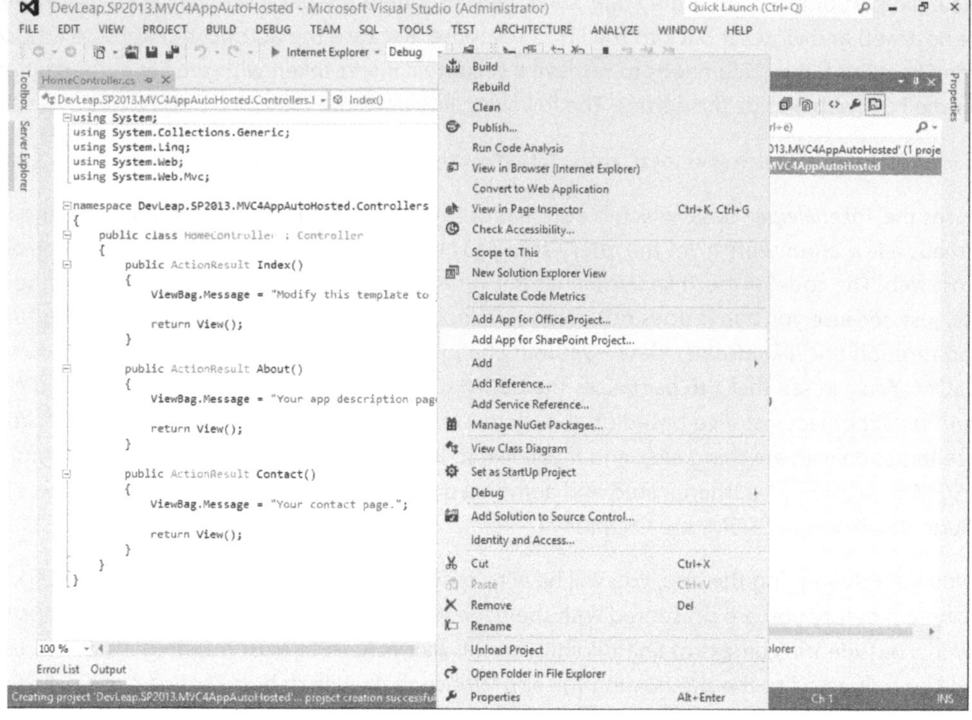

FIGURE 8-24 The menu item for creating a SharePoint app from an already existing ASP.NET website.

Important Do not choose a .NET version greater than 4.0 because, at the time of this writing, ASP.NET 4.5 is not supported by the autohosted apps environment on Windows Azure. Of course, this might change in the future.

Next, provide the URL of the host web, on Office 365 or SharePoint Online, for publishing the already existing ASP.NET website. Once you do, a new SharePoint app project will be added to the solution and some new references will be added to the ASP.NET web project. The name of the SharePoint app project will be the same of the ASP.NET web project, ending with the *.SharePoint* suffix. Moreover, the action will add a *TokenHelper* class to the ASP.NET web project, in order to support the SharePoint 2013 authentication and authorization environment. Now, the ASP.NET web project is the UI for the SharePoint app project. In fact, if you open the property grid of the SharePoint app, you can see that the MVC4 project is configured in the Web Project property of the app. See Figure 8-25 for details.

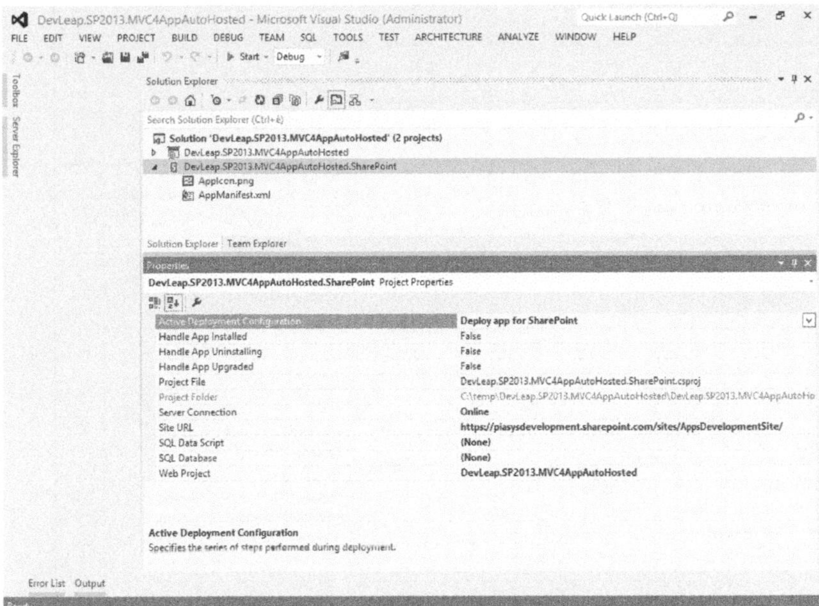

FIGURE 8-25 The property grid of the SharePoint autohosted app with the Web Project property in evidence.

Handling a SQL Azure database

As you can see from Figure 8-25, there are also properties for configuring a SQL Database project and a SQL Data script. Suppose the example autohosted app uses a custom SQL Azure database on the back end for storing contacts data. In this case, you can add a new SQL Server database to the current solution. To do so, right-click the solution and choose Add | New Project | SQL Server Database Project. Open the properties of the database project and configure its target platform to SQL Azure.

More Info If you do not configure the target platform to SQL Azure, Visual Studio will advise you and change it for you, as soon as you wire the SQL Database project to the SharePoint app. In fact, the only database platform supported by autohosted apps is SQL Azure.

Now add a new table for holding contacts to the database project (Add | New Item | Table) and configure some fields. For the sake of simplicity, in addition to the *Id* primary key field, configure just the following text fields: ContactDescription, ContactPhone, and ContactEmail. The final layout of the table will be similar to Figure 8-26.

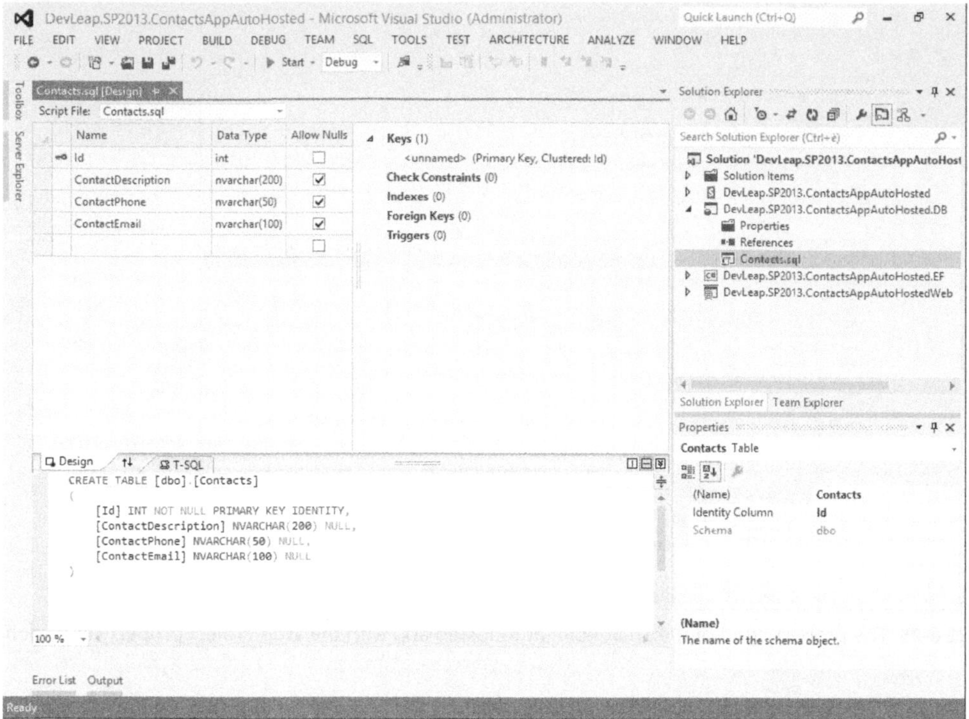

FIGURE 8-26 The designer of the Contacts table defined in the SQL Azure database.

Now you can configure the SQL Database project as the target database for the SharePoint app simply by selecting the new database project in the SQL Database property of the SharePoint app project.

To autopopulate the database with sample data, you can add an SQL script to the project and configure it in the SQL Data Script property of the SharePoint app. In real scenarios, you will probably use this script to autopopulate lookup tables, as well as to execute any other SQL script that you will need to commit just after having created the SQL Azure database.

Listing 8-13 provides the code excerpt you can use to retrieve an instance of a *SqlConnection* object for accessing the SQL Azure database—for example, for using it with Entity Framework. In fact, you cannot configure the connection string directly in the web.config file of your autohosted app, because while writing your app you won't know where the SQL Azure database will be deployed. To solve this issue, the SharePoint Client Object Model provides you with a class named *AppInstance*, which has a method called *TryGetAppDatabaseConnectionDirect* that accepts the current *ClientContext* instance and a couple of output arguments for trying to retrieve the current database connection.

LISTING 8-13 The .NET code to retrieve the *SqlConnection* object of a SQL Azure database for an autohosted app

```
SqlConnection connection;
Boolean isReadOnly;

var contextToken = TokenHelper.GetContextTokenFromRequest(
HttpContext.Current.Request);
var hostWeb = request["SPHostUrl"];

using (var clientContext = TokenHelper.GetClientContextWithContextToken(
    hostWeb, contextToken, request.Url.Authority)) {
        AppInstance.TryGetAppDatabaseConnectionDirect(clientContext,
            out connection, out isReadOnly);

        // This code block closes the connection in case of usage with Entity
        // Framework
        if (connection.State != System.Data.ConnectionState.Closed) {
            connection.Close();
        }
}
```

While working locally, the SQL Azure database will be deployed on your local machine under a connection string like the following:

```
Data Source=(localdb)\Projects;Initial Catalog=DevLeap.SP2013.ContactsAppAutoHosted.
DB;Integrated Security=True;Pooling=False;Connect Timeout=30;ApplicationIntent=ReadWrite
```

While on Windows Azure, the connection string will map to a real SQL Azure environment. Now you are free to use the database from any kind of code for accessing the database, such as direct *System.Data.SqlClient* objects, Entity Framework, or whatever else you like. In the companion source code, you will find a complete code example of using Entity Framework for accessing the Contacts entities, rendering the output in a read-only grid. Take a look at the result in Figure 8-27.

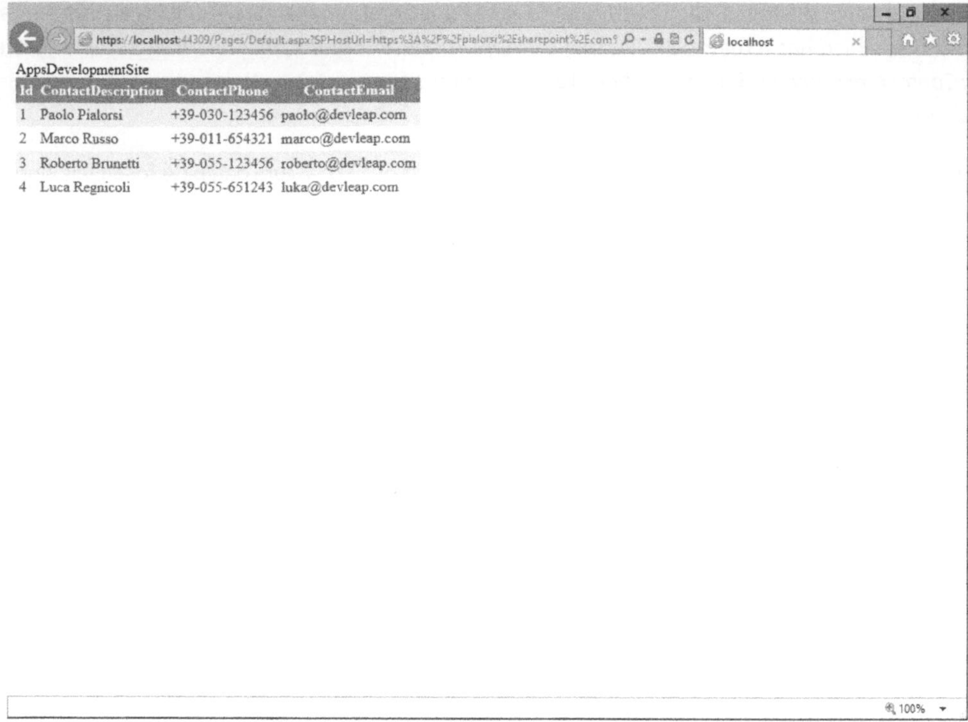

FIGURE 8-27 The sample SharePoint app based on SQL Azure rendering the list of Contacts entities.

The SharePoint *Chrome* control

As shown in Figure 8-27, the output is extremely simple, leaving a great deal of room for improvement to the UI and UX. For example, the app is missing a command bar to interact with the SharePoint environment, as well as a Back button to return to the host web. Such UI components were provided by default for SharePoint-hosted apps. You could create chrome to mimic a SharePoint-hosted app, but you don't have to: SharePoint provides a control called a *Chrome control*, which renders based on some HTML/JavaScript/CSS code and can be included in any SharePoint app page. Listing 8-14 provides the source code of the Default.aspx page of an autohosted app with the *Chrome* control in place.

LISTING 8-14 The Default.aspx page of the autohosted app with the *Chrome* control in place

```
<%@ Page Language="C#" AutoEventWireup="true" CodeBehind="Default.aspx.cs"
Inherits="DevLeap.SP2013.ContactsAppAutoHostedWeb.Pages.Default" %>
<!DOCTYPE html PUBLIC "-//W3C//DTD XHTML 1.0 Transitional//EN"
"http://www.w3.org/TR/xhtml1/DTD/xhtml1-transitional.dtd">
<html xmlns="http://www.w3.org/1999/xhtml">
<head runat="server">
    <title>Contacts Autohosted App with Chrome</title>
    <script type="text/javascript"
        src="//ajax.aspnetcdn.com/ajax/4.0/1/MicrosoftAjax.js"></script>
    <script type="text/javascript"
        src="//ajax.aspnetcdn.com/ajax/jQuery/jquery-1.7.2.min.js"></script>
    <script type="text/javascript">
        "use strict";

        var hostweburl;

        //load the SharePoint resources
        $(document).ready(function () {
            //Get the URI decoded URL.
            hostweburl =
                decodeURIComponent(
                    getQueryStringParameter("SPHostUrl")
            );

            // The SharePoint js files URL are in the form:
            // web_url/_layouts/15/resource
            var scriptbase = hostweburl + "/_layouts/15/";

            // Load the js file and continue to the
            //   success handler
            $.getScript(scriptbase + "SP.UI.Controls.js", renderChrome)
        });

        // Callback for the onCssLoaded event defined
        //  in the options object of the chrome control
        function chromeLoaded() {
            // When the page has loaded the required
            //  resources for the chrome control,
            //  display the page body.
            $("body").show();
        }
```

```
        //Function to prepare the options and render the control
        function renderChrome() {
            // The Help, Account and Contact pages receive the
            //   same query string parameters as the main page
            var options = {
                "appIconUrl": "../AppIcon.png",
                "appTitle": "Contacts Autohosted App with Chrome",
                "appHelpPageUrl": "Help.html?"
                    + document.URL.split("?")[1],
                // The onCssLoaded event allows you to
                //  specify a callback to execute when the
                //  chrome resources have been loaded.
                "onCssLoaded": "chromeLoaded()",
                "settingsLinks": [
                    {
                        "linkUrl": "Account.html?"
                            + document.URL.split("?")[1],
                        "displayName": "Account settings"
                    },
                    {
                        "linkUrl": "Contact.html?"
                            + document.URL.split("?")[1],
                        "displayName": "Contact us"
                    }
                ]
            };

            var nav = new SP.UI.Controls.Navigation(
                                    "chrome_placeholder",
                                    options
                                );
            nav.setVisible(true);
        }

        // Function to retrieve a query string value.
        // For production purposes you may want to use
        //  a library to handle the query string.
        function getQueryStringParameter(paramToRetrieve) {
            var params =
                document.URL.split("?")[1].split("&");
            var strParams = "";
            for (var i = 0; i < params.length; i = i + 1) {
                var singleParam = params[i].split("=");
                if (singleParam[0] == paramToRetrieve)
                    return singleParam[1];
            }
        }
    </script>
</head>
```

```
<body>
    <form id="form1" runat="server">
        <div id="chrome_placeholder"></div>
        <div style="margin: 10px;">
            <h1 class="ms-accentText">Contacts App</h1>
            <h2 class="ms-accentText">The list of Contacts</h2>
            <div id="MainContent">

                <asp:GridView ID="gridContacts" runat="server" CellPadding="4"
                    ForeColor="#333333" GridLines="None">
                    <AlternatingRowStyle BackColor="White" />
                    <EditRowStyle BackColor="#2461BF" />
                    <FooterStyle BackColor="#507CD1" Font-Bold="True"
                    ForeColor="White" />
                    <HeaderStyle BackColor="#507CD1" Font-Bold="True"
                    ForeColor="White" />
                    <PagerStyle BackColor="#2461BF" ForeColor="White"
                        HorizontalAlign="Center" />
                    <RowStyle BackColor="#EFF3FB" />
                    <SelectedRowStyle BackColor="#D1DDF1" Font-Bold="True"
                        ForeColor="#333333" />
                    <SortedAscendingCellStyle BackColor="#F5F7FB" />
                    <SortedAscendingHeaderStyle BackColor="#6D95E1" />
                    <SortedDescendingCellStyle BackColor="#E9EBEF" />
                    <SortedDescendingHeaderStyle BackColor="#4870BE" />
                </asp:GridView>
            </div>
        </div>
    </form>
</body>
</html>
```

The code contains a couple of JavaScript inclusions in the header of the page. Taken from the official Microsoft CDN, these JavaScript files support jQuery and AJAX. Next, an explicit script injects the JavaScript file SP.UI.Controls.js from the source host web URL. Moreover, the script prepares the *Chrome* control for rendering, providing the ID of a *DIV* control that will be the placeholder for the *Chrome* control, as well as a set of options. These options define the title, icon, help page URL, and additional Settings menu links for rendering in the *Chrome* control. Compare Figure 8-28 with Figure 8-27 to fully appreciate the results of this makeover. Notice the custom items in the Settings menu, as well as the Back button to return to the host site.

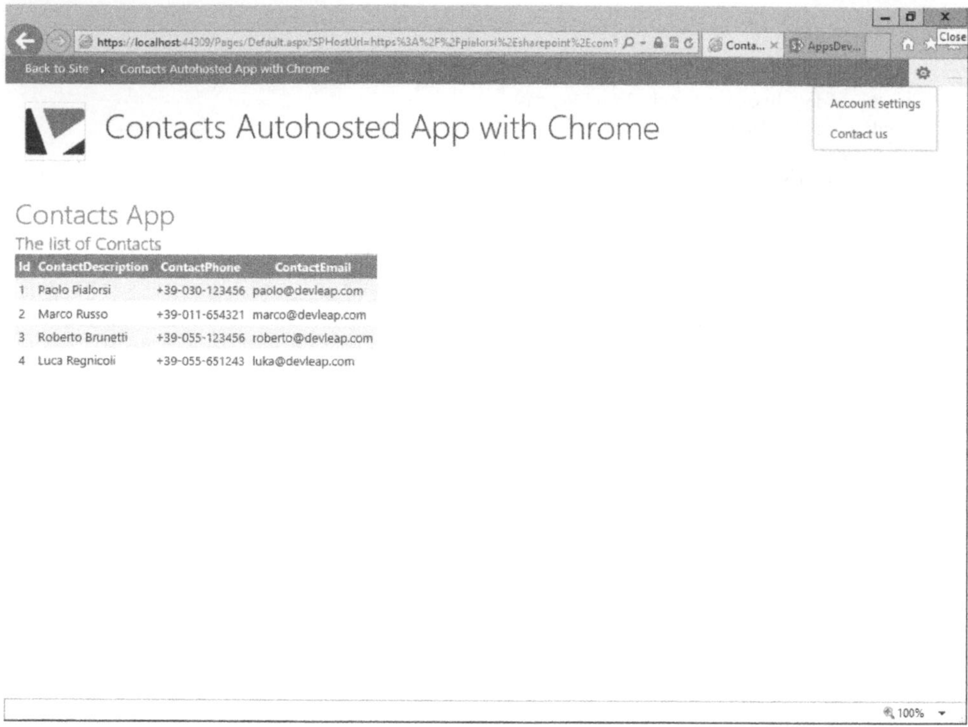

FIGURE 8-28 The Default.aspx page of the autohosted app, with the *Chrome* control in action.

One last thing to emphasize about the *Chrome* control is that when you change the design of the host site, the app site will reflect the same choices because the *Chrome* control loads its styles dynamically.

Provider-hosted apps

A provider-hosted app is almost like an autohosted app, except it uses a third-party provider for hosting the web application rather than Windows Azure websites. The third-party provider can manually provision Windows Azure or can be based on anything else, even an on-premises server farm of your own. On its second page, the Visual Studio wizard for creating a provider-hosted app asks you to choose between using Windows Azure Access Control Services (ACS) for authentication and authorization, rather than using a high-trust configuration based on a private certificate and asymmetric keys exchange (see Figure 8-29). The first choice is suitable when your app will be used on sites hosted on Office 365. The second choice, High Trust, is suitable for on-premises scenarios and will be discussed later, in the "Security infrastructure" section.

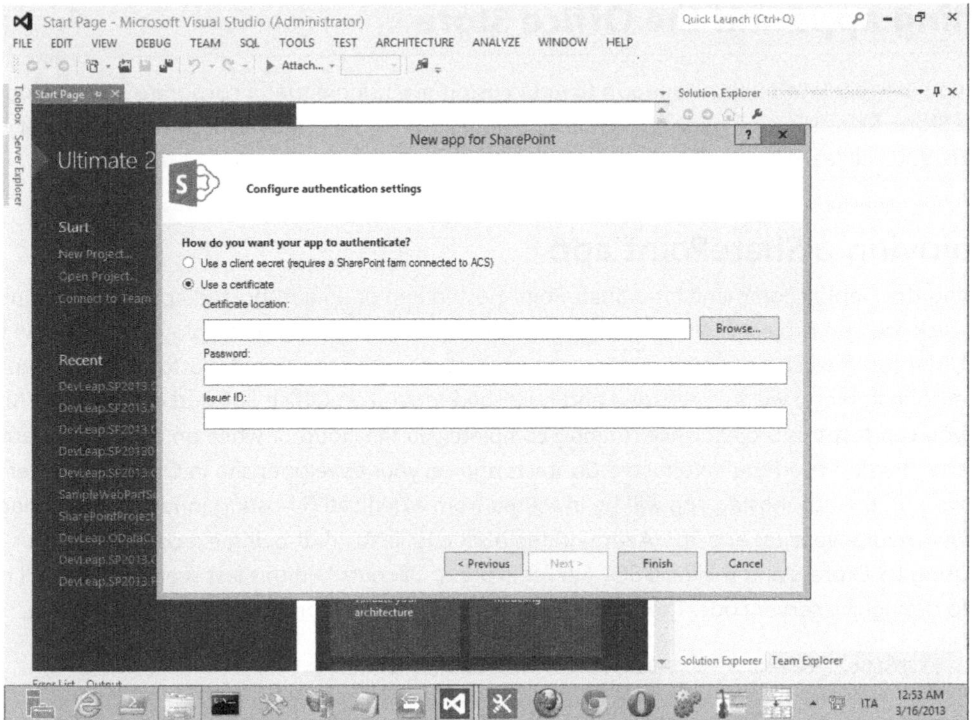

FIGURE 8-29 The second step of the wizard for creating a provider-hosted app.

Behind the scenes, the only difference between an autohosted app and a provider-hosted app is a line in the AppManifest.xml file. An autohosted app has the following piece of XML in the *AppPrincipal* element:

```
<AppPrincipal>
    <AutoDeployedWebApplication/>
  </AppPrincipal>
```

while a provider-hosted app contains this:

```
<AppPrincipal>
    <RemoteWebApplication ClientId="*" />
  </AppPrincipal>
```

As you can see, the *ClientId* attribute has a value of * (that is, *any*) because you will have to provide the real value for this data during the publishing phase only. While developing and debugging, you will not need it. Instead, you will use the *localhost* site hosted by IIS Express. (Again, the "Security infrastructure" section provides more detail.)

Publishing apps and the Office Store

Now you are ready to publish your app to your customers, using either a corporate app catalog or the Office Store. Regardless of which you choose, you need to prepare the proper output files first. In this section, you will learn how to achieve these results.

Deploying a SharePoint app

Invoking the Deploy command for a SharePoint-hosted app or an autohosted app is easy: simply right-click the app project in Visual Studio Solution Explorer and click the Deploy command on the menu. The result will be a complete deployment of your app on the target platform. For example, your autohosted app will be packaged and published for you on Office 365 and on Windows Azure. Now you can test this project while running completely in the cloud or while on the target platform. Suppose you deployed the autohosted Contacts app on your developer site in Office 365. After deployment, the autohosted app will be executed from a dedicated hosting infrastructure, using Windows Azure websites and SQL Azure on the back end, instead of being executed from your localhost using IIS Express and the local SQL Server Express. Of course, in this last scenario, you will not be able to debug the server code. The URL of your app will become something like the following:

```
https://52b8b0c7-78da-4a07-9d2b-3190e07625f5.o365apps.net/
```

As you can see, the URL references the Office 365 autohosted apps environment (*o365apps.net*), and every app installation receives a unique GUID-based host name. If you want to remove the app, you can invoke the Retract menu item, still available by right-clicking the app project in Solution Explorer, or you can explicitly remove it from the target host site.

Publishing a SharePoint app

When you're ready to publish your app, right-click the SharePoint app project in Solution Explorer and choose Publish from the menu to open the publishing wizard. For SharePoint-hosted and autohosted apps, the wizard only allows you to click the Finish button to create the package for publishing. The result will be an APP file placed inside the app.publish subfolder of the Debug or Release folder of the project, depending the compilation type you are using.

Important When publishing a final release of your app, compile it in release mode. Do not publish the APP file taken from the Debug folder; publishing software compiled in debug mode is a very bad practice for security and performances reasons. Because the publishing wizard opens the destination folder for you by default, as long as you publish the app while in release mode, you should be safe.

The APP file is an ordinary ZIP file, but with .app extension instead. In fact, if you change the file extension from .app to .zip and you explore the content, you will find files and folders describing the app for publishing. For an autohosted app, for instance, you'll see the AppIcon.png file, the AppManifest.xml file, a DACPAC file for provisioning the database on SQL Azure, a ZIP file for provisioning the website onto Windows Azure websites (if necessary), resource files, and so on. For SharePoint-hosted apps, you will see the AppIcon.png file, the AppManifest.xml, and the resources files, as well as a WSP file, which will be used for provisioning all the SharePoint artifacts onto the app website. Figure 8-30 compares the outline of two APP files: one for a SharePoint-hosted app (on the left) and one for an autohosted app (on the right).

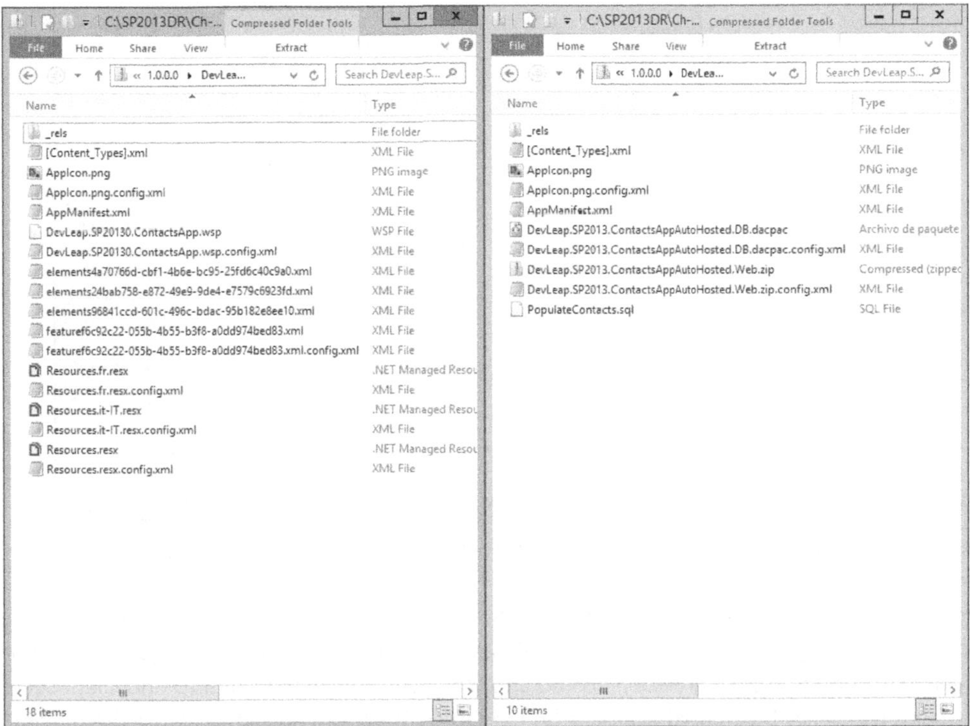

FIGURE 8-30 The contents of a SharePoint-hosted app's APP file (left) and an autohosted app's APP file (right), once renamed into ZIP.

In either case, you can manually upload the resulting APP file to a developer site for testing, publish it to a corporate app catalog, or submit it to the Office Store to make it publicly available.

While publishing a provider-hosted app, you are presented with a rich wizard. The first page asks you to select or create a new publishing profile (see Figure 8-31). It even offers you options for multiple profiles for testing, staging, production, and so on.

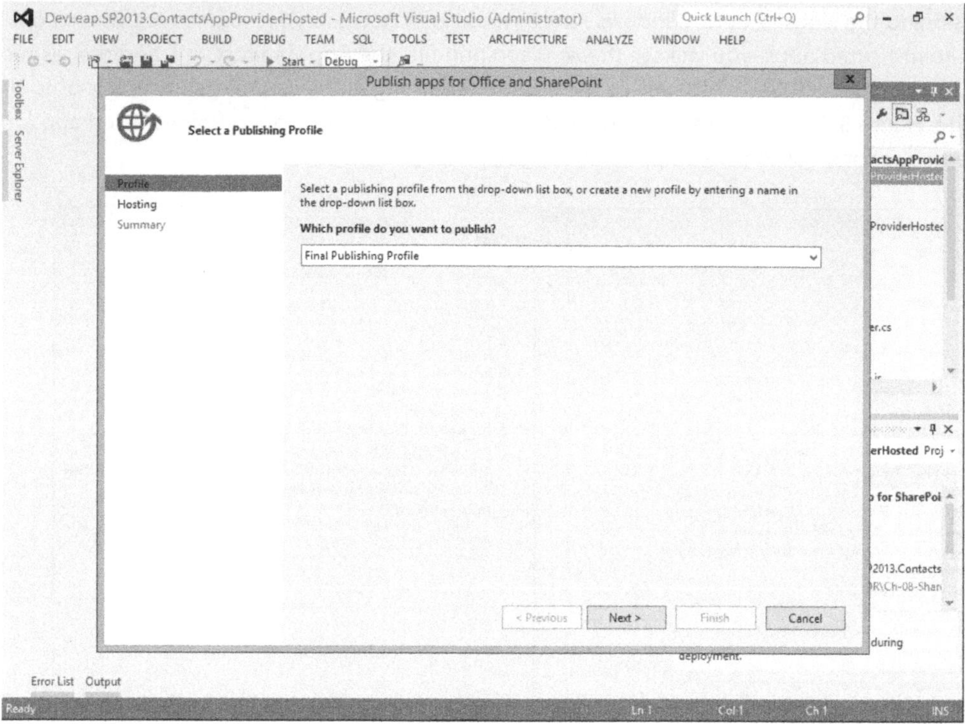

FIGURE 8-31 The first step of the publishing wizard for publishing a provider-hosted app.

The second page (Figure 8-32) asks you to provide information about the hosting environment, including the URL of the target site, the client ID, and the client secret for secure communication between SharePoint and the provider-hosted app. You can retrieve the client ID and client secret values from the Seller Dashboard available on the Office Store, or you can generate them from the target host site. (For more information, see the "Security infrastructure" section later in the chapter.

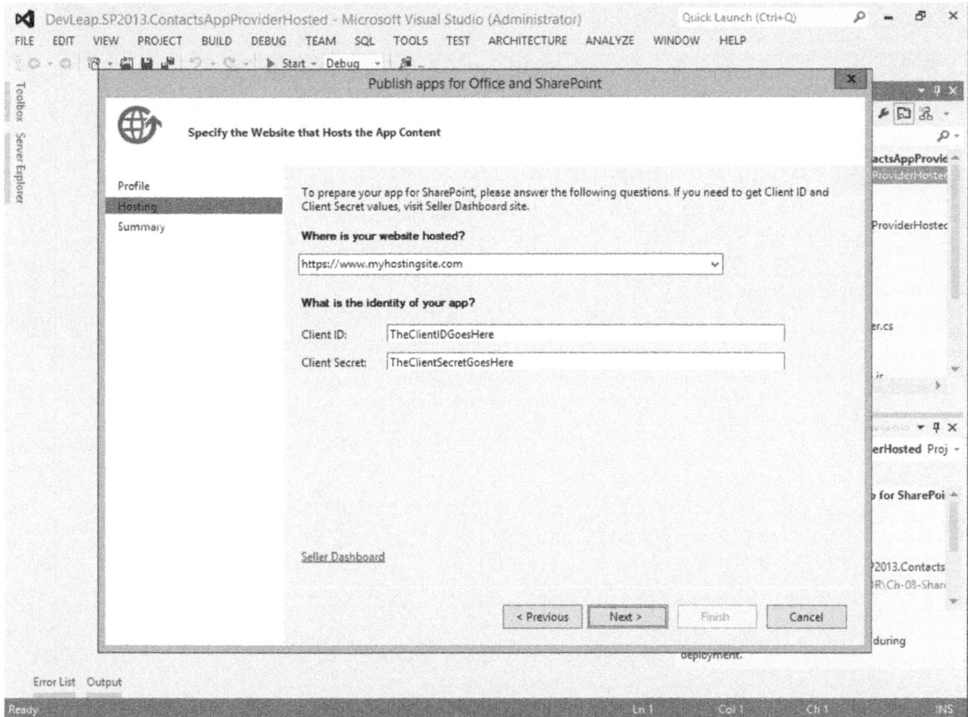

FIGURE 8-32 The second step of the publishing wizard for publishing a provider-hosted app.

The last page is just a recap of your settings. This time, the result of the publishing wizard will be a set of files: an APP file for publishing the app, a DEPLOY file (web deploy file) for the website deployment, and a ZIP file with the contents of the website.

The corporate app catalog

To publish an app to the corporate app catalog, you need to have the URL of the corporate app catalog site collection configured for your current web application or tenant, as well as a set of authorized credentials for publishing apps. Then you can simply upload the APP file to the catalog into the Apps For SharePoint library. The results will be similar to the corporate app catalog in Figure 8-33. In the section "App management configuration and deployment," you will learn how to configure an app catalog on your farm.

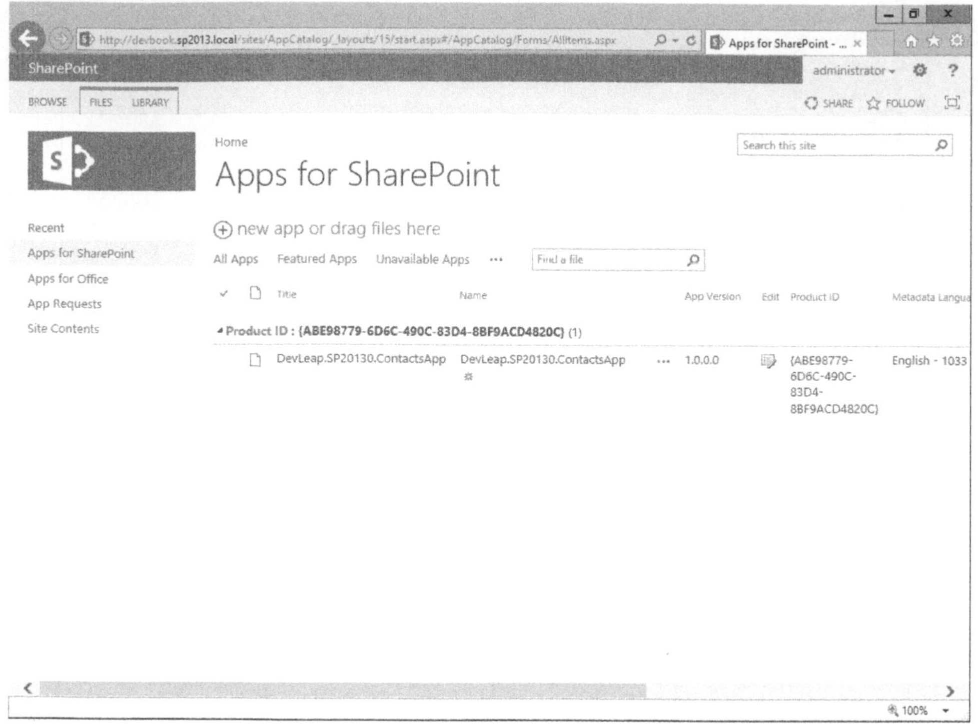

FIGURE 8-33 The list of apps for SharePoint published in a corporate app catalog.

Once you have configured a corporate app catalog for a web application or tenant, and you have published some apps on it, you can add an app to a target site by clicking Site Contents, and then Add An App. You can then choose apps published through the corporate app catalog by browsing a specific category of apps called From Your Organization. Figure 8-34 shows how the apps are presented to the end user. Notice that, for the sake of completeness, the app catalog in the figure also contains an autohosted app, which is not available in an on-premises scenario. Thus, the app catalog highlights this issue and does not allow the user to install that app.

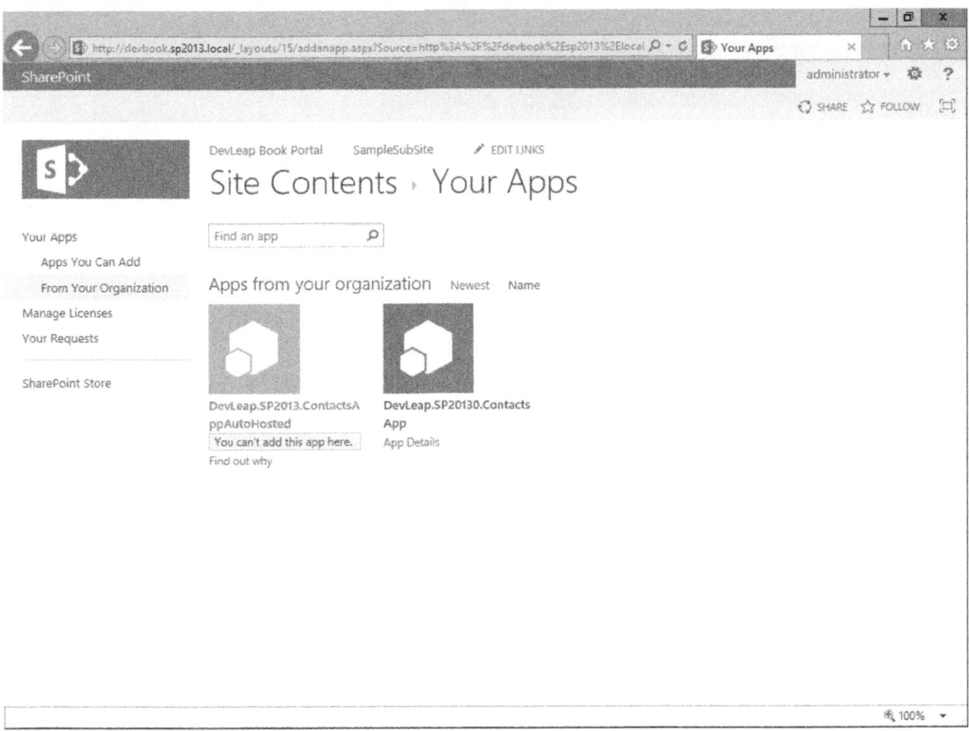

FIGURE 8-34 The user's view of the apps in a corporate app catalog.

If you are a farm administrator, you will be able to monitor app installation and usage from SharePoint Central Administration (SPCA).

The Office Store

What if you want to make your apps available for the entire world? In that case, you need to rely on the Office Store provided by Microsoft (*http://www.office.com/store*). To do so, you first need to create a seller account for publishing apps. With a valid and enabled account, you can access the Seller Dashboard at *https://sellerdashboard.microsoft.com*. There, after logging in with a valid Windows Live ID, you will be able to submit an app, manage your already submitted apps, register client IDs, and monitor metrics of selling and downloads of your apps. Figure 8-35 shows the first step for creating an app profile. You have to choose whether you are publishing an app for Office or SharePoint, or an app for Windows Azure. Note, however, that the Seller Dashboard is the same for both types of apps.

More Info For further information about how to create a seller account, read the document "How to: Create or edit your seller account in the Microsoft Seller Dashboard," available on MSDN online at *http://msdn.microsoft.com/en-us/library/office/apps/jj220034.aspx*.

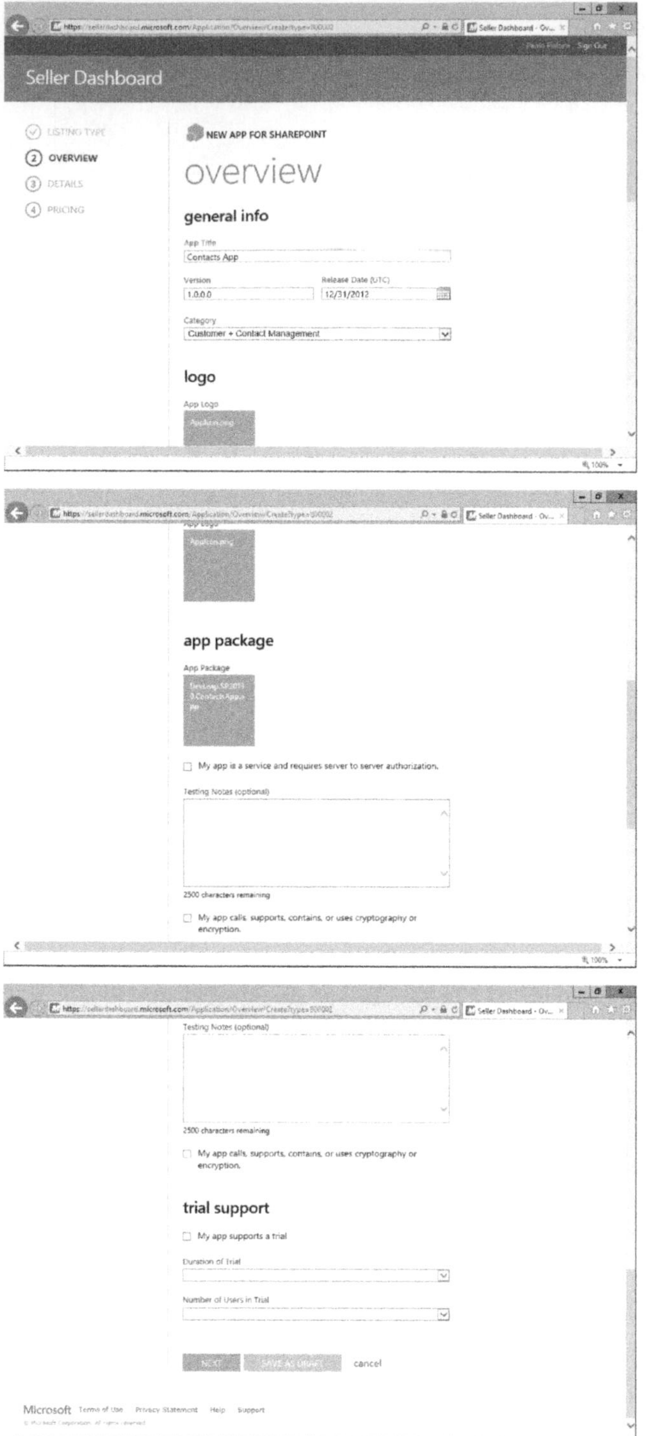

FIGURE 8-35 The first page of the wizard for submitting an app to the Office Store through the Seller Dashboard.

Click Next to go to the page for providing information about the app (title, version number, logo, category, screen shots, target markets, trial periods, and so on). As shown in Figure 8-36, during this phase you also must provide the APP file package.

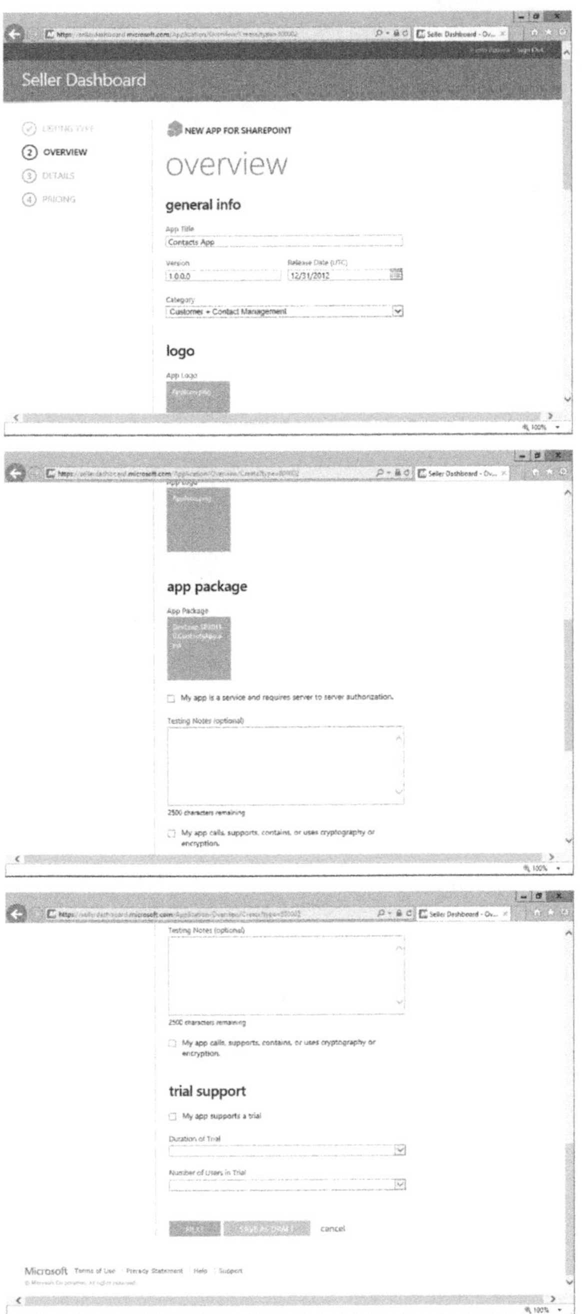

FIGURE 8-36 The second page of the wizard for submitting an app to the Office Store through the Seller Dashboard.

On the third page (Figure 8-37), you can provide descriptive information, up to five screen shots with a fixed size of 512×384 pixels, license information, and so on.

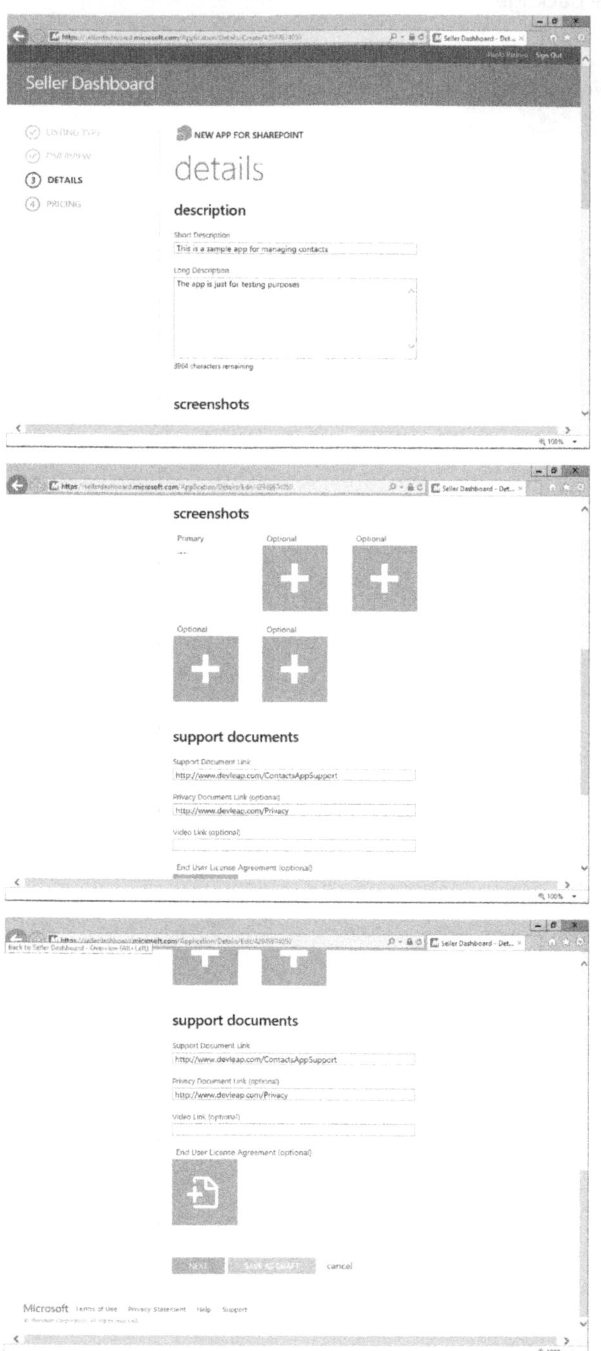

FIGURE 8-37 The third page of the wizard for submitting an app to the Office Store through the Seller Dashboard.

On the wizard's last page, shown in Figure 8-38, you can configure the price for your app or choose to make it freely available.

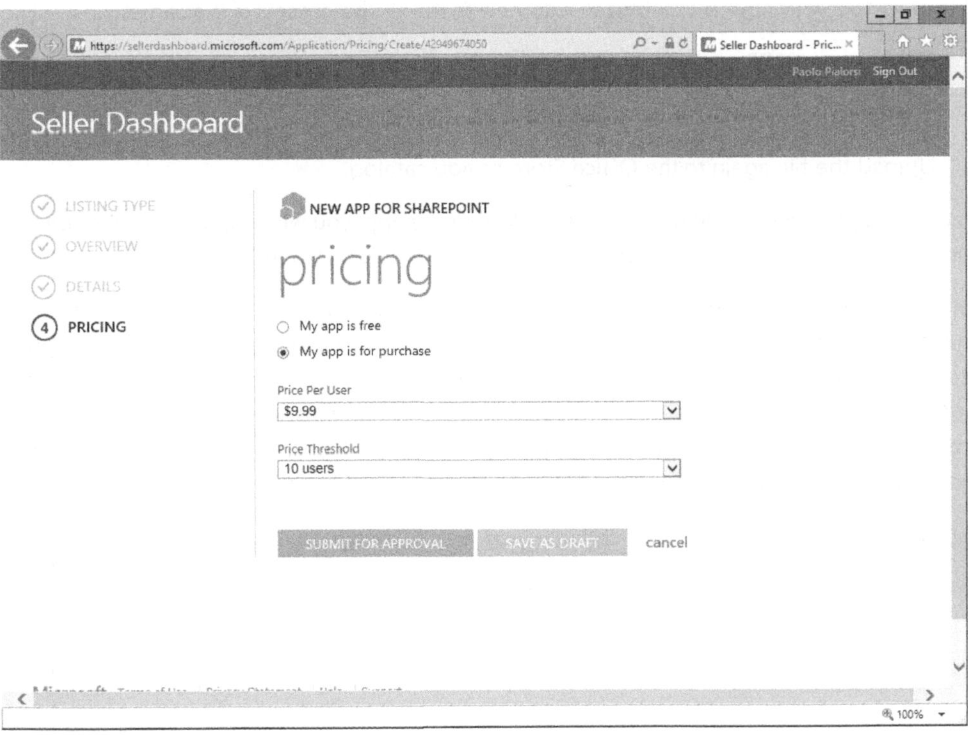

FIGURE 8-38 The last step for submitting an app to the Office Store through the Seller Dashboard.

Note You must provide your app's price on a per-user bases, but you can also specify the maximum number of user licenses that a customer can buy. If a customer buys a number of user licenses higher than the price threshold you set, he or she will pay only for the number of licenses configured in the Price Threshold field. Imagine you configure a price of $9.99 with a price threshold of 10 (as in Figure 8-38). Then, if a customer buys 20 copies of your app, he or she will pay only $99.90 (the price of 10 licenses), but will have the right to use up to 20 licenses.

Your app will be verified and checked against an approval process based on the rules outlined at the following URL: *http://msdn.microsoft.com/en-us/library/office/apps/jj220035*. Upon approval completion, your app will be available worldwide either on Office 365 or on-premises (as long as the farm administrators of the on-premises farm have enabled the capability to freely install apps from the Office Store).

As a seller, you will be able to monitor how your app sells on the market, as well as your revenues in the case of for-purchase apps.

Upgrading apps

The app model of SharePoint also provides a standard path for upgrading your apps. Whether you need to upgrade your app to fix a bug or add new features, the process is the same:

1. Create a new APP package with a new version number.
2. Change that information in AppManifest.xml file.
3. Upload the file again to the Office Store or app catalog.

Upon changing the version number and republishing the app, you will have a new subfolder in the app.publish folder. From there you will be able to get the new upgraded APP file.

For apps published through the Office Store, however, you will need to submit the new and updated version for approval before publishing to the end users. For apps published through a corporate app catalog, you simply update the APP file in the catalog's target Apps For SharePoint library. Regardless of the publishing environment you are using, existing installations will not be upgraded automatically. Instead, end users who have installed the app will be informed by the environment that a newer version is available, as shown in Figure 8-39.

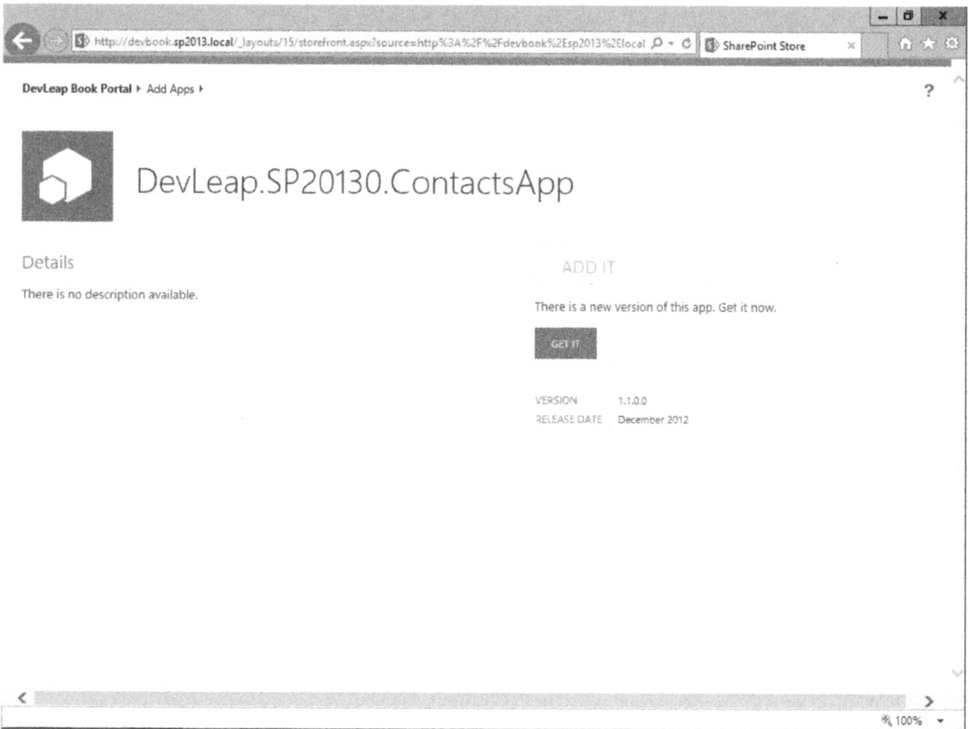

FIGURE 8-39 The notification of an available upgrade for an installed app.

Authorized users can upgrade the app by clicking the Get It button. During the upgrade process, the user will have to trust the app again. In fact, the upgraded version could have changed the permissions requirements. During the upgrade process, the app will show an informational message while on the Site Contents page.

The upgrade process for SharePoint-hosted apps is simple and easy. For autohosted apps, the upgrade of the Windows Azure website is handled on the Azure platform. The upgrade process for provider-hosted apps also involves the external publishing infrastructure, so be careful while upgrading these apps. In fact, you should not upgrade a provider-hosted app site introducing breaking changes, unless you are absolutely sure that all of your existing customers and users have already upgraded the app on their SharePoint environments. Usually, in these cases it would be better to keep different versions of the app online, on the provider side, to support customers who are reluctant to upgrade to the new versions of your app.

App management configuration and deployment

While you work on Office 365, the entire environment and application software is provided as a service, ready to use, according to the Software as a Service (SaaS) offering model. However, also having an on-premises farm that's fully functional and capable of supporting SharePoint apps can be very useful, especially while working in a development environment. In this section, you will learn how to configure a SharePoint 2013 on-premises farm to provide full support for the new app model. This section will assume that you already have a SharePoint 2013 farm ready for the app environment configuration.

First, you will need to configure the required service applications: the Subscription Settings service and the App Management service. To do so, you can use SPCA, or you can run a PowerShell script, as in Listing 8-15.

LISTING 8-15 A PowerShell script for configuring the services required for running the app model on-premises

```
Add-PSSnapin Microsoft.SharePoint.PowerShell -erroraction SilentlyContinue

$subSettingstName = "Subscription Settings Service"
$subSettingstDatabaseName = "SP2013_Farm_SubSettingsDB"
$appManagementName = "App Management Service"
$appManagementDatabaseName = "SP2013_Farm_AppManagementDB"

Write-Host "Creating Subscription Settings Service and Proxy..."
$subSvc = New-SPSubscriptionSettingsServiceApplication -ApplicationPool
$saAppPoolName
  -Name $subSettingstName -DatabaseName $subSettingstDatabaseName
$subSvcProxy = New-SPSubscriptionSettingsServiceApplicationProxy
  -ServiceApplication $subSvc
Get-SPServiceInstance | where-object {$_.TypeName -eq $subSettingstName} |
  Start-SPServiceInstance > $null
```

```
Write-Host "Creating App Management Service and Proxy..."
$appManagement = New-SPAppManagementServiceApplication -Name $appManagementName
  -DatabaseServer $databaseServerName -DatabaseName $appManagementDatabaseName
  -ApplicationPool $saAppPoolName
$appManagementProxy = New-SPAppManagementServiceApplicationProxy
  -ServiceApplication $appManagement -Name "$appManagementName Proxy"
Get-SPServiceInstance | where-object {$_.TypeName -eq $appManagementName} |
  Start-SPServiceInstance > $null
```

The very beginning of the script declares four literal variables that you can configure based on your naming conventions. The script simply creates the Subscription Settings service application, together with its proxy, and starts an instance of the service on the current server. The same happens for the App Management service application.

To configure the App Management service for supporting apps, first create a web application for hosting apps. To define such a web application, you need to determine the host name that will be used for that web application. For example, you could decide to install all the apps under a top-level domain dedicated to hosting apps (something like *company-apps.com*), or you could host apps in a subdomain of the main domain of your on-premises farm (something like *apps.company.com*). The former scenario is the one recommended by Microsoft in official product deployment guidelines. Configure your DNS accordingly by creating a catchall CNAME record in a new top-level domain or a subdomain in the already existing domain. The CNAME record should map to the host name where the apps will be installed. For example, in case your domain and host name is *company.com*, the CNAME will be for * or for **.apps*, respectively, and should map to *company.com*.

Next, create a new web application for hosting the apps and the app websites. Once again, you can use SPCA or PowerShell. Listing 8-16 demonstrates the PowerShell method.

LISTING 8-16 A PowerShell script for creating the web application for hosting apps

```
Add-PSSnapin Microsoft.SharePoint.PowerShell -erroraction SilentlyContinue

$PortalAppName = "Apps Portal Host"
$PortalAppPort = 80
$PortalAppPool = "AppsAppPool"
$PortalAppPoolUsername = "SHAREPOINT\SPContent"
$PortalAppDatabaseName = "SP2013_Farm_WSS_Content_Apps_Portal"
$PortalAppProxyGroup = "IntranetProxyGroup"

$appPoolAccount = Get-SPManagedAccount -Identity $PortalAppPoolUsername -EA 0
if($appPoolAccount -eq $null)
{
    Write-Host "Please supply the password for the Service Account..."
    $appPoolCred = Get-Credential $PortalAppPoolUsername
    $appPoolAccount = New-SPManagedAccount -Credential $appPoolCred -EA 0
}
$appPoolAccount = Get-SPManagedAccount -Identity $PortalAppPoolUsername -EA 0
```

```
# Creates a new claims-based NTLM (default) authentication provider
$ap = New-SPAuthenticationProvider

# Create the Portal Host
New-SPWebApplication -Name $PortalAppName -Port $PortalAppPort
  -ApplicationPool $PortalAppPool -ApplicationPoolAccount $appPoolAccount
  -DatabaseName $PortalAppDatabaseName -AuthenticationProvider $ap
  -ServiceApplicationProxyGroup $PortalAppProxyGroup

# Create the Portal Root Site Collection
$PortalRootOwner = "SHAREPOINT\Administrator"
$PortalRootName = "Apps Portal"

$PortalRootTemplate = Get-SPWebTemplate "STS#1"

New-SPSite -Url "http://sp2013srv01/" -OwnerAlias $PortalRootOwner -Template
$PortalRootTemplate -Name $PortalRootName
```

The script creates a new web application on the default server host name using the default configuration for claims-based authentication, and creates a root site collection based on the Blank Site template (STS#1). Again, the variables defined at the beginning of the script should be configured according to your farm and naming conventions.

To finalize the configuration of the services, you should configure the app domain name and the app prefix, which will be the name of the domain used for the autogenerated host names for hosting apps, as well as the prefix used while generating the host names. You can do that from SPCA by choosing Apps and then Configure Apps URLs in the App Management section. You can also still use PowerShell, executing the following two lines of code:

```
Set-SPAppDomain company-apps.com
Set-SPAppSiteSubscriptionName -Name "apps" -Confirm:$false
```

In the first line, you configure the domain name, which in the example is a top-level domain with a value of *company-apps.com*. While in the second line, you configure the prefix, which is "*apps*". Thus, the resulting apps URLs will be something like this:

```
http://apps-{UniqueID}.company-apps.com/sites/{ParentSiteName}/{AppName}/
```

Important For security reasons, it is strongly suggested to host apps under a secured site, which provides its content via HTTPS. For testing and development purposes, however, you can host apps in your development environment in a site published over HTTP. Moreover, when registering autohosted apps or provider-hosted apps, either on-premises or on the Seller Dashboard of the Office Store, you are obliged to provide a URL over HTTPS.

To complete the installation of your environment, you should configure an app catalog for providing corporate apps to your users. To do that, you need to have a corporate catalog site collection available in your web application or tenant. The template to use is APPCATALOG#0, and you can create it using the *New-SPSite* cmdlet or SPCA. Still using PowerShell, you can configure a site for being the app catalog using the following syntax:

```
Update-SPAppCatalogConfiguration -Site "http://www.company.com/sites/AppCatalog" -Force:$true
-SkipWebTemplateChecking:$true
```

The URL of the site collection passed to the cmdlet will determine the target web application or tenant for the command. Otherwise, you can use SPCA, navigate to the Apps page, and select the Manage App Catalog menu item in the App Management group. There you will be able to create a corporate app catalog site collection from scratch and associate it with the target web application or tenant.

Security infrastructure

The last topic to cover in this chapter is the security infrastructure behind the scenes of the SharePoint app model. As you know, every SharePoint app uses an app principal, which represents the identity of the app and determines the app's authorizations for accessing resources. This security environment uses the Security Token Service (STS) available in SharePoint, SAML (Security Assertion Markup Language) tokens, and the OAuth access tokens. The whole environment is based on the claims-based authentication model, which is the default authentication model in SharePoint 2013.

Important Apps are not supported in SharePoint web applications configured with classic mode authentication.

The hosting method you choose for your app determines how it handles authentication. For example, SharePoint-hosted apps run on an app web, which is a subsite of the host web. When working in app websites, you can take advantage of *internal authentication*, which allows your app code to use the CSOM and REST for accessing both the app web and the host web, without requiring explicit app authentication code. (Of course, you still will need explicit permissions.) On the contrary, autohosted and provider-hosted apps run on external, remote websites. In these cases, your code will need to use *external authentication*, which is explicit authentication based on Windows Azure ACS or a server-to-server (S2S) trust relationship. To be authenticated and authorized for accessing resources, autohosted and provider-hosted apps require OAuth access tokens. The access tokens can contain information about the app only, or can carry information about a user identity inside a context token.

In all hosting cases, you can use policies within your code to enforce authorizations for both the user and the app. When an app calls SharePoint using the CSOM or REST from client-side code, for example, both the user and the app need to adhere to the required permissions. If either of them misses the proper permissions, the app code will fail with an access-denied exception. When an autohosted or provider-hosted app executes server-side code, your policy needs to enforce authorization for the app only. You must explicitly enable this scenario in the app's AppManifest.xml file by setting the *AllowAppOnlyPolicy* attribute to *true* in the *AppPermissionsRequests* element. Only site collection administrators can grant use of the app-only policy. If the app-only policy is granted and the app already has tenant-scoped permissions, then the user must be a tenant administrator to grant use of the app-only policy. Finally, to use this capability in server-side code, you will need to invoke the *GetAppOnlyAccessToken* method of the *TokenHelper* class for retrieving a special app-only access token. Behind the scenes, all app-only requests are made by SHAREPOINT\APP, which is a special user that cannot be used during explicit authentication, almost like SHAREPOINT\SYSTEM.

All these scenarios are possible thanks to the OAuth protocol and Windows Azure ACS. In Chapter 20, "Claims-based authentication, federated identities, and OAuth," you will learn more about OAuth, ACS, user and app authentication, and the internals of the security infrastructure of SharePoint 2013. For now, however, simply understand that every single time you register an autohosted or provider-hosted app in SharePoint, you will need to provide a client ID and client secret information for securing the authentication and providing a valid and secure access token. When working with autohosted apps, the Office 365 environment must create this information and configure the remote web application to use them. When you work with provider-hosted apps, it is your responsibility to configure the client ID and the client secret in the remote web application. In fact, you have explicit configuration settings to provide while publishing the app, as you have already seen in Figure 8-32. There are also some application pages for managing app principals:

- **/_layouts/15/AppRegNew.aspx** Allows manual registration of a new app, providing the client ID and client secret, as well as the remote domain and redirect URL for the target app
- **/_layouts/15/AppPrincipals.aspx** Enumerates all the registered apps, together with their unique client IDs
- **/_layouts/15/AppInv.aspx** Allows you to retrieve app registration information (title, domain, and redirect URL) based on a provided client ID

When publishing your apps through the Office Store, you must create a client ID and client secret through a wizard on the Seller Dashboard of the Office Store. As shown in Figure 8-40, the first page of the wizard asks you to specify the client ID and the client secret.

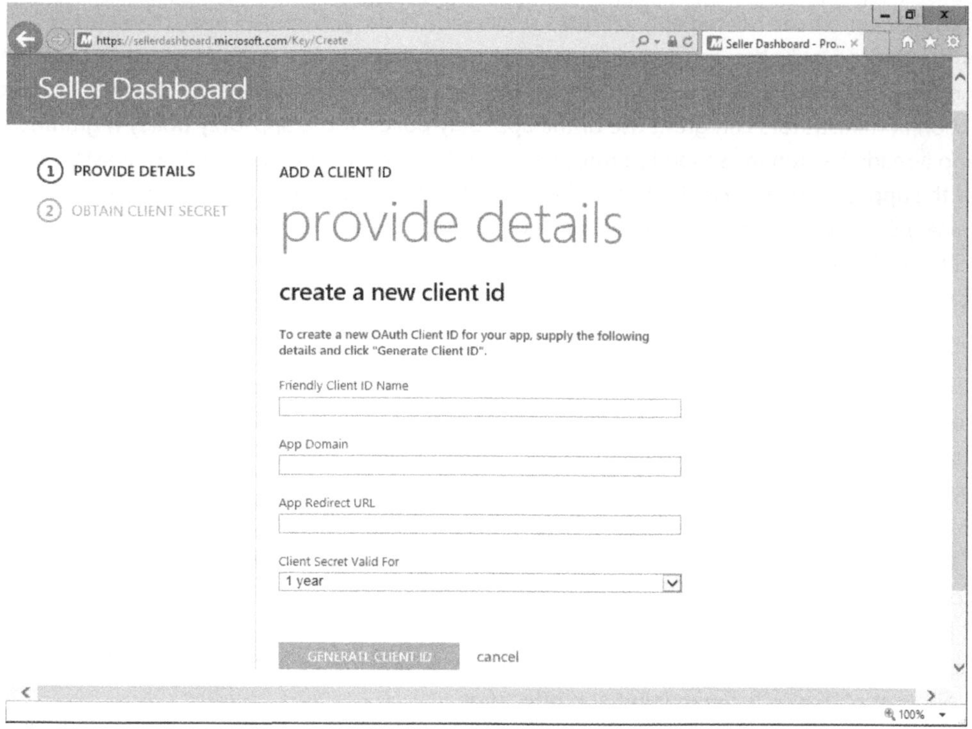

FIGURE 8-40 The first page of the wizard for creating a client ID and a client secret.

After you click the Generate Client ID button, you can review and make note of your settings from the wizard's recap page, as shown in Figure 8-41.

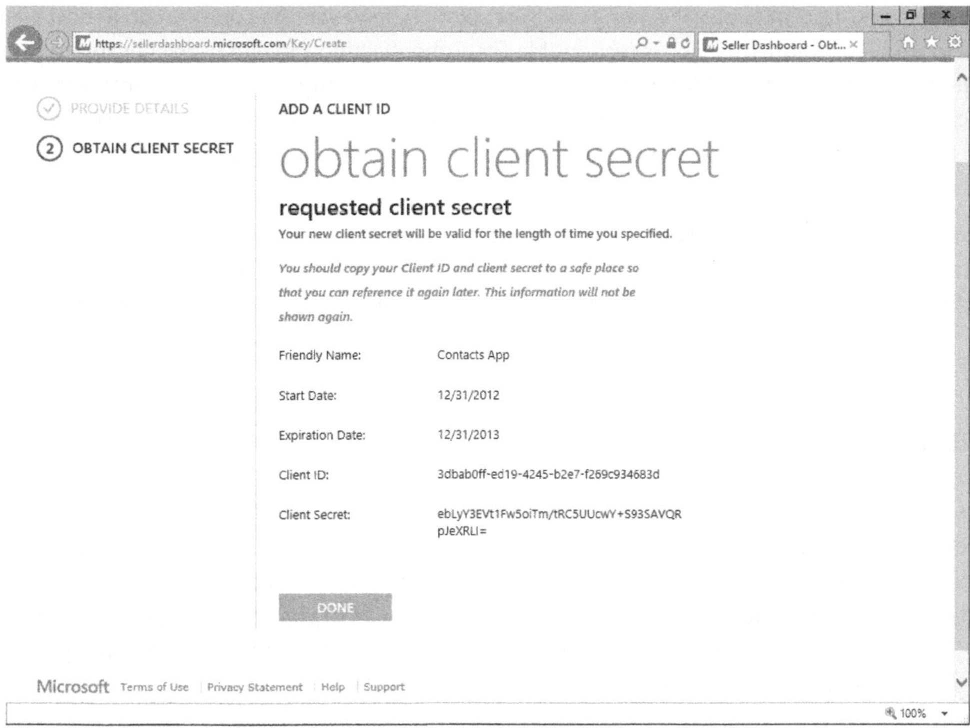

FIGURE 8-41 The recap page of the Seller Dashboard displays your newly created client ID and client secret.

As you can see, the screen provides all the security information (client ID and client secret) and urges you to copy the details to a safe place. For security reasons, you will never be able to come back to this screen after clicking the Done button. If you lose your client ID or client secret, you can't retrieve them—you must recreate them from scratch.

More Info For further details about configuring app principals and OAuth, read the document "Tips and FAQs: OAuth and remote apps for SharePoint 2013," which is available on MSDN online at *http://msdn.microsoft.com/en-us/library/fp179932.aspx*.

If you cannot rely on OAuth and ACS for authenticating an app principal, you can use S2S authentication, which requires you to configure a trust relationship between SharePoint and your app. This rarely used scenario works only on-premises and uses a certificate, to whose private key the app code should have access. This is a high-trust scenario, because the app is trusted by SharePoint but still has a restricted set of permissions. It is not a full-trust solution, in which the code can do almost everything. Moreover, a high-trust app is responsible for authenticating the end users, because it cannot use the capability of OAuth 2.0 and ACS to transfer the user identity through the context token. To configure this scenario, you will need to provide the app with an X.509 certificate, as well as execute some PowerShell scripts to register the certificate and the trust on the SharePoint side.

More Info For further details about configuring a high-trust scenario, read the document "How to: Create high-trust apps for SharePoint 2013 using the server-to-server protocol (advanced topic)," available at *http://msdn.microsoft.com/en-us/library/fp179901.aspx*.

Summary

In this chapter, you learned a great deal about the architecture of SharePoint apps. Specifically, you learned the differences between SharePoint-hosted, autohosted, and provider-hosted apps, as well as how to develop them. Then you explored the internals of the AppManifest.xml file of SharePoint apps. You discovered how to deploy and publish an app, either on a corporate app catalog or on the Office Store. Lastly, you examined the workings of the security infrastructure of the SharePoint app model. Now you are ready to create your own apps and publish them.

CHAPTER 9

The new SharePoint REST API

Another important introduction in Microsoft SharePoint 2013 is the REST (Representational State Transfer) API. The REST API gives any platform access to many key objects, properties, and methods that were previously available only via the Client Object Model for Microsoft .NET, Microsoft Silverlight, and JavaScript. In fact, the new API provides a rich set of REST URIs that you can access via HTTP and XML/JSON (JavaScript Object Notation) for consuming nearly every capability of the Client Object Model. All you need is a third-party technology capable of consuming REST services. In this chapter, you will learn about the architecture of this new REST API, as well as how to manage the most common tasks for everyday programming needs.

Introducing the REST API

The overall architecture of the REST API is based on the *client.svc* WCF service, which serves the classic Client Object Model, but implements an OData-compliant endpoint, too.

More Info OData stands for Open Data Protocol, and you can read more about it at *http://www.odata.org/*.

You can access the REST API at the relative URL *_api/* of any SharePoint site. For example, to access the API targeting the root site collection of a target web application, you can open your browser and navigate to a URL such as the following:

```
http://devbook.sp2013.local/_api/site
```

where *devbook.sp2013.local* in the example is the host name of a sample web application. The previous URL is just an alias to the real URL, which is

```
http://devbook.sp2013.local/_vti_bin/client.svc/site
```

As you can see, the real URL corresponds to *client.svc*, which was discussed in Chapter 7, "Client-side technologies." It is just an additional RESTful endpoint that publishes the capabilities of the classic Client Object Model through the OData protocol. By browsing to such a URL, you will see that the result is an XML representation—based on the ATOM protocol—of information about the current site collection. (When using Internet Explorer, be sure to disable the feed-reading view in the browser's content properties.) At the beginning of the ATOM response, there is a list of links targeting many additional URLs for accessing information and APIs related to the current site collection. At the end of the response, there are some properties specific to the current site collection.

Here are some other commonly used URLs of APIs, which are useful while developing on SharePoint:

- ***http://devbook.sp2013.local/_api/web*** Use to access the information about the target website.
- ***http://devbook.sp2013.local/_api/web/lists*** Use to access the collection of lists in the target website.
- ***http://devbook.sp2013.local/_api/web/lists/GetByTitle('Title of the List')*** Use to access the information of a specific list instance, selected by title.
- ***http://devbook.sp2013.local/_api/search*** Use to access the Search query engine.

As you can see, the root of any relative endpoint is the *_api/* trailer, which can be followed by many API targets (as the following section will illustrate) and correspond to the most common artifacts of SharePoint. As with many REST services, you can communicate with this REST API not only by the browser, invoking URLs with the HTTP *GET* method, but also by using a client capable of communicating over HTTP and parsing ATOM or JSON responses. In fact, depending on the HTTP *Accept* header provided within the request, the REST service will provide ATOM (*Accept: application/atom+xml*) or JSON (*Accept: application/json;odata=verbose*) answers. By default, REST service responses are presented by using the ATOM protocol, according to the OData specification.

Depending on the HTTP method and headers (*X-Http-Method*) you use, you can take advantage of various capabilities of the API, taking advantage of a complete CRUDQ (create, read, update, delete, and query) set of methods. The available HTTP methods and headers are:

- ***GET*** These requests typically represent read operations, which apply to objects, properties, or methods, which return information.
- ***POST*** Without any additional *X-Http-Method* header, this method is used for creation operations. For example, you can use *POST* to post a file to a library, to post an item to a list, or to post a new list definition for creation in a target website. While invoking *POST* operations against a target object, any property that is not required and is not specified in the HTTP invocation will be set to its default value. If you provide a value for a read-only property, you will get an exception.
- ***PUT*, *PATCH*, and *MERGE*** These requests are used for update operations. You can use *PUT* to update an object. While invoking *PUT* operations, you should specify all writable properties. If any property is missing, the operation could fail or could set the missing properties back to their default values. The *PATCH* and *MERGE* operations are based on the *POST* method, with the addition of an *X-Http-Method* header with a value of *PATCH* or *MERGE*. They are equivalent, and you should always use the former, because the latter is provided for backward compatibility only. Like *PUT*, *PATCH* and *MERGE* handle update operations. The big

difference is that with *PATCH* and *MERGE*, any writeable property that is not specified will retain its current value.

- ***DELETE*** These requests are for deleting an item and can be implemented with *POST*, plus the additional *X-Http-Method* header with a value of *DELETE*. If you invoke this operation against recyclable objects, SharePoint will move them to the Recycle Bin.

Listing 9-1 demonstrates how to use the new REST API. The sample is intentionally written using a legacy programming language, specifically VBScript in a .vbs file, to demonstrate that the REST APIs are available to any platform and any technology landscape. The code reads the title of a list instance in a target website.

LISTING 9-1 A sample VBScript file for reading the title of a list instance in a target website using the REST API

```
Dim xmlResponse 'As Microsoft.XMLDOM
Dim xmlHttp 'As Microsoft.XMLHTTP
Dim titleNode 'As Microsoft.Msxml.IXMLDOMNode

Set xmlResponse = CreateObject("Microsoft.XMLDOM")
Set xmlHttp = CreateObject("Microsoft.XMLHTTP")

xmlHttp.Open "GET", "http://devbook.sp2013.local/_api/web/lists/
GetByTitle('DevLeap%20Contacts')", false
xmlhttp.setRequestHeader "Content-Type", "application/xml"
xmlHttp.Send

xmlResponse.async = false
xmlResponse.LoadXml xmlHttp.responseText
xmlResponse.SetProperty "SelectionLanguage", "XPath"
xmlResponse.SetProperty "SelectionNamespaces", _  xmlns:a='http://www.
w3.org/2005/ Atom'" & _
    " xmlns:d='http://schemas.microsoft.com/ado/2007/08/dataservices'" & _
    " xmlns:m='http://schemas.microsoft.com/ado/2007/08/dataservices/metadata'"

Set titleNode = xmlResponse.SelectSingleNode("/a:entry/a:content/" & _
    "m:properties/d:Title/text()")

MsgBox titleNode.Text

Set title = Nothing
Set xmlResponse = Nothing
Set xmlHttp = Nothing
```

The sample code invokes a *GET* method to begin creating and configuring a *Microsoft.XMLHTTP* object for requesting a specific list instance by title. The result will be an XML (ATOM) representation of the list information, which will look like the excerpt in Listing 9-2. Near the end of Listing 9-2, notice the XML node with a qualified name value of *d:title*. Highlighted in bold, this represents the *Title* property of the list, and it is associated with a namespace that has a prefix value of *d*. The namespace URI of that namespace is *http://schemas.microsoft.com/ado/2007/08/dataservices* and corresponds to the well-known ADO.NET Data Services namespace URI.

LISTING 9-2 An excerpt of the XML (ATOM) representation of the list information of a specific list instance

```
<?xml version="1.0" encoding="utf-8"?>
<entry xml:base="http://devbook.sp2013.local/_api/"
xmlns="http://www.w3.org/2005/Atom"
  xmlns:d="http://schemas.microsoft.com/ado/2007/08/dataservices"
  xmlns:m="http://schemas.microsoft.com/ado/2007/08/dataservices/metadata"
  xmlns:georss="http://www.georss.org/georss"
  xmlns:gml="http://www.opengis.net/gml"
  m:etag="&quot;7&quot;">
  <id>http://devbook.sp2013.local/_api/Web/Lists(guid'bb72c030-20d0-47a6-b290-
f4f60e873d70')</id>
  <category term="SP.List"
scheme="http://schemas.microsoft.com/ado/2007/08/dataservices/scheme"/>
  <link rel="edit" href="Web/Lists(guid'bb72c030-20d0-47a6-b290-f4f60e873d70')"/>
  <link rel="http://schemas.microsoft.com/ado/2007/08/dataservices/related/
FirstUniqueAncestorSecurableObject" type="application/atom+xml;type=entry"
title="FirstUniqueAncestorSecurableObject" href="Web/Lists(guid'bb72c030-20d0-
47a6-b290-f4f60e873d70')/FirstUniqueAncestorSecurableObject"/>
  <link rel="http://schemas.microsoft.com/ado/2007/08/dataservices/related/
RoleAssignments" type="application/atom+xml;type=feed" title="RoleAssignments"
href="Web/Lists(guid'bb72c030-20d0-47a6-b290-f4f60e873d70')/RoleAssignments"/>

  <!-- List of link elements omitted for the sake of brevity -->

  <title/>
  <updated>2013-01-07T06:03:56Z</updated>
  <author>
    <name/>
  </author>
  <content type="application/xml">
    <m:properties>
      <d:AllowContentTypes m:type="Edm.Boolean">true</d:AllowContentTypes>
      <d:BaseTemplate m:type="Edm.Int32">10001</d:BaseTemplate>
      <d:BaseType m:type="Edm.Int32">0</d:BaseType>
      <d:ContentTypesEnabled m:type="Edm.Boolean">true</d:ContentTypesEnabled>
      <d:Created m:type="Edm.DateTime">2012-11-25T23:02:56Z</d:Created>
      <d:DefaultContentApprovalWorkflowId m:type="Edm.Guid">00000000-0000-0000-
0000-000000000000</d:DefaultContentApprovalWorkflowId>
      <d:Description></d:Description>
      <d:Direction>none</d:Direction>
      <d:DocumentTemplateUrl m:null="true"/>
      <d:DraftVersionVisibility m:type="Edm.Int32">0</d:DraftVersionVisibility>
      <d:EnableAttachments m:type="Edm.Boolean">true</d:EnableAttachments>
      <d:EnableFolderCreation m:type="Edm.Boolean">false</d:EnableFolderCreation>
      <d:EnableMinorVersions m:type="Edm.Boolean">false</d:EnableMinorVersions>
      <d:EnableModeration m:type="Edm.Boolean">false</d:EnableModeration>
      <d:EnableVersioning m:type="Edm.Boolean">false</d:EnableVersioning>
      <d:EntityTypeName>DevLeap_x0020_ContactsList</d:EntityTypeName>
      <d:ForceCheckout m:type="Edm.Boolean">false</d:ForceCheckout>
      <d:HasExternalDataSource m:type="Edm.Boolean">false
</d:HasExternalDataSource>
      <d:Hidden m:type="Edm.Boolean">false</d:Hidden>
      <d:Id m:type="Edm.Guid">bb72c030-20d0-47a6-b290-f4f60e873d70</d:Id>
```

```
      <d:ImageUrl>/_layouts/15/images/itgen.png</d:ImageUrl>
      <d:IrmEnabled m:type="Edm.Boolean">false</d:IrmEnabled>
      <d:IrmExpire m:type="Edm.Boolean">false</d:IrmExpire>
      <d:IrmReject m:type="Edm.Boolean">false</d:IrmReject>
      <d:IsApplicationList m:type="Edm.Boolean">false</d:IsApplicationList>
      <d:IsCatalog m:type="Edm.Boolean">false</d:IsCatalog>
      <d:IsPrivate m:type="Edm.Boolean">false</d:IsPrivate>
      <d:ItemCount m:type="Edm.Int32">4</d:ItemCount>
      <d:LastItemDeletedDate m:type="Edm.DateTime">2012-11-30T00:39:15Z
</d:LastItemDeletedDate>
      <d:LastItemModifiedDate m:type="Edm.DateTime">2012-11-30T00:39:15Z
</d:LastItemModifiedDate>
<d:ListItemEntityTypeFullName>SP.Data.DevLeap_x0020_ContactsListItem
</d:ListItemEntityTypeFullName>
      <d:MultipleDataList m:type="Edm.Boolean">false</d:MultipleDataList>
      <d:NoCrawl m:type="Edm.Boolean">false</d:NoCrawl>
      <d:ParentWebUrl>/</d:ParentWebUrl>
      <d:ServerTemplateCanCreateFolders
        m:type="Edm.Boolean">true</d:ServerTemplateCanCreateFolders>
      <d:TemplateFeatureId m:type="Edm.Guid">743feab9-3136-4e92-862f-
c554a63fdaa1</d:TemplateFeatureId>
      <d:Title>DevLeap Contacts</d:Title>
    </m:properties>
  </content>
</entry>
```

You can achieve the same goal with any other programming or scripting language capable of communicating over HTTP and managing ATOM or JSON answers. For example, consider Listing 9-3, which is written in C#: the click event handler of a *Button* control within a Microsoft Windows Store app for Windows 8 consumes the collection of lists available in a target website, using the *HttpClient* class of the Windows Runtime. Notice the code for creating an *HttpClient* instance configured to use integrated security and to accept JSON responses (highlighted in bold).

More Info For further information about developing Windows Store Apps for Windows 8, consult *Build Windows 8 Apps with Microsoft Visual C# and Visual Basic Step by Step*, by Luca Regnicoli, Paolo Pialorsi, and Roberto Brunetti (Microsoft Press, 2013).

LISTING 9-3 A Windows Store app consuming the collection of lists of a site collection using the REST API

```
private async void DownloadLists_Click(object sender, RoutedEventArgs e) {
    List<String> listsTitles = new List<string>();

    HttpClientHandler handler = new HttpClientHandler();
    handler.UseDefaultCredentials = true;
    HttpClient client = new HttpClient(handler);
    client.DefaultRequestHeaders.Add("Accept", "application/json;odata=verbose");
    HttpResponseMessage response = await client.GetAsync(
        "http://devbook.sp2013.local/_api/web/lists");

    String jsonString = await response.Content.ReadAsStringAsync();
    JsonObject o = JsonObject.Parse(jsonString);

    foreach (var i in o.FirstOrDefault().Value.GetObject()
        .FirstOrDefault().Value.GetArray()) {
        JsonObject item = i.GetObject();
        if (!item["Hidden"].GetBoolean())
            listsTitles.Add(item["Title"].GetString());
    }

    this.ListOfLists.ItemsSource = listsTitles;
}
```

Eventually, and for testing purposes, you can also play with tools like Fiddler Composer (*http://www.fiddler2.com*) in order to test the behavior and the responses provided by the REST API.

API reference

Every method offered by the REST API can be invoked using a reference URL, which is made according to the schema illustrated in Figure 9-1.

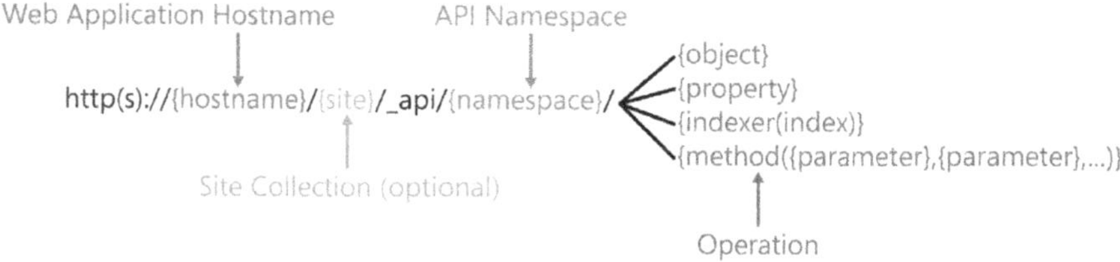

FIGURE 9-1 The schema of the URL of any REST API published by SharePoint 2013.

The protocol moniker can be *http* or *https*, depending on the web application configuration. The *{hostname}* argument is clearly the host name—which will eventually include the fully qualified domain name—of the target web application. The subsequent *{site}* is the target site collection and is optional, because you could target the root site collection. Following the *_api* trailer is a *{namespace}* argument that corresponds to one of the target families of APIs. Table 9-1 lists some of the main available namespaces. The URL ends with a reference to an *{object}*, a specific *{property}*, an *{indexer}*, or a *{method}* call. Indexers will be followed by a numeric *{index}* argument, while method calls could be followed by *{parameter}* arguments. For some operations, the arguments can be provided as a JSON object in the HTTP *POST* request body, as well.

TABLE 9-1 The main namespaces available in URLs of the REST API

Namespace	Target
site	The current site collection. Can be used to browse site collection properties and configuration, and corresponds to the *Microsoft.SharePoint.Client.Site* class of the Client-Side Object Model (CSOM).
web	The current website. Can be used to browse website properties, configuration, and contents, and corresponds to the *Microsoft.SharePoint.Client.Web* class of the CSOM.
SP.UserProfiles.PeopleManager	The APIs for working with the User Profile service within the context of the current user, and corresponds to the *Microsoft.SharePoint.Client.UserProfiles.PeopleManager* class of the CSOM.
ContextInfo	Retrieves the context of the current session, which corresponds to the serialization of an object of type *Microsoft.SharePoint.SPContextWebInformation*.
search	The search engine of SharePoint. Can be used to search content and suggestions.
publishing	The publishing engine. Can be used to manage the publishing capabilities.
social.feed	The social capabilities. Includes operations for accessing social feeds, followers, followed contents, and so on.

The REST API offers about 2,000 classes and more than 6,000 members, which are available throughout the hierarchy of objects of the CSOM, using the preceding namespaces as root objects. The first three namespaces are easy to manage and understand, because you simply need to reference the corresponding CSOM types and compose the request URLs. For example, the *Site* class of the *Microsoft.SharePoint.Client* namespace offers a property with name *Owner* and type *User*. Using the REST API, you can invoke the *GET* verb to retrieve the following URL:

```
http://devbook.sp2013.local/_api/site/owner
```

Moreover, for invoking the *GetWebTemplates* method, which accepts the *culture* parameter, you can invoke the following URL:

```
http://devbook.sp2013.local/_api/site/GetWebTemplates(1033)
```

The value *1033* provided is the en-US culture. Consult the CSOM online reference (*http://msdn.microsoft.com/en-us/library/ee544361.aspx*) to see all the available properties, methods, and members in general.

Notice that for security reasons, all the operations that modify data will require a security form digest with a name of *X-RequestDigest* in the HTTP request headers. To retrieve the value needed for this header, you have a couple of options:

- Working in JavaScript, inside a web page directly hosted in SharePoint or a SharePoint-hosted app, you can retrieve the value of the digest from a hidden INPUT field with an ID value of *__REQUESTDIGEST*. For example, using jQuery, you can reference the field with the following syntax: *$("#__REQUESTDIGEST").val()*.
- Working in any other context, you can invoke (using the *POST* method) the *ContextInfo* namespace and retrieve the form digest value from the ATOM or JSON response. By default, the form digest retrieved through this method will expire in 1,800 seconds.

Listing 9-4 shows the JSON output of the *ContextInfo* method invocation. The form digest value is highlighted in bold.

LISTING 9-4 The JSON output of the *ContextInfo* method invocation

```
{
  "d": {
    "GetContextWebInformation": {
      "__metadata": {
        "type":"SP.ContextWebInformation"
      },
    "FormDigestTimeoutSeconds":1800,
    "FormDigestValue":"0x8B48E76BAF6C86A17CCEC50F9A29E7CBB85816B883417C52C10C67
    FB19760517B774CD71E43517635386DE585E92A0262779824E5E0C7ECA905436A048AC85AC,
    08 Jan 2013 01:11:57 -0000",
    "LibraryVersion":"15.0.4420.1017",
    "SiteFullUrl":"http://devbook.sp2013.local",
    "SupportedSchemaVersions": {
      "results": [
        "14.0.0.0",
        "15.0.0.0"
      ]
    },
    "WebFullUrl":"http://devbook.sp2013.local"
    }
  }
}
```

Listing 9-5 provides a code excerpt of a Windows Store app for Windows 8 that invokes the *EnsureUser* method of a target website, providing a value for the form digest HTTP header after extracting that value from the *ContextInfo* method.

LISTING 9-5 A code excerpt for invoking the *EnsureUser* method of a target website via the REST API

```
private async void EnsureUser_Click(object sender, RoutedEventArgs e) {
    HttpClientHandler handler = new HttpClientHandler();
    handler.UseDefaultCredentials = true;
    HttpClient client = new HttpClient(handler);
    client.DefaultRequestHeaders.Add("Accept", "application/json;odata=verbose");
    HttpResponseMessage response = await client.PostAsync(
    "http://devbook.sp2013.local/_api/ContextInfo", null);
    String jsonString = await response.Content.ReadAsStringAsync();
    JsonObject o = JsonObject.Parse(jsonString);

    var info = o.FirstOrDefault().Value.GetObject().FirstOrDefault().Value;
    String digest = String.Empty;
    if (info != null) {
        digest = info.GetObject()["FormDigestValue"].GetString();
    }

    client.DefaultRequestHeaders.Add("X-RequestDigest", digest);
    response = await client.PostAsync(
      "http://devbook.sp2013.local/_api/web/EnsureUser('SampleUser01')", null);

    if (!response.IsSuccessStatusCode) {
        throw new Exception("Error while invoking EnuserUser method!");
    }
}
```

The other namespaces (*search*, *publishing*, and *social.feed*, for instance) provide some useful operations for managing the search engine, the publishing capabilities, and the social feeds.

Querying data

Another useful capability of the new REST API is the support for OData querying. Every time you invoke an operation that returns a collection of entities, you can also provide an OData-compliant set of query string parameters for sorting, filtering, paging, and projecting that collection. For example, imagine querying the list of items available in a document library. The URL would be:

```
http://hostname/_api/web/lists/GetByTitle('Documents')/Items
```

In case you are interested in the list of files in the root folder of the library, the corresponding URL is:

```
http://hostname/_api/web/lists/GetByTitle('Documents')/RootFolder/Files
```

According to the OData specification, you can append the following querying parameters to the URL:

- ***$filter*** Defines partitioning criteria on the current entity set. For example, you can provide the query string argument *$filter=substringof('LINQ',Name)%20eq%20true* to retrieve documents with *LINQ* in their file name.
- ***$select*** Projects only a subset of properties (fields) of the entities in the current entity set. For example, you can provide a value of *$select=Name,Author* to retrieve only the file name and the author of every file in the entity set.
- ***$orderby*** Sorts data returned by the query. You can provide query string arguments with a syntax like *$sort=TimeLastModified%20desc,Name%20asc* to sort files descending by *TimeLastModified* and ascending by *Name*.
- ***$top*** Selects the first *N* items of the current entity set. Use the syntax *&top=5* to retrieve only the first five entities from the entity set.
- ***$skip*** Skips the first *N* items of the current entity set. Use the syntax *$skip=10* to skip the first 10 entities of the entity set.
- ***$expand*** Automatically and implicitly resolves and expands a relationship between an entity in the current entity set and another related entity. For example, you can use the syntax *$expand=Author* to retrieve the author of a file.

As you have already seen in the previous example, the arguments provided to an OData query must be URL encoded because they are passed to the query engine via REST, through the URL of the service. Space characters must be converted into *%20*, for example, and any other nonalphanumeric characters must be converted into their corresponding encoded values.

In the previous examples, you saw just a quick preview of the available functions and operators for filtering entities with OData. Table 9-2 provides the full list of the available logical operations defined in the OData core specification. You can also read the official core documentation of OData at *http://www.odata.org/media/30002/OData.html*. The operators in bold are supported by the SharePoint 2013 REST API.

TABLE 9-2 The logical operations available in the OData core specification

Operator	Description	Example
eq	Equal	*/Suppliers?$filter=Address/City eq 'Redmond'*
ne	Not equal	*/Suppliers?$filter=Address/City ne 'London'*
gt	Greater than	*/Products?$filter=Price gt 20*
ge	Greater than or equal	*/Products?$filter=Price ge 10*
lt	Less than	*/Products?$filter=Price lt 20*
le	Less than or equal	*/Products?$filter=Price le 100*
and	Logical and	*/Products?$filter=Price le 200 and Price gt 3.5*
or	Logical or	*/Products?$filter=Price le 3.5 or Price gt 200*
not	Logical negation	*/Products?$filter=not endswith(Description,'milk')*

There are also some arithmetic operators, which are listed in Table 9-3.

TABLE 9-3 The arithmetic operators available in the OData core specification

Operator	Description	Example
add	Addition	*/Products?$filter=Price add 5 gt 10*
sub	Subtraction	*/Products?$filter=Price sub 5 gt 10*
mul	Multiplication	*/Products?$filter=Price mul 2 gt 2000*
div	Division	*/Products?$filter=Price div 2 gt 4*
mod	Modulo	*/Products?$filter=Price mod 2 eq 0*

None of the arithmetic operators defined in the OData core specification are supported by the SharePoint 2013 REST API. While defining a query, you can compose operators using parentheses—*()*—to group elements and define precedences. For example, you can write the following:

```
/Products?$filter=(Price sub 5) gt 10
```

Lastly, in queries for partitioning data, you can also use functions for strings, dates, math, and types. Table 9-4 provides the full list of functions available in the OData specification. Again, the operators highlighted in bold are those supported by SharePoint 2013 REST API.

TABLE 9-4 The functions available in the OData core specification for querying entities

Function	Description	Example
bool substringof(string searchString, string searchInString)	Returns a Boolean value stating whether the value provided in the first argument is a substring of the second argument. Can be used as a replacement for the contains method.	*substringof('Alfreds',CompanyName)*
bool endswith(string string, string suffixString)	Returns a Boolean value declaring whether the string provided in the first argument ends with the string provided in the second argument.	*endswith(CompanyName,'Futterkiste')*
bool startswith(string string, string prefixString)	Returns a Boolean value declaring whether the string provided in the first argument starts with the string provided in the second argument.	*startswith(CompanyName,'Alfr')*
int length(string string)	Returns an integer value representing the length of the string provided as the argument.	*length(CompanyName) eq 19*
int indexof(string searchIn-String, string searchString)	Returns an integer value representing the index of the string provided in the second argument, which is searched within the string provided in the first argument.	*indexof(CompanyName,'lfreds') eq 1*
string replace(string searchInString, string search-String, string replaceString)	Replaces the string provided in the second argument with the string provided in the third argument, searching within the first string argument.	*replace(CompanyName,' ', '') eq 'AlfredsFutterkiste'*
string substring(string string, int pos)	Returns a substring of the string provided in the first argument, starting from the integer position provided in the second argument.	*substring(CompanyName,1) eq 'lfreds Futterkiste'*
string substring(string string, int pos, int length)	Returns a substring of the string provided in the first argument, starting from the integer position provided in the second argument and stopping after a number of characters provided in the third integer argument.	*substring(CompanyName,1, 2) eq 'lf'*

Function	Description	Example
string tolower(string string)	Returns a string that is the lowercase conversion of the string provided as the string argument.	*tolower(CompanyName) eq 'alfreds futterkiste'*
string toupper(string string)	Returns a string that is the uppercase conversion of the string provided as the string argument.	*tolower(CompanyName) eq 'alfreds futterkiste'*
string trim(string string)	Returns a string trimmed of spaces, based on the string provided as the argument.	*trim(CompanyName) eq 'Alfreds Futterkiste'*
string concat(string string1, string string2)	Returns a string that is the concatenation of the two string arguments provided.	*concat(concat(City,', '), Country) eq 'Berlin, Germany'*
int day(DateTime datetimeValue)	Returns an integer that corresponds to the day of the datetime value provided as the argument.	*day(BirthDate) eq 8*
int hour(DateTime datetimeValue)	Returns an integer that corresponds to the hours of the datetime value provided as the argument.	*hour(BirthDate) eq 1*
int minute(DateTime datetimeValue)	Returns an integer that corresponds to the minutes of the datetime value provided as the argument.	*minute(BirthDate) eq 0*
int month(DateTime datetimeValue)	Returns an integer that corresponds to the month of the datetime value provided as the argument.	*month(BirthDate) eq 12*
int second(DateTime datetimeValue)	Returns an integer that corresponds to the seconds of the datetime value provided as the argument.	*second(BirthDate) eq 0*
int year(DateTime datetimeValue)	Returns an integer that corresponds to the year of the datetime value provided as the argument.	*year(BirthDate) eq 1948*
double round(double doubleValue)	Returns a double number that is the rounded value of the double value provided as the argument.	*round(Freight) eq 32*
decimal round(decimal decimalValue)	Returns a decimal number that is the rounded value of the decimal value provided as the argument.	*round(Freight) eq 32*
double floor(double doubleValue)	Returns a double number that is the floor value of the double value provided as the argument.	*floor(Freight) eq 32*
decimal floor(decimal datetimeValue)	Returns a decimal number that is the floor value of the decimal value provided as the argument.	*floor(Freight) eq 32*
double ceiling(double doubleValue)	Returns a double number that is the ceiling value of the double value provided as the argument.	*ceiling(Freight) eq 33*
decimal ceiling(decimal datetimeValue)	Returns a decimal number that is the ceiling value of the decimal value provided as the argument.	*ceiling(Freight) eq 33*
bool IsOf(type value)	Returns a Boolean value stating if the target entity is of the type provided as the argument.	*isof('NorthwindModel.Order')*
bool IsOf(expression value, type targetType)	Returns a Boolean value stating if the expression provided as the first argument, is of the type provided as the second argument.	*isof(ShipCountry,'Edm.String')*

Based on all the information provided in previous paragraphs, you should now be able to understand the following query:

```
http://devbook.sp2013.local/_api/web/lists/GetByTitle(Documents')/RootFolder/Files?$expand=Autho
r&$select=Name,Author,TimeLastModified&$sort=TimeLastModified%20desc,Name&$skip=20&$top=10&$filt
er=substringof('Chapter',Name)%20eq%20true
```

You can disassemble and decode the query string parameters with the information provided in Table 9-5.

TABLE 9-5 The sample query string parameters explained

Query part	Explanation
$expand=Author	Expand the related object author while retrieving the documents.
$select=Name,Author,TimeLastModified	Retrieve the fields *name*, *author*, and *time last modified*.
$sort=TimeLastModified desc,Name	Sort the output descending by *TimeLastModified* and ascending by *Name*.
$skip=20	Skip the first 20 items of the result set (the first two pages of 10 items).
$top=10	Retrieve only the first 10 items of the result set (the third page of 10 items).
$filter= substringof('Chapter',Name) eq true	Retrieve only files with a file name that contains the literal Chapter.

More Info For quick testing and definition of OData queries, you can use LINQPad, which is a smart tool available at the following URL: *http://www.linqpad.net*.

If you are working with the .NET Framework, the OData client library already creates such queries for you, allowing you to write LINQ queries on the consumer side. If you are working with any other development technology, however, you do need to understand and write this kind of queries.

Managing data

Creating, updating, deleting, and otherwise managing entities using OData and the REST API is relatively simple as long as you remember a few rules. First, as you've already seen, you must provide the *X-RequestDigest* HTTP header whenever you want to change some data. Second, when managing lists and lists items, you need to avoid concurrency conflicts by specifying an additional HTTP header with the name *IF-MATCH*, which assumes a value called *ETag*. To avoid concurrency conflicts, read the *ETag* value by retrieving the target entity (list or list instance) with a *GET* method. The *ETag* value will be included in the response HTTP headers and in the response content, regardless of whether it is formatted in ATOM or JSON. Listing 9-6 includes a sample set of HTTP response headers returned by SharePoint 2013 while selecting a list instance via the REST API. The *ETag* header is highlighted in bold.

Note The *IF-MATCH* header applies only to lists and list items and can assume a value of * for situations where you do not care about concurrency and merely want to force your action.

LISTING 9-6 A sample set of HTTP response headers returned while querying a list instance via the REST API

```
HTTP/1.1 200 OK
Cache-Control: private, max-age=0
Transfer-Encoding: chunked
Content-Type: application/json;odata=verbose;charset=utf-8
Expires: Mon, 24 Dec 2012 11:17:56 GMT
Last-Modified: Tue, 08 Jan 2013 11:17:56 GMT
ETag: "7"
Server: Microsoft-IIS/8.0
X-SharePointHealthScore: 0
SPClientServiceRequestDuration: 31
X-AspNet-Version: 4.0.30319
SPRequestGuid: e6c0f29b-cb1a-2004-1a5f-42027001734d
request-id: e6c0f29b-cb1a-2004-1a5f-42027001734d
X-FRAME-OPTIONS: SAMEORIGIN
Persistent-Auth: true
X-Powered-By: ASP.NET
MicrosoftSharePointTeamServices: 15.0.0.4420
X-Content-Type-Options: nosniff
X-MS-InvokeApp: 1; RequireReadOnly
Date: Tue, 08 Jan 2013 11:17:56 GMT
```

The code excerpt of the JavaScript function in Listing 9-7 updates the title of an item using the REST API and provides a value for the *ETag* parameter.

LISTING 9-7 A sample code excerpt to update the title of a list item using JavaScript and the REST API

```
var hostweburl;
var appweburl;
var eTag;

// This code runs when the DOM is ready and creates a context object
// which is needed to use the SharePoint object model
$(document).ready(function () {
    //Get the URI decoded URLs.
    hostweburl = decodeURIComponent(getQueryStringParameter("SPHostUrl"));
    appweburl = decodeURIComponent(getQueryStringParameter("SPAppWebUrl"));

    var scriptbase = hostweburl + "/_layouts/15/";
    $.getScript(scriptbase + "SP.RequestExecutor.js", execCrossDomainRequest);
});

function execCrossDomainRequest() {
    var contextInfoUri = appweburl + "/_api/contextinfo";
    var itemUri = appweburl +
"/_api/SP.AppContextSite(@target)/web/lists/GetByTitle('Documents')/Items(1)?@
target='" + hostweburl + "'";
```

```
    var executor = new SP.RequestExecutor(appweburl);

    // First request, to retrieve the form digest
    executor.executeAsync({
        url: contextInfoUri,
        method: "POST",
        headers: { "Accept": "application/json; odata=verbose" },
        success: function (data) {
            var jsonObject = JSON.parse(data.body);
            formDigestValue =
            jsonObject.d.GetContextWebInformation.FormDigestValue;
            updateListItem(formDigestValue, itemUri);
        },
        error: function (data, errorCode, errorMessage) {
            var errMsg = "Error retrieving the form digest value: "
                + errorMessage;
            $("#error").text(errMsg);
        }
    });
}

function updateListItem(formDigestValue, itemUri) {
    var executor = new SP.RequestExecutor(appweburl);
    var newContent = JSON.stringify({ '__metadata':
{ 'type': 'SP.Data.Shared_x0020_DocumentsItem' }, 'Title': 'Changed by REST API'
});

    // Second request, to retrieve the ETag of the target item
    executor.executeAsync({
        url: itemUri,
        method: "GET",
        headers: { "Accept": "application/json; odata=verbose" },
        success: function (data) {
            $("#message").text('ETag: ' + data.headers["ETAG"]);
            eTag = data.headers["ETAG"];
            internalUpdateListItem(formDigestValue, itemUri, eTag, newContent);
        },
        error: function (data, errorCode, errorMessage) {
            var errMsg = "Error retrieving the eTag value: "
                + errorMessage;
            $("#error").text(errMsg);
        }
    });
}

function internalUpdateListItem(formDigestValue, itemUri, eTag, newContent) {
    var executor = new SP.RequestExecutor(appweburl);
```

```
    // Third request, to change the title of the target item
    executor.executeAsync({
        url:
            appweburl +
"/_api/SP.AppContextSite(@target)/web/lists/GetByTitle('Documents')/Items(1)?@
target='" + hostweburl + "'",
        method: "POST",
        body: newContent,
        headers: {
            "Accept": "application/json;odata=verbose",
            "content-type": "application/json;odata=verbose",
            "content-length": newContent.length,
            "X-RequestDigest": formDigestValue,
            "X-HTTP-Method": "MERGE",
            "IF-MATCH": eTag
        },
        success: function (data) {
            $("#message").text('Item successfully updated!');
        },
        error: function (data, errorCode, errorMessage) {
            var errMsg = "Error updating list item: "
                + errorMessage;
            $("#error").text(errMsg);
        }
    });
}

// Function to retrieve a query string value.
// For production purposes you may want to use
// a library to handle the query string.
function getQueryStringParameter(paramToRetrieve) {
    var params =
        document.URL.split("?")[1].split("&");
    var strParams = "";
    for (var i = 0; i < params.length; i = i + 1) {
        var singleParam = params[i].split("=");
        if (singleParam[0] == paramToRetrieve)
            return singleParam[1];
    }
}
```

Executing as soon as the DOM document is ready, Listing 9-7 first configures both the app web URL and the host web URL. Then it configures a scripting file (SP.RequestExecutor.js), which will be discussed in the "Cross-domain calls" section, which follows. After startup, the sample code requests the *ContextInfo* via a *POST* request, in order to extract a valid value for the form digest. If your code runs inside a SharePoint-hosted app, you can simply read the form digest value from the current page (a hidden field with name __REQUESTDIGEST). After retrieving the form digest, the sample gets the item to update, in order to access its *ETag* value. Lastly, the code runs a *POST* request against the target item URI, providing the JSON serialization of the changes to apply, the form digest, and the *ETag*.

Later, in the "Common REST API usage" section, you will see many samples based on the basic concepts demonstrated here. For now, however, notice that the JavaScript code for invoking the REST API uses an object of type *SP.RequestExecutor* to invoke the service endpoints, instead of a classic *jQuery.Ajax* method. In the next section, "Cross-domain calls," you will learn how it works.

One last thing to understand about data management is how the REST API behaves in case of a concurrency conflict. Remember, providing the *ETag* value simply enables you to identify and manage conflicts; it does not prevent you from experiencing them, unless you provide a value of * for the *IF-MATCH* header. For example, imagine that while you're executing the code of Listing 9-7, someone else changes the same target item, confirming the updates before the execution of your code. In a real scenario, you should retrieve the *ETag* value as soon as the user starts editing the target item, and you should provide it back to the server while saving your changes. Thus, you could have a short-term concurrency conflict. Every time someone changes an item and saves it, the *ETag* value will change. It is a numeric value, and it will increment by 1 unit. If a conflict does occur, the update or delete action will fail, and your HTTP request will get back a 412 HTTP status code, which is the Precondition Failed status. Moreover, in the response body, you will find an XML or JSON representation of the error. For example, the JSON response error message will look like the following excerpt:

```
{"error":{"code":"-1, Microsoft.SharePoint.Client.ClientServiceException","message":{"lang":"en-US","value":"The request ETag value '\"4\"' does not match the object's ETag value '\"5\"'."}}}
```

You can find this object serialized inside the *data* argument of the function invoked if the HTTP request fails due to a concurrency conflict, and the *errorCode* variable will assume a value of *-1002*. In your custom code, you should catch this kind of exception and prompt the user with a concurrency conflict error, and eventually download the update item from SharePoint to let the user compare data and make a choice.

Cross-domain calls

When developing SharePoint apps, you typically need to make cross-domain JavaScript calls between the app web and the host web. Because the domain of the app web is always different from the domain of the host web, however, this can cause complications. Specifically, browsers prohibit this kind of behavior by default in an effort to avoid cross-domain attacks and their related security issues. Luckily, SharePoint 2013 provides a JavaScript library to help you satisfy the browsers and keep the calls flowing: the SP.RequestExecutor.js library.

Found in the _layouts/15 folder of every SharePoint site, the SP.RequestExecutor.js library provides out-of-the-box capabilities to make cross-domain calls against trusted and registered domains. When you instantiate the library's *SP.RequestExecutor* type in your client-side code, it uses a hidden *IFRAME* element, together with some *POST* messages and a proxy page (*AppWebProxy.aspx*) to enable you to make highly secure calls—even cross-domain calls.

In Listing 9-7, the startup code adds a reference to the library for making cross-domain calls. Then it creates an instance of the *SP.RequestExecutor* type, providing the URL of the app web in the object constructor. Behind the scenes, the object injects an IFrame rendering the *AppWebProxy.aspx* page, which calls the host web. When the call to the host web completes, the client instance of the *SP.RequestExecutor* retrieves the result from the IFrame and provides it to the calling app. Figure 9-2 diagrams this process.

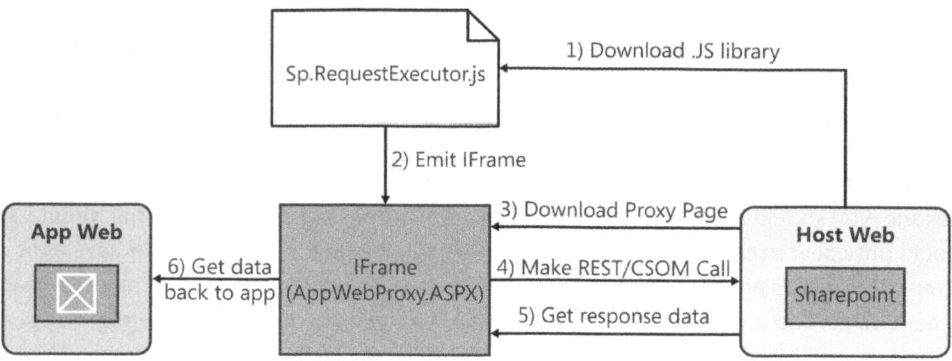

FIGURE 9-2 The steps of a cross-domain call using the SP.RequestExecutor.js library.

To use the SP.RequestExecutor.js library while invoking the REST API, you need to create an instance of the *SP.RequestExecutor* type. In addition, you must invoke the *executeAsync* method and provide the necessary arguments, including the following:

- ***url*** Represents the target URL of the REST API. While using the code from an app web, you can provide a reference to the host web using the *SP.AppContextSite()* function, as illustrated in Listing 9-7.
- ***method*** Defines the HTTP method to use while invoking the target URL.
- ***body*** Declares the content of the message body that will be posted to the target URL, just in case you will have message content to send.
- ***headers*** Allows defining a list of HTTP headers to provide while invoking the target URL. As you can see from Listing 9-7, here you can provide such headers as *Accept*, *X-RequestDigest*, *X-HTTP-Method*, *IF-MATCH*, and so on.
- ***success*** Is the pointer to a function that will be invoked in case of a successful call.
- ***error*** Is the pointer to a function that will be invoked in case of a failed call.

Security

By default, the REST API requires that the consumers act in an authenticated session for security purposes. The authenticated session can be gained through Windows integrated security, browser-based direct authentication (in the case of a SharePoint-hosted app), or using OAuth (in any other situation).

In the case of integrated security, you need to enable the automatic flow of integrated security credentials in the HTTP client library you will use. For example, if you're working in JavaScript within a web browser and using SharePoint-hosted app or application pages, the flow of integrated security credentials will be automatic. On the contrary, when working in a Windows Store app for Windows 8, you must request permission for the enterprise authentication capability in the AppManifest.xml file of the app.

If you want to use OAuth—suppose you're executing JavaScript code within a autohosted or provider-hosted app on a third-party site—you first need to retrieve and store the access token provided during the OAuth handshake. Then you must provide that access token to every request to the REST API, embedded in a dedicated *Authorization* HTTP header. The JavaScript code excerpt in Listing 9-8 configures that HTTP header using an access token stored in a hypothetical *accessToken* variable.

LISTING 9-8 A code excerpt for invoking the REST API with OAuth authentication

```
jQuery.ajax({
  url: "http://hostname/_api/contextinfo",
  type: "POST",
  headers: {
    "Authorization": "Bearer " + accessToken,
    "accept": "application/json;odata=verbose",
    "contentType": "text/xml"
  },
})
```

In addition, you can enable anonymous access to read-only operations of the REST API, in case you want to publish your contents to the public Internet. To configure this capability, you will need to edit the Anonymous permission of the target website. Figure 9-3 shows the configuration panel for setting this option. You can find the panel by choosing Site Settings | Site Permissions | Anonymous Access.

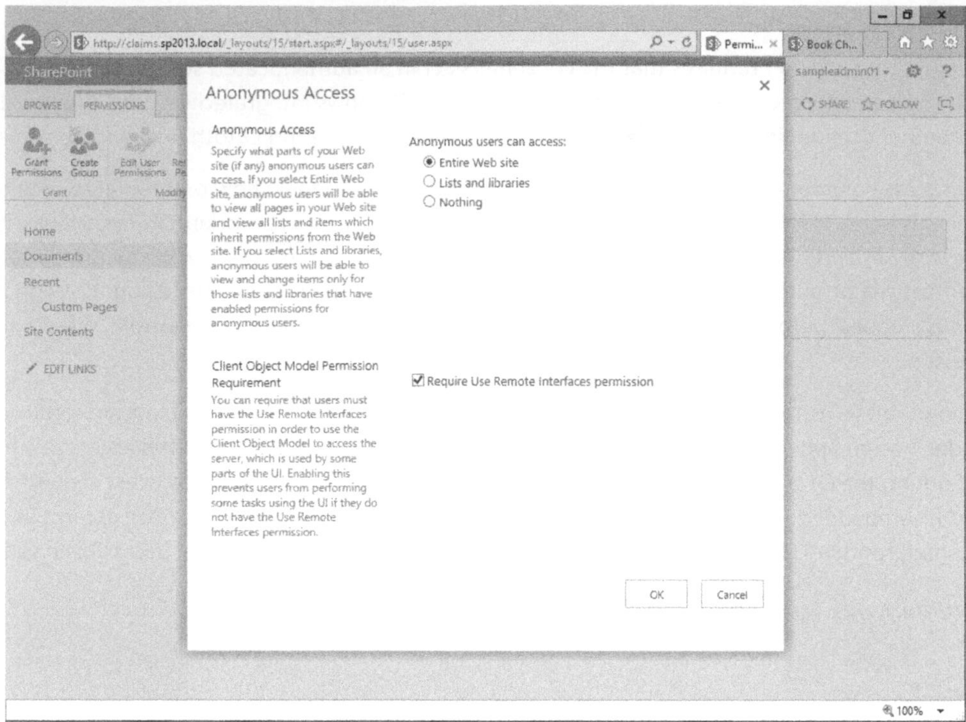

FIGURE 9-3 The UI for configuring anonymous access to the REST API.

If you turn off Require Use Remote Interfaces Permission, all anonymous users will be able to invoke the read-only operations of the REST API. Only authorized users can change this option, but they may do so from the web interface, working within PowerShell, or using the CSOM.

Common REST API usage

For the remainder of the chapter, you will learn how to use the REST API while executing common and useful tasks. All the code samples are provided in JavaScript and run in a SharePoint app that uses cross-domain calls. Thus, you will be able to reuse all the code excerpts illustrated by simply copying and pasting the code and adapting the values of the arguments and HTTP headers provided to the methods.

> **Important** The code samples come from a SharePoint-hosted app, so they do not need to provide an OAuth access token. Please refer to the "Security" section earlier in the chapter if you need to use the code sample from an autohosted or a provider-hosted app.

For the sake of simplicity, all the code samples also assume that you have the set of global and predefined variables illustrated in Listing 9-9, together with some common startup code.

LISTING 9-9 A code excerpt for the startup phase of the code samples illustrated in the current section

```
var hostweburl;
var appweburl;
var eTag;
var formDigestValue;

$(document).ready(function () {
    // Get the URI-decoded URLs.
    hostweburl = decodeURIComponent(getQueryStringParameter("SPHostUrl"));
    appweburl = decodeURIComponent(getQueryStringParameter("SPAppWebUrl"));

    var scriptbase = hostweburl + "/_layouts/15/";
    $.getScript(scriptbase + "SP.RequestExecutor.js", retrieveFormDigest);
});

// Function to retrieve a query string value.
// For production purposes you may want to use
// a library to handle the query string.
function getQueryStringParameter(paramToRetrieve) {
    var params =
        document.URL.split("?")[1].split("&");
    var strParams = "";
    for (var i = 0; i < params.length; i = i + 1) {
        var singleParam = params[i].split("=");
        if (singleParam[0] == paramToRetrieve)
            return singleParam[1];
    }
}

function retrieveFormDigest() {
    var contextInfoUri = appweburl + "/_api/contextinfo";
    var executor = new SP.RequestExecutor(appweburl)

    executor.executeAsync({
        url: contextInfoUri,
        method: "POST",
        headers: { "Accept": "application/json; odata=verbose" },
        success: function (data) {
            var jsonObject = JSON.parse(data.body);
            formDigestValue =
            jsonObject.d.GetContextWebInformation.FormDigestValue;
        },
        error: function (data, errorCode, errorMessage) {
            var errMsg = "Error retrieving the form digest value: "
                + errorMessage;
            $("#error").text(errMsg);
        }
    });
}
```

All the code samples illustrated in the next sections will behave as event handlers for HTML *Button* input elements.

Creating a new list

To create a new list instance via the REST API and JSON, you first need to prepare a JSON representation of the list to create. Then you must send it through AJAX, including the *X-RequestDigest* HTTP header. Listing 9-10 provides a function for this.

LISTING 9-10 A JavaScript function for creating a list instance using the REST API

```
function createNewList() {
    var executor = new SP.RequestExecutor(appweburl);
    var operationUri = appweburl +
        "/_api/SP.AppContextSite(@target)/web/lists?@target='" +
        hostweburl + "'";

    var bodyContent = JSON.stringify({
            '__metadata': { 'type': 'SP.List' },
            'AllowContentTypes': true,
            'BaseTemplate': 100,
            'ContentTypesEnabled': true,
            'Description': 'Custom List created via REST API',
            'Title': 'RESTCreatedList'
    });

    executor.executeAsync({
        url: operationUri,
        method: "POST",
        headers: {
            "Accept": "application/json;odata=verbose",
            "content-type": "application/json;odata=verbose",
            "content-length": bodyContent.length,
            "X-RequestDigest": formDigestValue,
        },
        body: bodyContent,
        success: function (data) {
            var jsonObject = JSON.parse(data.body);
        },
        error: function (data, errorCode, errorMessage) {
            var jsonObject = JSON.parse(data.body);
            var errMsg = "Error: " + jsonObject.error.message.value;
            $("#error").text(errMsg);
        }
    });
}
```

Notice that Listing 9-10 creates the list in the host web; your app will need specific permissions to accomplish this task.

Creating and updating a list item

Now imagine that you want to add one or more items to the list you just created. The code will be similar to Listing 9-10, but you will need to define the JSON structure of a list item. Moreover, you will need to change the URI of the operation in order to map to the collection of items of the target list. Listing 9-11 shows the necessary code.

LISTING 9-11 A JavaScript function for creating a list item in a list instance using the REST API

```
function createNewListItem() {
    var executor = new SP.RequestExecutor(appweburl);
    var operationUri = appweburl +
"/_api/SP.AppContextSite(@target)/web/lists/GetByTitle('RESTCreatedList')/Items"
+ "?@ target='" + hostweburl + "'";

    var bodyContent = JSON.stringify({
            '__metadata': { 'type': 'SP.Data.RESTCreatedListListItem' },
            'Title': 'Item created via REST API'
    });

    executor.executeAsync({
        url: operationUri,
        method: "POST",
        headers: {
            "Accept": "application/json;odata=verbose",
            "content-type": "application/json;odata=verbose",
            "content-length": bodyContent.length,
            "X-RequestDigest": formDigestValue,
        },
        body: bodyContent,
        success: function (data) {
            var jsonObject = JSON.parse(data.body);
        },
        error: function (data, errorCode, errorMessage) {
            var jsonObject = JSON.parse(data.body);
            var errMsg = "Error: " + jsonObject.error.message.value;
            $("#error").text(errMsg);
        }
    });
}
```

Notice the value assigned to the *type* property of the *__metadata* of the target item. It defines the data type name corresponding to a list item of the current list. Listing 9-11 assumes a value of *SP.Data.RESTCreatedListListItem*.

Updating an already existing item is almost the same as creating a new one, except that you need to provide the *ETag* value in the request headers and to synchronize the execution of parallel operations. Listing 9-12 shows an example that changes the *title* property of an existing list item.

LISTING 9-12 A JavaScript function for updating a list item in a list instance using the REST API

```
function updateListItem() {
    var executor = new SP.RequestExecutor(appweburl);
    var operationUri = appweburl +
"/_api/SP.AppContextSite(@target)/web/lists/GetByTitle('RESTCreatedList')/" +
"Items(1)?@target='" + hostweburl + "'";
    var bodyContent = JSON.stringify({
            '__metadata': { 'type': 'SP.Data.RESTCreatedListListItem' },
            'Title': 'Item changed via REST API'
    });

    // Retrieve the ETag value
    executor.executeAsync({
        url: operationUri,
        method: "GET",
        headers: { "Accept": "application/json; odata=verbose" },
        success: function (data) {
            $("#message").text('ETag: ' + data.headers["ETAG"]);
            eTag = data.headers["ETAG"];

            // Invoke the real update operation
            executor.executeAsync({
                url: operationUri,
                method: "POST",
                headers: {
                    "Accept": "application/json;odata=verbose",
                    "content-type": "application/json;odata=verbose",
                    "content-length": bodyContent.length,
                    "X-RequestDigest": formDigestValue,
                    "X-HTTP-Method": "MERGE",
                    "IF-MATCH": eTag
                },
                body: bodyContent,
                success: function (data) {
                    $("#message").text("Operation completed!");
                },
                error: function (data, errorCode, errorMessage) {
                    var jsonObject = JSON.parse(data.body);
                    var errMsg = "Error: " + jsonObject.error.message.value;
                    $("#error").text(errMsg);
                }
            });
        },
        error: function (data, errorCode, errorMessage) {
            var jsonObject = JSON.parse(data.body);
            var errMsg = "Error retrieving the eTag value: " +
                jsonObject.error.message.value;
            $("#error").text(errMsg);
        }
    });
}
```

Note that Listing 9-12 uses a nested *SP.RequestExecutor* instance, which will run just after successful completion of the external operation invocation.

Deleting an existing list item

What if you want to recycle one or more of the items you created in the previous examples? One more time, you need to provide the *ETag* value of the current item, as shown in Listing 9-13.

LISTING 9-13 A JavaScript function for deleting a list item in a list instance using the REST API

```
function deleteListItem() {
    var executor = new SP.RequestExecutor(appweburl);
    var operationUri = appweburl +
"/_api/SP.AppContextSite(@target)/web/lists/GetByTitle('RESTCreatedList')/" +
"Items(1)?@target='" + hostweburl + "'";

    // Retrieve the eTag value
    executor.executeAsync({
        url: operationUri,
        method: "GET",
        headers: { "Accept": "application/json; odata=verbose" },
        success: function (data) {
            $("#message").text('ETag: ' + data.headers["ETAG"]);
            eTag = data.headers["ETAG"];

            // Invoke the real update operation
            executor.executeAsync({
                url: operationUri,
                method: "POST",
                headers: {
                    "Accept": "application/json;odata=verbose",
                    "content-type": "application/json;odata=verbose",
                    "X-RequestDigest": formDigestValue,
                    "X-HTTP-Method": "DELETE",
                    "IF-MATCH": eTag
                },
                success: function (data) {
                    $("#message").text("Operation completed!");
                },
                error: function (data, errorCode, errorMessage) {
                    var jsonObject = JSON.parse(data.body);
                    var errMsg = "Error: " + jsonObject.error.message.value;
                    $("#error").text(errMsg);
                }
            });
        },
        error: function (data, errorCode, errorMessage) {
            var jsonObject = JSON.parse(data.body);
            var errMsg = "Error retrieving the eTag value: " +
                jsonObject.error.message.value;
            $("#error").text(errMsg);

    }
    });
}
```

Listing 9-13 uses an HTTP *POST* method, along with an *X-HTTP-Method* header with a value of *DELETE*. If you want to force the deletion, however, you can provide a value of * for the *ETag* header.

Querying a list of items

A common and useful operation is querying of a list of items. As shown in the "Querying data" section earlier in the chapter, you simply need to invoke an endpoint providing an OData query as a set of query string parameters. If you're working in JavaScript on the client side, however, the result will be a collection of items presented in JSON format. Listing 9-14 demonstrates how to query the items in a hypothetical list of contacts.

LISTING 9-14 A JavaScript function for querying a list of contacts using the REST API

```
function queryListItems() {
    var executor = new SP.RequestExecutor(appweburl);
    var operationUri = appweburl +
    "/_api/SP.AppContextSite(@target)/web/lists/GetByTitle('Sample%20Contacts')/"
+ "Items?@target='" + hostweburl + "'&$filter=Company%20eq%20'DevLeap'";

    executor.executeAsync({
        url: operationUri,
        method: "GET",
        headers: { "Accept": "application/json;odata=verbose" },
        success: function (data) {
            var jsonObject = JSON.parse(data.body);
            $("#result").empty();

            for (var i = 0; i < jsonObject.d.results.length; i++) {
                var item = jsonObject.d.results[i];
                $("#result").append("<div>" + item.Title + "</div>");
            }
        },
        error: function (data, errorCode, errorMessage) {
            var jsonObject = JSON.parse(data.body);
            var errMsg = "Error: " + jsonObject.error.message.value;
            $("#error").text(errMsg);
        }
    });
}
```

The HTTP request for querying items is a *GET*; it does not require a form digest, and it will suffice that the app and the current user both have permissions to read the target list. The response is a JSON serialized array of items that is browsed by code.

Creating a new document library

Most SharePoint solutions use documents and document libraries; Listing 9-15 shows you how to create a document library via the REST API.

LISTING 9-15 A JavaScript function for creating a document library via the REST API

```
function createNewLibrary() {
    var executor = new SP.RequestExecutor(appweburl);
    var operationUri = appweburl +
        "/_api/SP.AppContextSite(@target)/web/lists?@target='" +
        hostweburl + "'";

    var bodyContent = JSON.stringify( {
            '__metadata': { 'type': 'SP.List' },
            'AllowContentTypes': true,
            'BaseTemplate': 101,
            'ContentTypesEnabled': true,
            'Description': 'Custom Library created via REST API',
            'Title': 'RESTCreatedLibrary'
        });

    executor.executeAsync({
        url: operationUri,
        method: "POST",
        headers: {
            "Accept": "application/json;odata=verbose",
            "content-type": "application/json;odata=verbose",
            "content-length": bodyContent.length,
            "X-RequestDigest": formDigestValue,
        },
        body: bodyContent,
        success: function (data) {
            var jsonObject = JSON.parse(data.body);
        },
        error: function (data, errorCode, errorMessage) {
            var jsonObject = JSON.parse(data.body);
            var errMsg = "Error: " + jsonObject.error.message.value;
            $("#error").text(errMsg);
        }
    });
}
```

The procedure is almost identical to that for creating a custom list. The only difference is that here you provide a *BaseTemplate* value compliant with a document library. The example provides a value of *101*, which corresponds to a generic document library. When you successfully create the library, you will get back a JSON serialization of its definition in the success event.

Uploading or updating a document

Once you have one or more document libraries, you can use the REST API to upload documents into them. Listing 9-16 uploads an example XML file into a document library. The URL of the operation for adding the new file is highlighted in bold, as well as the HTTP headers that are required for the correct and secure execution of the operation.

LISTING 9-16 A JavaScript function for uploading a document into a document library via the REST API

```
function uploadFile() {
    var executor = new SP.RequestExecutor(appweburl);
    var operationUri = appweburl + "/_api/SP.AppContextSite(@target)/web/lists/"
        + "GetByTitle('Documents')/RootFolder/Files/Add" +
        "(url='SampleFile.xml',overwrite=true)?@target='" + hostweburl + "'";

    var xmlDocument = "<?xml version='1.0'?><document>" +
        "<title>Uploaded via REST API</title></document>";

    executor.executeAsync({
        url: operationUri,
        method: "POST",
        headers: {
            "Accept": "application/json;odata=verbose",
            "content-type": "text/xml",
            "content-length": xmlDocument.length,
            "X-RequestDigest": formDigestValue,
        },
        body: xmlDocument,
        success: function (data) {
            var jsonObject = JSON.parse(data.body);
            $("#message").text("Operation completed!");
        },
        error: function (data, errorCode, errorMessage) {
            var jsonObject = JSON.parse(data.body);
            var errMsg = "Error: " + jsonObject.error.message.value;
            $("#error").text(errMsg);
        }
    });
}
```

If you want to update an already published file, you can use a procedure like the one illustrated in Listing 9-17.

LISTING 9-17 A JavaScript function for updating a document into a document library via the REST API

```
function updateFile() {
    var executor = new SP.RequestExecutor(appweburl);
    var operationUri = appweburl +
        "/_api/SP.AppContextSite(@target)/web/" +
        "GetFileByServerRelativeUrl('/sites/AppsDevelopmentSite/" +
        "Shared%20Documents/SampleFile.xml')/$value?@target='" +
        hostweburl + "'";

    var xmlDocument = "<?xml version='1.0'?><document>" +
        "<title>File updated via REST API</title></document>";

    executor.executeAsync({
        url: operationUri,
        method: "POST",
        headers: {
            "Accept": "application/json;odata=verbose",
            "content-type": "text/xml",
            "content-length": xmlDocument.length,
            "X-HTTP-Method": "PUT",
            "X-RequestDigest": formDigestValue,
        },
        body: xmlDocument,
        success: function (data) {
            $("#message").text("Operation completed!");
        },
        error: function (data, errorCode, errorMessage) {
            var jsonObject = JSON.parse(data.body);
            var errMsg = "Error: " + jsonObject.error.message.value;
            $("#error").text(errMsg);
        }
    });
s}
```

As you can see, the REST endpoint for the operation is the *$value* of the file, and the file will be overridden by what it will be posted by the page.

Document check-in and checkout

Another vital component of many business-level solutions is the ability to control document versioning through the check-in and checkout capabilities of SharePoint. Listing 9-18 shows you how to check out a document, while Listing 9-19 handles check-in.

LISTING 9-18 A JavaScript function for checking out a document from a document library via the REST API

```
function checkOutFile() {
    var executor = new SP.RequestExecutor(appweburl);
    var operationUri = appweburl +
        "/_api/SP.AppContextSite(@target)/web/" +
        "GetFileByServerRelativeUrl('/sites/AppsDevelopmentSite/" +
        "Shared%20Documents/SampleFile.xml')/CheckOut()?@target='" +
        hostweburl + "'";

    executor.executeAsync({
        url: operationUri,
        method: "POST",
        headers: {
            "Accept": "application/json;odata=verbose",
            "X-RequestDigest": formDigestValue,
        },
        success: function (data) {
            var jsonObject = JSON.parse(data.body);
            $("#message").text("Operation completed!");
        },
        error: function (data, errorCode, errorMessage) {
            var jsonObject = JSON.parse(data.body);
            var errMsg = "Error: " + jsonObject.error.message.value;
            $("#error").text(errMsg);
        }
    });
}
```

LISTING 9-19 A JavaScript function for checking in a document into a document library via the REST API

```
function checkInFile() {
    var executor = new SP.RequestExecutor(appweburl);
    var operationUri = appweburl +
        "/_api/SP.AppContextSite(@target)/web/" +
        "GetFileByServerRelativeUrl('/sites/AppsDevelopmentSite/" +
        "Shared%20Documents/SampleFile.xml')/CheckIn?@target='" +
        hostweburl + "'";

    var bodyContent = JSON.stringify({
            'comment': 'Checked in via REST',
            'checkInType': 1
        });
```

```
    executor.executeAsync({
        url: operationUri,
        method: "POST",
        headers: {
            "Accept": "application/json;odata=verbose",
            "Content-type": "application/json;odata=verbose",
            "Content-length": bodyContent.length,
            "X-RequestDigest": formDigestValue,
        },
        body: bodyContent,
        success: function (data) {
            var jsonObject = JSON.parse(data.body);
            $("#message").text("Operation completed!");
        },
        error: function (data, errorCode, errorMessage) {
            var jsonObject = JSON.parse(data.body);
            var errMsg = "Error: " + jsonObject.error.message.value;
            $("#error").text(errMsg);
        }
    });
}
```

The checkout phase simply requires an operation URI to be invoked via HTTP *POST*. On the contrary, the check-in phase requires posting some arguments, which in the current example are presented as a JSON object. This posted JSON object represents the arguments for the classic and standard *CheckIn* method of the CSOM.

Deleting an existing document

The last action related to management of single files is the deletion of a document. As shown at the beginning of this chapter, to delete a document, you need to make an HTTP *POST* request to the service, providing an *ETag* for security validation rules and an HTTP header of type *X-HTTP-Method* with a value of *DELETE*. Listing 9-20 demonstrates the process.

LISTING 9-20 A JavaScript function for deleting a document from a document library via the REST API

```
function deleteFile() {
    var executor = new SP.RequestExecutor(appweburl);
    var operationUri = appweburl + "/_api/SP.AppContextSite(@target)/web/" +
        "GetFileByServerRelativeUrl('/sites/AppsDevelopmentSite/" +
        "Shared%20Documents/SampleFile.xml')?@target='" +
        hostweburl + "'";

    executor.executeAsync({
        url: operationUri,
        method: "POST",
        headers: {
            "Accept": "application/json;odata=verbose",
            "X-HTTP-Method": "DELETE",
            "X-RequestDigest": formDigestValue,
            "IF-MATCH": "*", // Discard concurrency checks
        },
        success: function (data) {
            $("#message").text("Operation completed!");
        },
        error: function (data, errorCode, errorMessage) {
            var jsonObject = JSON.parse(data.body);
            var errMsg = "Error: " + jsonObject.error.message.value;
            $("#error").text(errMsg);
        }
    });
}
```

Notice that Listing 9-20 retrieves the file itself as an *SP.File* object, instead of the bare content (*$value*) of the file. The code then deletes that file without performing a concurrency check.

Querying a list of documents

Querying a list of documents from a document library is almost the same as querying a list of items. The main difference is the URL of the endpoint, which targets the *Files* collection instead of the *Items* collection. Furthermore, every file of a document library is an object of type *SP.File*, not *SP.ListItem*.

LISTING 9-21 A JavaScript function for querying files from a document library via the REST API

```
function queryDocuments() {
    var executor = new SP.RequestExecutor(appweburl);
    var operationUri = appweburl +
        "/_api/SP.AppContextSite(@target)/web/lists/" +
        "GetByTitle('Documents')/RootFolder/Files?@target='" +
        hostweburl + "'";

    executor.executeAsync({
        url: operationUri,
        method: "GET",
        headers: { "Accept": "application/json;odata=verbose" },
        success: function (data) {
            var jsonObject = JSON.parse(data.body);
            $("#message").empty();

            for (var i = 0; i < jsonObject.d.results.length; i++) {
                var item = jsonObject.d.results[i];
                $("#message").append("<div>" + item.Name + "</div>");
            }
        },
        error: function (data, errorCode, errorMessage) {
            var jsonObject = JSON.parse(data.body);
            var errMsg = "Error: " + jsonObject.error.message.value;
            $("#error").text(errMsg);
        }
    });
}
```

Notice also that the HTTP query uses an HTTP *GET* method and provides only the *Accept* HTTP header, without requiring any other extended header or information.

More Info For further details about the types and members available in the REST API, consult the official reference of the *SP* namespace of the Client-Side Object Model for JavaScript (JSOM). You can find the official reference at *http://msdn.microsoft.com/en-us/library/ee557057.aspx.*

Summary

In this chapter, you learned about the new REST API introduced in SharePoint 2013. You examined the architecture and the capabilities of this new tool, which can be consumed either by .NET or SharePoint apps, as well as from any third-party platform. In addition, you learned how to implement the REST API in real projects with JavaScript, addressing a set of common scenarios.

CHAPTER 10

Remote event receivers

New to Microsoft SharePoint 2013, remote event receivers allow you to connect external software and apps to your SharePoint solutions. Through a remote event receiver, you can link to SharePoint any external software that's capable of providing services based on a specific and predefined SOAP (Simple Object Access Protocol) service contract. You should not, however, consider remote event receivers as alternatives to Business Connectivity Services (BCS). While BCS allows consuming data from external data sources, remote event receivers allow an external system to subscribe to specific events that will occur on the SharePoint side. The external system can be an ERP, a line-of-business (LOB) system, a custom SharePoint app, or a third-party solution. Furthermore, you can implement remote receivers using potentially any programming language, as long as it is capable of providing a SOAP endpoint to receive events. Throughout this chapter, you will investigate remote event receiver architecture, capabilities, security considerations, and implementation details.

Architecture of remote event receivers

The architecture of remote event receivers uses SOAP as the protocol for communicating across the wire, because it is the most open, standard protocol for implementing cross-platform dialogs. On the SharePoint side, the remote event receiver employs a Microsoft Windows Communication Foundation (WCF) proxy for calling the remote endpoint. While working in Microsoft .NET, you can also implement the remote event receiver side of the dialog using WCF. And, as you'll learn in the "A sample remote event receiver" section, Microsoft Visual Studio 2012 provides an item template and wizard-assisted procedure for this purpose. For now, however, you'll concentrate on learning about the architecture and capabilities of remote event receivers.

More Info To understand the architecture of remote event receivers, you should have a good knowledge of WCF and .NET server-side programming. If you aren't familiar with these topics, take a lap around WCF architecture and service implementation by reading *Windows Communication Foundation 4 Step by Step*, by John Sharp (Microsoft Press, 2010). You can also have a quick look at the following online article on MSDN: *http://msdn.microsoft.com/en-us/library/ms731082.aspx*.

The new remote event receivers introduced in SharePoint 2013 are similar to the event receivers that were available in SharePoint 2010. These are still available in SharePoint 2013, but they are provided mainly for backward compatibility, even if an occasional project could still benefit from their implementation. Classic and local event receivers are suitable only in on-premises and sandboxed solutions, while remote event receivers are a better choice for Microsoft Office 365 solutions and SharePoint apps.

More Info If you need further details about classic event receivers, consult the previous version of this book: *Microsoft SharePoint 2010 Developer Reference*, by Paolo Pialorsi (Microsoft Press, 2011).

Architecture and contracts

A remote event receiver is just a remote SOAP endpoint that adheres to a specific service contract. In Figure 10-1, you can see the functional schema of remote event receivers in SharePoint 2013.

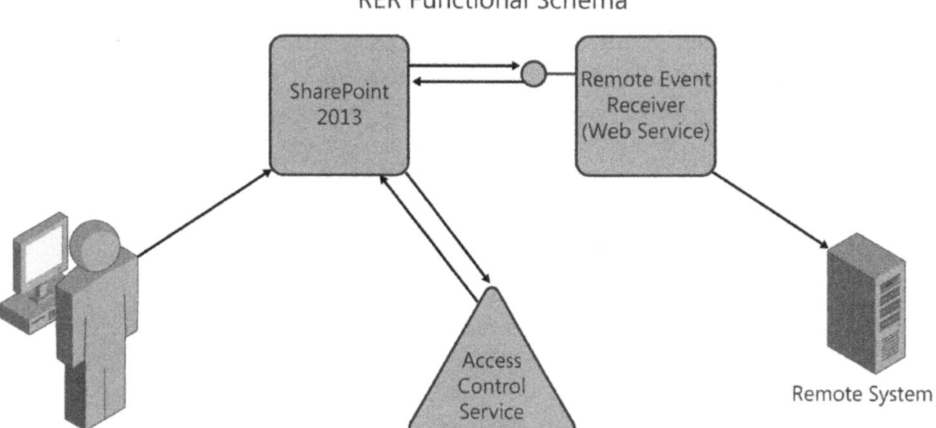

FIGURE 10-1 The functional schema of remote event receivers.

A remote event receiver is registered for handling events related to a list item, a list, a website, an app, a BCS entity, or a security configuration. Whenever an event related to a registered target occurs, the SharePoint 2013 remote event receiver environment raises a remote call to a SOAP endpoint published by a third-party remote system. Any authentication and authorization task is implemented using the Windows Azure ACS for Microsoft Office 365 (or the OAuth protocol in on-premises deployment scenarios). As you will learn in the "Security Infrastructure" section of this book, the OAuth protocol manages only app authentication and authorization, while standard user authentication and authorization are managed by the standard security infrastructure of SharePoint. You can also configure an app that publishes a remote event receiver to run in a so-called *high-trust*, or *server-to-server (S2S)*, configuration, which was introduced in Chapter 8, "SharePoint apps," and will be explained in detail in Chapter 20, "Claims-based authentication, federated identities, and OAuth."

Listing 10-1 outlines the service contract of remote event receivers, which is applied regardless of whether the target SharePoint 2013 environment is online or on-premises.

LISTING 10-1 The service contract of the remote event receiver services

```
[ServiceContract(Namespace="http://schemas.microsoft.com/sharepoint/remoteapp/")]
public interface IRemoteEventService {

    [OperationContract]
    SPRemoteEventResult ProcessEvent(SPRemoteEventProperties properties);

    [OperationContract(IsOneWay = true)]
    void ProcessOneWayEvent(SPRemoteEventProperties properties);
}
```

As you can see, the service contract defines just two operations, which correspond to the notification of a synchronous event and an asynchronous one-way event. The *ProcessEvent* operation handles synchronous events, while *ProcessOneWayEvent* is for asynchronous processing. Both the operations accept an argument of type *SPRemoteEventProperties*, which defines all the useful information for implementing the remote event receiver business logic. Listing 10-2 shows the definition of the *SPRemoteEventProperties* type.

LISTING 10-2 The definition of type *SPRemoteEventProperties*, which is the argument provided to the remote event receiver operations

```
[DataContract(Name="RemoteEventProperties",
    Namespace="http://schemas.microsoft.com/sharepoint/remoteapp/")]
public class SPRemoteEventProperties {
    [DataMember]
    public SPRemoteAppEventProperties AppEventProperties { get; internal set; }
    [DataMember]
    public string ContextToken { get; internal set; }
    [DataMember]
    public Guid CorrelationId { get; internal set; }
    [DataMember]
    public int CultureLCID { get; internal set; }
    [DataMember]
    public SPRemoteEntityInstanceEventProperties
        EntityInstanceEventProperties { get; set; }
    [DataMember]
    public string ErrorCode { get; internal set; }
    [DataMember]
    public string ErrorMessage { get; internal set; }
    [DataMember]
    public SPRemoteEventType EventType { get; internal set; }
    [DataMember]
    public SPRemoteItemEventProperties ItemEventProperties { get; internal set; }
    [DataMember]
    public SPRemoteListEventProperties ListEventProperties { get; internal set; }
    [DataMember]
    public SPRemoteSecurityEventProperties SecurityEventProperties { get;
        internal set; }
    [DataMember]
    public int UICultureLCID { get; internal set; }
    [DataMember]
    public SPRemoteWebEventProperties WebEventProperties { get; internal set; }
}
```

The *SPRemoteEventProperties* class is a data contract serializable type and thereby transferable across the wire within the SOAP request for remote event receivers. Moreover, the type provides properties for transferring all the useful information about the current context, the event that is happening, and the related event outcome, just in case of a synchronous event. Table 10-1 shows a detailed list of the main members of the *SPRemoteEventProperties* type.

TABLE 10-1 The main members of the *SPRemoteEventProperties* type

Member	Description
AppEventProperties	A complex property providing information about the app that is the target of the remote event receiver, in case the remote event receiver is related to a SharePoint app
ContextToken	A property of type *String* representing the OAuth content token of the current request
CorrelationId	The correlation ID of the current request, presented as a *GUID* property
CultureLCID	An *Integer* property providing the LCID of the current culture
EntityInstanceEventProperties	A complex property providing information about a BCS entity that is the target of the remote event receiver, in case the remote event receiver is related to a BCS entity set
ErrorCode	A read-only *String* property to access an error code
ErrorMessage	A read-only *String* property to access an error message
EventType	A property of type *SPRemoteEventType*, which defines the kind of event described by the remote event receiver
ItemEventProperties	A complex property providing information about a SharePoint item that is the target of the remote event receiver, in case the remote event receiver is related to an item
ListEventProperties	A complex property providing information about a SharePoint list that is the target of the remote event receiver, in case the remote event receiver is related to a list
SecurityEventProperties	A complex property providing information about a SharePoint security principal that is the target of the remote event receiver, in case the remote event receiver is related to a security principal
UICultureLCID	An *Integer* property providing the LCID of the current UI culture
WebEventProperties	A complex property providing information about a SharePoint website that is the target of the remote event receiver, in case the remote event receiver is related to a website

When the operation invoked is the synchronous one, the result is of type *SPRemoteEventResult*. This type provides information to SharePoint 2013 about the remote event outcome. Table 10-2 lists the main members for the *SPRemoteEventResult* type.

TABLE 10-2 The main members of the *SPRemoteEventResult* type

Member	Description
ChangedItemProperties	A property that allows changing the values of the fields of the target item of a synchronous event. For example, you can use it to change a field of an item when the target item is going to be added or updated.
ErrorMessage	A *String* property to provide a descriptive error message to SharePoint when the synchronous remote event receiver needs to abort the current operation.
RedirectUrl	A property that provides the *String* value of the URL to which you want to redirect the target user's browser as a result of an error raised from the remote event receiver. This property is deprecated, and you should avoid using it, unless you need to support backward compatibility.
Status	An enumerated type (*SPRemoteEventServiceStatus*) that allows synchronous events to abort the current operation. The available values are *CancelNoError*, *CancelWithError*, *CancelWithRedirectUrl*, and *Continue*. By default, this property assumes the value of *Continue*.

The *SPRemoteEventResult* type is serializable through data contract serialization, as well.

Scopes and types of receivers

SharePoint 2013 supports about 70 different types of events that you can raise. Depending on the type of event and the operation invoked, a remote event receiver can assume different scopes. Events with names ending in *-ed* are typically asynchronous events and are handled by the *ProcessOneWayEvent* operation, even if they can be executed synchronously, too. If an *-ed* event is executed synchronously, the invoked operation will be *ProcessEvent*. The *ProcessEvent* operation also handles all the events with names ending in *-ing*; these are synchronous events as well.

As a handy reference, this section lists all available events, divided by scope. Table 10-3 details events related to single list items.

TABLE 10-3 Events related to a list item

List item event type	Description
ItemAdding	An item of a list is going to be added.
ItemUpdating	An item of a list is going to be updated.
ItemDeleting	An item of a list is going to be deleted.
ItemCheckingIn	An item of a list is going to be checked in.
ItemCheckingOut	An item of a list is going to be checked out.
ItemUncheckingOut	An item of a list is going to be unchecked out.
ItemAttachmentAdding	An attachment of an item of a list is going to be added.
ItemAttachmentDeleting	An attachment of an item of a list is going to be deleted.
ItemFileMoving	A file of a library is going to be moved.
ItemVersionDeleting	A version of a file of a library is going to be deleted.
ItemAdded	An item of a list has been added.
ItemUpdated	An item of a list has been updated.
ItemDeleted	An item of a list has been deleted.
ItemCheckedIn	An item of a list has been checked in.
ItemCheckedOut	An item of a list has been checked out.
ItemUncheckedOut	An item of a list has been unchecked out.
ItemAttachmentAdded	An attachment of an item of a list has been added.
ItemAttachmentDeleted	An attachment of an item of a list has been deleted.
ItemFileMoved	A file of a library has been moved.
ItemFileConverted	A file of a library has been converted.
ItemVersionDeleted	A version of a file of a library has been deleted.

Table 10-4 illustrates events related to lists.

TABLE 10-4 Events related to a list

List event type	Description
FieldAdding	A field is going to be added to a list definition.
FieldUpdating	A field of a list definition is going to be updated.
FieldDeleting	A field of a list definition is going to be deleted.
FieldAdded	A field has been added to a list definition.
FieldUpdated	A field of a list definition has been updated.
FieldDeleted	A field of a list definition has been deleted.
ListAdding	A list instance is going to be added.
ListDeleting	A list instance is going to be deleted.
ListAdded	A list instance has been added.
ListDeleted	A list instance has been deleted.

A third family of events corresponds to those defined for actions related to a website. Table 10-5 enumerates these.

TABLE 10-5 Events related to a website

Web event type	Description
SiteDeleting	A site collection is going to be deleted.
WebDeleting	A website instance is going to be deleted.
WebMoving	A website instance is going to be moved.
WebAdding	A website instance is going to be added.
SiteDeleted	A site collection has been deleted.
WebDeleted	A website instance has been deleted.
WebMoved	A website instance has been moved.
WebProvisioned	A website instance has been provisioned.

Lastly, SharePoint provides events for app management, BCS entities, and security, which are defined in Table 10-6.

TABLE 10-6 Events related to security, apps, and BCS entities

Others EventType	Description
GroupAdding	A group is going to be added.
GroupUpdating	A group is going to be updated.
GroupDeleting	A group is going to be deleted.
GroupUserAdding	A user is going to be added to a group.
GroupUserDeleting	A user is going to be deleted from a group.
RoleDefinitionAdding	A role definition is going to be added.

Others EventType	Description
RoleDefinitionUpdating	A role definition is going to be updated.
RoleDefinitionDeleting	A role definition is going to be deleted.
RoleAssignmentAdding	A role is going to be assigned to a target principal.
RoleAssignmentDeleting	A role is going to be removed from a target principal.
InheritanceBreaking	Permissions inheritance is going to be broken.
InheritanceResetting	Permissions inheritance is going to be reset.
GroupAdded	A group has been added.
GroupUpdated	A group has been updated.
GroupDeleted	A group has been deleted.
GroupUserAdded	A user has been added to a group.
GroupUserDeleted	A user has been deleted from a group.
RoleDefinitionAdded	A role definition has been added.
RoleDefinitionUpdated	A role definition has been updated.
RoleDefinitionDeleted	A role definition has been deleted.
RoleAssignmentAdded	A role has been assigned to a target principal.
RoleAssignmentDeleted	A role has been removed from a target principal.
InheritanceBroken	Permissions inheritance has been broken.
InheritanceReset	Permissions inheritance has been reset.
AppInstalled	A SharePoint app has been installed.
AppUpgraded	A SharePoint app has been upgraded.
AppUninstalling	A SharePoint app is going to be uninstalled.
EntityInstanceAdded	A BCS entity instance has been added.
EntityInstanceUpdated	A BCS entity instance has been updated.
EntityInstanceDeleted	A BCS entity instance has been deleted.

You can implement and provision remote event receivers within a SharePoint app to implement custom event-handling capabilities that are related to the contents of the app website of an app, and you can also implement and provision them independently from a SharePoint app. While the remote event receivers defined in an app can be accessed both on-premises and on Office 365, remote event receivers that are not part of an app are more suitable for on-premises environments because they require some extra work during deployment.

A sample remote event receiver

Now that you know the various kinds of remote event receivers that are available, you'll create a simple remote event receiver. Imagine that you have a SharePoint app for managing orders of products. Whenever a new order is inserted in a SharePoint list of orders, you want a SharePoint app to be activated through a remote event receiver to perform an action on a LOB system.

A detailed implementation of the LOB system on the back end of the remote event receiver is out of scope for the current sample. Instead, let's start with creating a custom SharePoint app that simply intercepts the remote events. For example, you can define an autohosted app targeting an Office 365 environment, following the procedure you learned in Chapter 8. Then you can add a new *Order* content type, a list definition, and a list instance, which is based on the *Order* content type.

Important A remote event receiver works only in cases when the target SharePoint environment is capable of communicating via SOAP over HTTP/HTTPS with the remote event receiver service endpoint. As you learned in Chapter 8, if you are developing a remote event receiver for an on-premises deployment, you cannot create an autohosted app. For an on-premises scenario, your only options are SharePoint-hosted and provider-hosted apps. Moreover, for developing a remote event receiver in a SharePoint-hosted app, you will need to deploy an external website, too, because the SharePoint app website cannot publish the SOAP service endpoint for the remote event receiver. Meanwhile, you can easily invoke and eventually debug a remote event receiver defined in a provider-hosted app. In an on-premises scenario, that provider-hosted app will have to be defined as a high-trust app, unless you do not use Windows Azure ACS.

On the contrary, if you plan to deploy and debug an app for Office 365, you can choose between an autohosted and a provider-hosted model. Nevertheless, by default you will not be able to debug it on your local installation of Microsoft Internet Information Services (IIS) Express, because IIS Express is not accessible from Office 365. However, you can use the Windows Azure Service Bus to communicate between Office 365 and your local environment. The Microsoft Office Developer Tools for Visual Studio 2012 provide a set of tools for configuring remote debugging of remote event receivers through the Windows Azure Service Bus.

For further details about using the Windows Azure Service Bus for this purpose, please read the article "Debugging Remote Event Receivers with Visual Studio," which is available at *http://blogs.msdn.com/b/officeapps/archive/2013/01/03/debugging-remote-event-receivers-with-visual-studio.aspx.*

Lastly, consider that if you deploy the remote event receiver on your local development environment (for example, using IIS Express) or in a provider-hosted environment, and you want to publish the app via HTTPS, you will need to use an SSL certificate published by a trusted Certification Authority; otherwise, SharePoint will refuse to communicate with your remote event receiver because of certificate validation issues.

For the sake of completeness, you should provide some custom code to insert items in the newly defined list of orders. For example, you could define in the Default.aspx page of the app some HTML form fields to insert a new order item instance. Listing 10-3 provides an excerpt of the HTML code for defining such a form. Here, the order content type is made of the fields *Title*, *OrderId*, *OrderStatus* (admitted values are *Inserted*, *Approved*, *Shipped*, *Completed*), and *CustomerId*.

LISTING 10-3 The basic ASPX code of the Default.aspx page of the app, for adding new order items

```
<form id="form1" runat="server">

    <div id="chrome_placeholder"></div>

    <div style="margin-left: 20px;">
        Order Title: <asp:TextBox ID="OrderTitle" runat="server" /><br />
        Order ID: <asp:TextBox ID="OrderID" runat="server" /><br />
        Order Status:
        <asp:DropDownList ID="OrderStatus" runat="server">
            <asp:ListItem Value="Inserted" Text="Inserted" />
            <asp:ListItem Value="Approved" Text="Approved" />
            <asp:ListItem Value="Shipped" Text="Shipped" />
            <asp:ListItem Value="Completed" Text="Completed" />
        </asp:DropDownList><br />
        Customer ID: <asp:TextBox ID="CustomerID" runat="server" /><br />
        <asp:Button ID="InsertOrder" runat="server" Text="Insert Order!"
            OnClick="InsertOrder_Click" />

        <br /> <br />

        <asp:Button ID="RefreshOrders" runat="server" Text="Refresh Orders"
            OnClick="RefreshOrders_Click" />

        <br /> <br />

        <asp:GridView ID="gridOrders" runat="server" />

    </div>
</form>
```

As you can see from the code, the Default.aspx page provides both a form for inserting a new order item and a *GridView* control for showing the items in the list of orders. The .NET code behind the buttons for inserting a new item and for showing the list of items is based on the Client-Side Object Model (CSOM); you can find the full sample code in the companion samples for this chapter. Please refer to Chapter 7, "Client-side technologies," for further details about working with the CSOM.

After creating the SharePoint app and configuring the content type, list definition, and data management business logic, right-click the SharePoint app project (the one with the AppManifest.xml file in it) and select Add | New Item | Remote Event Receiver, as shown in Figure 10-2.

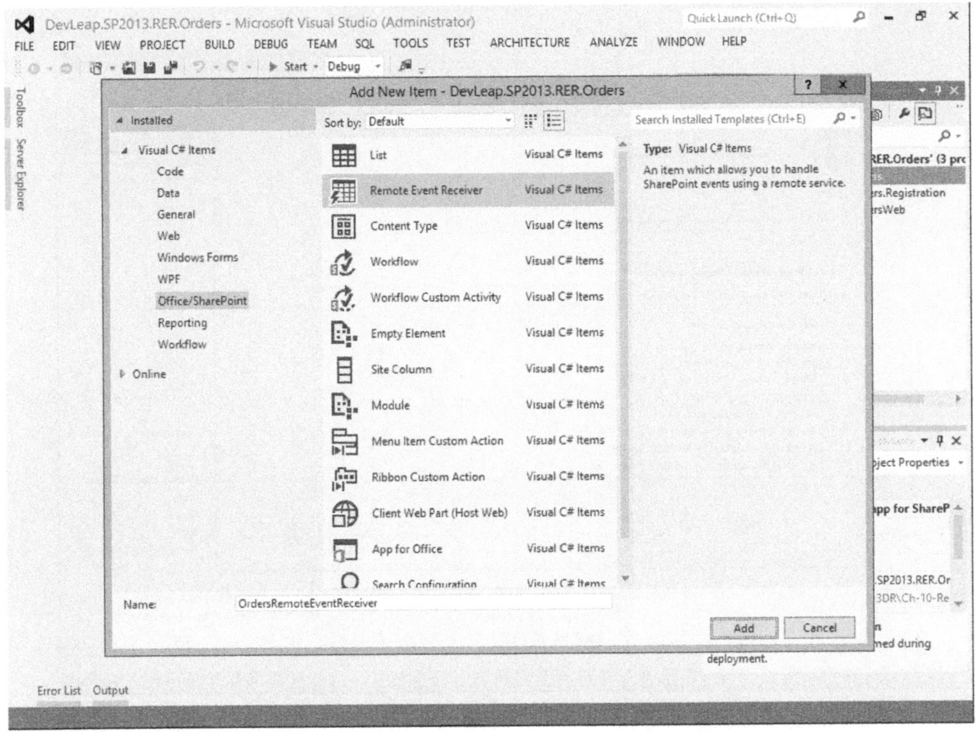

FIGURE 10-2 Visual Studio 2012 while adding a new remote event receiver.

When you click the Add button, Visual Studio launches a wizard (see Figure 10-3) that asks you to provide information about the scope of the event receiver and the type of events you want to trap.

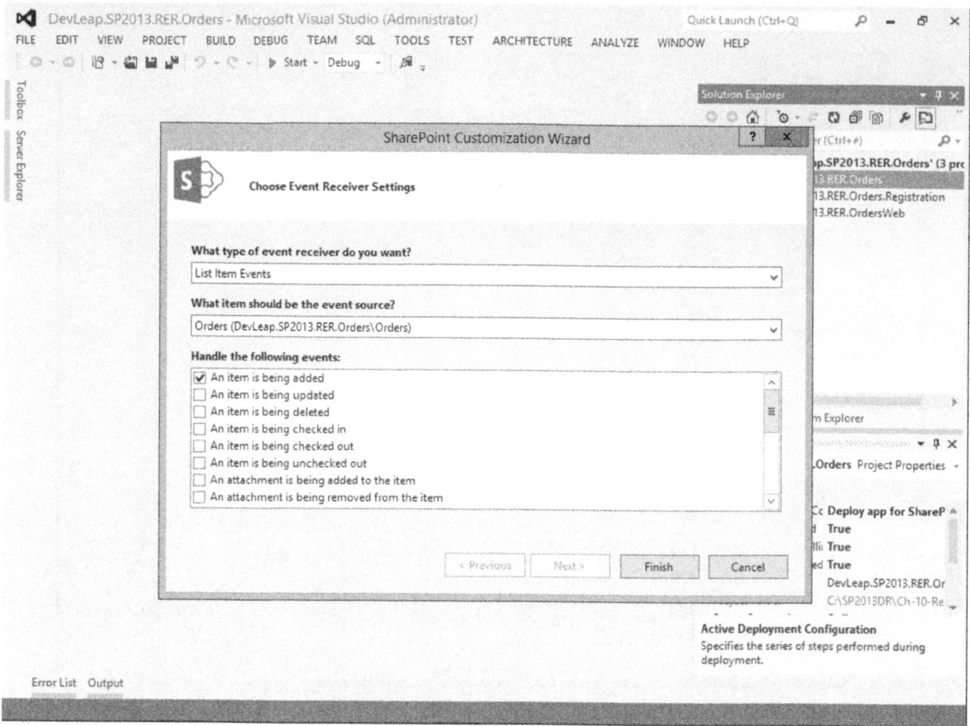

FIGURE 10-3 The wizard for configuring a new remote event receiver.

For example, select a remote event receiver targeting List Item Events, selecting the Orders list you previously created in the SharePoint app, and choosing events of type An Item Is Being Added and An Item Was Added, which correspond to the *ItemAdding* and *ItemAdded* event types, respectively. When you click Finish, the Visual Studio wizard adds not only a feature element to the target SharePoint app project, but also a WCF service to the web project.

Listing 10-4 provides the source code of the class implementing the WCF service, which corresponds to the remote event receiver.

LISTING 10-4 The basic remote event receiver implementation generated by the wizard of Visual Studio 2012

```
using System;
using System.Collections.Generic;
using System.Linq;
using System.Text;
using Microsoft.SharePoint.Client;
using Microsoft.SharePoint.Client.EventReceivers;

namespace DevLeap.SP2013.RER.OrdersWeb {
    public class OrdersRemoteEventReceive : IRemoteEventService {
        public SPRemoteEventResult ProcessEvent(SPRemoteEventProperties
        properties) {
            SPRemoteEventResult result = new SPRemoteEventResult();

            using (ClientContext clientContext =
                TokenHelper.CreateRemoteEventReceiverClientContext(
                properties)) {
                if (clientContext != null) {
                    clientContext.Load(clientContext.Web);
                    clientContext.ExecuteQuery();
                }
            }
            return result;
        }

        public void ProcessOneWayEvent(SPRemoteEventProperties properties) {
        }
    }
}
```

As you can see, the source code of the autogenerated remote event receiver handles the *ProcessEvent* method of the *IRemoteEventService* service contract. Moreover, it creates a new *ClientContext* instance of the CSOM, using the argument of type *SPRemoteEventProperties* provided to the remote event receiver operation. Notice the static method *CreateRemoteEventReceiver ClientContext* of the *TokenHelper* class, which creates a *ClientContext* instance based on the *ContextToken* property of the argument. Within the code of the remote event receiver, you can access, using the CSOM, the whole SharePoint host website and the app website, as well as their content and lists of items, in accordance with the permissions configured for you app. For more information on how to use the CSOM for interacting with SharePoint, see Chapter 7.

For the sake of simplicity, imagine that you want to retrieve information about the just-added item. You can access the argument of type *SPRemoteEventProperties* that's provided, and retrieve the properties of the currently managed item through the *ItemEventProperties* property. Listing 10-5 provides an example of this procedure.

LISTING 10-5 Sample implementation of the *ProcessEvent* operation of the remote event receiver

```
public SPRemoteEventResult ProcessEvent(SPRemoteEventProperties properties) {
    SPRemoteEventResult result = new SPRemoteEventResult();

    if (properties.EventType == SPRemoteEventType.ItemAdding) {
        using (ClientContext clientContext =
            TokenHelper.CreateRemoteEventReceiverClientContext(properties)) {

            if (clientContext != null) {
                if ((String)properties.ItemEventProperties
                .AfterProperties["DevLeapOrderStatus"] == "Completed") {
                    result.Status = SPRemoteEventServiceStatus.CancelWithError;
                    result.ErrorMessage =
                    "Order cannot be inserted as 'Completed'";
                }
                else {
                    String newTitle = String.Format("{0} - Added on {1}",
                        (String)properties.ItemEventProperties
                        .AfterProperties["Title"],
                        DateTime.Now);
                    result.ChangedItemProperties["Title"] = newTitle;
                }
            }
        }
    }

    return result;
}
```

As you can see in the code highlighted in bold in Listing 10-5, to access a field of the target item, you can query by field name the *AfterProperties* or *BeforeProperties* indexer properties of the *ItemEventProperties* property, which is available in the argument of type *SPRemoteEventProperties* received by the remote event receiver operation. Whether you query *AfterProperties* or *BeforeProperties* depends on the kind of event you are handling. For example, if you are managing the *ItemAdding* event, you will have only the *AfterProperties* values. If you are handling the *ItemUpdating* event, however, you will have both the *AfterProperties* and the *BeforeProperties values.*

In Listing 10-5, the synchronous event (the *ProcessEvent* operation) first checks the *EventType* property of the argument received. If *EventType* is of type *SPRemoteEventType.ItemAdding*, then it checks the *DevLeapOrderStatus* field of the target item. If the field has a value of *Completed*, the remote event receiver raises an error back to the SharePoint environment. To raise an error, you simply need to provide a value other than *Continue* for the *Status* property of the return value of the operation, which is of type *SPRemoteEventResult*. The sample raises an error and provides a description for that error in the *ErrorMessage* property of the operation result.

Just for the sake of example, in Listing 10-5, if the target order item passes the validation rule, the remote event receiver changes the *Title* field of the current order item, appending text with a value of *- Added on*, followed by the current date and time. Notice that, in order to change the field value, the remote event receiver implementation configures the *ChangedItemProperties* property of the operation result.

More Info You may be wondering why the sample code does not use the CSOM to change the field value. The answer is simple: you cannot change an item during the *ItemAdding* event, because the item still does not exist in the content database. Thus, you should not be able to retrieve it from the target list using the CSOM. Moreover, if you are trapping another event—not the *ItemAdding event*, but, for example, the *ItemUpdating* event—changing the target item via the CSOM will raise another remote event receiver event, and you will put your code in an infinite loop, blocking the app. Moreover, while executing multiple updates on the same item, because of the loop, you could get multiple concurrency exceptions, too.

If you want to add another event to an already defined remote event receiver, you can simply click the event receiver element in Solution Explorer in Visual Studio 2012 and change the properties in the property grid, where you will find a *Boolean* property for each available event. Figure 10-4 shows the UI for managing this task.

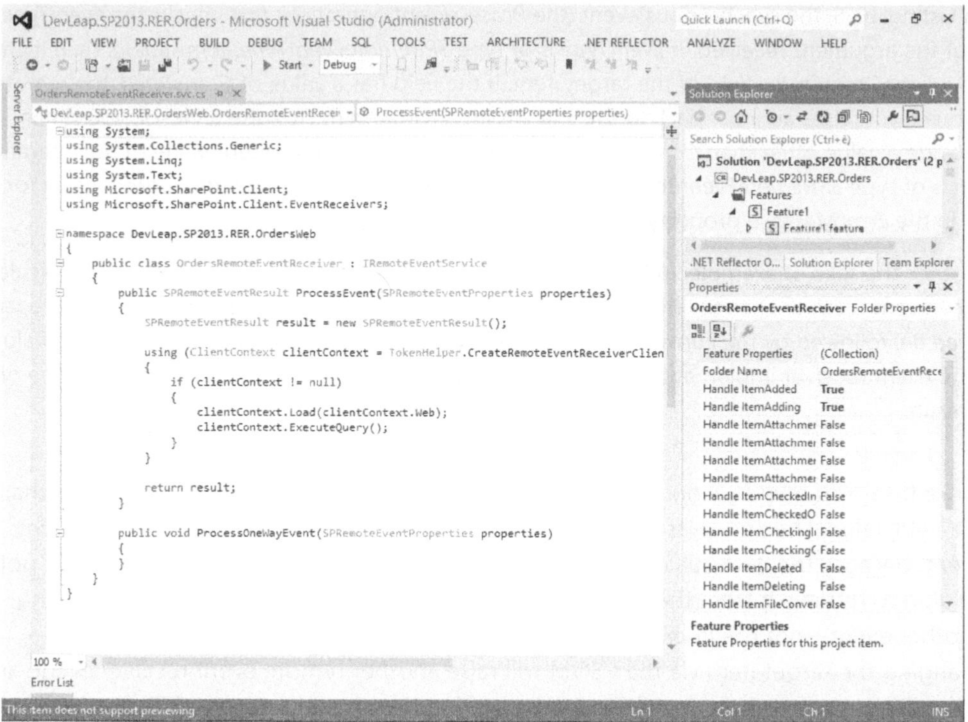

FIGURE 10-4 The property grid of an instance of a remote event receiver.

Now put a breakpoint in the remote event receiver service code, start the SharePoint app by pressing F5 in Visual Studio 2012, add a new order to the target list of orders using the form provided in the Default.aspx page, and see the events being raised in the service code. You will see both the *ItemAdding* event, raised in the *ProcessEvent* operation, and the *ItemAdded* event, raised in the *ProcessOneWayEvent* operation.

Listing 10-6 contains a sample of the *ProcessOneWayEvent* operation handling the *ItemAdded* event. As you can see, the event retrieves the target item by ID, using the CSOM, and changes its Title field by appending the literal value - *ItemAdded Event Raised*.

LISTING 10-6 Sample implementation of the *ProcessOneWayEvent* operation of the remote event receiver

```
public void ProcessOneWayEvent(SPRemoteEventProperties properties) {
    if (properties.EventType == SPRemoteEventType.ItemAdded) {
        using (ClientContext clientContext =
            TokenHelper.CreateRemoteEventReceiverClientContext(properties)) {
            if (clientContext != null) {
                List ordersList = clientContext.Web.Lists.GetByTitle("Orders");
                ListItem orderItem =
                    ordersList.GetItemById(
                    properties.ItemEventProperties.ListItemId);

                String newTitle = String.Format("{0} - ItemAdded Event Raised",
                    (String)properties.ItemEventProperties.
                    AfterProperties["Title"]);
                orderItem["Title"] = newTitle;
                orderItem.Update();
                clientContext.ExecuteQuery();
            }
        }
    }
}
```

Deployment and registration

To deploy remote event receivers, you need to provision a specific feature element that declares the name, the event to handle, the URL of the service, the ordinal sequence of the event, and the type of source for the event. When you add and configure a new remote event receiver in Visual Studio 2012, Visual Studio defines such a feature element behind the scenes. Listing 10-7 details the XML source of that feature element for the example remote event receiver you defined.

LISTING 10-7 The feature element for provisioning a remote event receiver handling *ItemAdding* and *ItemAdded* events

```xml
<?xml version="1.0" encoding="utf-8"?>
<Elements xmlns="http://schemas.microsoft.com/sharepoint/">
  <Receivers ListTemplateId="10101">
    <Receiver>
      <Name>OrdersRemoteEventReceiverItemAdding</Name>
      <Type>ItemAdding</Type>
      <SequenceNumber>10000</SequenceNumber>
      <Url>~remoteAppUrl/OrdersRemoteEventReceiver.svc</Url>
    </Receiver>
    <Receiver>
      <Name>OrdersRemoteEventReceiverItemAdded</Name>
      <Type>ItemAdded</Type>
      <SequenceNumber>10000</SequenceNumber>
      <Url>~remoteAppUrl/OrdersRemoteEventReceiver.svc</Url>
    </Receiver>
  </Receivers>
</Elements>
```

Listing 10-8 shows the complete definition of the *Receivers* element, which can contain multiple remote event receiver registrations for the same target object.

LISTING 10-8 The feature element of type *Receivers*, which defines one or more remote event receiver declarations

```xml
<Receivers
  ListTemplateId = "Text"
  ListTemplateOwner = "Text"
  ListUrl = "Text"
  RootWebOnly = "TRUE" | "FALSE"
  Scope = "Site" | "Web">
  <Receiver>
    <Name />
    <Type />
    <SequenceNumber />
    <Url />
    <Synchronization> Synchronous | Asynchronous </Synchronization>
    <Data />
    <Filter />
  </Receiver>
</Receivers>
```

The *Receivers* feature element belongs to the *http://schemas.microsoft.com/sharepoint* namespace. It is composed of a set of attributes, and accepts one or more *Receiver* child elements. Table 10-7 lists each available attribute, along with a brief explanation.

TABLE 10-7 The attributes of the *Receivers* element

Attribute	Description
ListTemplateId	Numeric value that defines the ID of the list definition to which the event receivers apply. It can assume any of the values defined in the *SPListTemplateType* enumeration, or it can assume a custom *ListTemplateId* of a custom list definition created with Visual Studio 2012.
ListTemplateOwner	GUID value that corresponds to the ID of the feature that provisioned the list template, if the list template is registered through a feature. Otherwise, it can be the name of the site definition that declares the current list template to which the event receivers apply.
ListUrl	Attribute that specifies the URL of the list instance to which the event receivers apply. Can assume the form of lists/orders, in case the target list name is Orders.
RootWebOnly	*Boolean* attribute to declare if the event receivers apply only to the root web.
Scope	Attribute that can assume the value of *Site* or *Web*. It defines the scope of the event receivers—they target either the site collection or the current web.

You can manually define feature elements provisioning remote event receivers. Although it is easier to let Visual Studio do the job for you, in some circumstances you may need to manually change the automatically generated files. For example, you can define whether an event will be synchronous or asynchronous using the *Synchronization* child element of the *Receiver* element. By default, all the *-ing* events are synchronous and all the *-ed* events are asynchronous, but you can configure any *-ed* event to be synchronous simply by setting the *Synchronization* child element of the *Receiver* tag to a value of *Synchronous*. If you provision an *-ing* event as synchronous, be careful that the *ProcessEvent* operation is raised on the service side, instead of the default *ProcessOneWayEvent* operation.

Lastly, the *Url* child element of the *Receiver* element is usually configured by Visual Studio 2012 as a URL relative to the app website, thanks to the *~remoteAppUrl* token at the beginning of the URL value. However, you can configure whatever URL you like and need. For example, if your app is running in a testing environment with a specific public URL, you can simply replace the autogenerated URL with a real, direct URL of your own.

You can also manage and register the remote event receivers by using code based on the Server Object Model. Listing 10-9 shows sample code for browsing all the already registered remote event receiver instances, as well as for adding a new remote event receiver definition.

LISTING 10-9 A sample code excerpt for browsing and adding remote event receivers to a target list

```
using (SPSite site = new SPSite("http://devbook.sp2013.local/")) {
    using (SPWeb web = site.OpenWeb()) {
        SPList targetList = web.Lists.TryGetList("Orders");

        // Browse all the already defined remote event receivers
        foreach (SPEventReceiverDefinition rer in targetList.EventReceivers) {
            Console.WriteLine("RER Name: {0}\nType: {1}\nSequence Number: {2}" +
                "\nUrl: {3}\nSynchronization: {4}",
                rer.Name,
                rer.Type,
                rer.SequenceNumber,
                rer.Url,
                rer.Synchronization
                );
            Console.WriteLine("**********************************");
        }

        // Add a new remote event receiver definition
        targetList.EventReceivers.Add(
            SPEventReceiverType.ItemAdding,
            "http://services.devleap.com/MyCustomRER.svc");
    }
}
```

Notice that the *EventReceivers* property of the *SPList* type serves both the remote event receivers and the local in-process event receivers. In this chapter, the latter are not discussed, because they are not suitable for a cloud scenario like Office 365. However, while browsing all the registered event receivers by code, you should pay attention about what you get out from the *EventReceivers* property.

Lastly, consider that a remote event receiver can also be registered using the CSOM, as you will learn in the next section.

App-related receivers

So far, you've seen remote event receivers defined inside and deployed through apps for trapping events related to the contents of a SharePoint app. Remote event receivers can also handle events that rely on the app life cycle itself rather than on data inside an app. For example, *AppInstalled*, *AppUpgraded*, and *AppUninstalling* are raised whenever an app is installed, upgraded, or uninstalled, respectively. The *AppInstalled* event is useful for provisioning custom content or configurations while installing an app. The *AppUninstalling* event handles the opposite scenario, and can save custom data before decommissioning the app website and before any data stored inside the app website is completely lost. The *AppUpgraded* event is handy for managing upgrades of data—for example, when an app upgrade needs to change data structures and sample data already provisioned with a previous version of the app.

The architecture and the SOAP contract of an app-related remote event receiver are exactly the same for any other remote event receiver. However, while trapping these events, you will receive a property with the name *AppEventProperties* and type *SPRemoteAppEventProperties*, available in the argument of type *SPRemoteEventProperties* provided to the *ProcessEvent* operation, which gives you information about the current app. Listing 10-10 provides the definition of the *SPRemoteAppEventProperties* type.

LISTING 10-10 The definition of the *SPRemoteAppEventProperties* type

```
[DataContract(Name="RemoteAppEventProperties",
    Namespace="http://schemas.microsoft.com/sharepoint/remoteapp/")]
public class SPRemoteAppEventProperties {
    [DataMember]
    public Uri AppWebFullUrl { get; private set; }
    [DataMember]
    public string AssetId { get; private set; }
    [DataMember]
    public string ContentMarket { get; private set; }
    [DataMember]
    public Uri HostWebFullUrl { get; private set; }
    [DataMember]
    public Version PreviousVersion { get; private set; }
    [DataMember]
    public Guid ProductId { get; private set; }
    [DataMember]
    public Version Version { get; private set; }
}
```

Table 10-8 details the members of the *SPRemoteAppEventProperties* type.

TABLE 10-8 The members of the *SPRemoteAppEventProperties* type

Member	Description
AppWebFullUrl	A property of type *URI* that provides the URL of the app website of the current app
AssetId	A *String* property providing the asset ID of the current app
ContentMarket	A *String* property providing the source market of the current app
HostWebFullUrl	A property of type *URI* that provides the URL of the host website of the current app
PreviousVersion	A property of type *Version*, declaring the previous version of the current app if an upgrade is occurring
ProductId	A *GUID* property providing the product ID of the current app, which is also defined in the AppManifest.xml file of the app
Version	A property of type *Version*, declaring the current version of the current app

To register an app-related event, you can manually edit the AppManifest.xml file of your app. Inside the *Properties* element of the AppManifest.xml file, you can add three elements corresponding to the three kinds of available events. The sample AppManifest.xml file in Listing 10-11 configures all three event receivers.

LISTING 10-11 A sample AppManifest.xml file for configuring all the available app-related event receivers

```
<?xml version="1.0" encoding="utf-8" ?>
<!--Created:cb85b80c-f585-40ff-8bfc-12ff4d0e34a9-->
<App xmlns="http://schemas.microsoft.com/sharepoint/2012/app/manifest"
     Name="DevLeapSP2013REROrders"
     ProductID="{00d890ef-ff24-4f35-b6b6-1528e526cf39}"
     Version="1.0.0.0"
     SharePointMinVersion="15.0.0.0">
  <Properties>
    <Title>DevLeap.SP2013.RER.Orders</Title>
    <StartPage>~remoteAppUrl/Pages/Default.aspx?{StandardTokens}</StartPage>
<InstalledEventEndpoint>~remoteAppUrl/AppEventReceiver.svc
</ InstalledEventEndpoint><UpgradedEventEndpoint>~remoteAppUrl/AppEventReceiver.
svc</UpgradedEventEndpoint> <UninstallingEventEndpoint>~remoteAppUrl/
AppEventReceiver.svc</UninstallingEventEndpoint>
  </Properties>

  <AppPrincipal>
    <RemoteWebApplication ClientId="*" />
  </AppPrincipal>

  <AppPermissionRequests AllowAppOnlyPolicy="true" />

</App>
```

Notice the three elements (highlighted in bold) for defining the URI of the remote service for handling *AppInstalled*, *AppUpgraded*, *AppUninstalling*. You can achieve the same result by editing the properties of the SharePoint app project. Figure 10-5 shows the property grid of a sample app project; the three properties are outlined in red.

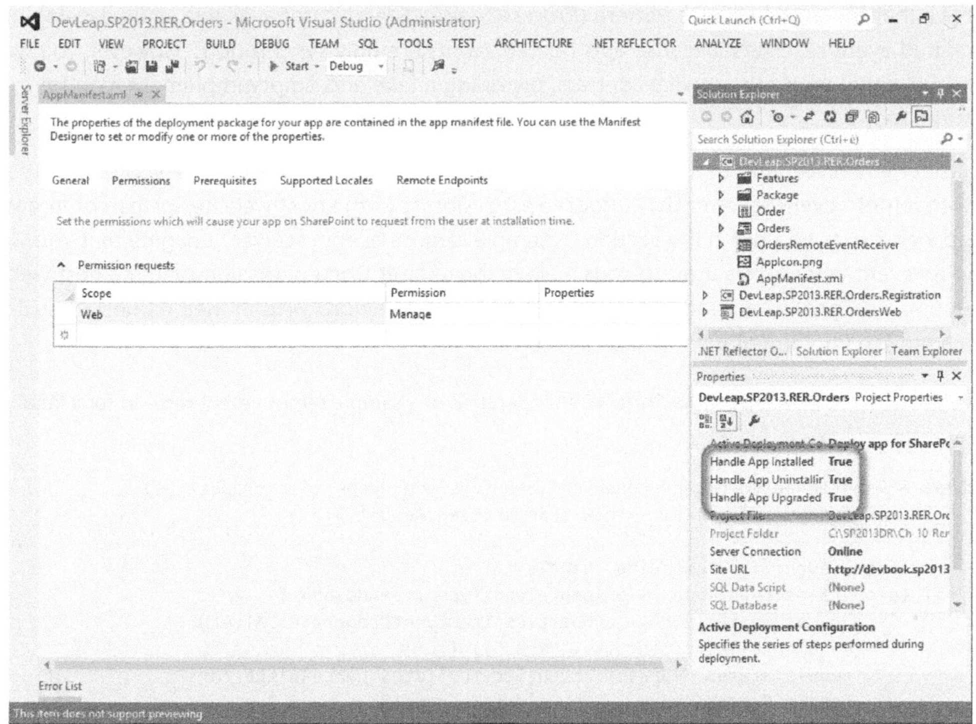

FIGURE 10-5 The properties for configuring app-related event receivers in a SharePoint app project.

When you enable an app-related event by setting its property value to *true*, Visual Studio adds a service file called AppEventReceiver.svc to the app web project. In the code of the service, you will be able to implement your custom receiver. Listing 10-12 illustrates a sample remote event receiver handling app-related events.

LISTING 10-12 A code excerpt of the *ProcessEvent* operation of a sample app-related remote event receiver

```
public SPRemoteEventResult ProcessEvent(SPRemoteEventProperties properties) {
    SPRemoteEventResult result = new SPRemoteEventResult();

    if (properties.EventType == SPRemoteEventType.AppInstalled ||
        properties.EventType == SPRemoteEventType.AppUpgraded ||
        properties.EventType == SPRemoteEventType.AppUninstalling) {

        // Do something with your app-related events

    }
    return (result);
}
```

Notice that the asynchronous pattern (*ProcessOneWayEvent*) is not available while developing app-related event receivers, because app-related events are only synchronous. However, you will have to fully implement the service contract, providing a fake and empty implementation for this operation, too.

Consider a real scenario for using an app-related event receiver. For example, you could provision a custom remote event receiver that targets a list or library in the host website, instead of targeting the app website, as you did in the section "A sample remote event receiver." Imagine that you want to trap an event whenever a user uploads a file in the default Documents library in the host website of your app. The goal of this receiver is to block files with the word *virus* in their name. Listing 10-13 shows a sample implementation of such a receiver.

LISTING 10-13 A code excerpt of the *ProcessEvent* operation of a sample remote event receiver for a library

```
public SPRemoteEventResult ProcessEvent(SPRemoteEventProperties properties) {
    SPRemoteEventResult result = new SPRemoteEventResult();

    // If the event is ItemAdding, handle it
    if (properties.EventType == SPRemoteEventType.ItemAdding) {
        String documentFileUrl = properties.ItemEventProperties.AfterUrl;
        if (documentFileUrl.Contains("virus")) {
            result.Status = SPRemoteEventServiceStatus.CancelWithError;
            result.ErrorMessage = "Invalid file name!";
        }
    }
    return (result);
}
```

As you can see, the implementation of this decoy receiver is really simple. If you attempt to upload a file whose name contains the keyword *virus* into the Documents library, the receiver will block it. Figure 10-6 illustrates how the standard UI of SharePoint behaves in this situation.

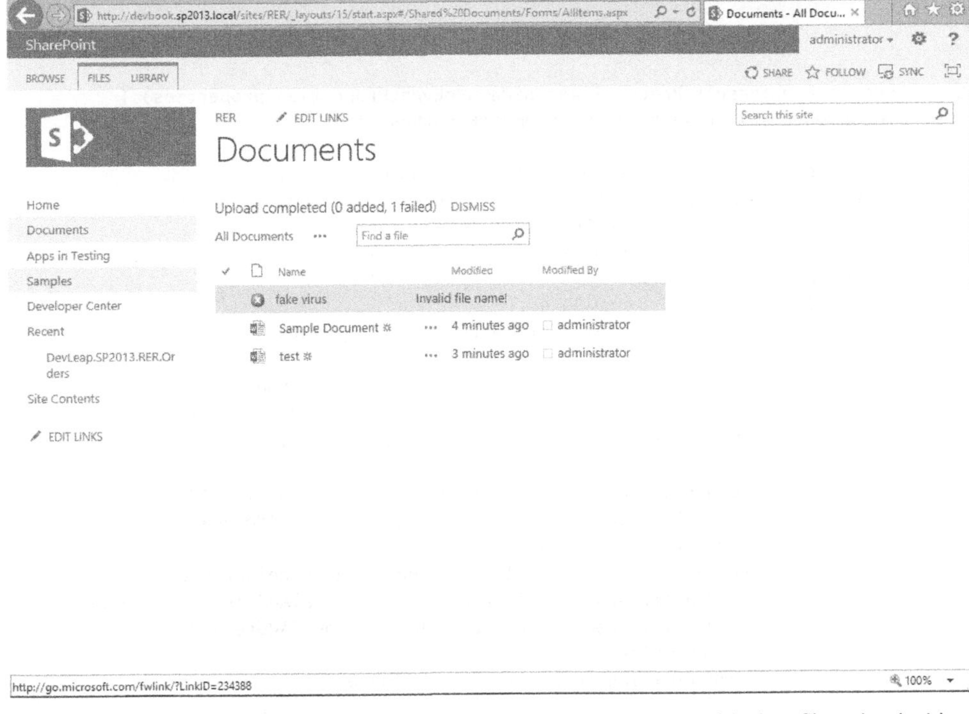

FIGURE 10-6 The standard UI of SharePoint when a remote event receiver blocks a file upload with an error message.

The interesting part of this example, however, is the registration of the remote event receiver. In fact, to register the receiver, you need to link the service with the target library, using the CSOM, within the *AppInstalled* event. In addition, of course, you will need to remove it from the list of configured receivers when the app is uninstalled (via the *AppUninstalling* event). Listing 10-14 provides sample code for an app-related event receiver that handles these tasks.

LISTING 10-14 A code excerpt of an app-related receiver for registering remote event receivers for a library in the host website

```
public SPRemoteEventResult ProcessEvent(SPRemoteEventProperties properties) {
    SPRemoteEventResult result = new SPRemoteEventResult();

    // Configure a remote event receiver for a document library
    if (properties.EventType == SPRemoteEventType.AppInstalled) {
        using (ClientContext clientContext = TokenHelper.
            CreateAppEventClientContext(
            properties, false)) {
            if (clientContext != null) {
                List documentsLibrary = clientContext.Web.Lists.
                GetByTitle("Documents");
                // Define the remote event receiver configuration
                EventReceiverDefinitionCreationInformation receiverDefinition =
                    new EventReceiverDefinitionCreationInformation();

                receiverDefinition.EventType = EventReceiverType.ItemAdding;
                receiverDefinition.ReceiverName = "DocumentItemAddingReceiver";
                receiverDefinition.ReceiverUrl =
                    String.Format("{0}://{1}/DocumentLibraryReceiver.svc",
                        OperationContext.Current.Channel.LocalAddress.Uri.Scheme,
                        OperationContext.Current.Channel.LocalAddress.Uri.
                        Authority);
                receiverDefinition.SequenceNumber = 10000;

                // Add it to the target library and save on SharePoint
                // asynchronously
                documentsLibrary.EventReceivers.Add(receiverDefinition);
                clientContext.ExecuteQuery();
            }
        }
    }
    // Remove the remote event receiver definition while uninstalling
    else if (properties.EventType == SPRemoteEventType.AppUninstalling) {
        using (ClientContext clientContext = TokenHelper.
            CreateAppEventClientContext(
            properties, false)) {
            if (clientContext != null) {


                // Search for the remote event receiver to remove
                List documentsLibrary = clientContext.Web.Lists.
                GetByTitle("Documents");
                clientContext.Load(documentsLibrary.EventReceivers);
                clientContext.ExecuteQuery();

                List<EventReceiverDefinition> toDelete =
                    new List<EventReceiverDefinition>();
```

```
                // Keep track of the remote event receiver instances to remove
                foreach (EventReceiverDefinition rer in documentsLibrary.
                EventReceivers) {
                    if (rer.ReceiverName == "DocumentItemAddingReceiver") {
                        toDelete.Add(rer);
                    }
                }

                // Effectively remove them
                if (toDelete.Count > 0) {
                    foreach (EventReceiverDefinition rer in toDelete) {
                        rer.DeleteObject();
                    }
                    clientContext.ExecuteQuery();
                }
            }
        }
    }
    return (result);
}
```

Notice that, in order to register a remote event receiver, your app needs to have at least the right of type *Manage* on the target website, which is the host website.

Callback capability

Another interesting and advanced feature available through remote event receivers is the callback capability, diagrammed in Figure 10-7.

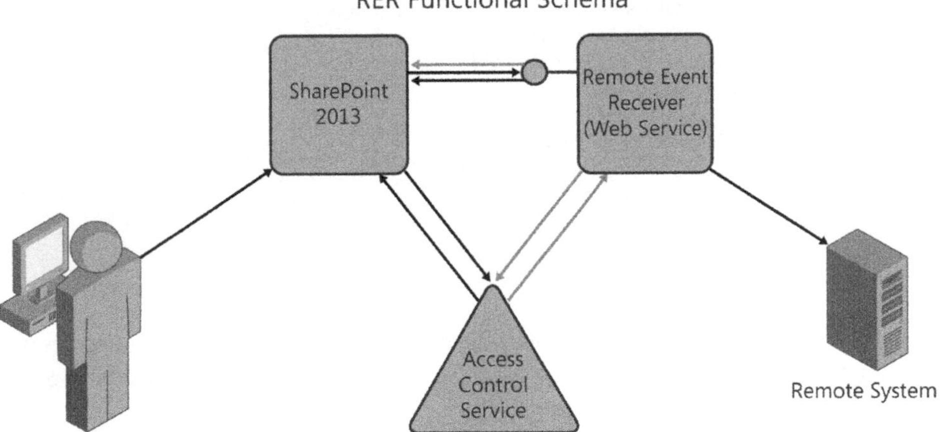

FIGURE 10-7 The functional schema of remote event receivers with callback capabilities.

The substantial difference from a classic scenario is that a remote event receiver using callback capabilities can acquire an app-related OAuth token if the remote event receiver is hosted by an app that runs on a farm in the cloud, like Office 365, or on-premises, but with OAuth properly configured.

More Info For further details about configuring an on-premises SharePoint 2013 farm for using ACS and OAuth, you can read the following blog post from Steve Peschka: *http://blogs.technet.com/b/speschka/archive/2012/07/23/setting-up-an-oauth-trust-between-farms-in-sharepoint-2013.aspx*.

Otherwise, you can configure your on-premises app using an S2S (high-trust) security configuration, avoiding the need for the OAuth protocol. Through the acquired token, the remote event receiver can call back the SharePoint environment, typically requesting content or performing some management tasks. Listing 10-15 shows a code excerpt of an event handled by the *ProcessEvent* operations, which are consequently asynchronous.

LISTING 10-15 A code excerpt of the *ProcessEvent* operation of a sample app-related remote event receiver

```
public void ProcessOneWayEvent(SPRemoteEventProperties properties) {
    if (properties.EventType == SPRemoteEventType.ItemAdded) {
        using (ClientContext clientContext =
            TokenHelper.GetS2SClientContextWithWindowsIdentity(new
            Uri(properties.ItemEventProperties.WebUrl),
            System.Security.Principal.WindowsIdentity.GetCurrent())) {
            if (clientContext != null) {
                List ordersList = clientContext.Web.Lists.GetByTitle("Orders");
                ListItem orderItem = ordersList.GetItemById(
                    properties.ItemEventProperties.ListItemId);

                String newTitle = String.Format("{0} - ItemAdded Event Raised",
                    (String)properties.ItemEventProperties.
                    AfterProperties["Title"]);
                orderItem["Title"] = newTitle;
                orderItem.Update();

                clientContext.ExecuteQuery();
            }
        }
    }
}
```

In the highlighted lines, the sample retrieves a client context instance and communicates with the SharePoint host website, modifying some data. The client context is acquired using an S2S (also known as high-trust) deployment instead of OAuth.

Security

From a security viewpoint, remote event receivers use the standard security infrastructure of SharePoint 2013 and SharePoint apps. Thus, if you create a remote event receiver within a SharePoint app, then that remote event receiver will execute its code like any other content of the app. For example, if you create or modify an item of a list or library from within an event receiver, and then you check the Created By or Last Modified By fields, you will find something like the information illustrated in Figure 10-8.

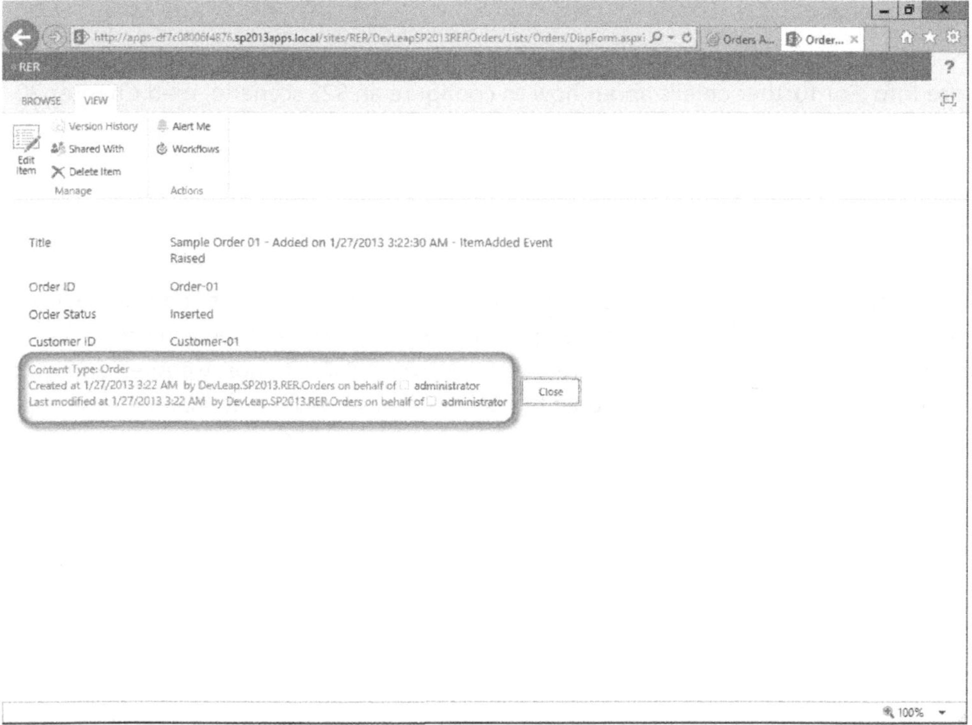

FIGURE 10-8 The properties of an item created and managed by a custom remote event receiver within a SharePoint app.

Notice that both the Created By and Last Modified By properties declare that the actions have been executed by the app *DevLeap.SP2013.RER.Orders*, on behalf of the current user, which in Figure 10-8 is the administrator.

If you save the context token and later execute a scheduled task with app-only credentials, the Last Modified By field will be related to the app only, without referencing a user on whose behalf the app is working.

Moreover, when SharePoint invokes a remote event receiver, it provides to it a rich set of information within the argument of type *SPRemoteEventProperties*. If you need to create a *ClientContext* instance for talking with the source SharePoint site, you can use either the *CreateRemoteEventReceiverClientContext* method of the *TokenHelper* class or the *GetS2SClientContextWithWindowsIdentity* method of the *TokenHelper* class. Both these methods give back a configured and ready-to-use *ClientContext* of the CSOM. The *CreateRemoteEventReceiverClientContext* method creates a *ClientContext* instance specifically for a remote event receiver running in a classic autohosted or provider-hosted scenario. The *GetS2SClientContextWithWindowsIdentity* method creates a *ClientContext* instance for an S2S (high-trust) scenario.

More Info For further details about how to configure an S2S scenario, read Chapter 20.

Summary

In this chapter, you learned about the architecture of remote event receivers and how they work. You saw how to develop and provision a sample remote event receiver. Then you considered such advanced scenarios as app-related event receivers, receivers related to host websites, and callback-enabled receivers. Lastly, you learned about the security infrastructure that underpins the implementation and execution of remote event receivers.

PART IV

Extending SharePoint

CHAPTER 11

Developing Web Parts

Since its early editions, Microsoft SharePoint has been famous and popular for the capability to compose pages through Web Parts. First introduced in SharePoint Team Services 2001, Web Parts are simply user-customizable regions hosted by a SharePoint webpage; they have been widely adopted by the market over the years. With Microsoft .NET 2.0, the infrastructure for Web Parts moved from SharePoint to the official ASP.NET web development platform, making the use of Web Parts possible in many kinds of ASP.NET applications. As reliable as ever, Web Parts are still available in SharePoint 2013 and can be useful in many solutions, especially when working on-premises.

To users, a Web Part is simply a piece of a webpage that they can customize from a web browser interface. For example, users can even add and remove Web Parts from pages (often called Web Part pages) by choosing Web Parts from a server gallery or from an online public gallery.

For developers, a Web Part is a class that defines code for rendering its content in the browser, for handling custom configuration, layout, positioning, and so on, within the SharePoint or ASP.NET environment. More importantly, developers can reuse Web Parts in many different pages and sites, simplifying custom solution development, deployment, and maintenance. In fact, many SharePoint solutions are based on a set of custom Web Parts that are referenced in pages.

This chapter explains how Web Parts work and how to develop custom Web Parts, as well as more advanced topics about Web Part development.

Web Part architecture

A Web Part is an ASP.NET custom control that inherits from the base class *WebPart* from the *System.Web.UI.WebControls.WebParts* namespace. To be able to fully use a Web Part in a page, you need to define a *WebPartZone* control, which is a container for a set of Web Parts. The *WebPartZone* control provides a common rendering pattern to all its constituent Web Parts. Another fundamental control in the Web Parts architecture is the *WebPartManager*, which handles all the tasks related to Web Part lifetime management—such as loading and unloading them, as well as serializing and deserializing their state within the current page and connecting Web Parts into Web Part zones. SharePoint has its own *WebPartZone* controls that give you the ability to define a set of SharePoint-specific rendering zones, such as the *WebPartZone* class for standard Web Part rendering and the *EditorZone* class to render parts responsible for editing other Web Parts. (Editor Parts will be covered later in this chapter.) Also, the *WebPartManager* control has been redefined in SharePoint into a custom implementation called *SPWebPartManager*, which handles some specific activities exclusively available in

SharePoint. In order to take advantage of these controls, SharePoint also provides a custom page type called *WebPartPage* (available in the *Microsoft.SharePoint.WebPartPages* namespace) that includes a preconfigured and unique instance of an *SPWebPartManager* control and the main Web Part zones, which are useful for rendering a page made of Web Parts. Figure 11-1 illustrates the overall architectural schema of such a page.

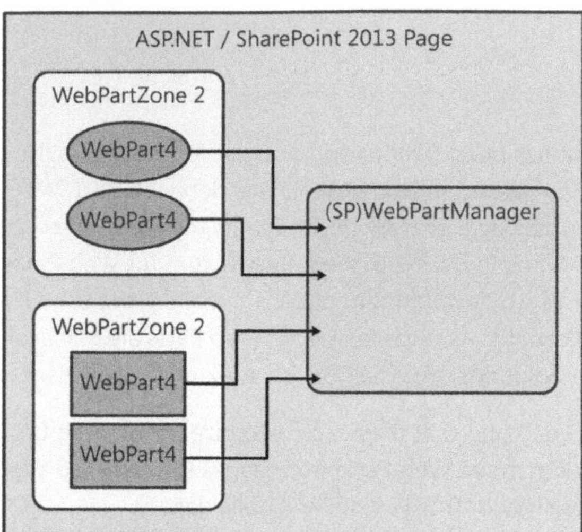

FIGURE 11-1 Overall architecture of a Web Part page in SharePoint and ASP.NET.

In everyday solutions, you will mainly work with Web Parts, and you will rarely have to directly interact with *WebPartZone* controls and the *WebPartManager* control.

A Hello World Web Part

It's time to start developing your first Web Part. Microsoft Visual Studio 2012 provides some project templates (Silverlight Web Part and Visual Web Part) and utilities that can help you to rapidly develop custom Web Parts. Suppose that you need to develop a Hello World Web Part that simply welcomes the current user, writing his or her name and the current *DateTime* value in the browser. You will begin creating a new project of type SharePoint 2013 - Empty Project. This project template simply starts with a set of assembly references, useful for developing any kind of SharePoint solution, and with a predefined deployment configuration. When you create a new SharePoint project, Visual Studio asks you for the URL of the website where it will deploy the solution. It also asks you what kind of deployment you want to build (farm solution or sandboxed solution). For this example, choose a farm solution deployment. You will see more about deployment later, in the "Web Part deployment" section. For now, you need to concentrate on the Web Part itself.

To develop your sample Web Part, you need to add a new file item of type Web Part to the project. Name the new item HelloWorldWebPart. A new class file is added, together with a set of configuration files, which will be discussed later. Figure 11-2 shows the project layout after you have added the Web Part item.

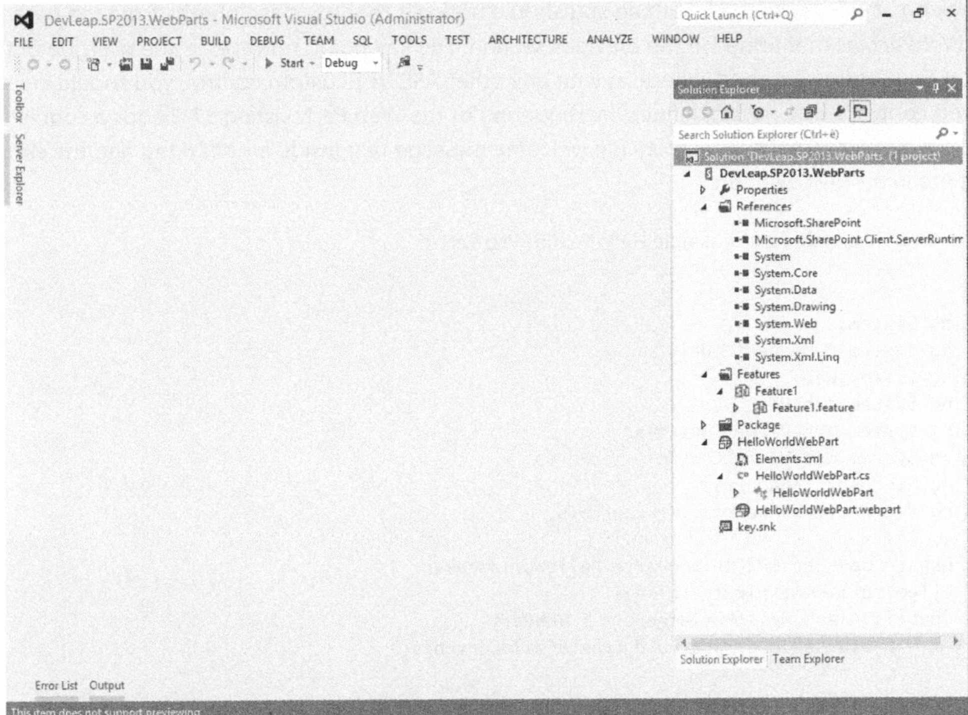

FIGURE 11-2 The project layout of the sample Web Part solution.

Listing 11-1 displays the content of the HelloWorldWebPart.cs file, just after you add the Web Part item to the project.

LISTING 11-1 The startup class file for the Hello World Web Part

```
using System;
using System.ComponentModel;
using System.Web;
using System.Web.UI;
using System.Web.UI.WebControls;
using System.Web.UI.WebControls.WebParts;
using Microsoft.SharePoint;
using Microsoft.SharePoint.WebControls;

namespace DevLeap.SP2013.WebParts.HelloWorldWebPart {
    [ToolboxItemAttribute(false)]
    public class HelloWorldWebPart : WebPart  {
        protected override void CreateChildControls()
        {
        }
    }
}
```

Looking at this code, the first thing you should notice is that the class inherits from the base class *WebPart*, as mentioned in the previous section. The key point, however, is the override of the *CreateChildControls* method, where, as with any other ASP.NET custom control, you should create the web control's tree, which defines the rendering of the Web Part. Listing 11-2 adds a couple of instances of *LiteralControl* to display the welcome message text inside an *<h1>* tag and the current date time in a <div> element.

LISTING 11-2 The code for the sample Hello World Web Part

```
using System;
using System.ComponentModel;
using System.Web;
using System.Web.UI;
using System.Web.UI.WebControls;
using System.Web.UI.WebControls.WebParts;
using Microsoft.SharePoint;
using Microsoft.SharePoint.WebControls;

namespace DevLeap.SP2010.WebParts.HelloWorldWebPart {
    [ToolboxItemAttribute(false)]
    public class HelloWorldWebPart : WebPart  {
        protected override void CreateChildControls()
        {
            SPWeb currentWeb = SPControl.GetContextWeb(HttpContext.Current);
            String currentUserName = currentWeb.CurrentUser.LoginName;
            this.Controls.Add(new LiteralControl(String.Format(
                "<h1>Welcome {0}!</h1>", currentUserName)));
            this.Controls.Add(new LiteralControl(String.Format(
                "<div>Current DateTime: {0}</div>", DateTime.Now)));
        }
    }
}
```

At the beginning of the *CreateChildControls* method implementation, the code also requests the current *SPWeb* instance from the *SPControl* class, through the current *HttpContext*, so it can get the current user's login name.

More Info For further details about the *SPWeb* and *SPControl* classes, refer to Chapter 5, "Server Object Model."

As you can see from this introductory example, to be a good Web Part developer, you first need to be a good ASP.NET developer. At the same time, every ASP.NET developer should be very comfortable developing Web Parts.

Figure 11-3 presents the output of the Hello World Web Part, inserted into the home page of a web application.

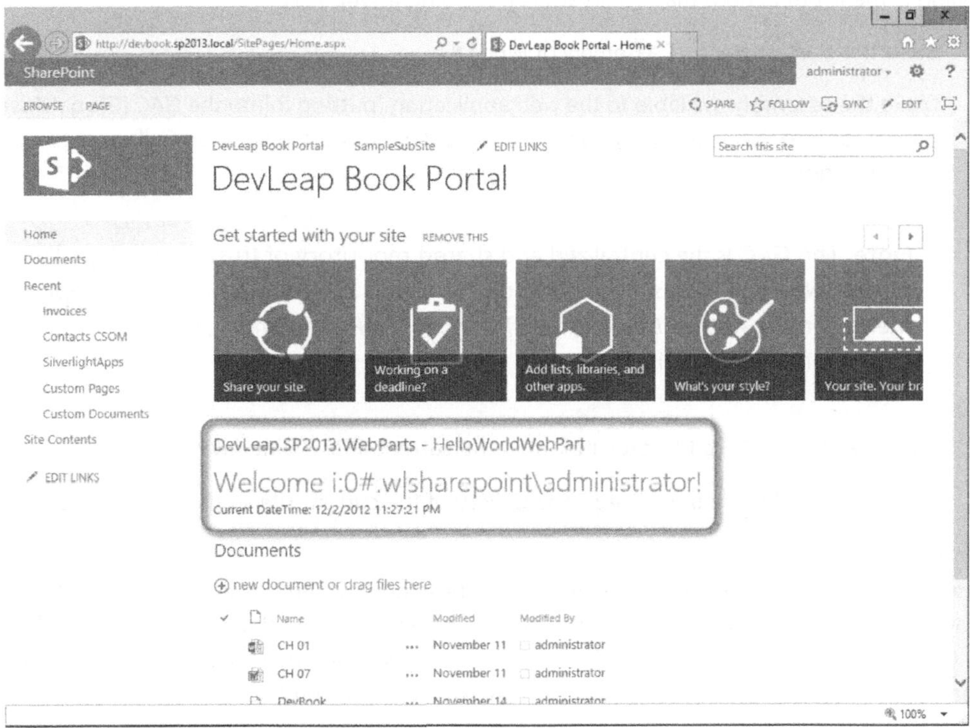

FIGURE 11-3 The output of the Hello World Web Part within a SharePoint 2013 site.

Note Another way of implementing a Web Part is to inherit from the class *WebPart* of namespace *Microsoft.SharePoint.WebPartPages*; however, this class internally inherits from the ASP.NET *WebPart* base class and is primarily provided for backward compatibility with older versions of SharePoint. If you decide to inherit your Web Parts from the SharePoint *WebPart* base class, these Web Parts will target *only SharePoint sites*; you cannot use them in standard ASP.NET websites. By using the SharePoint custom base class, you can take advantage of some additional functionalities that are not available in standard Web Part infrastructure. Although these additional capabilities have extremely limited uses, their few benefits will be discussed at the end of this chapter.

Web Part deployment

Following is the list of actions that occurs while deploying a Web Part:

1. Build the class into a .NET assembly of type DLL.
2. Make the assembly available to the web application (putting it into the GAC [Global Assembly Cache], or into the web application local bin folder, or into the Solution Gallery of the current site collection).

> **Note** The GAC is the centralized and shared repository of trusted and digitally signed .NET assemblies. For further details about .NET development and deployment, consult *Applied Microsoft .NET Framework Programming*, by Jeffrey Richter (Microsoft Press, 2002).

3. Authorize the Web Part to execute within the current SharePoint environment.
4. Load the Web Part into the Web Parts Gallery of the current site so that it is available to the end user.

Visual Studio 2012 makes it easy to complete all these deployment steps. Simply select Build | Deploy Solution to automatically deploy the Web Part on the website that you configured while creating the project. Behind the scenes, Visual Studio packages a Web Part solution package (WSP) for you and deploys it on the target environment, following the previously outlined steps.

Take a look at these steps from a practical perspective. Building the .NET assembly is trivial, so I will not cover it here; however, consider that if you ever want to put it into the GAC, you need to give it a strong name (including the name, version, culture, and public key token). Fortunately, Visual Studio 2012 does this for you, automatically adding a set of signing keys to the project. Putting the assembly into the GAC or web application bin folder is also trivial for any .NET developer. Conversely, installing the assembly into the Solution Gallery of the current site collection requires you to know about sandboxed solutions. However, in SharePoint 2013, you should prefer developing apps instead of using sandboxed solutions, in particular when they are used for deploying custom code—and a Web Part is mainly made of custom code. Thus, the deployment of a Web Part through a sandboxed solution will not be covered in this book.

To authorize the Web Part to execute within the SharePoint environment, you need to add a specific configuration item into the web.config file of the current web application, declaring the Web Part as a *SafeControl* object. At the end of this chapter, you can find more details about the *SafeControls* configuration section. Listing 11-3 presents an excerpt of the custom configuration that you need to apply.

LISTING 11-3 The custom configuration needed to make the Hello World Web Part safe for SharePoint

```
<?xml version="1.0" encoding="UTF-8" standalone="yes"?>
<configuration>
  <SharePoint>
    <!-- Removed for the sake of simplicity -->
    <SafeControls>
      <!-- Here there are many other SafeControls -->
      <SafeControl Assembly="DevLeap.SP2013.WebParts, Version=1.0.0.0,
      Culture=neutral, PublicKeyToken=cba640f292988abf"
      Namespace="DevLeap.SP2013.WebParts.HelloWorldWebPart" TypeName="*"
      Safe="True" SafeAgainstScript="False" />
    </SafeControls>
    <!-- Removed for the sake of simplicity -->
</configuration>
```

Making the Web Part available in the Web Part Gallery requires that you add the Web Part definition to the current site collection. This definition is a .webpart file that Visual Studio 2012 automatically generates when you add a Web Part item to a project. Listing 11-4 illustrates the default content of this file in the example.

LISTING 11-4 The .webpart file to deploy the Hello World Web Part

```
<?xml version="1.0" encoding="utf-8"?>
<webParts>
  <webPart xmlns="http://schemas.microsoft.com/WebPart/v3">
    <metaData>
<type name="DevLeap.SP2013.WebParts.HelloWorldWebPart.HelloWorldWebPart,
$SharePoint.Project.AssemblyFullName$" />
      <importErrorMessage>$Resources:core,ImportErrorMessage;<importErrorMessage>
    </metaData>
    <data>
      <properties>
        <property name="Title" type="string"> DevLeap.SP2013.WebParts -
HelloWorldWebPart</property>
        <property name="Description" type="string">My WebPart</property>
      </properties>
    </data>
  </webPart>
</webParts>
```

The key aspect of the .webpart file is the declaration of the type (a .NET type) corresponding to the current Web Part. Notice that a single .webpart file can declare many Web Parts, even if by default Visual Studio 2012 creates a .webpart file for each Web Part definition. The type name of the Hello World Web Part is declared as a full name (namespace plus class name), together with the containing assembly name. In this code example, the assembly name is defined using an alias (*$SharePoint.Project.AssemblyFullName$*), which Visual Studio 2012 will automatically replace with the real assembly name during the deployment process.

In addition, the .webpart file declares the default values for some of the properties of the Web Part. For instance, you can see that the *Title* and *Description* properties of the Web Part are defined as custom *property* elements within a *properties* wrapper element.

You can change the values of these properties as well as define some other properties by simply editing the .webpart file in Visual Studio. Table 11-1 provides a list of the most useful properties that you can define.

TABLE 11-1 Some of the main configurable properties of a .webpart file

Property name	Description
Title	Defines the title of the Web Part. The title will be shown to the end user in the Web Parts Gallery as well as when the Web Part is inserted in a page, and it will be the default title of a newly inserted Web Part.
Description	Describes the current Web Part. This will be shown to the end user in the Web Parts Gallery and when the Web Part is inserted in a page.
TitleIconImageUrl	Specifies the URL to an image used to represent the Web Part in its title bar. The default value is an empty string ("").
CatalogIconImageUrl	Specifies the URL to an image used to represent the Web Part in the Web Parts Catalog, which is the catalog for browsing available Web Part controls during Web Part insertion within a target page. The default value is an empty string ("").
ChromeType	Defines the type of border that frames the Web Part. It can assume the following values (the default value is *Default*): ■ ***Default*** Inherits its behavior from the containing Web Part zone ■ ***TitleAndBorder*** Displays a title bar with a border ■ ***None*** Will not display a border or title bar ■ ***TitleOnly*** Displays a title bar without a border ■ ***BorderOnly*** Displays a border without a title bar
ChromeState	Determines whether the Web Part will appear minimized or normal (not minimized).
AllowClose	Defines whether the Web Part can be closed by an end user.
AllowConnect	Defines whether the Web Part can be connected to another by an end user.
AllowEdit	Defines whether the Web Part can be edited by an end user.
AllowHide	Defines whether the Web Part can be hidden by an end user.
AllowMinimize	Defines whether the Web Part can be minimized by an end user.
AllowZoneChange	Defines whether the Web Part can be moved between different Web Part zones by an end user.
ExportMode	Allows defining if the current Web Part configuration can be exported for reuse on another website.

Listing 11-5 demonstrates how you can customize the .webpart file for the Hello World Web Part sample: by adding a *CatalogImageUrl* property to provide a custom image for the Web Part, by changing the *ChromeType* property, and by enabling editing through the *AllowEdit* property.

LISTING 11-5 The .webpart file to deploy the configured Hello World Web Part

```
<?xml version="1.0" encoding="utf-8"?>
<webParts>
  <webPart xmlns="http://schemas.microsoft.com/WebPart/v3">
    <metaData>
      <type name="DevLeap.SP2013.WebParts.HelloWorldWebPart.HelloWorldWebPart,
          $SharePoint.Project.AssemblyFullName$" />
      <importErrorMessage>$Resources:core,ImportErrorMessage;
</importErrorMessage>
    </metaData>
    <data>
      <properties>
        <property name="Title" type="string"> DevLeap.SP2013.WebParts -
HelloWorldWebPart</property>
        <property name="Description" type="string">
          Custom WebPart to welcome end user</property>
        <property name="CatalogIconImageUrl"
          type="string">/_layouts/images/ICTXT.GIF</property>
        <property name="AllowEdit" type="bool">true</property>
        <property name="ChromeType" type="chrometype">TitleAndBorder</property>
      </properties>
    </data>
  </webPart>
</webParts>
```

Figure 11-4 illustrates the output of the customized Hello World Web Part. You can also customize the group in which the Web Part will be presented to the end user within the Web Part Gallery. To achieve this result, you need to edit the Elements.xml file related to the Web Part and change the value of the *Group* property defined in that XML file. Notice the custom category, the custom icon in the Web Parts Catalog, the customized description, and the customized *ChromeType* property (*TitleAndBorder*).

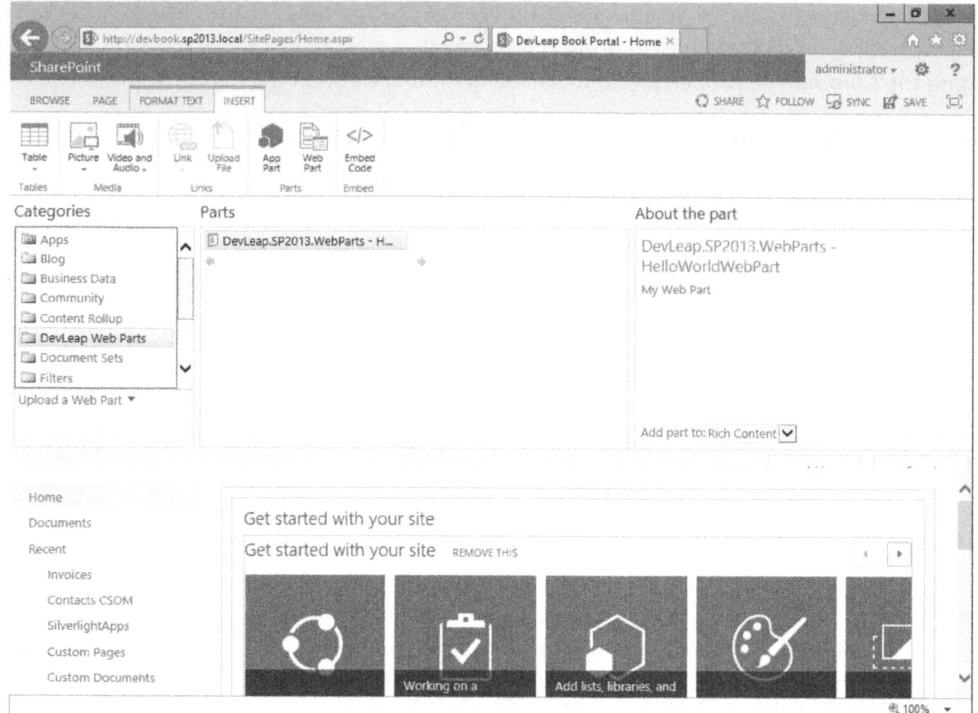

FIGURE 11-4 The output of the customized Hello World Web Part within a SharePoint 2013 site.

As you will see in the "Configurable Web Parts" section later in the chapter, developers can also define Web Part properties that are customizable by site owners or site members with the appropriate permissions. Such properties will be configurable with default values while deploying Web Parts—in exactly the same way as the standard Web Part properties just described.

Real Web Parts

Of course, real Web Parts are a little bit more complex than the Hello World example, and are equipped with a richer set of controls and behaviors. In this section, you will explore two kinds of Web Parts: classic Web Parts made of custom code, and Visual Web Parts, which are designed using the graphical designer of Visual Studio 2012.

Classic Web Parts

A standard classic Web Part is a control that is made up of a set of ASP.NET controls, interacts with the end user through events, and controls behavior. In this section, you will build a data entry Web Part that will collect data from the end user and insert that data into a target SharePoint list. The core engine of this Web Part will use the SharePoint Server Object Model as the means to insert items into the target list. The UI will be built using ASP.NET server controls.

Imagine that you have a target list of requests for contacts available in your SharePoint site, and you want to collect users' requests using your custom Web Part implementation. Name the Web Part *InsertRequestForContactWebPart* and create a SharePoint project in Visual Studio 2012 to host it. Next, choose a farm solution project type. The Web Part provides a small set of fields (for the reason of the request for contact and for requesting the user's full name and email address) to describe the request. These fields correspond to the Requests for Contacts target list that you manually defined in the current website.

Note In Chapter 3, "Data provisioning," you learned how to programmatically define and provision data structures of lists like Requests for Contacts. In an actual professional solution, you will probably need to define the list, as well as the Web Parts working on it, in a common SharePoint solution that you will be able to deploy "at once."

Internally, the Web Part will have a set of ASP.NET controls that correspond to the input fields, and will use the SharePoint Server Object Model (see Chapter 5, "Server Object Model," for further details) to insert the new item into the list. Listing 11-6 displays the whole implementation of the Web Part, while Figure 11-5 shows its final output.

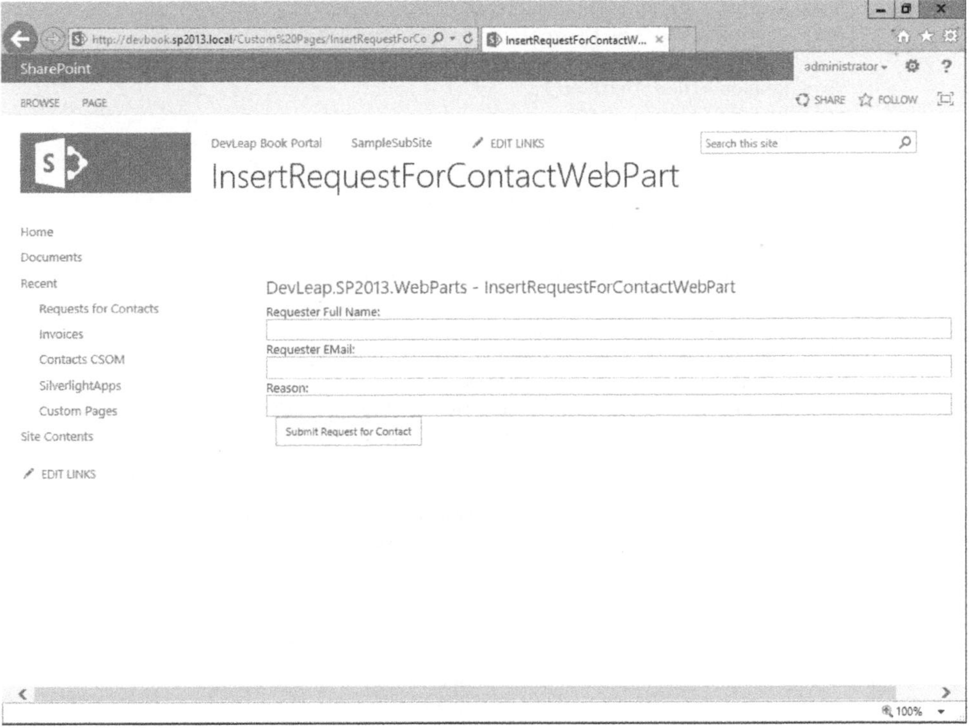

FIGURE 11-5 The output of the *InsertRequestForContactWebPart* within a SharePoint 2013 site.

LISTING 11-6 The whole implementation of the *InsertRequestForContactWebPart*

```
namespace DevLeap.SP2013.WebParts.InsertRequestForContactWebPart {
    [ToolboxItemAttribute(false)]
    public class InsertRequestForContactWebPart : WebPart {
        protected TextBox RequesterFullName;
        protected TextBox RequesterEMail;
        protected TextBox Reason;
        protected Button SubmitRequestForContact;
        protected Label ErrorMessage;

        protected override void CreateChildControls() {
            this.RequesterFullName = new TextBox();
            this.RequesterFullName.Columns = 100;
            this.RequesterFullName.MaxLength = 255;
            this.Controls.Add(new LiteralControl("<div>Requester Full Name: "));
            this.Controls.Add(this.RequesterFullName);
            this.Controls.Add(new LiteralControl("</div>"));

            this.RequesterEMail = new TextBox();
            this.RequesterEMail.Columns = 100;
            this.RequesterEMail.MaxLength = 100;
            this.Controls.Add(new LiteralControl("<div>Requester EMail: "));
            this.Controls.Add(this.RequesterEMail);
            this.Controls.Add(new LiteralControl("</div>"));

            this.Reason = new TextBox();
            this.Reason.Columns = 100;
            this.Reason.MaxLength = 255;
            this.Controls.Add(new LiteralControl("<div>Reason: "));
            this.Controls.Add(this.Reason);
            this.Controls.Add(new LiteralControl("</div>"));

            this.SubmitRequestForContact = new Button();
            this.SubmitRequestForContact.Text = "Submit Request for Contact";
            this.Controls.Add(new LiteralControl("<div>"));
            this.Controls.Add(this.SubmitRequestForContact);
            this.SubmitRequestForContact.Click +=
                new EventHandler(SubmitRequestForContact_Click);
            this.Controls.Add(new LiteralControl("</div>"));

            this.ErrorMessage = new Label();
            this.ErrorMessage.ForeColor = System.Drawing.Color.Red;
            this.Controls.Add(new LiteralControl("<div>"));
            this.Controls.Add(this.ErrorMessage);
            this.Controls.Add(new LiteralControl("</div>"));
        }

        void SubmitRequestForContact_Click(object sender, EventArgs e) {
            SPWeb web = SPControl.GetContextWeb(HttpContext.Current);
```

```
            try {
                SPList targetList = web.Lists["Requests for Contacts"];
                SPListItem newItem = targetList.Items.Add();
                newItem["Reason"] = this.Reason.Text;
                newItem["Requester full name"] = this.RequesterFullName.Text;
                newItem["Requester email"] = this.RequesterEMail.Text;
                newItem.Update();
            }
            catch (IndexOutOfRangeException) {
                this.ErrorMessage.Text =
                    "Cannot find list \"Requests for Contacts\"";
            }
        }
    }
}
```

In Listing 11-6, the code highlighted in bold declares the *protected* variables that hold the ASP.NET server controls. The code inside the *CreateChildControls* method override instantiates these controls. In particular, notice the binding between the *Click* server-side event of the button named *SubmitRequestForContact* and the *SubmitRequestForContact_Click* method. Within this last event-handling method, you create a new instance of an *SPListItem* representing a single contact request, compile its fields, and then feed the *SPList* instance with this new item.

Starting from this second example, it's easy to imagine that you can build whatever you need, using some ASP.NET code and custom controls, together with some .NET code. For instance, you can develop a Web Part that allows the user to interact with a back-end database, or you can define a Web Part that talks with an external SOAP service provided by a third party. As you let your creativity wander, keep in mind that SharePoint is a strong and secure environment—thus, every kind of customization or solution must be approved and authorized. Later, in the "Deployment and versioning" section, you will learn about the security aspects of developing and deploying custom SharePoint Web Parts that comply with the security infrastructure of SharePoint.

Visual Web Parts

Listing 11-6 defines all the ASP.NET server controls that make up the Web Part, using a lot of custom .NET code. Designing a Web Part by code is not always convenient, however, because in some scenarios you need to declare UI attributes (such as CSS styles), control positioning and alignment, and so on. In addition, writing and maintaining all the code and controls you create inside a Web Part can be difficult.

Luckily, Visual Studio 2012 offers an out-of-the-box solution for this problem: the Visual Web Part item template defines a Web Part that loads its UI from a custom ASCX control. This kind of Web Part internally creates a dynamic partial class of your Web Part, providing the .NET code for creating what you design in the designer. Listing 11-7 shows the core implementation of a Visual Web Part that is called *VisualInsertRequestForContactWebPart*. The invocation of method *InitializeControl* takes care of loading all the .NET code for defining the UI of the Web Part, which will be designed in the visual designer of Visual Studio 2012.

LISTING 11-7 The basic implementation of the *VisualInsertRequestForContactWebPart*

```
namespace DevLeap.SP2013.WebParts.VisualInsertRequestForContactWebPart {
    [ToolboxItemAttribute(false)]
    public class VisualInsertRequestForContactWebPart : WebPart {
        public VisualInsertRequestForContactWebPart() {
        }

        protected override void OnInit(EventArgs e) {
            base.OnInit(e);
            InitializeControl();
        }

        protected void Page_Load(object sender, EventArgs e) {
        }
    }
}
```

In the Web Part source code, you need to place not only the code related to the dynamic loading of the UI, but also the event handlers and custom procedures. You can assign all the other aspects of the controls' tree in the ASCX file, as shown in Listing 11-8.

LISTING 11-8 The ASCX file for the *VisualInsertRequestForContactWebPart*

```
<%@ Assembly Name="$SharePoint.Project.AssemblyFullName$" %>
<%@ Assembly Name="Microsoft.Web.CommandUI, Version=15.0.0.0, Culture=neutral,
PublicKeyToken=71e9bce111e9429c" %>
<%@ Register Tagprefix="SharePoint" Namespace="Microsoft.SharePoint.WebControls"
Assembly="Microsoft.SharePoint, Version=15.0.0.0, Culture=neutral, PublicKeyToke
n=71e9bce111e9429c" %>
<%@ Register Tagprefix="Utilities" Namespace="Microsoft.SharePoint.Utilities"
Assembly="Microsoft.SharePoint, Version=15.0.0.0, Culture=neutral, PublicKeyToke
n=71e9bce111e9429c" %>
<%@ Register Tagprefix="asp" Namespace="System.Web.UI" Assembly="System.Web.
Extensions, Version=4.0.0.0, Culture=neutral, PublicKeyToken=31bf3856ad364e35" %>
<%@ Import Namespace="Microsoft.SharePoint" %>
<%@ Register Tagprefix="WebPartPages" Namespace="Microsoft.SharePoint.
WebPartPages" Assembly="Microsoft.SharePoint, Version=15.0.0.0, Culture=neutral,
PublicKeyToken=71e9bce111e9429c" %>
<%@ Control Language="C#" AutoEventWireup="true" CodeBehind="VisualInse
rtRequestForContactWebPart.ascx.cs" Inherits="DevLeap.SP2013.WebParts.
VisualInsertRequestForContactWebPart.VisualInsertRequestForContactWebPart" %>
<p>
    Requester full name:
    <asp:TextBox ID="RequesterFullName" runat="server" Columns="100"
        MaxLength="255"></asp:TextBox>
</p>
```

```
<p>
    Requester email:
    <asp:TextBox ID="RequesterEMail" runat="server" Columns="100"
MaxLength="100"></asp:TextBox>
</p>
<p>
    Reason:
    <asp:TextBox ID="Reason" runat="server" Columns="100" MaxLength="255" />
</p>
<asp:Button ID="SubmitRequestForContact" runat="server"
    onclick="SubmitRequestForContact_Click" Text="Submit Request for Contact" />
<br />
<br />

<asp:Label ID="ErrorMessage" runat="server" ForeColor="Red" Visible="False" />
```

Of course, the benefit of having an ASCX file instead of standard .NET code is that an ASCX file can be defined using the Visual Studio 2012 designer, as shown in Figure 11-6.

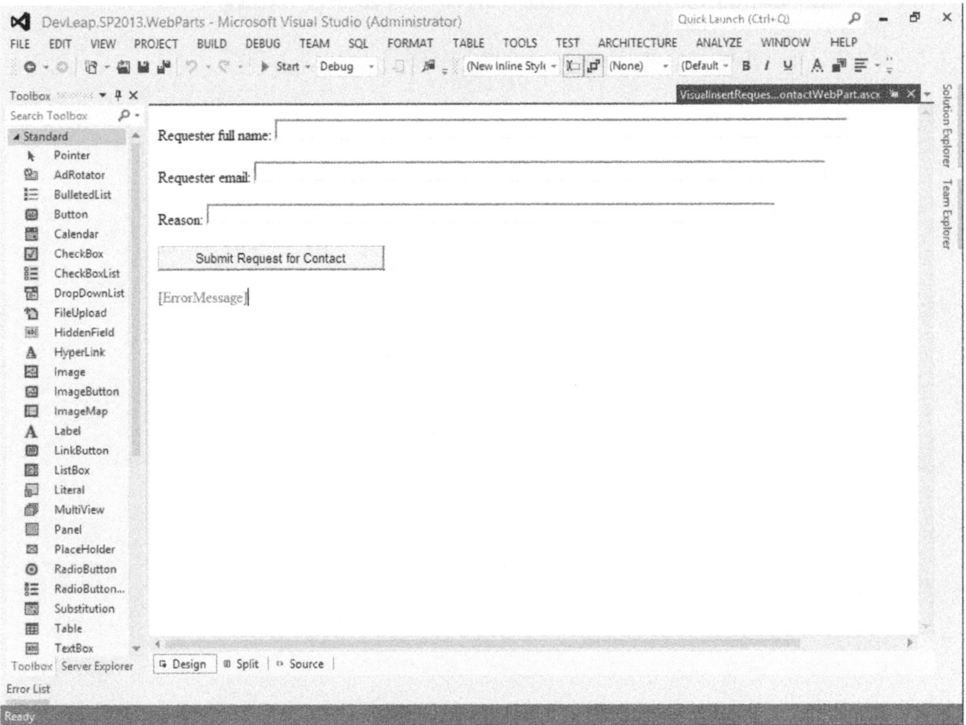

FIGURE 11-6 The visual layout of the ASCX file of the *VisualInsertRequestForContactWebPart* in the Visual Studio 2012 designer.

Configurable Web Parts

In the previous examples, you used a predefined target list for inserting items. In real-world SharePoint solutions, however, authorized users can configure Web Parts. In this section, you will see how to develop configurable Web Parts and how to present a user-friendly interface for Web Part configuration.

Configurable parameters

The first step in creating configurable Web Parts is to define the properties that can be altered. To do so, you simply need to declare a public property in the Web Part class definition, tagging the property with the *WebBrowsableAttribute* attribute and optionally with the *PersonalizableAttribute* attribute. Listing 11-9 shows a Web Part that declares a configurable property.

LISTING 11-9 A Web Part that provides a configurable property

```
Namespace DevLeap.SP2013.WebParts.ConfigurableInsertRequestForContactWebPart {
    [ToolboxItemAttribute(false)]
    public class ConfigurableInsertRequestForContactWebPart : WebPart {
        [WebBrowsable(true)]
        [Personalizable(PersonalizationScope.Shared)]
        public String TargetListTitle { get; set; }

        //
        // CreateChildControls code omitted ...
        //

        void SubmitRequestForContact_Click(object sender, EventArgs e) {
            SPWeb web = SPControl.GetContextWeb(HttpContext.Current);

            try {
                SPList targetList = web.Lists[this.TargetListTitle];

                SPListItem newItem = targetList.Items.Add();
                newItem["Reason"] = this.Reason.Text;
                newItem["Requester full name"] = this.RequesterFullName.Text;
                newItem["Requester email"] = this.RequesterEMail.Text;
                newItem.Update();
            }
            catch (IndexOutOfRangeException) {
                this.ErrorMessage.Text =
                   "Cannot find list \"Requests for Contacts\"";
            }
        }
    }
}
```

The *WebBrowsableAttribute* class instructs the Web Part infrastructure that the property has to be made available in the configuration panel for the Web Part, which is called the *tool pane*. This attribute accepts a *Boolean* parameter named *Browsable* that is assigned a value of *true* when the attribute is declared through its default constructor. The *PersonalizableAttribute* class declares that the property can be personalized and defines the scope of the personalization. It accepts a scope of type *User*, which means that the property can be personalized on a per-user basis, or a scope of type *Shared*, which means the property personalization will be shared between all users.

Some other useful attributes can help you better define the configurable property, improving the end-user experience. For instance, you can define a custom category for the property by tagging it with the *CategoryAttribute* attribute. You can change the caption of the property by tagging it with the *WebDisplayAttribute* attribute, and you can change the tooltip shown to the end user by tagging the property with the *WebDescriptionAttribute* attribute. You can provide a default value for the property via the *DefaultValueAttribute* attribute. Listing 11-10 displays a complete definition for the *TargetListTitle* property.

LISTING 11-10 A Web Part that provides a configurable property, with all the useful attributes

```
[WebBrowsable(true)]
[Personalizable(PersonalizationScope.Shared)]
[WebDescription("Title of the Target list")]
[WebDisplayName("Target list")]
[Category("Data Foundation")]
public String TargetListTitle { get; set; }
```

Figure 11-7 illustrates the UI presented to the user by a configurable property.

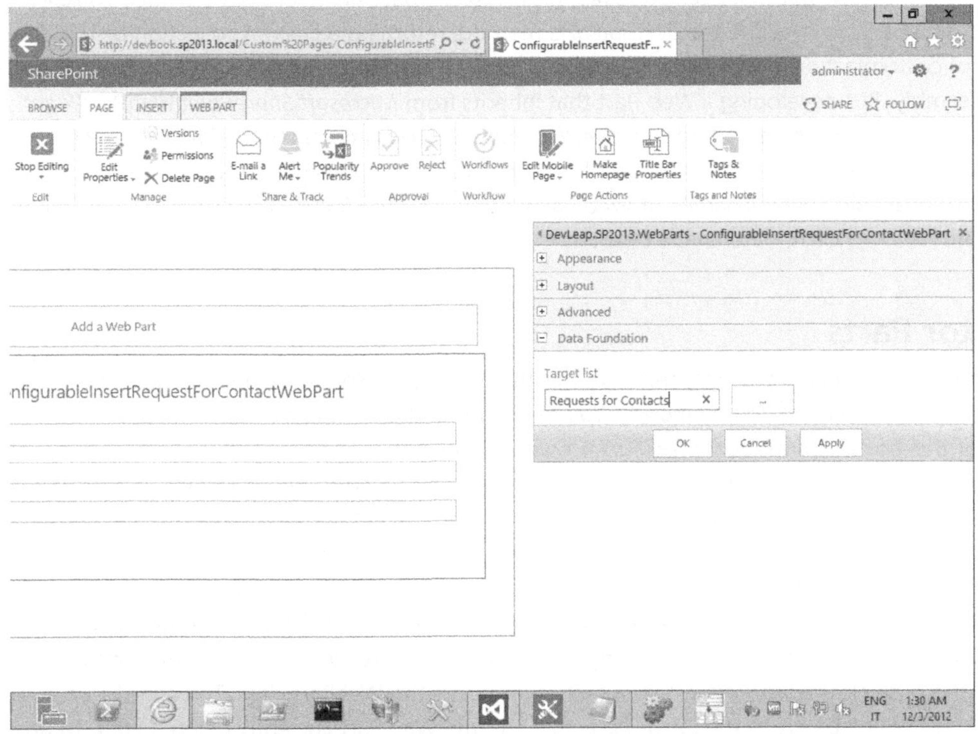

FIGURE 11-7 The tool pane of the sample Web Part.

The Web Part editor area in Figure 11-7 is provided by the SharePoint infrastructure and is based on a set of SharePoint-specific classes, called *Tool Parts*, which can be customized by user code. By default, SharePoint provides a *WebPartToolPart* class that provides the UI for editing the standard properties of Web Parts (title, chrome type, size, and so on) and a *CustomPropertyToolPart* class, which automatically allows editing custom properties.

Table 11-2 covers how the *CustomPropertyToolPart* class usually behaves when rendering custom properties.

TABLE 11-2 The standard behavior of the *CustomPropertyToolPart* class while rendering custom properties

Custom property type	Behavior
Boolean	Renders a check box
Enum	Renders a drop-down list
Integer	Renders a text box
String	Renders a text box
DateTime	Renders a text box

You can implement custom Tool Part classes by simply inheriting from the *ToolPart* base abstract class provided by the *Microsoft.SharePoint.WebPartPages* namespace. To make a custom Tool Part available to SharePoint, however, you need to inherit the Web Part class from the *Microsoft.SharePoint.WebPartPages.WebPart* base abstract class provided by SharePoint, instead of using the common *System.Web.UI.WebControls.WebParts.WebPart* base abstract class provided by ASP.NET. To do so, you need to override the *GetToolParts* method, returning a custom collection of Tool Parts. This kind of customization works only in SharePoint, due to the dependency on the Microsoft.SharePoint.dll assembly. But developing a Web Part that inherits from *Microsoft.SharePoint.WebPartPages.WebPart* is not considered a best practice. You should always implement ASP.NET Web Parts, which inherit from *System.Web.UI.WebControls.WebParts.WebPart*, unless you really need any of the few features available only in SharePoint Web Parts; this will be the focus of the section "The SharePoint-specific *WebPart* class," later in the chapter.

Editor Parts

Listing 11-10 defined a property that requires the end user to configure the Web Part manually, typing the target list name autonomously. You made use of the standard behavior of SharePoint and the out-of-the-box *CustomPropertyToolPart*. However, even if it were possible to publish such a Web Part, you would probably agree that this is not a user-friendly and error-free approach. A better solution is to provide a drop-down list with all the lists available in the current website, thereby avoiding typographical errors and the consequent time-consuming debugging tasks. To customize the configuration UI of the Web Parts this way, you can create custom classes called Editor Parts, provided by the Web Part infrastructure of ASP.NET. *Editor Parts* are controls hosted in a specific *WebPartZone* control called *EditorZone*. They are nearly the same as standard Web Parts, except that they inherit from the base class *EditorPart* instead of inheriting from the *WebPart* class. This specific base class provides the link between the Editor Part itself and the Web Part currently being edited. To provide a Web Part with a custom Editor Part, you need to override the implementation of the *IWebEditable* interface, which is implemented by the Web Part base class. Listing 11-11 provides the definition of this interface.

LISTING 11-11 The *IWebEditable* interface definition

```
public interface IWebEditable {
    EditorPartCollection CreateEditorParts();
    object WebBrowsableObject { get; }
}
```

The interface declares a method with the name *CreateEditorParts* that should return a collection of Editor Parts that support Web Parts with a wide set of Editor Parts. The interface also defines a public read-only property to get a reference to the configurable object that the Editor Parts will target. Usually, the *WebBrowsableObject* property returns the current Web Part instance (*this*). Listing 11-12 displays the new implementation of the custom Web Part.

LISTING 11-12 The new custom Web Part, implementing the *IWebEditable* interface

```
namespace DevLeap.SP2013.WebParts.EditorInsertRequestForContactWebPart {
    [ToolboxItemAttribute(false)]
    public class EditorInsertRequestForContactWebPart : WebPart {
        [WebBrowsable(false)]
        [Personalizable(PersonalizationScope.Shared)]
        public Guid TargetListID { get; set; }

        //
        // CreateChildControls code omitted ...
        //

        void SubmitRequestForContact_Click(object sender, EventArgs e) {
            SPWeb web = SPControl.GetContextWeb(HttpContext.Current);

            try {
                SPList targetList = web.Lists[this.TargetListID];
                SPListItem newItem = targetList.Items.Add();
                newItem["Reason"] = this.Reason.Text;
                newItem["Requester full name"] = this.RequesterFullName.Text;
                newItem["Requester email"] = this.RequesterEMail.Text;
                newItem.Update();
            }
            catch (IndexOutOfRangeException) {
                this.ErrorMessage.Text =
                    "Cannot find list \"Requests for Contacts\"";
            }
        }
```

```
        public override EditorPartCollection CreateEditorParts() {
            RequestForContactEditorPart editorPart =
                new RequestForContactEditorPart();
            editorPart.ID = this.ID + "_RequestForContactEditorPart";
            EditorPartCollection editorParts =
              new EditorPartCollection(base.CreateEditorParts(),
              new EditorPart[] { editorPart });
            return editorParts;
        }
        public override object WebBrowsableObject {
            get { return(this); }
        }
    }
}
```

In Listing 11-12, the property *TargetListTitle* of type *String* has been changed into the property *TargetListID* of type *Guid* so that it can store the unique ID of the target list, and that ID is used to look up the list instance in the *SubmitRequestForContact_Click* event handler. The code in the listing also turns off the *WebBrowsable* attribute on the property to hide it from the standard property grid of the Web Part editor. This property will be handled using the custom Editor Part.

Important If you do not turn off the *WebBrowsable* attribute of a property that is also configurable through a custom Editor Part, your end user will have both the custom Editor Part and the standard property grid for editing that property, provided by the *CustomPropertyToolPart* of SharePoint. This is, of course, confusing for the end user and should be avoided.

Next, the code overrides the *CreateEditorParts* method to invoke the base class method implementation and to add a custom Editor Part, named *RequestForContactEditorPart*, to the collection of available Editor Parts of the current Web Part. Notice also the definition of a custom ID for the Editor Part instance, based on the uniqueness of the current Web Part ID, to make the Editor Part ID unique as well.

EditorPart is a base abstract class that provides some virtual or abstract methods and properties that are useful for managing the editing of the target Web Part. For instance, every class inherited from *EditorPart* has a *WebPartToEdit* property that references the Web Part instance that the Editor Part is currently editing. There are also a couple of abstract methods, called *ApplyChanges* and *SyncChanges*, that can be used to save any changes to the Web Part currently being edited, and to load the current configuration from it, respectively.

Listing 11-13 gives you an opportunity to evaluate the implementation of the *RequestForContactEditorPart* class.

LISTING 11-13 The *RequestForContactEditorPart* class implementation

```
public class RequestForContactEditorPart : EditorPart {
    protected DropDownList targetLists;

    protected override void CreateChildControls() {
        this.targetLists = new DropDownList();

        SPWeb web = SPControl.GetContextWeb(HttpContext.Current);
        foreach (SPList list in web.Lists) {
            this.targetLists.Items.Add(new ListItem(list.Title,
            list.ID.ToString()));
        }

        this.Title = "Request for Contact EditorPart";
        this.Controls.Add(new LiteralControl("Select the target List:<br>"));
        this.Controls.Add(this.targetLists);
        this.Controls.Add(new LiteralControl("<br> <br>"));
    }

    public override bool ApplyChanges() {
        EnsureChildControls();
        EditorInsertRequestForContactWebPart wp =
            this.WebPartToEdit as EditorInsertRequestForContactWebPart;
        if (wp != null) {
            wp.TargetListID = new Guid(this.targetLists.SelectedValue);
        }
        return (true);
    }

    public override void SyncChanges() {
        EnsureChildControls();
        EditorInsertRequestForContactWebPart wp =
            this.WebPartToEdit as EditorInsertRequestForContactWebPart;
        if (wp != null) {
            ListItem selectedItem =
                this.targetLists.Items.FindByValue(wp.TargetListID.ToString());
            if (selectedItem != null) {
                this.targetLists.ClearSelection();
                selectedItem.Selected = true;
            }
        }
    }
}
```

As with any other Web Part, an Editor Part must create its controls graph to render its content. In Listing 11-13, the *CreateChildControls* method override creates a drop-down list and binds it to the collection of lists of the current website.

Then, the *ApplyChanges* method override saves the currently selected list ID into the *TargetListID* property of the current Web Part instance. Similarly, the *SyncChanges* method override autoselects the list with ID equal to the current *TargetListID* property value in the drop-down list. Figure 11-8 depicts the output of the custom Editor Part.

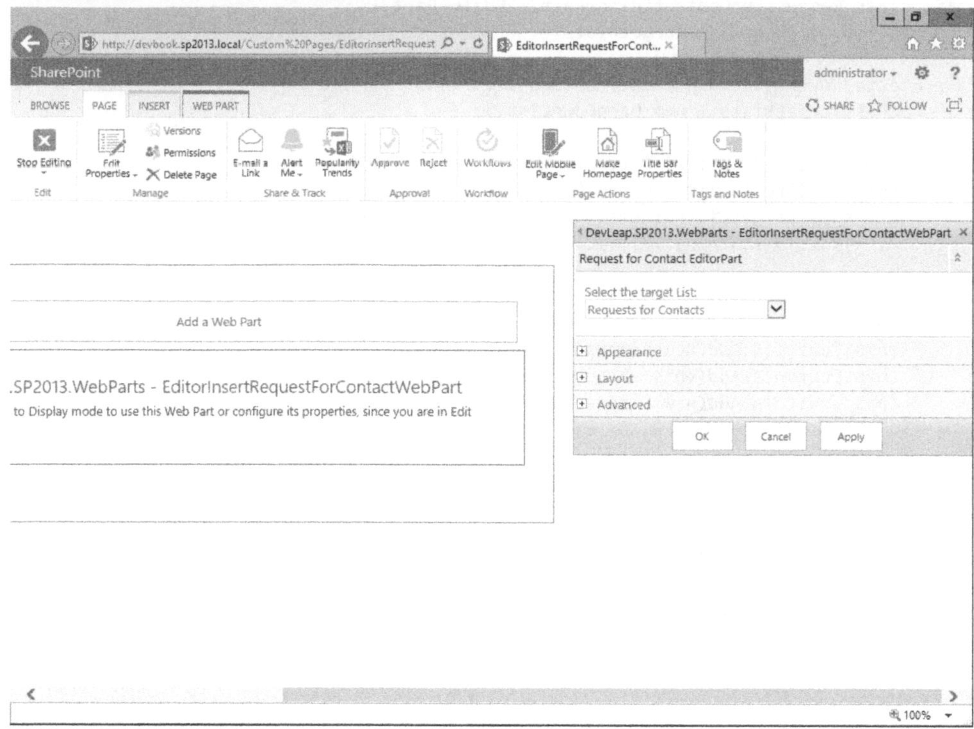

FIGURE 11-8 The configuration panel of the sample Web Part, with the Editor Part in place.

In an actual SharePoint solution, all of the Web Parts will typically provide a rich and complete set of configuration parameters, configurable and customizable through custom Editor Parts.

Handling display modes

During the course of developing real-world Web Parts, sooner or later you will probably face the need to change the rendering of your custom Web Parts, based on the status of the page that hosts them. A page hosting one or more Web Parts can be rendered in display mode (when the end user is browsing the site), in design mode (when the user can design the page layout), or in edit mode (when the end user is configuring or customizing the page and its controls).

To query the page display mode and render a Web Part accordingly, you need to query the *DisplayMode* property of the *WebPartManager* (*SPWebPartManager* in SharePoint). The sample Web Part in Listing 11-14 adapts its rendering based on the current *DisplayMode* property of the *WebPartManager* class.

LISTING 11-14 A Web Part rendering its content relative to the current page *DisplayMode* property of the *WebPartManager* class

```
protected override void CreateChildControls() {
    if (this.WebPartManager.DisplayMode == WebPartManager.BrowseDisplayMode) {
        // Page display mode
        // Render standard content
    }
    else if (this.WebPartManager.DisplayMode == WebPartManager.DesignDisplayMode)
{
        // Page design mode
        this.Controls.Add(new LiteralControl("<div>
           Please move to Display mode to use this Web Part.</div>"));
    }
    else if (this.WebPartManager.DisplayMode == WebPartManager.EditDisplayMode) {
        // Page edit mode
        this.Controls.Add(new LiteralControl("<div>
           Please move to Display mode to use this Web Part or configure its
           properties, since you are in Edit mode.</div>"));
    }
}
```

Any class inheriting from *WebPart* has a shortcut property referencing the current *WebPartManager* instance. Through this property, you can check the *DisplayMode* and many other context properties. You can also use the *WebPartManager* to subscribe to events related to *DisplayMode* changes. For instance, you can monitor the *DisplayMode* status with the *DisplayModeChanging* and *DisplayModeChanged* events.

Custom Web Part verbs

Another Web Part customization capability that is sometimes useful is the definition of custom Web Part verbs. *Web Part verbs* are menu items that are displayed in the Web Part menu, as shown in Figure 11-9.

To configure custom verbs, you need to override the read-only *Verbs* property provided by the base *WebPart* class. This property returns a *WebPartVerbCollection* and can be used to completely redefine the menu of a Web Part. Verbs are objects of type *WebPartVerb* and can be of three different kinds:

- **Server-side** Verbs that require a *POST*-back to carry out their job; they work on the server side
- **Client-side** Verbs that simply use JavaScript syntax to do their job; they work on the client side
- **Client and server-side** Verbs that first execute some client-side JavaScript, and then can execute some server-side code, unless the client-side code cancels the request

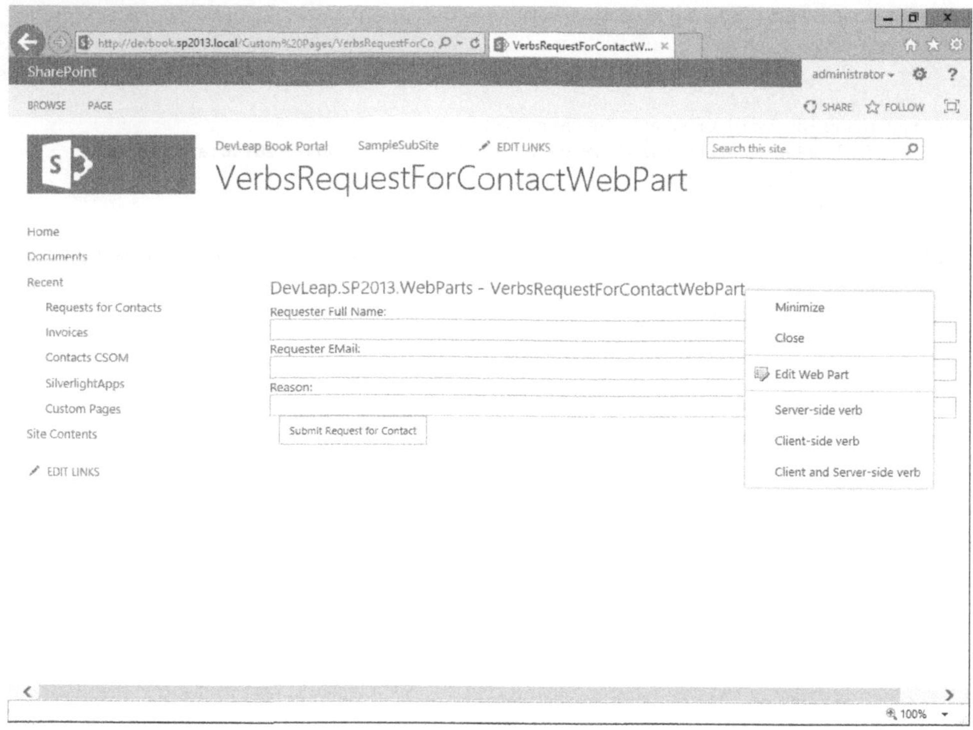

FIGURE 11-9 Sample custom verbs rendered in a custom Web Part.

Listing 11-15 presents an excerpt of the sample Web Part, which supports all three kinds of custom verbs.

LISTING 11-15 A custom Web Part with custom verbs

```
public override WebPartVerbCollection Verbs {
    get {
        WebPartVerb serverSideVerb = new WebPartVerb("serverSiteVerbId",
           handleServerSideVerb);
        serverSideVerb.Text = "Server-side verb";
        WebPartVerb clientSideVerb = new WebPartVerb("clientSideVerbId",
           "javascript:alert('Client-side Verb selected');");
        clientSideVerb.Text = "Client-side verb";
```

```
            WebPartVerb clientAndServerSideVerb = new
                WebPartVerb("clientAndServerSideVerbId",
                handleServerSideVerb,
                "javascript:alert('Client-side Verb selected');");
            clientAndServerSideVerb.Text = "Client and Server-side verb";
            WebPartVerbCollection newVerbs = new WebPartVerbCollection(
                new WebPartVerb[] {
                    serverSideVerb, clientSideVerb, clientAndServerSideVerb,
                }
                );
            return (new WebPartVerbCollection(base.Verbs, newVerbs));
        }
    }

    protected void handleServerSideVerb(Object source, WebPartEventArgs args) {
        EnsureChildControls();

        this.GenericMessage.Text = "You raised a server-side event!";
    }
```

The interesting aspect of this sample code is the implementation of the *Verbs* property, where you manually define and configure verbs, and then add them to the resulting collection of Web Part verbs.

Usually, custom verbs are defined in Intranet/extranet solutions to provide support for custom functionalities, such as refreshing content, opening custom pop-up windows, and so forth. In general, they are not used in web content management (WCM) solutions, because the user experience is usually different in these public-facing Internet sites.

Connectable Web Parts

A Web Part is defined as *connectable* when it can be connected with another Web Part, within the same page, in a provider-consumer relationship. Connectable Web Parts are useful for creating filters and master-detail pages, where one Web Part—the provider—typically renders a selectable list of items or a single master item, and other Web Parts—the consumers—render filtered contents based on the provider's current item. What happens behind the scenes is that the provider and the consumer share some data, based on a shared communication contract. As a concrete example, you will see how to develop a provider Web Part that offers a selectable list of product categories, and a consumer Web Part that shows the products belonging to the currently selected category.

First, to develop the sample connectable Web Parts solution, you need to define a data source. For the sake of simplicity, Listing 11-16 example uses an XML data source file, containing both categories and products, so you don't need to have access to a DBMS to build the example.

LISTING 11-16 The XML data source file for the connectable Web Parts sample

```
<?xml version="1.0" encoding="utf-8" ?>
<store>
  <categories>
    <category id="FOOD" description="Food" />
    <category id="BEV" description="Beverages" />
    <category id="APPAREL" description="Shoes and Dresses" />
    <category id="UTILS" description="Utilities and Tools" />
  </categories>
  <products>
    <product code="P01" description="Meat" categoryId="FOOD" price="15.00" />
    <product code="P02" description="Filet" categoryId="FOOD" price="18.00" />
    <product code="P03" description="Biscuits" categoryId="FOOD" price="4.00" />
    <product code="P04" description="Olive Oil" categoryId="FOOD" price="35.00"
/>
    <product code="P05" description="Chips" categoryId="FOOD" price="3.00" />
    <product code="P06" description="Water" categoryId="BEV" price="0.50" />
    <product code="P07" description="Red Wine" categoryId="BEV" price="7.00" />
    <product code="P08" description="White Wine" categoryId="BEV" price="9.00" />
    <product code="P09" description="Beer" categoryId="BEV" price="3.50" />
    <product code="P10" description="Weiss Bier" categoryId="BEV" price="4.00" />
    <product code="P11" description="Cap" categoryId="APPAREL" price="45.00" />
    <product code="P12" description="T-Shirt" categoryId="APPAREL" price="12.00"
/>
    <product code="P13" description="Coat" categoryId="APPAREL" price="210.00" />
    <product code="P14" description="Screwdriver" categoryId="UTILS" price="7.00"
/>
    <product code="P15" description="Hairdryer" categoryId="UTILS" price="31.00"
/>
  </products>
</store>
```

The provider Web Part that shows the categories will render a grid containing all the product categories, along with a link button that allows users to select a specific category. The products (or consumer) Web Part will render a grid of products, filtered by the selected category. The provider and the consumer need to share a *communication contract*, which is an interface that will be implemented by the provider and consumed by the consumer. Thanks to the smart architecture of ASP.NET connectable Web Parts, you can define that interface freely, without any constraints on its properties, methods, and signature. In addition, a typical interface for connecting Web Parts defines only properties that correspond to the data shared between provider and consumer. Listing 11-17 shows the interface defined for this example.

LISTING 11-17 The communication contract shared between the provider and the consumer Web Parts

```
public interface ICategoriesProvider {
    String CategoryId { get; }
}
```

To make the connection available, you need to implement the interface in a custom type and include a public method in the provider Web Part that returns an instance of that type. Then, to make SharePoint and ASP.NET aware that the method can be assumed as a connection provider, you decorate it with the *ConnectionProviderAttribute* attribute. Listing 11-18 contains an excerpt of an example implementation of the provider Web Part.

LISTING 11-18 An excerpt of the provider Web Part

```
public class CategoriesWebPart : WebPart, ICategoriesProvider {

    [WebBrowsable(true)]
    [Personalizable(true)]
    public String XmlDataSourceUri { get; set; }

    protected GridView gridCategories;

    protected override void CreateChildControls() {
        // ... code omitted ...
    }

    public String CategoryId {
        get {
                if (this.gridCategories.SelectedIndex >= 0) {
                    return (this.gridCategories.SelectedDataKey.Value as String);
                }
                else {
                    return (String.Empty);
                }
        }
    }
    [ConnectionProvider("Category")]
    public ICategoriesProvider GetCategoryProvider() {
        return (this);
    }

    // ... code omitted ...
}
```

As shown in Listing 11-18, the interface is generally implemented directly in the provider Web Part, returning an instance of the Web Part through the method decorated with the *ConnectionProvider* attribute. The *GetCategoryProvider* method simply returns *this* (the instance of the current Web Part), and is marked as *ConnectionProvider*, with a specific name for the data provided. That name will be shown to the end user while connecting Web Parts.

The other side of this connection—the consumer Web Part—looks like Listing 11-19.

LISTING 11-19 An excerpt of the consumer Web Part

```
public class ProductsWebPart : WebPart {

    [WebBrowsable(true)]
    [Personalizable(true)]
    public String XmlDataSourceUri { get; set; }
    protected ICategoriesProvider _provider;
    protected GridView gridProducts;
    protected String categoryId;
    [ConnectionConsumer("Products of Category")]
    public void SetCategoryProvider(ICategoriesProvider categoriesProvider) {
        this._provider = categoriesProvider;    }

    protected override void OnPreRender(EventArgs e) {
        if (this._provider != null) {
            this.categoryId = this._provider.CategoryId;
            if (!String.IsNullOrEmpty(this.categoryId)) {
                this.EnsureChildControls();
                // ... code omitted ...
            }
            else {
                this.Controls.Add(new LiteralControl(
                   "Please select a Product Category"));
            }
        }
        else {
            this.Controls.Add(new LiteralControl(
               "Please connect this Web Part to a Categories Data Provider"));
        }
            base.OnPreRender(e);
    }

    protected override void CreateChildControls() {
     // ... code omitted ...
    }
}
```

As its name implies, the consumer Web Part consumes the data presented by the provider Web Part through a specific public method, named *SetCategoryProvider*, which is decorated with the *ConnectionConsumerAttribute* attribute.

SharePoint automatically matches the provider method, marked as *ConnectionProvider*, and the consumer method, marked as *ConnectionConsumer*, invoking the former to get a reference to the provider instance, and the latter to set the reference. This way, the consumer, which is in its own On*PreRender* event method, will be able to check if a reference to a specific data provider exists, and, if so, will query it to get back the currently selected product category.

Figure 11-10 shows the output of these Web Parts connected in a common Web Part page.

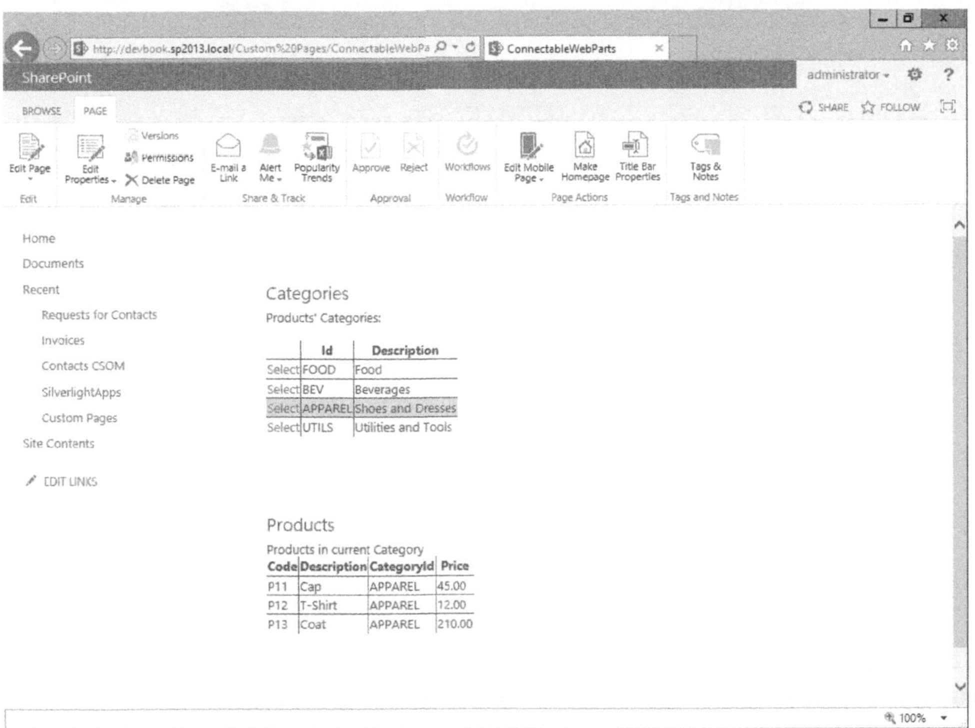

FIGURE 11-10 The output of the connected Web Parts within a SharePoint 2013 Web Part page.

Note It is strategic to query the data provider in the *OnPreRender* method of the consumer Web Part, instead of, for instance, invoking it in the *CreateChildControls* method. In fact, in the *CreateChildControls* method stage, the provider Web Part shouldn't be ready to provide the currently selected item, while in the *OnPreRender* stage, the current selection, if any, will be available.

Figure 11-11 shows the configuration interface natively provided by SharePoint to connect a couple of connectable Web Parts.

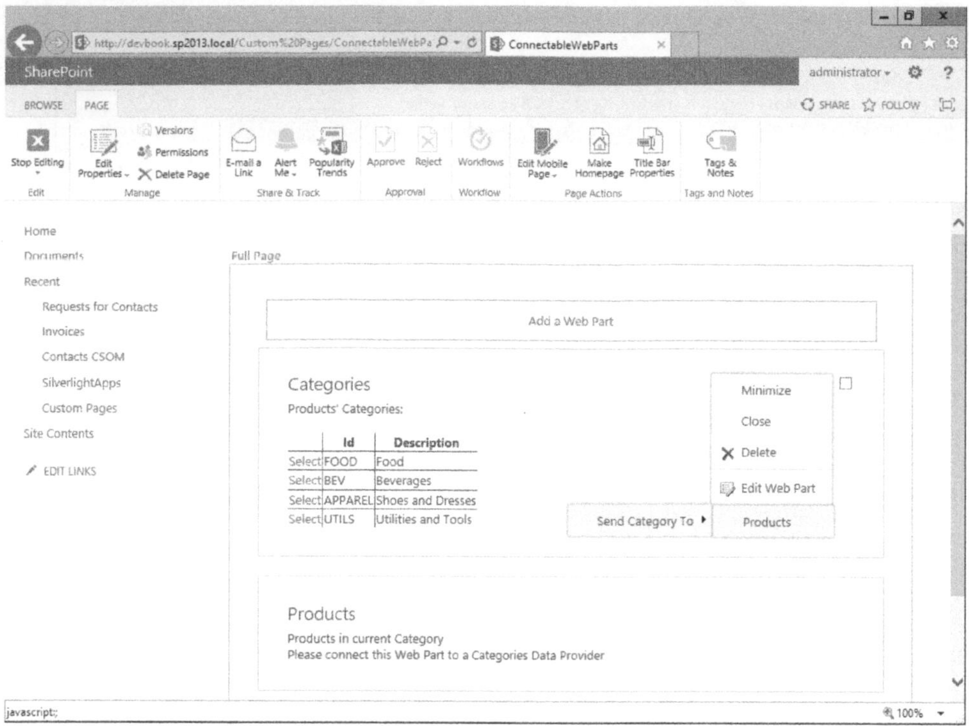

FIGURE 11-11 The native interface of SharePoint to connect a couple of connectable Web Parts.

Notice in Figure 11-11 how the Send Category To menu item goes into the Products Web Part item. The *Category* word is defined in the constructor of the *ConnectionProviderAttribute* in Listing 11-18.

In the interest of being thorough, Table 11-3 lists the configurable properties of *ConnectionProviderAttribute* and *ConnectionConsumerAttribute*. Some of these properties can be configured only through the constructors of these attributes.

TABLE 11-3 The configurable properties of *ConnectionProviderAttribute* and *ConnectionConsumerAttribute*

Property name	Description
AllowsMultipleConnections	In both attributes, indicates whether the connection point allows multiple connections.
ConnectionPointType	Represents a *Type* corresponding to the *ConnectionPoint* between the provider and the consumer. Generally, it is automatically assigned; however, it can be created and assigned using a custom type.
DisplayName	Represents the user-friendly name of the connection, used also in the browser UI when connecting Web Parts.
ID	Defines the unique ID of a connection provider and allows a provider to publish multiple unique connections, as well as a consumer to specify its target provider.

As is evident from the properties shown in Table 11-3, you can define a provider Web Part that provides data to multiple consumers, which can prove useful. As an example, if you build custom dashboards—typically for business intelligence solutions—you might have a provider Web Part that supplies the currently selected product, business unit, or whatever you need to monitor, and a set of consumer Web Parts that show detailed information about the currently selected item.

SharePoint by itself provides some native interfaces that correspond to Web Parts connection contracts, as listed in Table 11-4. These interfaces are considered obsolete, however, and you should rely on them only when you need to provide backward compatibility in your Web Parts.

TABLE 11-4 The SharePoint native connectable interfaces

Interfaces	Description
ICellProvider, ICellConsumer	Contract to provide or consume a single value, like a field or a cell.
IRowProvider, IRowConsumer	Contract to provide or consume a single row or a set of rows.
IListProvider, IListConsumer	Contract to provide or consume an entire list of items.
IFilterProvider, IFilterConsumer	Contract to provide or consume a filter in a master-detail scenario.
IParametersInProvider, IParametersInConsumer	Contract to provide or consume a set of parameters for a Web Part. In this situation, the consumer gives the values of the parameters to the provider.
IParametersOutProvider, IParametersOutConsumer	Contract to provide or consume a set of parameters for a Web Part. In this situation, the provider gives the values of the parameters to the consumer.

More Info Sometimes, you'll come across situations in which you would like to connect a provider Web Part, based on a specific provider contract interface, to a consumer Web Part that can't directly consume that contract, but can consume a different interface. The infrastructure of connectable Web Parts allows you to define *interface transformers*, which allow you to connect incompatible interfaces. This book does not cover this topic; however, it is **important** to be aware of its existence. You can find further details about this topic at *http://msdn.microsoft.com/en-us/library/ms469765.aspx*.

Deployment and versioning

In SharePoint 2013, you can deploy a Web Part in three locations:

- **The Solution Gallery** This allows deploying Web Parts in a sandboxed environment. Although introduced in SharePoint 2010, it is now deprecated in SharePoint 2013. Thus, this chapter will not cover it.

- **The bin directory of the hosting web application** Using this deployment, you can release a Web Part locally to a specific web application, with local maintenance and configuration.
- **The GAC** Code libraries and Web Parts are deployed here so that they can be shared by all the web applications in the current server farm. Code installed in the GAC has full-trust rights on the hosting server.

Regardless of which deployment location you choose, a Web Part is deployed through a .webpart file that's either included in a SharePoint solution or manually deployed by an authorized user. However, deployment includes not only installing from scratch, but also upgrading from one version to another.

To upgrade a Web Part, one useful suggestion is to release upgrades only through strongly named assemblies. A strongly named assembly can be checked against its signature when .NET loads it, to prevent tampering. In addition, the strong name also declares the assembly version clearly, better supporting upgrade paths.

Note The .NET Common Language Runtime (CLR) checks the digital signature of a strongly named assembly whenever it loads such an assembly deployed in the bin directory of the hosting application. However, the signature of an assembly deployed in the GAC is checked only when it's inserted into the GAC. This behavior may sound strange, but only administrators (local or domain) can add assemblies to the GAC. If an administrator inserts an assembly into the GAC, and that assembly has a valid signature, then only another user with administrative rights could change (tamper with) that binary file. So, unless your administrators become hackers, that situation should never happen!

If your upgrade process involves only internal code modification without changes to any public property of the Web Part, and you did not change the assembly version, you can simply substitute the assembly in the deployment location. If you changed some of the public properties of the Web Part, you need to adapt older versions of your Web Part to the last version. If a Web Part page or a wiki page contains an old instance of your Web Part, as soon as someone opens the page, the old Web Part will load, and SharePoint infrastructure will look for its assembly and type. If you replaced the old one with a new version, however, SharePoint will not find the old assembly, and the type load will fail. Similarly, if you renamed, removed, or otherwise changed some properties, the serialization of the old Web Part will not match the new type.

To solve the assembly-versioning issue, you can use the .NET native assembly binding redirect infrastructure. By manually adding a few lines of XML to the web.config file of the web application, you can instruct the .NET CLR to load the new assembly in place of the old one. Listing 11-20 shows an example of assembly-binding redirect.

LISTING 11-20 An excerpt of a web.config file with an assembly-binding redirect directive

```
<runtime>
  <assemblyBinding xmlns="urn:schemas-microsoft-com:asm.v1">
    <dependentAssembly>
      <assemblyIdentity name="DevLeap.SP2013.VersionableWebPart"
        publicKeyToken="6acae404adfa82c3" culture="neutral" />
      <bindingRedirect oldVersion="1.0.0.0" newVersion="2.0.0.0" />
    </dependentAssembly>
  </assemblyBinding>
</runtime>
```

This small piece of XML declares that when the CLR needs to load the assembly with name *DevLeap.SP2013.VersionableWebPart* and a *PublicKeyToken* value of *6acae404adfa82c3*, and with neutral culture and version 1.0.0.0 (*oldVersion*), it should instead try to load version 2.0.0.0 (*newVersion*) of the same assembly. Of course, the new assembly must be available in the web application bin folder or in the GAC.

On the other hand, migrating properties from one Web Part version into another is not a trivial feat. If you are upgrading an old SharePoint native Web Part to an ASP.NET Web Part, you can override the *AfterDeserialize()* method to migrate properties from the old version to the new one. This method will be invoked the first time SharePoint loads a page with an older version of your Web Part in it. For subsequent loads, the Web Part will already be upgraded, and the *AfterDeserialize()* method will not be invoked again.

Keep in mind that when you are upgrading ASP.NET Web Parts, you cannot use this method. For versioning personalization data in ASP.NET Web Parts, you should instead use the *IVersioningPersonalizable* interface defined in the namespace *System.Web.UI.WebControls.WebParts*. Listing 11-21 shows the signature of this interface.

LISTING 11-21 The *IVersioningPersonalizable* interface for Web Part versioning

```
namespace System.Web.UI.WebControls.WebParts {
    public interface IVersioningPersonalizable {
        void Load(IDictionary unknownProperties);
    }
}
```

The only method defined in this interface is *Load*, which receives a list of all the unknown properties that should be deserialized, but for which the Web Part environment does not know where to store their values. You can implement this interface to migrate personalization while the framework loads the Web Parts.

For clarity, consider the simple Web Part in Listing 11-22, which has one customizable property.

LISTING 11-22 A very simple Web Part to show how Web Part versioning works

```
namespace DevLeap.SP2013.VersionableWebPart.CustomWebPart {
    [ToolboxItemAttribute(false)]
    public class CustomWebPart : WebPart {
        [WebBrowsable(true)]
        [Personalizable(true)]
        public String TextToRender { get; set; }

        protected override void CreateChildControls() {
            this.Controls.Add(new LiteralControl(this.TextToRender));
        }
    }
}
```

This Web Part is deployed within an assembly with the following strong name:

```
DevLeap.SP2013.VersionableWebPart, Version=1.0.0.0, Culture=neutral,
PublicKeyToken=6acae404adfa82c3
```

Now suppose that you define a new version of this Web Part, changing the assembly version, renaming the public property *TextToRender* to *TextToRenderTimes*, and adding a new property, *NumberOfTimes*. First, you need to define a corresponding binding redirect in the web.config file. Then you must install the new assembly into the GAC, and finally, you need to implement the versioning interface (*IVersioningPersonalizable*).

Listing 11-23 shows an example of a new Web Part that transparently migrates unknown properties.

LISTING 11-23 The second version of the simple Web Part from Listing 11-22

```
namespace DevLeap.SP2013.VersionableWebPart.CustomWebPart {

    [ToolboxItemAttribute(false)]
    public class CustomWebPart : WebPart, IVersioningPersonalizable {

        [WebBrowsable(true)]
        [Personalizable(true)]
        public String TextToRenderTimes { get; set; }

        [WebBrowsable(true)]
        [Personalizable(true)]
        public Int32 RepeatTimes { get; set; }
```

```
        protected override void CreateChildControls() {
            for (Int32 c = 0; c < this.RepeatTimes; c++) {
                this.Controls.Add(new LiteralControl(this.TextToRenderTimes));
            }
        }
        void IVersioningPersonalizable.Load(IDictionary unknownProperties) {
            foreach (DictionaryEntry entry in unknownProperties) {
                if (entry.Key.ToString() == "TextToRender") {
                    this.RepeatTimes = 1;
                    this.TextToRenderTimes = entry.Value.ToString();
                }
            }
        }
    }
}
```

The *Load* method of *IVersioningPersonalizable* receives a dictionary of all the unmatched properties, which lets you match or migrate them to the corresponding new property, if it exists.

Security: Safe controls and cross-site-scripting safeguards

From a security point of view, every Web Part acts in the context of the current user; thus, its security against SharePoint data is based on the current user's permissions. However, SharePoint data security may not be the ultimate measure of a secure solution. For example, an authorized user could insert a Web Part that represents a risk for the client browser or for the server environment hosting the SharePoint solution. Imagine what would happen if a user uploads a custom Web Part that consumes a lot of CPU resources (perhaps 100 percent) due to a bug or even malicious intent. Any SharePoint front-end server that loads and executes this Web Part would block any further functionality—or at least have its performance seriously degraded.

To avoid such issues, SharePoint provides *safe controls*. In fact, SharePoint will load and execute only authorized Web Parts, based on a list of *SafeControl* elements declared in the web.config file of the current web application. When you deploy a Web Part solution at the farm level, the Web Part class is marked as a *SafeControl* in the web.config file of the site where the control is deployed. If you try to load a page that hosts a Web Part or a control not marked as a *SafeControl*, the load will fail, but the SharePoint environment will remain stable and secure. Listing 11-24 contains an example of a *SafeControl* declaration for one of the Web Parts defined previously in this chapter.

LISTING 11-24 A *SafeControl* declaration for the *RSSFeedDynamicViewerWebPart* control

```
<SafeControl Assembly="DevLeap.SP2013.AdvancedWebParts, Version=1.0.0.0,
  Culture=neutral, PublicKeyToken=420cb6d9461e6c7c"
  Namespace="DevLeap.SP2013.AdvancedWebParts.CategoriesWebPart"
  TypeName="*" Safe="True" SafeAgainstScript="False" />
```

Notice that the *SafeControl* tag references the safe Web Part in terms of assembly, including its strong name, namespace, and type name. The *SafeControl* tag also defines a *SafeAgainstScript* attribute with a *Boolean* value that allows configuring a feature called Cross-Site-Scripting SafeGuard, which was introduced in SharePoint 2010.

Through this feature, only users with the role of designer or higher can customize Web Parts via configuration properties. This means that, by default, a site contributor cannot configure or customize Web Part properties, while prior to SharePoint 2010 that was possible.

Since SharePoint 2010, the Client Object Model is available even in the web browser, via JavaScript. Imagine what would happen if a malicious user configured a Web Part property with some JavaScript code, invoking the Client Object Model to delete or change some data on the server, and that custom property was used to render the output of the Web Part (for instance, a *Title* property). Of course, the Client Object Model acts in the context of the current user, so the injected JavaScript could do exactly what the current user can do. But what would happen if that same page were opened by a site collection administrator, for example? This new kind of cross-site-scripting (XSS) is natively blocked by the Cross-Site-Scripting SafeGuard feature. This feature impacts not only your new Web Parts, but also any Web Part developed by anyone else.

If—at your own risk—you want to continue to let a Web Part remain configurable, even by site contributors, you can change the *SafeAgainstScript* attribute of the *SafeControl* declaration for that Web Part. Figure 11-12 illustrates the UI provided by Visual Studio 2012 for changing this property.

A value of *True* instructs SharePoint to allow editing and configuration even by site contributors. There is also a new attribute, *RequiresDesignerPermissionAttribute*, which you can use to tag a property to make it configurable only by users with designer rights or higher. This last attribute overrides any configuration in the web.config file, so if you declare a control with *SafeAgainstScript* but also define a property marked with *RequiresDesignerPermissionAttribute*, that property will still not be configurable by a contributor, and will require at least a designer role, regardless of the web.config configuration.

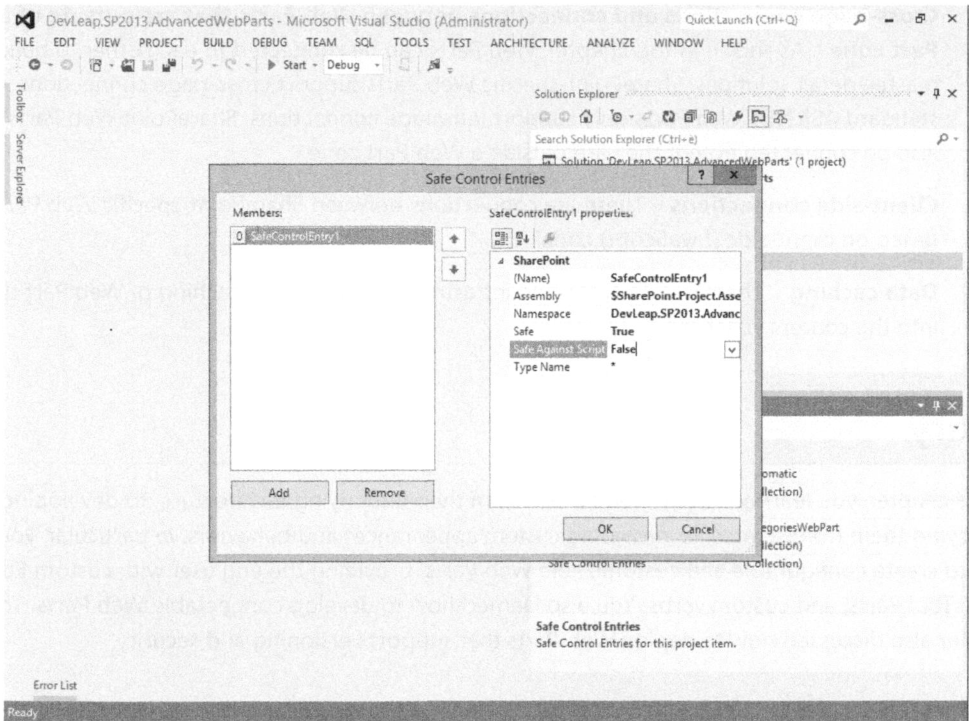

FIGURE 11-12 The Safe Control Entries property editor of a Web Part in Visual Studio 2012.

The SharePoint-specific *WebPart* class

As you learned at the beginning of this chapter, in SharePoint you have the capability to inherit Web Parts from a SharePoint-specific base class, instead of using the standard class provided by ASP.NET. The resulting Web Parts are still fully integrated with the ASP.NET Web Parts infrastructure, because the SharePoint *WebPart* class internally inherits from that of ASP.NET. These Web Parts can be used only in SharePoint. They have, however, a few additional capabilities that in very specific conditions make implementing SharePoint-specific Web Parts a beneficial choice:

- **Support for SharePoint Tool Parts** This provides support for Tool Parts, which were described in the "Configurable Web Parts" section.
- **Path or code replacement tokens** You can use these to inject tokens in the output HTML code of a SharePoint Web Part, and then have the SharePoint infrastructure replace them with their corresponding values. There are tokens for the current user name, the current locale ID of the website, and so on.

- **Cross-page connections and connections between Web Parts that are outside of a Web Part zone** As shown in this chapter, Web Parts can be connected to each other to build master-detail solutions. SharePoint-specific Web Parts support cross-page connections, while standard ASP.NET Web Parts only support intrapage connections. SharePoint Web Parts can also be connected even if they are outside a Web Part zone.
- **Client-side connections** These are connections between SharePoint-specific Web Parts, based on client-side (JavaScript) code.
- **Data caching** There is a data-caching infrastructure that allows caching of Web Part data into the content database.

Summary

In this chapter, you learned about Web Parts—from their underlying architecture, to developing and deploying them from scratch, to providing custom appearances and behaviors. In particular, you saw how to create configurable and customizable Web Parts, providing the end user with custom Editor Parts, Tool Parts, and custom verbs. You also learned how to develop connectable Web Parts. The chapter also discussed how to deploy Web Parts that support versioning and security.

CHAPTER 12

Customizing the UI

This chapter describes how to extend the UI of Microsoft SharePoint 2013. In particular, you will learn how to customize menus, ribbons, controls, and pages. This chapter is important if you want to be able to provide your users or customers with a custom UI that is compliant with the standard SharePoint behavior, while simultaneously satisfying the requirements of intranet and extranet solutions, as well as Internet publishing sites.

Custom actions

The first area of customization that you will address is creating custom actions in the standard SharePoint UI. Custom actions are features that can extend or change the standard behavior of any of the following items: menu items, link menus of administrative pages, and ribbons. The ribbon is important enough to warrant a dedicated section in this chapter (see "Ribbons"); all other custom actions will be covered here. As you may recall from Chapter 4, "SharePoint features and solutions," the types of custom action features that you can create are

- ***CustomAction*** Creates a new custom action to define a new control on a ribbon, a new menu item on a standard menu, or a new link on a settings page
- ***CustomActionGroup*** Creates a new group of custom actions for better usability from the perspective of the end user
- ***HideCustomAction*** Hides an existing custom action defined by another custom action or implemented by default in SharePoint

The following pages will delve into these items.

The *CustomAction* element

The definition of a *CustomAction* element requires the declaration of a feature element manifest, based on the XML structure, as illustrated in Listing 12-1.

LISTING 12-1 The *CustomAction* element structure

```
<CustomAction
  RequiredAdmin = "Delegated | Farm | Machine"
  ControlAssembly = "Text"
  ControlClass = "Text"
  ControlSrc = "Text"
  Description = "Text"
  FeatureId = "Text"
  GroupId = "Text"
  Id = "Text"
  ImageUrl = "Text"
  Location = "Text"
  RegistrationId = "Text"
  RegistrationType = "Text"
  RequireSiteAdministrator = "TRUE" | "FALSE"
  Rights = "Text"
  RootWebOnly = "TRUE" | "FALSE"
  ScriptSrc = "Text"
  ScriptBlock = "Text"
  Sequence = "Integer"
  ShowInLists = "TRUE" | "FALSE"
  ShowInReadOnlyContentTypes = "TRUE" | "FALSE"
  ShowInSealedContentTypes = "TRUE" | "FALSE"
  Title = "Text"
  UIVersion = "Integer">
    <UrlAction />
    <CommandUIExtension />
</CustomAction>
```

The *CustomAction* element is made of a set of attributes and accepts a couple of optional child elements. Table 12-1 describes each available attribute.

TABLE 12-1 The attributes supported by the *CustomAction* element

Attribute name	Description
RequiredAdmin	Optional *Text* attribute that specifies the rights required for the custom action to apply. Supported values are *Delegated*, *Farm*, and *Machine*.
ControlAssembly	Optional *Text* attribute used to declare a custom assembly full name, hosting a control for rendering the custom action with code running on the server side.
ControlClass	Used to declare a custom class, implementing a control for rendering the custom action with code running on the server side.
ControlSrc	Optional *Text* attribute that specifies the relative URL of an ASCX file that corresponds to the source of the custom action.
Description	Optional *Text* attribute with which you can provide a long description for the action.
FeatureId	Optional *Text* attribute that specifies the ID of the feature associated with the custom action.

Attribute name	Description
GroupId	Optional *Text* attribute that declares the group that will contain the custom action. For a complete reference of all the available groups and locations, refer to "Default Custom Action Locations and IDs," on MSDN online at *http://msdn.microsoft.com/en-us/library/bb802730.aspx*.
Id	Optional *Text* attribute that specifies the ID of the custom action. This can be a GUID or a string that uniquely identifies the custom action.
ImageUrl	Declares the relative URL of an image that represents an icon for the custom action.
Location	Specifies the location of the custom action. This is a value taken from a pre-defined list of locations or from a custom set of locations.
RegistrationId	Optional *Text* attribute that declares the ID of the target list, content type, or file type associated with the custom action.
RegistrationType	Optional *Text* attribute that declares the type of registration the action is targeting. *RegistrationType* works together with the *RegistrationId* attribute, and can assume one of the following values: *None, List, ContentType, ProgId*, or *FileType*.
RequireSiteAdministrator	Optional *Boolean* attribute that specifies whether the action will be displayed to all users or only to site administrators.
Rights	Optional *Text* attribute that defines the minimum set of rights required to view the current custom action. If it is not specified, the action will be visible to anyone. It can specify one or more rights, comma separated, selected from the list of available rights defined in the standard base permission of SharePoint. Possible values are *ViewListItems, ManageAlerts, ManageLists,* and so on. For a complete reference of all the base permissions available in SharePoint, refer to the document "SPBasePermissions Enumeration," at *http://msdn.microsoft.com/en-us/library/microsoft.sharepoint.spbasepermissions.aspx*.
RootWebOnly	Optional *Boolean* attribute, valid only for sandboxed solutions, that specifies if the action must be only on root websites.
ScriptSrc	Optional *Text* attribute that defines the relative URL of a script to download and execute. *ScriptSrc* works only in conjunction with a *Location* attribute with a value of *ScriptLink*. It is very useful whenever you need to reference external JavaScript source files for implementing custom behaviors.
ScriptBlock	Optional *Text* attribute that defines the ECMAScript source code of a script to execute. *ScriptBlock* works only in conjunction with a *Location* attribute with a value of *ScriptLink*.
Sequence	Optional *Integer* attribute that defines the ordinal position of the custom action, within its group.
ShowInLists	Deprecated optional *Boolean* attribute that specifies whether the action will be shown in the page for managing content types.
ShowInReadOnlyContentTypes	Optional *Boolean* attribute that specifies whether the action will be displayed only for the page for managing read-only content types.
ShowInSealedContentTypes	Optional *Boolean* attribute that specifies whether the action will be displayed only for the page for managing sealed content types.
Title	Required *Text* attribute to specify the title of the action. *Title* will be used in the UI to present the action to the end user.
UIVersion	Optional *Integer* value to define the version of the UI in which the action will be rendered.

In addition, a *CustomAction* tag can contain some child elements:

- ***UrlAction*** Defines a destination URL for when the end user clicks the custom action.
- ***CommandUIExtension*** Defines a complex UI extension, typically a ribbon. This will be discussed in the next section, "Ribbons."

The basic and most-used attributes are those for defining the ID, the title, the location (where you want the action to appear), and the registration type, together with the registration ID. For example, if you want your action to be displayed when the end user clicks the contextual menu of a document (also called the Edit Control Block [ECB] menu), you can define a custom action for the document libraries of a site like the one illustrated in Listing 12-2.

LISTING 12-2 A *CustomAction* targeting the ECB menu of items in a document library

```
<CustomAction
  Location="EditControlBlock"
  RegistrationType="List"
  RegistrationId="101"
  Id="DevLeap.CustomActions.DemoECB.SampleAction"
  Title="Sample Action"
  Description="Sample custom action.">
  <UrlAction Url="javascript:window.alert('You clicked the Sample Action!');"/>
</CustomAction>
```

The *Location* attribute specifies that the action will be shown in the ECB menu. The *RegistrationType* attribute targets a specific *List*, while the *RegistrationId* explicitly defines the list type (101 = "Document Library"). Notice the child element, *UrlAction*, which defines a destination URL for when the end user clicks the menu item. In this first example, the custom action simply shows an alert. Figure 12-1 depicts how the action looks in the web browser.

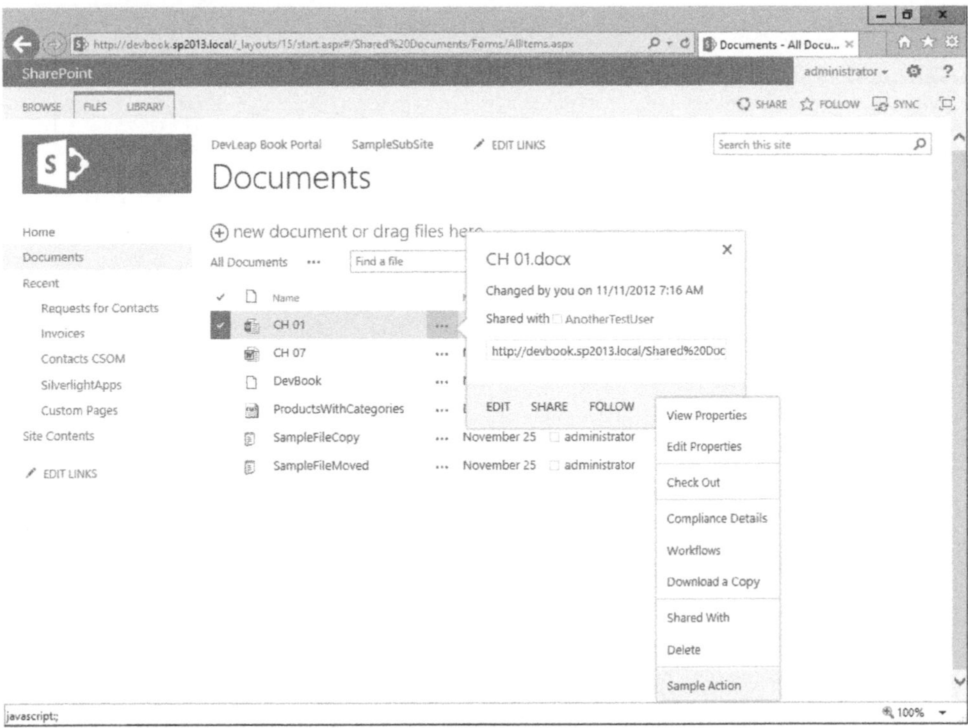

FIGURE 12-1 The custom action shown in the ECB of a document item.

Often, you need to define a custom action targeting not only a list, but also a specific content type, regardless of the list in which it is contained. For example, suppose that you have a custom content type defining a document of type *invoice* (call it *DevLeapInvoice*). This content type needs to have an identifying unique ID, which in this example will have a value of *0x010100DFCFE30E0795465F8973EF29B73F1551*.

The *DevLeapInvoice* content type has some custom metadata fields to define the invoice number, a description, and a status that can assume some predefined values (*Draft*, *Approved*, *Sent*, and *Archived*). Figure 12-2 illustrates the edit form of this kind of document.

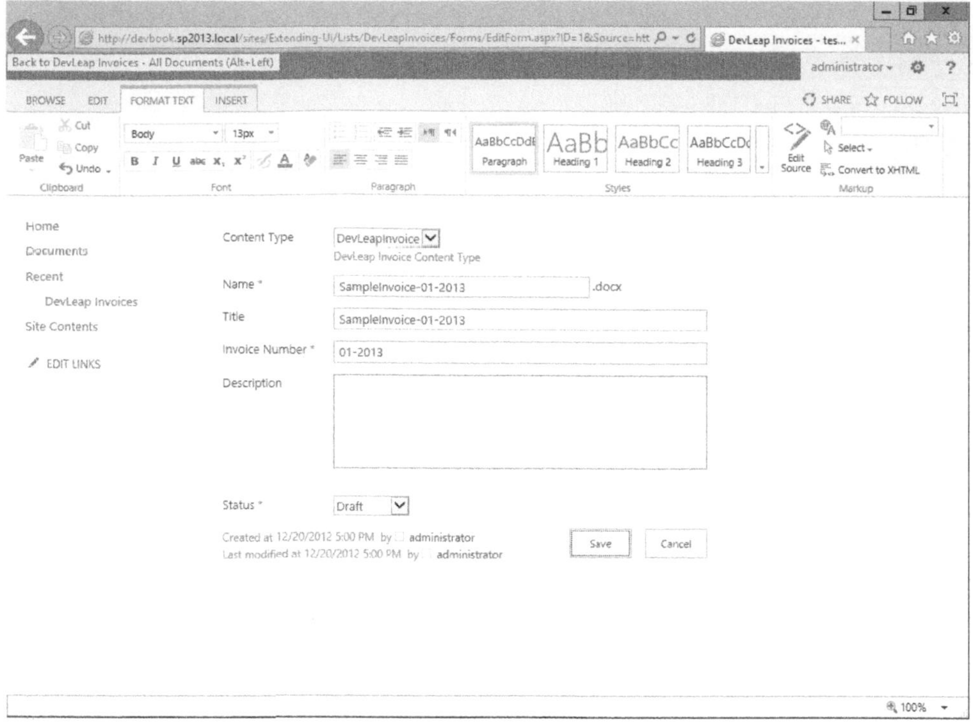

FIGURE 12-2 The edit form of a *DevLeapInvoice* item instance.

Listing 12-3 demonstrates a custom action, still targeting the ECB, that will be shown only in the ECB of items with a content type of *DevLeapInvoice*. The action allows archiving a single invoice, changing its Status field to a value of *Archived*.

LISTING 12-3 A *CustomAction* element targeting the ECB of items with a content type of *DevLeapInvoice*

```
<CustomAction
  Location="EditControlBlock"
  RegistrationType="ContentType"
  RegistrationId="0x010100DFCFE30E0795465F8973EF29B73F1551"
  Id="DevLeap.CustomActions.Invoices.Archive"
  Title="Archive Invoice"
  Rights="ViewListItems,EditListItems"
  Description="Archive this Invoice.">
  <UrlAction Url="~site/_layouts/DevLeap.SP2013.UIExtensions/
  DevLeapInvoiceChangeStatus.aspx?ItemId={ItemId}&amp;ListId={ListId}&amp;
  Status=Archived" />
</CustomAction>
```

The only substantial difference between Listing 12-3 and Listing 12-2 is the *RegistrationType* attribute, which now targets a *ContentType*, as well as the *RegistrationId*, which now defines the ID of the target content type instead of the ID of a list template. The code sample in Listing 12-3 also introduces the *Rights* attribute, with which you can archive invoices only to users who have the ViewListItems and EditListItems permissions assigned.

Additionally, the *UrlAction* child element defined in Listing 12-3 declares a URL of a custom application page, instead of a piece of JavaScript, as in Listing 12-2. The URL could also link to a custom page provided by a custom SharePoint 2013 app. In the "Application pages" section of this chapter, you will learn how to deploy custom application pages. For now, however, disregard the page itself and focus your attention on the *Url* attribute of the *UrlAction* element. This attribute can link to any kind of URL and can contain tokens that will be replaced by the environment during page rendering. These tokens are

- ***~site*** Website-relative (*SPWeb*) link
- ***~sitecollection*** Site collection–relative (*SPSite*) link
- ***~remoteAppUrl*** URL of the site hosting a SharePoint 2013 app, which installs a custom action
- ***{ItemId}*** Integer ID that represents the item within a list
- ***{ItemUrl}*** URL of the current item; works only for documents in libraries
- ***{ListId}*** ID (GUID) of the list on which the action is currently working
- ***{SiteUrl}*** URL of the website (*SPWeb*)
- ***{RecurrenceId}*** Recurrence index ID when related to recurring event items

Finally, you can use any valid JavaScript code block.

In Listing 12-3, the *Url* attribute uses the *{ItemId}* and *{ListId}* tokens because it targets the ECB menu of a single item, so it passes the item ID and list ID to the target page as *QueryString* parameters.

The ECB menu isn't the only location suitable for defining custom actions. Table 12-2 lists the most useful additional locations.

More Info For a complete list of all the available locations, refer to the document "Default Custom Action Locations and IDs," at *http://msdn.microsoft.com/en-us/library/bb802730.aspx*.

TABLE 12-2 The most useful locations for defining custom actions

Location	Group ID	Description
DisplayFormToolbar	*Not applicable*	Corresponds to the display form toolbar of lists
EditControlBlock	*Not applicable*	Corresponds to the per-item ECB menu
EditFormToolbar	*Not applicable*	Corresponds to the edit form toolbar of lists
Microsoft.SharePoint.SiteSettings	*Customization*	Look And Feel section of the Site Settings page
	Galleries	Galleries section of the Site Settings page
	SiteAdministration	Site Administration section of the Site Settings page
	SiteCollectionAdmin	Site Collection Administration section of the Site Settings page
	UsersAndPermissions	Users And Permissions section of the Site Settings page
Microsoft.SharePoint.StandardMenu	*ActionsMenu*	Actions menu in list and document library views
	ActionsMenuForSurvey	Site Actions menu for surveys
	NewMenu	New menu in list and document library views
	SiteActions	Site Actions menu
NewFormToolbar	*Not applicable*	Corresponds to the new form toolbar of lists
ViewToolbar	*Not applicable*	Corresponds to the toolbar in list views

Microsoft also documents the *Id* values for many of the previously defined custom actions, with which you can override standard menu items with custom items of your own.

The *CustomActionGroup* element

Another useful element for defining custom actions is *CustomActionGroup*. Using this element, you can define groups of actions; it is typically used when defining custom sections in the configuration pages, such as the Site Settings page or the pages of the Central Administration. In fact, you can also extend and override administrative pages, not only end-user UI elements. Listing 12-4 shows the structure of the *CustomActionGroup* element.

LISTING 12-4 The *CustomActionGroup* element structure

```
<CustomActionGroup
  Description = "Text"
  Id = "Text"
  Location = "Text"
  Sequence = "Integer"
  Title = "Text">
</CustomActionGroup>
```

The *CustomActionGroup* element is mainly descriptive (for the group it defines). It does not have any child elements because the only purpose of this element is to declare a new group, which will be referenced by other custom actions. Table 12-3 presents a brief description of the available attributes.

TABLE 12-3 The attributes supported by the *CustomActionGroup* element

Attribute name	Description
RequiredAdmin	Optional *Text* attribute that specifies the rights required for the custom action group to apply. Values supported are *Delegated, Farm*, and *Machine*.
Description	Optional *Text* attribute with which you can provide a long description for the action group.
Id	Required *Text* attribute that specifies the ID of the custom action group. It can be a GUID or a string that uniquely identifies the custom action group.
ImageUrl	Optional *Text* attribute that declares the relative URL of an image representing an icon for the custom action.
Location	Required *Text* attribute that specifies the location of the custom action group. *Location* is a value taken from a predefined list of locations or from a custom set of locations.
Sequence	Optional *Integer* value that defines the ordinal position of the custom action group within the set of groups.
Title	Required *Text* attribute that specifies the title of the action. *Title* will be used in the UI to present the action group to the end user.

Listing 12-5 illustrates how to use the *CustomActionGroup* element to define a new section in the Site Settings administrative page. Notice the *CustomAction* element that uses a value of *Microsoft.SharePoint.SiteSettings* for the *Location* attribute and the value of the custom action group's *Id* for the *GroupId* attribute.

LISTING 12-5 *CustomActionGroup* element extending the Site Settings administrative page

```
<CustomActionGroup
  Location="Microsoft.SharePoint.SiteSettings"
  Id="DevLeap.CustomActions.Invoices.Settings"
  Description="View Invoices Settings"
  Title="Invoices Management" />

<CustomAction
  Location="Microsoft.SharePoint.SiteSettings"
  GroupId="DevLeap.CustomActions.Invoices.Settings"
  Id="DevLeap.CustomActions.Invoices.SampleSettings"
  Title="Invoices Sample Settings Page"
  Description="Go to a custom page for managing Invoices' settings.">
  <UrlAction Url="~site/_layouts/DevLeap.SP2013.UIExtensions/InvoicesSettings.
aspx" />
</CustomAction>
```

Figure 12-3 shows the customized Site Settings administrative page in action.

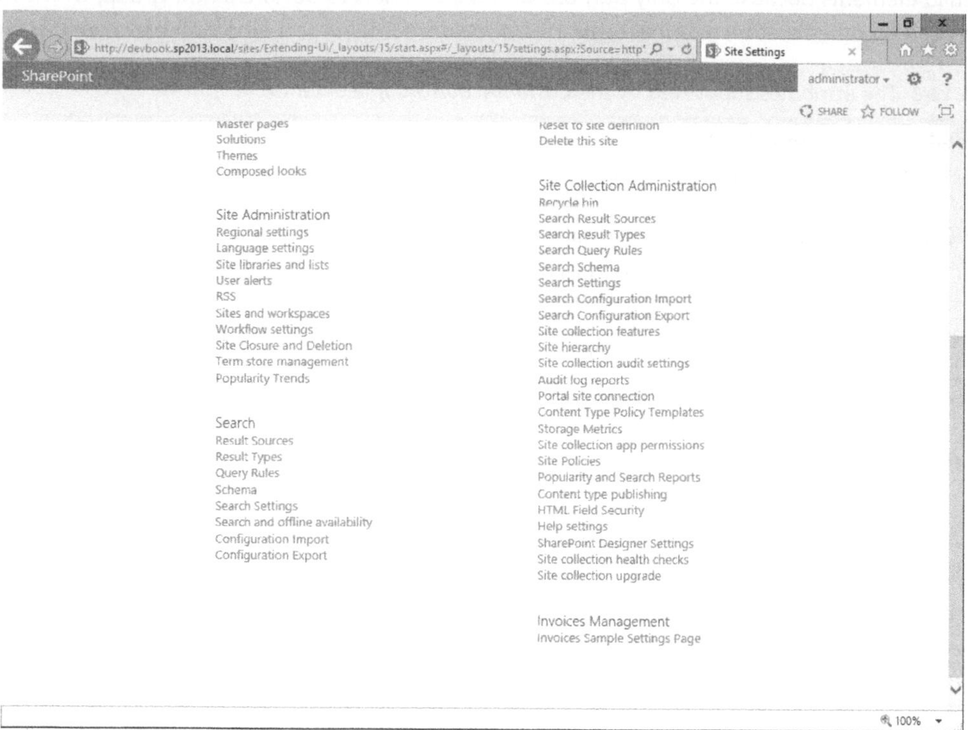

FIGURE 12-3 A customized Site Settings administrative page.

The *HideCustomAction* element

The last element available for customizing UI actions is *HideCustomAction*. Using this element, you can hide existing actions, regardless of whether they are standard, native actions or custom actions defined by you or someone else. Be aware, though, that not all native actions can be hidden. Listing 12-6 shows you the structure of the *HideCustomAction* element.

LISTING 12-6 The *HideCustomAction* element structure

```
<HideCustomAction
  GroupId = "Text"
  HideActionId = "Text"
  Id = "Text"
  Location = "Text">
</HideCustomAction>
```

This element simply defines the information about the action to hide. Table 12-4 gives you a brief explanation of the available attributes.

TABLE 12-4 The attributes supported by the *HideCustomAction* element

Attribute name	Description
GroupId	Optional *Text* attribute that specifies the group to which the action to hide belongs
HideActionId	Optional *Text* attribute that specifies the ID of the action to hide
Id	Optional *Text* attribute that specifies the ID of the current HideCustomAction element
Location	Optional *Text* attribute that specifies the location of the custom action to hide

Listing 12-7 presents an example of the *HideCustomAction* element being used to hide the Quick Launch menu item in the Look And Feel group of the Site Settings page.

LISTING 12-7 A sample *HideCustomAction* element declaration

```
<HideCustomAction
  Id="DevLeap.CustomActions.HideQuickLaunchFromSettings"
  Location="Microsoft.SharePoint.SiteSettings"
  GroupId="Customization"
  HideActionId="QuickLaunch" />
```

In Listing 12-7, the *Location*, *GroupId*, and *HideActionId* attributes correspond to those identifying the Site Theme action. Figure 12-4 shows the result of this action, comparing the page before applying the customization, and then after.

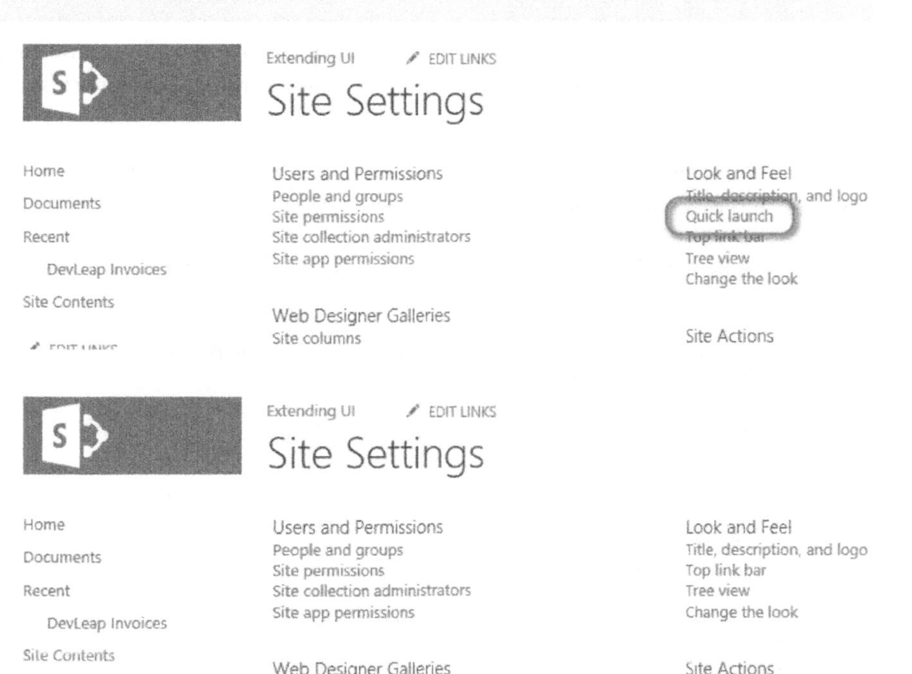

FIGURE 12-4 The Look And Feel group before (left) and after (right) hiding the Site Theme action.

Server-side custom actions

You can also create custom actions that define their content dynamically by using server-side code, instead of using an XML declaration. To define this kind of action, you need to declare a *CustomAction* element within a feature element manifest, providing a value for the *ControlAssembly* and *ControlClass* attributes. These attributes must reference the assembly and the full type name of a class inheriting from the base class *System.Web.UI.WebControls.WebControl* and building a specific set of controls inside the *CreateChildControls* method override. Listing 12-8 illustrates an example of a custom action referencing a custom *ControlClass* attribute.

LISTING 12-8 The custom action referencing a custom *ControlClass* attribute

```
<CustomAction
  Location="Microsoft.SharePoint.StandardMenu"
  GroupId="SiteActions"
  ControlAssembly="DevLeap.SP2013.UIExtensions, Version=1.0.0.0,
    Culture=neutral, PublicKeyToken=3b7c6076bf78362f"
  ControlClass="DevLeap.SP2013.UIExtensions.SwitchToMobileMode"
  Id="DevLeap.CustomActions.SwitchToMobileMode">
</CustomAction>
```

Note The values of both the *ControlAssembly* and the *ControlClass* attributes in Listing 12-8 must be defined on a single line of code.

The action targets the Site Actions menu (also known as the *gear menu*) and allows switching the site to mobile-rendering mode. Of course, you could write this action without a custom class, but this example gives you an idea of what's possible.

Listing 12-9 displays the sample implementation of the class, which is referenced in the *ControlClass* attribute, and which internally generates the menu item.

LISTING 12-9 The class referenced by the *CustomClass* attribute of the custom action of Listing 12-8

```
public class SwitchToMobileMode : System.Web.UI.WebControls.WebControl {
    protected override void CreateChildControls() {
        SPWeb web = SPControl.GetContextWeb(HttpContext.Current);
        MenuItemTemplate switchToMobile = new MenuItemTemplate();
        switchToMobile.Text = "Switch to Mobile view";
        switchToMobile.Description =
          "Switches the current site rendering mode to mobile";
        switchToMobile.ClientOnClickNavigateUrl =
          String.Format("{0}?Mobile=1", web.Url);

        this.Controls.Add(switchToMobile);
    }
}
```

Listing 12-9 illustrates that you can instantiate a *MenuItemTemplate* class, which represents a single menu item. You can then configure its descriptive properties, such as *Text, Description, ImageUrl*, and so on. However, the fundamental properties are those related to the behavior of the menu item within the UI. You can configure the *ClientOnClickNavigateUrl* property if you simply need to define a URL to navigate to when the user clicks the menu. Additionally, you can configure the *ClientOnClickScript* property to configure an ECMAScript code block to execute when the menu entry is clicked. Lastly, to set the control ID and parameter for a postback event, you can assign the *ClientOnClickUsingPostBackEvent* property. In this last scenario, you should handle the postback event yourself; for example, by implementing the *System.Web.UI.IPostBackEventHandler* interface in the control class. You can also configure the *ClientOnClickPostBackConfirmation* property to provide a confirmation message that will be displayed to the end user, just before handling the post-back event. Figure 12-5 shows the result of the sample in Listing 12-9.

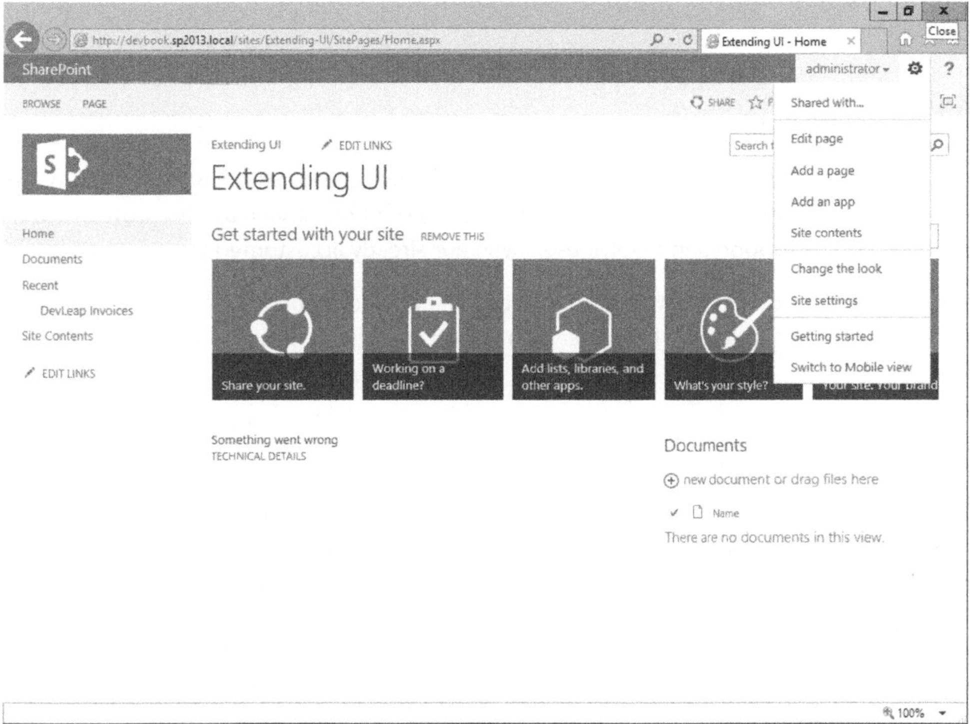

FIGURE 12-5 The custom action defined using a *MenuItemTemplate* class on the server side.

Another type of menu that you can instantiate within custom code is *SubMenuTemplate*, which represents the parent of a hierarchical menu.

Regardless of the type of menu items you define within your *CustomClass* implementation, it is mandatory to define the class as a *SafeControl* object for SharePoint. (Details about using *SafeControl* elements in web.config files were presented at the end of Chapter 11, "Developing Web Parts.")

Note While working with Microsoft Visual Studio 2012, Web Parts are automatically configured in the solution's manifest file as *SafeControl* items. However, the custom class shown in Listing 12-9, as well as any other control class that is not a Web Part, will not be automatically registered as a *SafeControl*. To force registration of the class as a *SafeControl*—using Visual Studio 2012—you can open the Feature Designer of any feature element of your package, such as the one defining the custom actions. There, in the property grid panel, you will find a Safe Control Entries property of type *collection* that will support you in configuring one or more custom *SafeControl* entries.

Ribbons

For end users, the ribbon is one of the most visible and evident features of SharePoint 2013. Having a web-based solution with a command bar that makes use of ribbons, such as Microsoft Office clients do, is a great way to support and involve users who are already accustomed to using such tools.

SharePoint 2013 provides a native set of ribbons, but any developer can define specific *CustomAction* elements to define his or her own ribbon commands, groups, and tabs. In this section, you will learn how.

Ribbon commands

Ribbon commands represent single items to place in a previously existing ribbon tab and group. For example, think about the code sample in Listing 12-3. The goal of that custom action was to allow archiving a single invoice, changing its Status field to a value of *Archived*. A better option, however, would be to give users the opportunity to archive multiple invoices at the same time. The ECB menu extended with Listing 12-3 applies only to a single item, while a ribbon command could be applied to multiple items simultaneously, improving usability and overall user experience.

To get familiar with ribbons, start with a simple example. Listing 12-10 presents a ribbon that displays an alert when it is clicked.

LISTING 12-10 A sample ribbon that shows an alert upon being clicked

```
<CustomAction
  RegistrationType="ContentType"
  RegistrationId="0x010100DFCFE30E0795465F8973EF29B73F1551"
  Id="DevLeap.CustomActions.Invoices.SampleRibbonCommand"
  Location="CommandUI.Ribbon.ListView">
  <CommandUIExtension>
    <CommandUIDefinitions>
      <CommandUIDefinition Location="Ribbon.Documents.Manage.Controls._children">
        <Button Id="SampleRibbonCommand"
                Alt="Shows an alert."
                Description="Shows an alert, just to make an example."
                Sequence="25"
                Command="ShowSampleAlert"
Image16by16="/_layouts/15/images/DevLeap.SP2013.UIExtensions/Baloon_16x16.png"
Image32by32="/_layouts/15/images/DevLeap.SP2013.UIExtensions/Baloon_32x32.png"
                LabelText="Show Alert"
                TemplateAlias="o1" />
      </CommandUIDefinition>
    </CommandUIDefinitions>
  <CommandUIHandlers>
    <CommandUIHandler Command="ShowSampleAlert"
                      CommandAction="javascript:
                      window.alert('This an alert from the ribbon');" />
    </CommandUIHandlers>
  </CommandUIExtension>
</CustomAction>
```

The *CustomAction* element is almost the same as in the previous section, but the *Location* attribute targets a location with a value of *CommandUI.Ribbon.ListView*, which corresponds to the ribbon menu of a *ListView* control. Then the action targets the *DevLeapInvoice* content type through its content type ID, as with the ECB custom action defined earlier. Thus, the ribbon command will show up only while *DevLeapInvoice* items are being worked on. However, instead of a *UrlAction* child element, now there is a *CommandUIExtension* element, which defines a ribbon item. In particular, it defines a set of *CommandUIDefinition* elements, wrapped in a *CommandUIDefinitions* parent element, together with one or more *CommandUIHandler* elements, wrapped by a *CommandUIHandlers* parent tag. A *CommandUIDefinition* element defines the UI behavior of the command with its *Location* attribute, which in the code sample has a value of *Ribbon.Documents.Manage.Controls._children* and declares that its child elements will be children of the Manage group of the Documents tab of the ribbon. In Listing 12-10, the command is represented as a *Button* element with a title, a description, a couple of images sized 16×16 pixels and 32×32 pixels, and so on. Also in Listing 12-10, the *Button* element has a *Sequence* attribute with a value of 25, which means it will render between the second and third button of the target ribbon group (Manage). For standard and native buttons, the *Sequence* attribute has a value that is a multiple of 10. Thus, the first button has a *Sequence* value of 10, the second has a *Sequence* value of 20, and so on.

Another interesting *Button* attribute is *TemplateAlias*, which defines the rendering behavior of the control. Native available templates are o1, which renders the 32×32 image form of the button, and o2, which renders the 16×16 image form. However, you can also define your own templates. Additionally, the *CommandUIHandler* element declares the code to execute when the commands are clicked. For example, in Listing 12-10, the *CommandAction* attribute of the *CommandUIHandler* element invokes a client-side *window.alert* method based on JavaScript. For mapping the *Button* to its handler, there is a *Command* attribute whose value corresponds to the *Command* attribute of the *CommandUIHandler* element. Figure 12-6 shows the results of Listing 12-10 in action.

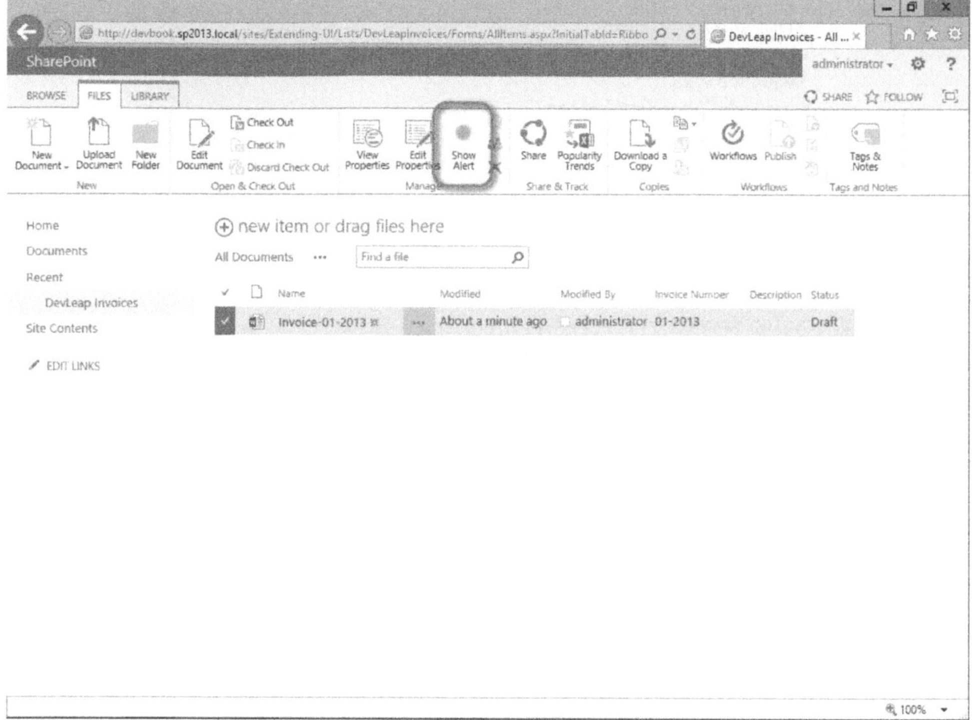

FIGURE 12-6 The custom ribbon command to show an alert in action.

The *CommandUIDefinition* element can host a rich set of child elements. Table 12-5 presents a quick list of all the supported child elements, taken from the official product documentation on MSDN (*http://msdn.microsoft.com/en-us/library/ff458373.aspx*).

TABLE 12-5 The child elements of the *CommandUIDefinition* element

Attribute name	Description
Button	Defines a push-button control. The main attributes are *Alt*, for alternate text; the *Command* to execute on click; *Description* and *LabelText*, for the UI; the various attributes to define 16×16 and 32×32 images, eventually cropped from an image map; the *TemplateAlias* and the *Sequence* position of the button in the owner group; and the various attributes to define tooltip text and images.
CheckBox	Defines a CheckBox control. *CheckBox* also has a *Command* attribute to execute when clicked, as well as layout attributes regarding *description*, images, and so on.
ColorPicker	Defines a ColorPicker control.
ComboBox	Defines a ComboBox control. *ComboBox* supports attributes for defining autocompletion; *the* command to execute on click; and the command to execute on open, close, and preview.
ContextualGroup	Defines a group of tabs that are presented when they are relevant. *ContextualGroup* allows defining a specific color to use while showing the group.
ContextualTabs	Contains groups of tabs that are conditionally present. *ContextualTabs* is the container of one or more *ContextualGroup* elements.
Controls	Contains elements that define controls. Controls can contain elements of type *Button*, *CheckBox*, *ComboBox*, *DropDown*, *FlyoutAnchor*, *GalleryButton*, *Label*, *MRUSplitButton*, *Spinner*, *SplitButton*, *TextBox*, and *ToggleButton*.
DropDown	Defines a control with which a user can select from a drop-down list. Supports most of the same attributes as the *ComboBox* element.
FlyoutAnchor	Defines the anchor point for a flyout menu. Supports attributes for defining the *command* to execute when the control is clicked, the various attributes for declaring images and tooltips, and the command to invoke for populating the menu dynamically.
Gallery	Defines a gallery. Supports attributes to define the dimensions of child items. *Gallery* is made up of a set of *GalleryButton* child elements.
GalleryButton	Defines a gallery button. These are almost like standard buttons, except that they allow defining the dimensions, according to the parent *Gallery*, and they support an *InnerHTML* attribute to define the HTML markup that illustrates the choice that the button represents.
Group	Defines a group of controls. Supports attributes for defining the description, the various images, and the *command* to execute when clicked.
Groups	Defines the groups of controls on a tab. Simply contains a set of child *Group* elements.
GroupTemplate	Defines the scaling behavior for controls in a Group element. *GroupTemplate* can host *Layout* child elements and offers a *ClassName* attribute for defining a CSS style sheet to apply to the group.
InsertTable	Defines a menu control for inserting a table that contains a variable number of cells. Provides a *Command* attribute for defining the code to execute when the table has to be inserted, as well as *CommandPreview* and *CommandRevert* attributes to preview and revert the effect of the command.
Label	Defines a *Label* control. Label supports a *ForId* attribute to declare the ID of the target control of the label, and some other attributes to define the images as well as the *LabelText* attribute.
MaxSize	Specifies the maximum size for a group of controls. *MaxSize* offers a *Size* attribute to define the maximum allowed size for the group of controls.
Menu	Defines a menu control. *Menu* supports only a *MaxWidth* attribute.
MenuSection	Defines a section of a menu. *MenuSection* can host child elements of type *Controls* and *Gallery*. It also offers a *DisplayMode* attribute to define the sizing of the items, and a *Scrollable* attribute to declare if the menu section can be scrolled.
MRUSplitButton	Defines a control that combines a button and a drop-down menu to display a list of the most recently used items. Provides some attributes to declare the code to execute for the purpose of populating the most recently used list, as well as to use when the user previews or reverts the selection, or effectively selects an item.

Attribute name	Description
QAT	Defines a quick-access toolbar. *QAT* supports some attributes to declare images and CSS classes, and hosts a *Controls* child element.
Ribbon	Contains elements that define the Server ribbon UI. *Ribbon* is the container of *Tabs* and *ContextualTabs* child elements. It supports many appearance attributes.
Scale	Defines how a group of controls on a tab is sized. *Scale* is the child of a *Scaling* element and supports *Size* and *PopupSize* attributes.
Scaling	Defines tab scaling. *Scaling* contains child elements of type *MaxSize* and *Scale*.
Spinner	Defines a spinner control. *Spinner* can contain a *Unit* child element and supports some appearance attributes, as well as a command to execute when the control is clicked.
SplitButton	Defines a control that combines a button and a drop-down menu. *SplitButton* can host a *Menu* child element. Supports many attributes to define various images, tooltips, and commands related to the drop-down menu.
Tab	Represents a Tab control. *Tab* defines a *CssClass* attribute to use while rendering the tab and the title to show in the tab. It is the container of the *Scaling* and *Groups* child elements.
Tabs	Contains elements that define tab controls. *Tabs* can host a set of *Tab* child elements.
TextBox	Defines a TextBox control. *TextBox* supports attributes for defining the appearance of the control, as well as a command to execute when it is clicked, and *MaxLength* to define the maximum length in characters.
ToggleButton	Defines a button that is used to switch states. *ToggleButton* supports attributes for defining the appearance of the control, as well as a command to execute when it is clicked.

Recall that the goal of this particular section is to have a ribbon with which a user can archive multiple items with content type *DevLeapInvoice* at the same time. Listing 12-11 shows the source code necessary.

LISTING 12-11 Source code for a ribbon that archives one or more items with a content type of *DevLeapInvoice*

```
<CustomAction
  RegistrationType="ContentType"
  RegistrationId="0x010100DFCFE30E0795465F8973EF29B73F1551"
  Id="DevLeap.CustomActions.Invoices.ArchiveRibbon"
  Location="CommandUI.Ribbon.ListView">
  <CommandUIExtension>
    <CommandUIDefinitions>
      <CommandUIDefinition
        Location="Ribbon.Documents.EditCheckout.Controls._children">
        <Button Id="InvoiceArchiveRibbonButton"
                Alt="Changes the status of the Invoice to Archived."
                Description="Change the status of the Invoice to Archived."
                Sequence="25"
                Command="ChangeInvoiceStatusToArchived"
                Image16by16=
```

```
"/_layouts/15/images/DevLeap.SP2013.UIExtensions/IconArchive_16x16.gif"
                Image32by32=
"/_layouts/15/images/DevLeap.SP2013.UIExtensions/IconArchive_32x32.gif"
                LabelText="Archive Invoices"
                TemplateAlias="o1" />
      </CommandUIDefinition>
    </CommandUIDefinitions>
    <CommandUIHandlers>
      <CommandUIHandler Command="ChangeInvoiceStatusToArchived"
                        EnabledScript="javascript:
                            function checkInvoicesSelected() {
                              // Check the number of selected items
                              var items =
                                SP.ListOperation.Selection.getSelectedItems();
                              return (items.length >= 1);
                            }
                            checkInvoicesSelected();"
                        CommandAction="javascript:
                            // Shared variables
                            var ctx;
                            var itemsToArchive;
                            var notifyId = '';

                            // Function that archives the selected items
                            function archiveInvoices() {

                              // Notify the end user about the work in progress
                              this.notifyId =
                                SP.UI.Notify.addNotification(
                                  'Archiving items...', true);

                              // Get the current ClientContext
                              this.ctx = new SP.ClientContext.get_current();

                              // Get the current Web
                              var web = this.ctx.get_web();

                              // Get the currently selected list
                              var listId =
                                SP.ListOperation.Selection.getSelectedList();
                              var sourceList = web.get_lists().getById(listId);

                              // Get the selected items and archive each of them
                              var items =
                                SP.ListOperation.Selection.getSelectedItems(
                                  this.ctx);

                              var item;
                              this.itemsToArchive = new Array(items.length);
                              for(var i in items) {
                                item = items[i];
```

```
                // Get each selected item
                var listItem = sourceList.getItemById(item.id);
                this.itemsToArchive.push(listItem);
                this.ctx.load(listItem);
              }

              // Effectively load items from SharePoint
              this.ctx.executeQueryAsync(
                Function.createDelegate(this, onQuerySucceeded),
                Function.createDelegate(this, onQueryFailed));
            }

            // Delegate called when server
            // operation is completed upon success
            function onQuerySucceeded(sender, args) {
              // Mark each item as Archived
              var item = null;
              do {
                item = this.itemsToArchive.pop();
                if (item != null) {
                  item.set_item('DevLeapInvoiceStatus',
                      'Archived');
                  item.update();
                }
              } while (item != null);

              // Effectively update items in SharePoint
              this.ctx.executeQueryAsync(
              Function.createDelegate(this, onUpdateSucceeded),
              Function.createDelegate(this, onQueryFailed));
            }

            // Delegate called when server
            // operation is completed upon success
            function onUpdateSucceeded(sender, args) {
              SP.UI.Notify.removeNotification(this.notifyId);
              SP.UI.ModalDialog.RefreshPage(
              SP.UI.DialogResult.OK);
            }

            // Delegate called when server
            // operation is completed with errors
            function onQueryFailed(sender, args) {
              alert('The requested operation failed: ' +
                args.toString());
            }
            archiveInvoices();" />
    </CommandUIHandlers>
  </CommandUIExtension>
</CustomAction>
```

Although Listing 12-11 is not short, it is actually quite simple. In fact, it takes advantage of the JavaScript Client-Side Object Model (JSOM)—which was presented in Chapter 7, "Client-side technologies"—within the code of the *CommandAction* attribute of the *CommandUIHandler* element. It creates a *ClientContext*, retrieves the selected items by using the *SP.ListOperation.Selection* class, and then updates them with a Status field value of *Archived*, invoking the asynchronous operation via the *executeQueryAsync* method of the *ClientContext*.

It is interesting to note that the ribbon is entirely defined in XML and JavaScript, without the need for any kind of server-side code. Thus, it will work asynchronously in the web browser without requiring a postback to the server. The only postback is required at the end of the update process, to refresh the list of items and reflect the applied changes. You can see the invocation of the *SP.UI.ModalDialog.RefreshPage* method in the *onUpdateSucceeded* method. You can also include the JavaScript code in an external JS file and reference it using a custom action with the *Location* attribute with a value of *ScriptLink*. Last but not least, remember that you can deploy such commands while working within a custom SharePoint 2013 app as well.

Another interesting aspect of Listing 12-11 is the attribute *EnabledScript* of the element *CommandUIHandler*. This attribute is invoked on the client side, and it contains another JavaScript script block to determine if the ribbon command must be enabled or disabled. Internally, the script checks the number of selected items and returns *true* only if there is at least one invoice selected in the result of the *SP.ListOperation.Selection.getSelectedItems()* method. As the sample code illustrates, the *SP.ListOperation.Selection.getSelectedItems()* method returns only the IDs of the selected items, not the items themselves.

To complete the example, the *Location* attribute of the *CommandUIDefinition* element declares where to locate the new ribbon. In this example, the ribbon is in the Open & Check Out group of the Documents tab, which has a location of *Ribbon.Documents.EditCheckout.Controls*. Thus, the new command has a *Location* value of *Ribbon.Documents.EditCheckout.Controls._children* to instruct the environment to show the item as a child of the Open & Check Out group.

Note You can find the complete list of locations in the document "Default Server Ribbon Customization Locations," which is available on MSDN at *http://msdn.microsoft.com/en-us/library/ee537543.aspx*.

The sample code of Listing 12-11 also uses the new notification area of SharePoint 2010, which will be discussed in the "Status bar and notification area" section. Figure 12-7 shows the ribbon command in action.

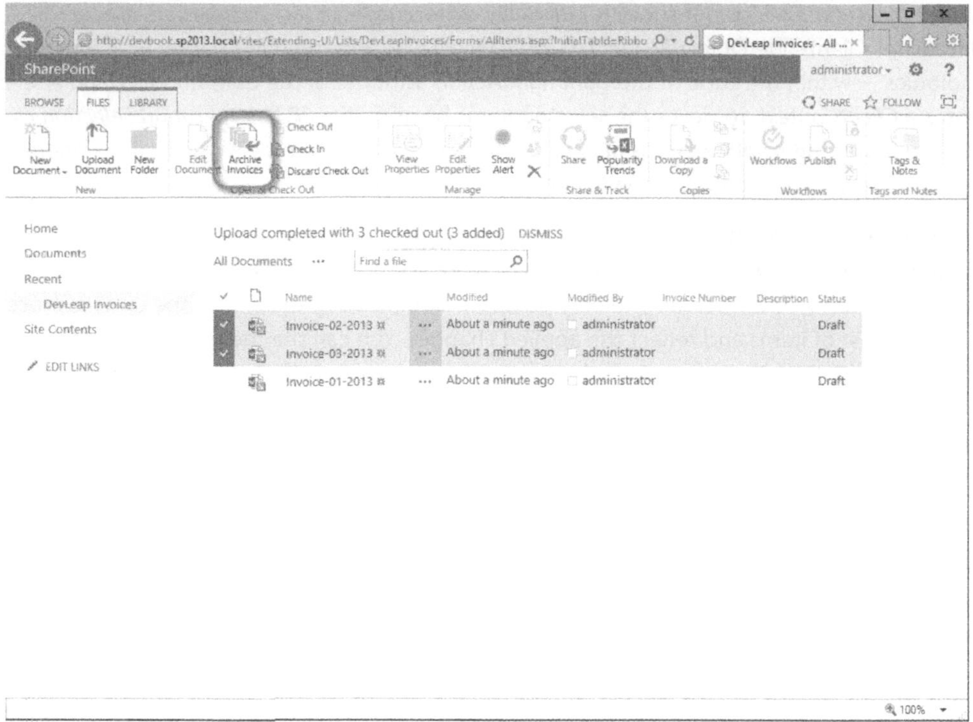

FIGURE 12-7 The custom ribbon command to archive multiple invoices simultaneously.

Finally, consider that inside the code of the *CommandAction* attribute, you can use substitution tokens that are replaced by the environment before executing the script. The available tokens are

- ***{ItemId}*** ID (GUID) taken from the list view
- ***{ItemUrl}*** Web-relative URL of the list item
- ***{RecurrenceId}*** ID of a recurrent item
- ***{SiteUrl}*** The fully qualified URL to the site
- ***{ListId}*** ID (GUID) of the list
- ***{ListUrlDir}*** Server-relative URL of the site plus the list's folder
- ***{Source}*** Fully qualified request URL
- ***{SelectedListId}*** ID (GUID) of the list that is currently selected from a list view
- ***{SelectedItemId}*** ID of the item that is currently selected from the list view

One last scenario to consider is the creation of a custom ribbon tab. In fact, if you have multiple commands to support your custom content, it is good habit to define a ribbon tab of your own, instead of extending an existing one. To define a new tab of ribbons, you need to use the *Tab*, *Scaling*,

Groups, and *Group* elements. Listing 12-12 demonstrates the declaration of a custom tab, which will show up only when selecting items with a content type of *DevLeapInvoice*. The tab will host three buttons that, for the sake of simplicity, just show an alert with a welcome message.

LISTING 12-12 A custom tab of ribbons for a content type of *DevLeapInvoice*

```
<CustomAction
  RegistrationType="ContentType"
  RegistrationId="0x010100DFCFE30E0795465F8973EF29B73F1551"
  Id="DevLeap.CustomActions.Invoices.Tab"
  Location="CommandUI.Ribbon.ListView">
  <CommandUIExtension>
    <CommandUIDefinitions>
      <CommandUIDefinition
        Location="Ribbon.Tabs._children">
        <Tab
          Id="DevLeap.CustomActions.Invoices.Tab.One"
          Title="Invoices"
          Description="This tab holds custom commands for Invoices."
          Sequence="1000">
          <Scaling
            Id="DevLeap.CustomActions.Invoices.Tab.One.Scaling">
            <MaxSize
              Id="DevLeap.CustomActions.Invoices.Tab.One.Scaling.MaxSize"
              GroupId="DevLeap.CustomActions.Invoices.Tab.One.GroupOne"
              Size="OneLargeTwoSmall"/>
            <Scale
              Id="DevLeap.CustomActions.Invoices.Tab.One.Scaling.Scale"
              GroupId="DevLeap.CustomActions.Invoices.Tab.One.GroupOne"
              Size="OneLargeTwoSmall" />
          </Scaling>
          <Groups Id="DevLeap.CustomActions.Invoices.Tab.Groups">
            <Group
              Id="DevLeap.CustomActions.Invoices.Tab.One.GroupOne"
              Description="This is the first group."
              Title="First Group"
              Sequence="52"
              Template="DevLeap.CustomActions.Invoices.RibbonTemplate">
              <Controls Id="Ribbon.CustomTabExample.CustomGroupExample.Controls">
                <Button
                  Id="DevLeap.CustomActions.Invoices.Tab.One.ButtonOne"
                  Command="ButtonOneCommand"
                  Sequence="10"
                  Description="First sample command."
                  Image32by32=
"/_layouts/15/$Resources:core,Language;/images/formatmap32x32.png"
                  Image32by32Left="-160"
                  Image32by32Top="-256"
                  LabelText="First sample command!"
                  TemplateAlias="customOne"/>
```

```
                <Button
                  Id="DevLeap.CustomActions.Invoices.Tab.One.ButtonTwo"
                  Command="ButtonTwoCommand"
                  Sequence="20"
                  Description="Second sample command."
                  Image16by16=
"/_layouts/15/$Resources:core,Language;/images/formatmap16x16.png"
                  Image16by16Left="-144"
                  Image16by16Top="-32"
                  LabelText="Second sample command!"
                  TemplateAlias="customTwo"/>
                <Button
                  Id="DevLeap.CustomActions.Invoices.Tab.One.ButtonThree"
                  Command="ButtonThreeCommand"
                  Sequence="30"
                  Description="Third sample command."
                  Image16by16=
"/_layouts/15/$Resources:core,Language;/images/formatmap16x16.png"
                  Image16by16Left="-96"
                  Image16by16Top="-128"
                  LabelText="Third sample command!"
                  TemplateAlias="customThree"/>
              </Controls>
            </Group>
          </Groups>
        </Tab>
      </CommandUIDefinition>
      <CommandUIDefinition Location="Ribbon.Templates._children">
        <GroupTemplate Id="DevLeap.CustomActions.Invoices.RibbonTemplate">
          <Layout
            Title="OneLargeTwoSmall"
            LayoutTitle="OneLargeTwoSmall">
            <Section Alignment="Top" Type="OneRow">
              <Row>
                <ControlRef DisplayMode="Large" TemplateAlias="customOne" />
              </Row>
            </Section>
            <Section Alignment="Top" Type="TwoRow">
              <Row>
                <ControlRef DisplayMode="Small" TemplateAlias="customTwo" />
              </Row>
              <Row>
                <ControlRef DisplayMode="Small" TemplateAlias="customThree" />
              </Row>
            </Section>
          </Layout>
        </GroupTemplate>
      </CommandUIDefinition>
    </CommandUIDefinitions>
```

```
      <CommandUIHandlers>
        <CommandUIHandler
          Command="ButtonOneCommand"
          CommandAction="javascript:window.alert('You pressed CommandOne!');" />
        <CommandUIHandler
          Command="ButtonTwoCommand"
          CommandAction="javascript:window.alert('You pressed CommandTwo!');" />
        <CommandUIHandler
          Command="ButtonThreeCommand"
          CommandAction="javascript:window.alert('You pressed CommandThree!');" />
      </CommandUIHandlers>
    </CommandUIExtension>
  </CustomAction>
```

Listing 12-12 first creates a new ribbon tab that declares a *Location* value of *Ribbon.Tabs._children*, with a *Title* value of *Invoices*. It also declares some scaling information, indicating how the ribbon will behave when the window is resized. Specifically, you must define a *MaxSize* element for each ribbon group, describing the rendering behavior at the maximum size. You also need to define at least one *Scale* element for each ribbon group, providing information about how to scale the contents of the group. Both the *MaxSize* and *Scale* elements use a *Size* attribute with a value that references the *Title* attribute of the *Layout* elements defined in the *CommandUIDefinition* element, with a *Location* value of *Ribbon.Templates._children*. In the current example, the *OneLargeTwoSmall* sizing layout describes a first *Section* element with one row, and a second *Section* element with two rows. The *Row* elements defined in the *Section* elements also declare a *TemplateAlias*, which the *Button* elements will reference. It is also important to notice the value of the *Location* attribute of the two *CommandUIDefinition* elements.

Notice the way that the images of the buttons are defined. For performance reasons, SharePoint 2013 uses CSS image sprites, which use images that are maps of multiple icons, rendered using CSS cropping. For example, there are two image files, named formatmap16x16.png and formatmap32x32.png, that contain a rich set of icons used for rendering buttons of ribbons and menus with a size of 16×16 pixels and 32×32 pixels, respectively. If you want to render a specific image, you need to reference the proper picture in the *Image16by16* or *Image32by32* attribute, depending on the size of the image you are looking for. Then you need to provide the location of the top and left corners of the image to crop, using the attributes *Image16by16Top* and *Image16by16Left*, or *Image32by32Top* and *Image32by32Left*. These attributes require a negative value for the offset. In Listing 12-12, the image URLs include the reference to the proper culture code, determined by querying the core resource strings. Figure 12-8 displays the output of Listing 12-12 as it appears in the web browser.

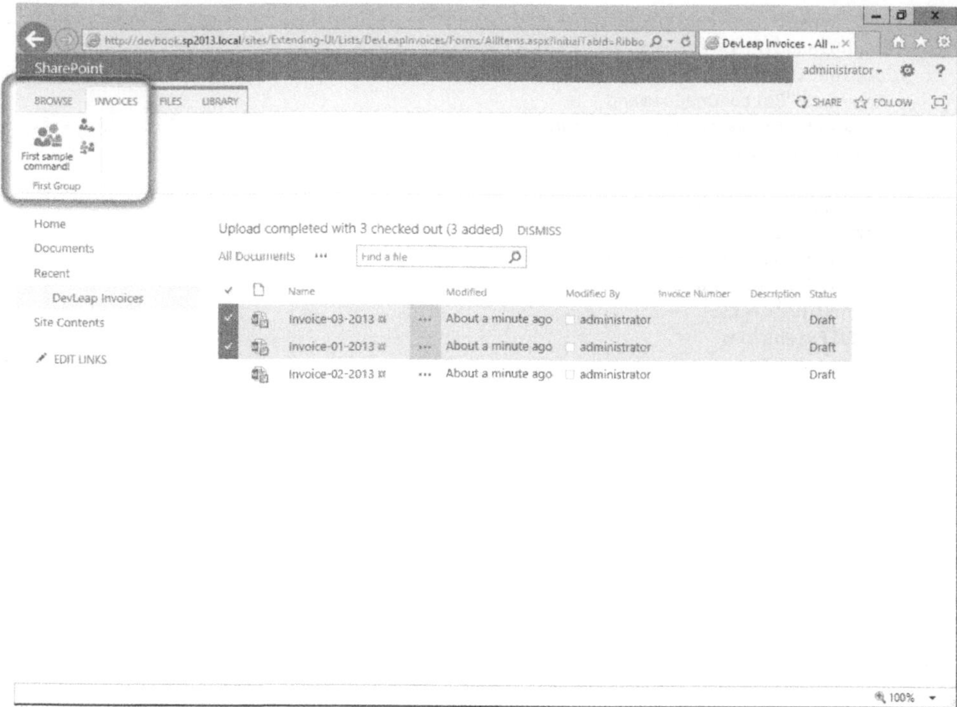

FIGURE 12-8 The custom tab of ribbons targeting the content type *DevLeapInvoice*.

Custom content

In the previous sections, some of the code listings referenced custom images and pages that were deployed on the farm together with the features that use them. In this section, you will learn how to use features to deploy this kind of custom content.

Images and generic content

The first types of content that you will probably need to deploy are custom images. By default, SharePoint stores images in the SharePoint15_Root\TEMPLATE\IMAGES folder and makes them available through a virtual directory named *_layouts/15/images/*.

Note SharePoint15_Root refers to the SharePoint root folder, which is typically located at C:\Program Files\Common Files\Microsoft Shared\Web Server Extensions\15.

Working with Visual Studio 2012, you can deploy custom images in the proper folder by right-clicking the project to open the menu shown in Figure 12-9, and then selecting Add | SharePoint "Images" Mapped Folder. This creates a folder named Images in your project. When you add an image file to this folder, the file will be automatically deployed in the SharePoint Images folder. To better organize files in the SharePoint folders, Visual Studio 2012 automatically creates a subfolder that uses the name of the current project and places the images there. For example, if your project name is *MyCustomProject*, and you add an image file with the name MyImage.jpg, then the image will be deployed under the path SharePoint15_Root\TEMPLATE\IMAGES\MyCustomProject\MyImage.jpg, and will be available through the relative URI *./_layouts/15/images/MyCustomProject/MyImage.jpg*.

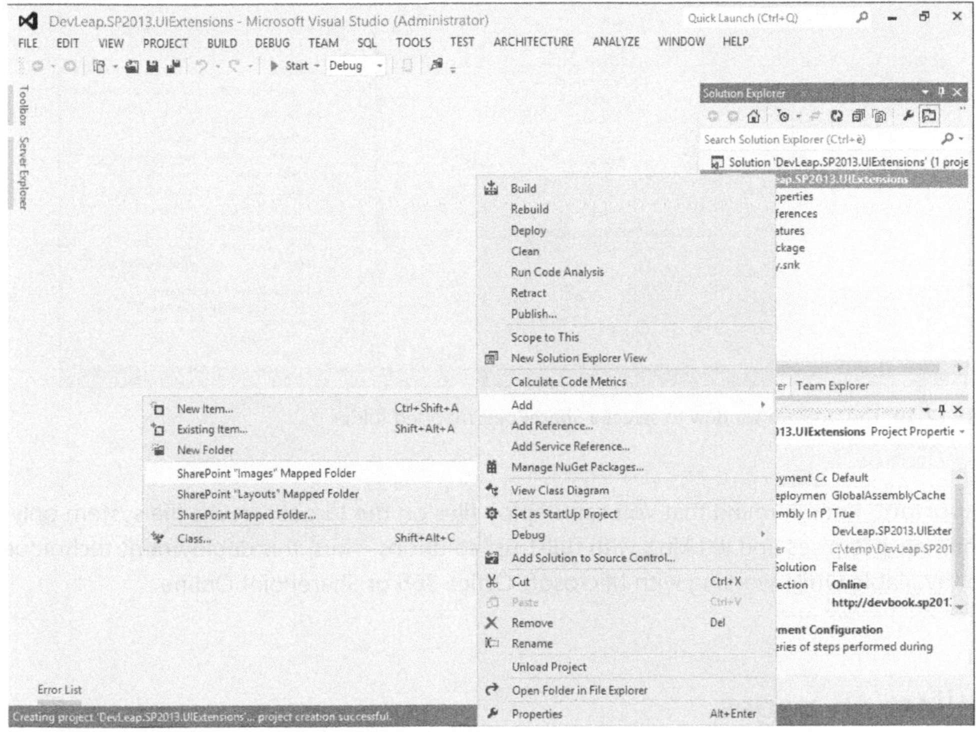

FIGURE 12-9 The menu item to add an image to the SharePoint15_Root\TEMPLATE\IMAGES folder.

If you need to deploy other kinds of generic content, such as ASCX controls, CSS files, JS files, and so on, select Add | SharePoint Mapped Folder from the project's contextual menu. You will be prompted with a pop-up window like the one shown in Figure 12-10. From there, you will be able to select any of the folders available under the SharePoint15_Root path.

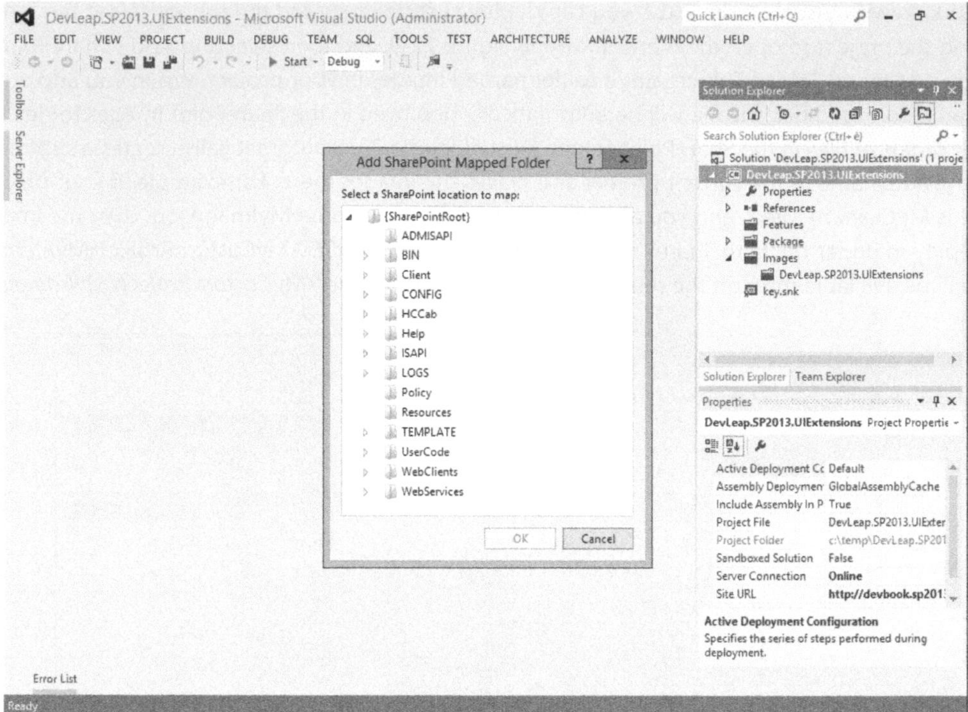

FIGURE 12-10 The pop-up window to select a SharePoint mapped folder.

Important Keep in mind that you can deploy files on the target server's file system only while on-premises and working with full-trust solutions. Thus, this deployment technique is not available while working with Microsoft Office 365 or SharePoint Online.

Application pages

Application pages are ASPX files that are available for all sites of a farm and deployed in the SharePoint15_Root\TEMPLATE\LAYOUTS folder. SharePoint makes them available through a virtual directory named *_layouts*. In general, these pages are defined to provide the UI for administrative tasks or to implement custom application pages that will be used to support custom solutions, which in this case do not include SharePoint apps that use a different page model (as discussed in Chapter 8, "SharePoint apps"). For example, Listing 12-3 contains a *UrlAction* element referencing a custom application page called *DevLeapInvoiceChangeStatus.aspx*.

To create such pages using Visual Studio 2012, you can simply add a new item to the project and then select an item of type Application Page, which is an ASPX file. A folder named Layouts will be added to the project, if it does not already exist. Within that folder, a subfolder will be created, using the name of your project. The new ASPX file will be placed in that subfolder. The ASPX file will define a standard ASP.NET page, which you will be able to define using standard ASP.NET controls, custom SharePoint controls, or custom controls of your own. By default, the page will have a *DynamicMasterPageFile* attribute with a value of *~masterurl/default.master*, but you can freely change this behavior. In addition, the *CodeBehind* attribute of the page will reference a code file declaring a custom ASP.NET page that will inherit from the *LayoutsPageBase* class, which is defined in the *Microsoft.SharePoint.WebControls* namespace and defines the base and common behavior for every application page. The *LayoutsPageBase* base class provides some useful properties to directly access the *SPWeb* and *SPSite* instances of the current context.

In Listing 12-3, the custom application page used in the *UrlAction* element was capable of changing the Status field of a single item with a content type of *DevLeapInvoice*, reading the target *ListId*, *ItemId*, and *Status* from the *QueryString*. Listing 12-13 reveals the source code behind that page.

LISTING 12-13 The source code behind the *DevLeapInvoiceChangeStatus.aspx* page used in Listing 12-3

```
using System;
using Microsoft.SharePoint;
using Microsoft.SharePoint.WebControls;
using System.Web;
using Microsoft.SharePoint.Utilities;

namespace DevLeap.SP2013.UIExtensions.Layouts.DevLeap.SP2013.UIExtensions {
    public partial class DevLeapInvoiceChangeStatus : LayoutsPageBase {
        protected void Page_Load(object sender, EventArgs e) {

            String itemId = this.Request.QueryString["ItemId"];
            String listId = this.Request.QueryString["ListId"];
            String status = this.Request.QueryString["Status"];

            if (!String.IsNullOrEmpty(itemId) &&
                !String.IsNullOrEmpty(listId) &&
                !String.IsNullOrEmpty(status)) {
                SPWeb web = this.Web;

                try {
                    try {
                      SPList list =
                        web.Lists[new Guid(this.Request.QueryString["ListId"])];
                      SPListItem item =
                        list.GetItemById(
                          Int32.Parse(this.Request.QueryString["ItemId"]));

                      web.AllowUnsafeUpdates = true;
                      item[FieldsIds.DevLeapInvoiceStatus_ID] = status;
                      item.Update();
                      SPUtility.Redirect(
                        list.DefaultViewUrl,
                        SPRedirectFlags.Default,
                        HttpContext.Current);
                    }
```

```
                finally {
                    web.AllowUnsafeUpdates = false;
                }
            }
            catch (ArgumentException) {
                throw new ApplicationException("Invalid List or Item ID!");
            }
        }
    }
  }
}
```

The ASPX code of the *DevLeapInvoiceChangeStatus.aspx* page is not terribly interesting because it has no content. However, a classic custom application page should define only the content regions to fill out the content placeholders defined in the master page used by the target site.

Important Application pages cannot be personalized or customized by the end user because they are defined on the file system. If you need to define custom pages that are also customizable, you need to refer to the next section.

Content pages, Web Part pages, and galleries

Sometimes you need to deploy pages that do not need to be shared and available on any site of your farm. Instead, you simply need to deploy a custom page or Web Part page to a single target site, eventually supporting customization by the end user or by using SharePoint Designer 2013.

To accomplish this task, you can use the *Module* feature element, which enables you to deploy an item into the content database of a target site. Listing 12-14 shows the structure of the *Module* element, together with its child elements.

LISTING 12-14 The structure of the *Module* feature element, together with its child elements

```
<Module
  HyperlinkBaseUrl = string
  IncludeFolders = "Text"
  List = "Integer"
  Name = "Text"
  Path = "Text"
  RootWebOnly = "TRUE" | "FALSE"
  SetupPath = "Text"
  Url = "Text">
```

```
  <File
    DocumentTemplateForList = string
    DoGUIDFixUp = "TRUE" | "FALSE"
    IgnoreIfAlreadyExists = "TRUE" | "FALSE"
    Level = Draft
    Name = string
    NavBarHome = "TRUE" | "FALSE"
    Path = string
    Type = "Ghostable" | "GhostableInLibrary"
    Url = string>
      <AllUsersWebPart />
      <BinarySerializedWebPart />
      <NavBarPage />
      <Property />
      <View />
      <WebPartConnection />
  </File>
</Module>
```

The code in Listing 12-14 is made up of a small set of attributes, while the core part is made of the child *File* element. Table 12-6 provides explanations of the main attributes of the *Module* element.

TABLE 12-6 The main attributes of the *Module* element

Attribute	Description
HyperlinkBaseUrl	Optional *Text* attribute that specifies an absolute URL to use as the base URL for hyperlinks.
List	Optional *Integer* attribute that specifies the type of the target list. The possible values are defined in the onet.xml file of the site template (more about this in Chapter 13, "Web templates").
Name	Required *Text* attribute that specifies the name of the module.
Path	Optional *Text* attribute that specifies the path of the physical files, relative to the feature's folder: SharePoint15_Root\TEMPLATE\FEATURES*FeatureName*.
RootWebOnly	Required *Boolean* attribute that specifies whether the files will be installed only on the top-level website of the current site collection.
SetupPath	Optional *Text* attribute that specifies the physical path to a folder within the SharePoint15_Root\TEMPLATE\FEATURES*FeatureName* folder that contains a file to include in the module.
Url	Optional *Text* attribute that specifies the virtual path of the folder in which to include the files to deploy. If *Path* is not specified, the value of *Url* will be used. If you provide a value that corresponds to a folder that does not exist, the folder will be created upon activation of the feature.

Moreover, Table 12-7 provides explanations of each attribute available for the *File* element.

TABLE 12-7 The attributes supported by the *File* element in a *Module* element

Attribute	Description
IgnoreIfAlreadyExists	Optional *Boolean* attribute that specifies whether to overwrite an already existing item (*true*) or not (*false*).
Name	Optional *Text* attribute that specifies the virtual path name for the file in the target site.
NavBarHome	Optional *Boolean* attribute that specifies whether to use the current content, in case it is a page, as the home link in the top navigation bar. In general it is used while defining custom site templates. For further details, see Chapter 13.
Path	Optional *Text* attribute that specifies the path of the physical file, relative to the feature's folder: SharePoint15_Root\TEMPLATE\FEATURES*FeatureName*.
Type	Optional *Text* attribute that specifies whether the file will be stored in a document library (*GhostableInLibrary*) or outside a document library (*Ghostable*).
Url	Required *Text* attribute that specifies the virtual path of the file in the target site. If the value of the *Name* attribute is specified, then it will be used as the virtual path. If the value of the *Path* attribute is not specified, the value of *Url* will be used instead.

Listing 12-15 shows how to deploy a custom image into the Site Assets library of a SharePoint site by using the *Module* feature.

LISTING 12-15 A *Module* feature to deploy an image into the Site Assets library of a SharePoint site

```
<?xml version="1.0" encoding="utf-8"?>
<Elements xmlns="http://schemas.microsoft.com/sharepoint/">
  <Module Name="SiteAssetsImage" Url="SiteAssets">
    <File IgnoreIfAlreadyExists="True"
          Path="SiteAssetsImage\DevLeap-Icon-48x48.png"
          Url="DevLeap-Icon-48x48.png"
          Type="GhostableInLibrary" />
  </Module>
</Elements>
```

You can also use the *Module* feature for deploying a content page, eventually to be made up of Web Parts. If you need to deploy an ASPX content page only, you can use an element manifest file, such as the one shown in Listing 12-16.

LISTING 12-16 A *Module* feature used to deploy a content page on a SharePoint site

```
<?xml version="1.0" encoding="utf-8"?>
<Elements xmlns="http://schemas.microsoft.com/sharepoint/">
  <Module Name="SampleContentPage">
    <File IgnoreIfAlreadyExists="True"
          Path="SampleContentPage\SampleContentPage.aspx"
          Url="SampleContentPage.aspx" />
  </Module>
</Elements>
```

The code in Listing 12-16 provisions a page with a URL value of *SampleContentPage.aspx* under the root of the target site, reading the page content from a file stored in the feature's folder, under the relative path *SampleContentPage\SampleContentPage.aspx*. Listing 12-17 presents the source code of that page.

LISTING 12-17 The source code of the page *SampleContentPage.aspx* provisioned in Listing 12-16

```
<%@ Page language="C#" MasterPageFile="~masterurl/default.master" %>

<asp:Content ID="Content1" ContentPlaceHolderId="PlaceHolderPageTitle"
runat="server">
    This is the SampleContentPage Title
</asp:Content>

<asp:Content ID="Content2" ContentPlaceHolderId="PlaceHolderPageTitleInTitleArea"
runat="server">
    This is the SampleContentPage Title in Title Area
</asp:Content>

<asp:Content ID="Content7" ContentPlaceHolderId="PlaceHolderPageDescription"
runat="server">
    This is the description of the SampleContentPage
</asp:Content>

<asp:Content ID="Content12" ContentPlaceHolderId="PlaceHolderMain"
runat="server">
    This is the main body of the SampleContentPage
</asp:Content>
```

If the page you are going to provision is a Web Part page, that means it is made up of Web Parts; the *File* element supports some child elements specifically available for including Web Parts in a Web Part page. Now consider the ASPX page illustrated in Listing 12-18. It defines a page that includes a *WebPartZone* control with an ID of *MainWebPartZone* placed in the *PlaceHolderMain* content region.

LISTING 12-18 A Web Part page provisioned through a *Module* feature

```
<%@ Page language="C#" MasterPageFile="~masterurl/default.master"
Inherits="Microsoft.SharePoint.WebPartPages.WebPartPage,
Microsoft.SharePoint,Version=15.0.0.0,Culture=neutral,PublicKeyToken=71e9bce111e
9429c" %>
<%@ Register Tagprefix="SharePoint" Namespace="Microsoft.SharePoint.WebControls"
Assembly="Microsoft.SharePoint, Version=15.0.0.0, Culture=neutral,
PublicKeyToken=71e9bce111e9429c" %>
```

```
<%@ Register Tagprefix="Utilities" Namespace="Microsoft.SharePoint.Utilities"
Assembly="Microsoft.SharePoint, Version=15.0.0.0, Culture=neutral,
PublicKeyToken=71e9bce111e9429c" %>
<%@ Register Tagprefix="WebPartPages" Namespace="Microsoft.SharePoint.
WebPartPages"
Assembly="Microsoft.SharePoint, Version=15.0.0.0, Culture=neutral,
PublicKeyToken=71e9bce111e9429c" %>
<%@ Import Namespace="Microsoft.SharePoint" %>
<%@ Assembly Name="Microsoft.Web.CommandUI, Version=15.0.0.0, Culture=neutral,
PublicKeyToken=71e9bce111e9429c" %>

<asp:Content ID="Content1" ContentPlaceHolderId="PlaceHolderPageTitle"
runat="server">
  <SharePoint:ListItemProperty ID="ListItemProperty1" Property="BaseName"
    maxlength="40" runat="server"/>
</asp:Content>

<asp:Content ID="Content12" ContentPlaceHolderId="PlaceHolderMain"
runat="server">
  <table cellpadding="4" cellspacing="0" border="0" width="100%">
    <tr>
      <td id="_invisibleIfEmpty" name="_invisibleIfEmpty" valign="top"
width="100%">
        <WebPartPages:WebPartZone runat="server" Title="loc:FullPage"
          ID="MainWebPartZone" FrameType="TitleBarOnly" />
      </td>
    </tr>
  </table>
</asp:Content>
```

Note The *@Register* directives at the top of Listing 12-18 must have the *Assembly* attribute defined on their own line.

The *Module* element defined in Listing 12-19 automatically provisions the page from Listing 12-18 into the library Site Pages, adding two Web Parts into the *WebPartZone* with ID *MainWebPartZone*. The key point is the inclusion of the *AllUsersWebPart* child elements in the *File* element. The first one defines an instance of the standard *ImageWebPart* of SharePoint. The second child element references the *HelloWorldWebPart* that was defined at the beginning of Chapter 11.

LISTING 12-19 The feature element manifest used to provision a Web Part page, together with some Web Parts

```
<?xml version="1.0" encoding="utf-8"?>
<Elements xmlns="http://schemas.microsoft.com/sharepoint/">
  <Module Name="SampleWebPartPage" Url="SitePages">
    <File IgnoreIfAlreadyExists="True"
          Path="SampleWebPartPage\SampleWebPartPage.aspx"
          Url="SampleWebPartPage.aspx"
          Type="GhostableInLibrary">
      <AllUsersWebPart WebPartZoneID="MainWebPartZone" WebPartOrder="1">
        <![CDATA[
          <WebPart xmlns="http://schemas.microsoft.com/WebPart/v2"
            xmlns:iwp="http://schemas.microsoft.com/WebPart/v2/Image">
              <Assembly>Microsoft.SharePoint, Version=15.0.0.0, Culture=neutral,
                PublicKeyToken=71e9bce111e9429c</Assembly>
              <TypeName>Microsoft.SharePoint.WebPartPages.ImageWebPart</TypeName>
              <FrameType>None</FrameType>
              <Title>$Resources:wp_SiteImage;</Title>
<iwp:ImageLink>/_layouts/images/homepageSamplePhoto.jpg</iwp:ImageLink>
              <iwp:AlternativeText>Home Page Sample Photo</iwp:AlternativeText>
          </WebPart>
        ]]>
      </AllUsersWebPart>
      <AllUsersWebPart WebPartZoneID="MainWebPartZone" WebPartOrder="2">
        <![CDATA[
          <webParts>
            <webPart xmlns="http://schemas.microsoft.com/WebPart/v3">
              <metaData>
                <type name="DevLeap.SP2013.WebParts. HelloWorldWebPart.
HelloWorldWebPart, DevLeap.SP2013.WebParts, Version=1.0.0.0, Culture=neutral,
PublicKeyToken=a7081b3b197bafe2" />
                <importErrorMessage>Cannot import this Web Part.
</importErrorMessage>
              </metaData>
              <data>
                <properties>
                  <property name="Title" type="string">Hello World Web Part
</property>
                </properties>
              </data>
            </webPart>
          </webParts>
        ]]>
      </AllUsersWebPart>
    </File>
  </Module>
</Elements>
```

Notice also that the syntax for declaring the two Web Parts is different. In fact, the former is a legacy Web Part that supports the old-style DWP Web Part deployment technique available since SharePoint 2003, while the latter uses the syntax of the new WEBPART deployment files available since SharePoint 2010.

Important You can insert and configure a Web Part instance within a Web Part page and then export it via the standard UI of SharePoint. The resulting file will contain all the XML information to support the configuration made through the UI. Now you can copy and paste this XML into an XML element file, having your Web Part properly configured in the project, without manually writing all the elements and attributes.

The *File* element supports some other child elements. For example, it supports the *View* child element, which can be used to instantiate a *ListView* into the target Web Part page. Additionally, it supports the *WebPartConnection* element to connect Web Parts directly during the provisioning process.

Keep in mind that extending a site using custom pages and custom content directly deployed into the content database is a habit that Microsoft started to discourage with SharePoint 2013. In fact, you should use the new app model available in SharePoint 2013, which Part III of this book, "Developing SharePoint apps," discusses.

Status bar and notification area

Found in the default master pages of SharePoint, the status bar and the notification area features are based on JavaScript code and a bit of extra markup. You can implement these tools within your pages easily with two JSOM classes. The *SP.UI.Notify* class manages the notification area, and the *SP.UI.Status* class manages the status bar. Table 12-8 describes the methods of the *SP.UI.Notify* class.

TABLE 12-8 The methods offered by the *SP.UI.Notify* class

Method	Description
addNotification	Used to add a notification to the notification area. Requires the text of the notification and a *Boolean* argument to specify if the notification will stay on the page until explicitly removed. *addNotification* returns an ID identifying the notification.
removeNotification	Removes a notification from the notification area. Requires the ID of the notification to remove.

To add a notification to the notification area, use the following:

```
var notifyId = SP.UI.Notify.addNotification("This is a Notification!", true);
```

To remove the notification, use this:

```
SP.UI.Notify.removeNotification(notifyId);
```

Table 12-9 describes the methods provided by the *SP.UI.Status* class.

TABLE 12-9 The methods offered by the *SP.UI.Status* class

Method	Description
addStatus	Adds a status to the status bar. Returns an ID identifying the status.
appendStatus	Appends text to an existing status message in the status bar.
removeAllStatus	Removes all the status messages from the status bar and hides the status bar.
removeStatus	Removes a status message from the status bar. Requires the ID of the status message that is being removed.
setStatusPriColor	Configures the color of the status bar.
updateStatus	Updates a status message. Requires the ID of the status message that is being updated.

To add a status message and turn the status bar red, for example, use the following code:

```
var statusId = SP.UI.Status.addStatus("Critical Status!");
SP.UI.Status.setStatusPriColor(statusId, 'red');
```

To remove the status message, you use this:

```
SP.UI.Status.removeStatus(statusId);
```

You can use these classes and methods whenever you need to interact with the end user, using the standard notification tools provided by SharePoint 2013. For example, the code in Listing 12-11 used the notification area to inform the end user about the process of archiving invoices. In Listing 12-20, a custom ribbon tab provides four commands to show and hide a notification message, as well as to show and hide a status message.

LISTING 12-20 The code of a custom ribbon tab that uses the *SP.UI.Notify* and *SP.UI.Status* classes

```
<?xml version="1.0" encoding="utf-8"?>
<Elements xmlns="http://schemas.microsoft.com/sharepoint/">
  <CustomAction
    RegistrationType="ContentType"
    RegistrationId="0x010100DFCFE30E0795465F8973EF29B73F1551"
    Id="DevLeap.CustomActions.Invoices.Notifications"
    Location="CommandUI.Ribbon.ListView">
    <CommandUIExtension>
      <CommandUIDefinitions>
        <CommandUIDefinition
          Location="Ribbon.Tabs._children">
          <Tab
            Id="DevLeap.CustomActions.Invoices.NotificationsTab"
            Title="Notification &amp; Status"
            Description="This tab holds commands for Status and Notifications."
            Sequence="1000">
            <Scaling
              Id="DevLeap.CustomActions.Invoices.NotificationsTab.Scaling">
              <MaxSize
```

```
Id="DevLeap.CustomActions.Invoices.NotificationsTab.One.Scaling.MaxSize"
GroupId="DevLeap.CustomActions.Invoices.NotificationsTab.GroupOne"
                Size="TwoLarge"/>
              <MaxSize
Id="DevLeap.CustomActions.Invoices.NotificationsTab.Two.Scaling.MaxSize"
GroupId="DevLeap.CustomActions.Invoices.NotificationsTab.GroupTwo"
                Size="TwoLarge"/>
              <Scale
Id="DevLeap.CustomActions.Invoices.NotificationsTab.One.Scaling.Scale"
GroupId="DevLeap.CustomActions.Invoices.NotificationsTab.GroupOne"
                Size="TwoLarge" />
              <Scale
Id="DevLeap.CustomActions.Invoices.NotificationsTab.Two.Scaling.Scale"
GroupId="DevLeap.CustomActions.Invoices.NotificationsTab.GroupTwo"
                Size="TwoLarge" />
            </Scaling>
            <Groups Id="DevLeap.CustomActions.Invoices.NotificationsTab.Groups">
              <Group
                Id="DevLeap.CustomActions.Invoices.NotificationsTab.GroupOne"
                Description="This is the Notification Area group."
                Title="Notification"
                Sequence="10"
Template="DevLeap.CustomActions.Invoices.RibbonTemplate.Notification">
                <Controls
Id="DevLeap.CustomActions.Invoices.NotificationsTab.GroupOne.Controls">
                  <Button
Id="DevLeap.CustomActions.Invoices.NotificationsTab.GroupOne.ShowNotification"
                    Command="ShowNotificationCommand"
                    Sequence="10"
                    Description="Show Notification command."
Image16by16="/_layouts/15/images/DevLeap.SP2013.UIExtensions/Baloon_16x16.png"
Image32by32="/_layouts/15/images/DevLeap.SP2013.UIExtensions/Baloon_32x32.png"
                    LabelText="Show Notification"
                    TemplateAlias="customOne"/>
                  <Button
Id="DevLeap.CustomActions.Invoices.NotificationsTab.GroupOne.HideNotification"
                    Command="HideNotificationCommand"
                    Sequence="20"
                    Description="Hide Notification command."
Image16by16="/_layouts/15/images/DevLeap.SP2013.UIExtensions/Baloon_16x16.png"
Image32by32="/_layouts/15/images/DevLeap.SP2013.UIExtensions/Baloon_32x32.png"
                    LabelText="Hide Notification"
                    TemplateAlias="customTwo"/>
                </Controls>
              </Group>
```

```
            <Group
              Id="DevLeap.CustomActions.Invoices.NotificationsTab.GroupTwo"
              Description="This is the Status Area group."
              Title="Status"
              Sequence="20"
              Template="DevLeap.CustomActions.Invoices.RibbonTemplate.Status">
              <Controls
Id="DevLeap.CustomActions.Invoices.NotificationsTab.
GroupTwo.Controls">
                <Button
Id="DevLeap.CustomActions.Invoices.NotificationsTab.GroupTwo.ShowStatus"
                  Command="ShowStatusCommand"
                  Sequence="30"
                  Description="Show Status command."
Image16by16="/_layouts/15/images/DevLeap.SP2013.UIExtensions/Baloon_16x16.png"
Image32by32="/_layouts/15/images/DevLeap.SP2013.UIExtensions/Baloon_32x32.png"
                  LabelText="Show Status"
                  TemplateAlias="customThree"/>
                <Button
Id="DevLeap.CustomActions.Invoices.NotificationsTab.GroupTwo.HideStatus"
                  Command="HideStatusCommand"
                  Sequence="40"
                  Description="Hide status command."
Image16by16="/_layouts/15/images/DevLeap.SP2013.UIExtensions/Baloon_16x16.png"
Image32by32="/_layouts/15/images/DevLeap.SP2013.UIExtensions/Baloon_32x32.png"
                  LabelText="Hide Status"
                  TemplateAlias="customFour"/>
              </Controls>
            </Group>
          </Groups>
        </Tab>
      </CommandUIDefinition>
      <CommandUIDefinition Location="Ribbon.Templates._children">
        <GroupTemplate
Id="DevLeap.CustomActions.Invoices.RibbonTemplate.Notification">
          <Layout
            Title="TwoLarge"
            LayoutTitle="TwoLarge">
            <Section Alignment="Top" Type="OneRow">
              <Row>
                <ControlRef DisplayMode="Large" TemplateAlias="customOne" />
                <ControlRef DisplayMode="Large" TemplateAlias="customTwo" />
              </Row>
            </Section>
          </Layout>
        </GroupTemplate>
      </CommandUIDefinition>
      <CommandUIDefinition Location="Ribbon.Templates._children">
        <GroupTemplate
Id="DevLeap.CustomActions.Invoices.RibbonTemplate.Status">
```

```
        <Layout
          Title="TwoLarge"
          LayoutTitle="TwoLarge">
          <Section Alignment="Top" Type="OneRow">
            <Row>
              <ControlRef DisplayMode="Large" TemplateAlias="customThree" />
              <ControlRef DisplayMode="Large" TemplateAlias="customFour" />
            </Row>
          </Section>
        </Layout>
      </GroupTemplate>
    </CommandUIDefinition>
  </CommandUIDefinitions>
  <CommandUIHandlers>
    <CommandUIHandler
      Command="ShowNotificationCommand"
      CommandAction="javascript:
        this.notifyId = SP.UI.Notify.addNotification(
          'Notification message ...', true);" />
    <CommandUIHandler
      Command="HideNotificationCommand"
      CommandAction="javascript:
        SP.UI.Notify.removeNotification(this.notifyId);" />
    <CommandUIHandler
      Command="ShowStatusCommand"
      CommandAction="javascript:
        this.statusId = SP.UI.Status.addStatus('Status message ...');
        SP.UI.Status.setStatusPriColor(this.statusId, 'red');" />
    <CommandUIHandler
      Command="HideStatusCommand"
      CommandAction="javascript:
        SP.UI.Status.removeStatus(this.statusId);" />
  </CommandUIHandlers>
</CommandUIExtension>
</CustomAction>  <CustomAction
  Location="ScriptLink"
  Id="DevLeap.CustomActions.Invoices.NotificationsTab"
  ScriptBlock="
    var notifyId = '';
    var statusId = '';
  "
  />
</Elements>
```

Take a look again at the last *CustomAction* element with a value of *ScriptLink* for the *Location* attribute. Notice that it instructs the SharePoint environment to include into the page the scripting code declared in the *ScriptBlock* attribute. As mentioned in Table 12-1, you can also reference an external script file, declaring the *ScriptSrc* attribute instead of the *ScriptBlock* attribute.

Dialog framework

Finally, you can extend the UI using the dialog framework of SharePoint 2013, which is provided by the class *SP.UI.ModalDialog* of the JSOM. Through this class, you can show pages inside modal dialog windows, and you can also pass information between the dialog window and the main window. Remember, the dialog framework was introduced with SharePoint 2010 and now is available mainly for backward compatibility. In fact, the new UI of SharePoint 2013 is almost free of dialogs, for a better user experience. Table 12-10 presents the main methods of the *SP.UI.ModalDialog* class.

TABLE 12-10 The main methods of the *SP.UI.ModalDialog* class

Method	Description
close	Closes the current dialog window and returns a result value of type SP.UI.DialogResult. The SP.UI.DialogResult type can assume a value of invalid, cancel, or OK.
commonModalDialogClose	Closes a modal dialog and returns a result value of type SP.UI.DialogResult and a custom return value of type Object. The SP.UI.DialogResult type can assume value of invalid, cancel, or OK.
commonModalDialogOpen	Opens a modal dialog and provides some input arguments, such as the URL of the content to show in the dialog, some options of type SP.UI.DialogOptions, a callback to a return function of type SP.UI.DialogCallback, and some extra arguments of type Object.
OpenPopUpPage	Opens a pop-up dialog page that provides some input arguments, such as the URL of the content to show in the pop-up page, a callback to a return function of type SP.UI.DialogCallback, and the width and height of the pop-up window.
RefreshPage	Reloads the current page for refreshing purposes.
showModalDialog	Shows a modal dialog that provides an input argument of type SP.UI.DialogOptions.
ShowPopupDialog	Shows a pop-up dialog that provides the URL of the content to show in the pop-up window.
showWaitScreenSize	Shows a wait screen that provides some input arguments, such as the title of the window, the message to show while waiting, a callbackFunc delegate to a return function, and the width and height of the window.
showWaitScreenWithNoClose	Does the same thing as showWaitScreenSize but without a close button in the upper-right corner of the window. This kind of window must be closed by custom code.

Take a look at how some of these methods work. Suppose that you want to extend the list of invoices, providing a custom ribbon command to open a pop-up window for changing the status of an item. Aside from the ribbon command definition, which by now should be familiar to you, consider the scripting code defined in Listing 12-21 that shows a custom application page to manage the invoice status.

LISTING 12-21 The scripting code used to show a modal dialog for changing the status of an invoice

```
// Function to open the dialog
function openChangeStatusDialog() {

  var ctx = SP.ClientContext.get_current();
  var selectedItem = SP.ListOperation.Selection.getSelectedItems(ctx)[0];
  var options = SP.UI.$create_DialogOptions();
  options.url = '{SiteUrl}/_layouts/DevLeap.SP2013.UIExtensions/' +
'DevLeapInvoiceChangeStatusDialog.aspx' + '?ListId=' +  SP.ListOperation.
Selection.getSelectedList() +  '&amp;ItemId=' + selectedItem.id;
  options.autoSize = true;
  options.dialogReturnValueCallback = Function.createDelegate(null,
dialogCloseCallback);
  this.dialog = SP.UI.ModalDialog.showModalDialog(options);
}

// Function to handle close callback
function dialogCloseCallback(result, returnValue) {
  if (result == SP.UI.DialogResult.OK) {
    window.alert('You clicked OK! And selected a status of: ' + returnValue);
  }
  if (result == SP.UI.DialogResult.cancel) {
    window.alert('You clicked Cancel!');
  }  SP.UI.ModalDialog.RefreshPage(result);
}
```

Listing 12-21 demonstrates that the custom function *openChangeStatusDialog* creates a variable of type *SP.UI.DialogOptions* and provides it to the *SP.UI.ModalDialog.showModalDialog* method. The *SP.UI.DialogOptions* class is made of some members that are useful when creating a dialog window. These members are

- ***url*** The URL of the resource to load in the dialog window.
- ***html*** Used this to include HTML content that you want to display in the dialog window (in case you don't want to provide a URL). The content must be provided as a DOM graph of nodes and not as a simple text value.
- ***title*** The title of the dialog window.
- ***args*** Optional arguments that can be passed to the dialog window.
- ***width*** The width of the dialog window.
- ***height*** The height of the dialog window.
- ***x*** The x-coordinate location of the upper-left corner of the dialog window.
- ***y*** The y-coordinate location of the upper-left corner of the dialog window.
- ***autoSize*** A *Boolean* value that specifies whether the dialog framework will handle autosizing of the dialog window, based on its content.

- ***allowMaximize*** A *Boolean* value that specifies whether the dialog window can be maximized.
- ***showMaximized*** A *Boolean* value that specifies whether the dialog window will be opened maximized or not.
- ***showClose*** A *Boolean* value that specifies whether the Close button will be shown or not.
- ***dialogReturnValueCallback*** A delegate to a callback function to invoke when the dialog window will be closed.

The callback function receives a *result* argument that allows determining whether the end user clicked the Cancel button or the OK button to close the dialog. In addition, it also takes a *returnValue* argument, in case the dialog window returns something to the main window. Notice that the code in Listing 12-21 defines the target URL of the dialog window, including in that URL the value of the *ListId* property of the current list and the *ItemId* property of the currently selected item, read using the Client-Side Object Model (CSOM). Figure 12-11 shows the dialog window in action.

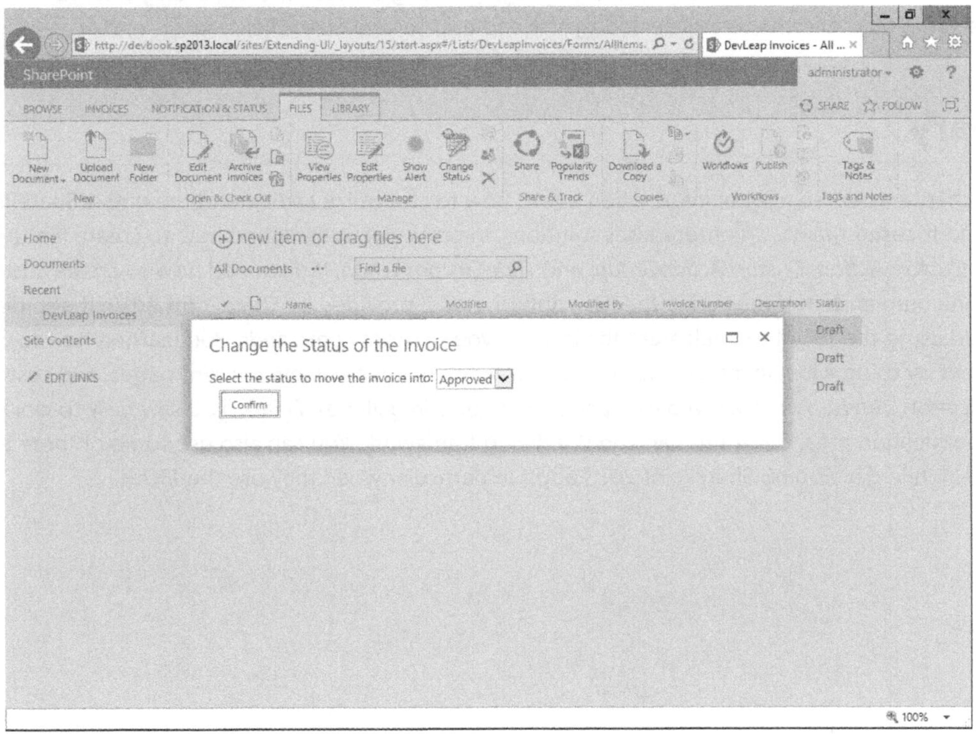

FIGURE 12-11 The dialog window to change the Status field of an invoice.

The target page is available in the source code samples, but it will not be explained here in detail because it is a standard application page, just like the one in Listing 12-17 However, one particularly interesting piece of code of the *DevLeapInvoiceChangeStatusDialog.aspx* page opened in the dialog window is the script used to close the dialog window itself, which gives feedback to the parent page. Listing 12-22 illustrates that code excerpt.

LISTING 12-22 The scripting code used to show a modal dialog for changing the status of an invoice

```
// In case we are in a PopUp dialog, we need to close it
if ((SPContext.Current != null) && SPContext.Current.IsPopUI) {
    this.Context.Response.Write("<script type='text/javascript'>window.
frameElement.commonModalDialogClose(1, '" + statusDropDown.SelectedValue +
"');</script>");
    this.Context.Response.Flush();
    this.Context.Response.End();
}
```

Notice that the current *SPContext* provides a property named *IsPopUI* to check if the current page is loaded in a pop-up dialog environment. If it is, the page writes to the ASP.NET *Response* object a small piece of JavaScript code to close the dialog, returning a status of *SP.UI.DialogResult.OK* (which has a value of 1) and the value selected by the end user for the Status field.

Summary

This chapter covered a lot of information about how to customize and extend the native SharePoint UI, and focused mainly on on-premises solutions. In particular, it described how to create features of type *CustomAction*, *CustomActionGroup*, and *HideCustomAction*. It discussed how to create custom ribbon commands and tabs using the new ribbon model provided by SharePoint 2010. It also discussed using the JSOM to implement the logic of your custom commands. You learned how to deploy content by using *Module* features so you can provision images, custom content pages, and custom application pages, as well as Web Part pages and items in galleries. Finally, you saw how to work with the notification area, the status bar, and the dialog framework. You can also use some of these techniques while developing SharePoint 2013 apps, in particular when they use the JSOM.

CHAPTER 13

Web templates

Providing your customers with packages of features that you activate selectively is a great way to extend Microsoft SharePoint to cover the requirements of most projects. Some situations, however, require a more robust solution: creating a ready-to-go site with predefined structure and content from the ground up, starting from a custom template.

For example, suppose you have to create an extranet site collection to host a set of websites, where each site represents the private extranet of a customer. Because every customer's site will have a common set of contents and features (for example, a library of orders, a library of invoices, and a discussion area), you might be tempted to base each site on one of the site models SharePoint provides for common scenarios, such as team site, blog, or community site. Don't do it. These templates are very broad, and you'd go crazy trying to manually provision the content using features. It's better to build your own new web template that defines the structure of a customer's extranet website, and then create every site instance starting from that template.

In this chapter, you will learn how to create, deploy, and manage these more complex site models.

The core techniques

SharePoint 2013 provides four main techniques for provisioning features and reusable site models:

- Site definitions
- Feature stapling
- Site templates
- Web templates

Before you can put them to work, you need to understand their differences and individual strengths.

A *site definition* is a site model defined on the file system and stored in the folder SharePoint15_Root\TEMPLATE\SiteTemplates of every front-end server. Saving files on the file system is an ancient habit that requires direct access to the servers in your server farm. Thus, it is not suitable for Microsoft Office 365 or SharePoint Online.

Feature stapling is a technique that enables you to customize existing site definitions by adding custom features to extend the site definition. The new features will also be included on all the new sites created using that specific site definition. Bear in mind, however, that feature stapling cannot be applied to already created sites. Once you deploy a site definition on the file system, changing its configuration is unsupported. This chapter will not cover feature stapling, because it is available mainly for backward compatibility and is not available in Office 365.

More Info For further details about feature stapling, you can read Vesa Juvonen's blog post at *http://blogs.msdn.com/b/vesku/archive/2010/10/14/sharepoint-2010-and-web-templates.aspx.*

A *site template* is an exported snapshot of an already existing site instance, with or without its content. You can use a site template, which is basically just a WSP package, to replicate a site instance from one environment to another, as long as the base site definition is available on the target environment, too. In addition, you can import site templates into Microsoft Visual Studio 2012 to create custom template projects. To save a site template from an already existing site instance, simply click Save Site As Template in the Site Actions menu group on the Site Settings page. The one exception, however, is that a site template cannot be created from a site in which publishing features are enabled, so it's only usable in team and collaboration sites.

Available since SharePoint 2010, a *web template* is a specific *WebTemplate* feature that you can create using Microsoft Visual Studio 2012 and provision using a sandboxed solution. A web template enables you to define a custom site model for future reuse. You can deploy web templates at the site collection level, through a sandboxed solution, or at the farm level using a full-trust WSP solution package. Because web templates can use a sandboxed solution for deployment, you can use them against Office 365 and SharePoint Online, too.

Site definitions

When creating custom site models, often a good way to start is by simply extending one of the site definitions provided in SharePoint 2013. To choose the right model to get started with, though, you need to know what the models are. The native site definitions are stored in the file system of the servers, specifically in the SharePoint15_Root\TEMPLATES\SiteTemplates folder. There, you will find a subfolder for every base site definition or group of site definitions. Whenever you create a new site collection or a new subsite under an existing site collection, SharePoint provides a list of all the available site templates, site definitions, and web templates from which you can choose the model to use for your new site. Figure 13-1 shows the standard page for choosing the template for a new subsite.

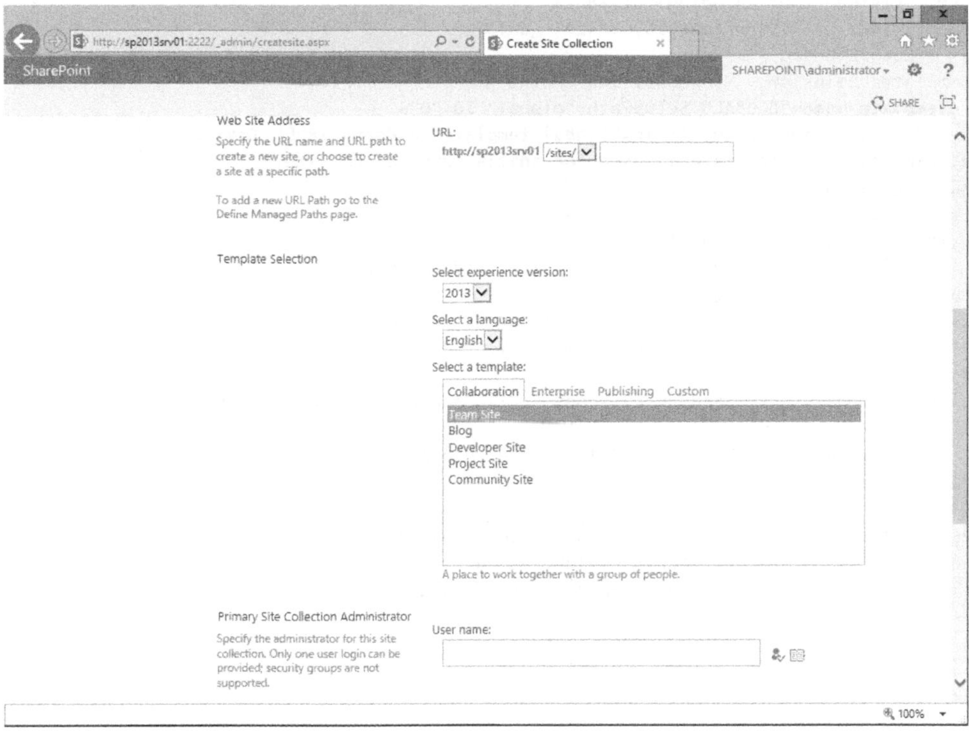

FIGURE 13-1 The standard page for choosing the template for a new subsite.

Behind the scenes, SharePoint loads the list of available models, reading all the available files with the prefix webtemp*.xml found in the SharePoint15_Root\TEMPLATE*IdCulture*\XML folder, where *IdCulture* corresponds to the currently selected language in the Create Site window. Regarding the *IdCulture* argument, 1033 stands for English (United States), 1040 stands for Italian, and so forth. The webtemp*.xml files enumerate one or more site models, together with their name, configuration, and folder. In Listing 13-1, the content of the main, standard webtemp.xml file is set for the English language.

LISTING 13-1 The content of the standard webtemp.xml file, set for English

```
<?xml version="1.0" encoding="utf-8"?>
<!-- _lcid="1033" _version="15.0.4420" _dal="1" -->
<!-- _LocalBinding -->
<Templates xmlns:ows="Microsoft SharePoint">
  <Template Name="GLOBAL" SetupPath="global" ID="0">
    <Configuration ID="0" Title="Global template" Hidden="TRUE" ImageUrl=""
Description="This template is used for initializing a new site." >
</Configuration>
  </Template>
  <Template Name="STS" ID="1">
    <Configuration ID="0" Title="Team Site" Hidden="FALSE"
ImageUrl="/_layouts/images/stts.png"
Description="A site for teams to quickly organize, author, and share
information. It provides a document library, and lists for managing
announcements,
calendar items, tasks, and discussions." DisplayCategory="Collaboration">
</Configuration>
    <Configuration ID="1" Title="Blank Site" Hidden="FALSE"
ImageUrl="/_layouts/
images/stbs.png"
Description="A blank site for you to customize based on your
requirements." DisplayCategory="Collaboration"
AllowGlobalFeatureAssociations="False"></Configuration>

    <!-- Code omitted for the sake of brevity -->

  </Template>

<!-- Code omitted for the sake of brevity -->

</Templates>
```

The file provides a list of *Template* items, each with a *Name* attribute and an optional *SetupPath* attribute. Each *Template* element is the parent of one or more *Configuration* elements, which provide a custom configuration for that specific template. For example, the STS template is available in three configurations: STS#0, STS#1, and STS#2. The syntax of *{TemplateName}#{Configuration ID}* is common in SharePoint. Table 13-1 lists the main available site definitions with the corresponding configurations, described as they are in SharePoint.

TABLE 13-1 Some of the main native site definitions available in SharePoint 2013

Title	Base definition	Configuration	Description
Team Site	STS	0	A site for teams to quickly organize, author, and share information.
Blank Site	STS	1	A blank site for you to customize, based on your requirements.
Document Workspace	STS	2	A site for colleagues to work together on a document.
Central Admin Site	CENTRALADMIN	0	A site for hosting the SharePoint Central Administration (SPCA) site. This template is hidden.
Blog	BLOG	0	A blog site.
Document Center	BDR	0	A site to centrally manage documents in your enterprise.
Records Center	OFFILE	1	A record management site.
Business Intelligence Center	BICenterSite	0	A site for presenting Business Intelligence Center.
Personalization Site	SPSMSITE	0	A site for delivering personalized views, data, and navigation from this site collection into My Site.
Publishing Portal	BLANKINTERNETCONTAINER	0	A starter site hierarchy for an Internet-facing site or a large intranet portal.
Enterprise Wiki	ENTERWIKI	0	A site for publishing knowledge that you capture and want to share across the enterprise.
Enterprise Search Center	SRCHCEN	0	A site for delivering the enterprise search center.
Basic Search Center	SRCHCENTERLITE	0	A site for delivering a basic search center.
Visio Process Repository	Visprus	0	A site for teams to quickly view, share, and store Microsoft Visio process diagrams.

The availability of some of these site definitions depends on your SharePoint 2013 license. For example, the Enterprise Search Center site requires you to have SharePoint Server 2013 Enterprise licensed and installed. By default, SharePoint 2013 includes a few other site definitions, but they are hidden and available only for backward compatibility. When you create a site instance by code, you can reference the site definition using the syntax *{TemplateName}#{Configuration ID}*. For example, *STS#0* means Team Site, *BLOG#0* means Blog Site, and so forth.

The webtemp*.xml files are just directories of site templates configurations. The actual configuration is included in an XML file named ONET.XML, which is located in the XML subfolder of every site definition. For example, consider the group of templates defined in the STS site definition. The corresponding ONET.XML file declares some common configuration items, such as the document templates, the list templates, the navigation bar groups, and the custom pages and Web Part pages to deploy. Then it defines some *Configuration* elements, each one corresponding to a specific configuration for the STS template. Listing 13-2 shows the ONET.XML file of the STS template, defining the configuration for STS#0.

LISTING 13-2 The ONET.XML file for the standard STS site template defining STS#0

```
<Configuration ID="0" Name="Default" MasterUrl="_catalogs/masterpage/v4.master">
  <Lists>
    <List FeatureId="00BFEA71-E717-4E80-AA17-D0C71B360101" Type="101"
      Title="$Resources:core,shareddocuments_Title;"
      Url="$Resources:core,shareddocuments_Folder;"
      QuickLaunchUrl="$Resources:core,shareddocuments_Folder;/Forms/AllItems.
aspx" />
    <List FeatureId="00BFEA71-6A49-43FA-B535-D15C05500108" Type="108"
      Title="$Resources:core,discussions_Title;"
      Url="$Resources:core,lists_Folder;/$Resources:core,discussions_Folder;"
      QuickLaunchUrl="$Resources:core,lists_Folder;/$Resources:core,discussions_
        Folder;/AllItems.aspx" EmailAlias="$Resources:core,discussions_
EmailAlias;" />
    <!-- Code omitted for the sake of brevity -->
  </Lists>
  <Modules>
    <Module Name="Default" />
  </Modules>
  <SiteFeatures>
    <!-- BasicWebParts Feature -->
    <Feature ID="00BFEA71-1C5E-4A24-B310-BA51C3EB7A57" />
    <!-- Three-state Workflow Feature -->
    <Feature ID="FDE5D850-671E-4143-950A-87B473922DC7" />
  </SiteFeatures>
  <WebFeatures>
    <!-- TeamCollab Feature -->
    <Feature ID="00BFEA71-4EA5-48D4-A4AD-7EA5C011ABE5" />
    <!-- MobilityRedirect -->
    <Feature ID="F41CC668-37E5-4743-B4A8-74D1DB3FD8A4" />
    <!-- WikiPageHomePage Feature -->
    <Feature ID="00BFEA71-D8FE-4FEC-8DAD-01C19A6E4053" />
  </WebFeatures>
</Configuration>
```

The configuration declares the list instances that will be created in the target site, the modules that will be provisioned (the pages that will be created), and the site-level and web-level features that will be activated. Additionally, consider that all of the site definitions inherit from a common and global definition named *GLOBAL*, which is defined in the SharePoint15_Root\TEMPLATE\GLOBAL folder. There, in the ONET.XML file in the XML folder, are defined all the base list templates and list types used by the other site definitions.

Custom site definitions

Assuming you are working on-premises, defining your own site definitions is simple. To manually create a custom site definition, copy an existing folder and change the ONET.XML file to select the list definitions to use for creating list instances, the modules to provision, and the features to activate. Next, define a custom webtemp*.xml file and copy it into the proper folder within SharePoint15_Root\TEMPLATES*IdCulture*\XML. You will be able to use the new definition after you recycle the application pool of your target web application, or after you execute *IISRESET*, which resets the entire Internet Information Services (IIS) environment.

Important Do not change any of the out-of-the-box site definitions, because changing such files and folders would lead you to an unsupported and probably unstable environment.

Try an example: copy the SharePoint15_Root\TEMPLATES\SiteTemplates\ENTERWIKI folder and name it MYENTERWIKI. Then open the ONET.XML file in the XML subfolder of MYENTERWIKI and change the Configuration section as you see fit. To add a Shared Documents list to the standard Enterprise Wiki site, for instance, add a *List* element to the *Lists* element of the *Configuration* tag in the ONET.XML file, like so:

```
<List FeatureId="00BFEA71-E717-4E80-AA17-D0C71B360101" Type="101"
  Title="$Resources:core,shareddocuments_Title_15;"
  Url="$Resources:core,shareddocuments_Folder;"
  OnQuickLaunch="TRUE" />
```

The values for the *FeatureId* and *Type* attributes are those corresponding to the base list definition of the document library, as it is declared in the *DocumentLibrary* feature in the SharePoint15_Root\TEMPLATES\FEATURES\DocumentLibrary folder.

To make the site template available for creating new site instances, you need to define a custom webtemp*.xml file; for example, call it webtempcustom.xml and copy it into the SharePoint15_Root\TEMPLATES\ldCulture\XML folder. Listing 13-3 shows the source code of such a file.

LISTING 13-3 The source code of the custom webtempcustom.xml file for the custom MYENTERWIKI site definition

```
<?xml version="1.0" encoding="utf-8"?>
<!-- _lcid="1033" _version="15.0.4420" _dal="1" -->
<!-- _LocalBinding -->
<Templates xmlns:ows="Microsoft SharePoint">
 <Template Name="MYENTERWIKI" ID="10001">
    <Configuration ID="0" Title="My Wiki Site" Hidden="FALSE"
   ImageUrl="/_layouts/15/images/wikiprev.png?rev=23" Description="A site for
a community to brainstorm and share ideas. It provides Web pages that can be
quickly edited to record information and then linked together through keywords"
DisplayCategory="DevLeap" >
    </Configuration>
 </Template>
</Templates>
```

Notice the *ID* value of *10001* used in the *Template* definition. In custom site templates, you should use values equal to or greater than 10000 for the *ID* attribute, to avoid overriding the IDs of native templates.

To use your new site definition named *MYENTERWIKI#0*, you now need to recycle the application pool of the target web application where you want to create a site based on this template. You can also reset IIS by invoking the *IISRESET* command to make the template available on all the web applications. Recycling the application pool or resetting the IIS process is required because SharePoint loads the site templates once at startup and then caches them for performance reasons. Figure 13-2 displays the new site template available in the list of templates.

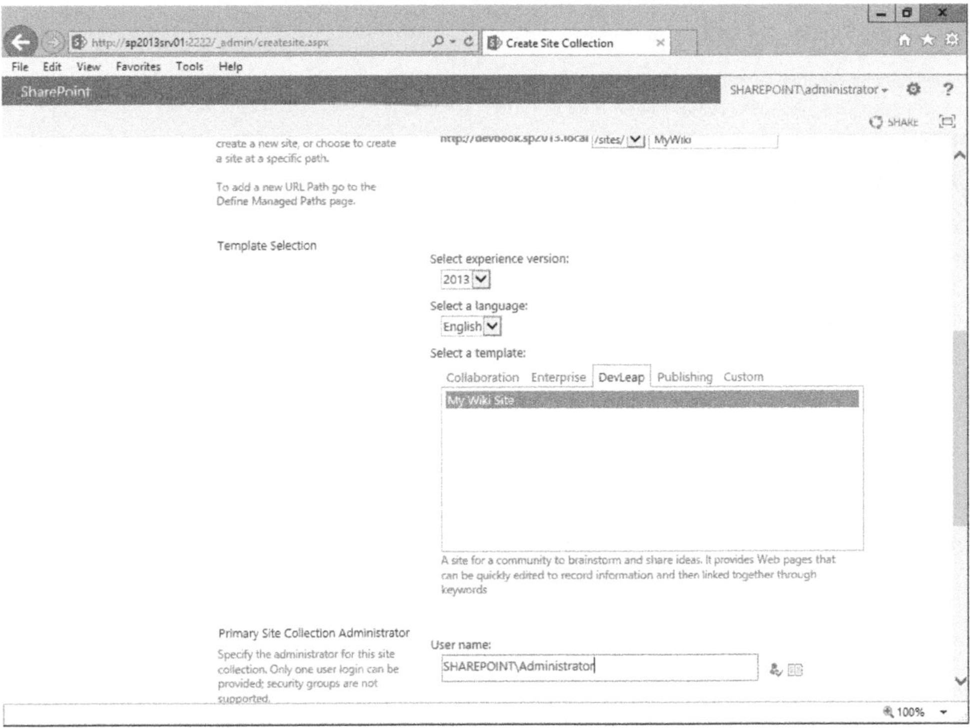

FIGURE 13-2 The standard page for choosing the template for a new subsite, with the new custom site definition.

Figure 13-3 illustrates the home page of a site created using the new My Wiki Site template, with the Shared Documents library at the top of the page.

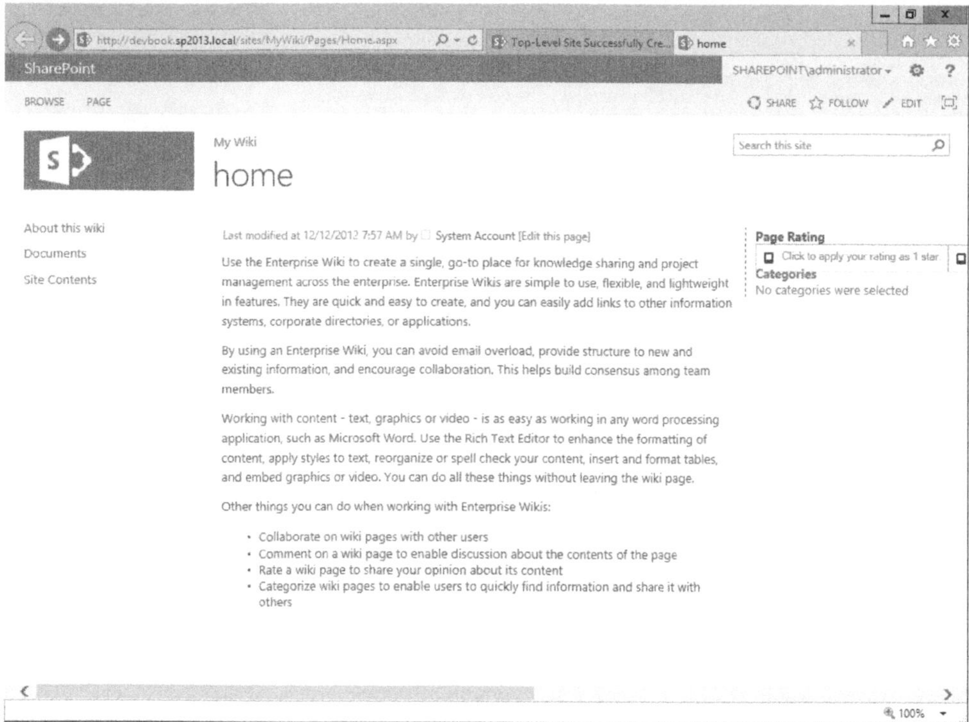

FIGURE 13-3 The home page of the site created using the custom My Wiki Site site definition.

To include a list view of the document library on the home page, you need to add a *View* element inside the *Module* element that is provisioning the Default.aspx page, in the ONET.XML file of your site definition. You'll learn more about this last topic in the next section.

Site definitions with Visual Studio

Manually creating site definitions is simple, but it is not always the best solution, nor is it considered a best practice. For example, the technique works only in an on-premises farm, and it requires great effort if you have many servers in a farm, because you must copy the files and folders to each server to use your custom site definition. Although you were able to use features already available in the farm for the My Enterprise Wiki example, quite often you will need to define a custom site template to take advantage of custom features and custom contents, which you need to deploy together with your site definition. To help you in such cases, Microsoft Visual Studio 2012 provides some item templates for creating a site definition from scratch. Figure 13-4 shows the Add New Item window of Visual Studio 2012, with the proper item template selected.

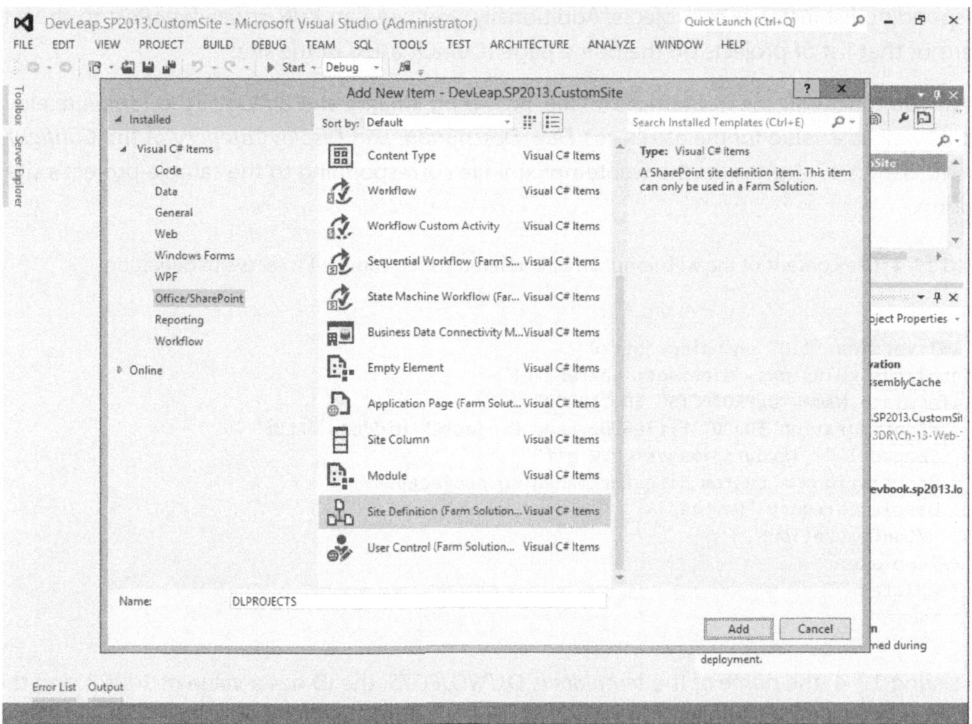

FIGURE 13-4 The Add New Item window of Visual Studio 2012 with the Site Definition item template highlighted.

Important Each time you define a project in Visual Studio, it builds and deploys an assembly. In general, however, a site definition is a codeless solution, unless you do not write custom code to support your custom features or you implement a custom feature receiver. Thus, in case you do not have custom code, you can simply exclude the assembly from being deployed and avoid having an empty assembly deployed on the farm. To exclude an assembly from deployment, you need to set the value of the Include Assembly In Package property for the current project to *False* using the Visual Studio property grid.

Once you choose the project template, Visual Studio 2012 prompts you with the common window, asking for the target site URL and the type of deployment (farm solution or sandboxed solution). For the site definition, your only choice is a farm solution deployment, because the site definition must be stored on the file system of the farm's servers. The sandboxed deployment is not available. The template project outline is made up of the minimal contents for defining a site definition: an ONET.XML file, a webtemp*.xml file, and a Default.aspx home page. To define your site definition, you simply need to add features (as you did in previous chapters), package the solution, and then deploy it.

For example, suppose that you want to deploy a new site definition for managing work projects, with a custom list definition, based on a new content type describing a project item and a corresponding list instance of projects. Additionally, you need an *XsltListViewWebPart* to show the content of that list of projects on the home page (Default.aspx) of the site.

First, you must edit the webtemp*.xml file, providing a name and an ID for the *Template* element, as well as a value for the attributes *Title*, *Description*, and *DisplayCategory* of the *Configuration* element. Listing 13-4 presents the webtemp*.xml file corresponding to the sample project's site definition.

LISTING 13-4 The content of the webtemp*.xml file related to the sample Projects site definition

```
<?xml version="1.0" encoding="utf-8"?>
<Templates xmlns:ows="Microsoft SharePoint">
  <Template Name="DLPROJECTS" ID="10002">
    <Configuration ID="0" Title="DevLeap Projects" Hidden="FALSE"
    ImageUrl="/_layouts/images/CPVW.gif"
    Description="A custom site for managing projects."
    DisplayCategory="DevLeap">
    </Configuration>
  </Template>
</Templates>
```

In Listing 13-4, the *name* of the *template* is *DLPROJECTS*, the ID has a value of *10002*, and the configuration ID is *0*, which means it is the first configuration. So, if you want to reference that site definition configuration by code, you should use the name *DLPROJECTS#0*.

Because the name assigned to the template is *DLPROJECTS*, the deployment location for ONET.XML, Default.aspx, and any other file of the site definition will target the folder SiteTemplates\DLPROJECTS. For example, because the ONET.XML file will be deployed in the XML folder of the site definition, its deployment location will be SiteTemplates\DLPROJECTS\Xml\. Visual Studio 2012 will carry this out for you.

Just after defining the webtemp*.xml file, you should work on the ONET.XML file, which is the main schema file for the custom site definition. You could define the Projects list within the ONET.XML file by using the *ListTemplate* element and a *List* instance element. Be aware that if you provision data through the ONET.XML file, you will not be able to extend or maintain it over the course of the site's lifetime. In fact, data provisioned with a site definition cannot be upgraded, and you would need to write custom code of your own to upgrade it. Instead, as you learned in Chapter 3, "Data provisioning," you could add the content type, list definition, and list instance defining the Projects data structure by using feature elements, which can be upgraded and maintained during the life cycle of your site. (You should already know how to manage this; if not, refer to Chapter 3 and Chapter 4, "SharePoint features and solutions.") In addition, if you use features, you can add feature activation directives to the ONET.XML file. For example, suppose you have a feature provisioning a new list instance of projects, based on a custom list definition and a custom content type. Listing 13-5 shows a sample ONET.XML deploying that list of projects, using a custom feature and the custom Default.aspx page.

LISTING 13-5 The content of the ONET.XML file related to the sample Projects site definition

```
<?xml version="1.0" encoding="utf-8"?>
<Project Title="DLPROJECTS" Revision="2" ListDir=""
         xmlns:ows="Microsoft SharePoint"
         xmlns="http://schemas.microsoft.com/sharepoint/">
  <NavBars>
  </NavBars>
  <Configurations>
    <Configuration ID="0" Name="DLPROJECTS">
      <Lists>
      </Lists>
      <SiteFeatures>
      </SiteFeatures>
      <WebFeatures>
        <Feature ID="13957dde-9510-4216-8e15-9b769ff73bcd" />
      </WebFeatures>
      <Modules>
        <Module Name="DefaultWithProjects" />
      </Modules>
    </Configuration>
  </Configurations>
  <Modules>
    <Module Name="DefaultWithProjects" Url="" Path="">
      <File Url="default.aspx" IgnoreIfAlreadyExists="TRUE">
        <View List="Lists/Projects" BaseViewID="1"
         WebPartZoneID="CentralZone" WebPartOrder="1">
          <![CDATA[
            <webParts>
              <webPart xmlns="http://schemas.microsoft.com/WebPart/v3">
                <metaData>
                  <type name="Microsoft.SharePoint.WebPartPages.
XsltListViewWebPart,
Microsoft.SharePoint,Version=15.0.0.0,Culture=neutral,
PublicKeyToken=71e9bce111e9429c" />
                  <importErrorMessage>Cannot import this Web Part.
                  </importErrorMessage>
                </metaData>
                <data>
                  <properties>
                    <property name="AllowConnect" type="bool">True</property>
                    <property name="ChromeType" type="chrometype">None</property>
                    <property name="AllowClose" type="bool">False</property>
                  </properties>
                </data>
              </webPart>
            </webParts>
          ]]>
        </View>
      </File>
    </Module>
  </Modules>
  <ServerEmailFooter>Email from DevLeap Projects Site</ServerEmailFooter>
</Project>
```

The first thing to notice in the ONET.XML file is the *Configuration* element, which corresponds to the one defined in the webtemp*.xml file. To use the content defined by your custom provisioning feature, you need to put a *Feature* element within the *WebFeatures* element. The feature provisioning the list instance of Project, together with site columns, content types, and list definition, is a web-scoped feature. Additionally, the feature provisions a *Module* element for the *Configuration*, referencing one of the available *Module* elements defined in the *Modules* section of the ONET.XML file.

The *Module* element provisions the Default.aspx page and also declares a *View* element, which includes a Web Part of type *XsltListViewWebPart* that renders the items of the list of projects, with the path Lists/Projects, into the *WebPartZone* control with ID *CentralZone*, defined in the source code of Default.aspx. Listing 13-6 illustrates the source code of the Default.aspx page provisioned with the custom site definition.

LISTING 13-6 The source of the Default.aspx page provisioned with the sample Projects site definition

```
<%@ Page language="C#" MasterPageFile="~masterurl/default.master"
Inherits="Microsoft.SharePoint.WebPartPages.WebPartPage,
Microsoft.SharePoint,Version=15.0.0.0,Culture=neutral,PublicKeyToken=71e9bce111e
9429c" %>
<%@ Register Tagprefix="SharePoint" Namespace="Microsoft.SharePoint.WebControls"
Assembly="Microsoft.SharePoint, Version=15.0.0.0, Culture=neutral, PublicKeyToke
n=71e9bce111e9429c" %>
<%@ Register Tagprefix="Utilities" Namespace="Microsoft.SharePoint.Utilities"
Assembly="Microsoft.SharePoint, Version=15.0.0.0, Culture=neutral, PublicKeyToke
n=71e9bce111e9429c" %>
<%@ Import Namespace="Microsoft.SharePoint" %>
<%@ Assembly Name="Microsoft.Web.CommandUI, Version=15.0.0.0, Culture=neutral,
PublicKeyToken=71e9bce111e9429c" %>
<%@ Register Tagprefix="WebPartPages" Namespace="Microsoft.SharePoint.
WebPartPages" Assembly="Microsoft.SharePoint, Version=15.0.0.0, Culture=neutral,
PublicKeyToken=71e9bce111e9429c" %>

<asp:Content ID="PageTitleContent" ContentPlaceHolderId="PlaceHolderPageTitle"
runat="server">
  <SharePoint:ProjectProperty ID="ProjectProperty2" Property="Title"
runat="server"/>
</asp:Content>

<asp:Content ID="SearchAreaContent" ContentPlaceHolderId="PlaceHolderSearchArea"
runat="server">
        <SharePoint:DelegateControl ID="DelegateControl1" runat="server"
                ControlId="SmallSearchInputBox" />
</asp:Content>
```

```
<asp:Content ID="MainContent" ContentPlaceHolderId="PlaceHolderMain"
runat="server">
        <table cellspacing="0" border="0" width="100%">
          <tr class="s4-die">
           <td class="ms-pagebreadcrumb">
                  <asp:SiteMapPath SiteMapProvider="SPContentMapProvider"
id="ContentMap" SkipLinkText="" NodeStyle-CssClass="ms-sitemapdirectional"
runat="server"/>
           </td>
          </tr>
          <tr>
           <td class="ms-webpartpagedescription"><SharePoint:ProjectProperty
             ID="ProjectProperty3" Property="Description" runat="server"/></td>
          </tr>
          <tr>
                <td>
                 <table width="100%" cellpadding="0" cellspacing="0"
                   style="padding: 5px 10px 10px 10px;">
                  <tr>
                   <td valign="top" width="100%">
                           <WebPartPages:WebPartZone runat="server"
                               FrameType="TitleBarOnly"
                               ID="CentralZone" Title="loc:CentralZone" />
                   </td>
                  </tr>
                 </table>
                </td>
          </tr>
        </table>
</asp:Content>
```

To deploy the site definition, you can simply select the Deploy command in Visual Studio. I suggest, however, that before you deploy the site definition, you change the deployment configuration from Default to No Activation in the project's properties, under the SharePoint properties page (see Figure 13-5). This will avoid activating the features in the deployment target site, as well.

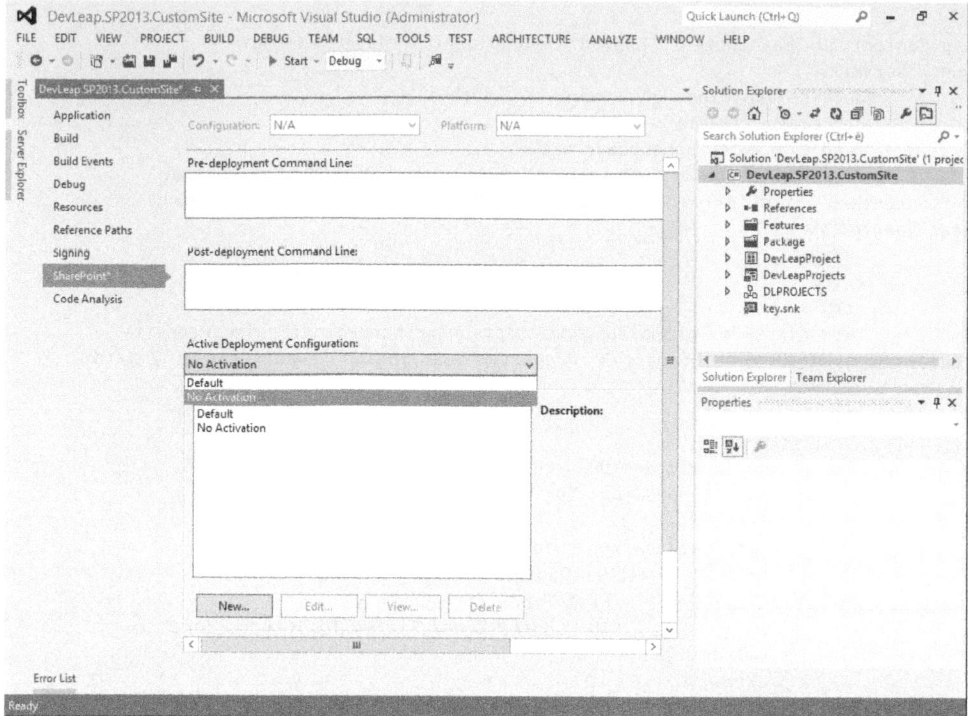

FIGURE 13-5 The properties window of the project for provisioning the sample site definition.

After deploying the site definition, you will find its corresponding folder in the SharePoint15_Root\TEMPLATES\SiteTemplates folder, and you will be able to create new site instances by using the new custom site template. Figure 13-6 displays the new site definition available in the list of creatable site definitions, while Figure 13-7 presents the home page of a site of projects created using the new site definition.

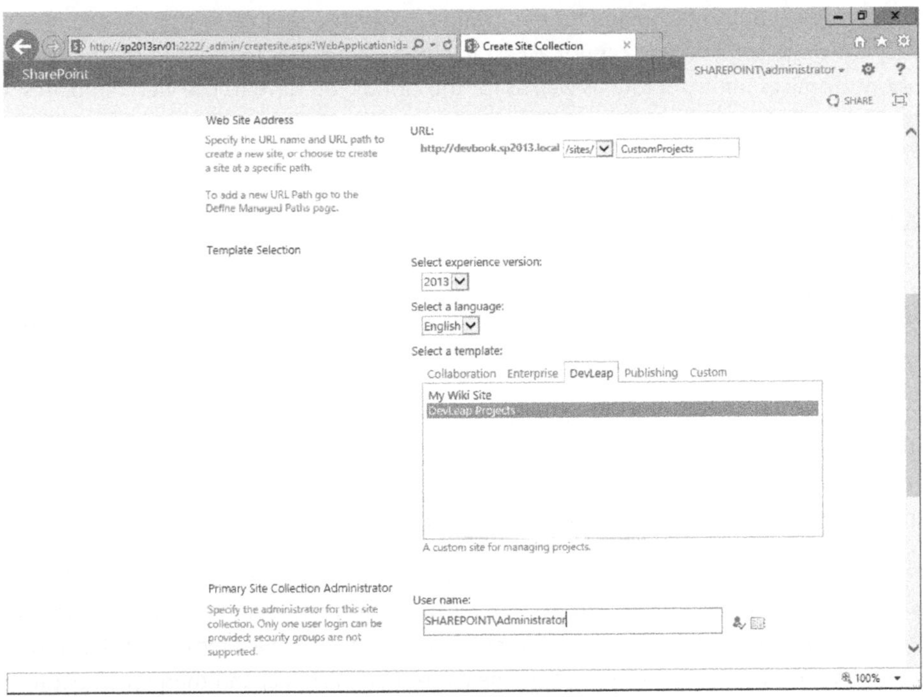

FIGURE 13-6 The sample site definition available as a model while creating a new site instance.

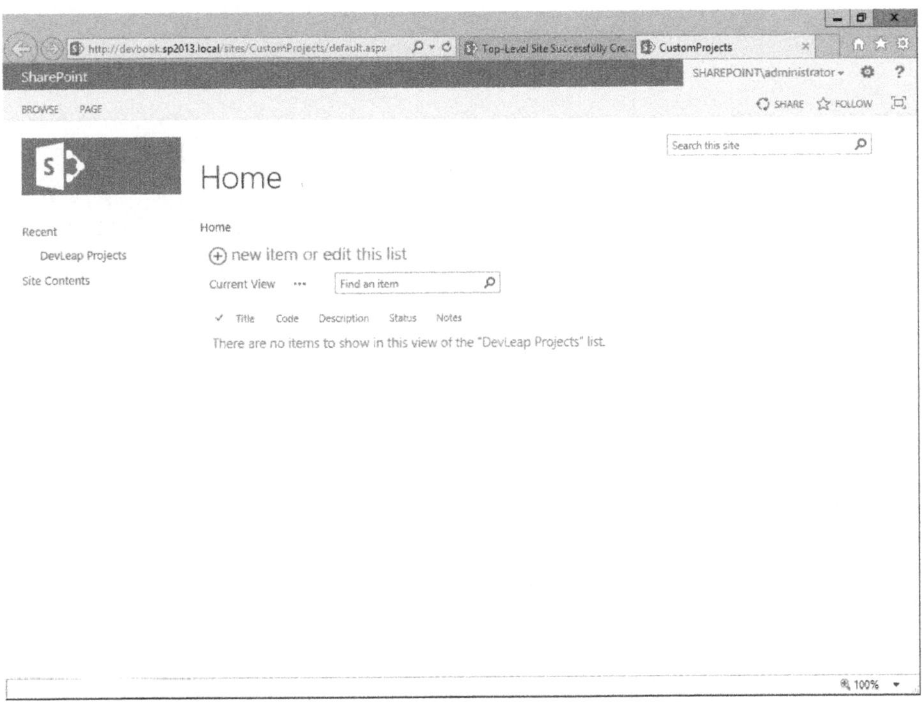

FIGURE 13-7 The home page of a site of projects created using the new sample site definition.

Finally, remember that this technique for deploying custom site templates with Visual Studio is available only on-premises, and you cannot access it within Office 365. In order to create site models suitable for on-premises infrastructure as well as for the cloud, you have to use web templates, which are discussed in the following section.

Site and web templates

When you create a new site instance from the UI of SharePoint, you are prompted to select a model, as shown previously in Figure 13-6. In addition to the site definitions you just learned about, the list of available site models contains web templates.

You can create a custom web template by exporting the definition of an existing site instance, with or without its content, and storing the result into the content database as a sandboxed solution. To export an existing site definition, you can use the web browser and navigate to the Save Site As Template page, located under the Site Actions group on the Site Settings page of the current website.

Regardless of how you save the web template, the result will be a WSP package with a feature element specifically introduced in SharePoint 2010 for managing deployment of custom web templates. The corresponding element is the *WebTemplate* element. To have a look at its structure, you can simply export an existing site instance, save the generated WSP file, and then rename it to CAB. You can then extract the element manifest declaring the *WebTemplate* feature. Listing 13-7 reveals the structure of the *WebTemplate* element.

LISTING 13-7 The *WebTemplate* element structure

```
<WebTemplate
  AdjustHijriDays = "Integer"
  AlternateCssUrl = "Text"
  AlternateHeader = "Text"
  BaseTemplateID = "Integer"
  BaseTemplateName = "Text"
  BaseConfigurationID = "Integer"
  CalendarType = "Integer"
  Collation = "Integer"
  ContainsDefaultLists = "TRUE" | "FALSE"
  CustomizedCssFiles = "Text"
  CustomJSUrl = "Text"
  Description = "Text"
  DisplayCategory = "Text"
  ExcludeFromOfflineClient = "TRUE" | "FALSE"
  ImageUrl = "URL"
  Locale = "Integer"
  Name = "Text"
  ParserEnabled = "TRUE" | "FALSE"
  PortalName = "Text"
  PortalUrl = "Text"
```

```
    PresenceEnabled = "TRUE" | "FALSE"
    ProductVersion = "Integer"
    QuickLaunchEnabled = "TRUE" | "FALSE"
    Subweb = "TRUE" | "FALSE"
    SyndicationEnabled = "TRUE" | "FALSE"
    Time24 = "TRUE" | "FALSE"
    TimeZone = "Integer"
    Title = "Text"
    TreeViewEnabled = "Text"
    UIVersionConfigurationEnabled = "TRUE" | "FALSE">
  </WebTemplate>
```

The *WebTemplate* element comprises a set of attributes, which are described in Table 13-2.

TABLE 13-2 The attributes supported by the *WebTemplate* element

Attribute name	Description
AdjustHijriDays	Optional *Integer* attribute that specifies the number of days to extend or reduce the current month in Hijri (Islamic) calendars used on the target website.
AlternateCssUrl	Optional *Text* attribute that specifies the URL for an alternative cascading style sheet (CSS).
AlternateHeader	Optional *Text* attribute that provides the name of a custom ASPX page. *AlternateHeader* defines a custom alternative header for provisioned pages. It should be available in the SharePoint15_Root\TEMPLATE\LAYOUTS folder.
BaseTemplateID	Required *Integer* attribute that specifies the ID of the parent site definition. *BaseTemplateID* contains the value of the *ID* attribute of the *Template* element in the webtemp*.xml file that defines the parent site definition.
BaseTemplateName	Required *Text* attribute that specifies the name of the parent site definition. *BaseTemplateName* contains the value of the *Name* attribute of the *Template* element in the webtemp*.xml file that defines the parent site definition.
BaseConfigurationID	Required *Integer* attribute that specifies the ID of the configuration of the parent site definition. *BaseConfigurationID* contains the value of the *ID* attribute of the *Configuration* element in the webtemp*.xml file that defines the parent site definition.
CalendarType	Optional *Integer* attribute that specifies the type of the default calendar type for calendars created on the target website.
Collation	Optional *Integer* attribute that specifies the collation to use for the target website.
ContainsDefaultLists	Optional *Boolean* attribute that specifies whether the parent site definition contains lists that are defined in the ONET.XML file of the GLOBAL site definition.
CustomizedCssFiles	Optional *Text* attribute that specifies custom CSS files.
CustomJSUrl	Optional *Text* attribute that provides a custom JavaScript file located in the SharePoint15_Root\TEMPLATE\LAYOUTS folder, which will be executed within the target website.
Description	Optional *Text* attribute that specifies a description for the site template.
DisplayCategory	Optional *Text* attribute that specifies the category in which the web template will appear in the SharePoint UI for creating a new site.
ExcludeFromOfflineClient	Optional *Boolean* attribute that specifies whether the site must be downloaded during offline client synchronization.

Attribute name	Description
ImageUrl	Optional *URL* address of the preview image of the model, which is displayed in the SharePoint UI for creating a new site.
Locale	Optional *Integer* attribute that specifies the locale ID of the language/culture for the target website.
Name	Required *Text* attribute that specifies the internal name of the web template.
ParserEnabled	Optional *Boolean* attribute that specifies whether the values of columns in document libraries will be automatically added to documents added to libraries of the target website.
PortalName	Optional *Text* attribute that provides the name of the portal associated with the website.
PortalUrl	Optional *Text* attribute that specifies the URL of the portal associated with the target website.
PresenceEnabled	Optional *Boolean* attribute that specifies whether online presence will be enabled for users of the target website.
ProductVersion	Optional *Integer* attribute that specifies the version of SharePoint Foundation used to create the web template.
QuickLaunchEnabled	Optional *Boolean* attribute that determines if the Quick Launch area will be enabled on the target website.
Subweb	Optional *Boolean* attribute that specifies whether the web template has been created from a child *Web* site or from the root *Web* site of a site collection.
SyndicationEnabled	Optional *Boolean* attribute that determines if RSS syndication will be enabled on the target website.
Time24	Optional *Boolean* attribute that specifies whether to use the 24-hour format to represents hours.
TimeZone	Optional *Integer* attribute that specifies the default time zone for the target website.
Title	Optional *Text* attribute that provides the title for the web template.
TreeViewEnabled	Optional *Text* attribute that specifies whether the tree view in the left navigation area of pages will be enabled. *TreeViewEnabled* can only take *TRUE* or *FALSE* text values.
UIVersionConfigurationEnabled	Optional *Boolean* attribute that specifies whether users can change the UI version of the target website.

Listing 13-8 shows an example of a *WebTemplate* instance, generated by exporting an instance of the sample site for managing projects, which you saw in the previous section.

LISTING 13-8 The *WebTemplate* element feature generated from the sample Projects site definition instance

```
<Elements xmlns="http://schemas.microsoft.com/sharepoint/">
  <WebTemplate AdjustHijriDays="0"
               AlternateCssUrl=""
               AlternateHeader=""
               BaseTemplateID="10002"
               BaseTemplateName="DLPROJECTS"
               BaseConfigurationID="0"
               CalendarType="1"
               Collation="25"
               ContainsDefaultLists="TRUE"
               CustomizedCssFiles=""
               CustomJSUrl=""
               ExcludeFromOfflineClient="FALSE"
               Locale="1033"
               Name="SampleProjects"
               ParserEnabled="TRUE"
               PortalName=""
               PortalUrl=""
               PresenceEnabled="TRUE"
               ProductVersion="4"
               QuickLaunchEnabled="TRUE"
               Subweb="TRUE"
               SyndicationEnabled="TRUE"
               Time24="FALSE"
               TimeZone="4"
               Title="SampleProjects"
               TreeViewEnabled="FALSE"
               UIVersionConfigurationEnabled="FALSE" />
</Elements>
```

Note in Listing 13-8 how the *WebTemplate* element references its parent site definition (*10002, DLPROJECTS#0*). In fact, all the three attributes—*BaseTemplateID*, *BaseTemplateName*, and *BaseConfigurationID*—reference the site definition created in the previous section. For this reason, Microsoft does not support changing or removing a site definition after having used it for creating sites. If a referenced site definition is changed or removed, elements such as the *WebTemplate* feature in Listing 13-8 will no longer work.

The easiest way to create a *WebTemplate* feature using Visual Studio is to design the site in the browser. Then you can save it as a template and export the resulting WSP package file, downloading it from the Solution Gallery page of the site collection. From there, you simply need to import the WSP file into Visual Studio 2012, creating a new project of type SharePoint 2013 - Import Solution Package. Now you can choose to define a sandboxed solution, because the *WebTemplate* feature has been implemented by Microsoft specifically to satisfy the requirement of deploying web templates through sandboxed solutions. Visual Studio will start a wizard that will prompt you to choose the WSP file, and then it will analyze the WSP file and generate a list of items that will be imported. In general, you should accept the proposed list unless you prefer to exclude some content from the web template. When you click the wizard's Finish button, you will have a new Visual Studio project, complete with a SharePoint package full of features and elements that correspond to the structure of the original site that was used to generate the web template.

To customize the web template project, you can manually open the imported ONET.XML file and change its contents. Figure 13-8 illustrates the interface of Visual Studio while an imported web template is being edited.

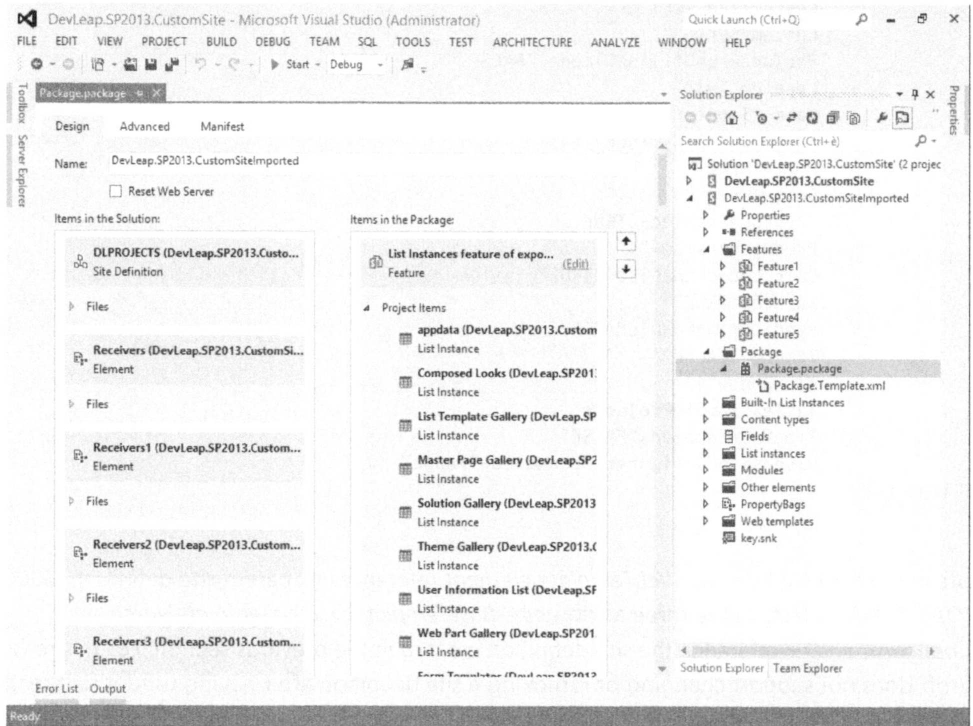

FIGURE 13-8 The Visual Studio project available for customizing an imported WSP file.

Visual Studio makes a lot of features and elements available, but the application needs only a few. The important elements are the list of projects and the custom home page.

Of course, you could also create a project for a web template from scratch, manually adding items to the corresponding folders and creating a project structure like the one shown in Figure 13-8.

Site definitions vs. web templates

It is important to understand that creating a site definition or a web template is an uncommon and complex task. In general, you should create features and solutions to deploy custom data structures and content. Features and solutions are more flexible, modular, and more easily maintained than site definitions or web templates, and they are typically the easiest to define.

If you decide that you need to create a new site model, you will need to choose between creating a site definition or a web template. In such situations, you should factor in the following:

- Deploying a web template requires only the proper rights to upload the WSP file into the solution gallery of the target site collection. A site definition requires physical access to the file system of the servers in the farm. In fact, a web template is a sandboxed solution.
- A site definition cannot be deployed in a cloud environment (SharePoint Online or Office 365), while a web template can be deployed and used in the cloud.
- A web template can be versioned without affecting existing site instances created from a previous version.
- When you change the pages defined in a web template, those changes will be available only in new sites, while changing the layout of pages provisioned through a site definition will also affect previously deployed sites. However, Microsoft recommends you not change a site definition after you have used it. Instead, for versioning or changing a site definition, you should use features stapling.
- A web template can do almost everything a site definition can. The only capabilities that are not available in a *WebTemplate* feature are module elements for provisioning pages, custom components to process files or security (*FileDialogPostProcessor* and *ExternalSecurityProvider*), *ServerEmailFooter* configuration for custom e-mail footers (which, however, are not that useful), feature stapling, and variations hierarchy.

Thus, the best practice is to favor web templates and avoid using site definitions, unless you really do need them.

Summary

In this chapter, you learned the difference between site definitions and web templates. You also learned how to create your own site definitions, both manually and with Visual Studio, and how to define a web template within Visual Studio 2012. Finally, you were presented with some important characteristics to consider when deciding whether to create a site definition or web template.

CHAPTER 14

Business Connectivity Services

Business Connectivity Services (BCS) is a fundamental service application of Microsoft SharePoint 2013. It provides capabilities to read and write data from external systems, such as line-of-business (LOB) applications, web services, databases, and any other external sources that offer a suitable connector. This chapter introduces the architecture of the service and examines some useful case studies.

Overview of BCS

BCS allows accessing external data by using a CRUDQ (create, read, update, delete, and query) approach. It is a service application that ships natively with any edition of SharePoint 2013, including SharePoint Foundation 2013. The edition of SharePoint you install, however, will determine the exact mix of features included. Figure 14-1 presents an architectural schema of BCS.

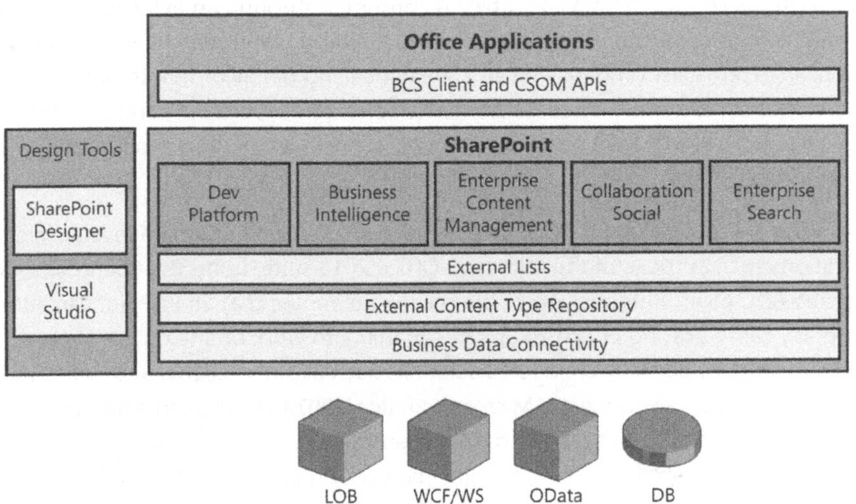

FIGURE 14-1 The architectural schema of the BCS application in SharePoint 2013.

The service is based on a core engine named Business Data Connectivity (BDC) that uses a runtime engine to connect with various data providers. The supported data providers are

- **LOB applications** Any LOB solutions that can be consumed through a specific connector or through one of the following providers

- **WCF/Web services** Any Simple Object Access Protocol (SOAP) web service or any Microsoft Windows Communication Foundation (WCF) service
- **OData** Any Open Data protocol–compliant data source service
- **Custom .NET assemblies** Custom Microsoft Windows .NET assemblies that will wrap any back-end data source
- **Database** Any database based on Microsoft SQL Server, Oracle, OLE DB data providers, or ODBC data providers

More Info For backward compatibility, you can also consume a custom connector, which is a custom-developed library for reading and writing data from any external data sources. If you are interested in this topic, read the document "Creating Custom Business Connectivity Services Connectors Using SharePoint Server 2010," which is available on MSDN at *http://msdn.microsoft.com/en-us/library/ff953161.aspx*. The best practice, however, is to use an established data provider.

Regardless of the type of data provider that you use, the BDC engine stores configurations and shapes of data sources in a dedicated repository, which is called External Content Type Repository and corresponds to a dedicated database file. SharePoint is a presentation layer for data managed using BCS, and every item that you read or write data from an external data source through BCS, that data corresponds to an external content type (ECT), which is consumed through an external list. SharePoint also provides several Web Parts out of the box for rendering, filtering, and searching data provided by BCS. In addition, an external list renders with an appearance and behavior that is almost the same as a standard SharePoint list of items. The capability to render external data in SharePoint as if it were internal data is a key feature of BCS; you can provide end users with a common experience for both internal and external data.

Also, if you have the SharePoint Server 2013 edition, you can consume BCS data (even offline) from client applications such as those of the Microsoft Office 2013 suite, using the Client-Side Object Model (CSOM) or the BDC Client Runtime, which is a client-side engine that SharePoint can automatically install on any client hosting Office 2013. The capability to work offline on the client side makes BCS very interesting for partially connected solutions such as smart clients and Office Business Applications. For example, you can connect a Microsoft Outlook 2013 client to an external list published through SharePoint and BCS, and take its data offline. This allows users to work with the data, even when disconnected from the network. The offline data will be saved in local storage on the client PC, within the current user profile folder. For security reasons, the data is also encrypted on the local folder of the end user. If the user changes any of the items while offline, when he or she goes back online, the BDC Client Runtime will be able to synchronize the client-side data cache with the server-side online data.

Important When working on a client, the BDC Client Runtime will connect directly to the data repository, without using SharePoint 2013 as an intermediary. Thus, if your repository is a database stored in a database management system (DBMS), the client will access the database directly; if the repository is accessed through a WCF/web service, the client will access the HTTP server directly. If you have any firewall between the client network and the server network, you will need to open the right TCP ports and protocols.

By default, the client accessibility and the offline capabilities are available only in Outlook 2013. However, the BDC Client Runtime is provided with an object model, which you can use from any .NET application. This means that you can write custom code in Microsoft Word 2013, Microsoft Excel 2013, and so on. You could also write some code in a custom .NET smart client of your own. An interesting aspect to note is that the offline data cache is unique on a per-user basis. Thus, offline data will be shared between multiple client applications, avoiding data duplication and concurrency conflicts within the same user's session.

To consume an external data source using BCS, you need to model the ECTs that you will use, together with a formal definition of the LOB system you are going to consume. This information can be defined with an XML file, built according to a BCS-specific XML schema. You can build the XML file by using a tool like SharePoint Designer 2013, Microsoft Visual Studio 2012, or any other XML editor. Depending on the type of data provider you plan to use, any of these applications could be useful. For example, SharePoint Designer 2013 is the ideal solution for modeling SQL Server–based solutions and WCF/web service–based solutions. Conversely, Visual Studio 2012 works very well with custom .NET assemblies and custom connectors. A generic XML editor is suitable for all the other situations.

Accessing a database

It's time to begin consuming some data using BCS. As an example, consider a SQL Server database containing some hypothetical records of a customer relationship management (CRM) system. Figure 14-2 shows the schema of the target database that accompanies this chapter. Notice that the Customers table contains a list of orders that consists of OrdersRows, which is related to a table of products.

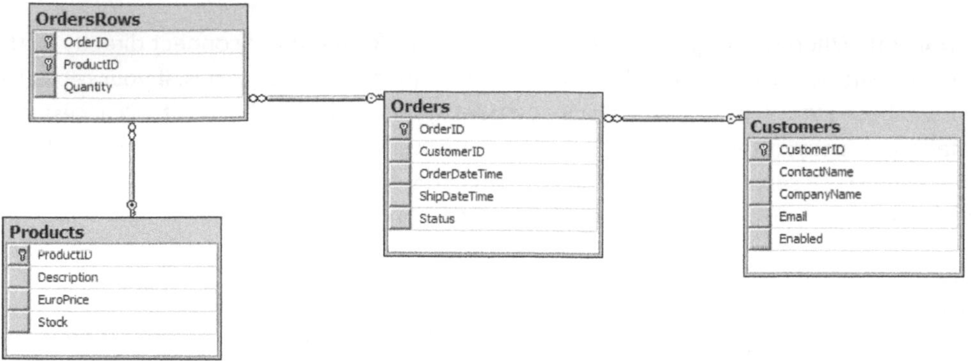

FIGURE 14-2 The schema of a sample CRM database that you will manage by using BCS.

As previously stated, the ideal tool for modeling a BCS connection to a DBMS is SharePoint Designer 2013. Start the application and open the target SharePoint site. Move to the External Content Types section in the Site Objects menu on the left side of the UI, as shown in Figure 14-3.

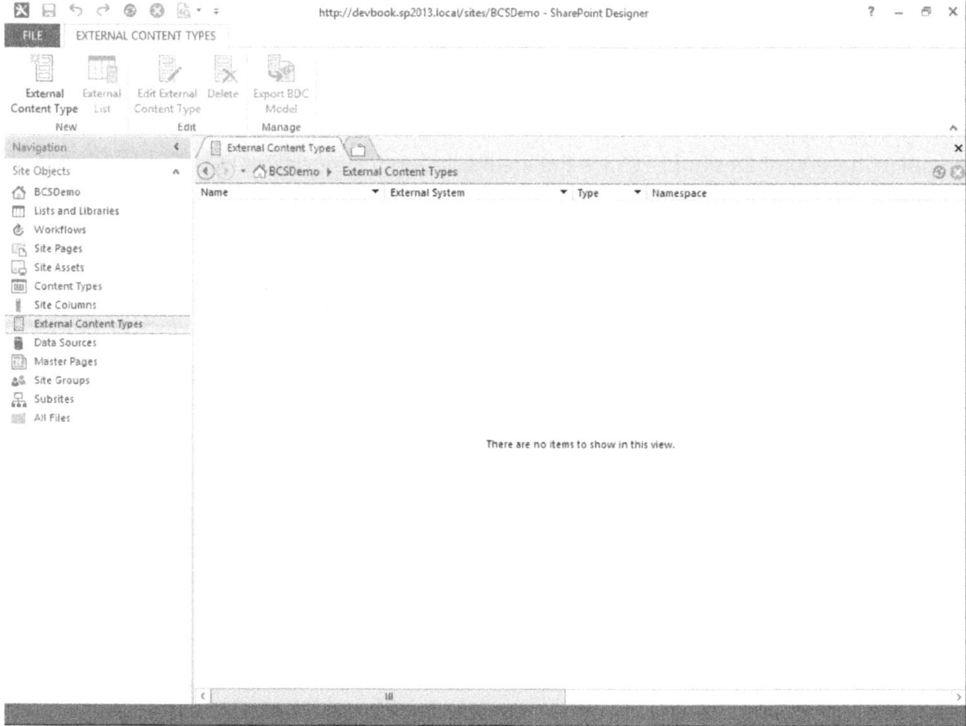

FIGURE 14-3 The Site Objects menu of SharePoint Designer 2013, shown with External Content Types highlighted.

To create a new ECT, on the ribbon, under the New group, click External Content Type. A window appears (see Figure 14-4), in which you will set up a *CRMCustomer* entity corresponding to the records in the *Customers* table of the target DBMS.

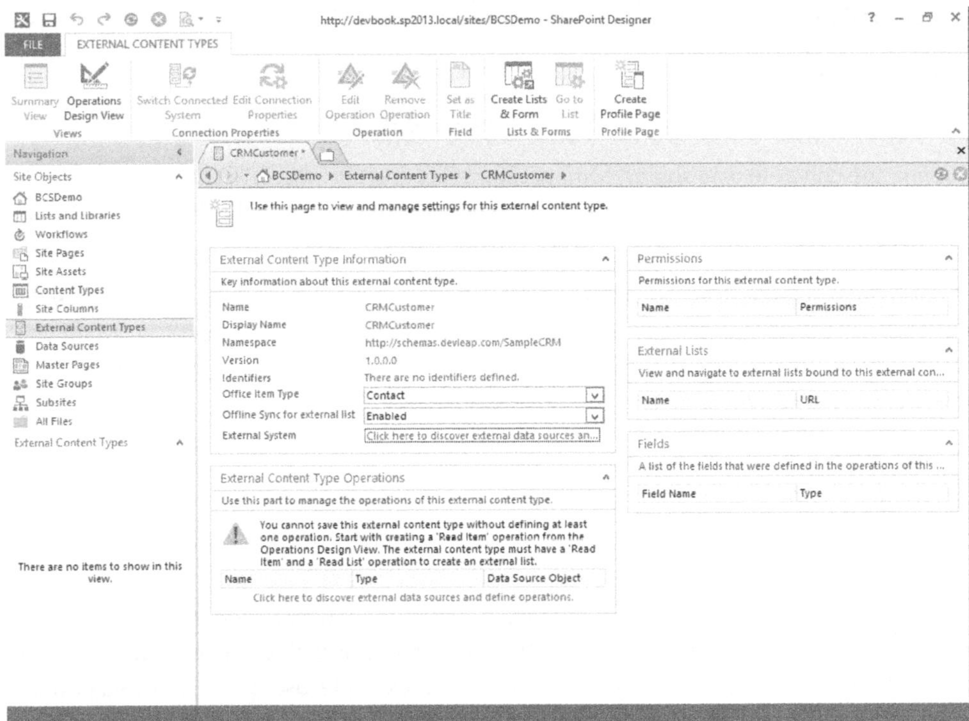

FIGURE 14-4 The window for creating a new ECT.

Specifically, you need to provide the following information:

- **Name** The name of the ECT.
- **Display Name** The name that will be used for displaying the ECT.
- **Namespace** The namespace, which can be any string, grouping ECTs of the same type or with a common data source.
- **Version** The version of the ECT.
- **Identifiers** The identifiers (defined via a wizard) that you will see in the upcoming pages.
- **Office Item Type** The behavior of the ECT when it will be presented in the office client UI. Possible values are Generic List, Appointment, Contact, Task, and Post. For example, for a Customers table, each Customer row can be mapped to a contact.
- **Offline Sync For External List** The capability to work offline.
- **External System** The concrete definition of the external data source. (This will be discussed shortly.)
- **External Content Type Operations** The operations available for the current ECT.

- **Permissions** The access permissions for the current ECT.
- **External Lists** The external lists where the current ECT is used.
- **Fields** The list of the fields declared for the current ECT.

To define the concrete data source configuration, click the Click Here To Discover External Data Sources And Define Operations link adjacent to External System, or click the Operations Design View ribbon command.

A second page appears. You can either click the Add Connection button to define a new data connection, or choose an existing data connection in the Data Source Explorer area. When you add a new connection, you must determine the type of data source to which you will connect. SharePoint Designer 2013 gives you three options:

- .NET Type
- SQL Server
- WCF Service

If you select SQL Server, a dialog box appears, in which you must provide the connection string information. You also need to configure an authentication method (this will be covered in depth in the next section). For the sake of simplicity, in the current example, use the default value Connect With User's Identity, which corresponds to a pass-through connection that will use the identity of the user at run time. If the web application is not configured to authenticate with Windows credentials, the NT Authority/Anonymous Logon account will be passed to the external system.

More Info For further details about BCS authentication and security infrastructure, read the document "Business Connectivity Services security tasks in SharePoint Server 2013," which is available on TechNet at *http://technet.microsoft.com/en-us/library/jj683116.aspx*.

After defining the connection string, you are presented with a list of tables, views, and stored procedures that are available in the external database. Right-click an item (table, view, or routine) in the Data Source Explorer window, and a contextual menu will appear, as shown in Figure 14-5. From this menu, you can add operations for managing data. Each operation corresponds to a method that will allow interaction with the data source. Using the SharePoint Designer 2013 interface, you can define the following operations:

- **Read Item** Corresponds to the method for reading a single row/item
- **Read List** Corresponds to the method for reading a list of rows/items
- **Create** Creates a new row/item
- **Update** Updates an already existing row/item
- **Delete** Deletes an already existing row/item

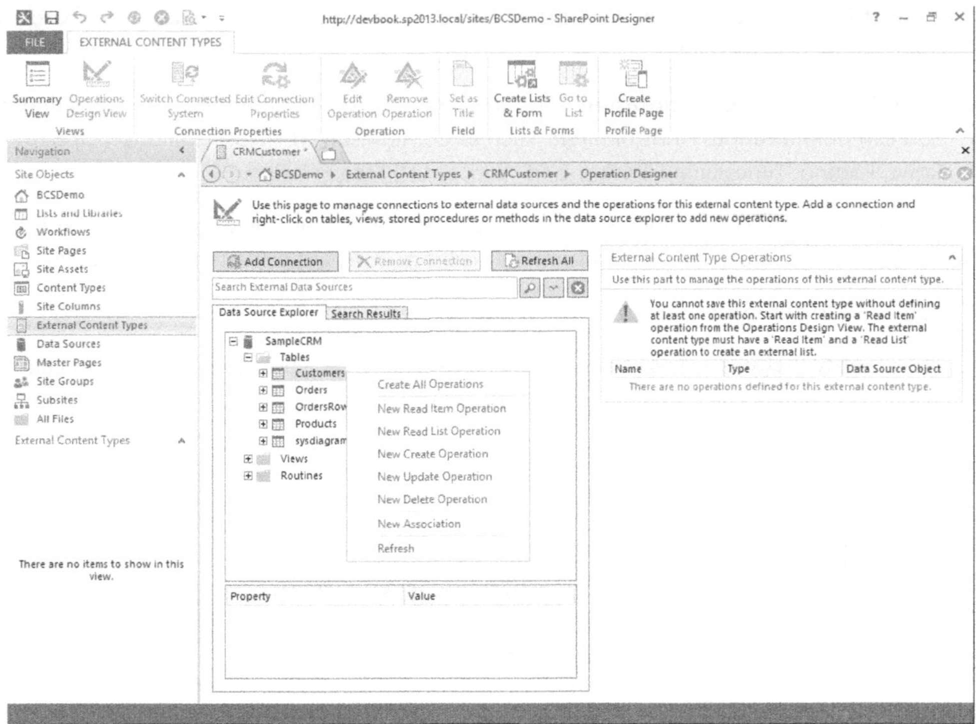

FIGURE 14-5 The Operations Designer window for an ECT.

In addition, the context menu contains a New Association command with which you can create a relationship between two ECTs in a master/detail fashion. This last topic is covered in the "Associating entities" section later in the chapter.

When you click the Create All Operations command at the top of the context menu, a wizard will guide you through three simple steps, and then create all the desired operations. The pages of the wizard are

- **Operation Properties** This gives a summary of what the wizard will do for you.
- **Parameters Configuration** Here, you can define all the fields of the ECT that you are creating. You must define an identifier field, but when using a SQL Server data source, SharePoint Designer 2013 can usually determine the identifier automatically, using the primary key of the table. If the primary key is composed with multiple columns, all of these columns will become required fields of the target ECT. If you choose to map the ECT to an Office type, you must satisfy some minimal requirements. For example, a contact of Office has to have a *LastName* property, and it is mandatory to map a field of the data source to that property. To do so, in the Properties section of the wizard, choose Office Property. From there, you can freely map all the fields that you like with their corresponding Office properties. You can also define

a field that will be used in the data picker and columns of type External Data for searching items while in SharePoint.

- **Filter Parameters Configuration** Use this page to define custom filters for selecting items. You can define various kinds of filters, such as Comparison Of Fields, Limitation Of Returned Rows, Paging, Timestamp Filtering, and Wildcard (*) Free Filtering.

Figure 14-6 depicts the main window for managing the ECT with all operations created and fields defined. Now you are almost ready for consuming the list of ECTs, but pay attention to two key points:

- You need to authorize users to consume the defined ECT.
- The identity that you will use to access the data source, depending on the authentication configuration you choose, will need to have access to the data source.

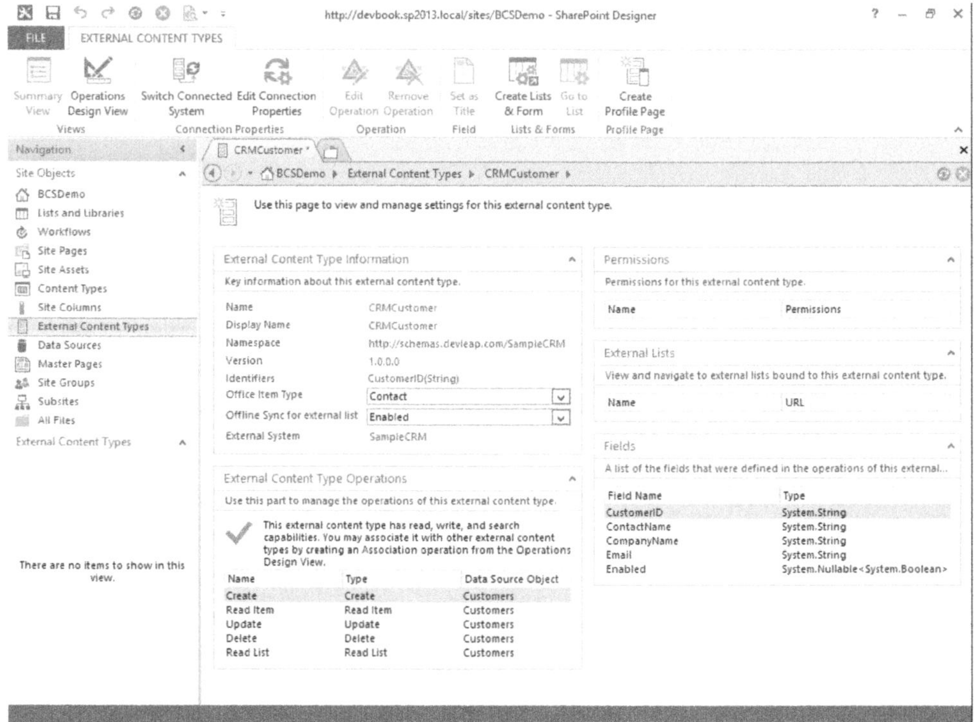

FIGURE 14-6 The window for creating a new ECT, completely configured.

Save the newly defined ECT by clicking the Save button in the upper-left corner. Then, open SharePoint Central Administration (SPCA) and browse to the management page of the BDC Services service application, as shown in Figure 14-7.

From this page, you can do the following:

- Manage all the ECTs, the configured external systems, and the BDC models that you have defined in the farm.
- Import an external model defined in another farm or with an external tool.
- Set user and group permissions for the entire metadata store or for a specific entity.
- Delete a previously defined ECT.
- Create, upgrade, or configure profile pages for an existing ECT. A profile page is a Web Part page for managing the contents of a specific ECT.

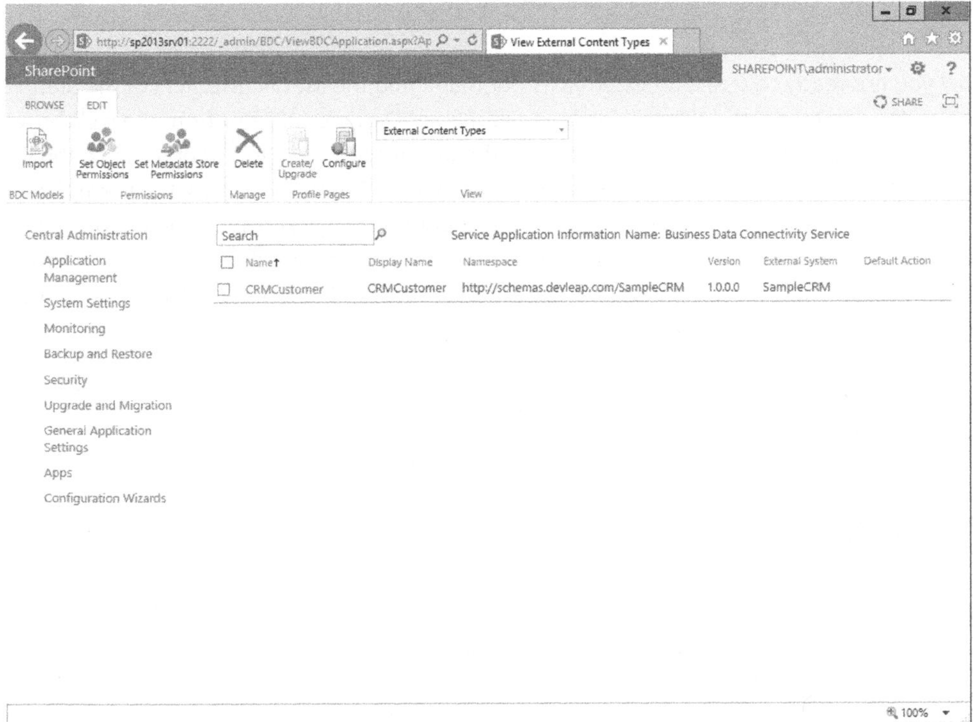

FIGURE 14-7 The SPCA page for managing BDC Services.

Select the *CRMCustomer* check box, and then on the ribbon, click Set Object Permission or select Set Metadata Store Permissions. In the window that appears, you can define permissions for a specific user or group. The available permission mask allows you to define four permissions:

- **Edit** Specifies whether the user can edit the external systems, a single external system, a single ECT, or an operation
- **Execute** Allows the user to execute CRUDQ operations against an ECT

- **Selectable In Clients** Allows the user to create external lists of the target ECT, use Business Data Web Parts, and select ECTs within the ECT picker
- **Set Permissions** Allows the user to set permissions on the target item (models, data sources, and ECTs)

You can propagate permissions on descendant items to work with a permission inheritance model.

The minimum requirement for viewing and managing ECT data is to have both the Selectable In Clients and the Execute permissions applied.

Important Remember that at least one user or group must be assigned the Set Permissions right to avoid creating unmanageable objects.

Now you are ready to create an external list for managing the list of customers of the *SampleCRM* database. You can create the external list from SharePoint Designer 2013 or from the web browser. For this exercise, use the web browser. Browse to the target site where you want to make the list available and choose the menu item to create a new list instance. Choose an External List template and create it. You will be asked to provide the standard properties of a new list (name and quick launch behavior) and the name for the ECT. Select the target ECT, and you are done. Figure 14-8 illustrates the result. Notice that the user experience is exactly the same as browsing a native list of SharePoint.

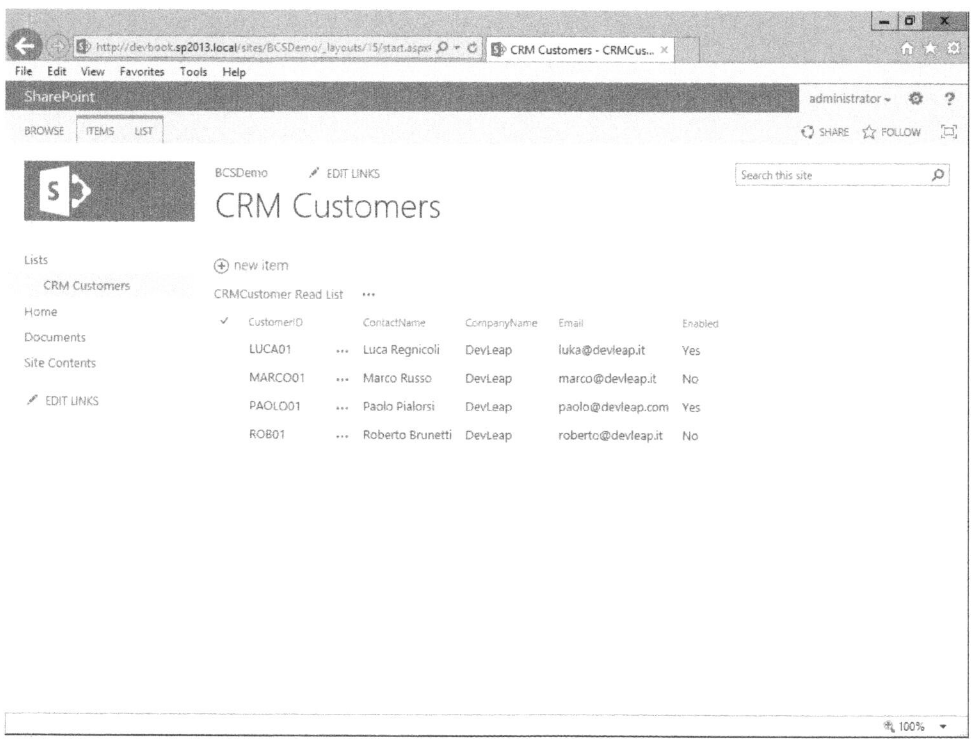

FIGURE 14-8 Browsing the Customers table through BCS in SharePoint 2013.

Note Depending on the authentication model you chose while creating the data source, you might receive an "Access denied by Business Data Connectivity" message. If you do, check the trace log of SharePoint, which by default is in the SharePoint15_Root\LOGS folder. You should find an exception with a *High* level of severity, a value of *Business Connectivity Services* in the *Area* field, and an error message stating that BCS received an Access Denied exception while trying to access SQL Server. In this case, you should give the proper permissions, from a SQL Server perspective, to the user who is trying to access the SQL Server database. With the default authentication configuration (Connect with User's Identity), the database connection will be opened, impersonating the user of the application pool, which by default in IIS 7.*x* and SharePoint 2013 is NT AUTHORITY\IUSR.

BDC authentication modes

The Business Data Connectivity engine provides several authentication modes through which you can access a target data source:

- **RevertToSelf** Disabled by default, this mode should be enabled at the service application level by a farm administrator. When configured, it allows for authenticating against the back-end data source using the application pool identity. You should never use this mode because it can make your environment unsafe. In SharePoint Designer 2013, it corresponds to BDC Identity mode.
- **PassThrough** Enabled by default, this mode applies impersonation and delegation of the current user's identity. If your web application uses Kerberos for authentication, the back-end data source will be accessed by the end user's identity, via delegation. If your web application uses NTLM, the back-end data source will be accessed by the application pool identity. In cases of security double-hop, which should be a common scenario in real farms, there will be authentication issues with NTLM, because of the lack of delegation capabilities. In SharePoint Designer 2013, it corresponds to the User's Identity mode.
- **WindowsCredentials** This mode uses the Secure Store service application for authenticating against the back-end data source using a set of Windows credentials. You'll learn more about how to configure this mode in the chapter. In SharePoint Designer 2013, it is the Impersonate Windows Identity mode.
- **RdbCredentials** This mode is almost the same as the WindowsCredentials mode. Although it still uses Secure Store service application, the credentials used to authenticate against the back-end data source are custom credentials instead of Windows ones. For example, the credentials can be SQL logins defined at the database level, in case of a SQL Server back-end data source. In SharePoint Designer 2013, it represents the Impersonate Custom Identity mode.

Figure 14-9 shows these modes presented by SharePoint Designer 2013 while a data source is being configured.

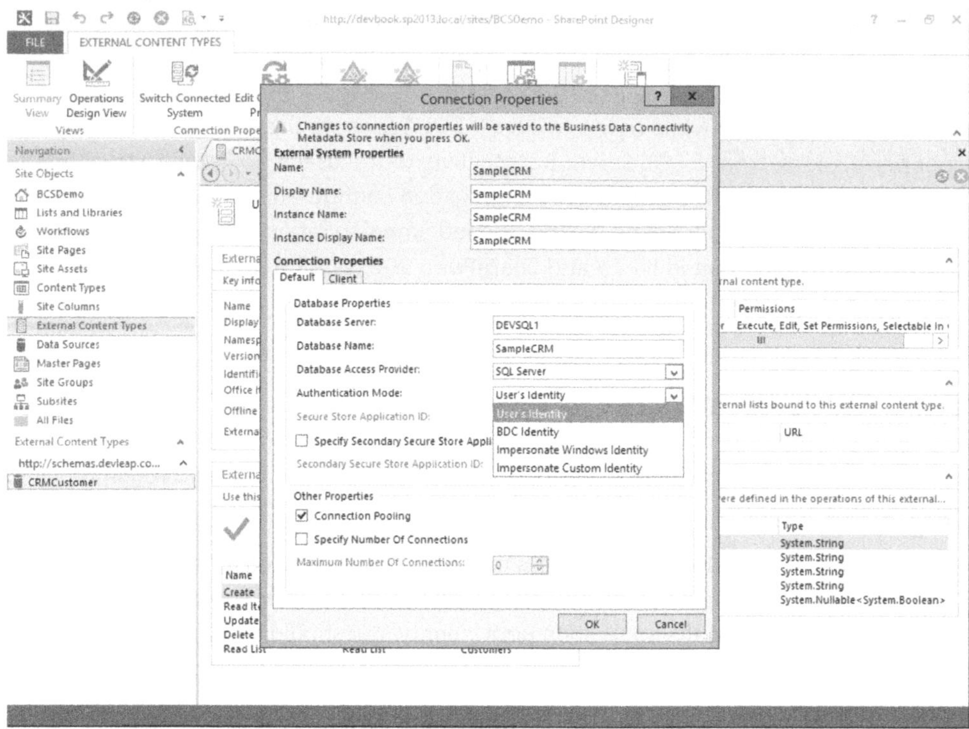

FIGURE 14-9 The connection properties of a BCS data source with the available authentication modes.

For the sake of clarity, consider an example of configuring a *WindowsCredentials* authentication mode. First, you will need to configure an application in the Secure Store Service administration page. Open SPCA, navigate to the Application Management section, and choose the Manage Service Application page. There, assuming you have already configured the BCS service and the Secure Store service, you have the opportunity to access the administration page of the Secure Store service. In case this is the first time you are using the Secure Store service, you will need to generate a new key for securely storing credentials. You can accomplish this task by clicking the Generate New Key ribbon button under the Key Management ribbon group. Providing a secure passphrase, you will be able to generate a new key. Then you can start creating a new application by clicking the New ribbon button in the Manage Target Application ribbon group. A wizard will ask you for some information about the target application. Figure 14-10 shows the first step of the wizard.

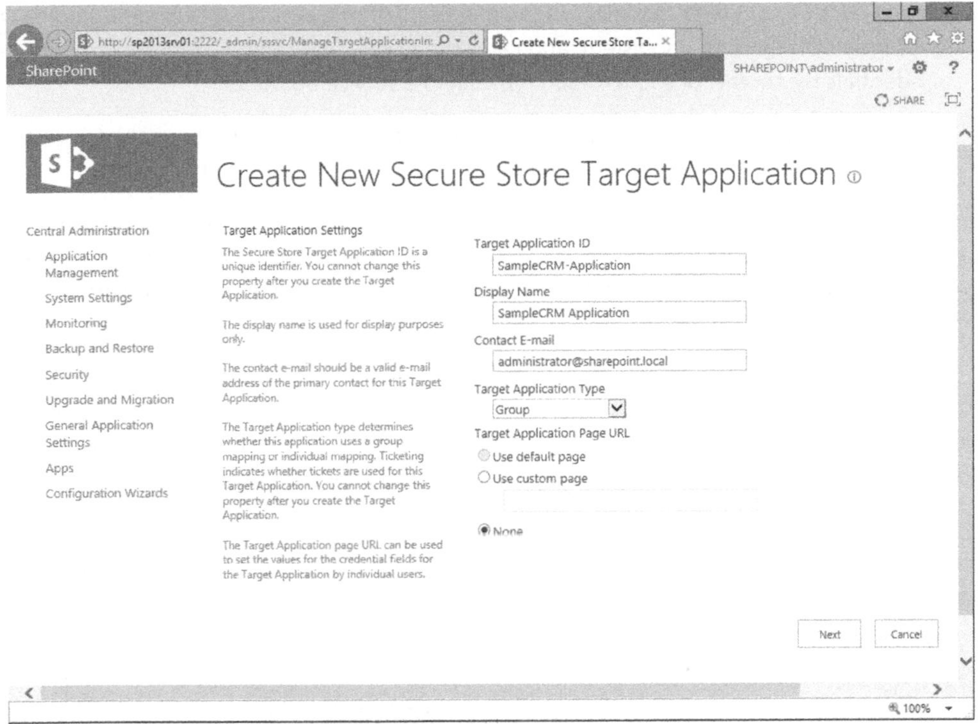

FIGURE 14-10 The first step of the Create New Secure Store Target Application wizard.

Through this first step, you can configure the target application ID, which is fundamental information that you will need to reference while configuring the BCS data source. Moreover, aside from some descriptive information, you will need to provide the target application type. The available values are:

- **Individual** Used for mapping each individual to a unique set of credentials on the external system
- **Individual Ticket** Used for mapping each individual to a unique set of credentials on the external system, and can issue tickets that can be redeemed later to get credentials by another account, which typically is a service account
- **Individual Restricted** Used for mapping individuals with restricted access to the calling context to a unique set of credentials on an external system
- **Group** Used for mapping all the members of one or more groups to a single set of credentials on the external system

- **Group Ticket** Used for mapping all the members of one or more groups to a single set of credentials on the external system, and can issue tickets that can be later redeemed to get credentials by another account, which typically is a service account
- **Group Restricted** Used for mapping members of one or more groups that have restricted access to the calling context to a single set of credentials on the external system

Suppose you want all the authenticated users to use a shared set of credentials for accessing the *SampleCRM* database. Thus, you should choose Group as the value for the target application type. Notice that you cannot change the target application type value after you have completed the configuration of a target application.

More Info For further details about configuring the Secure Store service, read the document "Configure the Secure Store Service in SharePoint 2013," which is available on TechNet, at *http://technet.microsoft.com/en-us/library/ee806866.aspx*.

After you configure these properties, click Next, and the wizard will prompt you with a screen like the one in Figure 14-11.

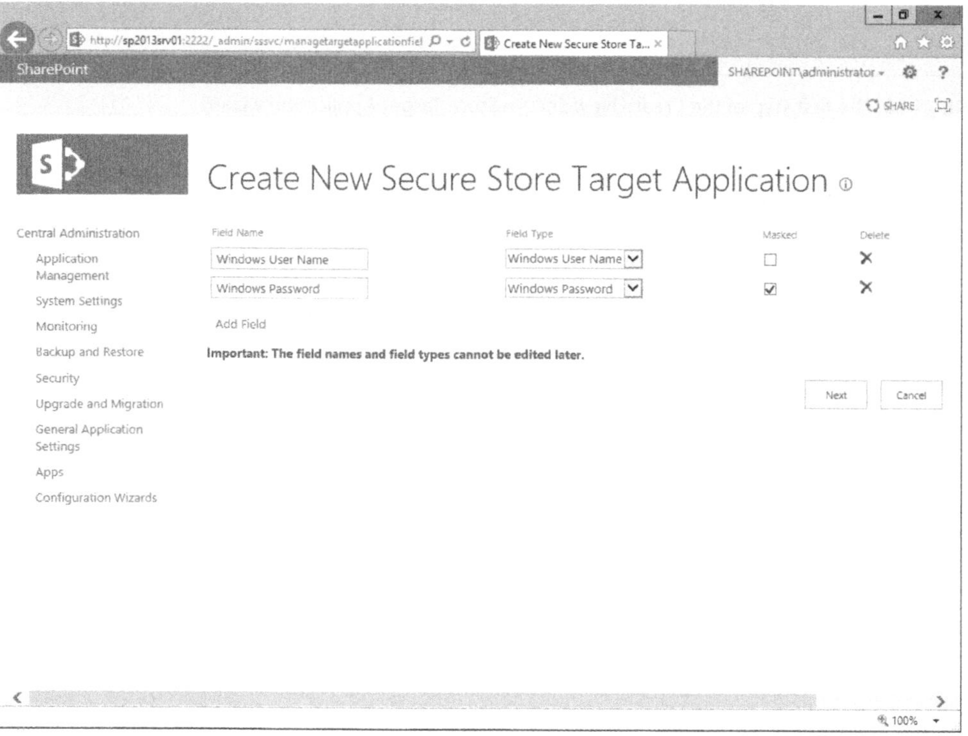

FIGURE 14-11 The second step of the Create New Secure Store Target Application wizard.

As you can see, the page allows for providing the fields describing the credentials that will be associated with each group of credentials. In the case of a set of Windows credentials, the fields will be Windows Username and Windows Password. The last step of the wizard, illustrated in Figure 14-12, asks for the administrators of the new target application, as well as for the users and groups that will be in target for the application.

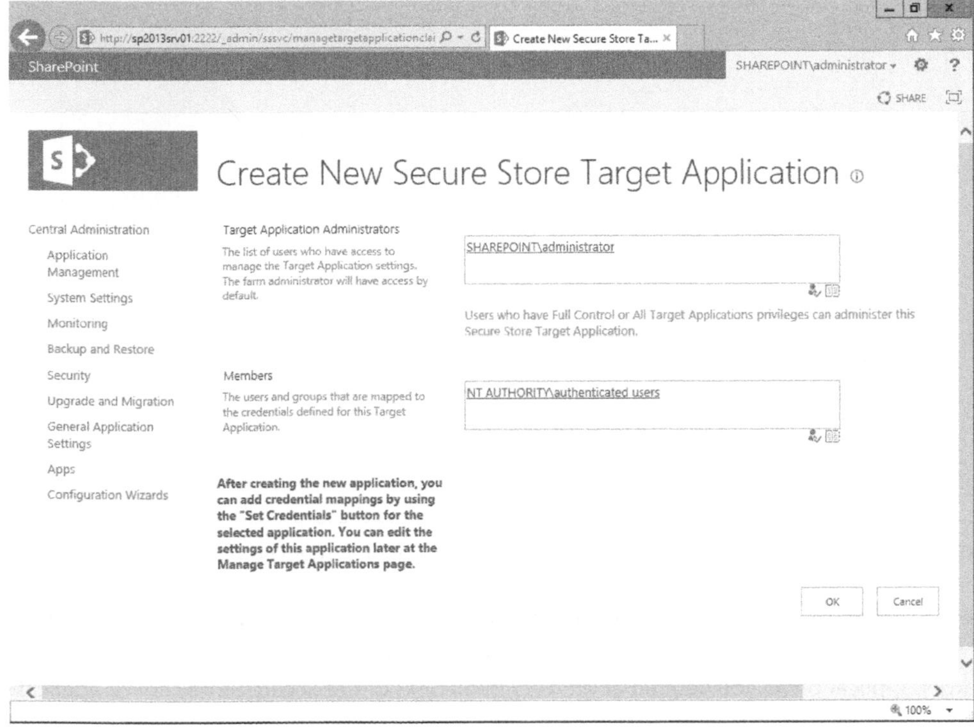

FIGURE 14-12 The last step of the Create New Secure Store Target Application wizard.

After you have created the target application, you need to configure a set of credentials for the target group. Click the Set ribbon button in the Credentials ribbon group after having selected the target application. Figure 14-13 shows the pop-up window for configuring the credentials.

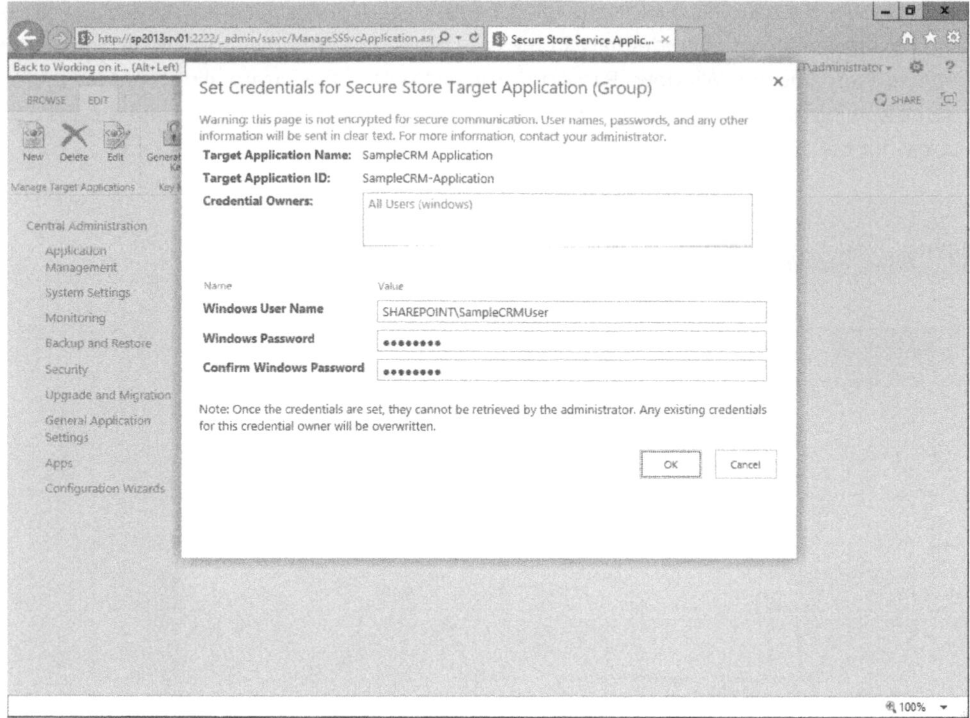

FIGURE 14-13 The Set Credentials For Secure Store Target Application (Group) pop-up window.

Now, in order to use the new Secure Store target application, you need to configure the data source in SharePoint Designer 2013. For example, select Impersonate Windows Identity and provide the target application ID you defined at the very beginning of the Secure Store service application.

BDC model file

You can export the ECT model created in the previous section by using SharePoint Designer 2013 or via the management page of the BCS service application. If you try to export the *Customer* ECT definition, an XML file with extension .bdcm (meaning *BDC model*) will be generated; it will look similar to Listing 14-1.

LISTING 14-1 The BDCM file that defines the *Customer* ECT retrieved from the *SampleCRM* database

```
<?xml version="1.0" encoding="utf-16" standalone="yes"?>
<Model xmlns:xsi="http://www.w3.org/2001/XMLSchema-instance"
xsi:schemaLocation="http://schemas.microsoft.com/windows/2007/BusinessDataCatalog
BDCMetadata.xsd" Name="CRMCustomer" xmlns="http://schemas.microsoft.com/
windows/2007/
BusinessDataCatalog">
  <AccessControlList>
    <AccessControlEntry Principal="sharepoint\administrator">
      <Right BdcRight="Execute" />
      <Right BdcRight="SetPermissions" />
      <Right BdcRight="SelectableInClients" />
    </AccessControlEntry>
  </AccessControlList>
  <LobSystems>
    <LobSystem Type="Database" Name="SampleCRM">
      <Properties>
        <Property Name="WildcardCharacter" Type="System.String">%</Property>
      </Properties>
      <AccessControlList>
        <!-- Code omitted for the sake of brevity -->
      </AccessControlList>
      <Proxy />
      <LobSystemInstances>
        <LobSystemInstance Name="SampleCRM">
          <Properties>
            <!-- Here is the database connection information -->
            <!-- Code omitted for the sake of brevity -->
          </Properties>
        </LobSystemInstance>
      </LobSystemInstances>
      <Entities>
        <Entity Namespace="http://schemas.devleap.com/SampleCRM"
        Version="1.0.0.0"
        EstimatedInstanceCount="10000" Name="CRMCustomer"
        DefaultDisplayName="CRMCustomer">
          <Properties>
            <Property Name="OutlookItemType"
            Type="System.String">Contact</Property>
          </Properties>
          <AccessControlList>
            <!-- Code omitted for the sake of brevity -->
          </AccessControlList>
          <Identifiers>
            <Identifier TypeName="System.String" Name="CustomerID" />
          </Identifiers>
          <Methods>
            <Method Name="Create" DefaultDisplayName="CRMCustomer Create">
              <Properties>
                <Property Name="RdbCommandType" Type="System.Data.CommandType,
                System.Data, Version=4.0.0.0, Culture=neutral,
                PublicKeyToken=b77a5c561934e089">Text</Property>
```

```
                <Property Name="RdbCommandText" Type="System.String">INSERT
INTO[dbo].[Customers]([CustomerID] , [ContactName] , [CompanyName] , [Email] ,
[Enabled])VALUES(@CustomerID , @ContactName , @CompanyName , @Email , @Enabled)
SELECT[CustomerID] FROM [dbo].[Customers] WHERE [CustomerID] = @CustomerID</
Property>
                <Property Name="BackEndObjectType"
                Type="System.String">SqlServerTable</Property>
                <Property Name="BackEndObject"
                  Type="System.String">Customers</Property>
                <Property Name="Schema" Type="System.String">dbo</Property>
              </Properties>
              <AccessControlList>
                <!-- Code omitted for the sake of brevity -->
              </AccessControlList>
              <Parameters>
                <Parameter Direction="In" Name="@CustomerID">
                  <TypeDescriptor TypeName="System.String" CreatorField="true"
                  IdentifierName="CustomerID" Name="CustomerID">
                    <Properties>
                      <Property Name="Size" Type="System.Int32">10</Property>
                    </Properties>
                    <Interpretation>
                      <NormalizeString FromLOB="NormalizeToNull"
                      ToLOB="NormalizeToEmptyString" />
                    </Interpretation>
                  </TypeDescriptor>
                </Parameter>
                <!-- Code omitted for the sake of brevity -->
              </Parameters>
              <MethodInstances>
                <MethodInstance Type="Creator" ReturnParameterName="Create"
                  ReturnTypeDescriptorPath="Create[0]" Default="true"
                  Name="Create" DefaultDisplayName="CRMCustomer Create">
                    <AccessControlList>
                      <!-- Code omitted for the sake of brevity -->
                    </AccessControlList>
                </MethodInstance>
              </MethodInstances>
            </Method>
            <!-- Code omitted for the sake of brevity -->
          </Methods>
        </Entity>
      </Entities>
    </LobSystem>
  </LobSystems>
</Model>
```

The main element of a BDCM file is the *Model* tag. This is the root element of the document, and it wraps an entire BDC model definition. *Model* has a dedicated *AccessControlList* element, and it defines one or more *LobSystem* definitions. A *LobSystem* element defines from an abstract viewpoint an external data source. A concrete data source is represented by a *LobSystemInstance* element, instead. Each ECT in a *LobSystem* is described by an *Entity* element, which declares a new ECT, together with its *Identifiers* and *Methods* elements. A single model in general defines a set of entities. Meanwhile, the *Method* elements are defined using single *Method* elements and are instantiated using elements of type *MethodInstance*. Each *MethodInstance* features a *Type* attribute, which defines the typology of method instance. Table 14-1 lists the available values for the *MethodInstance/@Type* attribute.

TABLE 14-1 The available values for the *MethodInstance/@Type* attribute

Type	Description
AccessChecker	Checks the permissions for the calling security principal related to a collection of entities.
AssociationNavigator	Retrieves a list of associated (related) entities from a single entity.
Associator	Associates an entity instance with another.
BinarySecurityDescriptorAccessor	Retrieves a list of bytes defining the permissions for a set of security principals, related to a specific entity instance.
BulkAssociatedIdEnumerator	Retrieves IDs of entities associated with another.
BulkAssociationNavigator	Retrieves destination entities that are associated with multiple specified entities.
BulkIdEnumerator	Supports the search engine of SharePoint during incremental updates. *BulkIdEnumerator* returns some version information for entities whose IDs are provided to the method.
BulkSpecificFinder	Retrieves a set of entities given a set of IDs.
ChangedIdEnumerator	Supports the search engine of SharePoint during incremental updates. *ChangedIdEnumerator* returns IDs of entities that were modified since a specified date/time.
Creator	Creates a new instance of an entity.
DeletedIdEnumerator	Supports the search engine of SharePoint during incremental updates. *DeletedIdEnumerator* returns IDs of entities that were deleted since a specified date/time.
Deleter	Deletes an entity instance.
Disassociator	Removes an association between an entity instance and another one.
Finder	Retrieves a list of entity instances, based on a set of filtering conditions that can be declared within the *Method* definition.
GenericInvoker	Invokes a specific method or task in the target system.
IdEnumerator	Supports the search engine. *IdEnumerator* retrieves the field values for the identifier fields of a list of entities.
Scalar	Returns a single scalar value from the external system.
SpecificFinder	Retrieves a specific instance of an entity, based on its corresponding identifier.
StreamAccessor	Returns a single stream of bytes from a specific entity instance. *StreamAccessor* can be used to retrieve images, videos, attachments, and so on that are related to a specific entity instance.
Updater	Updates an entity instance.

When you define a BDC model, regardless of the data provider you use on the back end, you end up defining a file such as the one shown in Listing 14-1 and using methods like the ones illustrated here. SharePoint Designer 2013 and Visual Studio 2012 support just the most frequently used method instance types, while the others should be defined manually in the BDCM file using an XML editor.

Offline capabilities

If you have SharePoint Server 2013, you can experience the offline capabilities offered by BCS. Browse to and select an external list, such as the one you created in the previous section. To connect your list to Outlook 2013 and make it available offline, on the ribbon, click Connect To Outlook (see Figure 14-14).

Note If you do not have the Connect To Outlook ribbon command available on the ribbon bar, please ensure that the site feature named Offline Synchronization For External Lists is activated and try again.

The Outlook offline capability is available because you defined the ECT with an Office Contact behavior. A temporary window appears, displaying the message "Preparing External List For Synchronization With Outlook."

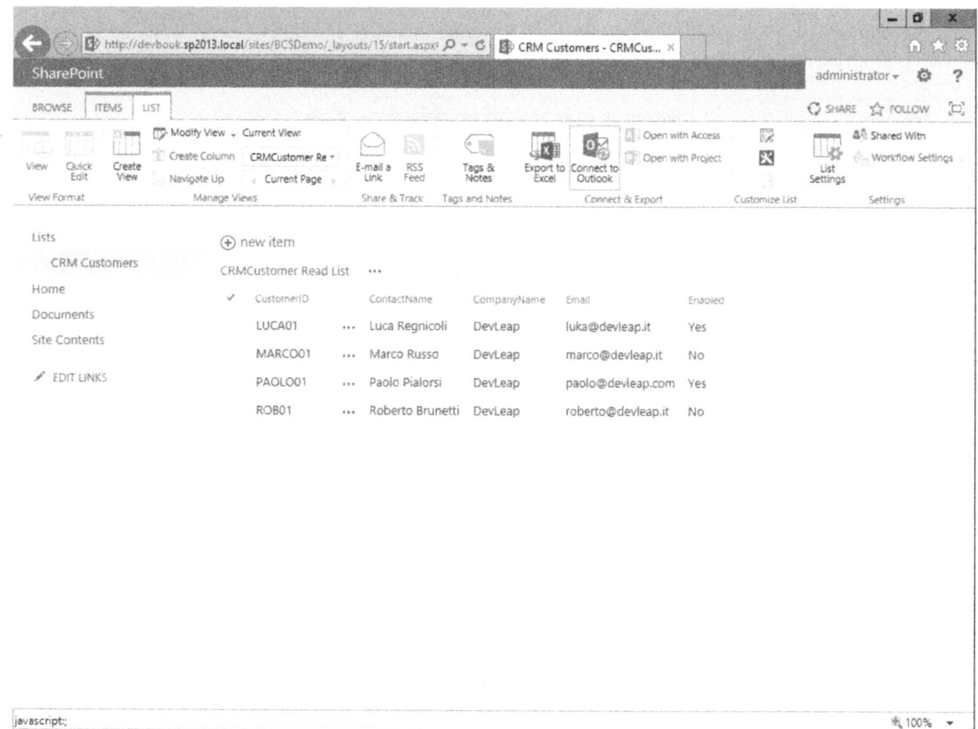

FIGURE 14-14 The ribbon of an external list with the Connect To Outlook command highlighted.

Next, an installer dialog window appears (Figure 14-15), asking the end user for permission to install the BDC Client Runtime on the client side (if it is not already installed) and to install the model schema for the entity that you are connecting with Outlook.

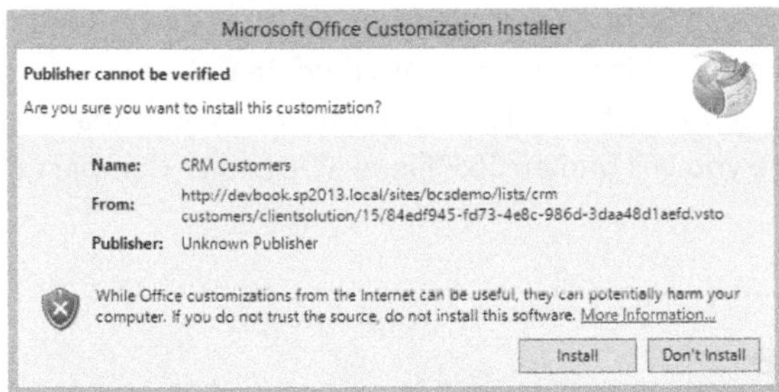

FIGURE 14-15 The pop-up dialog box that appears when installing the client model and consuming the ECT.

Click the Install button if the displayed information is acceptable; click Don't Install if it's not.

Figure 14-16 shows the final output of the offline list in Outlook 2013.

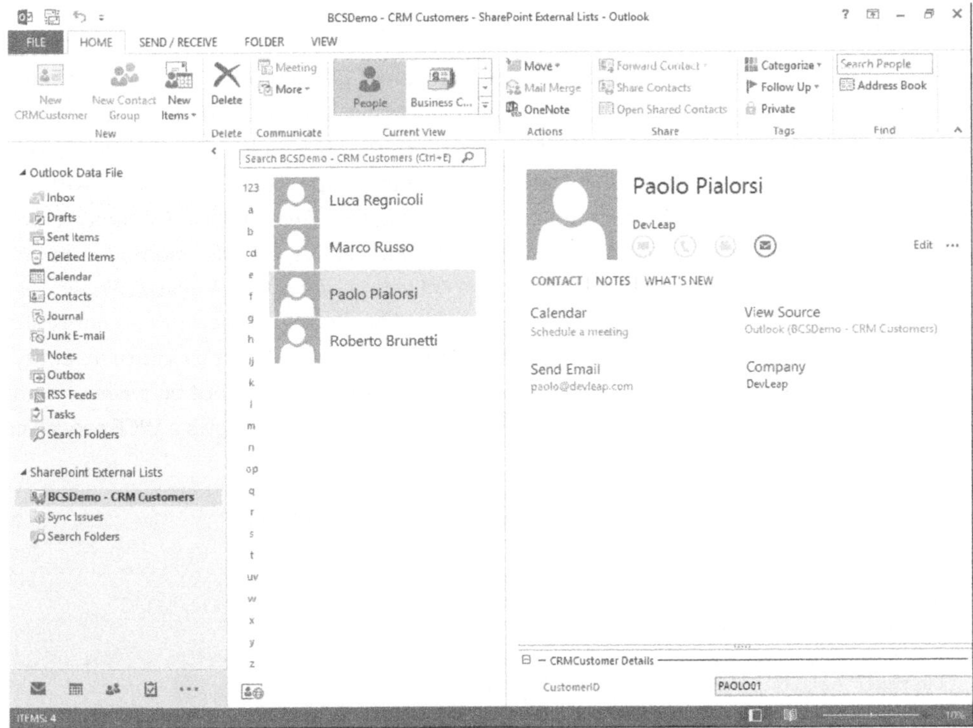

FIGURE 14-16 The list of contacts available in Outlook 2013 and corresponding to the list of customers.

Now you can browse and edit data either from SharePoint 2013 within the web browser or using Outlook 2013, or you can manage data directly in the database storage. Regardless of the interface you use for managing data, all your modifications will be sooner (online) or later (offline) synchronized with the back-end database.

As soon as you connect the list to the Microsoft Office client platform, the BDC Client Runtime creates a folder under the local user's profile path (which, for example, could be C:\Users*Your UserName*\AppData\Local\Microsoft\BCS), where the offline data is stored. Notice that the folder is green, meaning it is encrypted. There you will find an SDF file of SQL Server Compact Edition, as well as a PST offline cache file.

Accessing a WCF/SOAP service

Using the standard SharePoint 2013 UI for accessing data stored in a DBMS with CRUDQ support is undoubtedly interesting and challenging. For security and privacy reasons, however, many companies prefer to lock and secure their databases, preventing direct data access from clients or even servers. In these situations, articulated business solutions built on top of the database provide access to data filtered by business rules and security policies. Quite often, the business rules are exposed or published through SOAP services, eventually implemented using WCF.

The BCS support for connecting with SOAP services over HTTP (web services), optionally implemented with WCF, can also make these kinds of applications available in SharePoint. BCS can consume any SOAP service that offers the minimum set of operations that is mandatory for the WCF/web service connector of BCS. For a minimal implementation that is capable of reading data with a read-only approach, you need one SOAP operation corresponding to a *Finder* method instance type and another supporting the *SpecificFinder* type. From a SOAP perspective, a *Finder* method is an operation that optionally accepts some filters and returns a collection of entities. A *SpecificFinder* operation accepts an identifier and returns the corresponding entity. Specifically, every returned entity should have an identifying property, and the result of a *SpecificFinder* operation has to return an entity with at least the same properties as the result of the *Finder* operation. There cannot be a *Finder* method that returns more information than a *SpecificFinder* method. Listing 14-2 shows a WCF service contract satisfying these requirements.

LISTING 14-2 A WCF service contract satisfying the read-only requirements for WCF

```
[ServiceContract(Namespace = "http://schemas.devleap.com/CustomerService")]
public interface ICustomerService {
    [OperationContract]
    Customer GetCustomerById(String customerID);

    [OperationContract]
    Customers ListAllCustomers();
}
```

```
[DataContract(Name = "Customer", Namespace = "http://schemas.devleap.com/
Customers")]
public class Customer {
    [DataMember(Name = "CustomerID", Order = 1)]
    public String CustomerID { get; set; }

    [DataMember(Name = "ContactName", Order = 1)]
    public String ContactName { get; set; }

    [DataMember(Name = "CompanyName", Order = 1)]
    public String CompanyName { get; set; }

    [DataMember(Name = "Country", Order = 1)]
    public String Country { get; set; }
}

[CollectionDataContract(ItemName = "Customer", Name = "Customers", Namespace =
"http://schemas.devleap.com/Customers")]
public class Customers : List<Customer> {
    public Customers() : base() { }
    public Customers(IEnumerable<Customer> collection) : base(collection) { }
}
```

The sample contract uses a *Customer* entity and a *Customers* list of entities. These types are marked as serializable with the *DataContract* serialization engine used by WCF. The service contract publishes only two operations: *GetCustomerById* and *ListAllCustomers*. The former accepts the *customerID* (the identifier parameter) and returns a single *Customer* entity. The latter, for the sake of simplicity, does not expect any argument and returns a list of *Customer* instances.

If you would like to support a full CRUDQ scenario, you need to publish three more operations for the corresponding method types (*Creator, Updater, Deleter*). The *Creator* operation should accept the entity to create as input, and it should return the identifier of the created entity or the whole created entity. The *Updater* operation should accept the entity and, above all, its identifier. It is not required to return anything back to the caller, but it is not forbidden. The *Deleter* operation should accept the identifier of the entity to delete. A response is not required. Listing 14-3 demonstrates an extended WCF contract supporting the CRUDQ scenario.

LISTING 14-3 A WCF service contract satisfying the CRUDQ requirements for WCF

```
[ServiceContract(Namespace = "http://schemas.devleap.com/CustomerService")]
public interface ICustomerService {
    [OperationContract]
    Customer GetCustomerById(String customerID);

    [OperationContract]
    Customers ListAllCustomers();

    [OperationContract]
    Customer AddCustomer(Customer item);

    [OperationContract]
    Customer UpdateCustomer(Customer item);

    [OperationContract]
    Boolean DeleteCustomer(Customer item);
}
```

The internal code of a service that implements such a contract is trivial, and it will not be covered in this chapter. You will find a full sample implementation, however, in the code samples.

After you define a service contract and service implementation that adhere to the communication requirements, as well as publish the service through a dedicated endpoint, you can register a new ECT corresponding to the entity published by the service. The best tool for accomplishing this task is still SharePoint Designer 2013. The first part of the registration task is exactly the same as registering an external database. In the Data Source Explorer window, however, while adding a new connection for the external system behind the ECT, you need to select a new WCF Service data source type for the external data source. Figure 14-17 shows the WCF Connection dialog box for configuring a data source of type WCF Service.

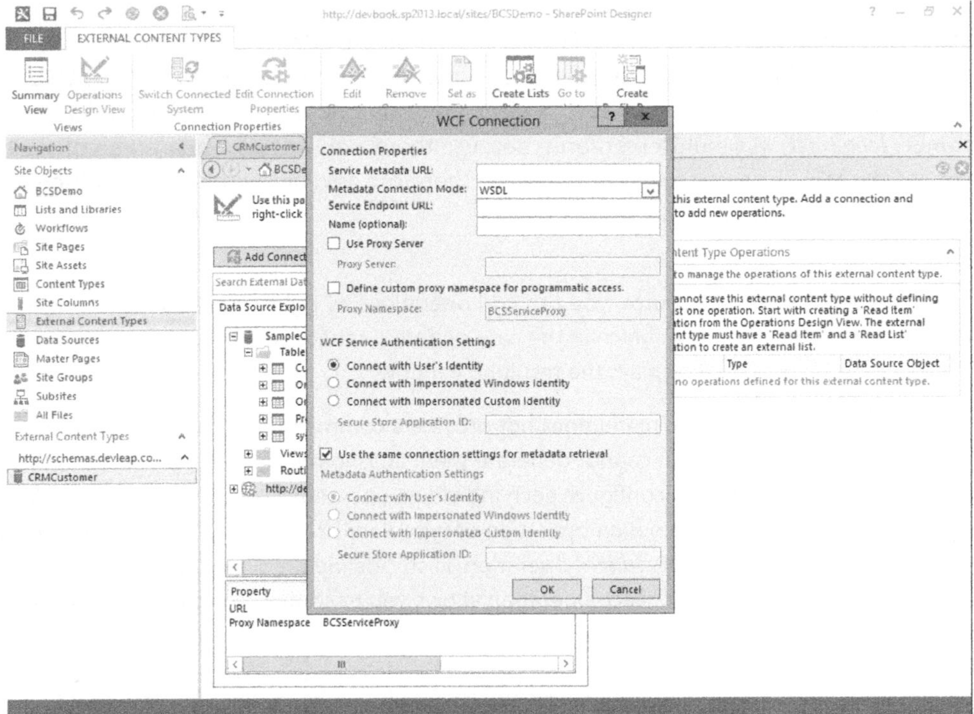

FIGURE 14-17 The WCF Connection dialog box for registering a WCF Service external data source.

The configuration information is as follows:

- **Service Metadata URL** This is the URL of the endpoint publishing the service's metadata.
- **Metadata Connection Mode** This is the type of metadata published by the service. The available values are WSDL and MetadataExchange (WS-MetadataExchange).
- **Service Endpoint URL** This is the URL of the endpoint publishing the service.
- **Name** This is an optional name for the service.
- **Use Proxy Server** This specifies an HTTP proxy to use for contacting the service endpoint.
- **Define Custom Proxy Namespace For Programmatic Access** This specifies a namespace for the autogenerated proxy code, in order to access the service proxy by custom code.
- **WCF Service Authentication Settings** This specifies the authentication technique to use while communicating with the external service.
- **Metadata Authentication Settings** This defines a specific authentication mode for retrieving the service metadata. This setting is optional.

After you register the external data source, you must define all the operations that you would like to support.

> **Note** While defining a WCF Service data source, if you provide a service or metadata address published by *localhost*, you will receive the following error message: "The URL should not loop back to the local host." In fact, you cannot use a loopback URL (for instance, *localhost*) in a multiserver farm, because there wouldn't be a guarantee of availability of the URL for every server of the farm. Therefore, you always need to publish services through qualified host names.

As with the SQL Server data source, you can add operations by right-clicking a SOAP operation in the Data Source Explorer window, which in the case of a WCF service will show you all the available SOAP operations. Figure 14-18 displays the resulting window.

Notice in Figure 14-18 that the menu does not provide a command for configuring all the operations in one shot. This is because it cannot generate them autonomously by simply reading the service metadata, so you need to configure each individual operation step by step. You should start by creating a *Finder* method, which is an operation of type *ReadList* . Then define a *SpecificFinder* method, which corresponds to a *ReadItem* operation. Lastly, define the *Create*, *Update*, and *Delete* operations, in case they're needed. Each operation allows you to configure the input and output arguments via a wizard interface.

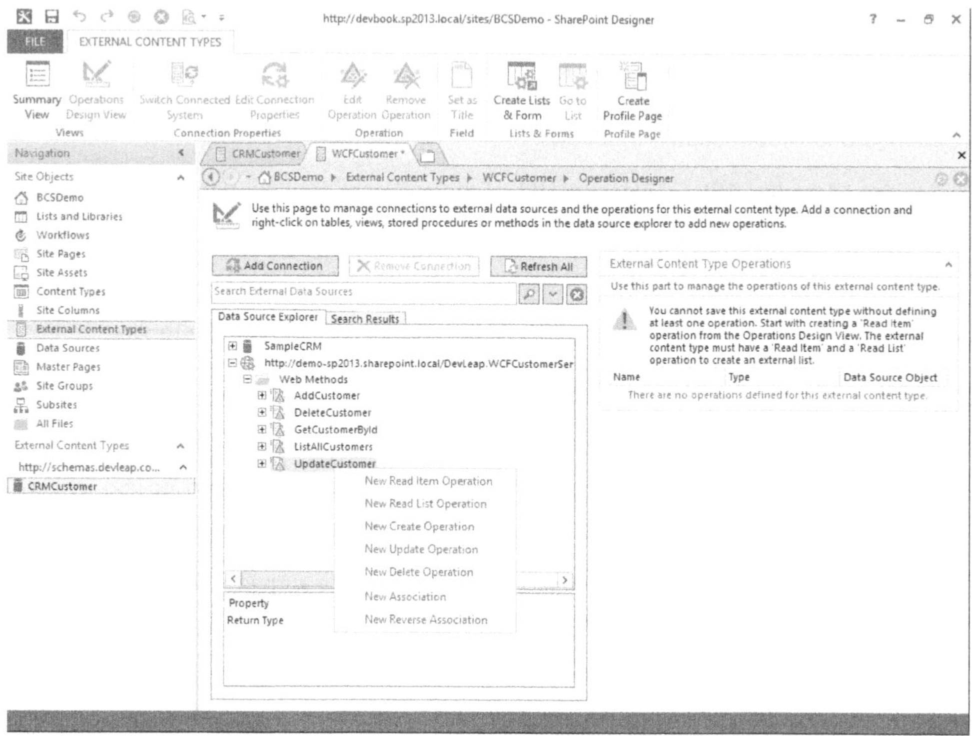

FIGURE 14-18 The Data Source Explorer window for the sample WCF Service data source.

During definition of the operation of type *ReadList*, you need to define the entity identifier in the Return Parameter Configuration wizard step. You should also define a field to show in the entity picker. For the purposes of the current example, you should define the *CustomerID* property of each *Customer* entity as the identifier field, and the *ContactName* property as the field to show in the picker. Figure 14-19 shows this wizard step.

Furthermore, when defining the operation of type *ReadItem*, you have to map the identifier property to the corresponding argument of the *SpecificFinder* method in the Input Parameters Configuration wizard step. Then, in the Output Parameters Configuration step, you must define the entity identifier in the output message, and any property mapping to the corresponding Office property, if you defined the ECT as an Office item type.

The same considerations about the entity identifier are valid for the operations of type *Create*, *Update*, and *Delete*.

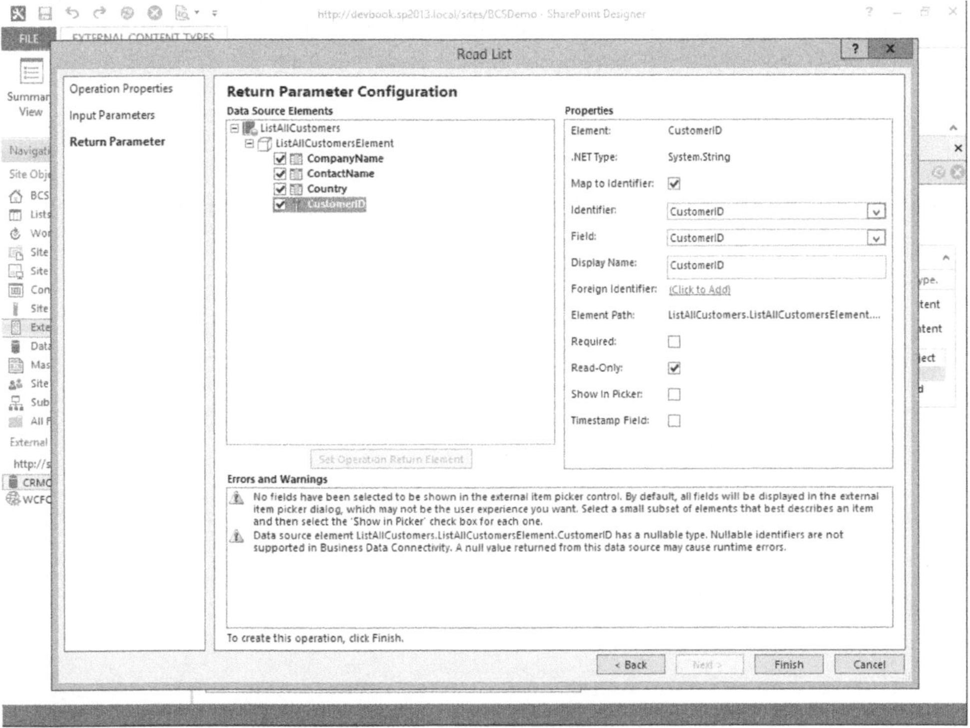

FIGURE 14-19 The Return Parameter Configuration wizard step that defines the *ReadList* operation.

When you finish configuring the ECT, save it, and then you can use it in external lists and Office clients, too.

Consuming OData services

One new capability of the BCS services introduced with SharePoint 2013 is support for OData services. OData stands for Open Data Protocol (see *http://www.odata.org*) and is an emerging technology for providing interoperable data-publishing services. A key feature of OData is that it is a web protocol for querying and updating data. Thus, you can use it to consume a complete CRUDQ experience. The data provided by an OData service can be published as an ATOM (XML) feed or using a JSON serialization format, both using the HTTP transport protocol.

To consume an OData service via BCS, you need to create a SharePoint 2013 app using Visual Studio 2012. In Chapter 8, "SharePoint apps," you learned how to create an app. For the sake of brevity, imagine here creating a SharePoint-hosted app for consuming a publicly available OData service like the one offered by Netflix (see *http://developer.netflix.com/docs/OData_Catalog*).

To consume an OData service, you simply need to add to the app a specific project item. In Figure 14-20, you can see that you need to right-click the SharePoint 2013 app project, select Add from the menu that appears, and then choose Content Types For An External Data Source.

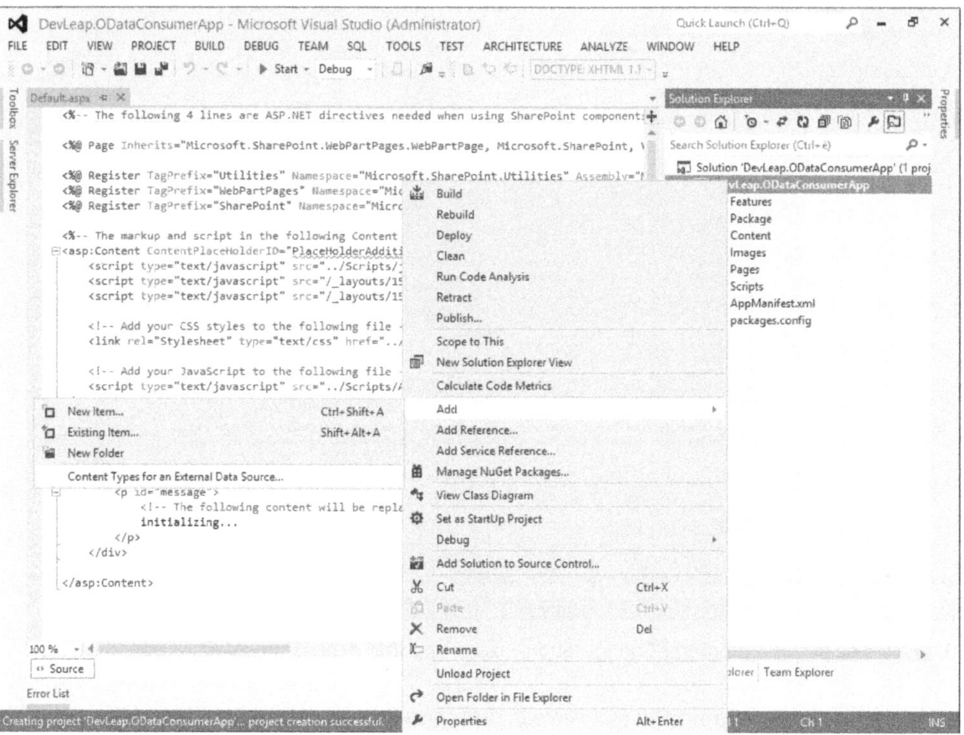

FIGURE 14-20 The Add | Content Types For An External Data Source menu item.

You will be prompted with a very brief wizard for providing the URL of the external OData service, which in the case of Netflix is *http://odata.netflix.com/Catalog/*, and the name to give to the data source. Figure 14-21 illustrates how this wizard step is made.

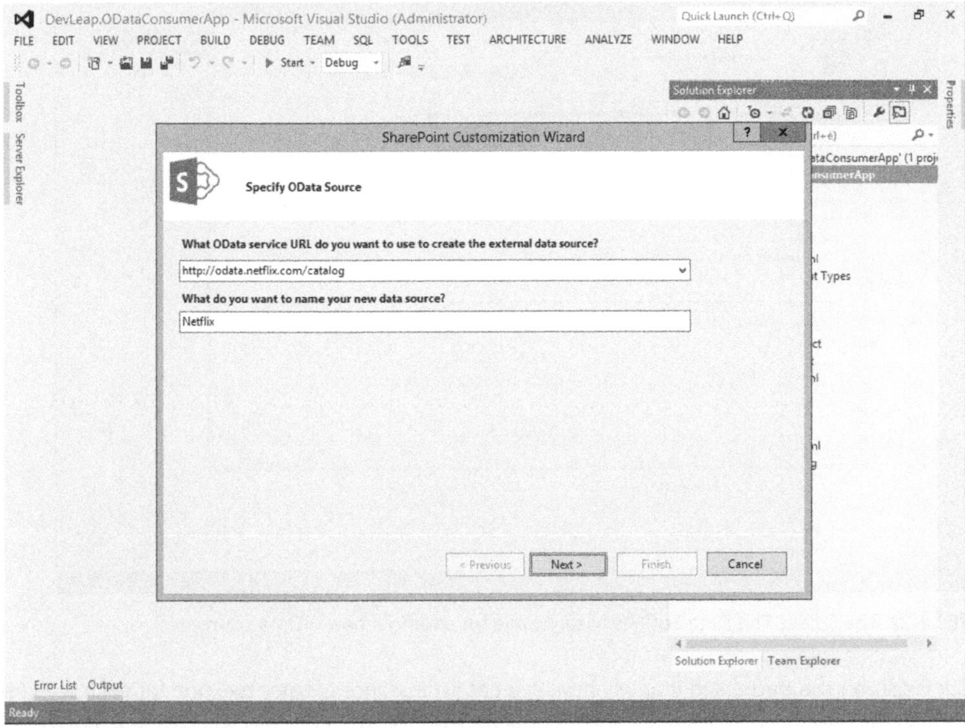

FIGURE 14-21 The Specify OData Source wizard page for adding a new OData source.

The next step is to choose the data lists to consume. Figure 14-22 shows how this last wizard step behaves. Notice that you can explicitly select the data lists you want to consume, and you can choose to automatically create external lists instances for every consumed data list in the target SharePoint app site.

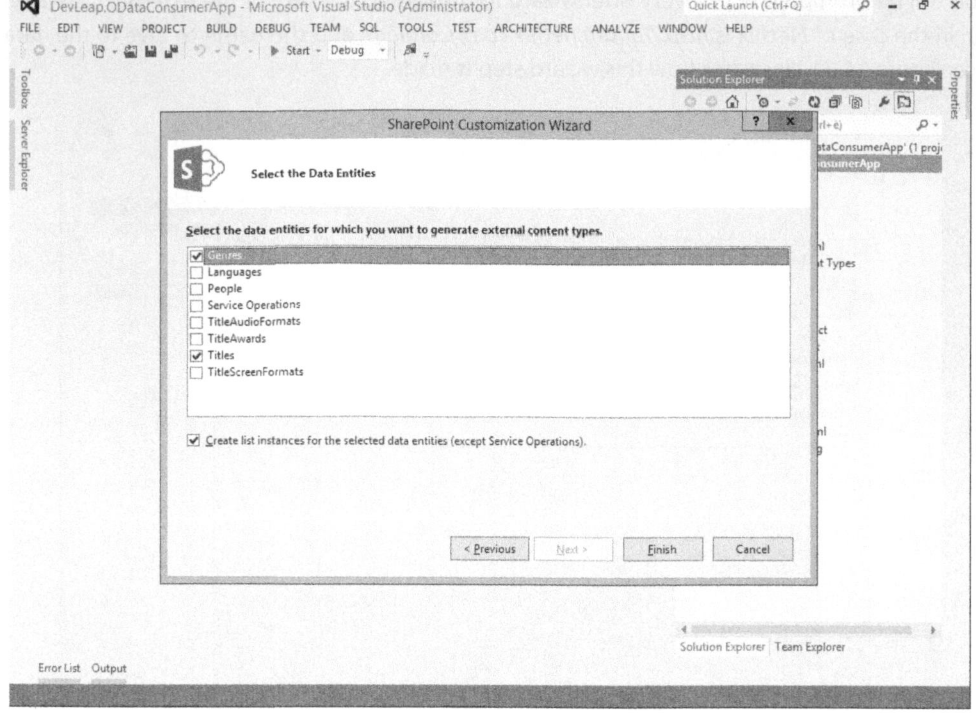

FIGURE 14-22 The Select The Data Entities wizard page for adding a new OData source.

Click Finish on the page, and you will have a set of list instance elements—one for each selected data entity—as well as an ECT file for every single data entity. The ECT files will define a model for each entity. Figure 14-23 displays the project outline, indicating the OData entities that have been created.

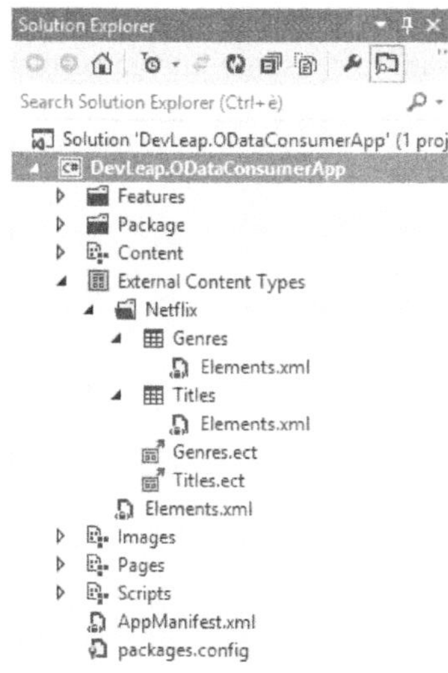

FIGURE 14-23 The outline of the SharePoint 2013 app after adding the ECTs from an OData service.

If you deploy the app or start debugging it, you will see that the target app's web will contain the external lists you defined. To check this result, you can simply navigate with your favorite browser to the corresponding URL. For example, to check the existence of the external list of titles consumed from Netflix, navigate to the URL *{app web URL}/Lists/Titles*. Figure 14-24 shows the results.

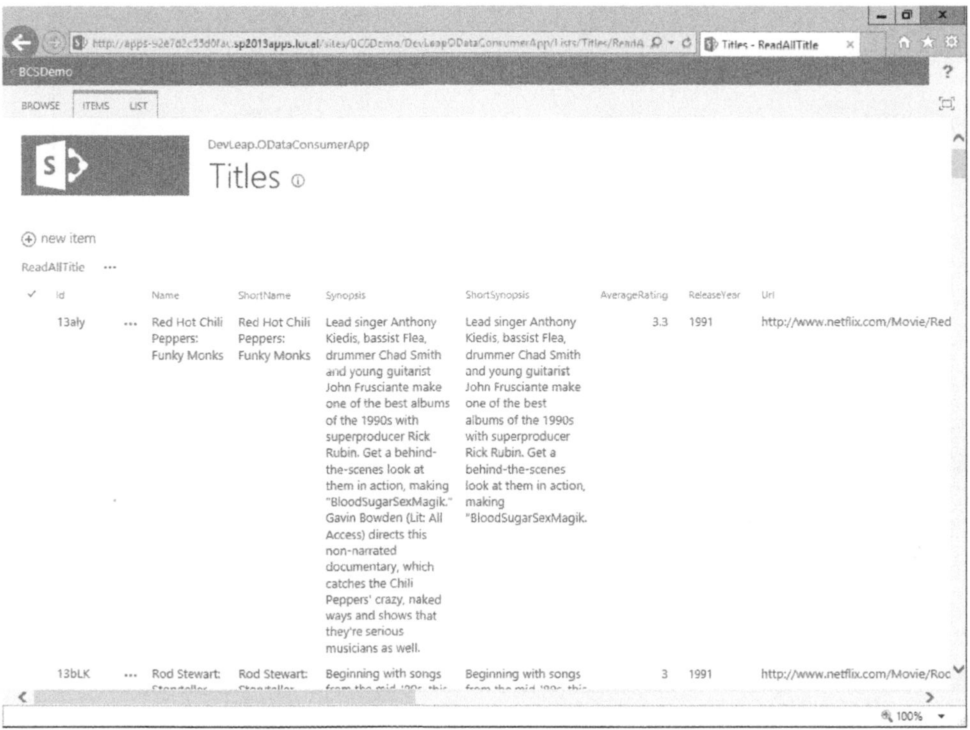

FIGURE 14-24 The list of titles from Netflix using the OData service connector for BCS.

.NET custom model

Another opportunity you have while defining BCS solutions is to develop a custom model in Visual Studio 2012. This capability is useful whenever you need to consume, and in particular index and search with the search engine, a third-party data source that is not directly accessible through a database connection or by using a web service. It is also useful when you need to use an intermediary proxy to aggregate data that will eventually be provided by non-homogeneous sources. A custom model is a .NET assembly compiled in Visual Studio 2012 and built starting from a Visual Studio template project of type SharePoint 2013 - Empty Project. This project type is by necessity a full-trust, farm-level solution that deploys its assembly into the Global Assembly Cache (GAC). Thus, you cannot use it in Office 365. In fact, the custom model is accessible from any web application and can be shared across the farm. Inside the .NET assembly, you can write any code you like, and you can use any kind of library, service, or data provider in order to read the target data source. From a BCS viewpoint, you define a BDCM file within Visual Studio 2012, and you model a set of entities that will correspond to the ECT that you want to design. Visual Studio 2012 provides the BCS Model Designer and a BDC Explorer window to support model definition. Figure 14-25 illustrates the model designer, together with the BDC Explorer toolbox.

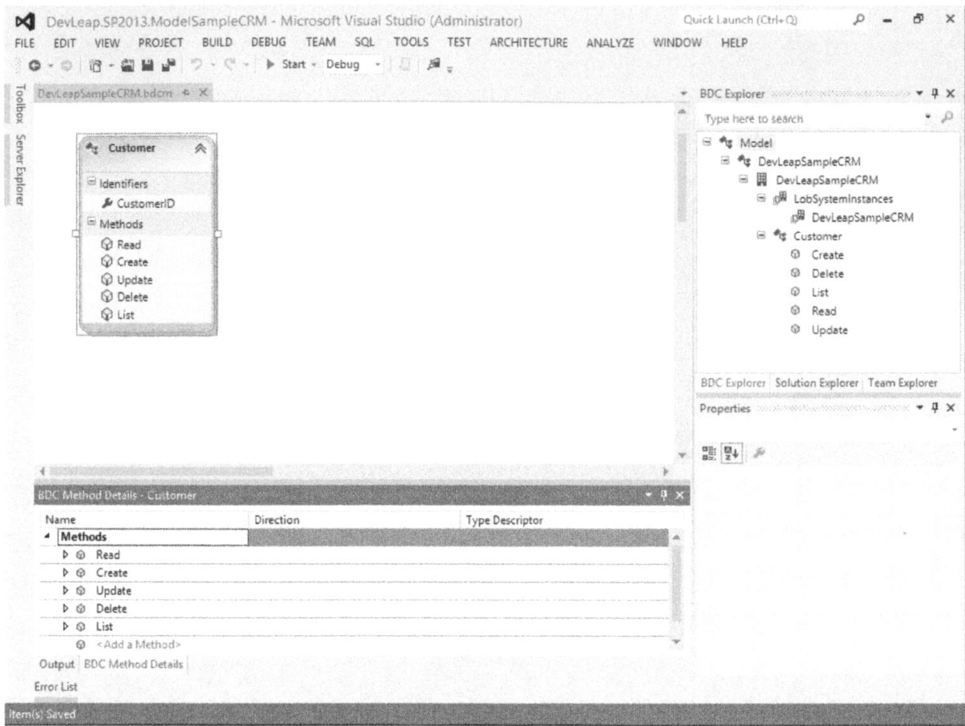

FIGURE 14-25 The BCS Model Designer available in Microsoft Visual Studio 2012.

The main goal of the model designer is to allow you to design entities and relationships (called *associations* in BCS) between entities. Each individual entity is made up of one or more identifier properties and some methods. The methods are defined and configured in terms of parameters, method instances, and filter descriptors using the BDC Method Details window. With the BDC Explorer, you can inspect the model by using the classic tree-view approach. The result of modeling is a BDCM file that you can manually import into SharePoint 2013. To do so, first deploy the corresponding assembly DLL into the GAC, and then use the BCS service application page in SPCA. Alternatively, you can take advantage of the automatic deployment provided by Visual Studio 2012, which uses a feature receiver (defined in class *ImportModelReceiver* of namespace *Microsoft.Office.SharePoint.ClientExtensions.Deployment*) for importing the file into the metadata catalog of BCS.

When you design a model in the graphical designer, Visual Studio 2012 automatically creates a code file called *{Entity}Service.cs* for each entity, where *{Entity}* corresponds to the name of the entity handled by that class file. Within that file, Visual Studio 2012 will place static methods corresponding to the method instances declared in the designer. In addition, you can use the designer to define the method instances and parameters for each designed method, as well as the data types of input, output, and return parameters.

To master the model design process, you should first define classes corresponding to all of the entities that you want to make available through the model. Then you should design the entities in the model designer and configure the methods that you want to make available. Remember that at the very least, you should define both a *Finder* and a *SpecificFinder* method. If you want to provide *Creator*, *Updater*, and *Deleter* methods, you can design them, too. In the accompanying code sample for this chapter, you will find a complete solution, which will be discussed in the next section.

Developing a custom model from scratch

In this section, you will use a step-by-step approach to learn how to design a simple model that publishes a list of customers read from the *SampleCRM* database (introduced previously in the "Accessing a database" section). In this example, however, you will read the customers using LINQ to Entities.

More Info LINQ to Entities is a topic that will not be covered in this book. If you would like to understand how it works, read the book *Programming LINQ in .NET Framework 4*, by Paolo Pialorsi and Marco Russo (Microsoft Press, 2010).

First, create a new SharePoint 2013 project of type SharePoint 2013 - Empty Project. Then add an item of type BCS Model (for example, name it *SampleCRMModel*). A window will appear with a preconfigured model designer, describing a *SampleCRMModel* model with a hypothetical *Entity1* item, together with both *Entity1.cs* and *Entity1Service.cs* classes. Remove the *Entity1* item from the model, as well as the related CS files.

Add an Entity Framework 5.0 model to the project (click Add | New Item | ADO.NET Entity Data Model) and define a link to the table of customers defined in the target *SampleCRM* SQL Server database. To make the Entity Framework 5.0 model work inside SharePoint, you need to change the web.config file of the target web application, deploy the EntityFramework.dll assembly into the BIN folder of the web application, and create the connection string for the external data source by code. This chapter will not cover details about how to manage these tasks, which are related to Entity Framework 5.0. Nevertheless, in the companion code samples, you will find all the code for consuming an external SQL Server database via Entity Framework 5.0 within a SharePoint 2013 site.

Next, add a new entity to the BCS model, giving it a name of *Customer*. The designer will generate a CustomerService.cs file for you. Add a new identifier for the *Customer* entity and name it *CustomerID*.

Now you need to configure at least two methods (see Figure 14-26). The *ReadList* method will correspond to a *Finder* method, while the *ReadItem* method will correspond to a *SpecificFinder method*. To add these methods, simply go to the BDC Method Details panel and select the option Add A Method, as well as the appropriate method type.

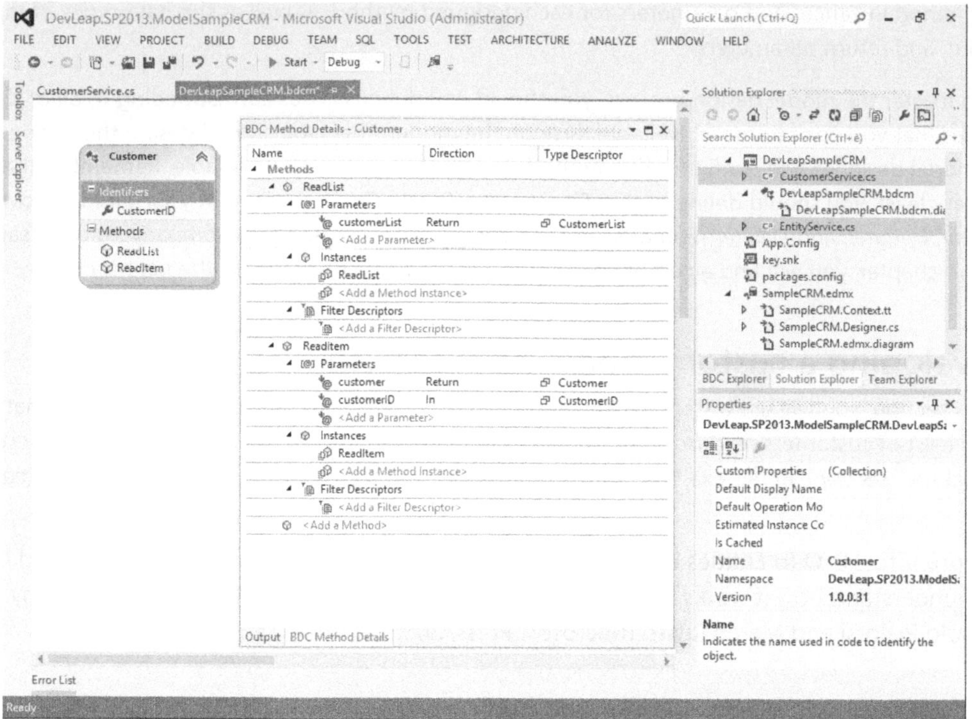

FIGURE 14-26 The BCS Model Designer showing the *Customer* ECT with its identifier and methods.

Start with the *ReadList* method. Select the method in the designer and show the BDC Method Details window, which by default appears in the bottom area of Visual Studio. If the window is not displayed, go to View | Other Windows to show it. As you can see, the *ReadList* method has a return parameter called *CustomersList*; click it. In the property grid, specify that the type name behind the *CustomersList* parameter will be the *List<Customer>* type, where the *Customer* type is the one generated by Entity Framework. Do the same thing for the *ReadItem* method, this time selecting a return value of type *Customer*. You can add other parameters, or you can stop modeling the entities here.

Now you are ready to implement the model code. Open the source code of the CustomerService.cs file, and notice that the designer defined the service code for you. Listing 14-4 shows this autogenerated code.

LISTING 14-4 The autogenerated CustomerService.cs file

```
public partial class CustomerService {
    public static Customer Read(string customerID) {
        throw new System.NotImplementedException();
    }

    public static IEnumerable<Customer> List() {
        throw new System.NotImplementedException();
    }
}
```

Replace the methods implementation with concrete code, and you will be ready to provide read-only data to BCS. Listing 14-5 shows you a concrete code implementation.

LISTING 14-5 The autogenerated CustomerService.cs file with a concrete code implementation

```
public partial class CustomerService {
    public static IEnumerable<Customer> ReadList() {
        SampleCRMEntities ctx = SampleCRMEntities.CreateContext();
        return (ctx.Customers);
    }

    public static Customer ReadItem(string customerID) {
        SampleCRMEntities ctx = SampleCRMEntities.CreateContext();
        return (ctx.Customers.FirstOrDefault(c => c.CustomerID == customerID));
    }
}
```

Notice that the static method *SampleCRMEntities.CreateContext* is part of the customization made to support Entity Framework 5.0 within SharePoint 2013. You can add also the *Creator*, *Updater*, and *Deleter* methods. To do so, click the Add A Method command menu item in the BDC Method Details window (illustrated previously in Figure 14-26). The *Creator* method accepts a parameter of type *Customer* with a direction value of *In*, and it returns a result of type *Customer* with a direction value of *Return*. The *Updater* method accepts at least a parameter of type *Customer* with a direction value of *In*, but it will not return anything. The *Deleter* method accepts a parameter of type *customerID* with a direction value of *In*, but it too does not return anything.

Listing 14-6 presents the final implementation of the CustomerService.cs file.

LISTING 14-6 The final CustomerService.cs implementation

```
public partial class CustomerService {
    public static IEnumerable<Customer> ReadList() {
        SampleCRMEntities ctx = SampleCRMEntities.CreateContext();
        return (ctx.Customers);
    }

    public static Customer ReadItem(string customerID) {
        SampleCRMEntities ctx = SampleCRMEntities.CreateContext();
        return (ctx.Customers.FirstOrDefault(c => c.CustomerID == customerID));
    }

    public static Customer Create(Customer newCustomer) {
        SampleCRMEntities ctx = SampleCRMEntities.CreateContext();
        ctx.Customers.Add(newCustomer);
        ctx.SaveChanges();

        return (newCustomer);
    }

    public static void Update(Customer customer) {
        SampleCRMEntities ctx = SampleCRMEntities.CreateContext();
        ctx.Customers.Attach(customer);
        ctx.SaveChanges();
    }

    public static void Delete(string customerID) {
        SampleCRMEntities ctx = SampleCRMEntities.CreateContext();
        ctx.Customers.Remove(ctx.Customers.FirstOrDefault
                (c => c.CustomerID == customerID));
        ctx.SaveChanges();
    }
}
```

After you finish designing your model, you can validate it by right-clicking the designer surface and selecting the Validate command. If your model is correctly defined, Visual Studio 2012 displays the message "Model validation completed with no errors" in the Output window.

Now you can deploy the model and consume it from your SharePoint 2013 sites.

Associating entities

Regardless of the type of data source provider you choose for designing your ECTs, it is important to know that you can define associations between entities of the same namespace or model. In fact, whenever you have entities with a relationship, you can design an association with which you can navigate through your data, moving across associations.

Depending on the tool that you use for designing your BCS models, you can define the following kind of associations:

- **One-to-many forward and/or reverse associations based on a foreign key** This models a classic 1-*n* relationship. An example of a one-to-many association is represented by a customer with his or her orders. It is based on a foreign key and can be modeled within SharePoint Designer 2013.
- **Many-to-many associations** These associations correspond to *n*-*n* relationships. An example of a many-to-many association is an association between customers and their interest areas. Customers can have multiple interest areas, and every interest area can have multiple interested customers.
- **Self-referential associations** These are associations that are self-referential for the same entity. An example could be a list of employees, where each employee is related to his or her manager, who is also an employee.
- **Multiple related ECTs** These associations allow modeling between one entity and multiple entities. An example could be an association table with multiple identifying foreign keys mapping to different tables, such as the description of a product in a multilanguage environment, where a description is identified by a product ID and a culture code, respectively corresponding to the product and culture used to identify the product description.

As an example, consider the *SampleCRM* database and the *CRMCustomer* ECT defined previously in the "Accessing a database" section. Add another ECT corresponding to the *Orders* table and call it *CRMOrder*. Each *Order* row is related to a specific *Customer* row, and the relationship is one-to-many, where *CRMCustomer* is the source and the related *CRMOrder* instances are the destinations. From within SharePoint Designer 2013, you can select the Operations Design View ribbon command of the destination ECT, and then click the Add Association menu item to create a new association.

Note In SharePoint Designer 2013, you always need to create an association starting from the destination entity, not from the source entity.

When you undertake adding a new association, a wizard appears that asks you to select the source ECT and the related identifier (see Figure 14-27).

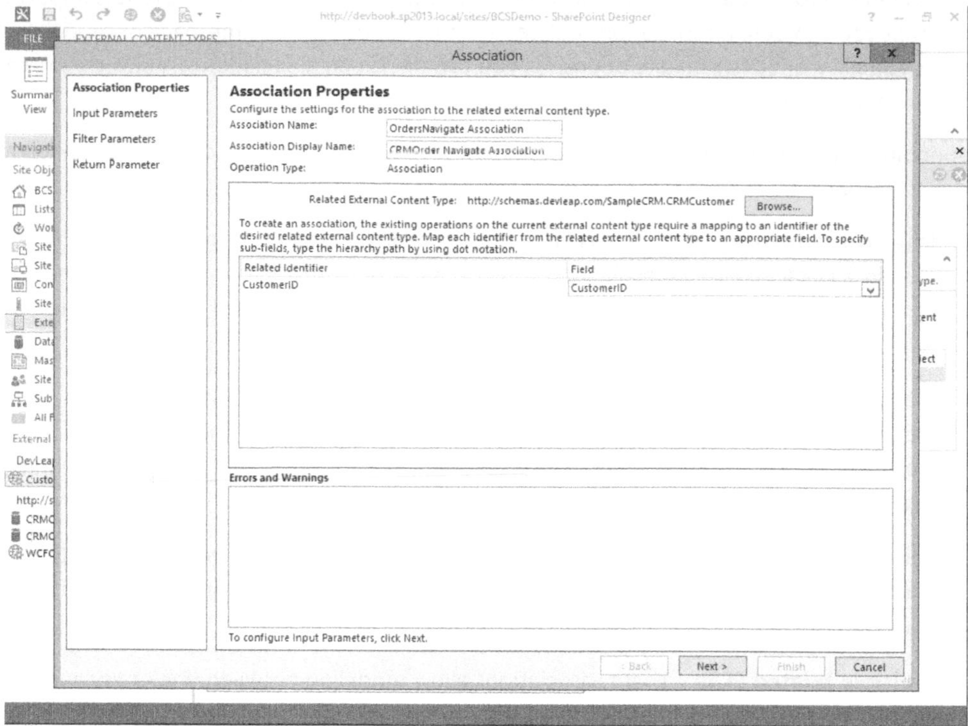

FIGURE 14-27 The first step of the wizard for creating an association between two ECT entities.

Then you need to select the parameters to provide to the association. An association is a particular kind of *MethodInstance* definition, as are, for example, *Associator*, *AssociationNavigator*, and *BulkAssociationNavigator*, which were described in Table 14-1. Thus, you have the ability to provide input parameters and filter parameters. The return type of the method is the related list of destinations.

You can use associations, for example, by using native Business Data Web Parts of SharePoint, creating pages that use the Business Data List and the Business Data Related List Web Parts. These Web Parts are available only in the Enterprise edition of SharePoint Server 2013. Figure 14-28 demonstrates the output of these Web Parts when configured to render *CRMCustomer* and related *CRMOrder* instances.

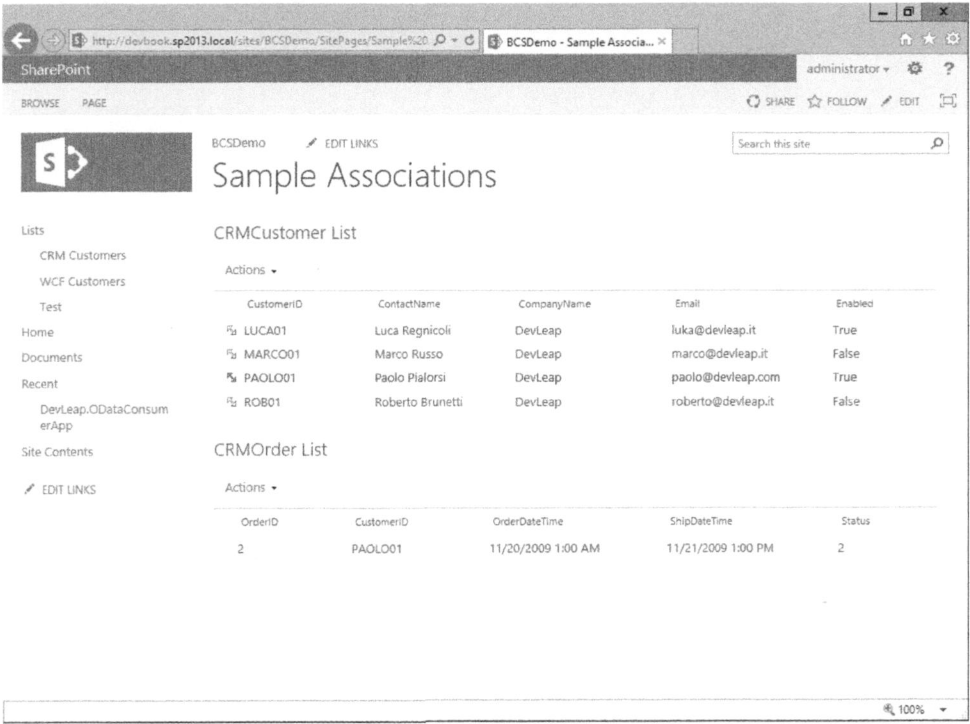

FIGURE 14-28 A Web Part page showing the output of Business Data List and Business Data Related List when connected.

If you need to define an association different from a one-to-many, based on a foreign key, you can use a text editor for the BDCM file or the Visual Studio 2012 BDC Model Designer.

Summary

In this chapter, you learned how BCS works on both the server and client side. You saw how to configure the most popular kinds of data source providers: DBMS, WCF/Web Service, OData, and the custom .NET model. You also read a quick overview of associations. You now have the basic elements to start using BCS in your real business solutions.

PART V

Developing workflows

CHAPTER 15

Windows Workflow Foundation

Part V, "Developing workflows," focuses on developing workflows and orchestrating business processes within Microsoft SharePoint 2013. First, in this chapter, you will learn about the architecture, capabilities, and functionality of Microsoft Windows Workflow Foundation (WF) 4.5, which serves as the basis of the new workflow engine of SharePoint 2013. To master the workflow engine of SharePoint 2013, you first need to understand the workflow engine of WF 4.5 itself. While subsequent chapters of Part V will cover workflows for SharePoint, this chapter delves into WF 4.5 alone.

Architecture of Windows Workflow Foundation 4.5

The latest version of the workflow engine from Microsoft, WF 4.5, is a rich set of libraries, types, and tools for creating custom workflow-based software solutions and is implemented with Microsoft .NET Framework 4.5. WF 4.5 is not a ready-to-use software or an application server available out of the box. With WF 4.5, you can't do anything unless you write custom code on top of the WF 4.5 engine. WF 4.5 is a tool for developers, not a software application for end users. You, as a developer, can create software applications providing workflow-based functionality using .NET 4.5 and WF 4.5.

Note To learn how SharePoint 2013 takes advantage of WF 4.5 to provide workflow-based capabilities to end users, see Chapter 16, "SharePoint workflow fundamentals."

In WF 4.5, every workflow is made of a set of activities or at least a single activity. An *activity* is the smallest unit of execution for a workflow and can be considered a single step of a workflow. Activities can be created by developers, or can be taken from the list of activities already available out of the box. Typically, a real workflow solution is made of activities available out of the box as well as custom developed ones. Whenever you need to implement a software application that uses WF 4.5, you should analyze the requirements of the target solution and define the custom activities necessary to implement that solution. Regardless of the number and type of custom activities you will develop, every workflow definition will be made of markup code defined using a syntax called XAML. When you run a workflow instance, you load the workflow definition, provide some input arguments, and allocate a thread for executing that workflow instance. Internally, the workflow engine will run every workflow instance with a maximum of one thread at a time.

WF 4.5 is based on the architecture shown in Figure 15-1. You can think of every application that uses WF 4.5 as a host application. Host applications access the WF runtime for loading and executing workflow instances, as well as the WCF (Windows Communication Foundation) runtime for communicating between the workflow instances and the outside. Every workflow instance can be persisted onto a dedicated persistence storage, and can also be monitored using out-of-the-box tools.

With Microsoft Visual Studio 2012, you can not only define workflows while developing custom solutions, but also use the native libraries of WF 4.5 to create custom workflow designers of your own. You can then include these workflow designers in your custom applications.

On the hosting side, you can also host and run workflow instances within Internet Information Services (IIS) and manage those instances using IIS management tools. You can also use Windows Server AppFabric, which provides some useful monitoring and management tools that extend the native capabilities of IIS.

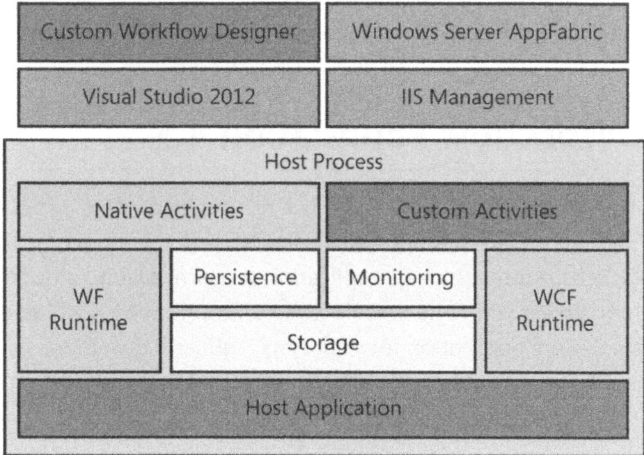

FIGURE 15-1 A simplified schema showing the architecture of a system with externalized authentication.

When you create a new workflow definition, you can choose between three workflow models that are available out of the box:

- **Sequence** Represents a sequential workflow in which you define an explicit entry point (start) and a well-known exit point (end). The workflow instances will be executed from the start to the end, stepping through multiple steps and following some branches, without the capability to step backward through the flow. The only way to step backward in a sequential workflow is to define multiple nested loops, but doing so would result in overly complex and difficult-to-manage workflows.
- **Flowchart** Defines a flow that behaves like a flow diagram; it can be traversed from start to finish, and specific conditions and rules can return the flow to previously completed steps.
- **State machine** Defines a state machine flow, which is made of a set of states and rules to transfer the flow. It is the most suitable solution for implementing human-interactive flows, because end-user behavior is unpredictable and nondeterministic.

Those are just basic examples of flow definitions. In reality, you can mix the three models within a single workflow definition. For example, you can create a flowchart workflow that internally is made of some sequences or state machines. You even can create workflow shapes of your own and plug them into the native infrastructure; however, flowcharts, sequences, and state machines can satisfy almost every need.

Listing 15-1 contains an example excerpt of XAML defining a sequential workflow that provides the typical "Hello world" message.

LISTING 15-1 The XAML code of a sample sequential workflow

```
<Activity mc:Ignorable="sap sap2010 sads" x:Class="WorkflowConsoleApplication1.
Workflow1"
    sap2010:ExpressionActivityEditor.ExpressionActivityEditor="C#"
 xmlns="http://schemas.microsoft.com/netfx/2009/xaml/activities"
 xmlns:mc="http://schemas.openxmlformats.org/markup-compatibility/2006"
 xmlns:sads="http://schemas.microsoft.com/netfx/2010/xaml/activities/debugger"
 xmlns:sap="http://schemas.microsoft.com/netfx/2009/xaml/activities/presentation"
 xmlns:sap2010="http://schemas.microsoft.com/netfx/2010/xaml/activities/
presentation"
 xmlns:scg="clr-namespace:System.Collections.Generic;assembly=mscorlib"
 xmlns:sco="clr-namespace:System.Collections.ObjectModel;assembly=mscorlib"
 xmlns:x="http://schemas.microsoft.com/winfx/2006/xaml">
  <TextExpression.NamespacesForImplementation>
    <sco:Collection x:TypeArguments="x:String">
      <x:String>System</x:String>
      <x:String>System.Collections.Generic</x:String>
      <x:String>System.Data</x:String>
      <x:String>System.Linq</x:String>
      <x:String>System.Text</x:String>
    </sco:Collection>
  </TextExpression.NamespacesForImplementation>
  <TextExpression.ReferencesForImplementation>
    <sco:Collection x:TypeArguments="AssemblyReference">
      <AssemblyReference>Microsoft.CSharp</AssemblyReference>
      <AssemblyReference>System</AssemblyReference>
      <AssemblyReference>System.Activities</AssemblyReference>

      <!-- Code omitted for the sake of brevity -->

    </sco:Collection>
  </TextExpression.ReferencesForImplementation>
  <Sequence>
    <WriteLine Text="Hello world!" sap2010:WorkflowViewState.IdRef="WriteLine_1"
/>
  </Sequence>
<sap2010:WorkflowViewState.IdRef>WorkflowConsoleApplication1.Workflow1_1</
sap2010:WorkflowViewState.IdRef>
  <sap2010:WorkflowViewState.ViewStateManager>

      <!-- Code omitted for the sake of brevity -->

  </sap2010:WorkflowViewState.ViewStateManager>
</Activity>
```

Aside from some infrastructural content, the real workflow definition is highlighted in bold and simply declares a sequence made of one activity of type *WriteLine*, which will write to the console window a welcome message with a text value of *Hello world!* Figure 15-2 shows the listing's graphical representation in the workflow designer available in Visual Studio 2012.

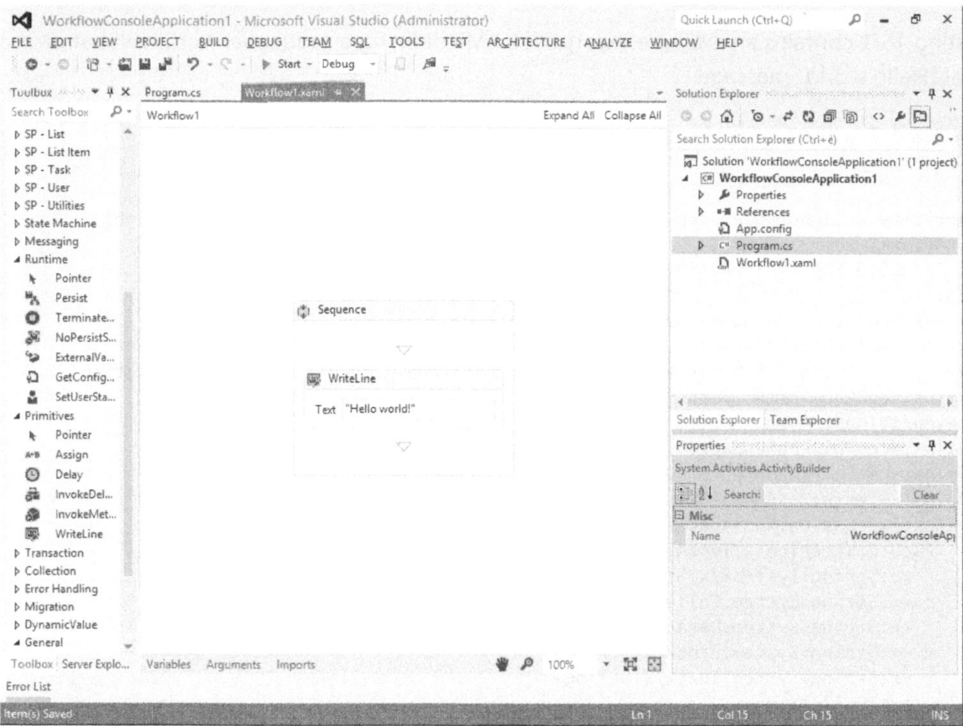

FIGURE 15-2 The graphical designer of Visual Studio 2012 presenting a sample workflow definition.

Furthermore, consider that with WF 4.5 you can also define a workflow simply by writing a few lines of code, aggregating instances of activities in an object graph defined as Microsoft C# or Visual Basic .NET source code. Listing 15-2 shows a code excerpt of a C#-based workflow.

LISTING 15-2 A sample sequential workflow only based on C# code

```
Sequence sequenceWorkflow = new Sequence {
    Activities = {
        new WriteLine { Text = "Hello world!" }
    }
};
```

Your first workflow project

To better understand how to define a workflow, try creating an extremely simple workflow definition corresponding to a flow for selecting a vacation destination. Imagine that you want to create, using WF 4.5, the workflow depicted as a flow diagram in Figure 15-3.

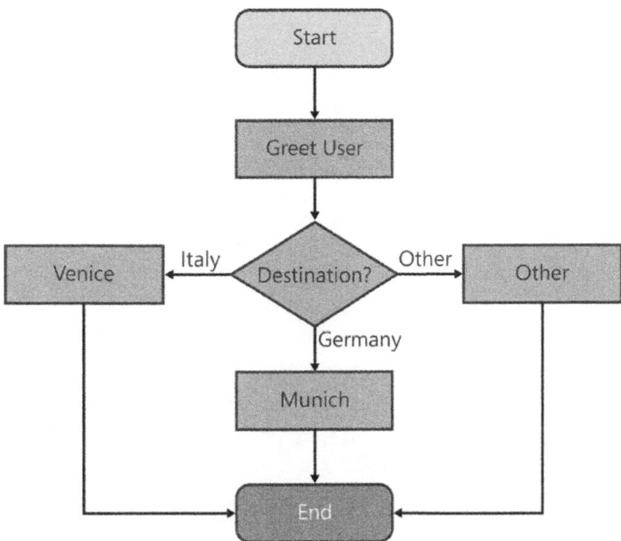

FIGURE 15-3 A flow diagram depicting a sample workflow outline.

To represent this workflow using WF 4.5, you can start by creating a sample Workflow project in Visual Studio 2012. Under the list of available project templates, you can find a group of workflow projects, where you can create one of the following:

- **Activity Designer Library** Represents a project template for creating a custom designer for a custom set of activities (discussed in Chapter 18, "Advanced workflows").
- **Activity Library** Represents a project template for creating a new set of custom activities (discussed later in this chapter and in Chapter 18).
- **WCF Workflow Service Application** Defines a project for hosting a workflow service, which will be published by a *WorkflowServiceHost* object. This topic will not be covered in detail in this book, because it is out of the scope of SharePoint 2013 workflows.
- **Workflow Console Application** Defines workflows that will run in the console environment of a Windows machine. It is a good option for practicing with WF 4.5 and for creating sample workflows.

For the example, start with a Workflow Console Application project template. You will be prompted with a blank design surface, and with a rich toolbox of activities on the left side of your screen. Figure 15-4 shows the Visual Studio 2012 interface just after the new project is created.

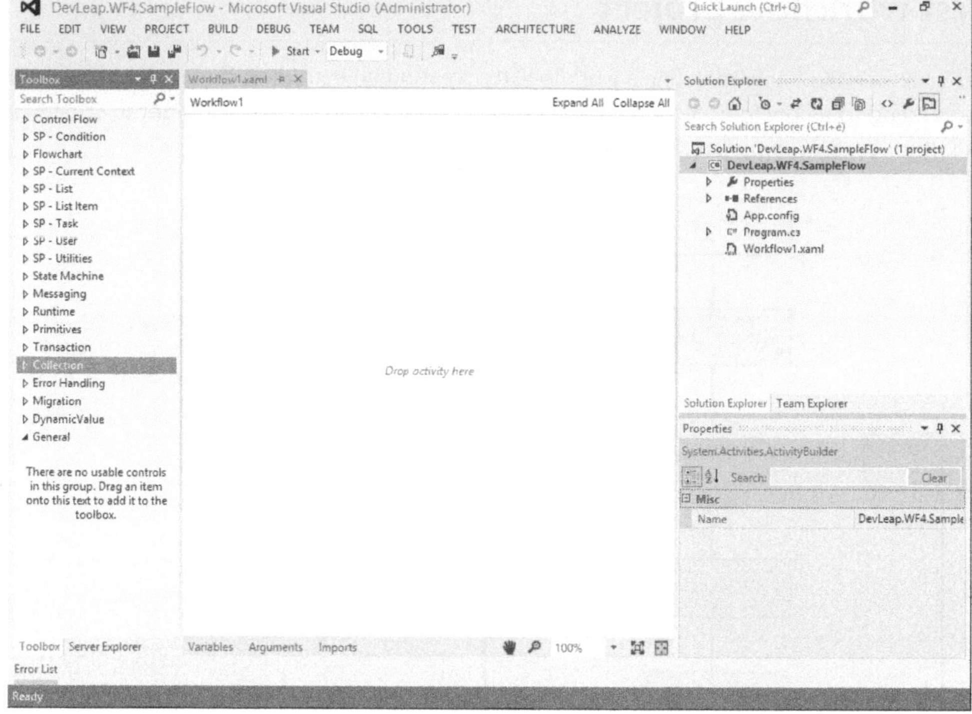

FIGURE 15-4 The outline of the sample workflow project in Visual Studio 2012.

To start designing your flow, drag an activity from the toolbox and drop it onto the workflow design surface. The following are the available groups of activities:

- **Control Flow** Activities for defining and controlling the flow of your processes. For example, in this group you can find activities like *DoWhile*, *ForEach*, *If*, *Parallel*, and so on.
- **Flowchart** Activities for defining a flowchart-based workflow. Such activities include *FlowChart*, *FlowDecision*, and *FlowSwitch*.
- **State Machine** Activities for defining state machine workflows. These activities include *StateMachine*, *State*, and *FinalState*.
- **Messaging** Activities for communicating with external systems, using SOAP (Simple Object Access Protocol), WCF, REST (Representational State Transfer) and HTTP, and so on. This is one of the richest groups of activities.
- **Runtime** Activities for persisting workflow status, terminating a workflow instance, executing a piece of flow without any persistence, and so on. These are the very core activities of WF 4.5.
- **Primitives** Activities to invoke external code, assign a value to a variable, wait for a delay, and perform other fundamental tasks.

- **Transaction** Activities like *TransactionScope*, *CompensableActivity*, *Compensate*, and *CancellationScope*, which are related to transactional tasks.
- **Collection** Activities for managing collections of items and variables. You can find activities for adding, removing, retrieving, and checking for the existence of items in a collection, and more.
- **Error Handling** Activities for handling errors, such as *TryCatch*, *Throw*, and *Rethrow*.
- **Migration** Activities to interoperate with previous versions of WF.
- **DynamicValue** Activities for managing dynamic values and types. For example, these include activities for managing JavaScript Object Notation (JSON) and OData content.

While working in an environment configured for developing SharePoint and Microsoft Office solutions, you will also find many other categories of activities, all with *SP* in their name. Chapter 17, "Developing workflows," will discuss them. This chapter, however, focuses on the standard and basic workflow engine of WF 4.5.

To create the workflow illustrated in Figure 15-3, you need to design a *FlowChart* activity. For instance, specify a value of *Vacation Flowchart* for its *DisplayName* property. Every *FlowChart* activity starts with a predefined startup point. Add a *WriteLine* activity to the flowchart and connect it to the green startup symbol. By clicking in the body of the *WriteLine* activity, you will be able to provide text to display on the console as a greeting message. Notice that here you can write any C# or Visual Basic expression. In fact, one of the main capabilities of the designer for WF 4.5 is the ability to configure activities using dynamic and code-based expressions. For the sake of simplicity, imagine the user provides the name of the destination to get the country as an input argument at the workflow startup. In a real workflow, you would probably use a custom activity for querying the user and for validating the provided input.

To declare an argument or variable, you can use the workflow designer. In the lower-left corner of the designer in Visual Studio 2012 are three tabs: Variables, Arguments, and Imports. The Variable tab enables you to define variables for holding values during execution of workflow instances. Variables can be scoped to define their lifetime and availability. The Arguments tab allows defining properties, input, output, or both input/output arguments that can be used to configure the workflow instances. With the Imports tab, you can define the assemblies that you want to reference in the code running within the workflow you are defining. To accept the *TargetCountry* argument, click the Arguments tab, and declare an input argument with name *TargetCountry* and type *String*.

Then design a *FlowSwitch<T>* activity with a value of *System.String* for the *T* to disambiguate. Connect the *FlowSwitch<T>* activity with the *WriteLine* activity you defined before and determine the behavior of the workflow, based on the content of the *TargetCountry* argument. To achieve this result, configure the *Expression* property of the *FlowSwitch<T>* activity in order to map it to the *TargetCountry* argument. Then, for the sake of simplicity, imagine that you want to use a *WriteLine* activity for each of the user's choices. According to the diagram in Figure 15-3, if the user provides a value of *Italy* for the *TargetCountry* argument, the workflow will suggest going to Venice; if the user provides a value of *Germany*, then the workflow will suggest visiting Munich; lastly, if the user provides any other value, the workflow will simply write "Other." Figure 15-5 illustrates the resulting flowchart definition.

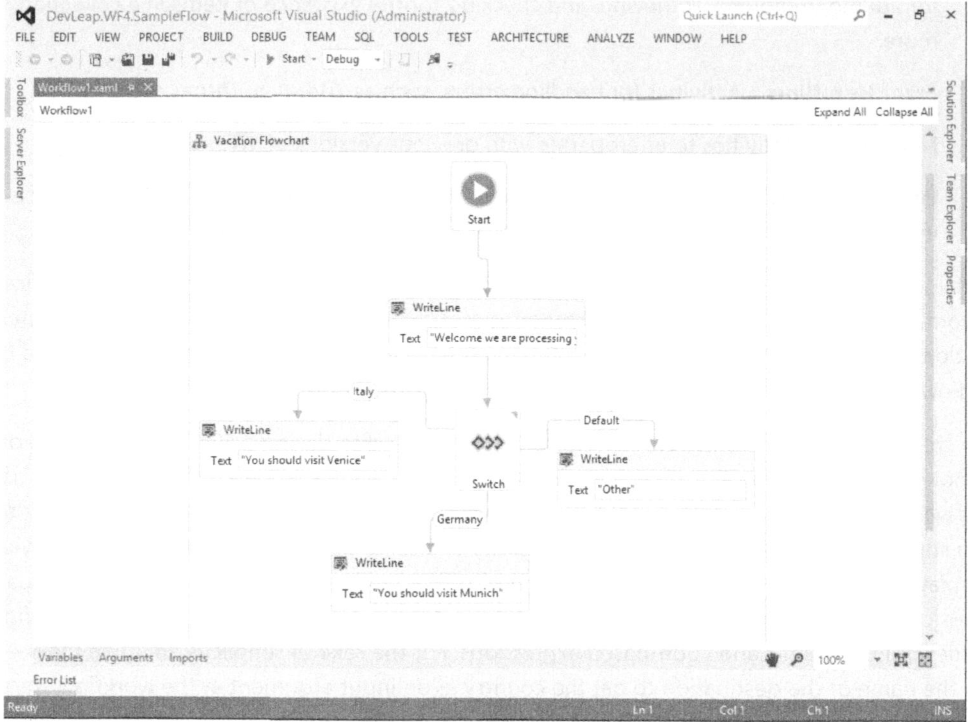

FIGURE 15-5 Outline of the sample workflow project in Visual Studio 2012.

To start debugging your new workflow definition, right-click the first *WriteLine* activity in the designer and select the Insert Breakpoint menu item from the Breakpoint menu. Now you can simply start playing the workflow in Visual Studio 2012 by pressing F5.

By default, the workflow instance starts with an empty value for the *TargetCountry* argument, and the flow will go through the default path (Other). You can configure a default value for this argument through the Arguments tab of the designer, or you can start the workflow providing an argument from outside the flow. In the next section, you will learn how to start a workflow providing some input arguments.

Hosting and execution

Out of the box, you have three available options for hosting and executing a workflow instance:

- *The WorkflowInvoker* class
- *The WorkflowApplication* class
- *The WorkflowServiceHost* class

The *WorkflowInvoker* class executes a single workflow instance using a single-threaded and synchronous model. The *WorkflowInvoker* execution engine assumes you want to execute a workflow instance that will run for a short time, without any kind of persistence storage. This option is suitable for quick and small workflows, which in general are simple, and which do not really need to be scalable, highly available, or asynchronous. The C# code excerpt in Listing 15-3 uses a *WorkflowInvoker* object to host and execute a workflow instance, based on the chapter's example workflow.

LISTING 15-3 Executing a workflow instance through a *WorkflowInvoker* object

```
Dictionary<String, Object> arguments = new Dictionary<String, Object>();
arguments.Add("TargetCountry", "Italy");

Activity instance = new VacationWorkflow();
WorkflowInvoker.Invoke(instance, arguments);
```

When using a *WorkflowInvoker* object, you can also include input arguments, within a variable of type *Dictionary<String, Object>*. In the code sample, the arguments provide a value for the *TargetCountry* argument.

Alternately, you can use an instance of the *WorkflowApplication* class, which allows hosting and executing a single workflow instance within an independent, scalable, asynchronous, and persistable runtime engine. In fact, the *WorkflowApplication* class internally uses a dedicated scheduler based on a thread pool. The scheduler can execute a workflow instance for a long time, even persisting its status into a back-end persistence storage if it becomes idle. The C# code excerpt in Listing 15-4 executes a workflow instance using a *WorkflowApplication* object, but is very basic. Later in this chapter, you will more thoroughly investigate workflow persistence.

LISTING 15-4 Executing a workflow instance using a *WorkflowApplication* object

```
ManualResetEvent rst = new ManualResetEvent(false);

Dictionary<String, Object> arguments = new Dictionary<string, object>();
arguments.Add("TargetCountry", "Italy");

Activity instance = new VacationWorkflow();
WorkflowApplication application = new WorkflowApplication(instance, arguments);

application.Completed = (WorkflowApplicationCompletedEventArgs e) => {
    rst.Set();
};

application.Run();
rst.WaitOne();
```

Notice that in Listing 15-4, the code waits for the workflow execution using an object of type *ManualResetEvent*. The workflow instance will be executed asynchronously, and the hosting application will have to wait for the background task to complete. Furthermore, while hosting a workflow instance within a *WorkflowApplication* object, you have the capability to suspend, unload, resume, or terminate a running workflow instance.

If the workflow you are implementing has to be published as a service, you have one last execution option. You can empower the *WorkflowServiceHost* class, which provides a hosting and execution infrastructure that internally uses the WCF engine and allows publishing of a workflow service. Such workflows can be defined within a web application and can be published using IIS or a custom self-hosting application. Not every workflow definition can be hosted within a *WorkflowServiceHost* object. To host a workflow definition as a workflow service, you need to design the workflow accordingly and use some specific activities that internally implement a WCF service contract.

Custom activities

As you know, every workflow definition is made of one or more activities. From a developer perspective, a workflow activity is just a piece of markup that aggregates already existing activities or is a custom class implementation. Using the Visual Studio 2012 workflow designer, you can easily implement a custom activity. To do so, open the chapter's sample project and add a new workflow project of type Activity Library.

In the new project, you will find a new project item with extension .xaml; this is an XML-based file that you will be able to design using the classic workflow designer and the toolbox of available out-of-the-box activities. Here, you can design a kind of subworkflow that you will be able to reuse many times in your own workflow definitions. However, this file can aggregate existing activities only, so its main purpose is to reuse existing elements, rather than to create completely new activities from scratch.

In a real business workflow solution, you will probably need to write some code to implement real activities from scratch. From an object-orientation viewpoint, a custom activity is just a class that inherits from the base class *System.Activities.Activity* or from one of the other types inheriting from that base class. Figure 15-6 displays the full hierarchy of types available for creating code-based activities.

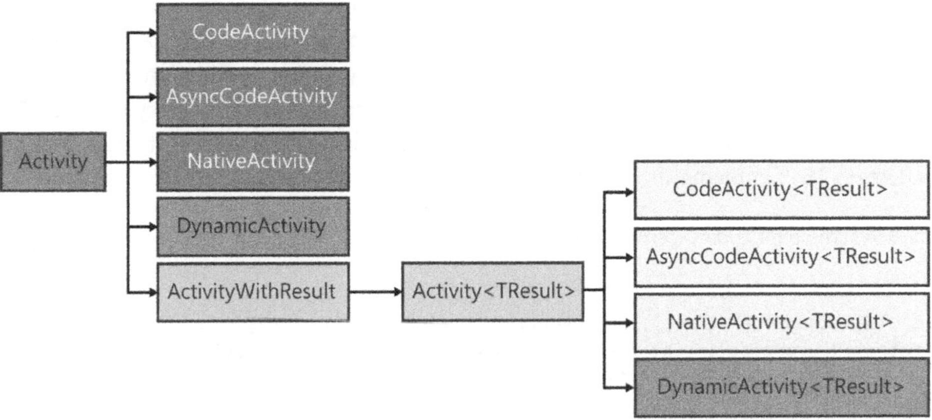

FIGURE 15-6 The hierarchy of types available for creating code-based custom activities.

For example, depending on the type of activity you want to implement, you can inherit from one of many available base classes, including the following:

- ***CodeActivity*** This is the base class to inherit from for creating a synchronous custom activity that provides some functionality implementing a code-based method called *Execute*, without necessarily providing a result.
- ***AsynCodeActivity*** This can be inherited to implement an asynchronous activity that can be used to execute code adhering to the asynchronous code execution pattern available in .NET and based on the *Begin/End{MethodName}* pair of methods. This kind of base class does not return a result value.
- ***NativeActivity*** This is the base class to inherit from for creating any kind of activity and can interact with the WF 4.5 runtime engine at any level. This base class does not return any result.
- ***CodeActivity<TResult>*** This can be inherited to implement a code-based activity that will provide a result of type *TResult*.
- ***AsynCodeActivity<TResult>*** This is the counterpart of the *AsyncCodeActivity*, and returns a result value of type *TResult*.
- ***NativeActivity<TResult>*** This is the same as the *NativeActivity*, but activities inheriting from this type will provide a result of type *TResult*.

In Figure 15-6, there are also some other types available, such as *DynamicActivity* and *DynamicActivity<TResult>*. These are sealed classes that are useful for creating custom activities and workflow instances directly in code, but not for creating custom activity types.

Now, think again about the simple vacation workflow example. In Figure 15-3, the workflow definition got the value of the *TargetCountry* argument from the list of input arguments of the workflow. A better option, however, is to include within the workflow definition some logic that queries the user for the target country, and then to provide some validation rules in the same workflow. To add this custom querying activity (call it *ReadLineActivity*), you first need to inherit from the *CodeActivity<TResult>* base class, because you will use some custom code to query the user. The result of type *TResult* will be a *System.String* and provide the user-specified target country to the workflow. Listing 15-5 implements such a custom activity.

LISTING 15-5 A sample C# code excerpt implementing a custom *ReadLineActivity*

```
public class ReadLineActivity : CodeActivity<String> {
    protected override string Execute(CodeActivityContext context) {
        return(Console.ReadLine());
    }
}
```

As you can see, the simple implementation reads a line from the console and returns the read value through the return value of the *Execute* method, which overrides the corresponding method of the *CodeActivity<String>* base class. Moreover, the *Execute* method receives an argument of type *CodeActivityContext*, which provides the current request context and which will be used later. Now, build the class library project, and open the workflow designer of the *VacationWorkflow* definition. Notice the new activity is waiting in the toolbox, ready to be inserted in the workflow definition.

After inserting the new activity, you can configure it. In the property grid of the designer, the custom activity provides a *Result* property. Delete the *TargetCountry* argument from the Arguments tab, and define a new *TargetCountry* variable of type *System.String* on the Variables tab of the workflow designer. Configure the *Result* property of the custom *ReadLineActivity* to return the read value into the *TargetCountry* variable. Figure 15-7 shows the new outline of the vacation workflow.

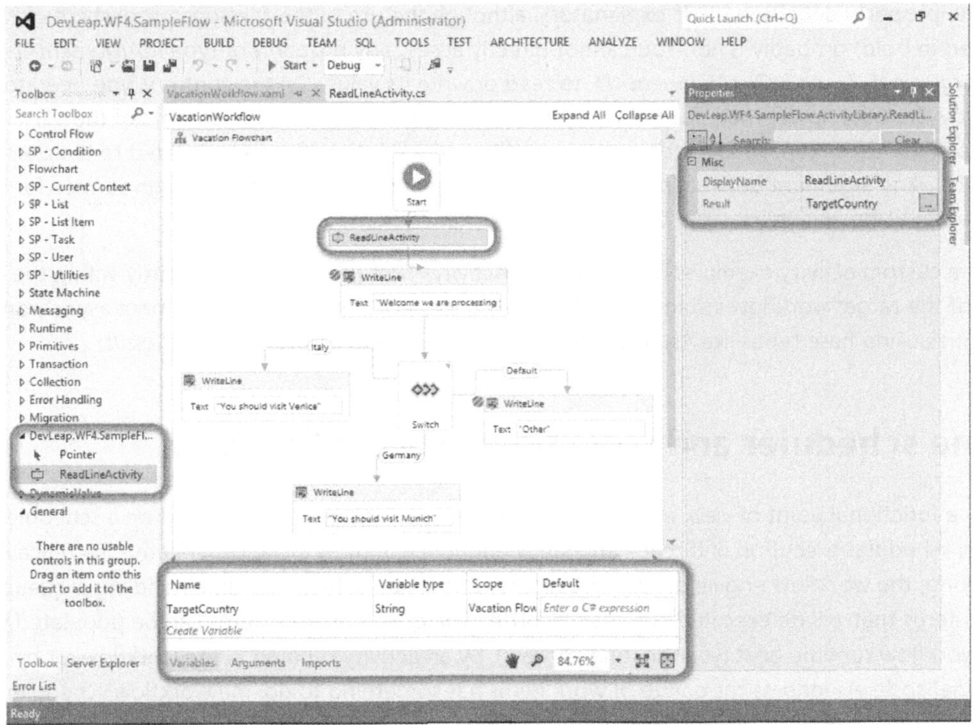

FIGURE 15-7 The workflow designer with the custom *ReadLineActivity* in place.

When defining custom activities, you not only provide result values, often you also need to accept configuration parameters and input/output arguments. In WF 4.5 custom activities, you can define as many arguments as you want simply by declaring properties of type *InArgument<T>*, *OutArgument<T>*, or *InOutArgument<T>*. As the type names imply, these types represent input, output, and input/output arguments. You can use these types for holding values that will be serialized and deserialized together with the workflow status and that you can use to change the behavior of your custom activities. Imagine that you want to define an input argument for the *ReadLineActivity*. This argument will be a string message that will prompt the workflow users before asking them for the target country value. Listing 15-6 provides a revised *ReadLineActivity* implementation.

LISTING 15-6 A sample C# code excerpt implementing a custom *ReadLineActivity* with an input argument

```
public class ReadLineActivity : CodeActivity<String> {
    public InArgument<String> Message { get; set; }

    protected override string Execute(CodeActivityContext context) {
        Console.WriteLine(this.Message.Get(context));
        this.Result = Console.ReadLine();
    }
}
```

The property definition is self-explanatory, although the use of the *Message* property (highlighted in bold) probably is not. You cannot directly access any property of type *InArgument<T>*, *OutArgument<T>*, or *InOutArgument<T>* to read or write its value. On the contrary, you need to employ the *Get* and *Set* methods provided for accessing their values in the context of the current activity execution, which is the argument of type *CodeActivityContext* provided to the *Execute* method. Any argument defined in this way will be available on the workflow design surface for configuration using an explicit value or an expression.

The custom activity examples based on *CodeActivity<TResult>* run synchronously within the execution of the target workflow instances. In Chapter 18, you will learn how to implement asynchronous activities using base types like *AsyncCodeActivity<TResult>* and *NativeActivity<TResult>*.

Runtime scheduler and workflow process life cycle

From a functional point of view, every workflow instance executes its steps based on a scheduler, which schedules execution of threads and steps during a workflow instance's lifetime. Technically speaking, the workflow engine of WF 4.5 executes one single activity per time handling a queue of work items that will be executed in a specific order. The queue of work items can be populated by the workflow runtime host (your hosting process), by an activity running in the workflow, or by some external code. As long as the queue of work items has something to do, the workflow scheduler schedules the execution of these work items, once per time in a single-threaded fashion. When the queue of work items is empty or when the currently running work item is handling a background task and there is nothing to do in the meantime, the workflow instance is idle. When a workflow instance is idle or between the executions of work items, you can persist the workflow state. When a workflow instance is idle, you can also unload that instance and reload it later when you have something to do.

Think about document approval workflows. There will be times when an approval workflow has to wait for end users' approval. It would be useless and dangerous to keep a pending workflow idle in memory just waiting for end users. You would consume resources (RAM and CPU) keeping alive a workflow instance that has nothing to do. Moreover, in the case of a hardware failure or system reboot, you would lose your workflow instance state if you kept it in memory only. On the contrary, if you save the workflow state periodically and you unload idle workflows from memory, you will be able to reload and resume them only when needed, and eventually use a multiserver infrastructure where workflows are loaded and resumed on the server when you have enough resources to manage their execution. Activities provided out of the box by WF 4.5 internally take advantage of this way of working. For activities that you implement, you should consider these issues and create the activities according to the behavior of the runtime scheduler of WF 4.5.

To better understand this topic, change the sample vacation workflow, adding a *Delay* activity between the *ReadLineActivity* and the first *WriteLine* activity. Any *Delay* activity instance accepts a *Duration* property, which represents the delay duration as a *TimeSpan* value. Figure 15-8 shows the new outline of the workflow definition.

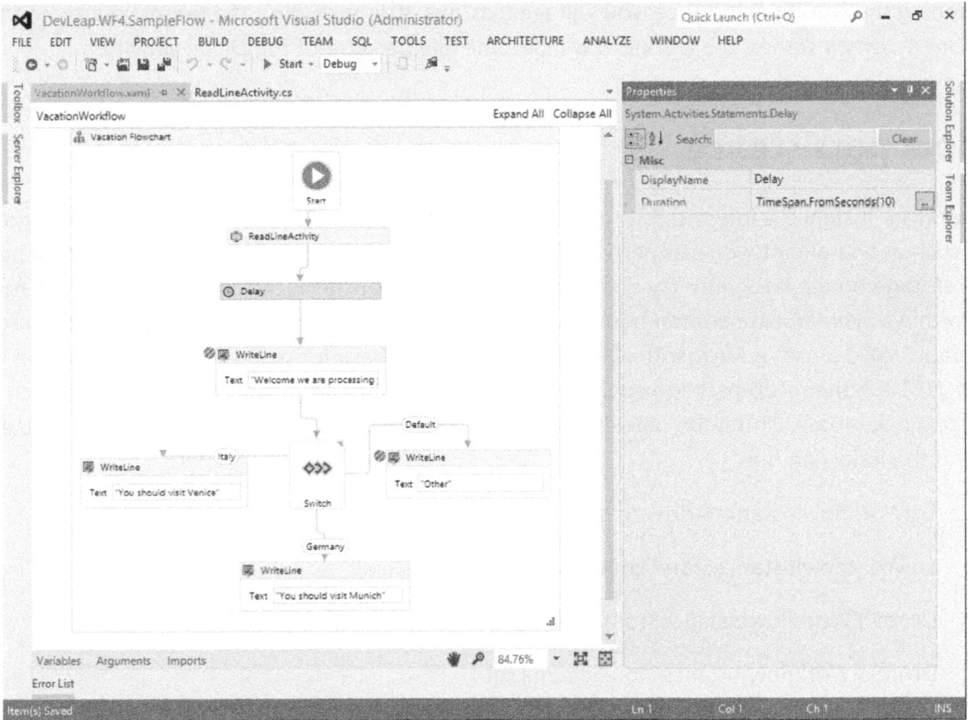

FIGURE 15-8 The workflow designer with the custom *Delay* activity in place.

Listing 15-7 contains a revised code excerpt for running the workflow instance using a *WorkflowApplication* class and intercepting the *Idle* event.

LISTING 15-7 Running the new workflow outline with a *Delay* activity

```
ManualResetEvent rst = new ManualResetEvent(false);

Activity instance = new VacationWorkflow();
WorkflowApplication application = new WorkflowApplication(instance);

application.Completed = (WorkflowApplicationCompletedEventArgs e) =>
{
    rst.Set();
};

application.Idle = (WorkflowApplicationIdleEventArgs e) =>
{
    Console.WriteLine("Workflow idle");
};

application.Run();
rst.WaitOne();
```

Running the workflow instance, you will see that, just after providing the target country to the *ReadLineActivity* instance, the workflow will become idle because of the *Delay* activity.

Workflow persistence

If a workflow instance is idle and it is running within a *WorkflowApplication* or a *WorkflowServiceHost* host, such as SharePoint, you can persist the workflow state as long as you have configured a persistence storage on the back end. Try configuring persistence for the vacation workflow sample running within a *WorkflowApplication* host. First, you need a properly configured persistence storage. By default, WF 4.5 uses a Microsoft SQL Server custom database for persistence storage. When you install .NET 4.5, the setup package copies onto your file system some SQL files for creating such a persistence database. Under the path %windir%\Microsoft.NET\Framework64\v4.0.30319\SQL\en, you will find the following files:

- SqlWorkflowInstanceStoreLogic.sql
- SqlWorkflowInstanceStoreSchema.sql
- DropSqlWorkflowInstanceStoreLogic.sql
- DropSqlWorkflowInstanceStoreSchema.sql

As you can deduce from their names, these files provide the T-SQL commands for creating or deleting the schemas and logic of persistence tables. There are multiple files because sometimes it is useful to create these tables and this logic within an already existing application-specific database, instead of creating a dedicated database. Because you have the source SQL files, you can execute them against any database, and you are free to use them in your own environment, too. These script files target SQL Server 2005 or higher. Run the SqlWorkflowInstanceStoreSchema.sql file first, and then run the SqlWorkflowInstanceStoreLogic.sql file. The first file creates the schemas for the tables, and the second one creates the business logic on top of these schemas.

With your persistence database ready, you next need to reference the assemblies System.Activities.DurableInstancing.dll and System.Runtime.DurableInstancing.dll within your target host application, and you need to change the code in order to use the persistence. Listing 15-8 demonstrates the revised hosting code.

LISTING 15-8 A sample C# code excerpt for hosting the vacation workflow with persistence storage configured

```
ManualResetEvent rst = new ManualResetEvent(false);

Activity instance = new VacationWorkflow();
WorkflowApplication application = new WorkflowApplication(instance);

SqlWorkflowInstanceStore store = new SqlWorkflowInstanceStore(
    "Server=DEVSQL1;Initial Catalog=WF45_PersistenceStorage;Integrated
Security=SSPI");
application.InstanceStore = store;

application.Completed = (WorkflowApplicationCompletedEventArgs e) =>
{
    rst.Set();
};

application.Idle = (WorkflowApplicationIdleEventArgs e) =>
{
    Console.WriteLine("Workflow Idle");
};

application.PersistableIdle = (WorkflowApplicationIdleEventArgs e) =>
{
    Console.WriteLine("Workflow PersistableIdle");
    return (PersistableIdleAction.Persist);
};

application.Run();
rst.WaitOne();
```

The code for configuring the persistence store is highlighted in bold, as is the *PersistableIdle* event handler, which will be raised as soon as the workflow instance is idle and ready for persistence. The event handler will be able to return a result of type *PersistableIdleAction*, which can assume the values *None*, *Persist*, or *Unload*. *None* does nothing, *Persist* instructs the *WorkflowApplication* instance to persist the workflow onto the target store, and *Unload* instructs the *WorkflowApplication* instance to persist and unload the workflow instance, to free resources.

Consider that the *SqlWorkflowInstanceStore* class used in Listing 15-8 is the default implementation of a persistence store service, which is provided out of the box by WF 4.5 and which stores the status of workflows in SQL Server. However, it is just a class inheriting from the *InstanceStore* abstract class, and you can implement a persistence storage service of your own. For example, on MSDN, you can find a sample for storing workflow data in a custom XML file (see *http://msdn.microsoft.com/en-us/library/ee829481.aspx*).

If you are wondering what will be saved into the persistence store, you could inspect the table [System.Activities.DurableInstancing].[InstancesTable] created within the persistence storage database. There you will find the serialized workflow instance state, which is not human readable and is mainly made of the following information:

- The list of work items to execute
- The list of bookmarks of the current workflow, which will be discussed in Chapter 17, "Claims-based authentication, federated identities, and OAuth."
- Variables, arguments, and all the instance data of the workflow instance
- Any pending callback, such as a timer
- Any custom data, because you can extend the persistence of WF 4.5 and provide some custom data to store in the persistence storage

Summary

In this chapter, you investigated the architecture of WF 4.5 and how to take advantage of WF 4.5 in your own software solutions. You also learned how to design a simple workflow, how to create a very basic custom activity, and how the workflow scheduler executes workflow instances and activities. Lastly, you saw how the out-of-the-box persistence storage system works in WF 4.5.

CHAPTER 16

SharePoint workflow fundamentals

For Microsoft SharePoint 2013, Microsoft completely redesigned the architecture of the workflow engine. Unlike previous versions of SharePoint (2007 and 2010), which were based on Microsoft Windows Workflow Foundation (WF) 3.0, the new 2013 engine supports WF 4.5. This chapter walks you through the architecture of this new engine. Along the way, you'll learn how to work with Workflow Manager 1.0, which provides a WF 4.5 server farm. You'll also learn how to create your own workflow from scratch.

The new architecture

A good way to understand the new architecture of workflow in SharePoint 2013 is to compare it to the existing WF 3.*x* architecture in SharePoint 2010 (Figure 16-1). This legacy workflow engine is still available in SharePoint 2013, mainly for backward compatibility, and a good understanding of its limits allows a better understanding of the architectural choices made in SharePoint 2013.

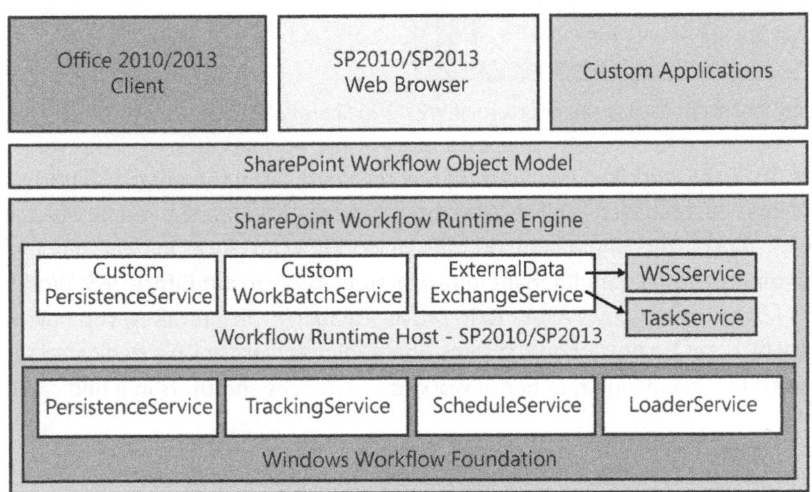

FIGURE 16-1 A simplified schema of the architecture of WF 3.*x* in SharePoint 2010 and 2013.

From a functional perspective, every workflow instance running on WF 3.*x* is hosted in SharePoint 2010/2013 and runs on a SharePoint server. When a running workflow instance interacts with an end user through custom pages or tasks, the workflow instance is executed within the process of a web front-end server. When a workflow instance executes some background tasks, it runs in the background timer service of SharePoint, through a dedicated timer job that will run every *n* minutes (by default, every 5 minutes) onto one dedicated application server. While a workflow instance is not running—for example, because it is waiting for an external event such as an approval from an end user—the instance gets persisted in the content database of the target site collection and is unloaded to keep the environment light and safe.

Such an architecture works great for simple and low-traffic scenarios. For a huge workflow infrastructure with thousands of running workflow instances, however, you cannot rely on executing instances within the same process that is providing web content to end users, nor can you rely on a single dedicated application server. Thus, in SharePoint 2013 you should take advantage of the new WF 4.5 engine (shown in Figure 16-2) and relegate WF 3.*x* to backward compatibility uses only.

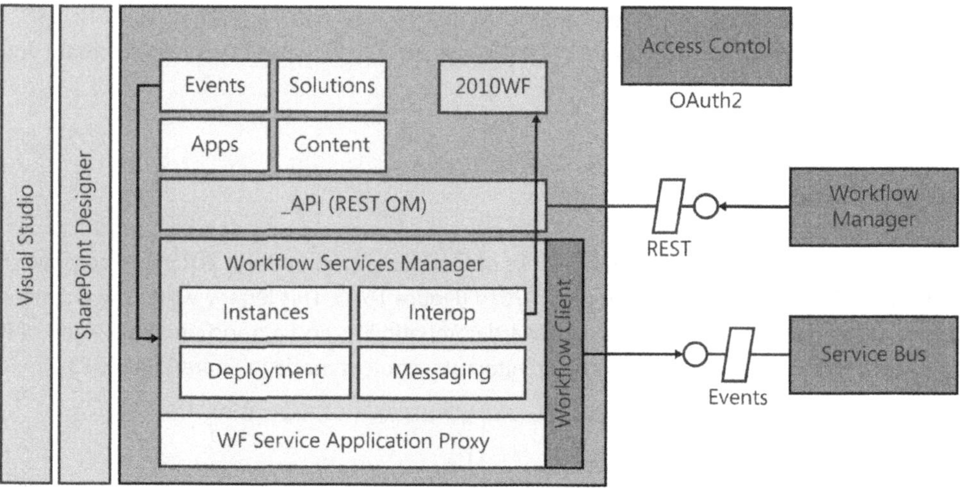

FIGURE 16-2 A simplified schema of the new architecture of WF 4.5 in SharePoint 2013.

As shown in Figure 16-2, the workflow engine now runs on a dedicated server farm, based on a new service called Workflow Manager 1.0. The Workflow Manager 1.0 engine has a highly scalable architecture, which allows executing a huge number of workflow instances in near–real time and using an external multiserver and multitenant infrastructure. In Microsoft Office 365, Workflow Manager is hosted on Microsoft Windows Azure to improve scalability. On-premises, you have to deploy a server farm, which can be hosted on the same SharePoint servers or on a dedicated set of servers, in case you need to serve a high number of workflow instances and users in a dedicated environment.

The Workflow Manager farm and the SharePoint 2013 farm communicate across the network, empowering the new Windows Azure Service Bus when communicating between SharePoint and Workflow Manager. In Office 365, the Windows Azure Service Bus will be provided by Windows Azure. On-premises, however, you will have to install the stand-alone version of the Service Bus, which can be installed together with Workflow Manager 1.0. Later in this chapter, you will learn how to deploy on-premises both Workflow Manager 1.0 and the Service Bus engine. On the other side, when Workflow Manager communicates with SharePoint 2013, it uses the new Representational State Transfer (REST) APIs, like any external SharePoint 2013 app.

The security infrastructure is enforced using OAuth 2.0 and Windows Azure Access Control Services (ACS) in Office 365, or, if you are on-premises, a local security (server-to-server, or S2S) trust between SharePoint 2013 and the local Workflow Manager.

Important To work properly, both the OAuth 2.0 and S2S configurations require you to have an instance of the User Profile service of SharePoint 2013 installed and configured. Thus, starting with SharePoint 2013, the new WF 4.5 workflow engine is available only on SharePoint Server Standard or Enterprise; it is no longer available on SharePoint Foundation. On the contrary, the legacy WF 3.*x* engine still works on SharePoint Foundation 2013.

On the SharePoint side of the architecture, there is also a service application proxy, which connects the SharePoint 2013 farm with the remote Workflow Manager 1.0 farm. To communicate with the remote Workflow Manager 1.0 farm, the service application proxy uses a Workflow Client 1.0 library, which provides the basic and primitive commands for interacting with the remote Workflow Manager 1.0 farm. Internally, the Workflow Services Manager component, which sits on top of the workflow service application proxy, provides capabilities to support workflow instance management, deployment, messaging, and interoperability with legacy SharePoint 2010 workflows.

SharePoint, on its own side, manages lists, libraries, items, documents, and all the events that can be of any interest for the workflow engine. Moreover, SharePoint saves and manages workflow associations, activities, and metadata configuration. Whenever an event of interest occurs for Workflow Manager, such as *itemAdded* or *itemUpdated*, the workflow service application proxy will inform Workflow Manager using a WCF-based communication channel, using the Service Bus and an event publish/subscribe model. This publish/subscribe model can also be accessed by apps and custom workflows, which can send activation messages through the Service Bus to the external Workflow Manager engine. One interesting thing to notice is that, thanks to the publish/subscribe event model offered by the Service Bus, if an event of interest for multiple target workflow instances occurs on the SharePoint side, the communication channel between SharePoint and Workflow Manager will deliver only one event notification. On the Workflow Manager side, the Service Bus will raise the event in every target workflow instance, via a multicast event-based system, reducing the traffic across the wire and allowing multiple subscribers for the same published event.

In this new architecture, you can associate a workflow definition either with an *SPWeb* object or an *SPList* instance. Starting with SharePoint 2013 and the new workflow architecture, a workflow association cannot be defined targeting an *SPContentType* object, however. Thus, SharePoint 2013 supports list workflows and site workflows only. Moreover, as it was in the previous version of the workflow engine, in 2013, a workflow instance can be started manually by an end user, or automatically upon specific events, such as an item creation or change. Furthermore, with the new engine, as with the old, you can start a workflow definition as many subsequent times against a specific item as you want, but you cannot start two concurrent instances of the same workflow definition against a unique target item.

As soon as a workflow association is started against a target item, the client side of the workflow service will inform the remote Workflow Manager using an event, which is defined accordingly to the publish/subscribe infrastructure defined. If there will be any workflow definition on the Workflow Manager side subscribed for that specific event happening, then a new workflow instance will be created. Moreover, as it was with SharePoint 2010 workflows, every workflow association relies on a workflow tasks list, as well as a workflow history list. The workflow tasks list holds the tasks related to the workflow processes, while the workflow history list stores history messages.

From a development perspective, an advanced user can create workflow definitions using either SharePoint Designer 2013 or Microsoft Visual Studio 2012. You can create workflows for both versions of the workflow engine using either tool.

The following are the main goals achieved with this new architecture:

- **Higher and better scalability** The new workflow engine is very scalable and highly performing.
- **Decoupling between SharePoint 2013 and Workflow Manager 1.0** The new Workflow Manager is completely independent from SharePoint 2013, so it can be run wherever you need, keeping SharePoint unaware of the real location of the workflow farm.
- **SharePoint app integration and support for cloud-ready workflows** You can develop apps that empower workflows in their internal implementation and that can run in the cloud (autohosted or provider-hosted), communicating with the remote SharePoint 2013 environment.
- **Markup-based workflow definition and better expressiveness** The workflow definitions are now mainly markup based, and to publish a new workflow definition you simply need to publish the XAML markup code—not libraries or .NET assemblies at the SharePoint farm level.
- **More power to SharePoint Designer 2013** Because of the previous point, SharePoint Designer 2013 is now more powerful and is the best choice to implement many of the workflows you will need. This opens the workflow engine to inexperienced users and nondevelopers.
- **Independence from cloud or on-premises deployment** The overall architecture is independent from the location of both the SharePoint 2013 farm (on-premises or on Office 365) and the Workflow Manager farm (on-premises or on Windows Azure).

Deployment of Workflow Manager 1.0

To start playing with the new Workflow Manager 1.0 engine, you can use Office 365, which is already configured and ready to use, or you can deploy the workflow engine on-premises. The new workflow engine is not configured by default, however; you need to download, install, and configure it before you can use it. If you plan to play with the new workflow engine simply on Office 365, skip ahead to the "Your first workflow with SharePoint Designer 2013" section. If you plan to deploy the workflow on-premises, read on here.

You can download the Workflow Manager 1.0 engine, as well as Workflow Client 1.0, from Microsoft through Web Platform Installer 4.5 (or later), which is available at *http://www.microsoft.com/web/downloads/platform.aspx*. Figure 16-3 displays the interface of Web Platform Installer 4.5 when installing Workflow Manager 1.0.

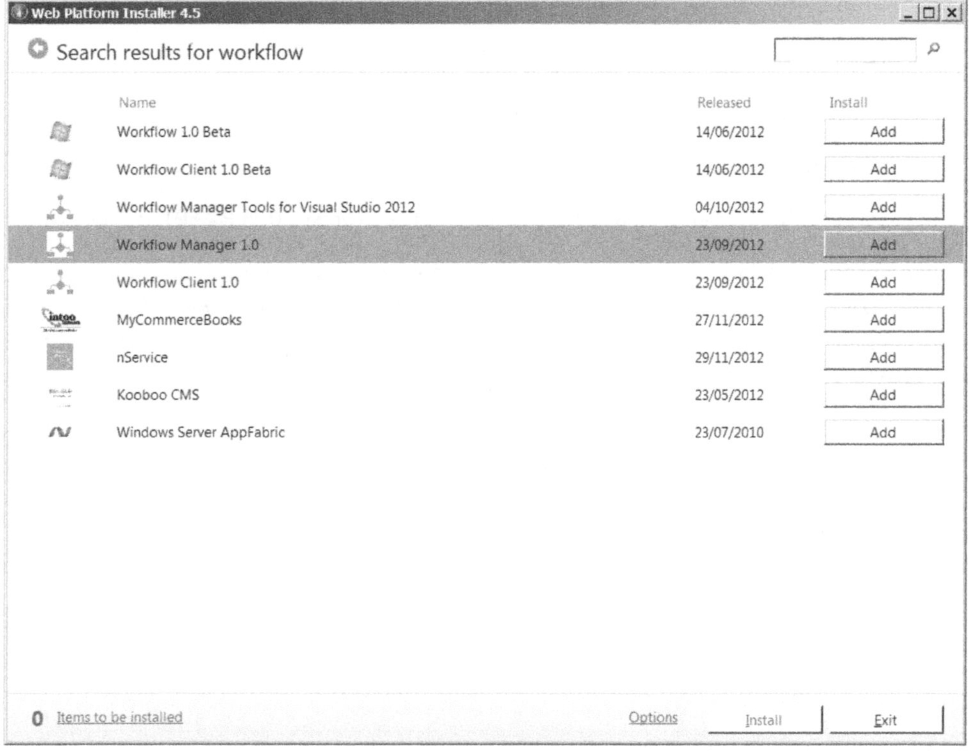

FIGURE 16-3 The Web Platform Installer UI during the installation of Workflow Manager 1.0.

More Info Be careful to download the right version of the product. In fact, via Web Platform Installer 4.5, you can download Workflow Manager 1.0 as well as the Workflow 1.0 beta 2version. However, the beta version is not supported on SharePoint 2013 RTM. Moreover, the Workflow Manager 1.0 package includes Workflow Client 1.0, and you do not need to download and install it separately.

In order to leverage the new workflow engine on-premises, you should install the February 2013 Cumulative Update of both Service Bus 1.0 and Workflow Manager 1.0. Moreover, you should install the March 2013 Public Update for SharePoint 2013. Lastly, you need to have the RTM version of the Office Developer Tools for Visual Studio 2012.

To install Workflow Manager 1.0, you need the following:

- .NET Framework 4.5
- Service Bus 1.0 (Plus February 2013 CU)
- Workflow Client 1.0 (Plus February 2013 CU)
- Windows PowerShell 3.0
- SQL Server 2008 R2 Service Pack 1 (SP1), SQL Server Express 2008 R2 SP1, or SQL Server 2012

If you are installing Workflow Manager 1.0 on the same servers where you are running the SharePoint 2013 farm, all these requirements will be already satisfied. Otherwise, if you plan to install Workflow Manager on-premises on a dedicated set of servers, you will have to install all of them, and you will have to install Workflow Client 1.0 only onto the SharePoint servers.

After you install Workflow Manager 1.0, you must run the Workflow Manager Configuration Wizard, which will walk you through the various configuration steps. The configuration wizard starts by asking if you want to configure a new Workflow Manager farm or if you want to join an already existing farm (Figure 16-4).

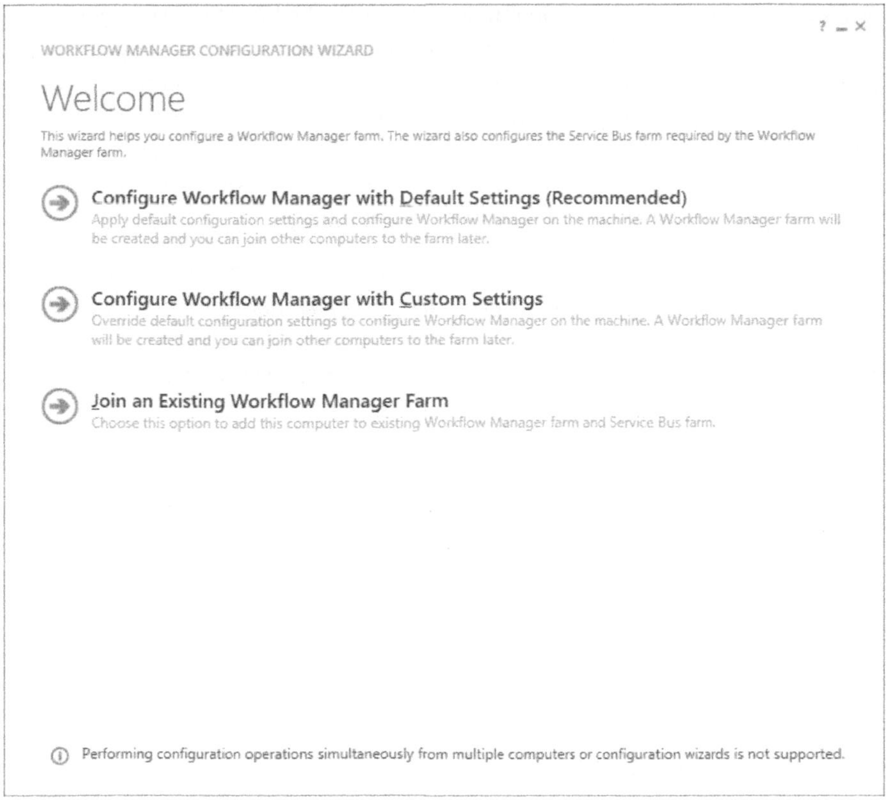

FIGURE 16-4 The first step of the Workflow Manager Configuration Wizard.

Choose to configure a new farm, and select the second option—Configure Workflow Manager With Custom Settings—which will allow you to personalize the farm configuration for your testing, development, or production environment.

Next, the wizard asks you to provide some configuration information about the Workflow Manager farm (Figure 16-5). You will have to provide information about the following:

- The target Microsoft SQL Server service instance and the database name for storing the Workflow Manager farm management data.
- The target Microsoft SQL Server service instance and the database name for storing workflow instance data.
- The target Microsoft SQL Server service instance and the database name for storing workflow resources.
- The account to use for running the Workflow Manager service instance. This should be a set of valid domain-level credentials, which will be authorized to log on as a service on the servers of the farm. You should avoid using any domain administrative account for this purpose. It would be better to create a dedicated service account.

- The certificates to use for securing communication across the Workflow Manager farm, as well as for securing configuration data. You can autogenerate these certificates by simply providing a shared secret, or you can provide the three certificates (communication, outbound signing, and configuration encryption) needed, choosing them from the current certificate store. In a real production environment, the best practice is to use manually created certificates, because you will have to trust them on all of the machines and services consuming the Workflow Manager farm, including the SharePoint 2013 farm.
- The TCP ports that will be used by Workflow Manager to publish its environment. By default, the ports configured are port 12290 for secure (HTTPS) management requests, and port 12291 for insecure (HTTP) management requests. In a development and testing environment, you can configure HTTP, too. In a production environment, however, you should avoid publishing Workflow Manager over HTTP for security reasons.
- The domain group that will determine the users authorized to manage the Workflow Manager farm. Again, you should create and configure a dedicated group, rather than use the automatically proposed group of domain administrators.

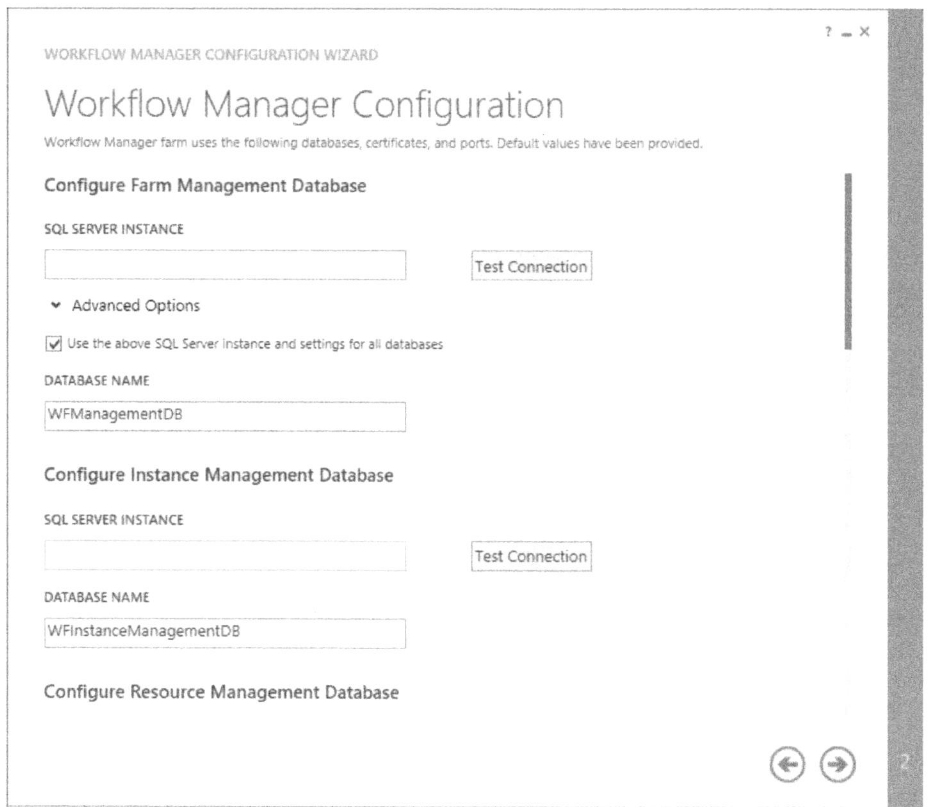

FIGURE 16-5 The second step of the Workflow Manager Configuration Wizard, for configuring the Workflow Manager farm.

After you configure the Workflow Manager farm, you must configure the Service Bus. Again, the wizard will drive you through the steps to accomplish this task. In particular, as you can see in Figure 16-6, you will be prompted for providing the following information:

- The target Microsoft SQL Server service instance and the database name for storing the Service Bus farm management data.
- The target Microsoft SQL Server service instance and the database name for storing the Service Bus gateway data.
- The target Microsoft SQL Server service instance and the database name for storing the Service Bus message container data.
- The account to use for running the Service Bus service instance. This should be a set of valid domain-level credentials, which will be authorized to log on as a service on the servers of the farm. Avoid using any domain administrative account for this purpose; create a dedicated service account instead.
- The certificates to use for securing communication with the Workflow Manager farm, as well as for securing configuration data. You can autogenerate these certificates simply by providing a shared secret, or you can provide the two certificates (for communication and configuration encryption) needed, choosing them from the current certificate store. In a real production environment, the best practice, once again, is to use manually created certificates, because you will have to trust them on all of the machines and services consuming the Workflow Manager farm, including the SharePoint 2013 farm.
- The TCP ports that will be used by the Service Bus to publish its environment. By default, the ports configured are port 9355 for secure (HTTPS) communication, port 9344 for network-level (TCP) communication, and port 9356 for message broker communication. It will be configured also a port range of five ports, by default starting on port 9000 and ending on port 9005, for internal farm communication between servers in the Service Bus farm.
- The domain group that will determine the users authorized to manage the Service Bus farm. Again, you should create and configure a dedicated group, rather than using the automatically proposed group of domain administrators.

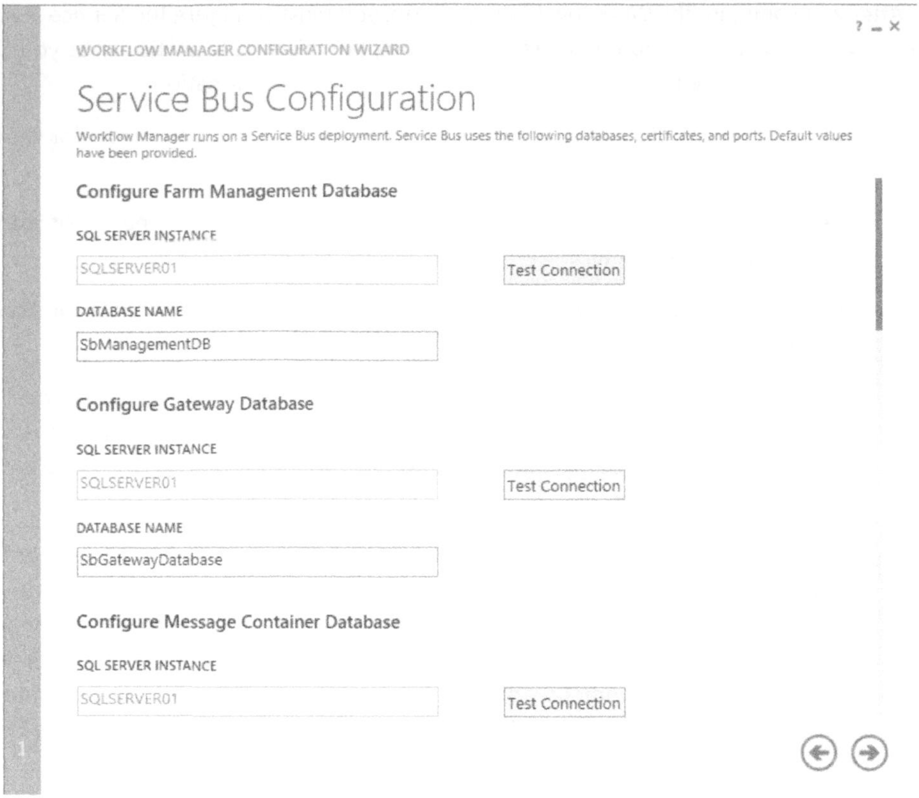

FIGURE 16-6 The main step of the Service Bus Configuration wizard for configuring the Workflow Manager farm.

The Workflow Manager Configuration wizard also allows you to generate a PowerShell script for automating the installation process, just in case you want to repeat the same installation process using that script. After configuring a first server in the farm, you will be able to add as many servers as you want. It will suffice to download and install Workflow Manager 1.0 on any target server and to run the Workflow Manager Configuration wizard, choosing to join an already existing farm.

After having configured the Workflow Manager farm, you will have a wide set of database files configured on the target Microsoft SQL Server database engine, including

- The Service Bus Gateway database
- The Service Bus Management database
- The Service Bus Message Container database
- The Workflow Manager Instance Management database
- The Workflow Manager Management database
- The Workflow Manager Resource Management database

While on your development environment, you need not give these database files special attention, but in a real production environment, you should consider including these databases in you disaster-recovery and high-availability plans.

More Info For further details about deploying a highly available Workflow Manager farm, read the article "Configuring a Highly Available Workflow in Workflow Manager 1.0," available on MSDN at *http://msdn.microsoft.com/en-us/library/windowsazure/jj193534.aspx.*

After you configure a Workflow Manager farm, you should have three services running on the target servers:

- Service Bus Gateway
- Service Bus Message Broker
- Workflow Manager Backend

The last step before you can use Workflow Manager in SharePoint 2013 is to link the Workflow Manager farm with the SharePoint 2013 farm. To accomplish this task, you simply need to execute the following PowerShell cmdlet:

```
Register-SPWorkflowService -SPSite 'http://devbook.sp2013.local/' -WorkflowHostUri 'http://
sp2013srv01:12291/' -AllowOAuthHttp -Force $wfproxy = Get-SPWorkflowServiceApplicationProxy
$wfproxy.RegisterWorkflowLifecycleManagementEnvironment()
```

Table 16-1 lists all of the arguments available for the *Register-SPWorkflowService* cmdlet.

TABLE 16-1 Arguments that you can provide to the *Register-SPWorkflowService* cmdlet

Argument	Description
SPSite	Specifies the target site collection to configure.
WorkflowHostUri	Specifies the full URL (including the port number) of the workflow service management endpoint.
AllowOAuthHttp	Enables support for OAuth over HTTP, instead of requiring HTTPS.
Force	Forces the current configuration, overwriting any already existing configuration settings and ignoring any errors.
PartitionMode	Allows connecting each subscription (tenant) to a dedicated workflow service instance. If not provided, every subscription will connect to a single and shared workflow service instance.
ScopeName	Specifies a name for identifying the SharePoint 2013 farm to the workflow service instance.

As already stated, in a development or testing environment, you could configure the Workflow Manager farm to use HTTP and port 12291, and not only HTTPS and port 12290. On the other hand, in a production environment, you should always configure HTTPS, and you should register as trusted the X.509 certificate used by the Workflow Manager farm on the SharePoint 2013 farm as well.

More Info For further details about managing SSL certificates between Workflow Manager 1.0 and SharePoint 2013, read the article "Installing Workflow Manager certificates in SharePoint Server 2013," available on TechNet at *http://technet.microsoft.com/en-us/library/jj658589.aspx*.

After linking the SharePoint 2013 farm with the Workflow Manager farm, you will be able to find a new service application proxy named Workflow Service Application Proxy under SharePoint Central Administration (SPCA), on the Manage Service Applications page. By clicking that service application proxy, you will be presented with a simple page stating that the workflow service is connected, as shown in Figure 16-7.

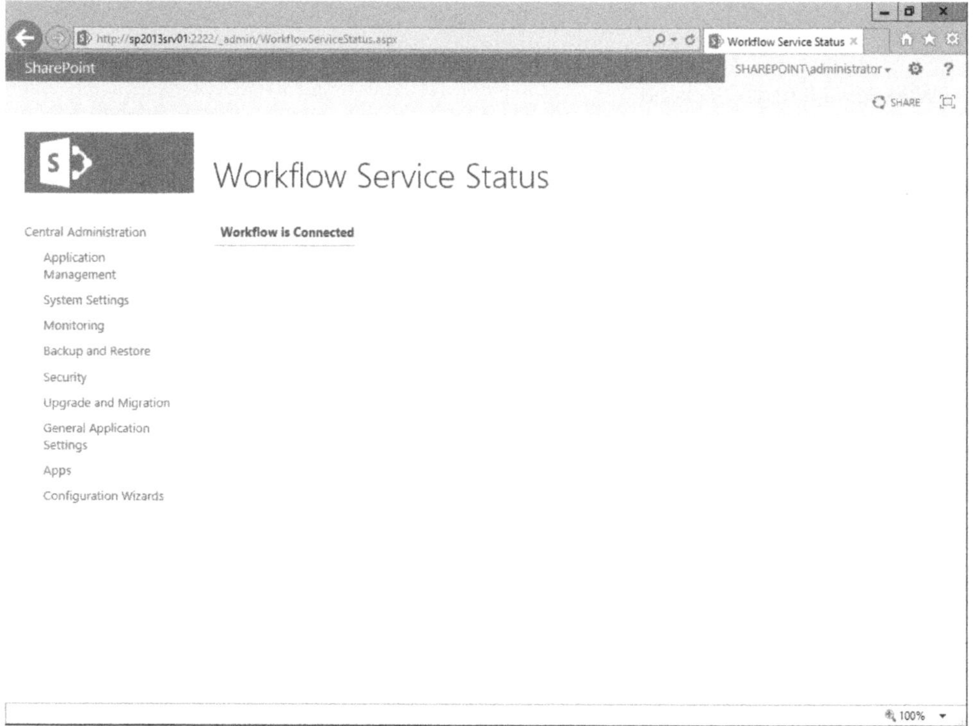

FIGURE 16-7 The service application proxy page of the Workflow Service Application Proxy.

One last test to check that the workflow service is properly configured and connected to SharePoint 2013 is to start a new instance of SharePoint Designer 2013 and access the site you just connected with the workflow service. Click the Workflows command on the left-hand accordion and add a new list workflow definition for any of the available lists or libraries—for example, choose the Documents library if it exists in the target site. In the Create List Workflow dialog box will be a drop-down list with a caption of Platform Type (see Figure 16-8).

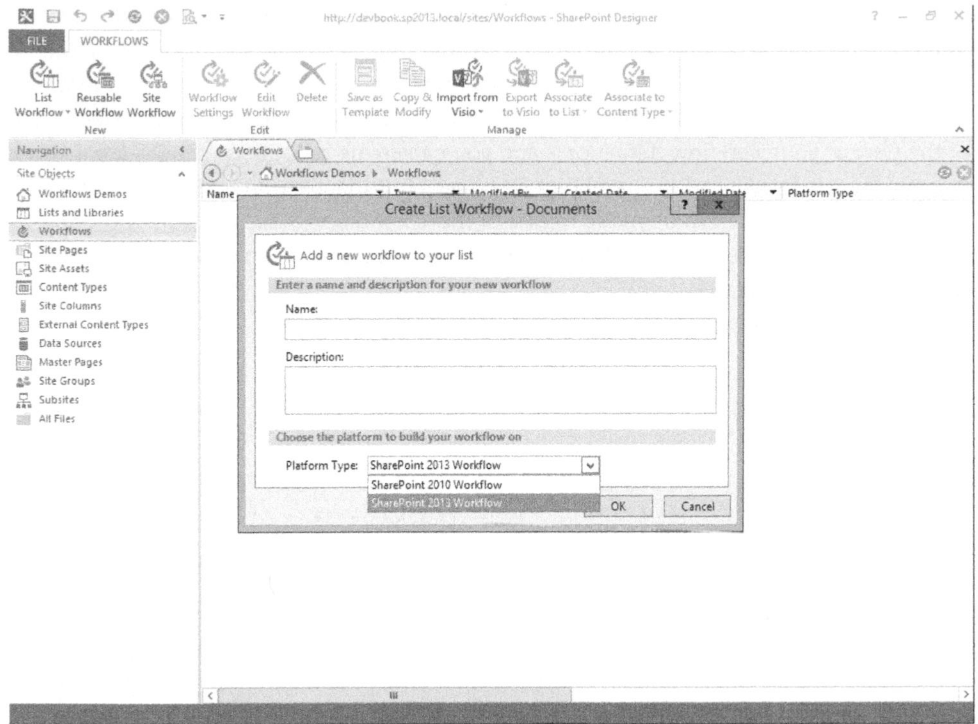

FIGURE 16-8 The dialog window for creating a new list workflow definition in SharePoint Designer 2013.

If this drop-down list provides you both SharePoint 2010 Workflow (WF 3.*x*) and SharePoint 2013 Workflow (WF 4.5), then you are ready to start creating workflows with the new workflow engine. If you see only SharePoint 2010 Workflow, you need to double-check your farm configuration.

Your first workflow with SharePoint Designer 2013

The best way to learn about a tool or technique is to see it in action, so in this section, you will create a SharePoint workflow from scratch with Microsoft SharePoint Designer 2013. For this exercise, imagine that you want to implement a sample approval workflow, which will assign an approval task to a target user as soon as a new document is uploaded to a target library.

To begin, open SharePoint Designer 2013 and connect to a target site configured for supporting the new workflow engine. Choose the Workflows section in the left-hand accordion and select the command to create a new List Workflow. For example, target the Documents library that is available by default in many site definitions, or create a new document library for using it as the target of your workflow definition. Choose the SharePoint 2013 workflow target platform.

SharePoint Designer 2013 will prompt you with a new design surface, which is made of stages. A *stage* is a piece of a workflow definition that allows grouping conditions and actions together. You can think of a stage as a state in a state machine workflow; you can go to a specific stage when a certain condition occurs, or you can repeat a stage until a condition ceases. Through stages, you can control the flow of your workflow definitions, and you can create repetitions. Stages are a new and fundamental feature introduced in SharePoint Designer 2013 thanks to the new workflow engine of SharePoint 2013. Each stage can be made of one or more conditions, steps, actions, or loops. On the top ribbon of SharePoint Designer 2013, as shown in Figure 16-9, you can choose to add any of these elements to the design surface.

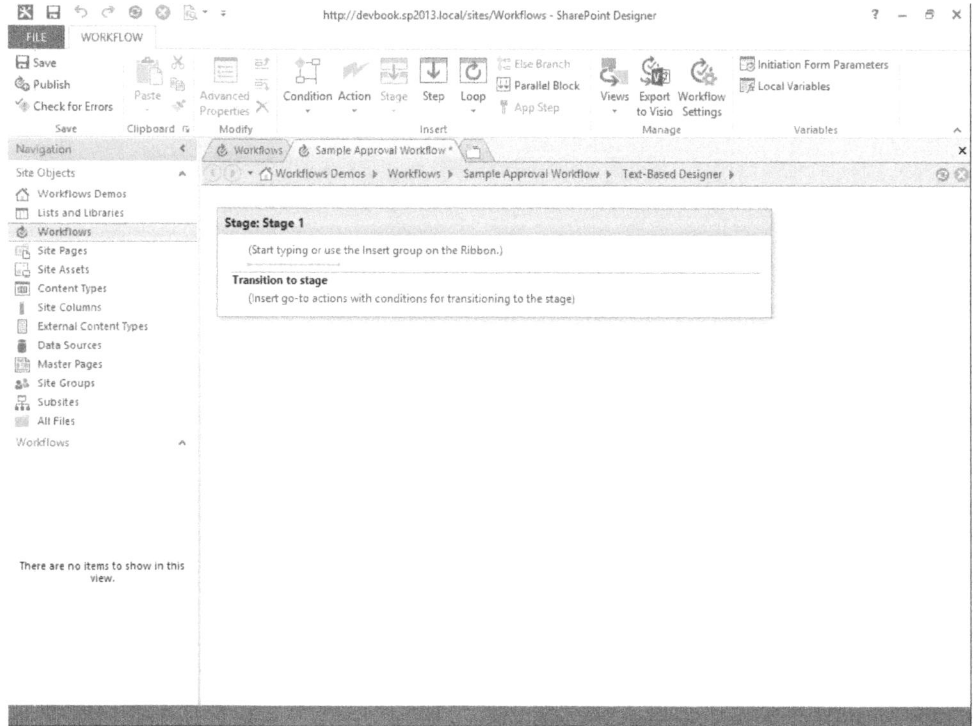

FIGURE 16-9 The workflow design surface of SharePoint Designer 2013.

When designing an approval workflow, you first must define some infrastructural variables and startup parameters, which will be used to configure any workflow instance. On the ribbon, click the Initiation Form Parameters button. You will be prompted with a dialog box like the one illustrated in Figure 16-10.

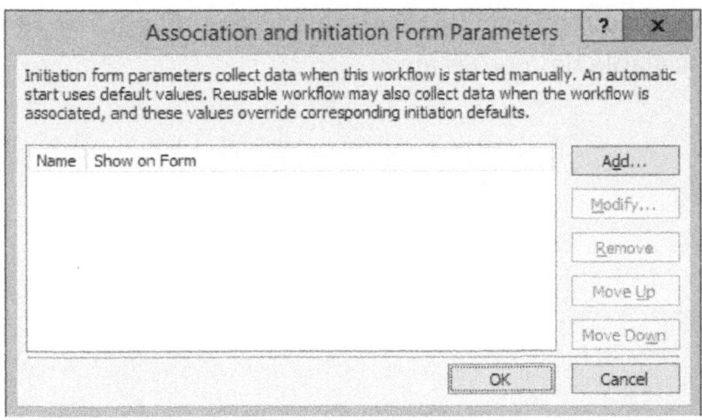

FIGURE 16-10 The Association And Initiation Form Parameters dialog box of SharePoint Designer 2013.

As in SharePoint 2010, in SharePoint 2013 a workflow definition can have an *association form*, which is used to configure the workflow association with its target. It can also have an *initiation form*, which is used to provide startup parameters to a specific workflow instance. An association or initiation parameter can assume several types of values:

- Single line of text
- Multiple lines of text
- Number (for example, 1, 1.0, or 100)
- Date and time
- Choice (menu to choose from)
- Yes/no (check box)
- Person or group
- Hyperlink or picture

You can define every parameter by providing a name, a description, an underlying data type, and an optional default value. Assume that the current approval workflow needs to define a default request-for-approval message during association, as well as a target approver (person or group) during initiation. Add a couple of parameters that fit these definitions and name them *ApprovalRequestMessage* and *TargetApprover*. As you define each parameter, the interface of the dialog box adapts to the target data type you choose. For example, while configuring the *TargetApprover* parameter as a field of type Person or Group, you are prompted with a designer for configuring the behavior of the *PeoplePicker* control that will be used.

Now you can define some variables by clicking the Local Variables ribbon command. The variables should have a name and a data type. The available data types are:

- *Boolean*
- *Date/Time*
- *Dictionary*
- *GUID*
- *Integer*
- *Number*
- *String*

First, define an *ApprovalOutcome* variable of data type *Boolean*. Now you are ready to design the real workflow. In order to ask to the *TargetApprover* subject to approve the document, add an action, evaluate its result, and change the status of the target document. The action for assigning a task to a target user is available in the Actions group. In Chapter 15, "Windows Workflow Foundation," you learned how to create a very simple activity from scratch by writing some custom code. From a SharePoint 2013 viewpoint, an action is a wrapper around one or more activities that makes them available as a human-readable statement. Table 16-2 lists the default actions available in SharePoint Designer 2013. Although they are not listed here, some legacy actions of SharePoint 2010 are still available (for backward compatibility) in SharePoint 2013 via the interop bridge.

TABLE 16-2 The default actions available in SharePoint Designer 2013

Action name	Description
Start a List Workflow	Starts a new list workflow instance based on the SharePoint 2010 workflow engine. You can provide some input parameters and choose the target item on which the workflow instance will be executed.
Start a Site Workflow	Starts a new site workflow instance based on the SharePoint 2010 workflow engine. You can provide some input parameters with which the workflow instance will be executed.
Add a Comment	Enables you to leave a comment on the workflow design surface.
Add Time to Date	Adds a specific time in minute, hours, days, or months to a date. The output is saved in a variable. The date to change can be a specific date, the current date, or a lookup value.
Build Dictionary	Builds a dictionary variable (key/values pairs). It is typically used for managing JavaScript Object Notation (JSON) data retrieved from an external Representational State Transfer (REST) service consumed over HTTP. The output is saved in a variable.
Call HTTP Web Service	Allows calling an external REST service over HTTP, using the verbs *GET*, *POST*, *PUT*, and *DELETE*. You can provide a variable (typically a dictionary) as an input request and get back a response variable, which can still be a dictionary. You can also collect variables for retrieving the HTTP response headers and the HTTP response status code.
Count Items in a Dictionary	Counts the number of items in a dictionary, storing the resulting number into a variable.

Action name	Description
Do Calculation	Performs a calculation across two numbers, specific or lookup, applying any of the following operations: plus, minus, multiply by, divide by, and module. The result is saved in a variable.
Get an Item from a Dictionary	Retrieves a specific item from a dictionary variable, storing the result in a variable.
Log to History List	Logs a message to the workflow history list.
Pause for Duration	Pauses the current workflow instance for a time interval in days, hours, and minutes.
Pause until Date	Pauses the current workflow instance until a specific date and time, which can be provided as an explicit value or can be read from a lookup value or variable.
Send an Email	Sends an email to a user or group of users. You can configure properties for To, CC, Subject (specific or lookup/calculated), and Message Body (with formatting and calculated fields). Internally, it uses the *SPUtility.SendMail* function via the Client-Side Object Model (CSOM).
Set Time Portion of Date/Time Field	Sets the time portion (hours and minutes) of a date or time field. It saves the result in a variable.
Set Workflow Status	Sets the status of the current workflow instance.
Set Workflow Variable	Sets the value of a variable of the current workflow instance.
Check In Item	Checks in an item in a target document library.
Check Out Item	Checks out an item from a target document library.
Copy Document	Copies a document from one document library to another.
Create List Item	Creates a new list item in a target list. You can provide field values for the new item.
Delete Item	Deletes an item from a list.
Discard Check Out Item	Discards changes and checks in an item that is checked out.
Set Field in Current Item	Sets the value of a specific field into the current item.
Translate Document	Translates a specific document in a particular language using the Machine Translation Service application introduced with SharePoint 2013 Server. The result is saved as a document in a specified target library.
Update List Item	Updates a list item in a target list. You can provide field values to update in the target item.
Wait for Event in List Item	Pauses the current workflow instance, waiting for a specified event. The event can be an *ItemAdded* or an *ItemUpdated* event. The result is stored in a variable.
Wait for Field Change in Current Item	Pauses the current workflow instance, waiting for a specific field of the current item to change its value.
Assign a Task	Assigns a task to a target person or group. You can define participants, title, description (with formatting and lookup), and due date. You can wait, pausing the workflow instance, for task completion. You can plan to send a reminder email and recurrent reminder emails. You can also define custom task outcome values.
Start a Task Process	Starts a task process with multiple task recipients. You can define task completion to be serial (one at a time) or parallel (all at once). You can pause the current workflow instance, waiting for all responses, the first response, a specific response, or the percentage of responses.
Extract Substring from End of String	Copies *n* characters from the end of a string and copies the result into a variable.

Action name	Description
Extract Substring from Index of String	Retrieves a substring from a provided string, starting at a specified character index, and copies the result into a variable.
Extract Substring from Start of String	Copies *n* characters from the beginning of a string and copies the result into a variable.
Extract Substring of String from Index with Length	Retrieves a substring from a provided string, starting at a specified character index, copying *n* characters and storing the result into a variable.
Find Interval Between Dates	Calculates the time interval in minutes, hours, or days between two dates and saves the result in a variable.
Find Substring in String	Searches for a substring in a specified string and returns the index of the substring's starting point, if any, into a result variable.
Replace Substring in String	Replaces a substring in a provided string and stores the result in a variable.
Trim String	Removes white spaces at the begging and end of a provided string value and stores the result in a variable.
Go to Stage	Defines the next stage to which the current workflow instance will go.

To monitor the outcome of actions and determine the flow of a process, you can use conditions. Table 16-3 lists the conditions available in SharePoint Designer 2013. Although not included here, some legacy SharePoint 2010 conditions are still available (for backward compatibility) via the interop bridge. In addition, in Chapter 18, "Advanced workflows," you will learn how to extend the list of conditions and actions by creating custom code in Visual Studio 2012.

TABLE 16-3 The conditions available in SharePoint Designer 2013

Condition name	Description
If Any Value Equals Value	Checks if a field value of the current item or of a lookup item equals a specific value
Created by a Specific Person	Checks if the current item has been created by a specific person
Created in a Specific Date Span	Checks if the current item has been created within a specific date and time interval
Modified by a Specific Person	Checks if the current item has been modified by a specific person
Modified in a Specific Date Span	Checks if the current item has been modified within a specific date and time interval
Person Is a Valid SharePoint User	Checks if a specific person is a valid SharePoint user
Title Field Contains Keywords	Checks if the Title field value of the current item contains a specific string value

Lastly, you can define loops (*Loop n Times and Loop with Condition* action), as well as parallel blocks, which are useful for creating real workflow and business processes.

For the sample approval workflow, you need to add a few more actions from Table 16-2. Assume that the approval process should not take more than five days from the creation of the target item to approve. Thus, insert an *Add Time to Date* action to add five days to the current date and time, and store the result in a variable. Next, add an action to assign an approval task to the target approver user, providing values for task recipients, title, description, and due date, and reading them from the current workflow variables. Now rename the current stage by clicking the stage title and providing a Title value of "Assign Approval Task."

Add a new stage and name it Check Approval Outcome. At the very end of the first stage, add a *Go to Stage* action, and set the target stage to the Check Approval Outcome stage. In the new stage, add a condition of type *If Any Value Equals Value*, and configure it to check the approval task outcome. If the task outcome is an approval, the workflow will set the workflow variable named *ApprovalOutcome* to a value of *Yes*; otherwise, it will set that variable to a value of *No*. Moreover, the workflow will save a message in the history list to track the approval result.

Lastly, the stage will read any comment from the approval task and save it into the *ApprovalComment* workflow variable. To complete the workflow definition, create the second stage to complete the workflow instance, configuring a *Go to Stage* action to go to the *End of Workflow* action. Figure 16-11 shows the resulting workflow definition.

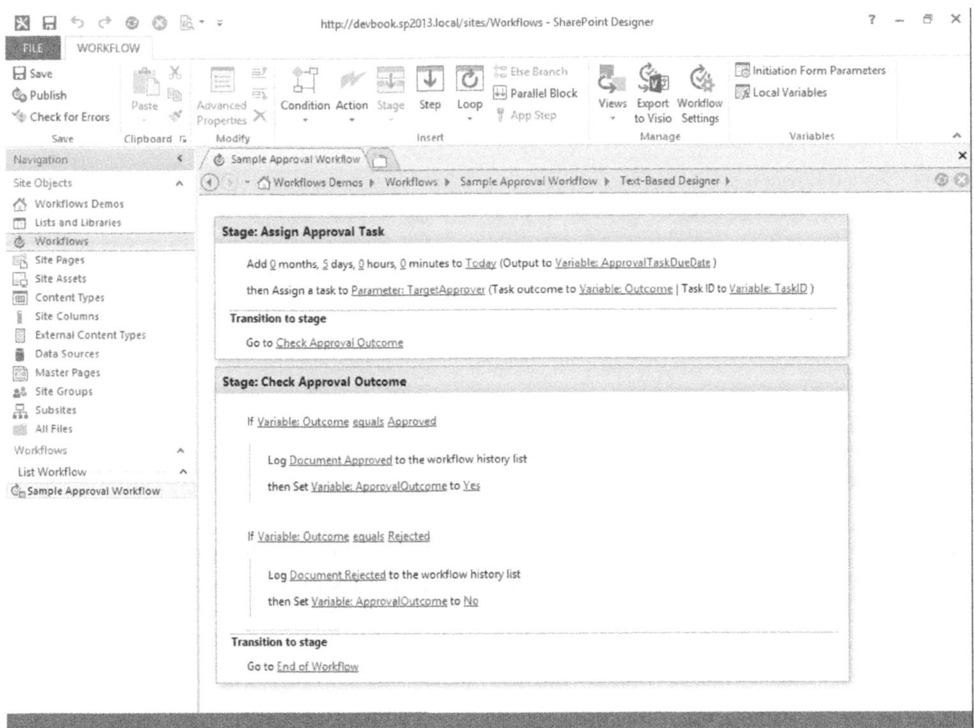

FIGURE 16-11 The approval workflow designed in SharePoint Designer 2013.

To test the example workflow, you need to save and publish it using the corresponding ribbon commands on the ribbon of SharePoint Designer 2013. As soon as you publish the workflow definition, you can browse to the target library, upload a document, and start a workflow instance. To start an instance, click the ECB (Edit Control Block) menu of the newly uploaded item and choose the Workflows menu item. As shown in Figure 16-12, you will be prompted with the list of all the available workflow definitions, grouped by target platform type (SharePoint 2010 workflows and SharePoint 2013 workflows). Start the example workflow and follow the process.

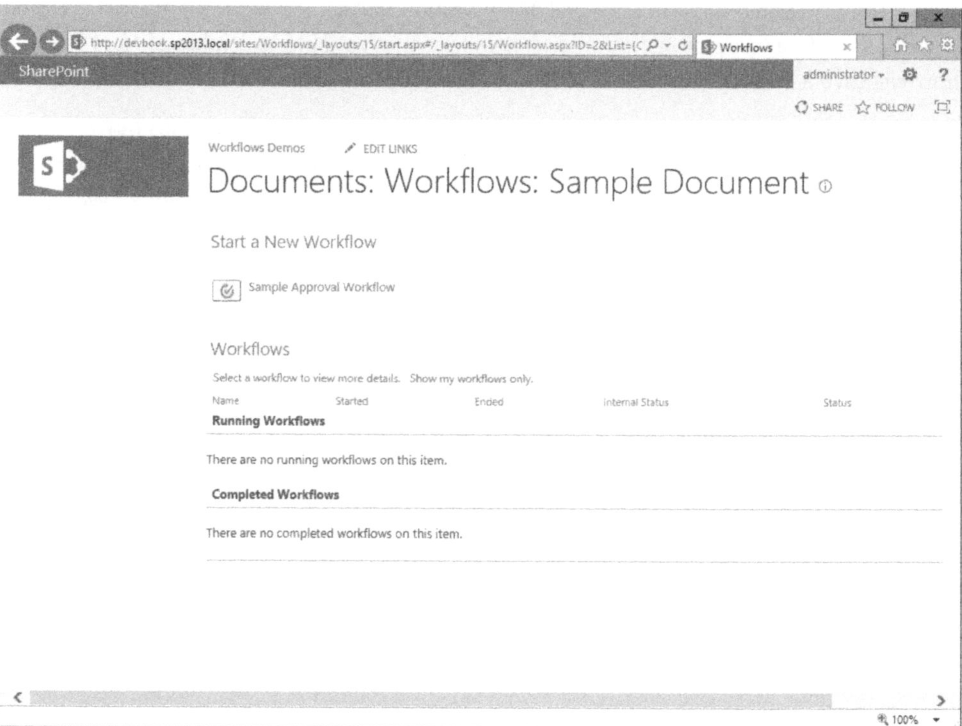

FIGURE 16-12 The page for starting a new workflow instance in SharePoint 2013.

Upon starting the workflow instance, you will be prompted with the initiation form, which asks you to provide the initiation parameters that were defined at the very beginning of the workflow design process. Those are the *ApprovalRequestMessage* and *TargetApprover* parameters. Figure 16-13 shows the initiation form autogenerated by SharePoint Designer 2013.

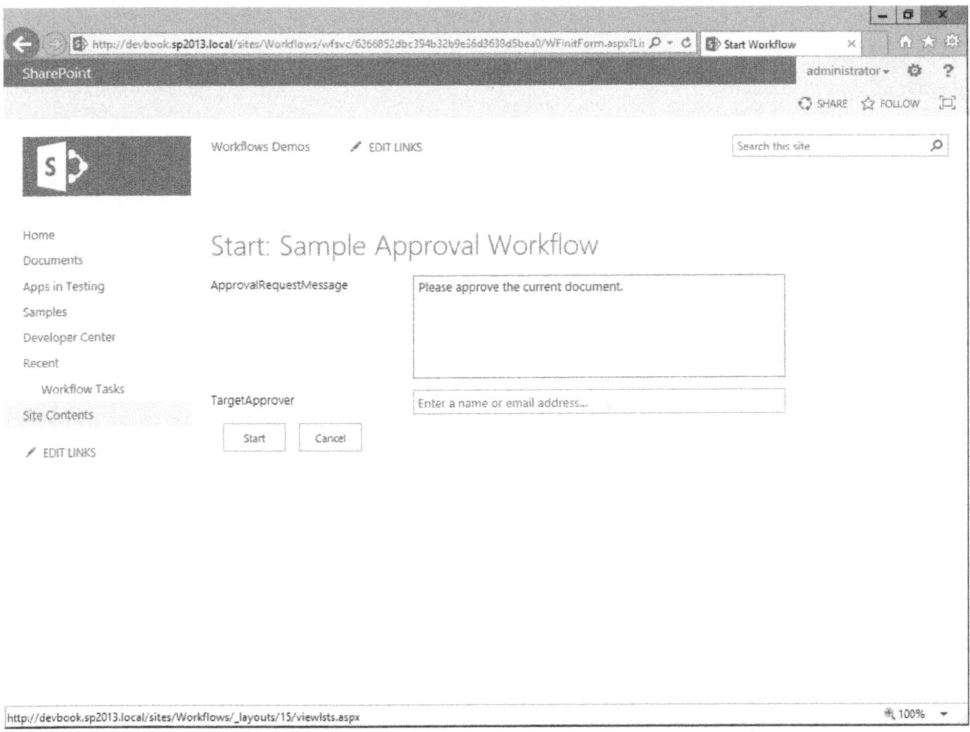

FIGURE 16-13 The initiation form of the sample document approval workflow.

Start the workflow instance and follow the process. Notice the default view of the current library now displays the name of the running workflow instance as the title of the workflow status field. This field presents the status of the running workflow instances and behaves like any other list field, enabling you to filter and sort values. You can export the field into such client platforms as the Office 2013 client, and it provides a direct entry point to the workflow status page, which contains information about the currently running workflow instance, the pending tasks, and the history list. Figure 16-14 highlights the workflow status field.

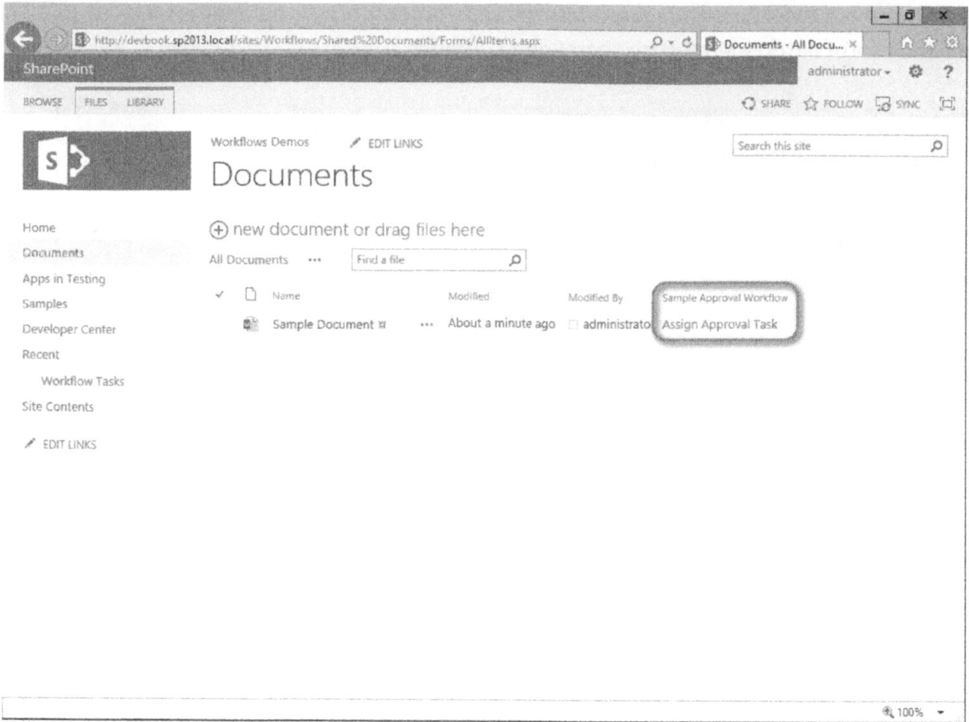

FIGURE 16-14 The document library view with the approval workflow status field outlined in red.

The workflow status page provides information about the workflow initiator, the start date and time, the last run date and time, the SharePoint internal status of the workflow instance, and the workflow status. Table 16-4 lists the possible values for the workflow internal status field, while Figure 16-15 highlights two workflow status fields on the workflow status page.

TABLE 16-4 The values available for the internal status field of a workflow instance

Status name	Description
NotStarted	Signals that the workflow instance has not started.
Started	Signals that the workflow instance has started and is running.
Suspended	Signals that execution of the workflow has been stopped, but may be resumed.
Canceling	Signals that the workflow instance has received a cancellation message.
Canceled	Signals that execution of the specified workflow instance is canceled.
Terminated	Terminates the running workflow instance and raises the *Completed* event in the host. Once the workflow is terminated, it cannot be resumed.
Completed	Signals that the workflow instance has finished running.
NotSpecified	Signals that no status has been specified.
Invalid	Signals that the workflow instance is in an invalid state.

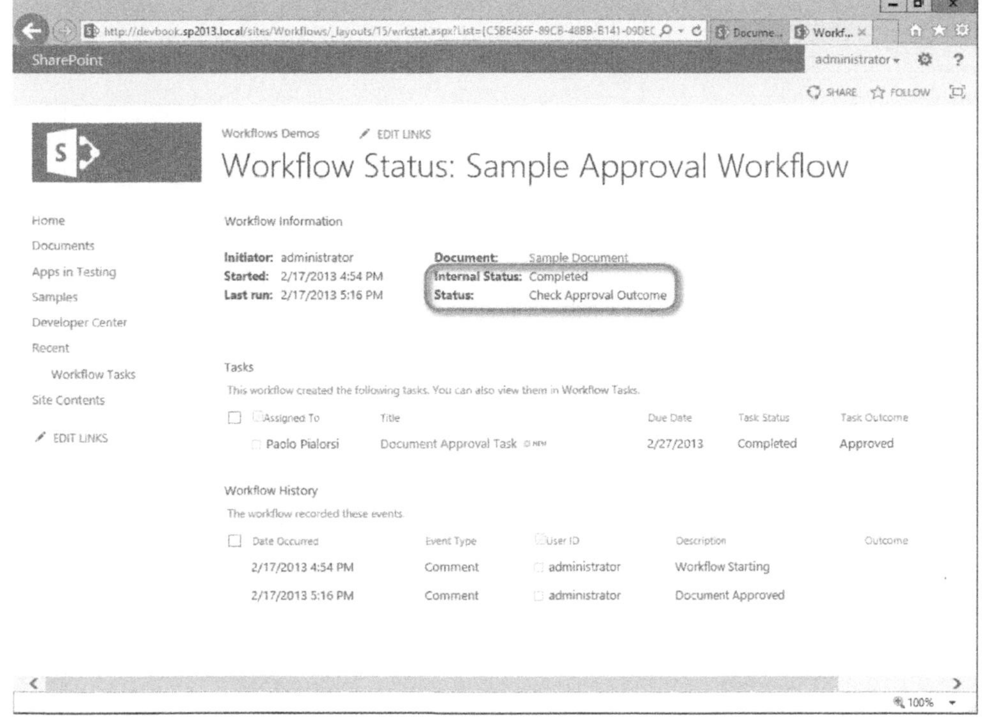

FIGURE 16-15 The two workflow status fields provided by the workflow status page.

Figure 16-16 shows the form for editing the approval task. To reach that form, simply click any task presented on the workflow status page, and then select the Edit Task command from the ECB menu. As you can see, aside from the standard task fields, there are a few commands in the bottom area of the form for approving or rejecting the document.

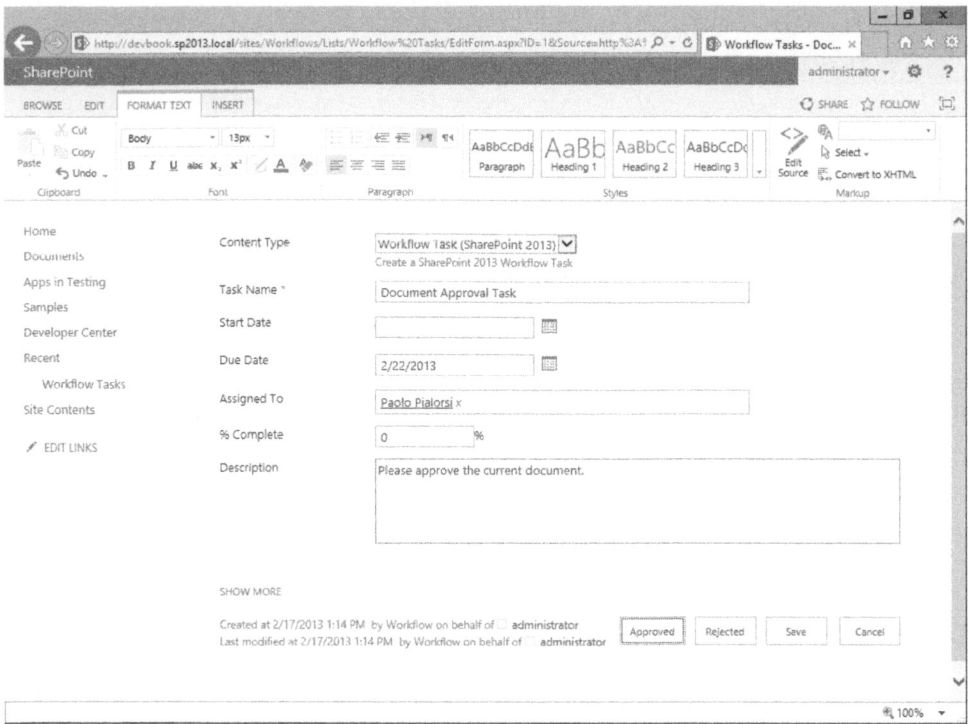

FIGURE 16-16 The approval task form provided by default in SharePoint 2013 for a workflow approval task.

In SharePoint, tasks like the one illustrated in Figure 16-16 are a fundamental part of a workflow process and, in general, are among the most frequently used techniques to interact with end users. Before SharePoint 2013, a user had to browse all the lists of tasks of every different site to manage his or her assigned tasks—a complex and time-consuming process. Luckily, SharePoint 2013 introduces the new Work Management Service Application, which enables you to aggregate tasks from multiple systems into a unique and central location. This location is the user's personal site and is provided through the User Profile service. Users can aggregate tasks from SharePoint 2013, Microsoft Exchange Server 2013, Microsoft Project Server 2013, and potentially any other provider that supports the Work Management Service Application. Thus, all the workflow tasks created by SharePoint 2013 workflows, regardless of the site where they were created, are aggregated and provided to the end users through a unique and consolidated UI, which improves usability and productivity of end users.

Back to SharePoint Designer 2013, you can experience one of the most brilliant features introduced in SharePoint 2013 workflows: the visual designer view. Click the Views ribbon command and choose Visual Designer view. Figure 16-17 shows the result.

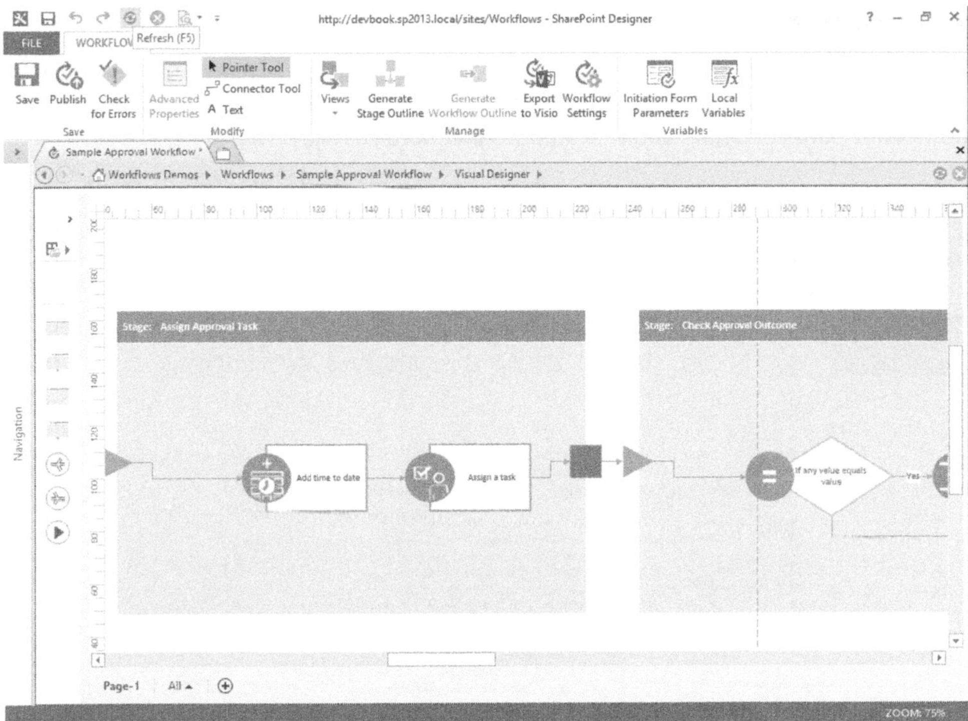

FIGURE 16-17 The approval workflow in the visual designer view in SharePoint Designer 2013.

You can click the Export to Visio ribbon command to export the workflow definition into a VSDX file of Microsoft Visio 2013. This capability is useful if you need to share the workflow process definition with someone who is not an experienced SharePoint user or designer, but rather a businessperson with only Visio 2013 installed on his or her machine. In Visio 2013, you will have exactly the same user experience you have in SharePoint Designer 2013 while in the Visual Designer view. Lastly, consider that, at a later time, you will be able to import into SharePoint Designer 2013 a workflow definition designed or edited in Visio 2013.

More about workflows

Now that you have defined a basic workflow sample, you can tackle some more advanced and useful topics. For example, you will see how exceptions are handled in workflows and how they are presented to end users. You will also learn how to create reusable workflows and how to manage versioning of workflows definitions.

Exception management

Consider exception management, for example. SharePoint Designer 2013 does not include any actions or conditions to implement *try...catch* blocks for business logic. Instead, you must consult the workflow status page for details about exceptions that occur, as shown in Figure 16-18.

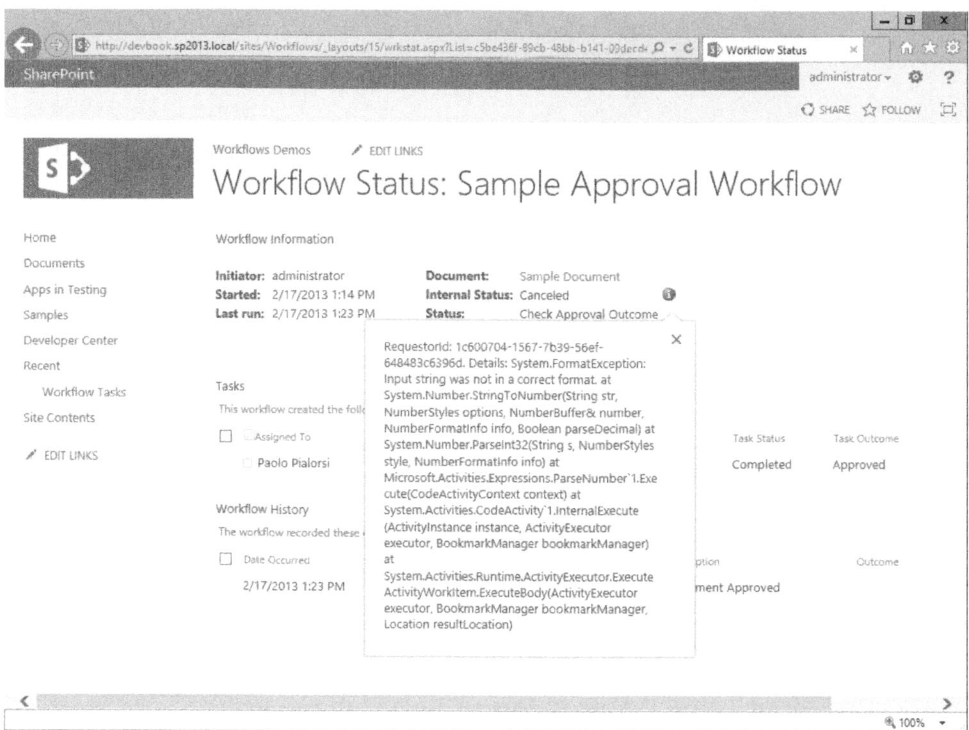

FIGURE 16-18 The workflow status page of a workflow instance that raised an exception while running.

As you can see, the stack trace message that pops up when you click the info icon is not completely user friendly and probably would be unintelligible to the average end user. Another common exception occurs if the user tries to start an instance of a workflow definition that is already running against the current item. The workflow instance will not start, because only a single instance of a workflow definition can be started against an item. The workflow instance will try to start, however, and will instantly fail with an internal status value of Terminated, providing a message like the one shown in Figure 16-19.

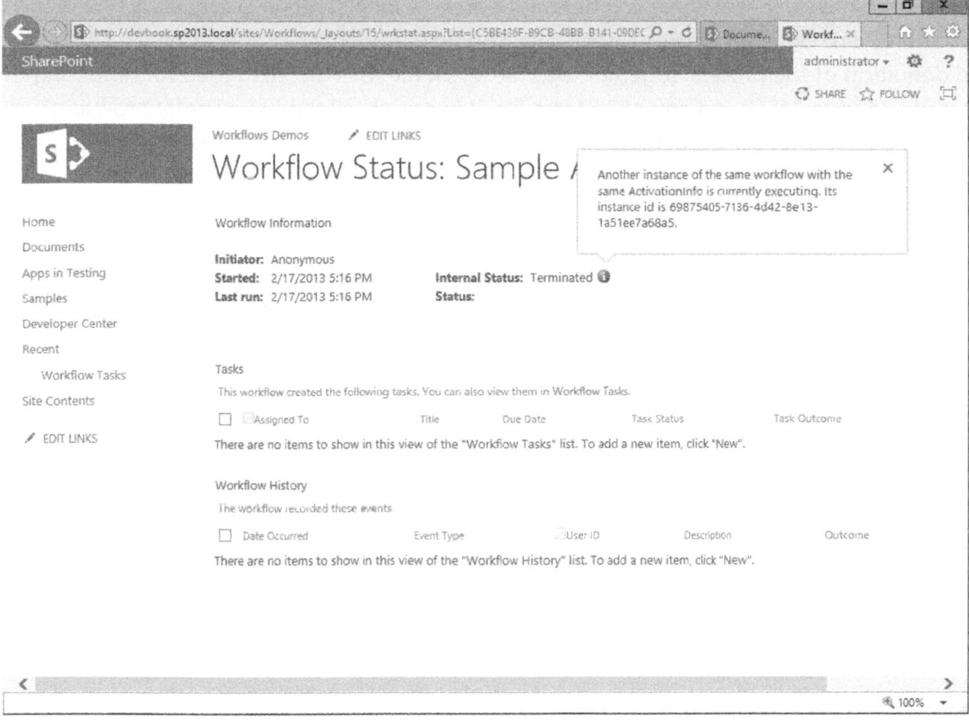

FIGURE 16-19 The workflow status page of a workflow instance that has been terminated because another instance of the same workflow definition is already running on it.

Reusable workflows

In SharePoint Designer 2013, you have the option to create a reusable workflow definition, which is almost the same as a classic list workflow, but you can reuse it by associating its definition with multiple targets. The design process is almost the same as the one for defining a classic list workflow as well. After saving and publishing the reusable workflow, however, you have to click the Associate To List ribbon command to effectively associate the workflow definition with a target. The association process starts your default web browser, after which you associate the workflow definition with its target using the web browser interface.

You can also save as a template a workflow definition created in SharePoint Designer 2013. A saved template is just a Windows SharePoint Services Solution Package (WSP) saved in the Sites Assets library of the current site and that you can download and reuse somewhere else.

> **Important** In Visual Studio 2012, you can import a saved WSP file using the project template called SharePoint 2013 - Import Reusable 2010 Workflow. However, be careful, because that project template works only with old-style WSP packages, which define SharePoint 2010 workflows. It does not handle SharePoint 2013 workflow definitions.

Remember, however, that when you define a workflow in SharePoint Designer 2013, behind the scenes SharePoint Designer creates a flowchart workflow model and produces only a XAML markup-based definition of the process, together with the VSDX file for Visio 2013 used for rendering the view illustrated in Figure 16-17, and any ASPX form file. You can check this behavior by browsing, using SharePoint Designer 2013, to the folder containing the source files of the workflow. In Figure 16-20 you can see the content of the folder representing the sample approval workflow.

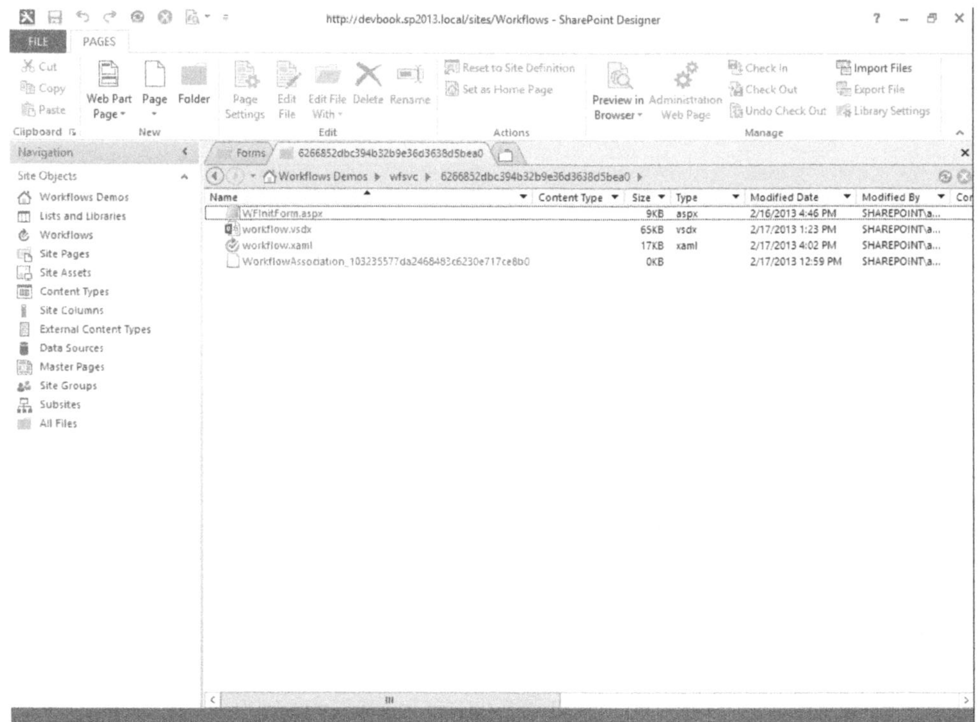

FIGURE 16-20 The content of the folder containing the sample approval workflow defined in SharePoint Designer 2013.

Versioning workflows

Starting with WF 4.5, the workflow engine of .NET Framework can manage versioning of workflow identities. From a SharePoint 2013 perspective, however, the versioning of a workflow definition remains unchanged. The Workflow Settings page, which is the page from which you associate a workflow definition with a target, gives you the option to remove an existing workflow association. When you remove one workflow definition, you must choose what will happen to the running instances of that workflow. Figure 16-21 shows the Remove Workflows page that is displayed when you choose to remove an association.

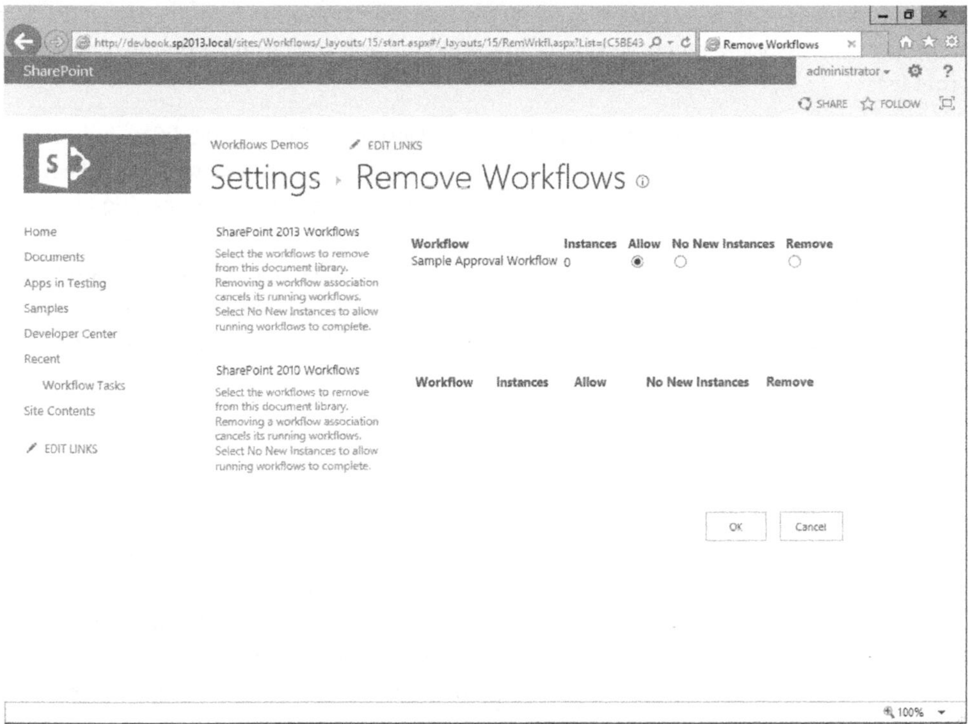

FIGURE 16-21 The Remove Workflows page for a list.

You have the option to force workflow association removal, interrupting any running instances, by selecting the Remove option. Otherwise, you can select the No New Instances option, which allows the running instances to complete, but disables the capability to create new instances of that workflow. Usually, these options are very useful when performing workflow maintenance or an upgrade. In fact, an idle workflow instance is persisted in the Workflow Manager database and will be reloaded in memory when execution starts again as the result of an event like a user's task change, a delay expiration, and so on.

When this occurs, you have no guarantee that the same workflow version will still be available in the current environment. For example, there could be a newer version, potentially different from the original one used during instance creation.

If you decide to forcibly remove the workflow association without waiting for any running instances to complete, the workflow engine of SharePoint will terminate running instances immediately, and thus avoid any kind of issues related to workflow versioning. Of course, you will lose any data or information status about the running workflow instances.

On the other hand, if you decide to prevent new instances of the workflow, but you leave all the running instances in their state, you will have the opportunity to wait for their completion. After all the running instances complete, you can forcibly remove the association from the target list. In the meantime, you can associate a new version of the workflow and start using it on the other items of the target list.

While working with workflows defined in SharePoint Designer 2013, the workflow publishing engine of SharePoint Designer 2013 will always upgrade existing workflow associations, keeping already running instances associated with the original workflow definition and starting the new instances using the new workflow definition. Moreover, be mindful that using the Remove Workflows page to remove a workflow association of a workflow definition that you defined in SharePoint Designer 2013 leaves the environment in an unstable state. In fact, you will still be able to associate that workflow definition to the target list, but you will no longer be able to edit its definition using SharePoint Designer.

Summary

Reading this chapter, you learned about the architecture of the new workflow engine of SharePoint 2013 by comparing it with the legacy SharePoint 2010 workflow engine. You learned how to deploy a Workflow Manager environment on-premises, and you saw how to connect a SharePoint 2013 farm on-premises with an external Workflow Manager. Then you created a simple approval workflow using SharePoint Designer 2013 in order to better understand how to design workflows based on markup, without writing any code. At the end of the chapter, you learned how errors, workflow statuses, and versioning are handled.

CHAPTER 17

Developing workflows

This chapter covers Microsoft SharePoint workflows from a developer perspective, discussing how to create real workflows using either SharePoint Designer 2013 or Microsoft Visual Studio 2012. As you learned in Chapter 16, "SharePoint workflow fundamentals," SharePoint Designer 2013 is a powerful authoring tool for workflows. Whenever you need to create real workflow solutions, consider SharePoint Designer 2013 first. If it does not satisfy your functional requirements, then consider using Visual Studio 2012 instead. You can either design the entire workflow solution within Visual Studio 2012, or you can create custom actions and conditions in Visual Studio while still defining the workflow in SharePoint Designer 2013 (see Chapter 18, "Advanced workflows," for details).

In this chapter, you will learn to create workflows, workflow forms, and SharePoint apps that use workflow features, as well as understand workflow implementation from a practical viewpoint. You'll begin by using SharePoint Designer.

Consuming REST services

The best way to appreciate the real potential of SharePoint Designer 2013 as a mature workflow authoring tool is to put it to work. In this section, you will use it to create a workflow solution that consumes services via HTTP, as well as Representational State Transfer (REST) and JavaScript Object Notation (JSON). Imagine that you need to create a site workflow that manages all the documents in a library. You can consume the REST API offered by SharePoint 2013 to retrieve the collection of documents, and then you can manage them through the REST API or by using the out-of-the-box activities of SharePoint Designer 2013.

Start SharePoint Designer 2013 and create a new site workflow definition called Documents Maintenance Workflow. Insert a *Call HTTP Web Service* action, and click the configuration link, which is available in the shape of the action, to access the Call HTTP Web Service dialog box, shown in Figure 17-1.

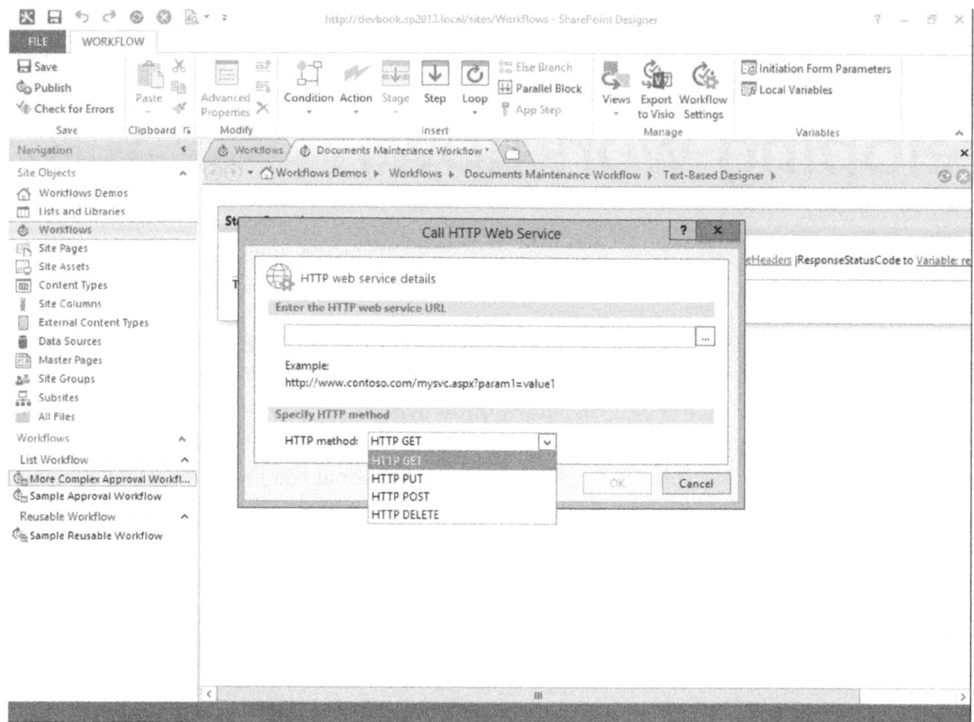

FIGURE 17-1 The dialog window for configuring the *Call HTTP Web Service* action of SharePoint Designer 2013.

Choose the *HTTP GET* request method and provide a URL that retrieves the ID and the Title of all the documents in the library with title Documents. For the example environment, use *http://devbook.sp2013.local/sites/Workflows/_api/web/Lists/GetByTitle('Documents')/Items?$select=ID,Title.*

After defining the HTTP method and the URL, you can configure the request headers, the request body, the response body, the response headers, and the response status code through some dedicated workflow variables. To properly compile the request headers, you add a *Build a Dictionary* action prior to the *Call HTTP Web Service* action and configure a variable of type *Dictionary* to hold the headers' values, including at least the *Accept* header for requesting a JSON response format (*application/json;odata=verbose*). To configure the request headers, right-click the *Call HTTP Web Service* action and choose the Properties menu. You will be prompted with a dialog box for configuring all the available properties of the *Call HTTP Web Service* action. There you will find the HTTP *RequestHeaders* property, as shown in Figure 17-2.

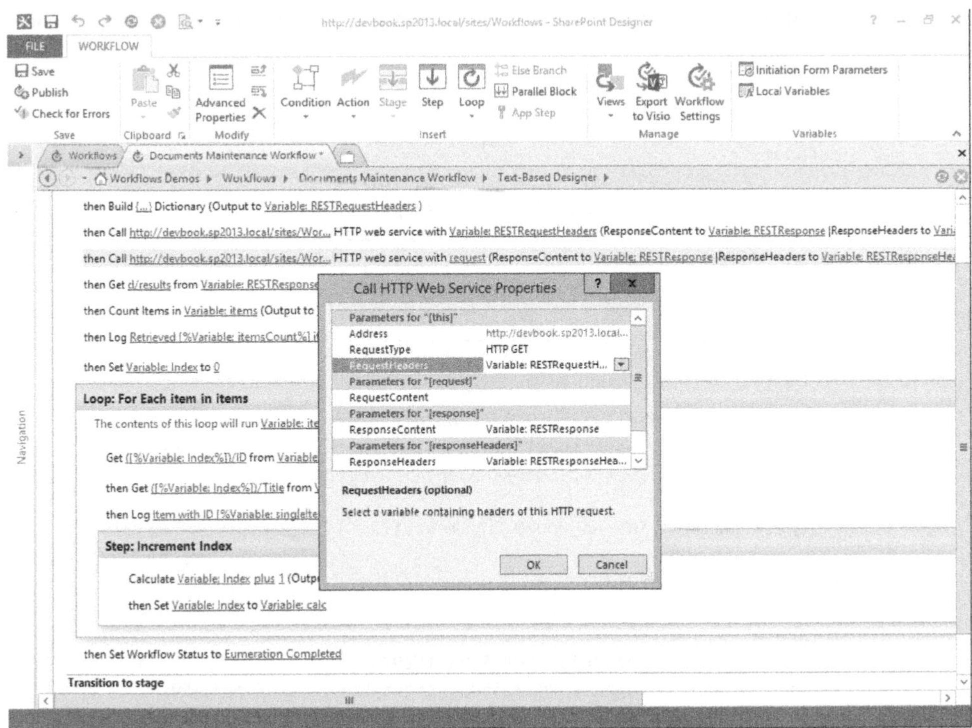

FIGURE 17-2 The dialog window for configuring the *Call HTTP Web Service* action during the configuration of the *RequestHeaders* property.

More Info As you learned in Chapter 9, "The New SharePoint REST API," the REST API uses the response headers to provide useful information such as the *ETag* of a single item. Thus, having the capability to collect the response headers of an HTTP request is fundamental in situations when you want to change the items via REST.

The variables for holding these values (request body, request headers, response body, and response headers) must be of type *Dictionary*, because they will keep a set of values. In particular, consider that the REST service will return JSON content according to the provided *Accept* request header. Listing 17-1 shows an excerpt of a sample JSON result.

LISTING 17-1 An excerpt of the JSON response provided by the REST API while querying the items of a library


```
{"d":
    {"results":
        [{"__metadata":
            {"id":"91f72d8d-cd93-4872-bc18-c2f612d15ad2",
            "uri":"http://devbook.sp2013.local/sites/Workflows/_api/Web/
                Lists(guid'c5be436f-89cb-48bb-b141-09decd4ed400')/Items(6)",
             "etag":"\"3\"",
             "type":"SP.Data.Shared_x0020_DocumentsItem"},
          "Id":6,
          "Title":"Invoice-03-2013",
          "ID":6},
         {"__metadata":
             {"id":"85e0058d-b111-483f-a2a2-423bbde1fa01",
              "uri":"http://devbook.sp2013.local/sites/Workflows/_api/Web/
                  Lists(guid'c5be436f-89cb-48bb-b141-09decd4ed400')/Items(7)",
              "etag":"\"2\"",
              "type":"SP.Data.Shared_x0020_DocumentsItem"},
          "Id":7,
          "Title":"Invoice-01-2013",
"ID":7},
         {"__metadata":
             {"id":"de91a68e-76df-4b39-b50f-5abab1529733",
              "uri":"http://devbook.sp2013.local/sites/Workflows/_api/Web/
                  Lists(guid'c5be436f-89cb-48bb-b141-09decd4ed400')/Items(8)",
              "etag":"\"2\"",
              "type":"SP.Data.Shared_x0020_DocumentsItem"},
          "Id":8,
          "Title":"Invoice-02-2013",
"ID":8}]
    }
}
```


As shown in Figure 17-3, the JSON response has a hierarchical structure.

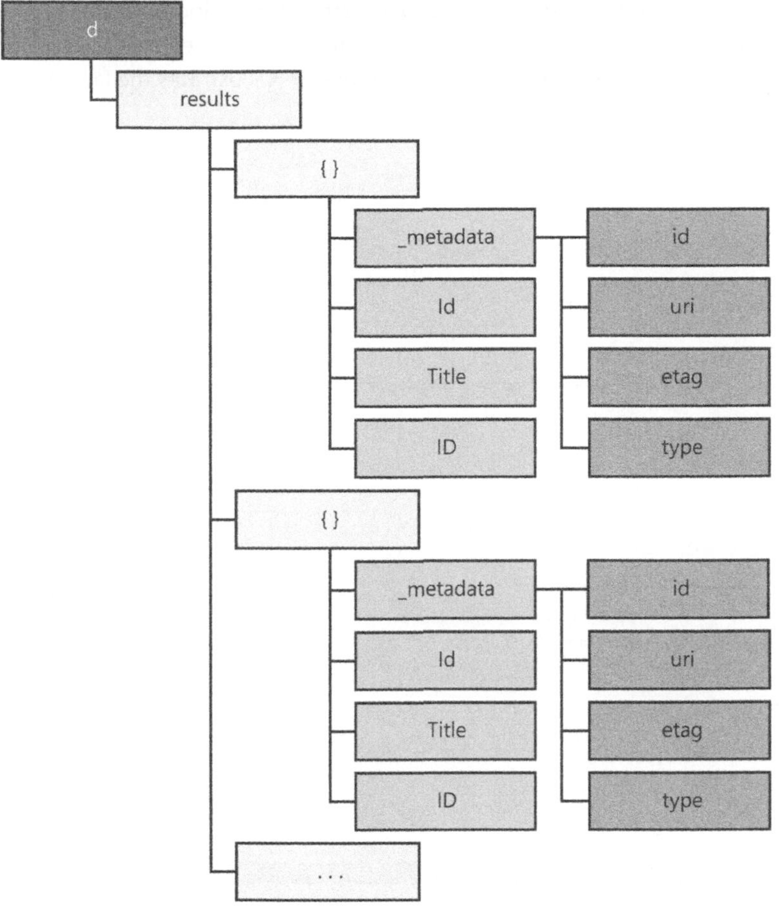

FIGURE 17-3 The hierarchical structure of a JSON response retrieved from a REST operation for enumerating the documents of a library.

To manage such a response within the workflow definition, you can use the *Get an Item from a Dictionary* action. For an input argument, provide the response content retrieved from the *Call HTTP Web Service* action, and configure the path according to the hierarchy illustrated in Figure 17-3. For example, to retrieve the collection of resulting items, you can provide a path value of *d/results*. To retrieve a single resulting item, provide a path value of *d/results[{Index}]*, where the *{Index}* parameter is a numeric indexer.

Now imagine that the goal of the maintenance workflow is to retrieve the title and ID of each document, in order to write them and the number of items retrieved to the workflow history list. To get the number of items, you can use the *Count Items in a Dictionary* action, providing as input the collection of items (*d/result*). To extract the ID and the title of every document, simply iterate through them. SharePoint Designer 2013 offers the Loop *n* Times construct to handle this task. First, retrieve the total number of items returned using the Count Items in a Dictionary action. Then you can loop *n* times, where the value of *n* will be the number of retrieved items. Using a local variable to hold the currently selected item index, you can browse all the returned items and retrieve the ID and title of each via a couple of *Get an Item from a Dictionary* actions. Figure 17-4 illustrates the layout for this workflow.

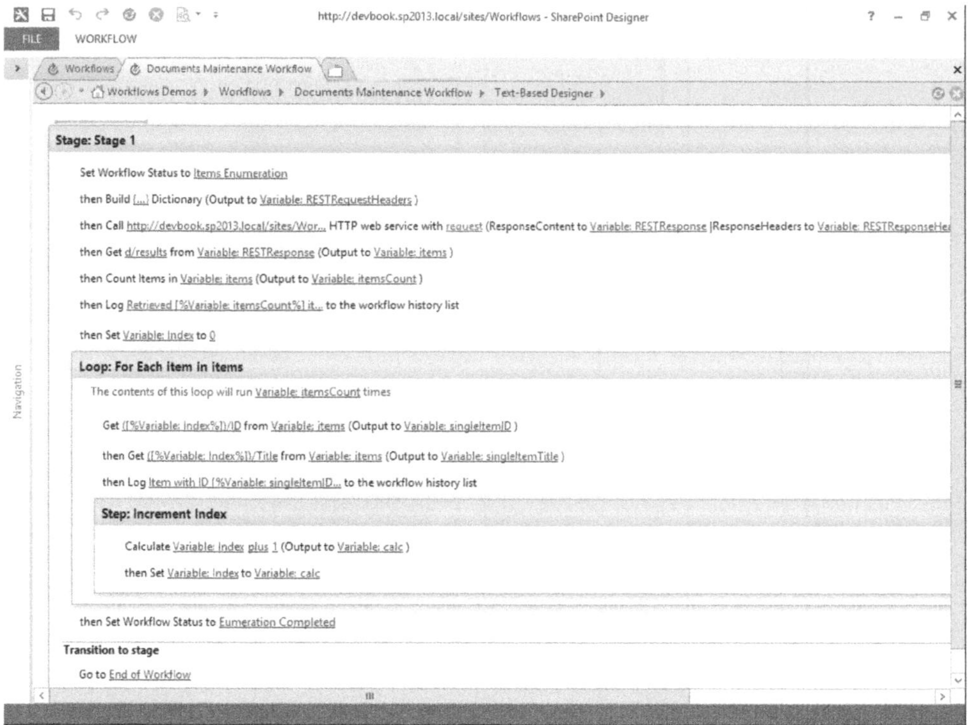

FIGURE 17-4 The structure of a sample workflow definition for enumerating the documents of a library.

Note that when looping through the resulting items, the *Index* variable increments in a dedicated inner step. If you save, publish, and execute such a workflow, you will see the workflow status page of the workflow instance, which illustrates the history list with the ID and title of the items retrieved (Figure 17-5).

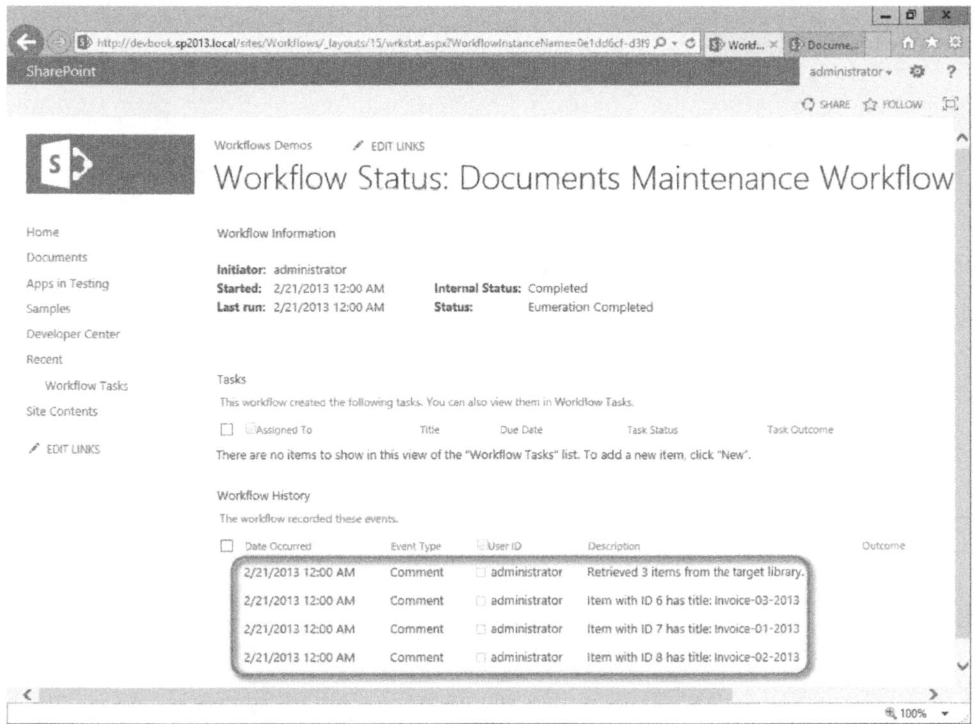

FIGURE 17-5 The workflow status page of a sample workflow definition.

By using the *Call HTTP Web Service* action and the other actions to manage dictionaries, you can invoke the native REST API available in SharePoint 2013, targeting your own farm or any other farm, as long as you provide the proper OAuth authentication HTTP headers. As you can see, SharePoint Designer 2013 is a powerful tool for creating workflows, but it's not the only one.

Visual Studio 2012 for creating workflows

Visual Studio 2012 offers its own advantages for creating workflow definitions. To get started with its creation wizard, launch Visual Studio 2012, create a new project of type SharePoint 2013 - Empty Project and choose to target a farm-level solution. Add a new item to the newly created project by right-clicking the project in Solution Explorer and selecting Add | New Item. Choose a new item of type Workflow, and name it MyFirstWorkflow. A wizard will ask you to provide some information about the workflow you are going to create (Figure 17-6).

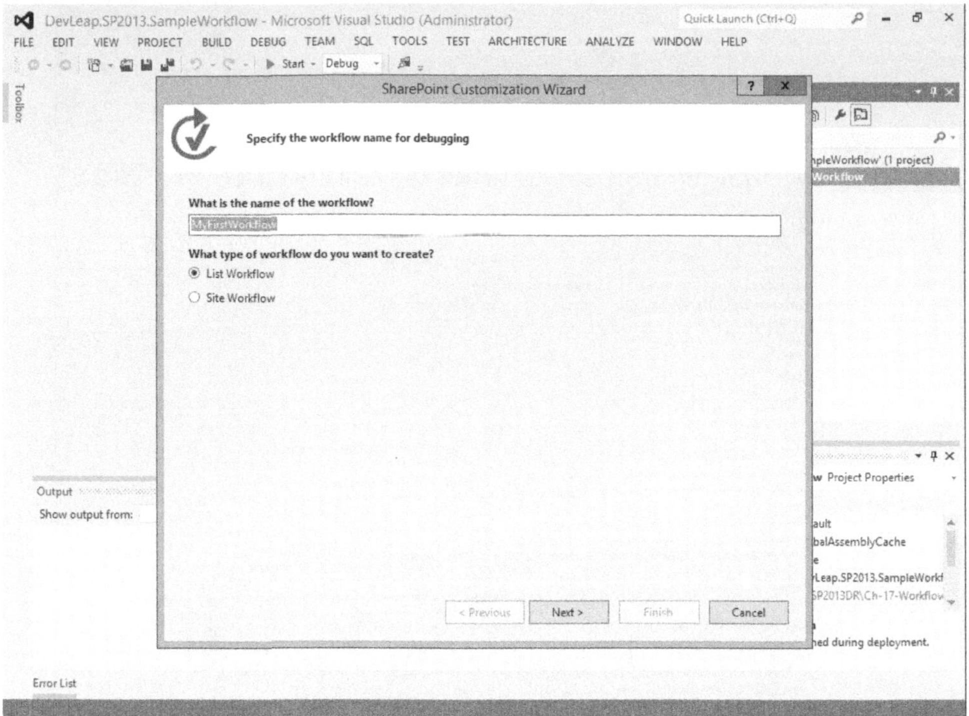

FIGURE 17-6 The first step of the wizard for creating a new workflow definition in Visual Studio 2012.

The first step of the wizard asks you to declare if the workflow will target a list or a site. The second step (Figure 17-7) then prompts you to select the target list if you decide to create a list workflow, as well as the target history list and task list. You can also decide to create a new history list and/or new tasks list. In this step, you can also decide whether to associate the workflow definition with a target. Later, during the provisioning of the workflow, you will provide the lists with which you will associate the workflow definition.

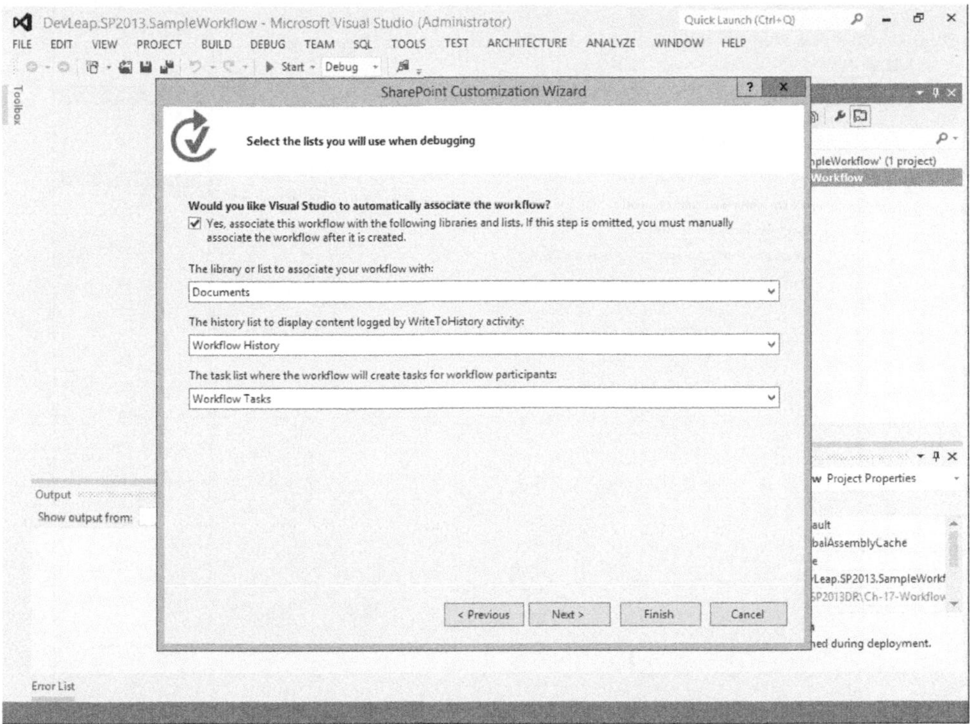

FIGURE 17-7 The second step of the wizard for creating a new workflow definition in Visual Studio 2012.

The third and last step of the wizard asks you to decide when and how the instances of the workflow definition will be created and started. The available options, as shown in Figure 17-8, are the following:

- A user manually starts the workflow.
- The workflow starts automatically when an item is created.
- The workflow starts automatically when an item is changed.

While developing a new workflow, you should usually choose to manually start the workflow, just because it is easier to debug a workflow and manually start its instances while the debugger is active, rather than having to create or change an item to fire new instances of the workflow definition.

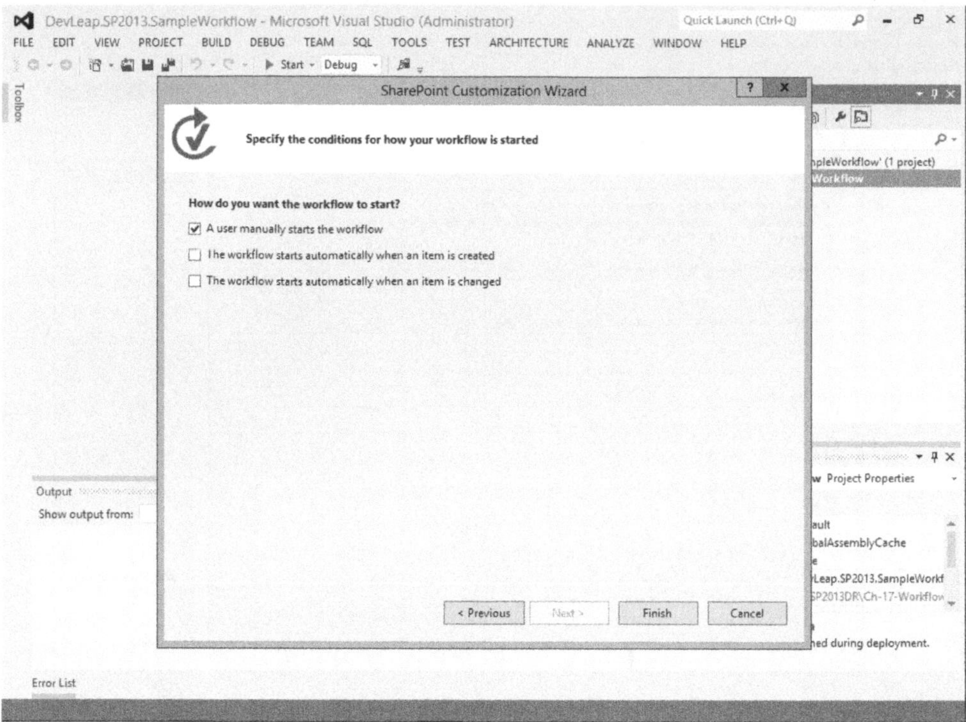

FIGURE 17-8 The third and last step of the wizard for creating a new workflow definition in Visual Studio 2012.

Keep in mind that all these options are mainly for debugging purposes. When you create a workflow definition in Visual Studio 2012, the resulting workflow will be available for association wherever you want to associate it. The result of this wizard will be a XAML file, together with a feature element and a SharePoint feature for provisioning the workflow. As you saw in Chapter 15, "Windows Workflow Foundation," a XAML workflow file created from scratch is a whiteboard—from a designer viewpoint. Even in this case, by opening the XAML file created, you will have a whiteboard, with just a *Sequence* activity designed on it. You can now use the toolbox provided by Visual Studio 2012 to define activities on the target design surface. In particular, in the activity toolbox that is available when you are in the designer, you will find many groups of SharePoint-related activities (see Figure 17-9). In Table 17-1, you can see the list of all the SharePoint-related activities available out of the box, divided into functional groups.

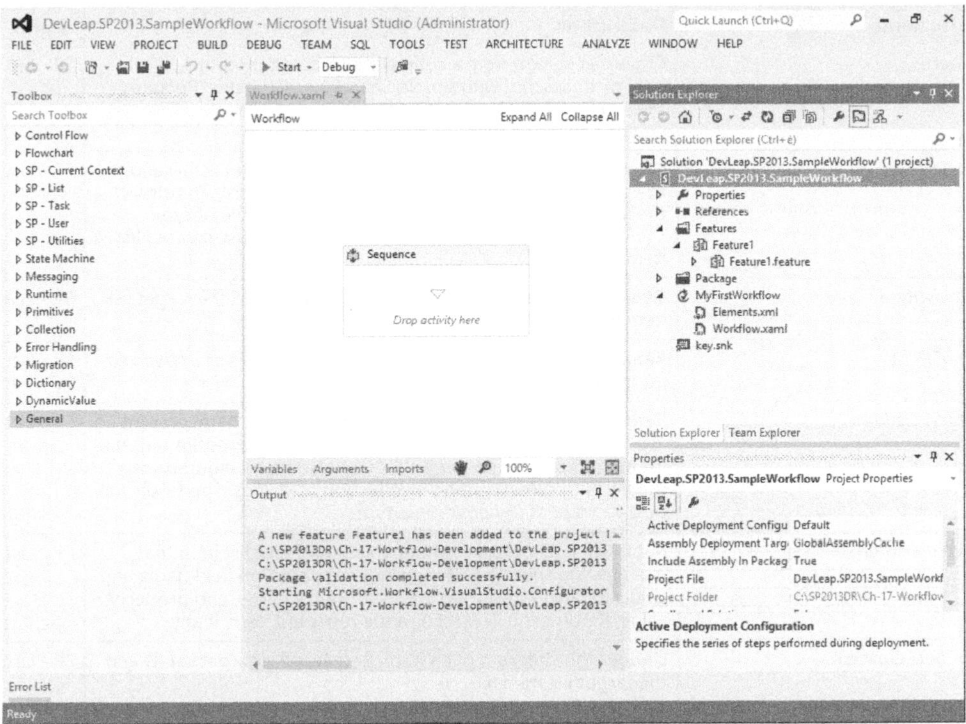

FIGURE 17-9 The whiteboard for designing workflows in Visual Studio 2012.

TABLE 17-1 The SharePoint-related activities available in Visual Studio 2012 workflows

Activity name	Description	Group
GetCurrentItemId	Retrieves the ID (*Int32*) of the current SharePoint list item on which a list workflow instance is running. Returns a value of type *Int32*.	SP - Current Context
GetHistoryListId	Retrieves the ID of the current SharePoint history list, if a history list is specified in the current workflow association. Returns a value of type *GUID*.	SP - Current Context
GetTaskListId	Retrieves the ID of the current SharePoint 2013 tasks list, if a tasks list is specified in the current workflow association. Returns a value of type *GUID*.	SP - Current Context
LookupWorkflowContextProperty	Returns the value of a specified workflow context property. Accepts the context variable name, which can be *Associator, Initiator, Association Name, Instance ID, Current Site URL, Current Item URL, List Name*, or *List ID*. Returns a *String* value.	SP - Current Context
WebUri	Returns the absolute URI of the SPWeb instance containing the currently running workflow instance. Returns a value of type *String*.	SP - Current Context
CheckInItem	Checks in a list item. Requires the ID of the target list and the ID of the target item. Optionally, also accepts a comment.	SP - List
CheckOutItem	Checks out a list item. Requires the ID of the target list and the ID of the target item.	SP - List

Activity name	Description	Group
CopyItem	Copies a file item from a source library to a target one. Works only with files, not with simple SharePoint list items. Requires the source list ID, item ID, target list ID, and a flag to allow overwriting the destination.	SP - List
CreateListItem	Creates a SharePoint list item. Requires the target list ID and the target field values as a *DynamicValue* property. Returns the ID of the created list item, as well as a variable of type *DynamicValue* with the metadata fields of the just-created list item.	SP - List
DeleteListItem	Deletes a list item. Requires the target list ID and the target list item ID.	SP - List
LookupSPList	Returns, as a *DynamicValue*, the list of properties of a specified list instance. Requires the target list ID.	SP - List
LookupSPListItem	Returns properties of a specified SharePoint list item, presenting the values in a *DynamicValue* variable. Requires the target list item ID and the target list ID. Can also be configured with the fields to retrieve, using a collection of strings. The result will be a variable of *DynamicValue* type.	SP - List
LookupSPListItemId	Returns the *ID* property of the first SharePoint list item that matches the specified filtering criteria, based on field name and value. Requires the target list ID, property name, and property value. Returns the ID (*Int32*) of the retrieved item, if any.	SP - List
UndoCheckOutItem	Undoes the checkout of an item. Requires the target list ID and the target list item ID.	SP - List
UpdateListItem	Updates one or more properties of a specified SharePoint list item. Requires the target list ID, list item ID, and list of properties and values to update as a *DynamicValue* variable.	SP - List
WaitForFieldChange	Waits for a specified field of a specified SharePoint list item to change to a specified value. Requires the target list ID, SharePoint list item ID, and field name and value, to monitor for the change event. Returns a *DynamicValue* field.	SP - List
WaitForItemEvent	Waits for a specified event happening on a specified item on which the workflow is running. Requires the target list ID, SharePoint list item ID, and event to wait for. The available events are *ItemAdded* and *ItemUpdated*. Returns the ID (*Int32*) of the item related to the event.	SP - List
CompositeTask	Runs a task process, assigning multiple tasks to multiple people in parallel or series, waits for tasks to complete, and calculates aggregate outcome. Accepts arguments for configuring approvers, email notification behavior, task content type, available outcome values, and so on. Returns an aggregated outcome in a variable.	SP - Task
SingleTask	Runs a single task process, assigning the task to a single person or to a group and waiting for task completion. Accepts arguments for configuring the task assignee, email notification behavior, task content type, available outcome values, and so on. Returns an outcome value in a variable, as well as the ID of the created task item.	SP - Task
LookupSPGroup	Retrieves the properties of a target group. Requires the principal ID (*Int32*) of the group and returns the properties as a variable of type *DynamicValue*.	SP - User
LookupSPGroupMembers	Retrieves the properties of members of a target group. Requires the principal ID (*Int32*) of the group and returns the properties as a variable of type *DynamicValue*.	SP - User

Activity name	Description	Group
LookupSPPrincipal	Returns properties of a target principal (that is, a user or a group). Requires the user name (*String*) of the target user or group and returns the properties as a variable of type *DynamicValue*. Optionally, can also add the principal to the current *SPWeb* instance, if it does not already exist in the current website.	SP - User
LookupSPPrincipalId	Returns the principal ID (*Int32*) of a user or a group, through its user name (*String*). Optionally, can also add the principal to the current *SPWeb* instance, if it does not already exist in the current website.	SP - User
LookupSPUser	Retrieves the properties of a target user. Requires the principal ID (*Int32*) of the user and returns the properties as a variable of type *DynamicValue*.	SP - User
AppOnlySequence	Is a container activity that executes all activities inside of its scope with the identity of the workflow, instead of using the identity of the workflow initiator user.	SP - Utilities
DelayUntil	Delays the execution of the workflow until a specified *DateTime* value, if that date and time has not already passed.	
Email	Sends an email message to SharePoint users. Requires email subject and body. Can optionally accept To, CC, BCC, and additional headers. The fields To, CC, BCC, and Additional Headers are collections of strings.	SP - Utilities
LookupSPChoiceFieldIndex	Returns the index of a specified value in a SharePoint Choice field.	SP - Utilities
TranslateDocument	Creates a translated copy of a document, copying the result into a specified target library. Uses SharePoint Translation Services and requires a preconfigured Machine Translation Service application. Requires the source list ID, the source document list item ID, the destination list ID, and the language to translate the document to.	SP - Utilities
WaitForCustomEvent	Waits for a custom event to be sent into the workflow. Requires the name of the event as a *String* value. It optionally returns the event result as a *String* value.	SP - Utilities
WorkflowInterop	Starts a SharePoint 2010 (Microsoft Windows Workflow Foundation [WF] 3.5) workflow instance. Accepts input arguments for configuring the workflow definition, the target list item, the startup parameters, and so on. Returns the GUID of the started workflow instance, and optionally a variable of type *DynamicValue* with the values of the variables of the target workflow instance at completion. Can be configured to wait for the workflow completion, suspending the current workflow instance.	SP - Utilities
WriteToHistory	Writes a comment to the workflow history list. Requires the input message as a *String* type.	SP - Utilities

The Workflow Manager infrastructure provides some additional activities that are useful while designing SharePoint 2013 workflows. Although these activities are not only for SharePoint workflows, they are surely useful when developing them. Table 17-2 lists these activities.

TABLE 17-2 The activities available in Visual Studio 2012 workflows with Workflow Manager

Activity name	Description	Group
GetS2SSecurityToken	Retrieves a server-to-server (S2S) security token as a variable of type *SecurityToken*. Can also retrieve an app-only S2S security token in case it's needed.	Messaging
HttpSend	Sends an HTTP request to a target web server. Can use any of the following verbs: *GET, POST, PUT, DELETE, PATCH, HEAD, COMMENT, OPTIONS, TRACE*, and *CONNECT*. Accepts arguments like the target URI, request content, request headers, response content, response headers, and response status code. Can also accept an argument of type *SecurityToken* if the connection will use an S2S secured communication.	Messaging
AddToDictionary<TKey, TValue>	Adds an item to a dictionary. Accepts a target dictionary, a key, and a value.	Collection
ClearDictionary<TKey, TValue>	Clears a target dictionary.	Collection
CountDictionary<TKey, TValue>	Count the number of items in a target dictionary.	Collection
DictionaryContains<TKey, TValue>	Checks if a target dictionary contains a specific value. Returns a *Boolean* value.	Collection
GetDictionaryValue<TKey, TValue>	Gets an item value from a dictionary, based on its key.	Collection
RemoveFromDictionary<TKey, TValue>	Removes an item from a dictionary, based on its key.	Collection
BuildDictionary<TKey, TValue>	Creates and initializes a new dictionary. Accepts the key and value pairs, and returns a new dictionary variable.	Collection
SplitKeyValuePair<TKey, TValue>	Splits key and value from a given key/value pair.	Collection
BuildDynamicValue	Builds a *DynamicValue* variable out of a set of paths and values. If the passed *DynamicValue* variable is null, then creates and initializes it. If not null, adds new properties to it.	DynamicValue
ContainsDynamicValueProperty	Returns *true* if a property is contained in a *DynamicValue* variable.	DynamicValue
CopyDynamicValue	Copies properties from one *DynamicValue* variable to another.	DynamicValue
CountDynamicValueItems	Returns the number of items in a *DynamicValue* variable.	DynamicValue
CreateDynamicValue	Creates one *DynamicValue* variable with a path that can be passed at run time.	DynamicValue
GetDynamicValueProperties	Get properties from a *DynamicValue* variable.	DynamicValue
GetODataProperties	Gets the value of multiple properties from an OData message provided as a *DynamicValue* variable.	DynamicValue
GetDynamicValueProperty<T>	Gets one property of a *DynamicValue* variable.	DynamicValue
IsEmptyDynamicValue	Returns *true* if a given input *DynamicValue* variable is empty.	DynamicValue
ParseDynamicValue	Parses JSON code into a *DynamicValue* variable.	DynamicValue

Now imagine that you want to create a simple workflow definition that targets a document library, retrieves the current item, checks out the document, and writes an item in the associated history list. Insert a *CheckOutItem* activity and configure it to check out the current item, configuring values of the *ListId* and *ItemId* properties with the values of the automatically provided values defined as *(current list)* and *(current item)*.

More Info The workflow designer in Visual Studio 2012 allows you to automatically choose the current target list ID and target item ID values by choosing the values *(current list)* and *(current item)*, where available.

Then add a *WriteToHistory* activity and configure its *Message* property to an explicit string value of *Document checked-out!*. Figure 17-10 illustrates the result in the workflow designer.

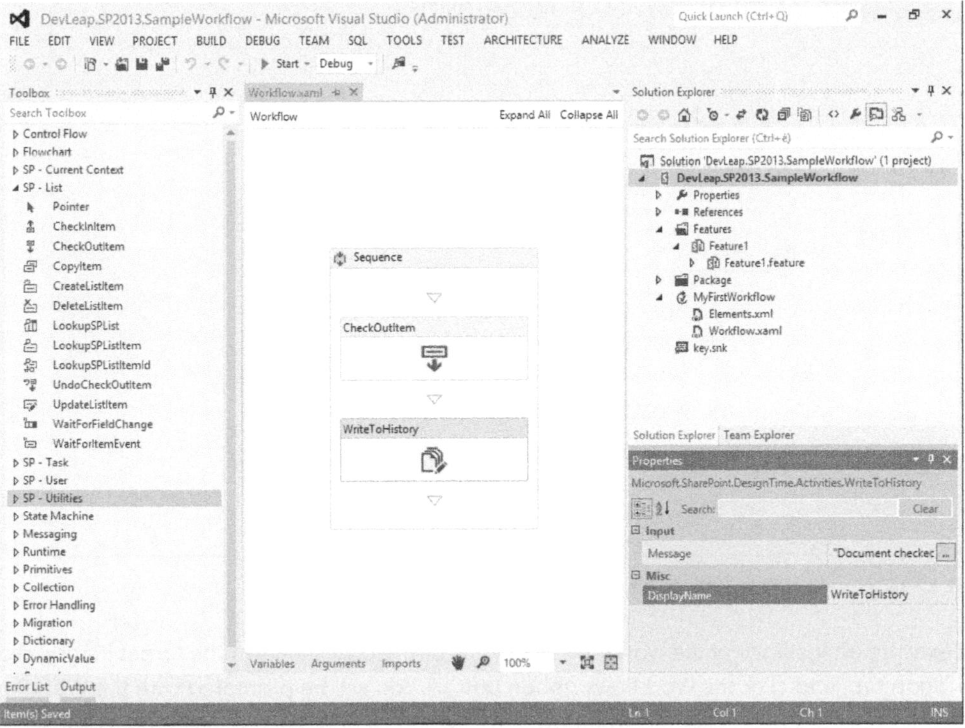

FIGURE 17-10 The sample workflow designed in Visual Studio 2012.

Notice that you have not defined any code. You simply configured the workflow definition using the designer and the properties of the defined activities with their underlying Microsoft C# or Visual Basic expressions. This is one of the key features of workflows in SharePoint 2013: they are markup based. You do not have to write any code, even if you define a workflow in Visual Studio 2012.

Note If you previously defined workflows with SharePoint 2010 and WF 3.5, you are probably familiar with the *CodeActivity* activity. With SharePoint 2013 and WF 4.5, this activity has been removed.

Now you are ready to build, deploy, and test your workflow definition. Right-click the project in Solution Explorer and select the Deploy menu item. Now open the browser and navigate to the Documents library. Open the Workflow Settings page, which is available on the Library ribbon tab, and check the available workflows. You should see the workflow you just deployed, as illustrated in Figure 17-11.

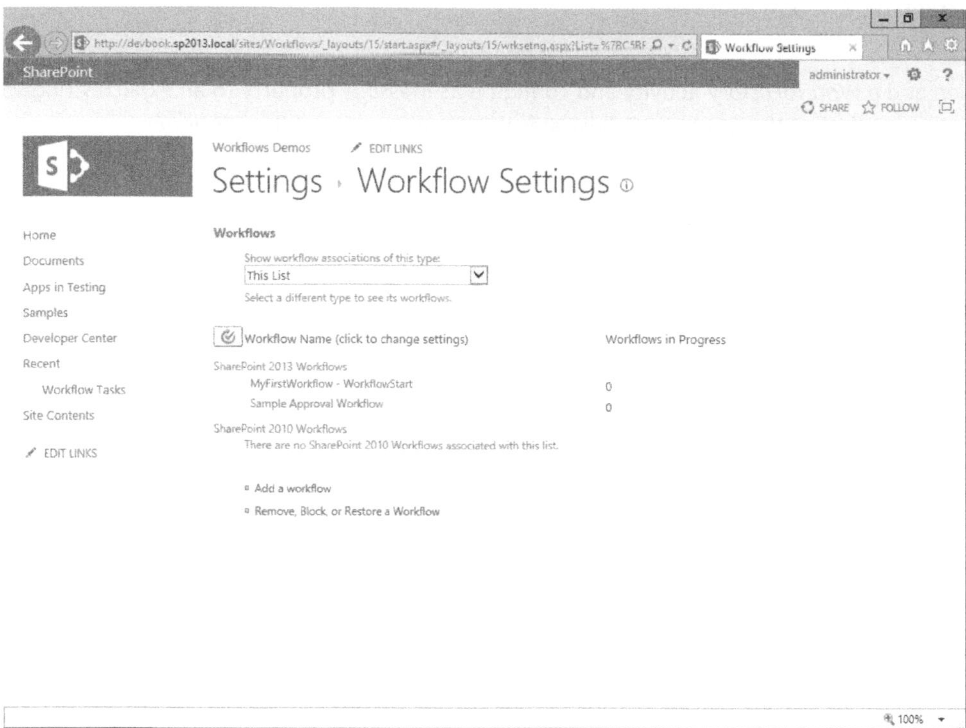

FIGURE 17-11 The Workflow Settings page of a document library.

To execute an instance of the workflow, select any of the documents in the target library, click the Files ribbon tab, and click the Workflows ribbon button. You will be prompted with the Workflows page of the selected item. Click the workflow name to start a new instance. As soon as you start the workflow, the target document becomes checked out. Click the ECB menu and select the Workflows menu item to access the Workflows page (Figure 17-12).

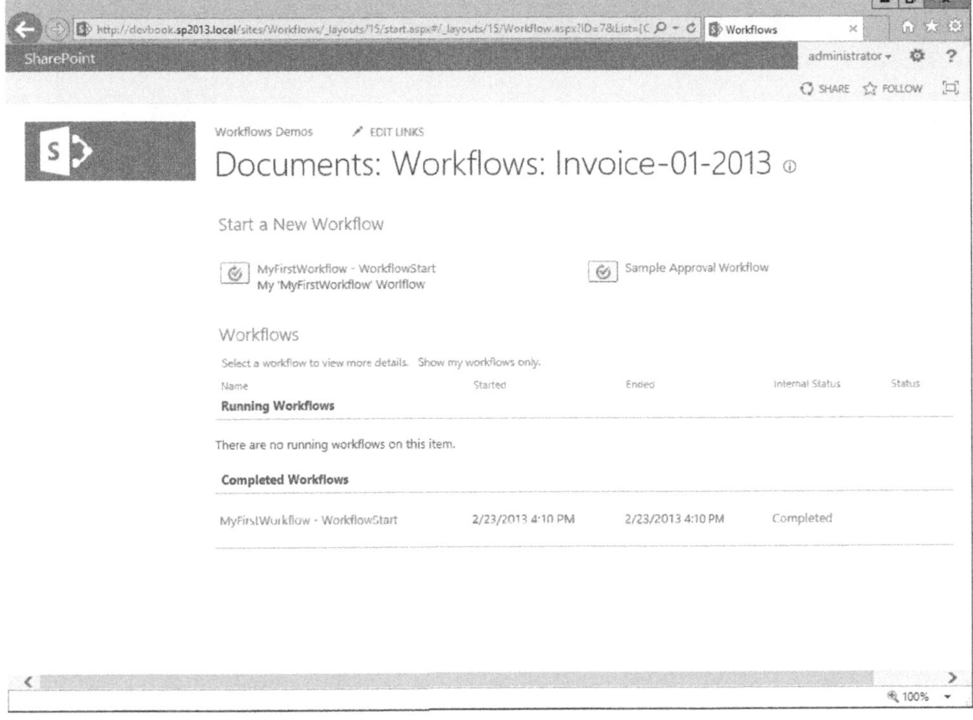

FIGURE 17-12 The Workflows page of a document item in a document library.

Click the Internal Status column, where you see a value of Completed, to access the Workflow Status page of that completed workflow instance. As shown in Figure 17-13, the workflow instance has an Internal State value of Completed, and the Workflow History list reports a single item with the description defined in the workflow definition in Visual Studio 2012.

The workflow instance you have just associated with the target library of orders does not provide a custom workflow status column. In fact, workflows created with Visual Studio 2012 by default do not provide implementation for such a column. Later in this chapter, in the "Workflow deployment" section, you will learn how to turn it on.

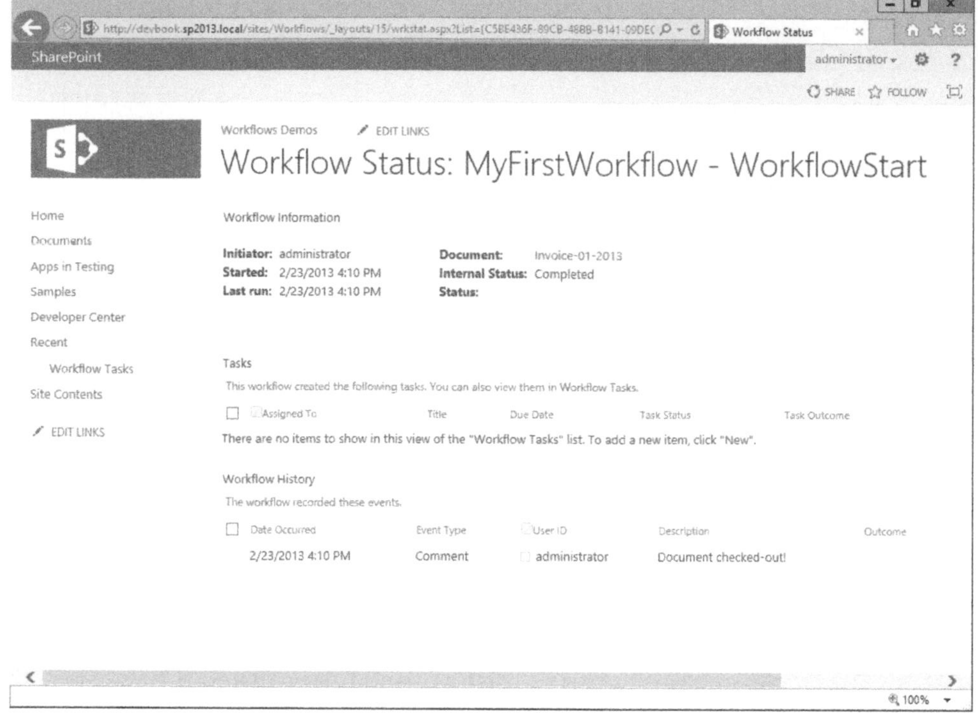

FIGURE 17-13 The Workflow Status page of a workflow instance executed against a specific document.

To test and debug your workflow definition, you can place a breakpoint within the designer on any of the activities you defined. Suppose you want to break and debug starting from the *GetCurrentListId* activity instance. Press F5 to start debugging the project. Visual Studio 2012 will deploy the workflow project to SharePoint, and will start a console process that acts as a Workflow Manager instance dedicated to debugging.

More Info The Workflow Manager instance dedicated to debugging corresponds to the process Microsoft.Workflow.TestServiceHost.exe, which by default is available in the folder C:\Program Files (x86)\Workflow Manager Tools\1.0. This process emulates a Workflow Manager. Visual Studio 2012, while debugging a workflow for SharePoint 2013, registers this emulator in SharePoint 2013, in order to intercept requests and debug workflow instances.

Starting a workflow instance while debugging will raise within Visual Studio 2012 any breakpoint you declared in the workflow definition. Figure 17-14 shows the console output of the Workflow Manager emulator.

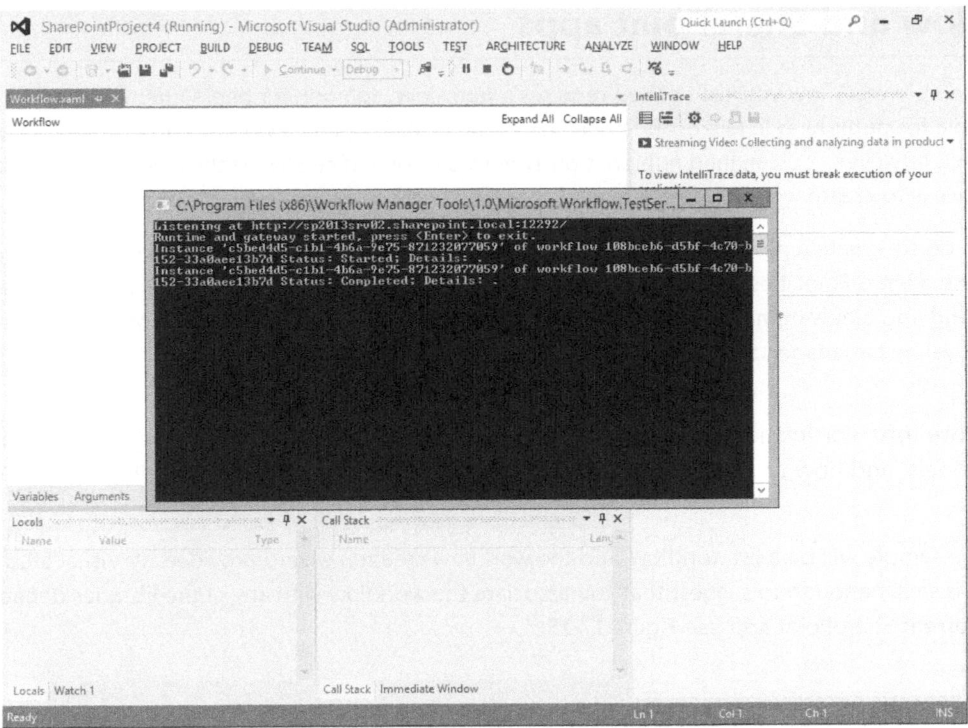

FIGURE 17-14 The console screen of the Workflow Manager emulator available for debugging SharePoint 2013 workflows within Visual Studio 2012.

Here is the output, in the console window, provided by the emulator after executing a sample workflow instance:

```
Listening at http://sp2013srv01.sharepoint.local:12292/
Runtime and gateway started, press <Enter> to exit.
Instance '866d65ba-4870-4ef7-8730-2d48eb8fa9d6' of workflow fb5b0c53-2f56-46a3-b3db-c07f0c13e591

Status: Started; Details: .
Instance '866d65ba-4870-4ef7-8730-2d48eb8fa9d6' of workflow fb5b0c53-2f56-46a3-b3db-c07f0c13e591

Status: Completed; Details: .
```

While debugging the workflow, expect to have a slow environment, because the overall debugging infrastructure is a little bit heavy to run and manage, and it is resource-consuming, too.

Workflow and SharePoint apps

The sample workflow you just defined requires a farm-level solution for deployment, so it is not suitable for publishing in Microsoft Office 365. If you instead define a workflow in a SharePoint app project, however, you can then publish it on-premises or on Office 365 via the cloud. Thus, the best practice is to create workflow definitions in apps, rather than in farm-level solutions.

To do so, create a new SharePoint 2013 app project—for instance, targeting an Office 365 tenant. Choose a SharePoint-hosted app, define a document library instance called Orders in the app website, and add a new item of type Workflow. Imagine that the library holds a set of orders that need approval by a manager, and name it OrdersWorkflow.

More Info For further details about creating a SharePoint 2013 app, the available hosting models, and how to add a document library instance, see Chapter 8, "SharePoint apps."

The sample will be a list workflow, and the workflow creation wizard provided by Visual Studio 2012 is smart enough to suggest that you associate the workflow with any of the libraries defined in the current SharePoint app (see Figure 17-15).

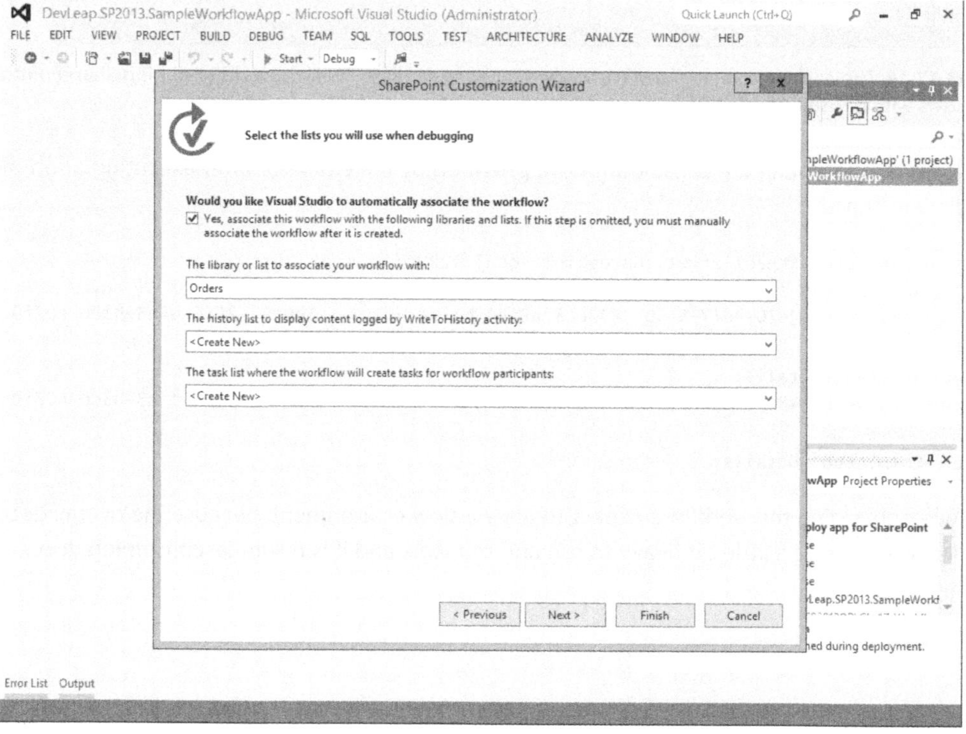

FIGURE 17-15 The wizard for creating a workflow definition in a SharePoint app, using Visual Studio 2012.

If the Workflow History list and the Workflows Tasks list are not already available in the SharePoint app, you can define them explicitly, or you can simply ask the wizard to create them for you in the target app website.

While a real approval workflow definition should handle such input arguments as the target approver and the approval request message, the sample approval workflow will define explicit and fake values for these arguments. Later, you will use an initiation form. For now, create variables for holding the *TargetApprover* (*String*), the *ApprovalRequestMessage* (*String*), the *ApprovalTaskId* (*Int32*), and the *ApprovalTaskOutcome* (*Int32*) values.

Insert a *SingleTask* activity instance into the sequence defining the workflow, and configure its properties by clicking the Configure link provided in the designer. You will be prompted with a pop-up configuration screen (see Figure 17-16), where you will be able to configure all the main properties of the task. As you will see, a *SingleTask* activity has many required properties. Table 17-3 lists the values configured in the current sample.

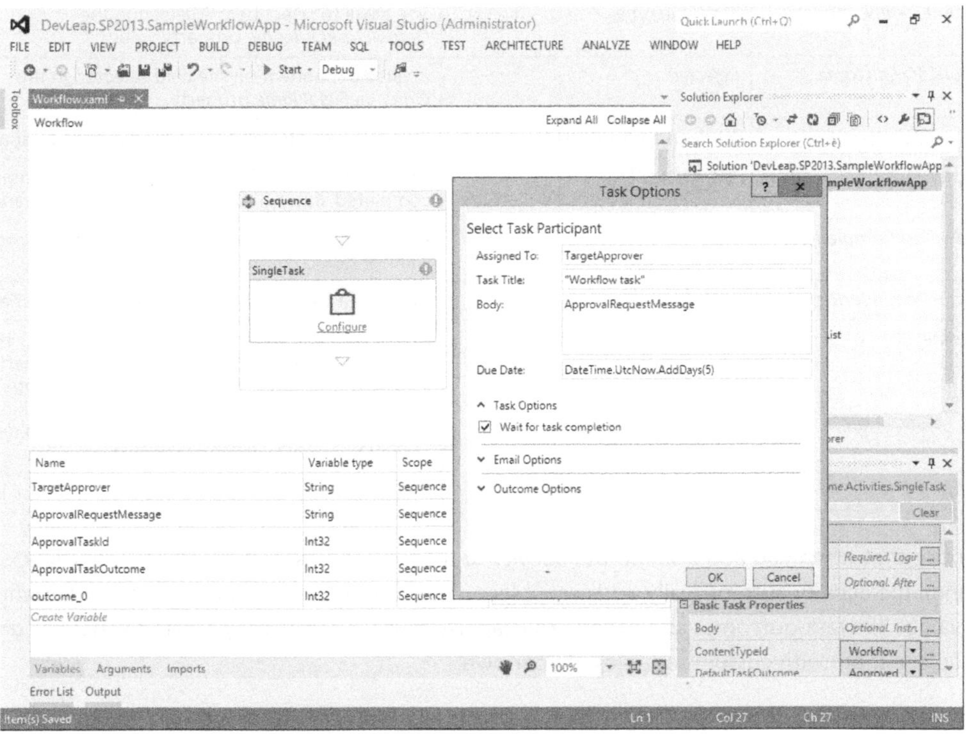

FIGURE 17-16 The Task Options designer provided by the *SingleTask* activity within Visual Studio 2012.

TABLE 17-3 The configuration of the main properties for the *SingleTask* activity

Property name	Value	Notes
AssignedTo	*TargetApprover*	An argument with a predefined value of *i:0#.w|sharepoint\\administrator* or *paolo@sp2013dr.onmicrosoft.com.* Later it will be taken from the workflow initiation form.
DueDate	*DateTime.UtcNow.AddDays(5)*	The number of days, which should be taken from the workflow initiation form.
Body	*ApprovalRequestMessage*	An argument with a predefined value of *Please approve this order.* Later it will be taken from the workflow initiation form.
ContentTypeId	*Workflow Task (SharePoint 2013)*	A *ContentTypeId* with a value of *0x0108003365C4474CAE8C42BCE396314E88E51F*, corresponding to the out-of-the-box *Workflow Task* (SharePoint 2013) content type. You can also provide a custom content type ID for a custom task, as described later, in the "Custom workflow tasks" section.
OutcomeFieldName	*Task Outcome*	The value to select before selecting the *DefaultTaskOutcome* property value.
DefaultTaskOutcome	*Rejected*	A value dependent on the field selected in the *OutcomeFieldName* property.
Title	*"Order Approval Task"*	An explicit value. You should read it from a variable.
CompletedStatus	*"Completed"*	The explicit value of the localized string describing the completed status. You should read it from a variable.
WaitForTaskCompletion	*True*	A *Boolean* value that instructs the workflow process to wait for task completion.
OverdueReminderRepeat	*Daily*	An explicit value. You should read it from a variable.
Outcome	*ApprovalTaskOutcome*	An output variable of type *Int32*. If the activity is configured with the *WaitForTaskCompletion* property with a value of *true*, upon task completion this property will provide the index of the task outcome value, taken from the available values defined for the field declared in the *OutcomeFieldName* property.
TaskId	*ApprovalTaskId*	The item ID of the task item created in the task lists.

Notice that when you add a *SingleTask* activity or a *CompositeTask* activity to the workflow designer, the activity automatically adds variables to the current context for holding fundamental field values like task outcomes and others. You can use these automatically created variables, or you can replace them with custom variables of your own.

Now you need to determine if the task outcome is an approval of the order or a rejection. Insert an *If* activity, which is available in the Control Flow group of native activities. In the condition, enter the following expression:

```
ApprovalTaskOutcome == 0
```

The 0 value corresponds to the *Approved* outcome value, which is the first value defined in the underlying field type. In the left branch, which is the one labeled as *Then*, insert a *WriteToHistory* activity, providing a value of *Approved* for the *Message* property. In the right branch, which is the one labeled as *Else*, insert another *WriteToHistory* activity, providing a value of *Rejected* for the *Message* property. The sample workflow definition is now complete. Take a look at the final workflow outline in Figure 17-17.

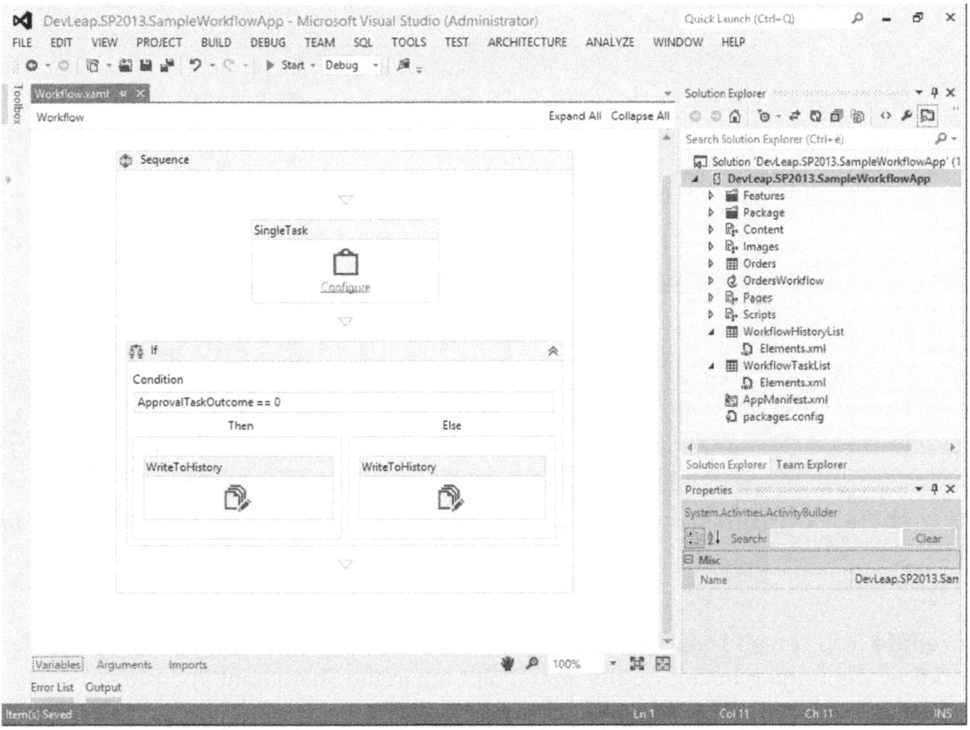

FIGURE 17-17 The outline of the sample order-approval workflow in the designer provided by Visual Studio 2012.

Now press F5 to deploy and debug the SharePoint app, or deploy it and then test it through the web browser as if you were an end user. If you debug the app by pressing F5, because the project contains a workflow definition, the Visual Studio 2012 debugger will start the Workflow Manager emulator, too. If you simply deploy and test the app from the browser, you will use the standard Workflow Manager. You will not, however, be able to raise breakpoints and step into the workflow definition unless you do not attach the Internet Information Services (IIS) worker process with the debugger. Moreover, consider that workflow debugging is allowed only in on-premises environments and cannot be done while targeting Office 365. If you try to debug a workflow project targeting Office 365, Visual Studio 2012 will raise a debug error, providing you the pop-up message shown in Figure 17-18.

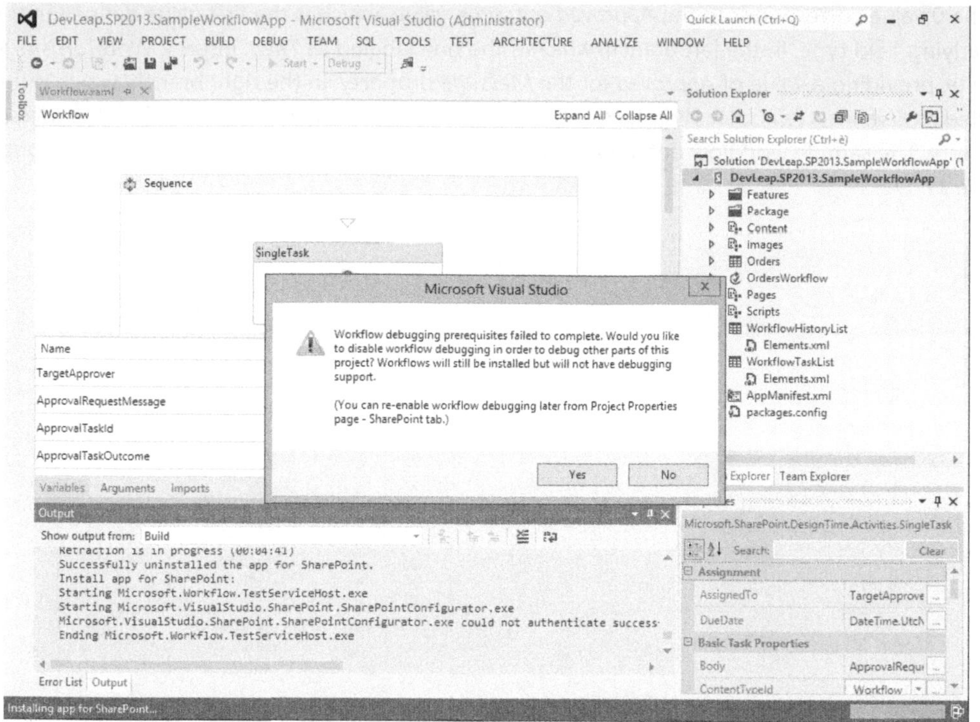

FIGURE 17-18 The pop-up error message raised by Visual Studio 2012 during the debugging of a workflow targeting Office 365.

More Info You can also enable or disable workflow debugging by changing the Enable Workflow Debugging option on the SharePoint tab in the SharePoint app project properties.

Figure 17-19 shows the Workflow Status page of the sample workflow definition while running on a target document.

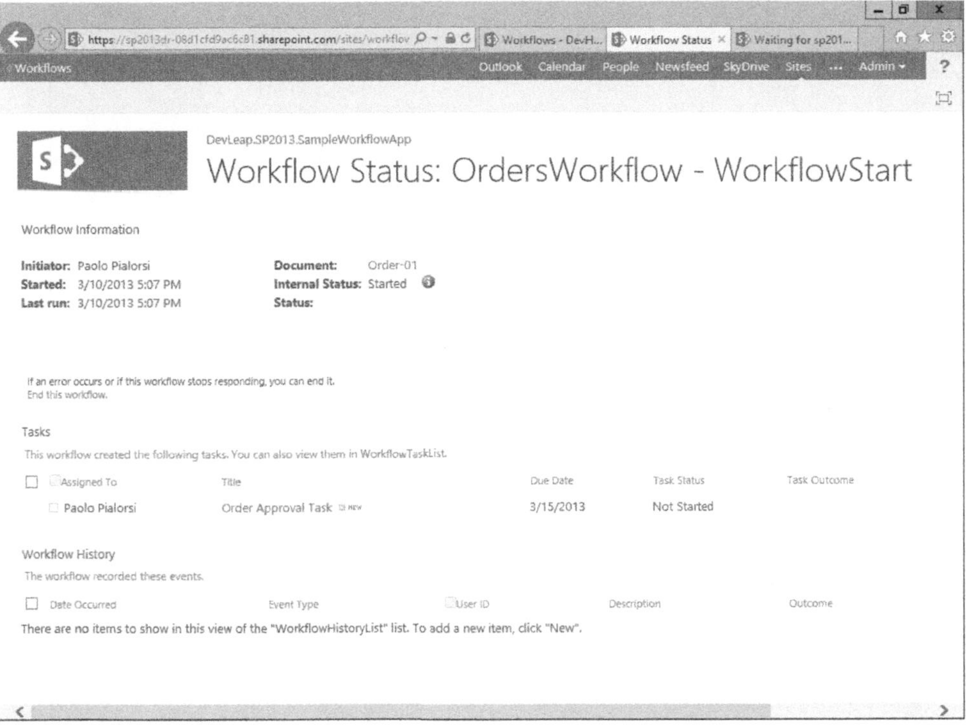

FIGURE 17-19 The Workflow Status page of a sample order-approval workflow defined in Visual Studio 2012.

Figure 17-20 shows the task form for completing the approval task. It is an ASP.NET form, which is almost the same as the one available while developing workflows in SharePoint Designer 2013. Moreover, consider that starting with SharePoint 2013, the workflow task forms cannot be created using Microsoft InfoPath Forms Services; the only option you have is to use ASP.NET forms.

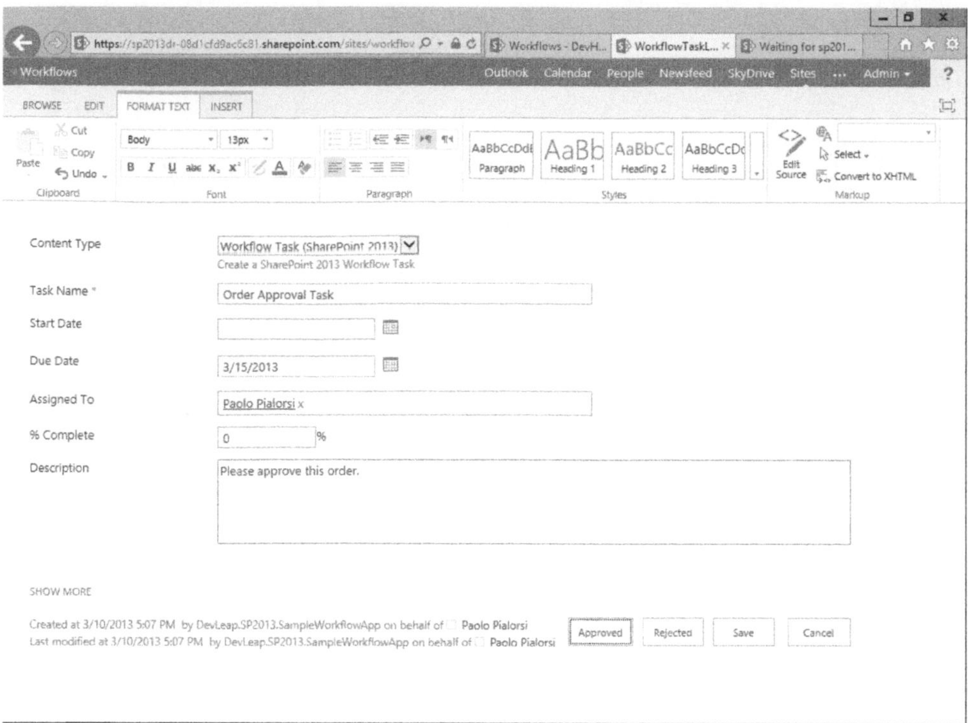

FIGURE 17-20 The ASP.NET task form for approving an order for the approval workflow for the sample orders.

Lastly, while a workflow created in a farm-level solution by default does not present the workflow status column, a workflow defined in a SharePoint app does present that column, as do workflows created with SharePoint Designer 2013.

Workflow forms

In this section, you will learn how to create custom workflow forms. To create a workflow association or initiation form, you can simply use Visual Studio 2012. Right-click the workflow element in Solution Explorer, and then choose to add a new item. From the resulting list of available items, choose a Workflow Initiation Form template type (see Figure 17-21). The suggested file name will be for an ASPX page file.

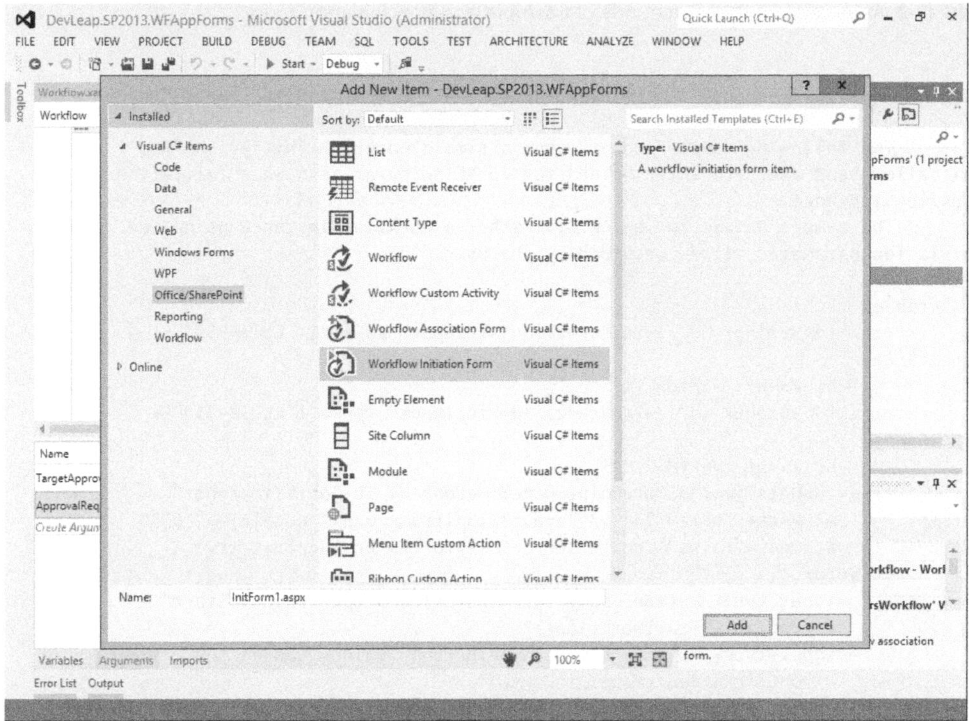

FIGURE 17-21 The Add New Item window for a workflow element in Visual Studio 2012.

After you add the Workflow Initiation Form item, Visual Studio prompts you with the source code of the ASPX page file, which will be placed in the Pages folder of the current SharePoint app project. The page is made of a *Content* control targeting the *PlaceHolderMain* region of the default master page of SharePoint. The *Content* control contains ASP.NET, HTML, and JavaScript code completely commented (and left there for the sake of providing an example of some of the most common ways of rendering input fields for initiation arguments of type *String*, *Integer*, and *DateTime)*. The ASPX file provides a couple of sample buttons to start the workflow instance or cancel the initiation. Lastly, at the end of the file is a small piece of JavaScript code that, using the Client-Side Object Model (CSOM) and the Workflow Services Manager client library, starts a new workflow instance providing the arguments configured by the user through the initiation form.

More Info The Workflow Services Manager client library is available in the JavaScript file sp.workflowservices.js, which is referenced in the PlaceHolderAdditionalPageHead region of the initiation form page.

Listing 17-2 shows an excerpt of the source code of the initiation form.

LISTING 17-2 An excerpt of the source code of a sample workflow initiation form

```
<asp:Content ID="Content4" ContentPlaceHolderId="PlaceHolderMain" runat="server">
<%--
        The following sample code creates a simple workflow initiation form
that allows end users to enter values for workflow parameters when initiating a
workflow instance.
        The sample JavaScript below will start a workflow instance using the
initiation parameter values provided by the user.
--%>
    <table>
        <tr><td>String:<br /><textarea id="strInput" rows="1" cols="50"">
</textarea>
            <br /><br /></td></tr>
        <tr><td>Integer:<br /><textarea id="intInput" rows="1" cols="50"">
</textarea>
            <br /><br /></td></tr>
        <tr><td>DateTime: <SharePoint:DateTimeControl ID="dateTimeInput"
            DatePickerFrameUrl="../_layouts/15/iframe.aspx" LocaleId="1033"
            DateOnly="false" runat="server"  /><br /><br /></td></tr>
        <tr><td>
            <input type="button" name="startWorkflowButton" value="Start"
                onClick="StartWorkflow()" />
            <input type="button" name="cancelButton" value="Cancel"
                onClick="RedirFromInitForm()" />
               <br />
        </td></tr>
    </table>
    <script type="text/javascript">
        // ---------- Start workflow ----------
        function StartWorkflow() {
            var errorMessage = "An error occurred when starting the workflow.";
            var subscriptionId = "", itemId = "", redirectUrl = "";
            var urlParams = GetUrlParams();

            if (urlParams) {
                //itemGuid = urlParams["ItemGuid"];
                itemId = urlParams["ID"];
                redirectUrl = urlParams["Source"];
                subscriptionId = urlParams["TemplateID"];
            }
            if (subscriptionId == null || subscriptionId == "") {
                // Cannot load the workflow subscription without a
                // subscriptionId, so workflow cannot be started.
                alert(errorMessage +
"  Could not find the workflow subscription id.");
                RedirFromInitForm(redirectUrl);
            }
```

```
else {
    // Set workflow in-arguments/initiation parameters
    var wfParams = new Object();
    var strInputValue = document.getElementById("strInput").value;
    if (strInputValue) {
        wfParams['strArg'] = strInputValue;
    }
    var intInputValue = document.getElementById("intInput").value;
    if (intInputValue) {
        var intValue = parseInt(intInputValue);
        if (intValue)
            wfParams['intArg'] = intValue;
    }
    var dateTimeInputValue = document.getElementById(
        "ctl00_PlaceHolderMain_dateTimeInput_dateTimeInputDate").
        value;
    if (dateTimeInputValue) {
        var dateTimeValue = new Date(document.getElementById(
            "ctl00_PlaceHolderMain_dateTimeInput_dateTimeInputDate").
            value);
        if (dateTimeValue)
            wfParams['dateTimeArg'] = dateTimeValue;
    }

    // Get workflow subscription and then start the workflow
    var context = SP.ClientContext.get_current();
    var wfManager = SP.WorkflowServices.WorkflowServicesManager.
        newObject(context, context.get_web());
    var wfDeployService = wfManager.getWorkflowDeploymentService();
    var subscriptionService = wfManager.
    getWorkflowSubscriptionService();
    context.load(subscriptionService);

    context.executeQueryAsync(
        function (sender, args) { // Success
            var subscription = null;

            // Load the workflow subscription
            if (subscriptionId)
                subscription = subscriptionService.
                getSubscription(subscriptionId);
            if (subscription) {
                if (itemId != null && itemId != "") {
                    // Start list workflow
                    wfManager.getWorkflowInstanceService()
                        .startWorkflowOnListItem(subscription,
                        itemId, wfParams);
                }
```

```
                    else {
                        // Start site workflow
                        wfManager.getWorkflowInstanceService()
                            .startWorkflow(subscription, wfParams);
                    }
                    context.executeQueryAsync(
                        function (sender, args) {
                            // Success
                            RedirFromInitForm(redirectUrl);
                        },
                        function (sender, args) {
                            // Error
                            alert(errorMessage + "  " +
                            args.get_message());
                            RedirFromInitForm(redirectUrl);
                        }
                    )
                }
                else {
                    // Failed to load the workflow subscription,
                    // so workflow cannot be started.
                    alert(errorMessage +
                        "  Could not load the workflow subscription.");
                    RedirFromInitForm(redirectUrl);
                }
            },
            function (sender, args) { // Error
                alert(errorMessage + "  " + args.get_message());
                RedirFromInitForm(redirectUrl);
            }
        )
    }
}

// ---------- Redirect from page ----------
function RedirFromInitForm(redirectUrl) {
    window.location = redirectUrl;
}
// ---------- Returns an associative array (object) of URL params -------
function GetUrlParams() {
    var urlParams = null;
    if (urlParams == null) {
        urlParams = {};
        var parts = window.location.href.replace
        (/[?&]+([^=&]+)=([^&]*)/gi,
            function (m, key, value) {
                urlParams[key] = decodeURIComponent(value);
        });
    }
    return urlParams;
}
</script>
</asp:Content>
```

The JavaScript code that starts the workflow instance is highlighted in bold. Note that you can define the initiation form any way you want, from a markup and design viewpoint. The only important thing is to start the workflow instance using the JavaScript code. Of course, having a code excerpt for handling all the most useful data types and for starting a workflow instance is a great aid.

To start the workflow providing input arguments, the JavaScript code retrieves the current *SP.ClientContext* instance. Through this, it gets a reference to a new instance of the *SP.WorkflowServices.WorkflowServicesManager* class, which will be explained in detail in Chapter 18. For now, it will suffice to know that the *WorkflowServicesManager* instance retrieves a reference to the types useful for resolving the current workflow definition. Using the *TemplateID* query string parameter, which will be provided to the initiation form by SharePoint, the JavaScript code retrieves the workflow definition associated with the current initiation form, and starts the workflow instance using either the *startWorkflow* method or the *startWorkflowOnListItem* method of the *WorkflowInstanceService* class, depending on the target of the workflow.

Important The *WorkflowInstanceService* type, which is used to start a workflow instance in the JSOM, provides two methods for starting a new workflow instance: *startWorkflow* and *startWorkflowOnListItem*. Which one you should use depends on the type of workflow definition you are starting. The *startWorkflow* method starts a site workflow and accepts the workflow subscription and the arguments. The *startWorkflowOnListItem* method starts a list workflow and accepts the workflow subscription, the target item ID (*Int32*), and the arguments.

Now go back to the *OrdersWorkflow* definition you designed in the previous section. To retrieve values provided through the initiation form, you need to define workflow arguments corresponding to the fields configured in the form. In the current OrdersWorkflow sample, delete the variables *ApprovalRequestMessage* and *TargetApprover* and replace them with a couple of arguments with the same name and type (*String*). You need to adapt the initiation form accordingly. Leave the String field in the page, deleting the Integer and DateTime sample code excerpts. Then change the JavaScript code to provide the right startup arguments. As you can see from reading the code highlighted in bold in Listing 17-3, a client-side *PeoplePicker* control has been inserted, which is new in SharePoint 2013. This new control allows selecting a user, a group, or a distribution list from the client code using JavaScript. This control will be used to retrieve the value for the *TargetApprover* argument.

More Info For further details about the client-side *PeoplePicker* control, you can read the article "How to: Use the client-side *PeoplePicker* control in apps for SharePoint," available on MSDN at the following URL: *http://msdn.microsoft.com/en-us/library/jj713593.aspx*. You can also consider the code sample available here: *http://code.msdn.microsoft.com/SharePoint-2013-Add-the-900e0742*.

LISTING 17-3 An excerpt of the source code of the OrdersWorkflow initiation form

```
<asp:Content ID="Content2" ContentPlaceHolderId="PlaceHolderAdditionalPageHead"
    runat="server">
    <script type="text/javascript" src="../_layouts/15/sp.runtime.js"></script>
    <script type="text/javascript" src="../_layouts/15/sp.js"></script>
    <script type="text/javascript" src="../_layouts/15/sp.workflowservices.js">
</script>

    <!-- Scripts added to support client-side PeoplePicker -->
    <script type="text/javascript" src="../Scripts/jquery-1.7.1.min.js"></script>
    <SharePoint:ScriptLink ID="ScriptLink1" name="clienttemplates.js"
    runat="server"
        LoadAfterUI="true" Localizable="false" />
    <SharePoint:ScriptLink ID="ScriptLink2" name="clientforms.js" runat="server"
        LoadAfterUI="true" Localizable="false" />
    <SharePoint:ScriptLink ID="ScriptLink3" name="clientpeoplepicker.js"
    runat="server"LoadAfterUI="true" Localizable="false" />
    <SharePoint:ScriptLink ID="ScriptLink4" name="autofill.js" runat="server"
        LoadAfterUI="true" Localizable="false" />
    <SharePoint:ScriptLink ID="ScriptLink6" name="sp.core.js" runat="server"
        LoadAfterUI="true" Localizable="false" />
    <script type="text/javascript"
        src="../Scripts/ClientSidePeoplePicker.js"></script>
</asp:Content>
<asp:Content ID="Content4" ContentPlaceHolderId="PlaceHolderMain" runat="server">
    <table>
        <tr>
            <td>
               Approval request message:<br />
               <textarea id="ApprovalRequestMessage" rows="5" cols="50">
               </textarea>
               <br /><br />
            </td>
        </tr>
        <tr>
            <td>
               Target Approver(s):<br />
               <div id="peoplePicker"></div>
               <br /><br />
            </td>
        </tr>
        <tr>
            <td>
               <input type="button" name="startWorkflowButton" value="Start"
                    onClick="StartWorkflow()" />
               <input type="button" name="cancelButton" value="Cancel"
                    onClick="RedirFromInitForm()" />
               <br />
            </td>
        </tr>
    </table>
```

```
<script type="text/javascript">
    // ---------- Start workflow ----------
    function StartWorkflow() {
        var errorMessage = "An error occured when starting the workflow.";
        var subscriptionId = "", itemId = "", redirectUrl = "";
        var urlParams = GetUrlParams();

        if (urlParams) {
            //itemGuid = urlParams["ItemGuid"];
            itemId = urlParams["ID"];
            redirectUrl = urlParams["Source"];
            subscriptionId = urlParams["TemplateID"];
        }
        if (subscriptionId == null || subscriptionId == "") {
            // Cannot load the workflow subscription without a
            // subscriptionId, so workflow cannot be started.
            alert(errorMessage +
            "  Could not find the workflow subscription id.");
            RedirFromInitForm(redirectUrl);
        }
        else {
            // Set workflow in-arguments/initiation parameters
            var wfParams = new Object();
            var approvalRequestMessageValue = $("#ApprovalRequestMessage").
            val();
            if (approvalRequestMessageValue) {
                wfParams['ApprovalRequestMessage'] =
                approvalRequestMessageValue;
            }
            var targetApproverValue = getUserKeys("peoplePicker");
            if (targetApproverValue) {
                wfParams['TargetApprover'] = targetApproverValue;
            }

            // Get workflow subscription and then start the workflow
            var context = SP.ClientContext.get_current();
            var wfManager = SP.WorkflowServices.WorkflowServicesManager.
            newObject(context, context.get_web());
            var wfDeployService = wfManager.getWorkflowDeploymentService();
            var subscriptionService = wfManager.
            getWorkflowSubscriptionService();
            context.load(subscriptionService);

            context.executeQueryAsync(
                function (sender, args) { // Success
                    var subscription = null;
                    // Load the workflow subscription
                    if (subscriptionId)
                        subscription = subscriptionService.
                        getSubscription(subscriptionId);
                    if (subscription) {
                        if (itemId != null && itemId != "") {
                            // Start list workflow
                            wfManager.getWorkflowInstanceService()
```

```
                                    .startWorkflowOnListItem(subscription,
                                    itemId, wfParams);
                            }
                            else {
                                // Start site workflow
                                wfManager.getWorkflowInstanceService()
                                    .startWorkflow(subscription, wfParams);
                            }
                            context.executeQueryAsync(
                                function (sender, args) {
                                    // Success
                                    RedirFromInitForm(redirectUrl);
                                },
                                function (sender, args) {
                                    // Error
                                    alert(errorMessage + "  "
                                    + args.get_message());
                                    RedirFromInitForm(redirectUrl);
                                }
                            )
                        }
                        else {
                            // Failed to load the workflow subscription,
                            // so workflow cannot be started.
                            alert(errorMessage +
                                "  Could not load the workflow subscription.");
                            RedirFromInitForm(redirectUrl);
                        }
                    },
                    function (sender, args) { // Error
                        alert(errorMessage + "  " + args.get_message());
                        RedirFromInitForm(redirectUrl);
                    }
                )
            }
        }

        // Code omitted for the sake of brevity ...

    </script>
</asp:Content>
```

Because the *OrdersWorkflow* definition targets a list workflow, the JavaScript code will use the *startWorkflowOnListItem* method, providing as arguments the workflow subscription ID corresponding to the current workflow definition, the ID of the current item taken from the query string, and a dictionary of arguments that will have to match the arguments defined in the workflow designer of Visual Studio 2012. The sample workflow initiation form will also resolve the selected target approver user key using some custom JavaScript code, which is a modified version of the code provided by MSDN for using the client-side *PeoplePicker control*. Listing 17-4 shows the JavaScript code for resolving the target approver.

LISTING 17-4 An excerpt of the JavaScript code to retrieve the user key provided by the client-side *PeoplePicker* control

```
// Run your custom code when the DOM is ready.
$(document).ready(function () {
    // Specify the unique ID of the DOM element where the picker will render.
    initializePeoplePicker('peoplePicker');
});

// Render and initialize the client-side PeoplePicker.
function initializePeoplePicker(peoplePickerElementId) {
    // Create a schema to store picker properties, and set the properties.
    var schema = {};
    schema['PrincipalAccountType'] = 'User,DL,SecGroup,SPGroup';
    schema['SearchPrincipalSource'] = 15;
    schema['ResolvePrincipalSource'] = 15;
    schema['AllowMultipleValues'] = false;
    schema['MaximumEntitySuggestions'] = 50;
    schema['Width'] = '280px';

    // Render and initialize the picker.
    // Pass the ID of the DOM element that contains the picker, an array of
    // initial
    // PickerEntity objects to set the picker value, and a schema that defines
    // picker properties.
    this.SPClientPeoplePicker_InitStandaloneControlWrapper(
        peoplePickerElementId, null, schema);
}

// Query the picker for user information.
function getUserKeys(peoplePickerElementId) {
    // Get the PeoplePicker object from the page.
    var peoplePicker = this.SPClientPeoplePicker.SPClientPeoplePickerDict
        [peoplePickerElementId + "_TopSpan"];

    // Get information about all users.
    var users = peoplePicker.GetAllUserInfo();
    var userInfo = '';
    for (var i = 0; i < users.length; i++) {
        var user = users[i];
        for (var userProperty in user) {
            userInfo += userProperty + ':  ' + user[userProperty] + '<br>';
        }
    }
    // We do not use the userInfo variable,
    // but just in case ... leave it here ...

    // Get user keys.
    var keys = peoplePicker.GetAllUserKeys();
    return(keys);
}
```

To test and check the arguments, you can add a couple of *WriteToHistory* activities for writing the two arguments to the Workflow History list.

However, to effectively use the initiation form, you will need to configure the workflow project item in the Visual Studio 2012 project. In Solution Explorer, click the OrdersWorkflow item to edit its properties using the standard property grid of Visual Studio 2012. There you will find a long list of properties, including one named *InitiationUrl*. Through the *InitiationUrl* property, you can define the ASPX page to use as the initiation form for your workflow. When you add an initiation form through Visual Studio 2012, it automatically adds the proper value to the workflow configuration.

Deploy the SharePoint app and start a workflow instance; you will be prompted with an initiation form like the one shown in Figure 17-22.

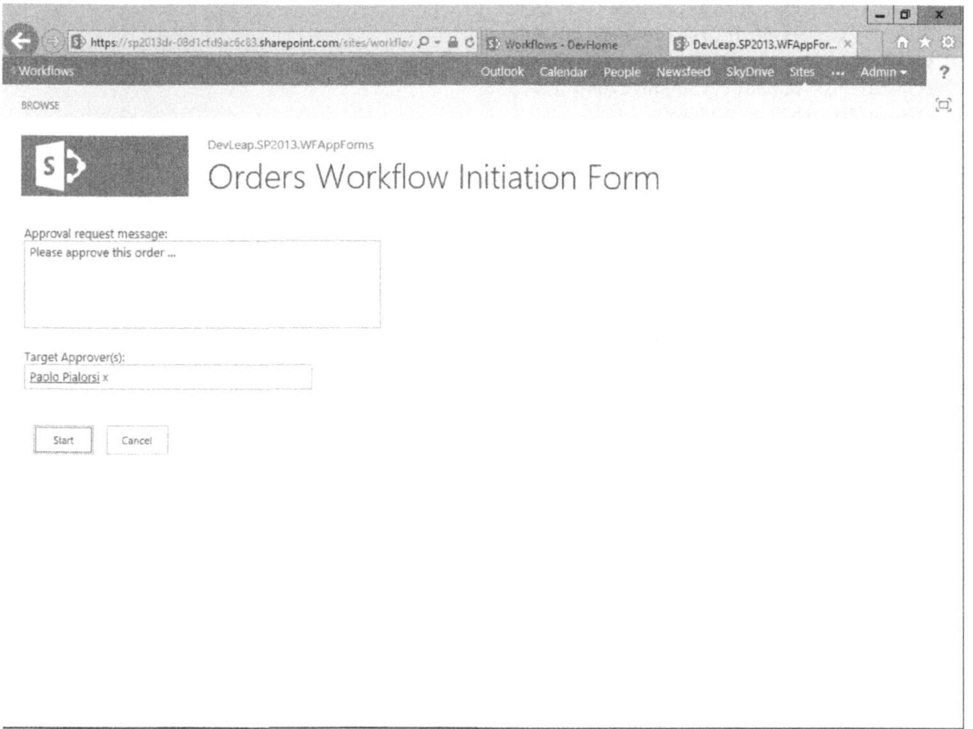

FIGURE 17-22 The workflow initiation form for the sample *OrdersWorkflow* definition in Visual Studio 2012.

The form displays a field for providing the content of the *ApprovalRequestMessage* argument, and the client-side *PeoplePicker* control for providing the value of the *TargetApprover* argument.

The workflow association form will be almost the same as the workflow initiation form. The only difference will be the JavaScript code behind the form. By using the association form, you will need to define the association, which in SharePoint 2013 is represented by a *WorkflowSubscription* type instance and its configuration properties. However, consider that in SharePoint 2013, many of the workflows you will develop in Visual Studio 2012 will be defined within SharePoint apps. Thus, the association of the workflow with its target list, library, or site will happen during the provisioning of the app, because end users usually do not configure lists, libraries, and the app website manually. Meanwhile, if you are developing a farm-level workflow, you may also need to create a custom workflow association form. In Chapter 18, you will learn how to publish a *WorkflowSubscription* instance, using the Workflow Services Manager client library, and write an association form page for a workflow defined in a farm-level solution.

Custom workflow tasks

You can further customize your workflows by creating custom tasks and defining custom task fields and custom task forms. To create a custom task, you first define a custom content type, inheriting from the basic *Workflow Task* (SharePoint 2013) content type.

More Info For details about how to create a custom content type, please refer to Chapter 3, "Data provisioning," as well as Chapter 8.

Within the custom content type definition, declare a site column for holding a custom task outcome, which will be the customization defined in the custom task. Listing 17-5 shows the source XML code declaring the new task content type.

LISTING 17-5 The XML code declaring the custom *OrderApprovalTask* content type

```
<?xml version="1.0" encoding="utf-8"?>
<Elements xmlns="http://schemas.microsoft.com/sharepoint/">
  <Field ID="{919DEB5B-FB24-49B8-93E1-0EDE24947F9F}"
         Name="OrderApprovalOutcome"
         StaticName="OrderApprovalOutcome"
         DisplayName="OrderApprovalOutcome"
         Type="OutcomeChoice"
         Required="FALSE"
         Group="DevLeap Site Columns">
    <CHOICES>
      <CHOICE>Approved</CHOICE>
      <CHOICE>To Review</CHOICE>
      <CHOICE>Rejected</CHOICE>
    </CHOICES>
  </Field>
```

```
  <!-- Parent ContentType: Workflow Task (SharePoint 2013)
(0x0108003365C4474CAE8C42BCE396314E88E51F) -->
  <ContentType
ID="0x0108003365C4474CAE8C42BCE396314E88E51F00D46A33DB74E44810A5A763715BB0F727"
               Name="OrderApprovalTask"
               Group="DevLeap Content Types"
               Description="Orders Approval Content Type"
               Inherits="FALSE"
               Version="0">
    <FieldRefs>
      <FieldRef ID="{919DEB5B-FB24-49B8-93E1-0EDE24947F9F}"
Name="OrderApprovalOutcome" />
    </FieldRefs>

    <XmlDocuments>
      <XmlDocument NamespaceURI="http://schemas.microsoft.com/sharepoint/v3/
contenttype/forms/url">
        <FormUrls xmlns="http://schemas.microsoft.com/sharepoint/v3/contenttype/
forms/url">
          <Display>Pages/OrderApprovalTaskForm.aspx</Display>
          <Edit>Pages/OrderApprovalTaskForm.aspx</Edit>
        </FormUrls>
      </XmlDocument>
    </XmlDocuments>

  </ContentType>
</Elements>
```

Notice that the custom task inherits from the *Workflow Task* (SharePoint 2013) content type (*0x0108003365C4474CAE8C42BCE396314E88E51F*), but it does not inherit the UI from the parent content type (attribute inherits with a value of *FALSE*). On the contrary, the *ContentType* element is configured to use a custom set of forms, which are configured as relative URLs mapping to custom ASPX pages defined in the Pages folder of the current SharePoint app project. Also notice that the custom site column for holding the task outcome is of type *OutcomeChoice*, which is a new SharePoint 2013 type defined for holding the outcome of a workflow task.

The custom ASPX page implementing the task form, which is illustrated in Listing 17-6, defines some custom UI elements and provides three buttons to approve, reject, or submit the order for review. Based on the JSOM, the code behind the page simply updates the current task item, which was retrieved using the *List* and *ID* query string arguments, and sets the *OrderApprovalOutcome* field according to the user's choice.

LISTING 17-6 The ASPX code of the custom workflow task form

```
<%@ Page language="C#" MasterPageFile="~masterurl/default.master"
Inherits="Microsoft.SharePoint.WebPartPages.WebPartPage, Microsoft.SharePoint,
Version=15.0.0.0, Culture=neutral, PublicKeyToken=71e9bce111e9429c" %>
<%@ Register Tagprefix="SharePoint" Namespace="Microsoft.SharePoint.WebControls"
Assembly="Microsoft.SharePoint, Version=15.0.0.0, Culture=neutral, PublicKeyToke
n=71e9bce111e9429c" %>
<%@ Register Tagprefix="Utilities" Namespace="Microsoft.SharePoint.Utilities"
Assembly="Microsoft.SharePoint, Version=15.0.0.0, Culture=neutral, PublicKeyToke
n=71e9bce111e9429c" %>
<%@ Register Tagprefix="WebPartPages" Namespace="Microsoft.SharePoint.
WebPartPages" Assembly="Microsoft.SharePoint, Version=15.0.0.0, Culture=neutral,
PublicKeyToken=71e9bce111e9429c" %>

<asp:Content ContentPlaceHolderId="PlaceHolderAdditionalPageHead" runat="server">
    <SharePoint:ScriptLink name="sp.js" runat="server" OnDemand="true"
LoadAfterUI="true" Localizable="false" />
    <script type="text/javascript" src="../Scripts/jquery-1.7.1.min.js"></script>
</asp:Content>

<asp:Content ContentPlaceHolderId="PlaceHolderMain" runat="server">

    <h1>Order Approval Task</h1>

    <WebPartPages:WebPartZone runat="server" FrameType="TitleBarOnly" ID="full"
Title="loc:full" />

    <table>
        <tr>
            <td>
               Please choose the outcome for the current task
            </td>
        </tr>
        <tr>
            <td>
                <input type="button" name="approveTaskOutcome" value="Approved"
                    onclick="setTaskOutcome('Approved');" />
                <input type="button" name="rejectTaskOutcome" value="Rejected"
                    onclick="setTaskOutcome('Rejected');" />
                <input type="button" name="toReviewTaskOutcome" value="To Review"
                    onclick="setTaskOutcome('To Review');" />
               <br />
            </td>
        </tr>
    </table>
```

```
    <script type="text/javascript">
        var ctx;
        var urlParams = null;

        function getUrlParams() {
            if (urlParams == null) {
                urlParams = {};
                var parts = window.location.href.
                replace(/[?&]+([^=&]+)=([^&]*)/gi, function (m, key, value) {
                    urlParams[key] = value;
                });
            }
            return urlParams;
        }

        function setTaskOutcome(outcome) {
            ctx = SP.ClientContext.get_current();
            var web = ctx.get_web();
            var tasksList = web.get_lists().getById(
                decodeURIComponent(getUrlParams()["List"]));
            var task = tasksList.getItemById(getUrlParams()["ID"]);
            task.set_item("OrderApprovalOutcome", outcome);
            task.set_item("Status", "Completed");
            task.update();

            ctx.executeQueryAsync(
                function (sender, args) {
                    redirFromInitForm();
                },
                function (sender, args) {
                    alert("Error while saving the task outcome: " +
                    args.get_message());
                }
            );
        }

        function redirFromInitForm() {
            window.location = decodeURIComponent(getUrlParams()["Source"]);
        }

    </script>
</asp:Content>
```

To use the new task content type, you could add to the app website a new list of tasks of this type. A better practice, however, is to use the wizard that adds a new workflow definition. By default, this wizard creates a tasks list for you; you should edit the list definition of that tasks list instead of creating a new one from scratch.

Open the Elements.xml file related to the tasks list and add a *ContentTypeBinding* element using a code excerpt like the one highlighted in bold in Listing 17-7.

LISTING 17-7 The code for provisioning the Workflow Tasks list, including a custom task content type

```
<?xml version="1.0" encoding="utf-8" ?>
<Elements xmlns="http://schemas.microsoft.com/sharepoint/">
  <ListInstance FeatureId="{f9ce21f8-f437-4f7e-8bc6-946378c850f0}"
                TemplateType="171"
                Title="WorkflowTaskList"
                Description="This list instance is used for workflow Task items."
                Url="Lists/WorkflowTaskList"
                RootWebOnly="FALSE" />

  <ContentTypeBinding ListUrl="Lists/WorkflowTaskList"
                      RootWebOnly="FALSE"
                      ContentTypeId="0x0108003365C4474CAE8C42BCE396314E88E51F"/>
  <ContentTypeBinding ListUrl="Lists/WorkflowTaskList"
                      RootWebOnly="FALSE"
ContentTypeId="0x0108003365C4474CAE8C42BCE396314E88E51F00D46A33DB74E44810A5A7637
15BB0F727"/>
</Elements>
```

The *ContentTypeBinding* element binds the custom content type to the tasks list definition available out of the box in SharePoint, and referenced through its *TemplateType* ID, which has a value of 171. In the current example, the content type ID of the custom task content type is the *ContentTypeBinding* element (highlighted in bold). Now, moving to the workflow definition, you can insert a *SingleTask* activity or a *CompositeTask* activity, and you can configure the task content type to match the new custom content type (see Figure 17-23).

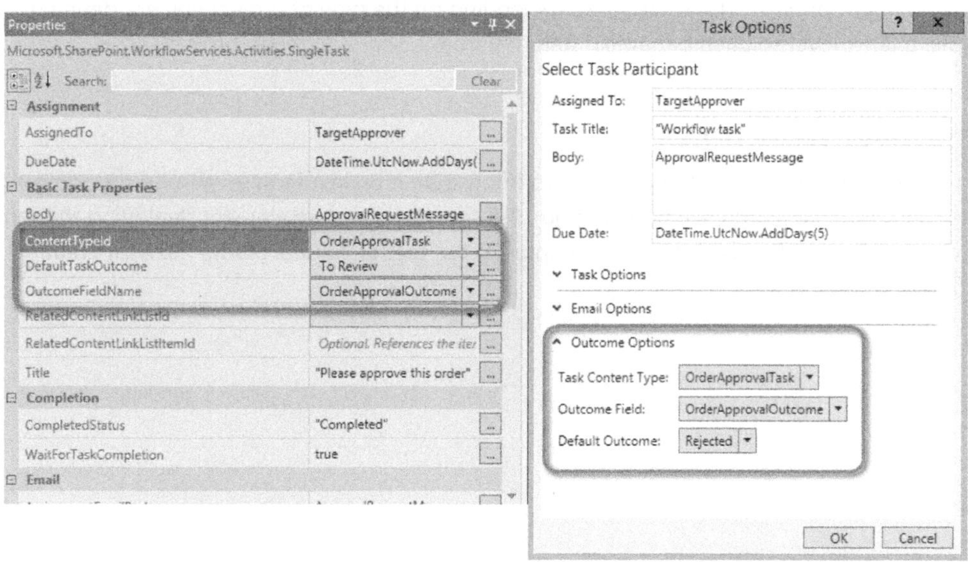

FIGURE 17-23 The property editors of a *SingleTask* activity configured for using a custom task content type.

You can configure the custom task using either the standard property grid of Visual Studio 2012 or the Task Options pop-up window available in the workflow designer.

Discussing the whole approval workflow is out of scope for this context. In short, you define the workflow process using whatever activities you like, and then deploy and test it. In Figure 17-24, you can see how the custom task form behaves in the web browser when the assignee edits it.

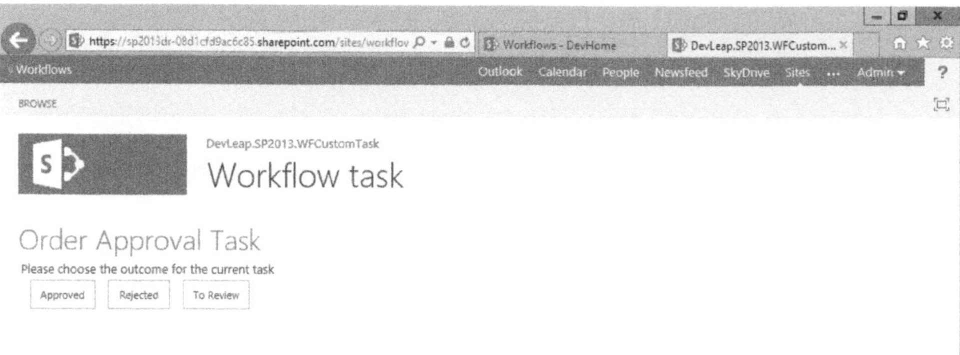

FIGURE 17-24 The custom workflow task form rendered in the web browser.

Workflow deployment

Now that you can develop a workflow definition, you're ready to delve into the workings of the workflow deployment process. This topic varies depending on the type of project you are defining. For example, a farm-level solution behaves differently from a SharePoint app project.

Farm-level workflow

When you deploy a project that includes a workflow definition in a farm-level solution, you can use the standard *Module* feature element. Listing 17-8 shows the feature element deploying the sample approval workflow defined earlier in the chapter, in the section "Visual Studio 2012 for creating workflows."

LISTING 17-8 The feature element file for deploying a sample workflow definition

```
<?xml version="1.0" encoding="utf-8" ?>
<Elements xmlns="http://schemas.microsoft.com/sharepoint/">
  <Module Name="MyFirstWorkflow" Url="wfsvc/5d8de52d6b344e0ba8d8da022449bb7b">
    <File Url="Workflow.xaml" Type="GhostableInLibrary"
        Path="MyFirstWorkflow\Workflow.xaml" DoGUIDFixUp="TRUE">
      <Property Name="ContentType" Value="WorkflowServiceDefinition" />
      <Property Name="isReusable" Value="true" />
      <Property Name="RequiresInitiationForm" Value="False" />
      <Property Name="RequiresAssociationForm" Value="False" />
      <Property Name="WSPublishState" Value="3" />
      <Property Name="WSDisplayName" Value="MyFirstWorkflow" />
      <Property Name="WSDescription" Value="My 'MyFirstWorkflow' Workflow" />
      <!-- If you change the name or Url of your custom initiation or association
form,
            remember to update the corresponding property value (InitiationUrl or
            AssociationUrl) to match the new web relative url.
      -->
      <Property Name="InitiationUrl"
      Value="wfsvc/5d8de52d6b344e0ba8d8da022449bb7b/MyFirstWorkflow/WFInitForm.
aspx" />
      <Property Name="AssociationUrl"
      Value="wfsvc/5d8de52d6b344e0ba8d8da022449bb7b/MyFirstWorkflow/WFAssocForm.
aspx" />
      <Property Name="RestrictToType" Value="List" />
      <Property Name="RestrictToScope" Value="{$ListId:Shared Documents;}" />
    </File>
    <File Url="WorkflowStartAssociation"
     Path="MyFirstWorkflow\WorkflowStartAssociation"
        Type="GhostableInLibrary">
      <Property Name="WSDisplayName" Value="MyFirstWorkflow - Workflow Start" />
      <Property Name="ContentType" Value="WorkflowServiceSubscription" />
      <Property Name="WSPublishState" Value="3" />
      <Property Name="WSEventType" Value="WorkflowStart" />
      <Property Name="WSEnabled" Value="true" />
      <Property Name="WSGUID" Value="a5fdbc8e-0132-4403-a919-74fcc088192d" />
      <Property Name="WSEventSourceGUID" Value="{$ListId:Shared Documents;}" />
      <Property Name="Microsoft.SharePoint.ActivationProperties.ListId"
          Value="{$ListId:Shared Documents;}" />
      <Property Name="HistoryListId" Value="{$ListId:Lists/Workflow History;}" />
      <Property Name="TaskListId" Value="{$ListId:Lists/Workflow Tasks;}" />
      <Property Name="StatusColumnCreated" Value="1" />
    </File>
    <File Path="MyFirstWorkflow\WFInitForm.aspx"
    Url="MyFirstWorkflow/WFInitForm.aspx" />
    <File Path="MyFirstWorkflow\WFAssocForm.aspx"
    Url="MyFirstWorkflow/WFAssocForm.aspx" />
  </Module>
  <ListInstance FeatureId="{2c63df2b-ceab-42c6-aeff-b3968162d4b1}"
                TemplateType="4501"
                Title="wfsvc"
                Description=
"This list instance is used by SharePoint to keep track of workflows. Do not
modify."
                Url="wfsvc"
                RootWebOnly="FALSE" />
</Elements>
```

The most interesting parts of the file are highlighted in bold. For example, the *Module* feature element provisions a pair of files with two content types:

- ***WorkflowServiceDefinition*** Represents a workflow definition, together with its configuration properties—for example, the target (list or site), and the *InitiationUrl* and *AssociationUrl* properties, if any.
- ***WorkflowServiceSubscription*** Declares an association between a *WorkflowServiceDefinition* and a target. This file defines the name, the activation type, the tasks list, the history list, and so on.

The workflow by itself is deployed in a folder relative to the wfsvc library. The folder will have a unique name. The workflow feature provisions the wfsvc library, which effectively holds the workflow definition files, which include the XAML file, the association file, any forms, and so on.

The file with content type *WorkflowServiceDefinition* supports many configurable properties. The most interesting are

- ***WSDisplayName*** Represents the display name of the workflow definition. It is visible to the end users when configuring new workflow associations.
- ***WSDescription*** Represents the description of the workflow definition. It is visible to the end users when configuring new workflow associations.
- ***InitiationUrl*** Represents the relative URL of the workflow initiation form, if any.
- ***AssociationUrl*** Represents the relative URL of the workflow association form, if any.
- ***RestrictToType*** Limits the available event source type for the workflow subscriptions based on the current workflow definition. The available values are *List*, *Site*, and empty or null, which behave the same.
- ***RestrictToScope*** Is a GUID value or an expression that will be processed by Visual Studio 2012 during packaging of the WSP file, which further restricts the scope of the current workflow definition. For example, if the *RestrictToType* property has a value of *List*, then this property can assume the value of the GUID of a specific list.

The default workflow-provisioning template available in Visual Studio 2012 does not use any initiation or association form. However, if you add a workflow initiation form or a workflow association form, Visual Studio 2012 will add the corresponding *Property* and *File* elements to the feature element file. By default, when you add a workflow initiation or association form while working in farm-level solutions, Visual Studio 2012 places the forms' files within the same folder that hosts the workflow definition.

The file with content type *WorkflowServiceSubscription* supports many other configurable properties. The most interesting are

- ***WSDisplayName*** Represents the display name of the workflow subscription. It is visible to the end users while starting a new workflow instance.

- ***WSEventType*** Defines the list of event types for which the workflow subscription is listening.
- **WSEnabled** Defines whether the current workflow subscription is enabled or not.
- ***WSEventSourceGUID*** Defines the unique ID (GUID) of the event source corresponding to the *WSEventType* value. Usually it is the ID of the target list or library if the workflow is a list workflow.
- ***ListId*** Defines the ID of the target list if the workflow is a list workflow.
- ***HistoryListId*** Defines the ID of the history list, if any.
- ***TaskListId*** Defines the ID of the tasks list, if any.
- ***StatusColumnCreated*** Declares whether the workflow subscription should have a workflow status column or not.

The supported values for the *WSEventType* property are

- ***WorkflowStart*** Allows the workflow to be manually started by an authenticated user with Edit Item permissions
- ***ItemAdded*** Starts the workflow when a new item is created
- ***ItemUpdated*** Starts the workflow when an item is updated

Workflow features use a dedicated feature receiver, declared in the *SPWorkflowPackageFeatureReceiver* class of the *Microsoft.SharePoint.WorkflowServices* namespace. This feature receiver accepts only features with a web scope, and if the workflow is properly configured, this feature receiver registers the workflow status column to the target list or library.

To accomplish the status column–registration task, you need to configure the *StatusColumnCreated* property of the *File* element with content type *WorkflowServiceSubcription*. Here is a code excerpt of the property to configure:

```
<Property Name="StatusColumnCreated" Value="1" />
```

A value of 1 instructs the feature receiver to create a status column with a name equal to the workflow association name. Any other value will not create the workflow status column.

By configuring all the properties illustrated in this section, you can determine the provisioning of your workflow definitions. Usually, the out-of-the-box provisioning files will suffice, but if necessary, you can edit the feature element file to adhere to your requirements.

SharePoint app workflow

When you deploy a workflow definition through a SharePoint app project, Visual Studio 2012 hides all the inner workings from you. The deployment is managed for you, and you simply have to configure a set of properties that determine the behavior of the deployment process. To edit these properties, click the workflow item in Solution Explorer and work through the property grid of Visual Studio 2012 (see Figure 17-25).

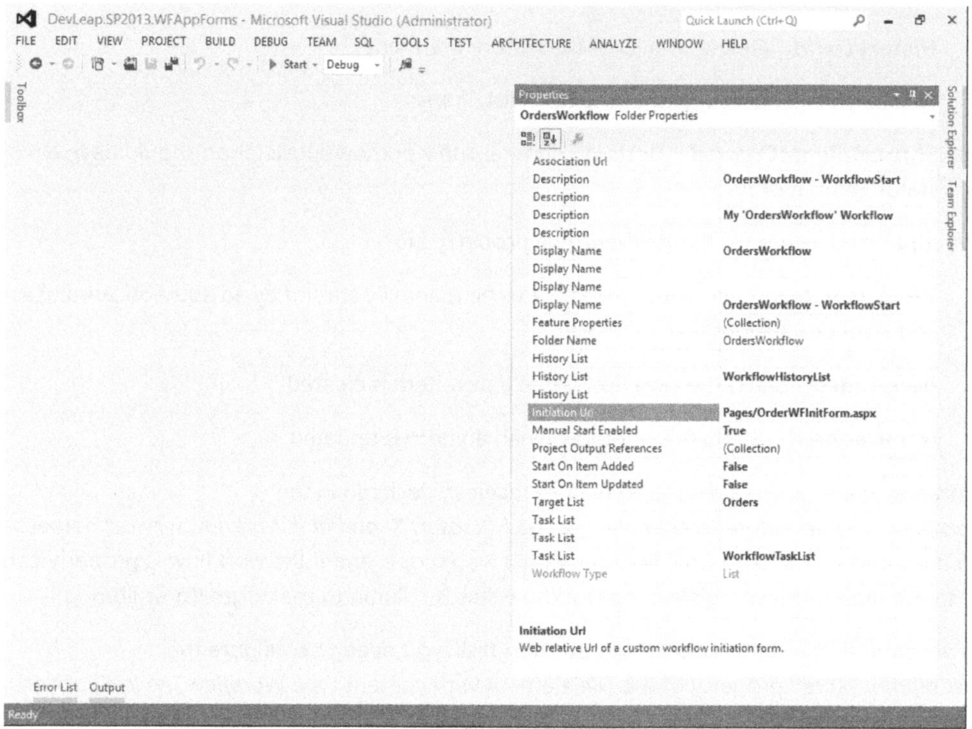

FIGURE 17-25 The property grid of a workflow defined in a SharePoint app in Visual Studio 2012.

As you can see, there are properties for managing all the most common configuration parameters, including description, display name, history list, tasks list, initiation and association form URLs, startup behavior, and target list. For instance, if you want to configure the workflow to start when a target item is added, you can simply change the value of the property *Start On Item Added* to *true*. Moreover, if you want to configure the URL of the initiation or association form, you need to choose or provide a value for the *Initiation Url* and *Association Url* properties.

Behind the scenes, the editor will configure some XML elements in a file named SharePointProjectItem.spdata, which is placed in the same folder as the XAML file with the source code of the workflow definition.

Flowcharts and state machines

So far, using Visual Studio 2012, you have designed only sequential workflows. However, you can also use flowcharts and state machines in SharePoint 2013 workflows. From an operational viewpoint, designing a flowchart or a state machine is not that different from creating a sequential workflow. You simply need to delete the *Sequence* activity, which is provided by default by Visual Studio 2012 within the workflow item template for SharePoint, and replace it with a *Flowchart* or *StateMachine* activity. For example, Figure 17-26 illustrates a sample flowchart-based approval workflow for SharePoint 2013 in the workflow designer.

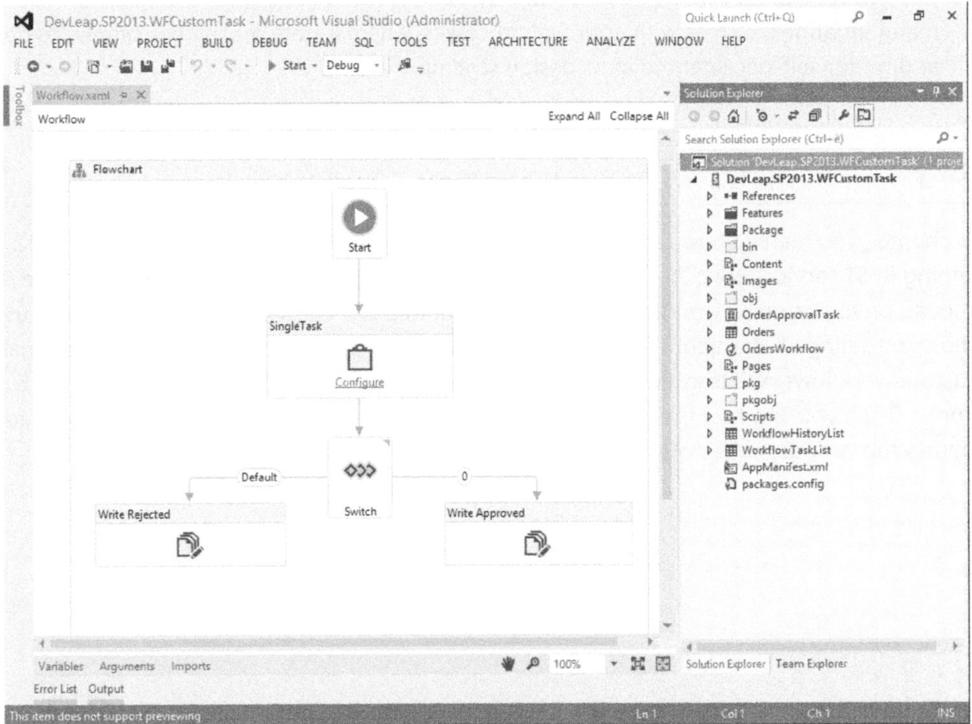

FIGURE 17-26 The workflow design surface of Visual Studio 2012 for a flowchart workflow.

More interesting than how to design the sequences, flowcharts, or state machines is when to use which kind of model. The answer depends on the functional requirements of your project:

- **Sequential workflow** A good option whenever you need to define a flow with clear starting and ending points, with a defined path to move from the beginning to the end, and without the need to step back in the flow process. For example, a sequential workflow is the right choice for defining maintenance processes, and is often used in site collection–level workflows.
- **Flowchart workflow** The right solution for implementing decision-based processes. Flowcharts are based on the idea of performing an action, evaluating the action result or a

condition, making a decision, performing another action, and so on. With a flowchart, you can come across the same portions of a flow process multiple times. It is a suitable option for defining approval processes with moderate interaction with end users, loops, and so on. Not by chance, SharePoint Designer 2013 creates workflows as flowcharts when you use its workflow designer.

- **State machine workflow** The best choice for modeling a human-interactive process, like a document approval process. The states of the state machine correspond to the phases of the process. The outcome of every approval phase corresponds to a transition rule, which defines the target state to go to. When the process is completed, the state machine can make a transition to the final state. Even if every state machine can be defined using a flowchart, there are many situations, such as with approval processes, where a state machine is simpler to design and better self-documented in its design schema.

Summary

In this chapter, you learned how to create advanced workflows using SharePoint Designer 2013, consuming REST services using the *Call HTTP Web Service* action and the *Dictionary* data type. Then you moved on to designing workflows using Visual Studio 2012. You saw how to implement custom workflows targeting an on-premises farm, as well as how to create SharePoint apps that internally use custom workflows. You learned how to create custom workflow forms, custom tasks, and custom task forms. Then you saw how the deployment process of a workflow works. The chapter ended by comparing the various models of workflow definitions available.

CHAPTER 18

Advanced workflows

In this chapter, you will learn about some advanced topics and new features introduced with Microsoft SharePoint 2013. The chapter will explain how you can create custom actions by using declarative activities, as well as by writing code-based activities. You will learn about workflow security and how to use Workflow Services Manager from the client side. If you are working with SharePoint workflows for the first time, you may wish to postpone a careful reading of the material until after you have more experience with standard workflow features. If you're comfortable with the basics of workflows and are ready to take your projects to the next level, however, read on now.

Custom actions

One of the main areas of extensibility for every workflow solution—not just SharePoint solutions—is developing custom activities. In Chapter 15, you learned the very basics of creating custom activities: simply defining a custom class that inherits from the *System.Activities.Activity* base class. Depending on your implementation, you may need to do more. In this section, you will learn how to develop custom activities targeting both SharePoint Designer 2013 and Microsoft Visual Studio 2012.

Let's start with some useful definitions. As you know, an *activity* is a building block of a workflow and represents the minimal unit of workflow execution. An *action* is a high-level wrapper of one or more activities to provide a human-readable statement within SharePoint Designer 2013 or another client platform. Because in SharePoint 2013 the Workflow Manager engine is open for integration, you can implement workflow designers of your own that consume the Workflow Services Manager services (the section "Workflow Services Manager" will explain how).

You can define a custom action two ways. You can work declaratively in Visual Studio 2012, simply using the designer without writing any code, to create a *declarative activity.* Alternately, you can create some custom code to define a *code activity* that will enable you to use the whole .NET development environment. The code-activity scenario is suitable only for on-premises farms, because it requires you to deploy your custom code using a full-trust solution.

Creating a declarative activity

To create a declarative activity, you must have a development environment with SharePoint 2013 Server and Workflow Manager installed locally. On the same machine that houses SharePoint 2013, you must also install Visual Studio 2012 Professional or higher, as well as the Microsoft Office Developer Tools for Visual Studio 2012.

Imagine that you want to create a custom activity for consuming a list of customers from an external Representational State Transfer (REST) or OData service. For example, you can consume the publicly available OData service for reading the well-known Northwind database, which is available at *http://services.odata.org/Northwind/Northwind.svc*. To begin, launch Visual Studio 2012, create a new project of type SharePoint 2013 - Empty Project, and choose to produce a sandboxed solution. Next, add a new item of type Workflow Custom Activity to the project. You will be prompted with a workflow activity designer that already includes a *Sequence* activity.

The order-approval workflow needs to retrieve some data about the target customer of the order; it does so by querying the Northwind OData service using the *CustomerID* field. The REST URI for retrieving the customer data is *http://services.odata.org/Northwind/Northwind.svc/Customers('ALFKI')?$select={CustomerID},CompanyName,ContactName,ContactTitle,Country.*

Replace the *{CustomerID}* argument with the *CustomerID* value of the customer to look up. Listing 18-1 shows the JavaScript Object Notation (JSON) result of the service invocation.

LISTING 18-1 The JSON response of the Northwind OData service during a query for a specific customer instance

```
{
  "d" : {
    "__metadata": {
    "uri":
    "http://services.odata.org/Northwind/Northwind.svc/Customers('ALFKI')",
    "type":"NorthwindModel.Customer"
  },
  "CustomerID": "ALFKI",
  "CompanyName": "Alfreds Futterkiste",
  "ContactName": "Maria Anders",
  "ContactTitle": "Sales Representative",
  "Country": "Germany"
  }
}
```

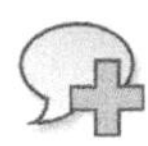

More Info To check the output of the service, you can use the Fiddler2 tool (*http://www.fiddler2.com/*). To view the JSON output format, remember to configure an *Accept* HTTP header with a value of *application/json*.

To implement the custom activity (call it *NWCustomerLookup*), you first need to create an input argument with name *CustomerID* to receive the ID of the customer to look for in the Northwind database. You also need a set of output arguments for holding the return values, which are all of type *String*; name them *CompanyName*, *ContactName*, *ContactTitle*, and *Country*.

To effectively contact the remote OData service, you can use the *HttpSend* activity, available in Visual Studio 2012. Simply provide the target URL, as well as the *Accept* HTTP header (*application/json*). To create the set of HTTP headers, use a *BuildDynamicValue* activity and put the output into a *responseHeaders* variable of type *DynamicValue*. You can place the response in a variable of type *DynamicValue*, as well. Table 18-1 shows the configuration provided to the main properties of the *HttpSend* activity.

TABLE 18-1 The configuration provided to the main properties of the *HttpSend* activity

Attribute name	Description	Value
Method	Defines the HTTP method or verb	*GET*
Uri	Defines the URI to contact; in this example, it will be dynamically calculated using the input argument *CustomerID*	*"http://services.odata.org/Northwind/Northwind.svc/Customers('" + CustomerID + "')?$select=CustomerID,CompanyName,ContactName,ContactTitle,Country*
RequestHeaders	Declares the HTTP request headers that will be used to contact the remote endpoint	*requestHeaders*
ResponseContent	Represents the response, as a variable of type *DynamicValue*, returned by the remote service	*responseContent*

By using the *GetDynamicValueProperties* activity, you can retrieve the fields and place them inside the specific output arguments. Figure 18-1 illustrates the outline of the custom declarative activity.

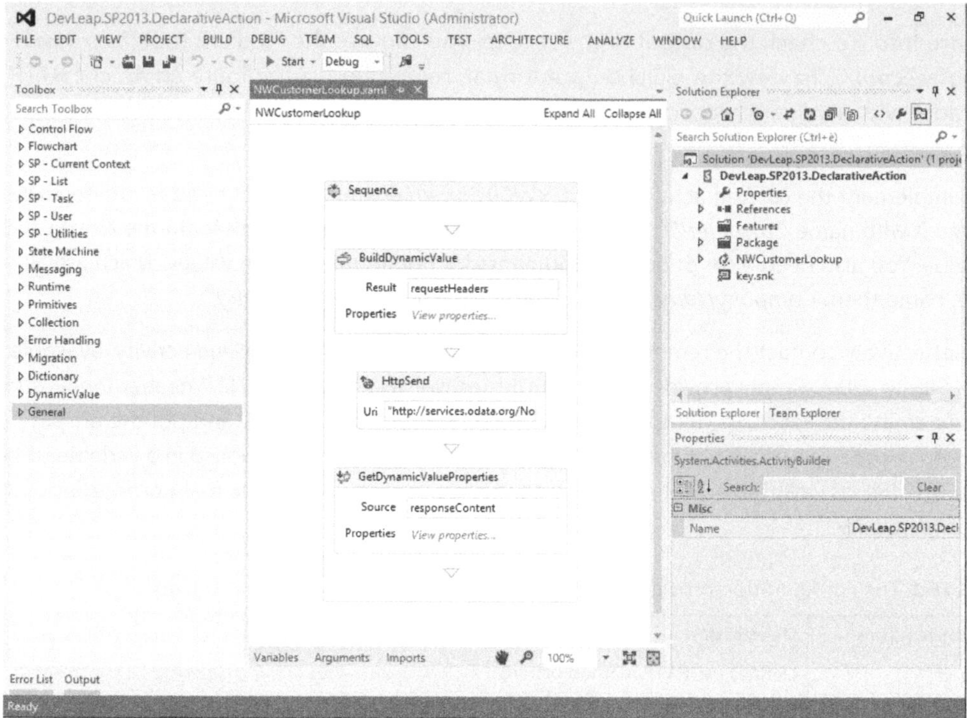

FIGURE 18-1 The outline of the custom declarative activity in the designer of Visual Studio 2012.

To deploy the custom activity, you need to do a little bit of work, which is covered in detail in the next section. For now, assume you have already deployed the custom declarative activity, and take a look at Figure 18-2 to see how the custom activity behaves in SharePoint Designer 2013.

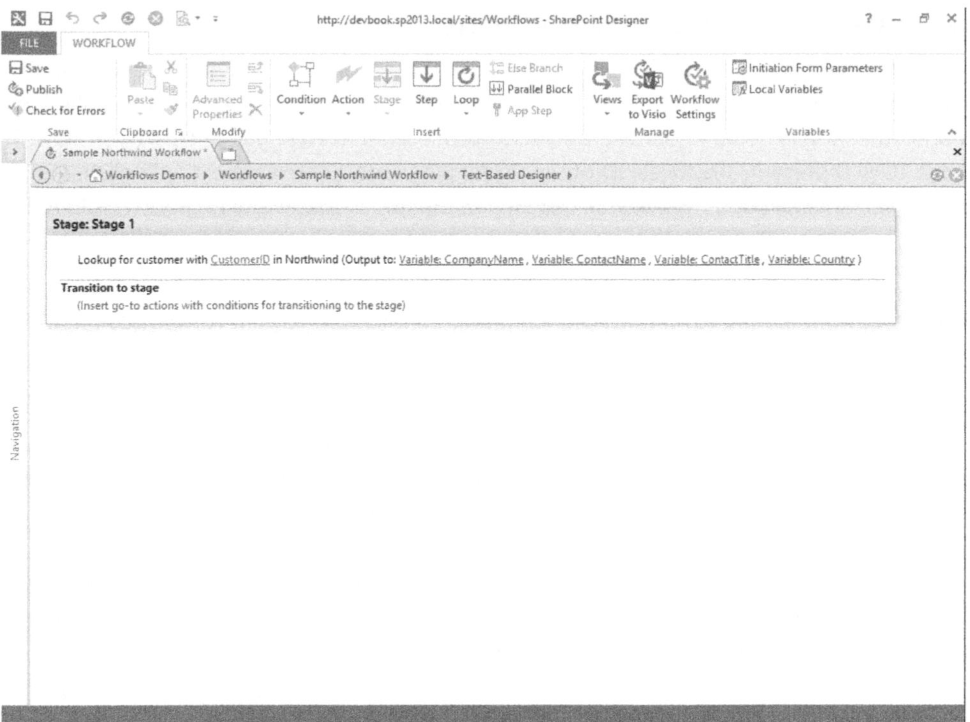

FIGURE 18-2 The custom declarative activity in the designer of SharePoint Designer 2013.

Important Whenever you deploy custom actions or custom activities for SharePoint Designer 2013, the client tool will need to refresh its local cache; otherwise, the new elements will not be available. Luckily, SharePoint Designer 2013 informs you about this issue. Nevertheless, you must manually clear the cache. To accomplish this task, simply delete the folder with path *user profile*\appdata\local\microsoft\websitecache*sitename*.

The sample illustrated in Figure 18-2 defines a simple site workflow, which is defined just to test the custom declarative activity. As you can see, the activity is described using the following sentence:

```
Lookup for customer with CustomerID in Northwind (Output to: Variable: CompanyName, Variable:
ContactName, Variable: ContactTitle, Variable: Country).
```

The *CustomerID* token represents an input argument, while the *CompanyName*, *ContactName*, *ContactTitle*, and *Country* arguments are the output values that will be saved in workflow variables. Notice that inserting the action in the designer will automatically create the target variables for holding the output values. In the next section, you will learn how to achieve this automatic behavior.

Deployment of declarative actions

From a deployment and provisioning viewpoint, workflow actions and activities are defined in specific files with an .actions4 extension, which vary by language and which can be installed onto the SharePoint servers in the folder SharePoint15_Root\TEMPLATE*Language LCID*\Workflow. The *Language LCID* represents the locale ID of the target language. For example, the English (LCID: 1033) version of the .actions4 files will be installed in the folder SharePoint15_Root\TEMPLATE\1033\Workflow.

Note SharePoint15_Root refers to the SharePoint root folder, which is typically located at C:\Program Files\Common Files\Microsoft Shared\Web Server Extensions\15.

In the same folder, you will also find some .actions files. However, those files are related to SharePoint 2010 and the legacy WF 3.*x* workflow engine, and you should not bother with them in this chapter. The .actions4 files can also be provisioned using sandboxed solutions, if you want to deploy custom declarative activities in Microsoft Office 365. Listing 18-2 shows a code excerpt of the default workflow15.actions4 file, which contains the same out-of-the-box actions you saw while making your first workflow with SharePoint Designer 2013 in Chapter 16, "SharePoint workflow fundamentals." Listing 18-2 defines the native *Set Field in Current Item* action.

LISTING 18-2 A code excerpt of the workflow15.actions4 file for defining an action

```
<Action Name="Set Field in Current Item"
  ClassName="Microsoft.SharePoint.WorkflowServices.Activities.SetField"
  AppliesTo="list" UsesCurrentItem="true" Category="List Actions">
  <RuleDesigner Sentence="Set %1 to %2">
    <FieldBind Field="FieldName" Text="field" Id="1"
        DesignerType="WritableFieldNames" DisplayName="Field" />
    <FieldBind Field="FieldValue" Text="value" Id="2"
        TypeFrom="FieldName" DesignerType="Dependent" DisplayName="Value" />
  </RuleDesigner>
  <Parameters>
    <Parameter Name="FieldName" Type="System.String, mscorlib" Direction="In"
        DesignerType="WritableFieldNames"
        Description="Field to set the value of." />
    <Parameter Name="FieldValue" Type="System.Object, mscorlib" Direction="In"
        DesignerType="Dependent" Description="Value to set the field to." />
  </Parameters>
</Action>
```

As you can see, the excerpt defines an *Action* element, which is the root element for any action definition. This element requires a *ClassName* attribute, which defines the underlying .NET type that effectively implements the action. The most common attributes of the *Action* element are illustrated in Table 18-2.

More Info For further details about the workflow configuration schemas in SharePoint 2013, you can read "WorkflowActions4 schema reference," available on MSDN at *http://msdn.microsoft.com/en-us/library/jj583378.aspx.*

TABLE 18-2 The main attributes for configuring a custom action in the .actions4 files

Attribute name	Description	Data type
__SolutionId	Specifies a GUID that the client application writes to the implementation-specific action. The server uses the GUID to help locate the assembly at workflow run time.	*xsd:string*
AppliesTo	Defines the target of the action. The available values are *site, list, doclib,* and *all.* They are all self-explanatory. Depending on the value provided to this attribute, the action will be visible and either available or not in the UI of SharePoint Designer 2013. It is a required attribute.	*xsd:string,* within a fixed set of available values: *site, list, doclib,* and *all.*
Assembly	Is the strong name (*Name, Version, Culture, PublicKeyToken*) of the assembly containing the type implementing the custom action.	*xsd:string*
Category	Provides the category where the action will show up in the UI of SharePoint Designer 2013.	*xsd:string*
ClassName	Is the fully qualified name of the class that implements the workflow action. It is a required attribute.	*xsd:string*
FunctionName	Specifies the name of a function to call. That function will be defined in the *ClassName* attribute, available in the assembly defined in the *Assembly* attribute.	*xsd:string*
Name	Is the descriptive name of the action, and is displayed in the UI of SharePoint Designer 2013. It is a required attribute.	*xsd:string*
SandboxedFunction	If *true*, calls a specific function defined in the class with name equal to the *ClassName* attribute. That class will be searched in the assembly with a strong name value equal to the content of the *Assembly* attribute. That assembly will by looked for in the solution with the ID value defined in the *__SolutionId* attribute.	*xsd:boolean*
ShapeImageUrl	Defines the URL of an image that will be used in the UI of SharePoint Designer 2013 to present the action.	*xsd:string*
UsesCurrentItem	Indicates whether the action targets a specific list item, or if it is suitable for a site workflow. If this attribute is configured with a value of *false* or is not configured, the action can be used in a site workflow. Otherwise, the action can only be used in a list workflow.	*xsd:boolean*

The main child elements of the *Actions* element are *RuleDesigner* and *Parameters*. The former defines the behavior of the custom action within SharePoint Designer 2013, and declares the sentence to prompt to the user designing the workflow, as well as any field to ask for. Reading Listing 18-2, you can see that the *RuleDesigner* element accepts a *Sentence* attribute, which defines a tokenized string. For example, the sentence for the *Set Field in Current Item* action is the following:

```
Set %1 to %2
```

where *%1* and *%2* correspond to two occurrences of children *FieldBind* elements. Every *FieldBind* element defines a field that matches a token in the sentence. The *FieldBind* element accepts a wide range of attributes, which are illustrated in Table 18-3.

TABLE 18-3 The main attributes for configuring the *FieldBind* element in the .actions4 files

Attribute name	Description	Data type
DesignerType	Defines the data type to use within the designer UI of SharePoint Designer 2013. The main available values are defined later in this section. It is a required attribute.	*xsd:string*
DisplayName	Represents the display name of the field in the UI of SharePoint Designer 2013.	*xsd:string*
EventCategory	Defines the event category type for instances of the *FieldBind* element with a *DesignerType* attribute with a value of *ListItemEvent* or *EventDropdown*.	*xsd:string*
Field	Declares the name of the field corresponding to the current *FieldBind* element. There will be a *Parameter* element (in the *Parameters* element section) with the *Name* attribute with the same value.	*xsd:string*
Id	Defines the numeric ID of the field, and will match the *%Id* token declared in the *Sentence* attribute of the *RuleDesigner* parent element.	xsd:positiveInteger
OperatorTypeFrom	When the *DesignerType* attribute has a value of *Operator*, declares the field from which the current field will retrieve its operator type.	*xsd:string*
Text	Declares the descriptive text used for presenting the field in the UI of SharePoint Designer 2013.	*xsd:string*
TypeFrom	When the *DesignerType* attribute has a value of *Dependent*, declares the field from which the current field will retrieve its type.	*xsd:string*

The *Parameters* element of the .actions4 file behaves similarly to the *RuleDesigner* element. In fact, the *Parameters* element is the parent of a set of *Parameter* elements, where each one describes a single parameter with a direction (input, output, or optional), name, type, and designer behavior. Table 18-4 lists the main attributes available for configuring each *Parameter* element.

TABLE 18-4 The main attributes for configuring the *Parameter* element in the .actions4 files

Attribute name	Description	Data type
Description	Defines the description of the current parameter.	*xsd:string*
DesignerType	Defines the data type to use within the designer UI of SharePoint Designer 2013. The main available values are defined later in this section. It is a required attribute.	*xsd:string*
Direction	Declares the direction (input, output, or optional) for the parameter.	xsd:string, within a fixed set of available values: In, Out, and Optional.
DisplayName	Represents the display name of the field in the UI of SharePoint Designer 2013.	*xsd:string*
InitialValue	Defines the initial and default value for the parameter.	*xsd:string*
Name	Defines the name of the parameter. The value of this attribute is used to reference the parameter in the *FieldBind* elements.	*xsd:string*
Type	Defines the underlying data type, represented as a .NET type with a name and container assembly.	*xsd:string*

Each *Parameter* element can be referenced by name in the *FieldBind* elements. In Listing 18-3, you can see the NWCustomerLookup.actions4 file, which defines the custom *NWCustomerLookup* declarative activity you created in the previous section.

LISTING 18-3 The content of the NWCustomerLookup.actions4 file for defining the *NWCustomerLookup* declarative activity

```
<Action Name="Northwind customer lookup"
  ClassName="DevLeap.SP2013.DeclarativeAction.NWCustomerLookup"
Category="DevLeap" AppliesTo="all">
  <RuleDesigner
 Sentence="Lookup for customer with %1 in Northwind (Output to: %2, %3, %4, %5)">
    <FieldBind Field="CustomerID" DesignerType="TextBox" Id="1" Text="CustomerID"
      DisplayName="CustomerID" />
    <FieldBind Field="CompanyName" DesignerType="ParameterNames" Id="2"
Text="CompanyName" DisplayName="CompanyName" />
    <FieldBind Field="ContactName" DesignerType="ParameterNames" Id="3"
Text="ContactName" DisplayName="ContactName" />
    <FieldBind Field="ContactTitle" DesignerType="ParameterNames" Id="4"
      Text="ContactTitle" DisplayName="ContactTitle" />
    <FieldBind Field="Country" DesignerType="ParameterNames" Id="5"
Text="Country" DisplayName="Country" />
  </RuleDesigner>
  <Parameters>
    <Parameter Name="CustomerID" Type="System.String, mscorlib" Direction="In"
      DesignerType="TextArea" Description="The ID of the customer to lookup" />
    <Parameter Name="CompanyName" Type="System.String, mscorlib" Direction="Out"
      DesignerType="ParameterNames"
Description="The ID of the customer to lookup" />
    <Parameter Name="ContactName" Type="System.String, mscorlib" Direction="Out"
      DesignerType="ParameterNames"
Description="The ID of the customer to lookup" />
    <Parameter Name="ContactTitle" Type="System.String, mscorlib" Direction="Out"
      DesignerType="ParameterNames"
Description="The ID of the customer to lookup" />
    <Parameter Name="Country" Type="System.String, mscorlib" Direction="Out"
      DesignerType="ParameterNames"
Description="The ID of the customer to lookup" />
  </Parameters>
</Action>
```

To deploy the current custom activity, you simply need to package the resulting WSP file and upload the sandboxed solution to the target site collection. Visual Studio 2012 already does this for you, and also creates an .actions4 file in the project. That .actions4 file will be almost empty, however, so you will have to compile it manually, and without any kind of IntelliSense or syntax check. In case you are creating a declarative activity within a sandboxed solution, the .actions4 file, the XAML file, and any other elements are deployed to the content database of the target site collection through a sandboxed solution. Because you don't need physical access to the file system of the target server farm, the declarative activities are the first choice for extending native activities in the context of a Office 365 cloud-hosted solution.

While compiling the .actions4 file, you must provide values for a variety of settings. For example, the *DesignerType* attribute accepts a long list of possible values. The most interesting and frequently used of these values are the following:

- ***TextBox*** Accepts a text value and presents a text box in the UI of the designer.
- ***Operator*** Allows for providing a set of values in a dedicated list of *Option* elements.
- ***Dependent*** Declares a field type that will retrieve its data type from another field, declared in a *TypeFrom* attribute.
- ***Dropdown*** Presents a drop-down list of values on the design surface.
- ***SinglePerson*** Provides a single-user lookup on the design surface.
- ***Date*** Provides a control for selecting a data value.
- ***TextArea*** Allows for setting a multiline text field.
- ***RestCall*** Defines the arguments of a REST/HTTP call.
- ***ParameterNames*** Creates a variable in the current workflow context, using the type and name of the current field or parameter.
- ***StringBuilder*** Provides a control for building a value of type *String*.
- ***Dictionary*** Allows for creating a collection of key/values pairs. Behind the scenes, it corresponds to a *DynamicValue* variable.
- ***Hide*** Prevents a field from being displayed on the design surface.
- ***ListItem*** Provides a lookup to a specific list item.
- ***CreateListItem*** Provides the UI for configuring the creation of a new list item.
- ***UpdateListItem*** Provides the UI for configuring the update of a list item.
- ***ItemProperties*** Provides the UI for configuring a set of fields for a list item.
- ***ChooseListItem*** Provides the UI for selecting a specific list item.
- ***DocLibNames*** Provides the UI for selecting a specific document library using a drop-down list of all the available document libraries.
- ***Email*** Provides the UI for defining an email address.
- ***Person*** Allows for providing a single person as the variable type.
- ***WorkflowParameters*** Provides a lookup to the workflow context parameters.
- ***Float*** Provides a numeric field or property of type *float*.
- ***Stages*** Provides a drop-down list for selecting a specific stage of the workflow definition.

Creating a code activity

A code activity, which is suitable only for on-premises scenarios, can be based on one or more code files. Let's start with a simple example of a custom credit card validator activity. You can inherit from the base *CodeActivity<T>*, where the type of *T* will be *Boolean* and will return *true* if the argument named *CreditCard*, which is of type *InArgument<String>*, represents a real credit card number.

Create a new Visual Studio 2012 project of type Activity Library and add a new item of type Code Activity with the name *CreditCardValidationActivity*. The code template for a code activity item already includes a property of type *InArgument<String>* and overrides the *Execute* method of the base *CodeActivity* class. Change the base class of the *CreditCardValidationActivity* class to inherit from *CodeActivity<Boolean>*, and refresh the signature of the method overriding the *Execute* method of the base class. Now you are ready to implement the business logic of the custom code activity. Listing 18-4 provides the code for implementing the custom activity, which internally uses the .NET 4.5 data validation framework to check the credit card number. For this purpose, you will need to reference the assembly *System.ComponentModel.DataAnnotations* with version 4.0.0.0.

More Info The sample code activity uses a publicly available algorithm for validating the credit card numbers, which is mainly a kind of CRC (cyclic redundancy check). Called LUHN after its inventor, the algorithm is documented at *http://en.wikipedia.org/wiki/Luhn_algorithm*. On the Internet, you will find tons of code samples for validating credit card numbers using this algorithm. Starting in .NET 4.5, however, you have an alternative: using a native class called *CreditCardAttribute*, which is available in the *System.ComponentModel.DataAnnotations* namespace and is useful for validating credit card numbers.

LISTING 18-4 The source code of the custom code activity for validating credit card numbers

```
using System;
using System.Collections.Generic;
using System.Linq;
using System.Text;
using System.Activities;
using System.ComponentModel.DataAnnotations;

namespace DevLeap.SP2013.CustomActivities {

    public sealed class CreditCardValidationActivity : CodeActivity<Boolean> {

        [RequiredArgument]
        public InArgument<String> CreditCard { get; set; }

        protected override bool Execute(CodeActivityContext context) {
            CreditCardAttribute cc = new CreditCardAttribute();
            return (cc.IsValid(this.CreditCard.Get(context)));
        }
    }
}
```

As you can see, the custom code activity itself is very simple, in order to keep the focus on implementation and deployment.

Deployment of code activities

You can define a real custom activity with all the arguments that you like, whether they are of type *InArgument<T>*, *OutArgument<T>*, or *InOutArgument<T>*. You can implement the business logic with as much complexity as you like, but sooner or later you will need to deploy the activity.

The first step is still the creation of an .actions4 file. Listing 18-5 contains the .actions4 file for the *CreditCardValidationActivity*.

LISTING 18-5 The content of the CreditCardValidationActivity.actions4 file for defining the *CreditCardValidationActivity*

```
<?xml version="1.0" encoding="utf-8" ?>
<WorkflowInfo Language="en-us">
  <Actions>
    <Action Name="Validate Credit Card"
        ClassName="DevLeap.SP2013.CustomActivities.CreditCardValidationActivity"
        Assembly="DevLeap.SP2013.CustomActivities, Version=1.0.0.0,
Culture=neutral, PublicKeyToken=bbaf2a8a1431fb28"
        Category="DevLeap" AppliesTo="all">
      <RuleDesigner Sentence="Validate credit card number %1 (Output to: %2)">
        <FieldBind Field="CreditCard" DesignerType="TextBox" Id="1"
Text="CreditCard" DisplayName="CreditCard" />
        <FieldBind Field="ValidationResult" DesignerType="ParameterNames" Id="2"
            Text="Result" DisplayName="Result" />
      </RuleDesigner>
      <Parameters>
        <Parameter Name="CreditCard" Type="System.String, mscorlib"
        Direction="In"
            DesignerType="TextArea" Description="The credit card number" />
        <Parameter Name="ValidationResult" Type="System.Boolean, mscorlib"
        Direction="Out"
            DesignerType="ParameterNames" Description="The validation result" />
      </Parameters>
    </Action>
  </Actions>
</WorkflowInfo>
```

As you can see, the file is almost the same as the one defined in Listing 18-3. However, this time, the *Action* element is wrapped in an *Actions* parent element, and the XML file has a *WorkflowInfo* root element. Moreover, the *Action* element declares the *Assembly* attribute, which references the strong name of the assembly providing the custom activity class. The assembly will need to be strongly named, because it will have to be deployed in the GAC (Global Assembly Cache) of the SharePoint servers. This time, the custom .actions4 file will go to the file system, not to the content database of the target site collection through a sandboxed solution.

While developing custom code activities, you must define a second XML file, called AllowedTypes.xml, which declares the types allowed for loading in the Workflow Manager engine. Listing 18-6 defines that file for the sample *CreditCardValidationActivity* class.

LISTING 18-6 The AllowedTypes.xml file defined for the *CreditCardValidationActivity*

```
<?xml version="1.0" encoding="utf-8" ?>
<AllowedTypes>
  <Assembly Name="DevLeap.SP2013.CustomActivities">
    <Namespace Name="DevLeap.SP2013.CustomActivities">
      <Type>CreditCardValidationActivity</Type>
    </Namespace>
  </Assembly>
</AllowedTypes>
```

The file is simple, and declares the assembly, namespace, and class name of the types allowed to run in the workflow engine.

The following are the steps for deploying the custom code activity to Workflow Manager.

1. Copy the assembly and the AllowedTypes.xml file into the following path locations:
   - %ProgramFiles%\Workflow Manager\1.0\Workflow\Artifacts
   - %ProgramFiles%\Workflow Manager\1.0\Workflow\WFWebRoot\bin
2. Restart the Workflow Manager engine (that is, the Workflow Manager Backend service).
3. To make the custom activity available in SharePoint 2013, copy the assembly into the GAC of all the involved SharePoint servers.
4. Add the .actions4 file to the path SharePoint15_Root\TEMPLATE*Language LCID*\Workflow.
5. Restart Internet Information Services (IIS) (execute an *IISReset*).
6. Clean the client-side cache of SharePoint Designer 2013.

In the case of multiserver deployment, you must execute the preceding steps on each server of the farm.

More Info For further details about deploying custom code-based activities, you can read the document "Defining and using custom code activities and types in a Workflow Manager 1.0 workflow," at *http://msdn.microsoft.com/en-us/library/windowsazure/jj193517(v=azure.10).aspx*.

Now you are ready to play with your new custom activity in SharePoint Designer 2013.

Because some of the files have to be copied outside of the SharePoint15_Root path (that is, C:\Program Files\Common Files\Microsoft Shared\Web Server Extensions\15), you cannot create an automated setup-and-deployment process that uses a WSP file. Unfortunately, you will need to create a PowerShell file, or something similar, to replicate and automate the installation process. Nevertheless, for the SharePoint side of the deployment, you can use a farm-level solution—which will be capable of deploying the assembly to the GAC—to copy the .actions4 file to the Workflow folder of SharePoint 2013, as well as to recycle the IIS application pool process.

After deploying the custom code activity, you will be able to find it in SharePoint Designer 2013, as shown in Figure 18-3 (see the red outline).

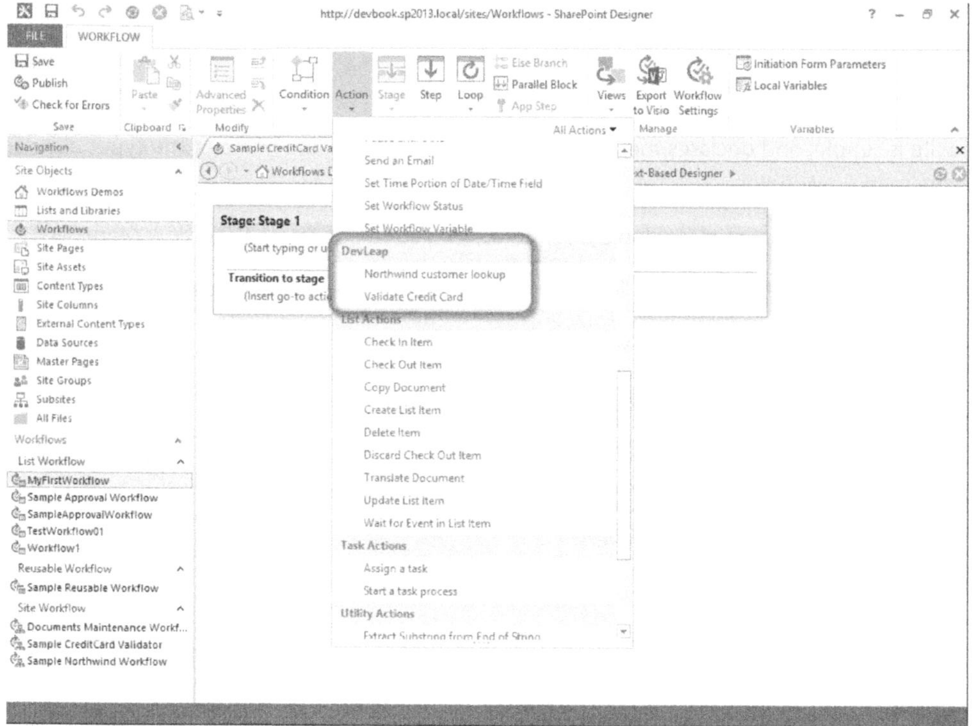

FIGURE 18-3 The custom code activity in the list of available actions in the designer of SharePoint Designer 2013.

Figure 18-4 shows the behavior of the custom code activity in SharePoint Designer 2013. From an end-user viewpoint, a custom activity is presented the same way whether it is declarative or code based. Behind the scenes, however, the deployment process is different, and the potentials are completely different, too. While a declarative action can use already existing actions only, a code-based activity can do whatever you want, because it uses custom code.

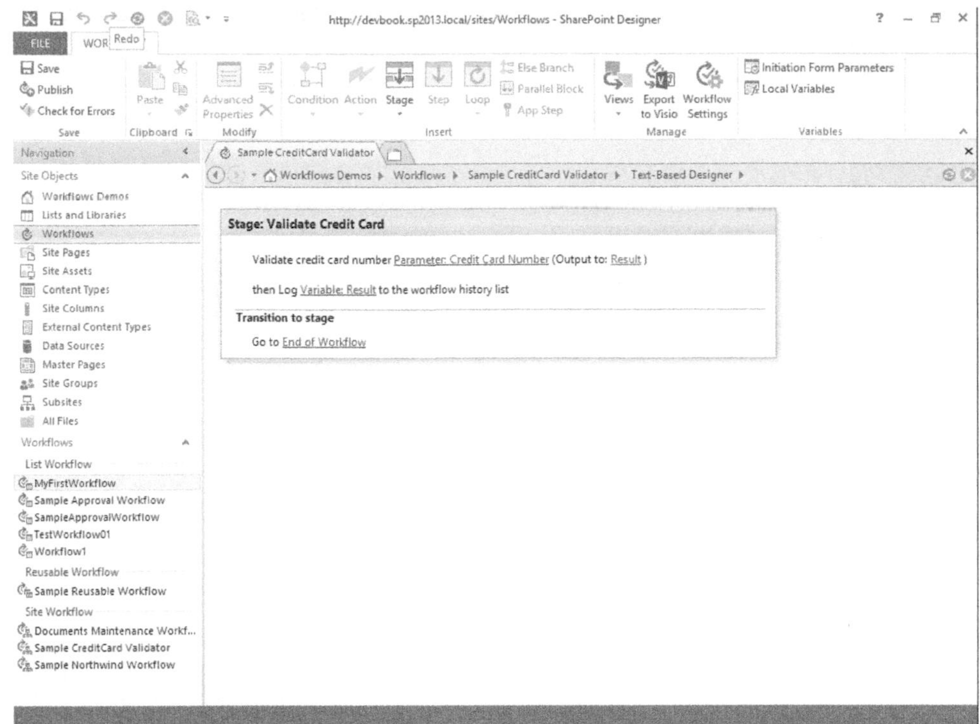

FIGURE 18-4 The custom code activity in the designer of SharePoint Designer 2013.

Security and workflow app principal

In SharePoint 2013, the workflow engine has been changed not only from an architectural viewpoint, but also from a security perspective.

In SharePoint 2010, the workflow instances run as the initiating user by default, or can run impersonating the publisher via the impersonation step, or can run acting with elevated privileges using some custom code. Now, in SharePoint 2013, workflows have their own identity, which is an app principal. To experience this behavior, open the web browser and navigate to the Site Settings page. There, under the Users And Permissions group of actions, click the Site App Permissions menu item. Figure 18-5 shows the output in the web browser.

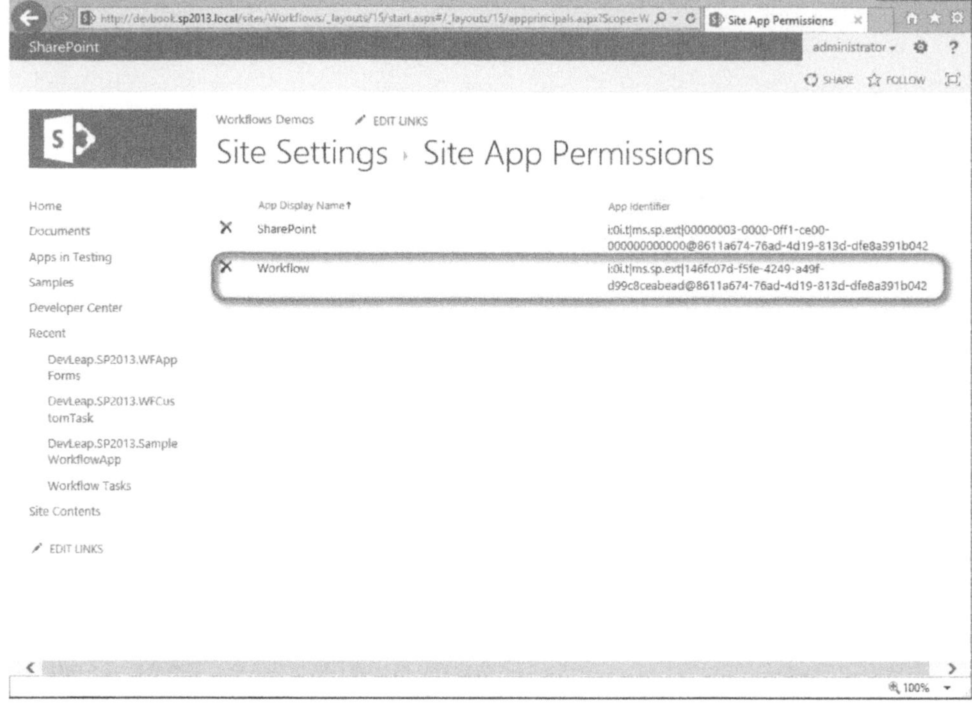

FIGURE 18-5 The Site App Permissions page of a SharePoint 2013 site with workflow definitions.

Notice the app outlined in red, which has a display name value of Workflow and a dedicated app identifier. This is the app identity that will be used by the workflow engine for performing operations. For the sake of completeness, notice that in the Site App Permission page there is also an app identifier for SharePoint itself. To better prove the existence of an app principal dedicated to the workflow engine, start a workflow instance of a workflow definition created with SharePoint Designer 2013, targeting, for example, the Documents library of the current site. Imagine starting an instance of the sample approval workflow defined in Chapter 16. That workflow definition creates a task. Open the task and check the Created At and Last Modified At fields (see Figure 18-6).

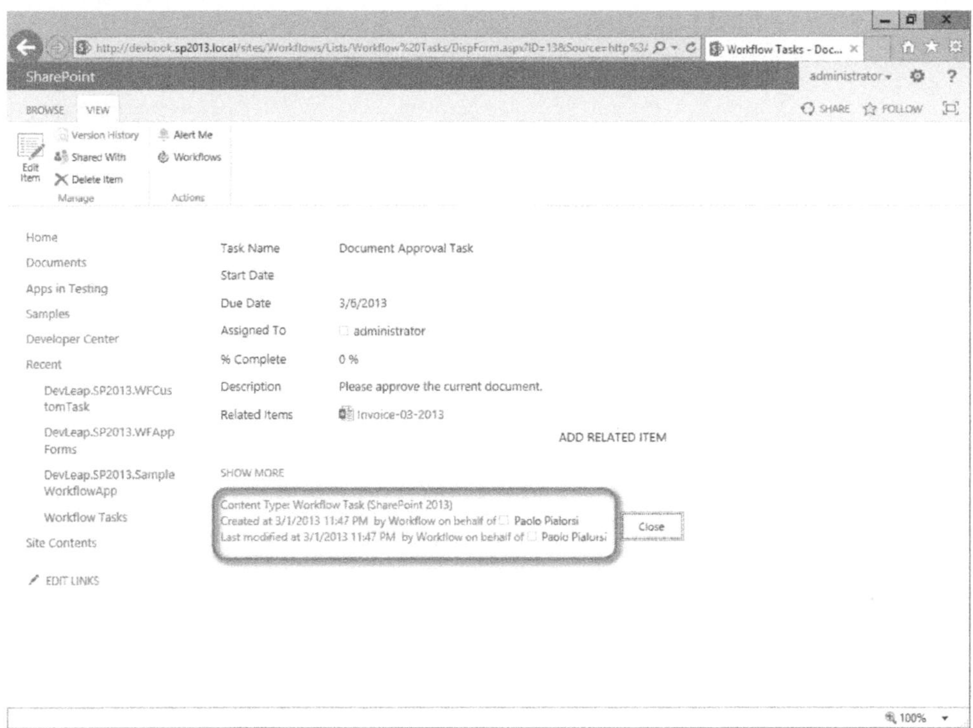

FIGURE 18-6 The display page of a task item created with a custom workflow definition.

As shown in Figure 18-6, the creator is "Workflow on behalf of Paolo Pialorsi" and the modifier is "Workflow on behalf of Paolo Pialorsi." What you have just seen makes clear that the workflow engine has its own identity and acts on behalf of the target users. By default, any workflow instance will act on behalf of the current user, and consequently, any update or item creation will be marked as illustrated in Figure 18-6. From an authorization viewpoint, the item creation or modification will be authorized only if the workflow app permission and the user permission both have the right to do so. If the user or the workflow do not have the permission to perform an operation, then that operation will fail.

Occasionally, you may need to implement a workflow for performing actions that users can't perform. For example, imagine an approval workflow that has to move a document from one library to another, where the target library is not directly accessible by the users of the workflow. In such situations, because of the authorization policy you have just seen, the file-move operation would fail. However, there is an option to execute a step with the identity of the workflow app only, without combining the workflow app identity with the user's identity. The result will be a kind of elevation of permissions, from the workflow app perspective. To achieve this, you can use the App Step capability, which is available in SharePoint Designer 2013. First of all, you need to activate a specific site feature called Workflows Can Use App Permissions from the Site Features page (Figure 18-7).

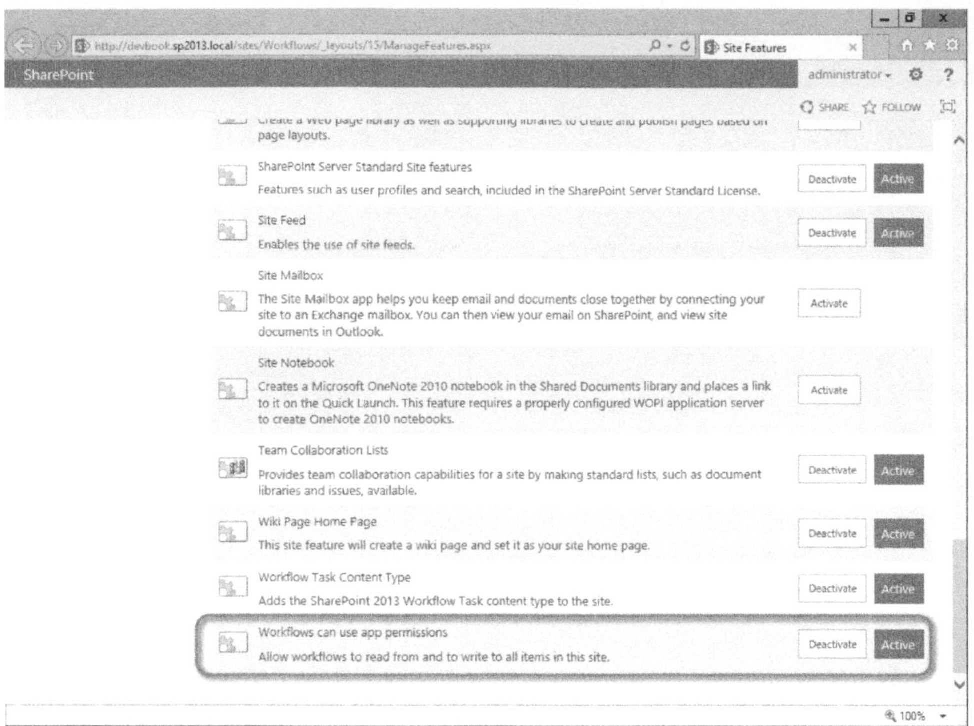

FIGURE 18-7 The Site Features page of a SharePoint 2013 site with the Workflows Can Use App Permissions feature highlighted.

Important If you activate the Workflows Can Use App Permissions feature while editing an existing workflow definition in SharePoint Designer 2013, you will need to close and restart SharePoint Designer 2013 to make it aware of the availability of the App Step capability.

After activating the feature, insert an app step into the target workflow definition by clicking the ribbon button highlighted in Figure 18-8.

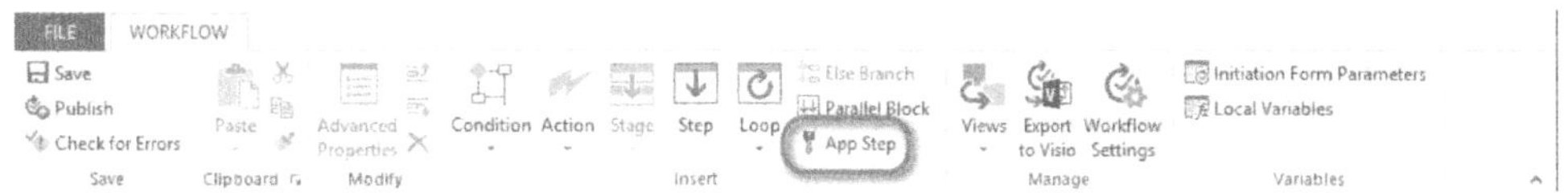

FIGURE 18-8 The App Step ribbon button available in SharePoint Designer 2013.

An app step is just a container of actions and conditions that will be executed under the workflow app identity only. In Figure 18-9, you can see the outline of a sample workflow definition, which creates a list item in a fake target list of contacts by using the standard workflow app principal combined with the user's identity. Then, using an app step, the workflow definition updates the just-created item by using the workflow app principal only.

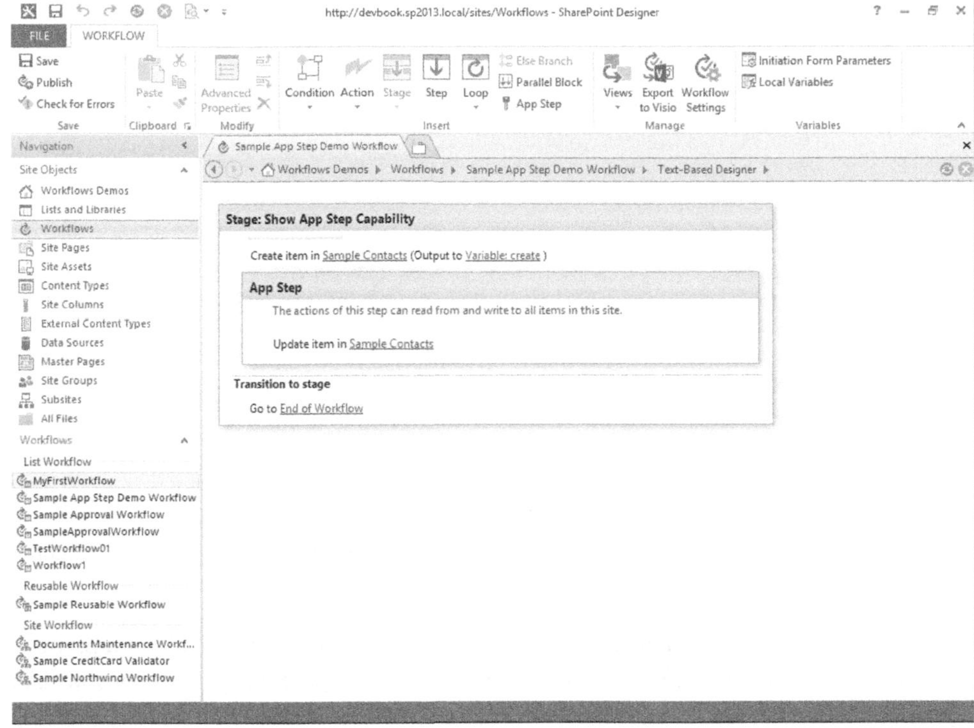

FIGURE 18-9 The outline of a sample workflow definition using an app step in SharePoint Designer 2013.

As you can imagine, showing the properties of the item created and then updated by an instance of this sample workflow definition reveals that the item was created by "Workflow on behalf of Paolo Pialorsi," as it was in the previous examples (see Figure 18-10). The same item was last modified by the workflow principal only, however.

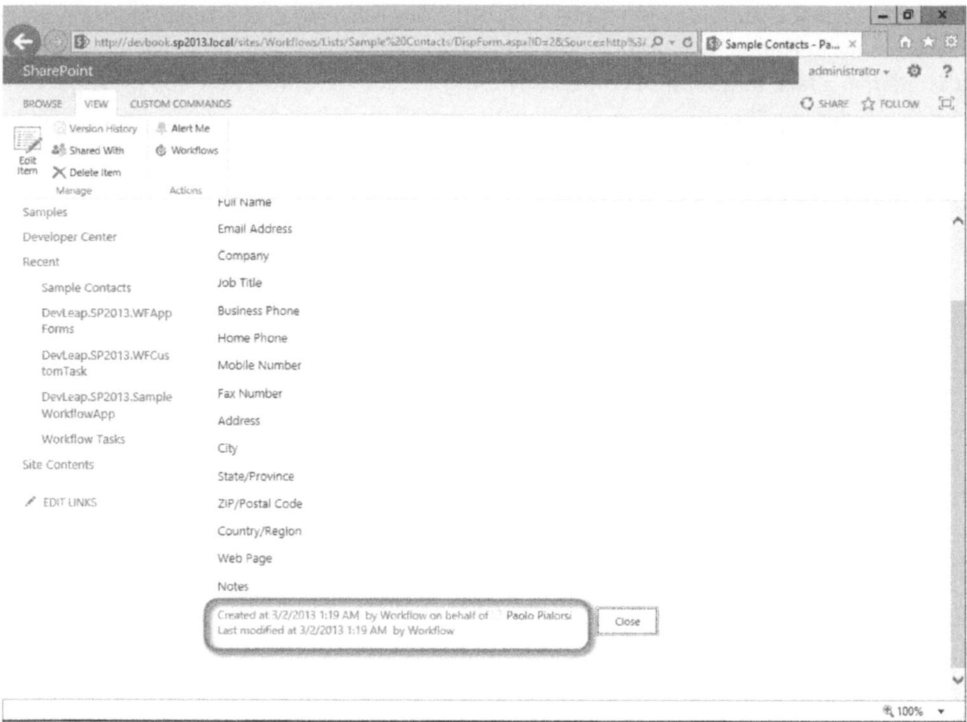

FIGURE 18-10 The security properties of an item created and updated by the sample workflow definition using the app step.

When you design a workflow definition that uses an app step, during the publishing phase, SharePoint Designer 2013 will warn you that you are publishing a potentially dangerous workflow (see Figure 18-11). In fact, the workflow app identity will have permissions to read and write any item in the target site. Thus, the app step provides a way of having a full elevation of privileges, and you should therefore use it carefully.

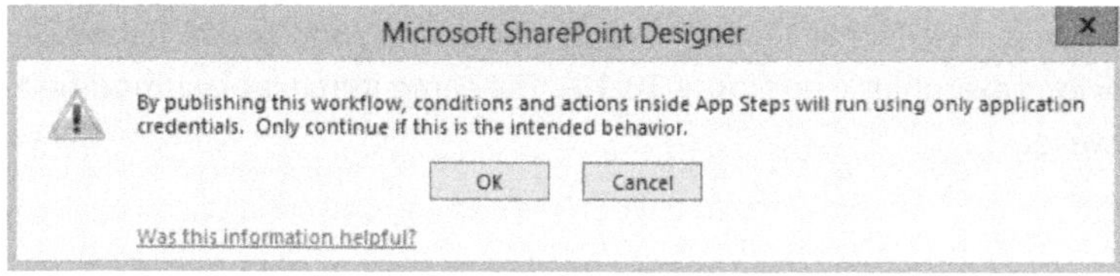

FIGURE 18-11 The warning prompted by SharePoint Designer 2013 while publishing a workflow definition that includes one or more app steps.

While developing workflows with Visual Studio 2012, the counterpart of the app step is the *AppOnlySequence* activity. As discussed in Chapter 17, "Developing workflows," the *AppOnlySequence* activity is a container activity that executes all activities inside of its scope with the identity of the workflow, instead of using the identity of the workflow initiator user.

When you create a workflow definition with Visual Studio 2012 inside a SharePoint app, the identity of that workflow will be the identity of the container app. Thus, any list or item inside the app website will be accessible for reading and writing to the workflow instances, too. Meanwhile, the contents in the host website will be accessible to the workflow definition only if the app has the proper permissions granted.

Starting from SharePoint 2013, you should create workflow definitions that target a site using SharePoint Designer 2013, in order to be able to use the same workflow definition and the new declarative model regardless of whether you are on-premises or on Office 365. When you are creating a custom SharePoint app, however, you should use a workflow definition created with Visual Studio 2012. In this last case, you should create workflow definitions that target the contents of your app website, not workflow definitions that write content of the host web. Because your app could be installed on any host web, you cannot make any assumptions about the data structures available in the host web. Nevertheless, under specific rights grants, you can also create a workflow that reads or writes content in the host web.

Workflow Services Manager

The new architecture of workflows in SharePoint 2013 introduces the Workflow Services Manager component, which (as you learned in Chapter 16, and in particular Figure 16-2) handles all the main tasks and activities related to the new workflow infrastructure. In SharePoint 2013, when you want to talk and interact with the workflow engine, you need to talk and interact with Workflow Services Manager, which will be the proxy to the Workflow Manager engine. Figure 18-12 depicts the main capabilities offered by Workflow Services Manager.

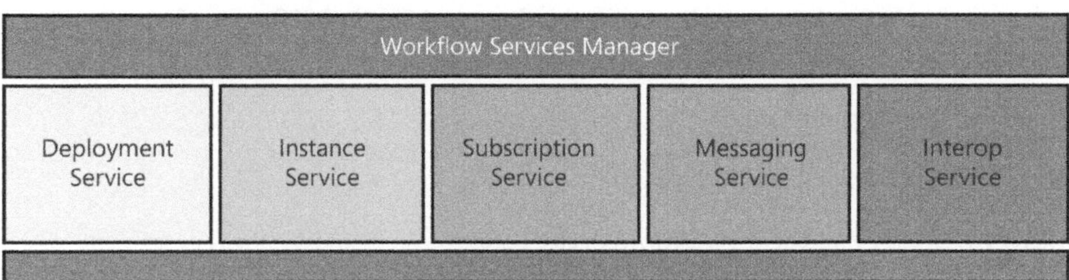

FIGURE 18-12 The main capabilities offered by Workflow Services Manager.

Workflow Services Manager provides a rich set of services and capabilities, which are

- **Deployment service** Enables saving, publishing, and updating properties of workflow definitions. It also offers methods for validating the XAML of workflow definitions.
- **Instance service** Enables managing and interacting with running workflow instances. It allows retrieving the list of running instances, a reference to a specific instance, and sending a direct message to a workflow instance.

- **Subscription service** Manages the associations between workflow definitions, deployed through the Deployment Service, and targets, which can be lists or sites.
- **Messaging service** Handles messaging from SharePoint to workflow instances via the Service Bus infrastructure.
- **Interop service** Allows executing legacy SharePoint 2010 and WF 3.*x* workflows from the new engine. It is fundamental to guarantee backward compatibility with workflows already defined in SharePoint 2010.

The goal of Workflow Services Manager is to provide a rich set of APIs, regardless of whether you are on the server side using the Server Side Object Model or on the client side using the Client-Side Object Model (CSOM), the JavaScript Client Object Model (JSOM), or REST. This rich set of APIs allows managing, deploying, provisioning, and communicating with workflow definitions and instances from any external SharePoint app, mobile device, custom tool, or whatever else.

More Info For more information about the server-side object model for Workflow Services Manager, consult *http://msdn.microsoft.com/en-us/library/microsoft.sharepoint.workflowservices.aspx*. To learn more about taking advantage of Workflow Services Manager from the CSOM, the JSOM, and REST, you should read the following protocol reference: *http://msdn.microsoft.com/en-us/library/hh660550.aspx*.

Using Workflow Services Manager

Let's investigate how to use this new API while working on the client side. To execute the necessary code excerpts, first create a new console application in Visual Studio 2012 and reference at least the following assemblies:

- Microsoft.SharePoint.Client.dll
- Microsoft.SharePoint.Client.Runtime.dll
- Microsoft.SharePoint.Client.WorkflowServices

To practice working with the Workflow Services Manager API, take a look at how to accomplish such common tasks as retrieving the workflow definitions associated with a target list or library, associating a workflow with a target, terminating a workflow, and publishing a custom workflow through XAML.

For example, Listing 18-7 enumerates the workflows associated with a specific target library.

LISTING 18-7 A CSOM code excerpt for retrieving the list of workflow definitions associated with a target library

```
private static void EnumerateWorkflowSubscriptions() {

    ClientContext ctx = new
ClientContext("http://devbook.sp2013.local/sites/Workflows/");
    Web web = ctx.Web;
    ctx.Load(web);
    List documents = web.Lists.GetByTitle("Documents");
    ctx.Load(documents);
    ctx.ExecuteQuery();

    WorkflowServicesManager wfManager = new WorkflowServicesManager(ctx, web);
    WorkflowSubscriptionService subscriptionService =
        wfManager.GetWorkflowSubscriptionService();
    ctx.Load(subscriptionService);
    WorkflowSubscriptionCollection subscriptions =
        subscriptionService.EnumerateSubscriptionsByList(documents.Id);
    ctx.Load(subscriptions);
    ctx.ExecuteQuery();

    foreach (var s in subscriptions) {
        Console.WriteLine("*****************************************");
        Console.WriteLine("Id: {0}", s.Id);
        Console.WriteLine("Name: {0}", s.Name);
        Console.WriteLine("DefinitionId: {0}", s.DefinitionId);
        Console.WriteLine("Enabled: {0}", s.Enabled);
        Console.WriteLine("EventSourceId: {0}", s.EventSourceId);
        Console.WriteLine("EventTypes");
        foreach (var e in s.EventTypes) {
            Console.WriteLine("EventType: {0}", e);
        }
        Console.WriteLine("ManualStartBypassesActivationLimit: {0}",
            s.ManualStartBypassesActivationLimit);
        Console.WriteLine("PropertyDefinitions");
        foreach (var p in s.PropertyDefinitions) {
            Console.WriteLine("Property: {0} - Value: {1}", p.Key, p.Value);
        }
        Console.WriteLine("StatusFieldName: {0}", s.StatusFieldName);
    }
}
```

Highlighted in bold, the code uses the Subscription service to retrieve the list of workflow subscriptions associated with the library with the title "Documents" in the target SharePoint site. Notice that the *WorkflowServicesManager* class must be created to provide the current instance of the *ClientContext*, as well as the target object of type *Web*. Through the *WorkflowServicesManager* class instance, you get access to the current Subscription service instance. In fact, the

WorkflowServicesManager type provides all the useful entry points for using the whole Workflow Services Manager engine. Table 18-5 lists the main members of the *WorkflowServicesManager* type.

TABLE 18-5 The main members of the *WorkflowServicesManager* type

Member name	Description
AppId	Read-only property to retrieve the ID of the currently associated workflow app
IsConnected	Read-only property to determine if the current Workflow Services Manager instance is connected with a back-end Workflow Manager infrastructure
ScopePath	Read-only property to retrieve the path to the current scope in the workflow host
WorkflowServiceAddress	Read-only property to retrieve the URI of the workflow manager host
GetWorkflowDeploymentService	Method to retrieve an instance of the *WorkflowDeploymentService* class
GetWorkflowInstanceService	Method to retrieve an instance of the *WorkflowInstanceService* class
GetWorkflowInteropService	Method to retrieve an instance of the *WorkflowInteropService* class
GetWorkflowMessagingService	Method, available only in the Server Object Model, to retrieve an instance of the *WorkflowMessagingService* class
GetWorkflowSubscriptionService	Method to retrieve an instance of the *WorkflowSubscriptionService* class

Each service type provides a rich set of methods and properties to manage deployment, instances, interoperability, subscriptions, and messaging.

For example in Listing 18-7, the code excerpt retrieves an instance of the *WorkflowSubscriptionService* class, in order to get the currently defined subscriptions for a target library, using the *EnumerateSubscriptionsByList* method. Each subscription is represented by an instance of the *WorkflowSubscription* type, which can be used not only for reading a subscription, but also for associating a new subscription to a target. Later in this section, you will learn more about creating workflow associations. In Table 18-6, you can see the main members of the *WorkflowSubscription* type.

TABLE 18-6 The main members of the *WorkflowSubscription* type

Member name	Description
DefinitionId	Property to get or set the ID (GUID) of the associated workflow definition.
Enabled	Property to define whether the current workflow subscription is active or not.
EventSourceId	Property to get or set the logical source instance name of the event. Usually corresponds to the GUID of the target list or site.
EventTypes	Property to get or set the list of events in target for the current subscription. The available values are *WorkflowStarting*, *ItemAdded*, and *ItemUpdated*.
ManualStartBypassesActivationLimit	Property to define whether multiple workflow instances can be started manually on the same list item at the same time. This property can be used for list workflows only.
Name	Property to get or set the descriptive name of the subscription.
PropertyDefinitions	Property to get a reference to a *Dictionary<String, String>* variable of key/value pairs of properties that represent the configuration of the subscription.

Member name	Description
StatusColumnCreated	Property of type *Boolean* to define whether the workflow association will have to create a custom workflow status column in the target list or library. It is available only on the Server Object Model.
StatusFieldName	Property to get or set the name (*String*) of the field representing the workflow status.
GetProperty	Method to read a property from the configuration properties of the subscription. It is available only on the Server Object Model.
SetProperty	Method to write a property to the configuration properties of the subscription.

Through an instance of the *WorkflowSubscriptionService* class and with objects of type *WorkflowSubscription*, you can do many things. For example, the code excerpt of a workflow association page in Listing 18-8 takes advantage of the JSOM implementation of Workflow Services Manager to associate a workflow definition with a target.

LISTING 18-8 A code excerpt taken from a workflow association page based on the JSOM

```
function associateWorkflow() {
    ctx = SP.ClientContext.get_current();
    wfManager = SP.WorkflowServices.WorkflowServicesManager.newObject(ctx,
ctx.get_web());
    var depService = wfManager.getWorkflowDeploymentService();
    subscriptionService = wfManager.getWorkflowSubscriptionService();
    ctx.load(subscriptionService);

    definitionId = $('input[name=WorkflowDefinition]').val();
    definitionName = $('input[name=WorkflowName]').val();
    taskListId = $('input[name=TaskListWF4').val();
    historyListId = $('input[name=HistoryList').val();
    allowManual = $('input[name=AllowManual').val();
    autoStartCreate = $('input[name=AutoStartCreate').val();
    autoStartChange = $('input[name=AutoStartChange').val();

    associatedListId = getUrlParams()["AssociatedList"];
    subscription = SP.WorkflowServices.WorkflowSubscription.newObject(ctx);
    subscription.set_definitionId(definitionId);
    subscription.set_name(definitionName);
    subscription.set_enabled(true);
    subscription.set_eventSourceId(associatedListId);
```

```
    // Define event types
    eventTypes = new Array();
    eventTypesIndex = 0;
    if (allowManual == "ON") {
        eventTypes[eventTypesIndex] = "WorkflowStart";
        eventTypesIndex = eventTypesIndex + 1;
    }
    if (autoStartCreate == "ON") {
        eventTypes[eventTypesIndex] = "ItemAdded";
        eventTypesIndex = eventTypesIndex + 1;
    }
    if (autoStartChange == "ON") {
        eventTypes[eventTypesIndex] = "ItemUpdated";
        eventTypesIndex = eventTypesIndex + 1;
    }
    subscription.set_eventTypes(eventTypes);

    // Configure Status Field Name
    subscription.set_statusFieldName("OrdersWorkflowStatus");
    subscription.setProperty("StatusColumnCreated", "1");

    // Configure properties
    subscription.setProperty("ApprovalTaskDueDays",
    $("#ApprovalTaskDueDays").val());
    subscription.setProperty("ApprovalRequestMessage",
        $("#ApprovalRequestMessage").val());
    subscription.setProperty("TargetApprover",  getUserKeys("peoplePicker"));

    // Workflow Tasks List
    subscription.setProperty("TaskListId", taskListId);

    // Workflow History List
    subscription.setProperty("HistoryListId", historyListId);

    // Publish the WorkflowSubscription
    subscriptionService.publishSubscriptionForList(subscription,
    associatedListId);

    ctx.executeQueryAsync(
        function (sender, args) {
            redirFromInitForm();
        },
        function (sender, args) {
            alert("Something went wrong while associating workflow: " +
                args.get_message());
            redirFromInitForm();
        }
    );
}
```

To create a new instance of the *WorkflowSubscription* type, Listing 18-8 configures all the main properties (highlighted in bold) described in Table 18-6. The most important part of the code excerpt is the invocation of the *publishSubscriptionForList* method, which accepts the subscription and the ID of the associated list or library. As you might guess from the name of the method, it is suitable only for publishing subscriptions for lists or libraries. If you want to publish a subscription for a site workflow, use the *publishSubscription* method instead.

Another interesting use case is the starting of a new workflow instance. First, to create a new instance of a workflow definition, use the *GetWorkflowInstanceService* method of the *WorkflowServicesManager* class to reference an object of type *WorkflowInstanceService*. Next, as you learned in Chapter 17, you can use the *StartWorkflow* or the *StartWorkflowOnListItem* methods. The *WorkflowInstanceService* class provides many other helpful members, as well. Table 18-7 lists the most commonly used methods.

TABLE 18-7 The main members of the *WorkflowInstanceService* type

Member name	Description
CancelWorkflow	Sends a cancel message to a specified workflow instance, permitting the instance to execute a cancellation scope.
CountInstances	Retrieves the count of all the instances of a specified subscription.
CountInstancesWithStatus	Retrieves the count of all the instances of a specified subscription that have a specific internal status. The internal status can assume any of the following values: *NotStarted*, *Started*, *Suspended*, *Canceling*, *Canceled*, *Terminated*, *Completed*, *NotSpecified*, and *Invalid*.
EnumerateInstancesForListItem	Retrieves the instances running on a specific list item; allows multiple overloads.
EnumerateInstancesForSite	Retrieves the instances running on a specific site.
GetDebugInfo	Retrieves debug information, in JSON format, about a workflow instance.
GetInstance	Retrieves a workflow instance by ID; allows multiple overloads.
ResumeWorkflow	Resumes a workflow instance that is suspended.
StartWorkflow	Starts a site workflow.
StartWorkflowOnListItem	Starts a list workflow.
SuspendWorkflow	Suspends a workflow instance that is executing.
TerminateWorkflow	Terminates a workflow instance forcefully by deleting it from memory. The instance is not allowed to execute a cancellation scope.

For example, Listing 18-9 contains a code excerpt of a function that forcibly terminates all the workflow instances running on the items of a target library.

LISTING 18-9 A CSOM code excerpt of a function that forcibly terminates all the workflow instances running on the items of a list

```
private static void TerminateAllWorkflowInstances() {
    ClientContext ctx = new ClientContext(
    "http://devbook.sp2013.local/sites/Workflows/");
    Web web = ctx.Web;
    ctx.Load(web);
    List documents = web.Lists.GetByTitle("Documents");
    ctx.Load(documents);
    ctx.ExecuteQuery();

    WorkflowServicesManager wfManager = new WorkflowServicesManager(ctx, web);
    WorkflowInstanceService instanceService = wfManager.
    GetWorkflowInstanceService();

    ListItemCollection items = documents.GetItems(
    CamlQuery.CreateAllItemsQuery());
    ctx.Load(items);
    ctx.ExecuteQuery();

    foreach (ListItem item in items) {
        WorkflowInstanceCollection instances =
            instanceService.EnumerateInstancesForListItem(documents.Id, item.Id);
        ctx.Load(instances);
        ctx.ExecuteQuery();

        foreach (var instance in instances) {
            if (instance.Status == WorkflowStatus.Started ||
                instance.Status == WorkflowStatus.Suspended)
                instanceService.TerminateWorkflow(instance);
        }
        ctx.ExecuteQuery();
    }
}
```

The *WorkflowDeploymentService* class is also interesting. Through this service, you can deploy and manage the workflow definitions. Table 18-8 lists its main methods.

TABLE 18-8 The main members of the *WorkflowDeploymentService* type

Member name	Description
DeleteDefinition	Deletes a workflow definition.
DeprecateDefinition	Marks a workflow definition as deprecated. Currently running workflow instances are allowed to complete, but new instances of the workflow definition are prevented from starting. This method is useful for performing workflow versioning.
EnumerateDefinitions	Retrieves workflow definitions from the workflow store.
GetDefinition	Retrieves a specific workflow definition from the workflow store.
GetDesignerActions	Retrieves the list of valid Workflow Manager Client 1.0 actions for the specified server.
PackageDefinition	Packages a workflow definition into a WSP file that will be saved in the Site Assets library of the current site.
PublishDefinition	Publishes a workflow definition to the workflow store.
SaveDefinition	Saves a workflow definition to the workflow store.
ValidateActivity	Validates a workflow activity against workflow definitions stored in the target workflow store.

Listing 18-10 shows a code excerpt of a sample procedure for publishing the XAML of a workflow definition to the workflow store.

LISTING 18-10 A CSOM code excerpt of a function that published the XAML of a workflow definition to the workflow store

```
private static void PublishXamlWorkflowToWorkflowStore(String xaml) {

    ClientContext ctx = new
    ClientContext("http://devbook.sp2013.local/sites/Workflows/");
    Web web = ctx.Web;
    ctx.Load(web);
    List documents = web.Lists.GetByTitle("Documents");
    ctx.Load(documents);
    ctx.ExecuteQuery();

    WorkflowServicesManager wfManager = new WorkflowServicesManager(ctx, web);
    WorkflowDeploymentService deploymentService =
        wfManager.GetWorkflowDeploymentService();

    var validationResult = deploymentService.ValidateActivity(xaml);
    ctx.ExecuteQuery();

    WorkflowDefinition definition = new WorkflowDefinition(ctx);
    definition.Xaml = xaml;
    definition.DisplayName = "Sample XAML based Workflow";
    definition.Description = "Workflow saved by code";
    deploymentService.SaveDefinition(definition);
    ctx.ExecuteQuery();
}
```

Listing 18-10 validates the XAML code, which is provided as an argument of type *String* to the sample *PublishXamlWorkflowToWorkflowStore* method, and then saves the workflow definition to the workflow store. After executing that code and providing a valid XAML workflow definition, you will find a new workflow definition available in SharePoint Designer 2013 for adding in the target SharePoint site.

The *WorkflowInteropService* class simply provides methods to start or cancel a legacy SharePoint 2010 and WF 3.*x* workflow instance. In particular, the *StartWorkflow* method accepts all the arguments useful to start a new workflow instance—which are the association name, the correlation ID, the target list ID, and the target item GUID—as well as any additional arguments or parameters for running the workflow. Meanwhile, the *CancelWorkflow* method accepts the GUID of the workflow instance to cancel. Lastly, the *WorkflowMessagingService* class, which is available only on the Server Object Model, provides the *PublishEvent* method, which allows publishing a message to the Service Bus, providing the GUID of the event source, the name of the event, and a collection of key/value pairs for providing a payload to the target subscribers of the event. Typically, the event source GUID should be the ID of the list, or of the site depending on the kind of workflow you are running, and the name of the event is the fully qualified name of the event.

Summary

In this chapter, you learned how to create custom activities, either declaratively or by writing code. You learned how to deploy both declarative and code-based activities, and you experimented with both of them. Then you saw how the new security infrastructure of workflows in SharePoint 2013 works, and how the authorization rules are applied. In particular, you saw how to use app steps, which are available in SharePoint Designer 2013, and the *AppOnlySequence* activity, which is available in Visual Studio 2012. Lastly, you learned about Workflow Services Manager by walking through some useful code excerpts for taking advantage of this powerful component from client code using the CSOM or the JSOM.

PART VI

Security infrastructure

CHAPTER 19

Authentication and authorization infrastructure

No real solution today can ignore the topics of authentication and authorization. Microsoft SharePoint 2013 takes security seriously and provides a modern and powerful set of tools, as well as a solid architecture, for supporting claims-based authentication and authorization. The native support for claims opens SharePoint 2013 to integration with third-party platforms as well as single-sign-on scenarios.

In this first chapter of Part VI, "Security infrastructure," you will dig into the main topics about authentication and authorization in SharePoint 2013. In particular, you will learn about claims-based authentication, as well as the old classic authentication mode, which is still available for the sake of backward compatibility. You will also learn how SharePoint authorizes users after having authenticated them. In the next chapter, you will focus on identity federation and OAuth.

Authentication infrastructure

Within its two authentication modes—classic and claims based—SharePoint 2013 supports three authentication methods:

- **Windows Authentication** Uses the Windows infrastructure, providing support for NTLM, Kerberos, Anonymous, Basic, and Digest authentication. X.509 Certificate Authentication is not supported, unless you manually configure users' certificate mapping rules within Internet Information Services (IIS). It works both in classic mode and claims-based mode.
- **Forms-Based Authentication (FBA)** Utilizes a username-and-password HTML form that queries a membership provider on the back end. By default, it includes providers for LDAP and SQL Server; however, you can develop custom providers of your own. FBA is based on the standard forms authentication provided by Microsoft ASP.NET, which resides at the very core of SharePoint. It works only in claims-based mode.
- **SAML Token-Based Authentication** Uses an external identity provider that supports SAML 1.1 and WS-Federation Passive profile. SAML token-based Authentication includes Microsoft Active Directory Federation Services (AD FS) version 2.0, LDAP, or custom third-party identity providers. It works only in claims-based mode.

You can configure each method against a web application or a zone using SharePoint Central Administration (SPCA), as shown in Figure 19-1. To reach the Create New Web Application page, simply open SPCA, click Application Management, and then click Manage Web Applications. There you will find a ribbon button for creating a new web application.

Note A SharePoint *zone* provides the ability to publish the same web application with multiple endpoints (URLs). Available since SharePoint 2007, the goal of this feature is to give you a method to share a common application configuration and common content databases between multiple IIS sites, which can each have specific configurations of authentication, authorization, security in general, and web.config files.

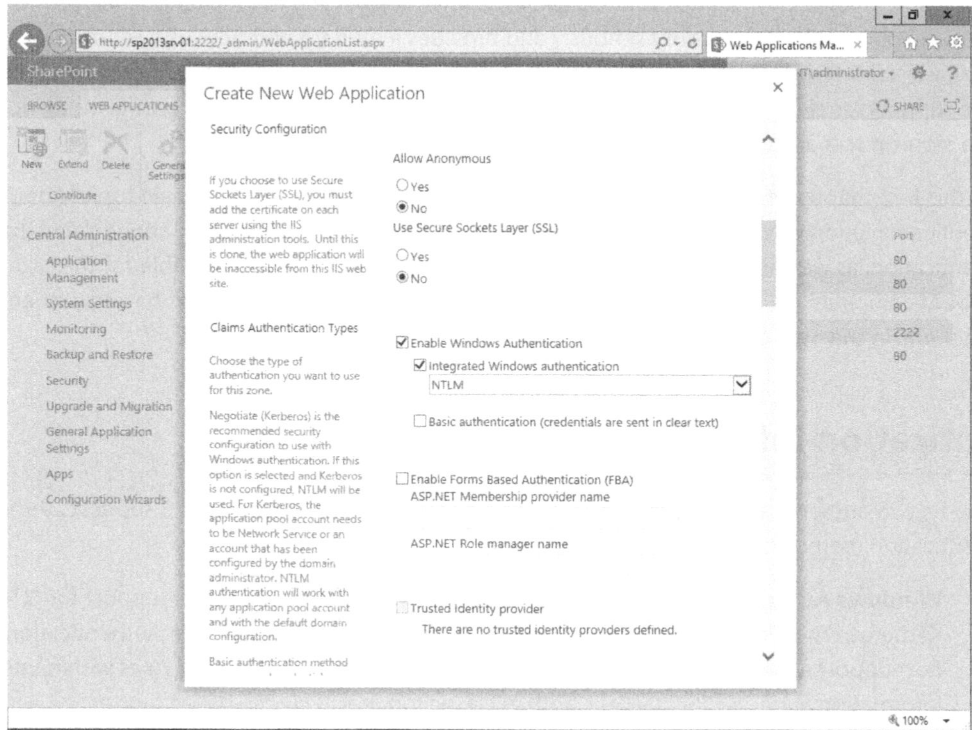

FIGURE 19-1 The UI provided by SPCA for configuring the authentication methods.

Starting with SharePoint 2013, the SPCA UI provides the settings for configuring claims-based authentication only. If you need to use classic authentication mode for backward compatibility, such as when running sites migrated from SharePoint 2010, then you must use PowerShell. This is only a temporary solution, however, because classic mode is deprecated and will be removed in future releases. Thus, when migrating an existing SharePoint solution to SharePoint 2013, you should carefully consider the task of migrating to claims-based authentication, too, if the source web application is not already claims based.

Note Remember that classic mode supports only Windows Authentication (that is, NTLM or Kerberos), while claims-based mode supports all the three available authentication methods.

In the following section, you will learn the main features of claims-based authentication.

Claims-based authentication

The claims-based authentication mode was introduced with SharePoint 2010. It employs the concept of *claims identity*, representing each user's identity as tokens made of claims. A claim is a statement, asserted by an issuer, about a subject, which is assumed to be true by the reader, due to a trust relationship between the reader and the issuer. The statement can be about any kind of information. For example, it could be the name, the identity, a role membership, a user preference, or anything else. Claims are issued by a claim provider and packaged into a *security token*, which is emitted by a security token service, which can also be an identity provider or can use an external identity provider. The *identity provider* is a service that authenticates the end users, based on a specific set of credentials. For example, an identity provider could be Microsoft Windows Live, Facebook, your Active Directory infrastructure with AD FS on top of it, and so on. The target of the security token is a *service provider*, which can be a website, a web service, or whatever else. The entity described by the security token is called *Subject*; in general, this is a user, a server, a service, or anything else that can have an identity of its own.

The power of claims-based authentication arises from the fact that claims-based identities are cross platform and can lead your solutions to provide single-sign-on capabilities on multiple platforms using a standard, secure, and reliable protocol. You can use claims to federate your company with customers, resellers, external service providers, and other third parties. Using claims-based authentication and external security token services and identity providers allows you to federate and trust external systems without duplicating users' credentials and passwords. Only the identity providers will manage credentials and passwords, while all the various service providers will trust the intermediary identity providers and the security tokens emitted by the security token services.

Each claim consists of a *ClaimType property*, which in general is a URI that uniquely defines the type of the claim; a *ClaimValue property*, which is the real content of the claim; and a *ClaimValueType property*, which defines the data type of the *ClaimValue property*. Each claim can also be described by some other information, such as the *Issuer* and the target *Subject properties*.

The capability to describe an identity as a set of claims (a set of true and trustable information) allows supporting any kind of authentication mechanism. In fact, with the claims-based mode, you can use Windows Authentication, but you can also use FBA or any third-party trusted identity provider.

If you use Windows Authentication in claims-based authentication mode, the Windows identities will be converted to a set of claims representing the current user. You can still take advantage of integrated authentication, because the Windows identity of the current user will be translated into claims at no cost to you. In addition, a Windows user authenticated using classic mode is almost the same as a user authenticated with claims-based mode, because internally in SharePoint the user identity is the same (an instance of type *SPUser*). On the back end, SharePoint 2013 always uses claims identities—regardless of the mode you selected on the front end—to communicate between the front-end servers and the servers (within the same farm) hosting service applications.

In your code, the current user's identity and principal will be instances of type *ClaimsIdentity* and *ClaimsPrincipal*, available in the assembly *Microsoft.IdentityModel* released with Windows Identity Foundation (WIF) 1.0.

Important Be careful: Microsoft .NET Framework 4.5 defines two new types for *ClaimsIdentity* and *ClaimsPrincipal* in the *System.Security.Claims* namespace in mscorlib.dll, and these are broadly available in all the .NET Framework 4.5. However, SharePoint 2013 uses the WIF 1.0 library, with the addition of an extension library (Microsoft.IdentityModel.Extensions.dll) for supporting OAuth and server-to-server authentication. Thus, the *ClaimsIdentity* and *ClaimsPrincipal* types used by SharePoint 2013 are those available in the old version of WIF, not the new one introduced in .NET 4.5. Chapter 20, "Claims-based authentication, federated identities, and OAuth," will cover this topic in depth.

Migrating from classic to claims-based mode

When you are migrating a SharePoint 2010 web application that uses classic-mode authentication to claims-based mode in SharePoint 2013, you can use the PowerShell cmdlet *Convert-SPWebApplication*. The syntax is as follows:

```
Convert-SPWebApplication -Identity <SPWebApplicationPipeBind>
    -To <String>
    [-Force <SwitchParameter>]
    [-RetainPermissions <SwitchParameter>]
```

where the *Identity* argument identifies the web application to convert. The *To* argument declares the target authentication mode, which by now can only assume the literal value of *Claims*. There is also an optional *Force* argument that is useful to keep permissions (*RetainPermissions*) while migrating. For example, if you want to migrate the web application published at the URL *http://migrated.intranet.local/* to claims-based authentication, you can use the following syntax:

```
Convert-SPWebApplication -Identity http://migrated.intranet.local
    -To Claims -RetainPermissions -Force
```

The command converts the web application's authentication mode to Windows Claims authentication mode, which is the most similar to Windows Classic, and migrates the user accounts in the content database to claims-encoded values, keeping their assigned permissions. To execute the migration, you must be a member of the *securityadmin* role of the target SQL Server database server, a member of the *db_owner* role of all the content databases that need to be upgraded, and a member of the Administrators group of the server on which you are running the PowerShell script.

Important After you convert a web application to claims-based authentication, you cannot revert it back to classic-mode authentication. Thus, you should plan the migration carefully and eventually test it in a testing environment before applying it in production.

After migration, check in the ULS (Unified Logging System) log for any user accounts that are no longer in the Active Directory database (defined in the converted content databases), because they will not be migrated.

If you want to convert only a subset of users to claims-based authentication, such as only those who use a specific content database, PowerShell can help. Specifically, use the *MigrateUsersToClaims* method provided by the *SPWebApplication* class. You can find further details about this method at *http://msdn.microsoft.com/en-us/library/jj171669.aspx.*

Claims-based authentication types

With claims-based mode, you can enable multiple authentication methods within the same zone. Thus, you can now have a unique zone—and a unique URL—to access your site, but your users will be able to choose between multiple authentication methods with which to provide their credentials.

When you configure claims-based mode with a unique authentication method, SharePoint will authenticate the end users directly with that unique method. However, if you configure multiple authentication methods, your users will be prompted to select their desired authentication method. Figure 19-2 depicts the authentication method selection page, configured to support both Windows Authentication and FBA.

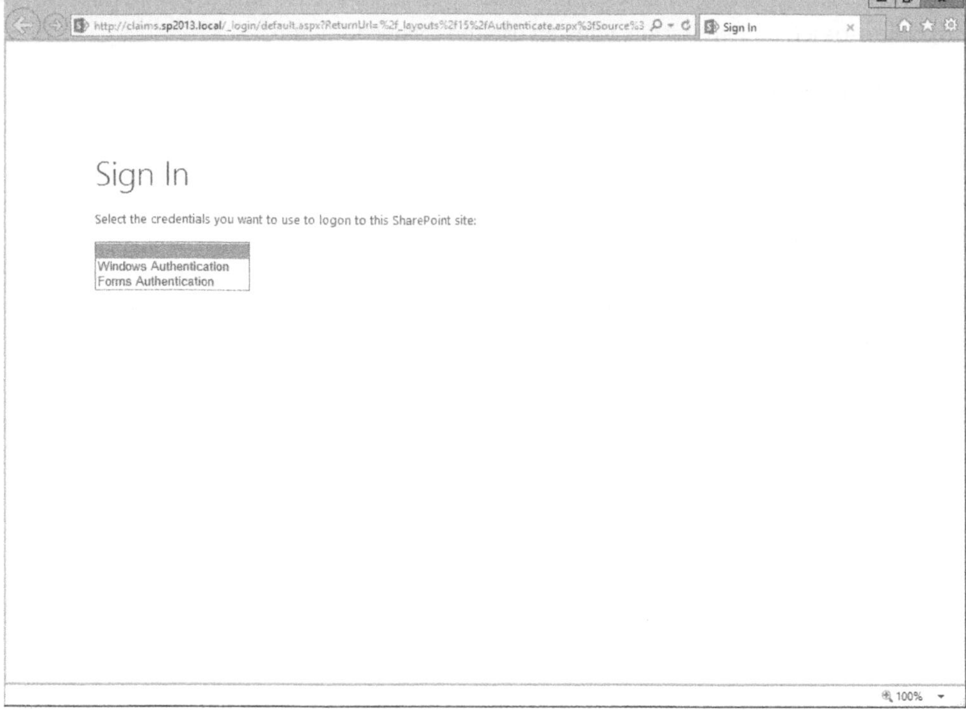

FIGURE 19-2 The Sign In page, on which end users select the authentication method when multiple authentication methods are configured on the same zone.

Behind the scenes, the authentication engine of SharePoint normalizes all the users' identities into *SPUser* instances, converting every identity into a set of claims. The users' identity normalization process involves invoking a native service application of SharePoint, called the Security Token Service (STS). Figure 19-3 shows a functional schema of the identity normalization process managed by SharePoint 2013. This section will cover Windows Authentication and FBA, while SAML-based authentication will be covered in the next chapter.

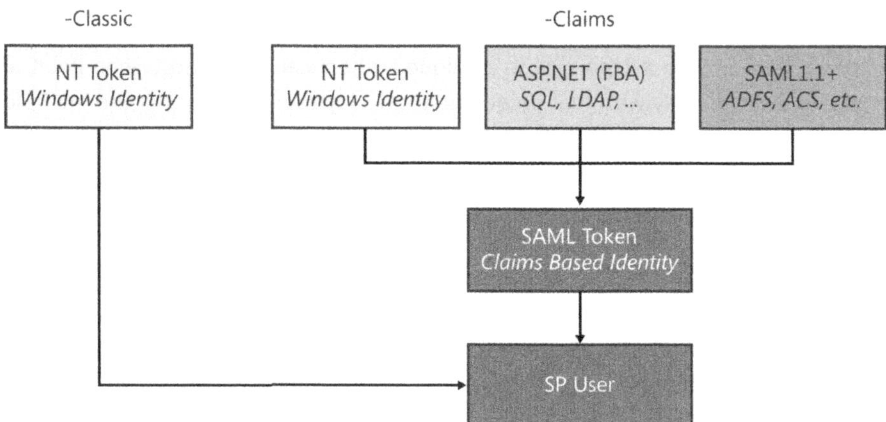

FIGURE 19-3 A functional schema of the identity normalization process managed by SharePoint 2013.

Windows authentication

In terms of capabilities, Windows Authentication is almost the same as the old-style classic mode. Backstage, however, the user's identity is translated into a set of claims. If you develop a custom control or Web Part for writing a user's identity, you will see that the current user's identity is a *ClaimsIdentity*. The set of claims that comprise the user's identity by default are

- ***http://schemas.xmlsoap.org/ws/2005/05/identity/claims/nameidentifier*** A claim with a value of type *String* that defines the user name.
- ***http://schemas.microsoft.com/ws/2008/06/identity/claims/primarysid*** A claim with a value of type *String* that defines the security identifier (SID) of the user.
- ***http://schemas.microsoft.com/ws/2008/06/identity/claims/primarygroupsid*** A claim with a value of type *String* that defines the SID of the primary group of the users.
- ***http://schemas.xmlsoap.org/ws/2005/05/identity/claims/upn*** A claim with a value of type *String* that defines the user principal name (UPN) of the user.
- ***http://schemas.microsoft.com/sharepoint/2009/08/claims/userlogonname*** A claim with a value of type *String* that defines the logon name of the user.
- ***http://schemas.microsoft.com/sharepoint/2009/08/claims/userid*** A claim with a value of type *String* that defines the user ID of the current user. For Windows Authentication, it assumes a value of *0#.w|{Username}*, where the string *0#.w|* is a trailer and *{Username}* is the user name of the user. The *w* stands for Windows Authentication.
- ***http://schemas.xmlsoap.org/ws/2005/05/identity/claims/name*** A claim with a value of type *String* that defines the name of the user, assuming a syntax like that of the previously described claim (*userid*).
- ***http://schemas.microsoft.com/sharepoint/2009/08/claims/identityprovider*** A claim with a value of type *String* that defines the name of the identity provider. For Windows Authentication, it assumes a value of *windows*. This is a SharePoint-specific claim.
- ***http://schemas.microsoft.com/office/2012/01/nameidissuer*** A claim with a value of type *String* describing the issuer of the *nameid* claim (see the *nameid* entry later in this list). This is a Microsoft Office–specific claim.
- ***http://sharepoint.microsoft.com/claims/2009/08/isauthenticated*** A claim with a value of type *String* and an inner value of *True* or *False*, used to indicate whether the current user is authenticated. This is a SharePoint-specific claim.
- ***http://schemas.microsoft.com/sharepoint/2009/08/claims/farmid*** A claim with a value of type *String* that defines the ID of the current SharePoint farm. This is a SharePoint-specific claim.
- ***http://schemas.microsoft.com/office/2012/01/upn*** A claim with a value of type *String* that describes the UPN of the current user. This is an Office-specific claim.

- ***http://schemas.microsoft.com/office/2012/01/nameid*** A claim with a value of type *String* that describes the unique name identifier of the current user. This is an Office-specific claim.
- ***http://sharepoint.microsoft.com/claims/2009/08/tokenreference*** A claim with a value of type *String* that defines a reference to the user token. This is a SharePoint-specific claim.
- ***http://sharepoint.microsoft.com/claims/2012/02/claimprovidercontext*** A claim with a value of type *String* that defines the context of the current user token. This is a SharePoint-specific claim usually corresponding to the URL of the context.
- ***http://schemas.microsoft.com/ws/2008/06/identity/claims/groupsid*** A claim with a value of type *String* that defines the SID of a group to which the current user belongs. A single *ClaimsIdentity* could contain many claims of this type, depending on the number of groups to which the current user belongs.
- ***http://schemas.microsoft.com/ws/2008/06/identity/claims/authenticationmethod*** A claim with a value of type *String* that defines the configured authentication method. When using Windows Authentication, it assumes a value of *http://schemas.microsoft.com/ws/2008/06/identity/authenticationmethod/windows.*
- ***http://schemas.microsoft.com/ws/2008/06/identity/claims/authenticationinstant*** A claim with a value of type *DateTime* that defines the date and time the token was issued.

To extract the value of the claims, you can use code such as in Listing 19-1.

LISTING 19-1 Extracting claims from a current user's identity

```
ClaimsIdentity ci = this.Page.User.Identity as ClaimsIdentity;
if (ci != null) {
    this.Controls.Add(new LiteralControl("<h2>Claims</h2>"));
    foreach (Claim c in ci.Claims) {
        this.Controls.Add(new LiteralControl(
            String.Format(
             "<div>ClaimType: {0} - ClaimValue: {1} - ClaimValueType: {2}</div>",
              c.ClaimType, c.Value, c.ValueType)));
    }
}
```

In this example, it suffices to cast the current user's identity (*this.Page.User.Identity*) to the *ClaimsIdentity* type of the *Microsoft.IdentityModel* namespace. Assuming the cast is successful, you will be able to enumerate the *Claims* property and extract each individual *Claim* instance.

Forms-Based Authentication

When you configure FBA, you gain the capability to authenticate your users against an external repository of users. By default, this can be an LDAP or Microsoft SQL Server database built using the standard SQL Membership Provider of ASP.NET. Of course, you can also develop custom membership providers of your own, querying any kind of users' repository. In the next section, you will learn how to configure SharePoint 2013 to support FBA with the standard SQL Membership Provider. For now, consider the default set of claims that make up the user's identity when using FBA:

- ***http://schemas.xmlsoap.org/ws/2005/05/identity/claims/nameidentifier*** The same as in Windows Authentication.
- ***http://schemas.microsoft.com/ws/2008/06/identity/claims/role*** A claim with a value of type *String* that defines the name of a role to which the current user belongs. There could be many claims of this type in a single *ClaimsIdentity*, depending on the number of roles to which the current user belongs.
- ***http://schemas.microsoft.com/sharepoint/2009/08/claims/userlogonname*** The same as in Windows Authentication.
- ***http://schemas.microsoft.com/sharepoint/2009/08/claims/userid*** A claim with a value of type *String* that defines the user ID of the current user. For FBA, it assumes a value of *0#.f|{MembershipProvider}|{Username}*, where the string *0#.f|* is a trailer, *{MembershipProvider}* is the name of the configured membership provider, and *{Username}* is the user name of the user. The *f* stands for FBA.

More Info For further details about login name encoding, please read the following Wiki page on TechNet: *http://social.technet.microsoft.com/wiki/contents/articles/13921.sharepoint-2013-and-sharepoint-2010-claims-encoding.aspx.*

- ***http://schemas.xmlsoap.org/ws/2005/05/identity/claims/name*** A claim with a value of type *String* that defines the name of the user, assuming a syntax like that of the previously described claim (*userid*).
- ***http://schemas.microsoft.com/sharepoint/2009/08/claims/identityprovider*** A claim with a value of type *String* that defines the name of the identity provider. For FBA, it assumes a value of *forms:{MembershipProvider}*, where *{MembershipProvider}* is the name of the configured membership provider. This is a SharePoint-specific claim.
- ***http://sharepoint.microsoft.com/claims/2009/08/isauthenticated*** A claim with a value of type *String* and an inner value of *True* or *False*, used to indicate whether the current user is authenticated. This is a SharePoint-specific claim.

- ***http://schemas.microsoft.com/sharepoint/2009/08/claims/farmid*** A claim with a value of type *String* that defines the ID of the current SharePoint farm. This is a SharePoint-specific claim.
- ***http://schemas.microsoft.com/office/2012/01/upn*** A claim with a value of type *String* that describes the UPN of the current user. This is an Office-specific claim.
- ***http://schemas.microsoft.com/office/2012/01/nameid*** A claim with a value of type *String* that describes the unique name identifier of the current user. This is an Office-specific claim.
- ***http://sharepoint.microsoft.com/claims/2009/08/tokenreference*** A claim with a value of type *String* that defines a reference to the user token. This is a SharePoint-specific claim.
- ***http://sharepoint.microsoft.com/claims/2012/02/claimprovidercontext*** A claim with a value of type *String* that defines the context of the current user token. This is a SharePoint-specific claim that usually corresponds to the URL of the context.

Configuring FBA with SQL Membership Provider

In this section, you will learn how to configure a SharePoint 2013 web application to support FBA against a SQL Server database. The process involves configuring and creating a SQL Server database, changing the web.config file of the target web application, SPCA, and SharePoint STS, configuring SQL Server permissions, configuring SharePoint, and enabling users and roles in SharePoint.

Configuring the SQL Server database

To configure SharePoint to support FBA with SQL Membership Provider, you first need to create a SQL Server database file that supports your environment. To help you, ASP.NET provides a tool called ASPNET_REGSQL.EXE, which is available in the Microsoft .NET Framework folder. You invoke ASPNET_REGSQL.EXE within the Microsoft Visual Studio command prompt, and it creates a SQL Server database file. The tool is organized as a wizard (see Figure 19-4) with four main pages:

- **Welcome screen** There is nothing more to do here than simply click the Next button.
- **Select A Setup Option** On this page, you select whether to configure a new database or to remove an existing one. Choose the Configure SQL Server For Application Services option.
- **Select The Server And Database** Here, you select the target SQL Server database server where the database file will be created, together with the authentication method that will be used to communicate with the server, and the name of the database file that will be created.
- **Confirm Your Settings** This is simply a summary of your settings.

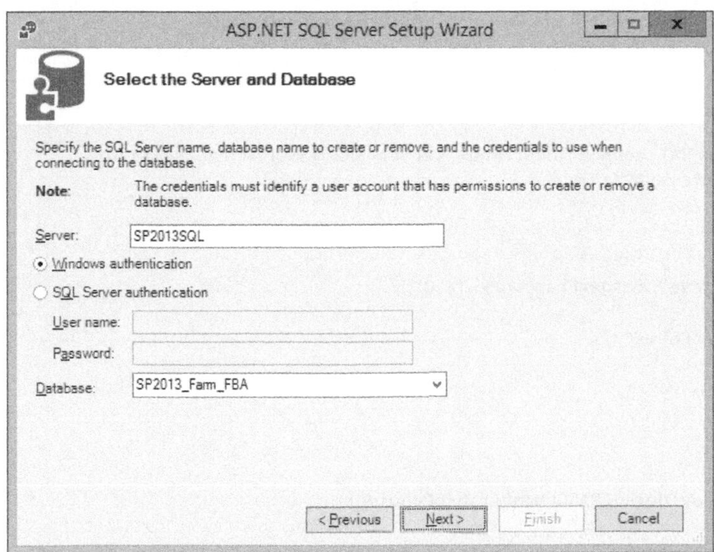

FIGURE 19-4 The Select The Server And Database page of the ASPNET_REGSQL.EXE wizard.

Note To learn more about FBA with a SQL Server database on the back end, consult *http://www.microsoft.com/en-us/download/details.aspx?id=34684.*

After you create the database, you need to configure some users and groups to use in SharePoint. For this purpose—and for the sake of simplicity—you can create a new ASP.NET Empty Website project in Visual Studio.

Important Remember that SharePoint 2013 is based on.NET Framework 4.5. Therefore, your website should be created using the same target version of .NET Framework to avoid issues with varying assembly versions.

You can configure the website by going to Project | ASP.NET Configuration, which brings up the ASP.NET Web Site Administration Tool. This is a well-known tool with which every ASP.NET developer should be familiar. From there, you can use the Security Setup Wizard to configure your site for supporting FBA using the previously created SQL database. You can also manually configure the web.config file, if you like. After completing this task, the web.config file of the sample site will look like the XML excerpt illustrated in Listing 19-2.

More Info If you are not familiar with the Web Site Administration Tool site, see the document "Web Site Administration Tool Overview," which is available on MSDN at *http://msdn.microsoft.com/en-us/library/yy40ytx0.aspx.*

LISTING 19-2 The web.config file of the sample site for configuring FBA in Visual Studio

```
<configuration>
  <connectionStrings>
    <add name="SharePointFBA" connectionString="server=SP2013SQL;database=SP2013_
Farm_FBA;integrated security=SSPI;"/>
  </connectionStrings>

  <system.web>
    <compilation debug="true" targetFramework="4.0" />

    <authentication mode="Forms" />

    <authorization>
      <deny users="?"/>
    </authorization>

    <membership defaultProvider="FBASQLMembershipProvider">
      <providers>
        <add connectionStringName="SharePointFBA" applicationName="/"
             passwordAttemptWindow="5" enablePasswordRetrieval="false"
             enablePasswordReset="false" requiresQuestionAndAnswer="true"
             requiresUniqueEmail="true" passwordFormat="Hashed"
             name="FBASQLMembershipProvider"
             type="System.Web.Security.SqlMembershipProvider, System.Web,
Version=4.0.0.0,Culture=neutral, PublicKeyToken=b03f5f7f11d50a3a" />
      </providers>
    </membership>

    <roleManager enabled="true" defaultProvider="FBASQLRoleManager">
      <providers>
        <add connectionStringName="SharePointFBA" applicationName="/"
             name="FBASQLRoleManager"
             type="System.Web.Security.SqlRoleProvider, System.Web,
Version=4.0.0.0, Culture=neutral, PublicKeyToken=b03f5f7f11d50a3a" />
      </providers>
    </roleManager>

  </system.web>
</configuration>
```

Note The type attribute values, as well as the connectionString attribute, in the preceding listing should appear on a single line in your code. They're wrapped here due to typographic constraints.

These configuration elements will be useful when configuring SharePoint 2013 for FBA. While you're in the Security Setup Wizard, you can also configure some users and groups, for testing purposes. In the sample code that accompanies this chapter, the following roles have been created:

- Admins
- Managers
- Users

In addition, the following users have been created:

- SampleAdmin01
- SampleManager01
- SampleUser01

As their names imply, each user belongs to the corresponding role. For example, you can give them a password value of Passw0rd!. You should test your authentication infrastructure by writing a couple of sample pages for logging in and logging out.

Configuring SharePoint web.config files

Now that you have a working configuration for you site, you are ready to apply that configuration to SharePoint. First, you need to locate the web.config file of the web application where you will configure FBA. By default, the root folder of a SharePoint web application is located in the C:\inetpub\wwwroot\wss\VirtualDirectories folder of every front-end server.

> **Note** For the sake of simplicity, if you are working in a lab environment, you could create a new web application by using SPCA or PowerShell, and configure it with the following steps. Otherwise, in a production environment, you should locate the web.config file of the real target web application.

Next, you need to copy the *connectionStrings/add* element that defines your SQL Server membership database into the *connectionStrings* element of the target web.config file. Be careful while editing the web.config file, and make a backup copy of it before applying any kind of change. If the *connectionStrings* section is missing, you must create it from scratch, adding it after the *configSections* element of the web.config file, as shown:

```
<connectionStrings>
  <add name="SharePointFBA" connectionString="server=SP2013SQL;database=SP2013_Farm_
FBA;integrated security=SSPI;"/>
</connectionStrings>
```

Then you need to locate the *Membership* and *RoleProvider* sections, within the *system.web* section of the target web.config file. There, you need to copy only the providers' configuration, without changing the default providers that were already configured by SharePoint. The result should look like the following:

```
<membership defaultProvider="i">
  <providers>
    <add name="i" type="Microsoft.SharePoint.Administration.Claims.
SPClaimsAuthMembershipProvider, Microsoft.SharePoint, Version=15.0.0.0, Culture=neutral,
PublicKeyToken=71e9bce111e9429c" />
    <add connectionStringName="SharePointFBA" applicationName="/"
          passwordAttemptWindow="5" enablePasswordRetrieval="false"
          enablePasswordReset="false" requiresQuestionAndAnswer="true"
          requiresUniqueEmail="true" passwordFormat="Hashed"
          name="FBASQLMembershipProvider"
          type="System.Web.Security.SqlMembershipProvider, System.Web, Version=4.0.0.0,
Culture=neutral, PublicKeyToken=b03f5f7f11d50a3a" />
  </providers>
</membership>
<roleManager defaultProvider="c" enabled="true" cacheRolesInCookie="false">
  <providers>
    <add name="c" type="Microsoft.SharePoint.Administration.Claims.SPClaimsAuthRoleProvider,
Microsoft.SharePoint, Version=15.0.0.0, Culture=neutral, PublicKeyToken=71e9bce111e9429c" />
    <add connectionStringName="SharePointFBA" applicationName="/"
          name="FBASQLRoleManager"
          type="System.Web.Security.SqlRoleProvider, System.Web, Version=4.0.0.0,
Culture=neutral, PublicKeyToken=b03f5f7f11d50a3a" />
  </providers>
</roleManager>
```

Note The *type* attribute values in the preceding listing should appear on a single line in your code. They're wrapped here due to typographic constraints.

In the previous example, the code highlighted in bold shows that SharePoint 2013 already has a default membership provider named *i* and a default role provider named *c*. These are the providers that manage the claims-based infrastructure.

After you have configured the web.config file of the target web application, you need to configure the web.config file of the SPCA web application in the same way, as well as the web.config file of the internal SharePoint STS. The SPCA web application must be configured so that you can manage users defined in the FBA database from within the administrative pages, as well. You can still find its web.config file in a folder in the C:\inetpub\wwwroot\wss\VirtualDirectories path of every front-end server. The STS web application needs to have access to the FBA database in order to retrieve claims and information about the authenticated users during identity normalization. You can find the STS service of SharePoint and its web.config file in the SharePoint15_Root\WebServices\SecurityToken folder.

Configuring SQL Server permissions

To take full advantage of the authentication infrastructure that you have just configured, the application pools of SharePoint need to have access to the SQL Server database you configured for FBA. Thus, you need to properly configure the database's permissions. This is a simple but fundamental task. To carry it out, you need to enable the Windows identities configured for the following:

- The SPCA application pool
- The STS application pool
- The application pool of the target web application

All three need the following database role memberships:

- aspnet_Membership_FullAccess
- aspnet_Roles_FullAccess

Configuring SharePoint

You are almost done. Now you simply need to configure the FBA providers—for example, through the SPCA interface. To access the list of available web applications, click Application Management, then click Manage Web Applications, and then choose the FBA target. On the ribbon, click the Authentication Providers command, and in the window that appears, click the Default Configuration link. The Edit Authentication configuration page will open.

Select the Enable Forms Based Authentication (FBA) check box, and provide the name for the membership provider and role provider to use. Figure 19-5 shows the configuration dialog box, completed with information based on the current sample scenario.

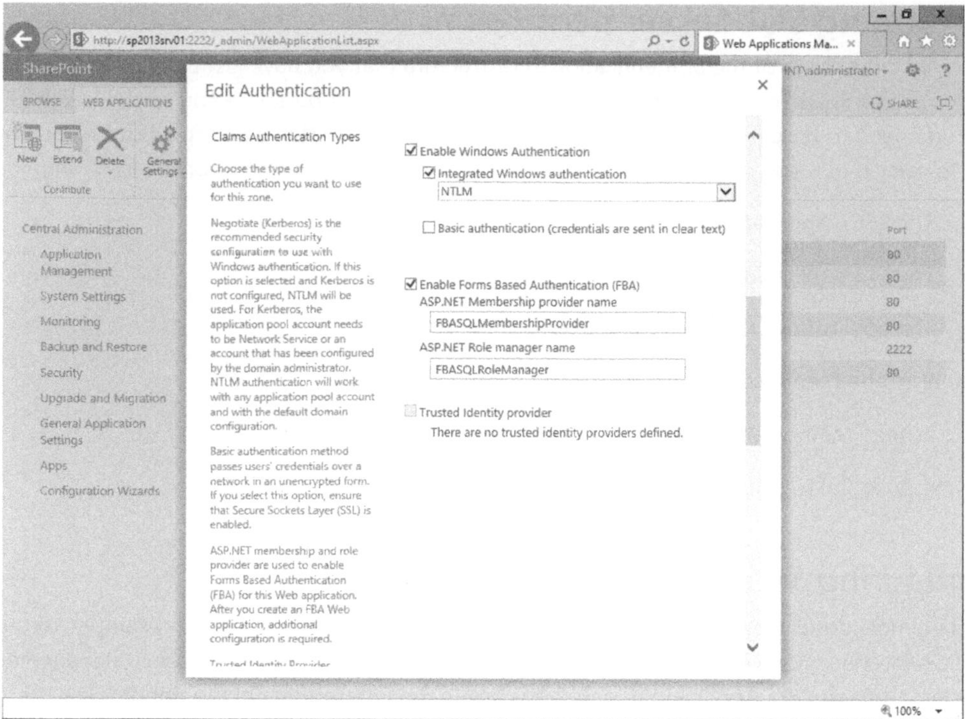

FIGURE 19-5 The Edit Authentication configuration page of SPCA.

Enabling FBA users or roles

The last step in configuring FBA is to enable some users or roles to access the site collections defined in your target web application. You can accomplish this task either from SPCA or from the People And Groups page of the target site.

Notice that if you now try to browse for users or roles, you will be able to browse both Windows and FBA users within the same browsing windows. From the perspective of SharePoint 2013, all the users are claims identities, regardless of the authentication provider that was used. Notice how searching for users in Figure 19-6 returns one result in the role repository of FBA and three more results in the security groups of Windows.

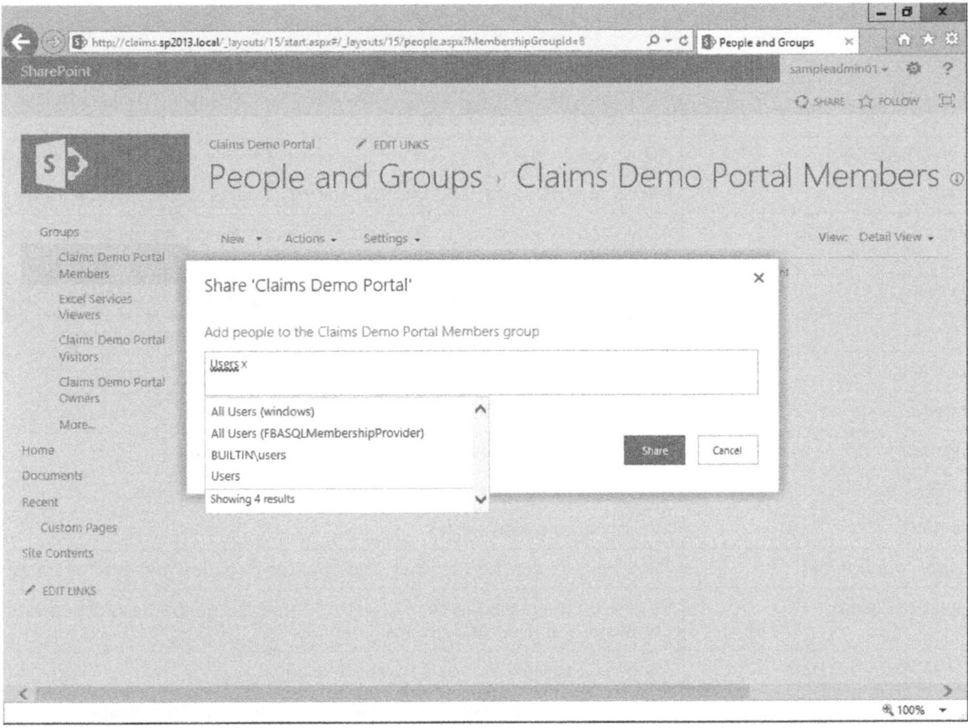

FIGURE 19-6 The Share dialog box with multiple authentication providers configured, during a search for users.

Authorization infrastructure

No matter which authentication mode and methods you choose, authorization in SharePoint is always managed the same way. This is a great feature that makes life easier for SharePoint administrators, because they do not need to care about the front-end authentication environment.

Authorization in SharePoint is based on *permission levels*, which are a formal definition of a set of permissions. Permission levels can be assigned to users (*SPUser*) or groups (*SPGroup*). Both *SPUser* and *SPGroup* inherit from *SPPrincipal*, which is the base class for every principal in SharePoint, including app principals, as you will learn in Chapter 20. The permission is the low-level item from an authorization viewpoint. SharePoint defines many permissions, and Table 19-1 presents the full list, in the same order as they are defined in the SharePoint management interface. Consider that these permissions cannot be customized or extended. However, it's unlikely that you would need to customize them because they cover a very wide range of needs.

TABLE 19-1 The list of permissions defined in SharePoint 2013

Permission	Description
Manage Lists	Allows you to create and delete lists, add or remove columns in a list, and add or remove public views of a list.
Override Check Out	Allows you to discard or check in a document that is checked out to another user.
Add Items	Allows you to add items to lists and add documents to document libraries.
Edit Items	Allows you to edit items in lists, edit documents in document libraries, and customize Web Part pages in document libraries.
Delete Items	Allows you to delete items from a list and documents from a document library.
View Items	Allows you to view items in lists and documents in document libraries.
Approve Items	Allows you to approve a minor version of a list item or document.
Open Items	Allows you to view the source of documents with server-side file handlers.
View Versions	Allows you to view past versions of a list item or document.
Delete Versions	Allows you to delete past versions of a list item or document.
Create Alerts	Allows you to create alerts.
View Application Pages	Allows you to view forms, views, and application pages, and enumerate lists.
Manage Permissions	Allows you to create and change permission levels on the website and assign permissions to users and groups.
View Web Analytics Data	Allows you to view reports on website usage.
Create Subsites	Allows you to create subsites such as team sites, meeting workspace sites, and document workspace sites.
Manage Web Site	Grants the ability to perform all administration tasks for the website, as well as manage content.
Add and Customize Pages	Allows you to add, change, or delete HTML pages or Web Part pages, and edit the website using a SharePoint Foundation–compatible editor.
Apply Themes and Borders	Allows you to apply a theme or borders to the entire website.
Apply Style Sheets	Allows you to apply a style sheet (CSS file) to the website.
Create Groups	Allows you to create a group of users that can be used anywhere within the site collection.
Browse Directories	Allows you to enumerate files and folders in a website using SharePoint Designer and WebDAV interfaces.
Use Self-Service Site Creation	Allows you to create a website using self-service site creation.
View Pages	Allows you to view pages in a website.
Enumerate Permissions	Allows you to enumerate permissions on the website, list, folder, document, or list item.
Browse User Information	Allows you to view information about users of the website.
Manage Alerts	Allows you to manage alerts for all users of the website.
Use Remote Interfaces	Allows you to use SOAP, WebDAV, the Client Object Model, or SharePoint Designer interfaces to access the website.
Use Client Integration Features	Allows you to use features that launch client applications. Without this permission, users will have to work on documents locally and upload their changes.
Open	Allows users to open a website, list, or folder in order to access items inside that container.

Permission	Description
Edit Personal User Information	Allows a user to change his or her own user information, including adding a picture.
Manage Personal Views	Allows you to create, change, and delete personal views of lists.
Add/Remove Personal Web Parts	Allows you to add or remove personal Web Parts on a Web Part page.
Update Personal Web Parts	Allows you to update Web Parts to display personalized information.

A permission level is made up of a set of permissions selected from the list in Table 19-1. SharePoint 2013 defines a default set of seven permission levels:

- **View Only** Allows the user to view pages, list items, and documents. Document types with server-side file handlers can be viewed in the browser but not downloaded.
- **Limited Access** Allows the user to view specific lists, document libraries, list items, folders, or documents when given permissions.
- **Read** Allows the user to view pages and list items, and download documents.
- **Contribute** Allows the user to view, add, update, and delete list items and documents.
- **Edit** Allows the user to add, edit, and delete lists, and view, add, update, and delete list items and documents.
- **Design** Allows the user to view, add, update, delete, approve, and customize pages.
- **Full Control** Gives the user full control.

Chapter 2, "SharePoint data fundamentals," showed how an out-of-the-box SharePoint site configures four groups of users: Excel Viewers, Site Visitors, Site Members, and Site Owners. To configure permission levels for such users, begin on the Site Permissions page, which you can access from the Settings menu (the gear at the top-right of the browser, just beside the user name) on the Site Settings page. Click the Permission Levels ribbon command to display a page in which you can create new permission levels. To create and configure groups, go to the People And Groups page, which you can reach through the Site Settings page.

When you enable anonymous access for a site, you will be able to configure permissions for anonymous users. Figure 19-7 shows the choices for anonymous access: Nothing (no access), Lists And Libraries (but only those for which anonymous users have been explicitly enabled), and Entire Web Site. This page also provides an option to determine whether anonymous users will be able to access remote client APIs anonymously. Consider that an anonymous user does not have any claim assigned, but he or she is still represented by a *ClaimsIdentity* and a *ClaimsPrincipal*, in case of claims-based authentication mode.

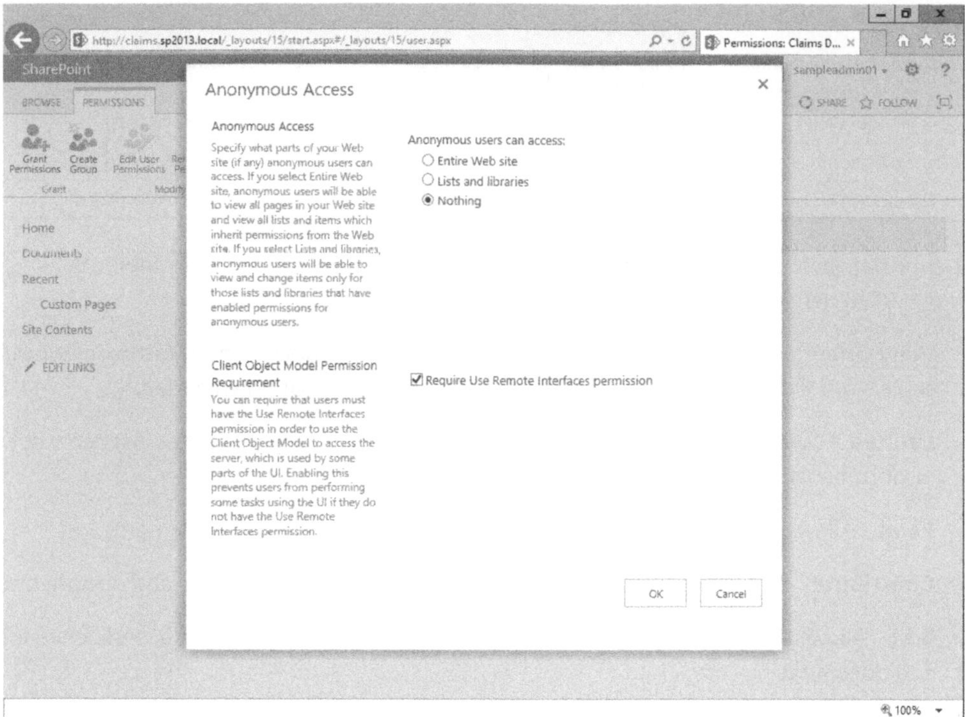

FIGURE 19-7 The Anonymous Access page for configuring anonymous access permissions.

Note Anonymous access can be configured from SPCA via the Authentication Providers page. You used this page earlier in this chapter to configure the authentication providers for a web application. You can follow the procedure shown at *http://technet.microsoft.com/en-us/library/ff608071.aspx#section2.*

After you define permission levels and assign them to users or groups, you can also override default permissions at the list or library level, or even at the single-item level. Because webpages are items, as are documents and general list items, you can configure permissions at the single-page level, too.

Summary

In this chapter, you learned how SharePoint 2013 authenticates and authorizes users. In particular, you saw that there are two authentication modes: claims-based mode, which is the default, and classic mode, which is available only in code and for backward compatibility. You can choose from three authentication methods: Windows Authentication, FBA, and using trusted identity providers, which will be explained in Chapter 20. You also walked through how to configure both the claims-based mode and FBA to authenticate users against a SQL Server database. Finally, you learned how SharePoint manages authorizations and permissions.

CHAPTER 20

Claims-based authentication, federated identities, and OAuth

This chapter takes a detailed look at claims-based authentication and the security infrastructure behind Microsoft SharePoint apps. After a general overview, it focuses on web-based and HTTP-based scenarios. You will learn how to use Microsoft Windows Identity Foundation (WIF) 4.5 (the official Microsoft claims-based framework) to implement a simple Security Token Service (STS), as well as how to register that STS in SharePoint 2013 so that you can share a common single-sign-on infrastructure between multiple SharePoint sites and even third-party sites. In addition, you will learn how to federate with Windows Azure Access Control Services (ACS). Lastly, the chapter covers OAuth for app authentication and authorization.

Claims-based authentication and WS-Federation

Today's software solutions always require user authentication and authorization. Quite often, however, each application implements its own authentication method, and users are obliged to remember and manage many different credentials. Think about a typical day in your life: you log on to your domain network when you turn on your computer; you log on to Facebook using its specific credentials; next, you log on to *http://www.live.com* using your Microsoft Account credentials; then, if you need to access your home banking system, you provide yet another set of credentials specific for that system; and so on. The list of examples could be very long, indeed.

The problem is evident: you and everyone else in today's digital world have too many sets of credentials to remember, manage, and keep safe. Wouldn't a better solution be to decouple applications and software solutions from their authentication environments, while taking advantage of a shared set of credentials? In the ideal digital world, you should authenticate once, at the very beginning of the day, and use a worldwide single-sign-on infrastructure.

Now consider the scenario of the emerging cloud-computing offerings. Quite often, you use some services on-premises, such as domain controllers, file servers, ERP, and so forth, as well as online services, such as Microsoft Office 365 (Office Web Apps, Microsoft Exchange Online, SharePoint Online, Microsoft Lync, and so on), Microsoft CRM Online, and some services built on top of the Windows Azure platform. Of course, users of your internal network's domain should authenticate on the internal network as well as online, and you should avoid multiplying users' credentials and authentications. In the ideal world, you should federate your internal network with the online services, providing a single-sign-on experience to your users, utilizing a federated trust between your network on-premises and the online services in the cloud.

Furthermore, from a developer's perspective, it is hard to implement the authentication and authorization logic for each and every software solution that a user implements. It would be better to externalize the authentication infrastructure, concentrating the software implementation on the business logic and rules, eventually providing a custom authorization environment only.

Many software solutions authenticate their users just because they need to authorize access to resources or functionalities based on users' identities. They do not really need, however, to collect and maintain users' credentials. From an authorization viewpoint, it suffices to have some information about the users to cluster them in groups or audiences and authorize access to resources based on their properties.

Pushed by these ideas, a few years ago the software market started working on the goal of defining an authentication infrastructure that could be externalized and that could identify every user as a digital identity. In Chapter 19, "Authentication and authorization infrastructure," you learned that a digital identity is essentially a set of claims. Remember that a claim is a statement that is asserted by an issuer about a subject; this statement is assumed to be true by the reader, due to a trust relationship between the reader and the issuer. The externalized authentication provider is generally defined as the *identity provider (IP)* and often publishes an STS. The application or software solution externalizing the authentication process is called the *service provider* or *relying party.* The consumer, who uses the service provider for authenticating with the IP, is generally called the *subject.* Figure 20-1 portrays an extremely simplified authentication architecture employed by a software solution that uses externalized authentication.

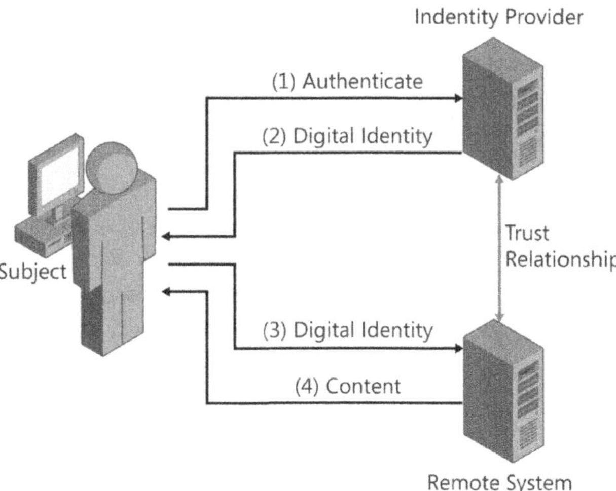

FIGURE 20-1 A simplified schema showing the architecture of a system with externalized authentication.

From a technology viewpoint, these concepts use such specifications as WS-Security, WS-Trust, and WS-*. The final goal of these specifications is to allow for implementing a token-based authentication and authorization system, in which third parties can issue tokens.

In December 2006, an international and multivendor working group defined a specification called Web Services Federation Language 1.1 (WS-Federation), which states its role is to define "mechanisms to allow different security realms to federate, such that authorized access to resources managed in one realm can be provided to security principals whose identities are managed in other realms."

Note If you are interested, you can download the full WS-Federation specification document from *http://specs.xmlsoap.org/ws/2006/12/federation/ws-federation.pdf.* There is also an updated version of the specification, called WS-Federation 1.2, available on the OASIS website, at *http://docs.oasis-open.org/wsfed/federation/v1.2/os/ws-federation-1.2-spec-os.pdf.*

From a practical viewpoint, WS-Federation defines extensions to the WS-Security and WS-Trust specifications, which support exchange of authentication and authorization claims between federated partners, identities brokering, and protection of claims during their transmission across partners. One of the most interesting features of WS-Federation is the capability to provide federation techniques that you can use in communication based on Simple Object Access Protocol (SOAP), via WS-Security and WS-Trust, as well as in web browser–based environments. The SOAP scenario is often called *active requestor*, while the scenario based on web browsers is referred to as *passive requestor*. From the perspective of SharePoint and web/HTTP, you should be most interested in the passive requestor scenario, because it is the only process that you can manage, as well as experience from a user viewpoint.

Note SharePoint 2013 uses the active (SOAP-oriented) scenario in the communication infrastructure of the service applications. Providing complete coverage of all the WS-Federation scenarios is beyond the scope of this book, however.

Figure 20-2 illustrates a sequence diagram related to the functional schema of WS-Federation in the passive requestor scenario.

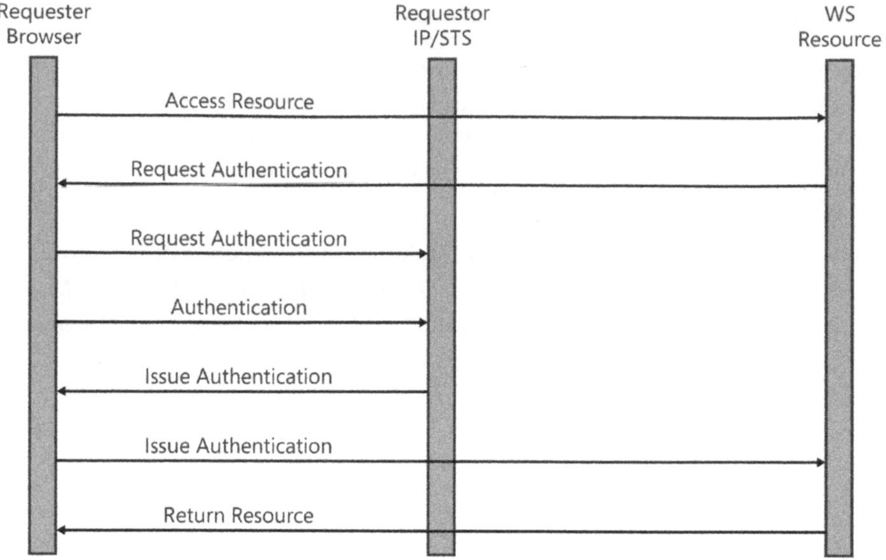

FIGURE 20-2 The sequence diagram of WS-Federation for the passive requestor scenario.

In Figure 20-2, the passive requestor scenario walks through the following steps:

1. The web browser (subject) sends a request for a resource to the service provider.
2. The service provider returns a request for authentication and redirects the browser to the IP/STS of the IP.
3. The end user authenticates within the IP/STS.
4. If the credentials are valid, the IP/STS issues a token and returns it to the browser.
5. The browser sends (via automatic HTTP *POST*) the issued token to the service provider.
6. The service provider receives the issued token and validates it against the list of trusted IPs. If the token was issued by a trusted IP, it marks the end user as authenticated and eventually authorizes the subject based on the claims presented in the security token.
7. If the user recognized by the IP/STS is valid and authorized, the SP accepts the request and returns the originally requested resource.

The term *passive* derives from the fact that the web browser is unconsciously and automatically redirected to the IP/STS, and then automatically sends the token via *POST* to the SP. Thus, the browser is passive during the authentication process.

If you share the same IP/STS for two or more sites, such as sharing your Microsoft Account across multiple sites, once an end user has authenticated with the IP/STS, he or she will be able to obtain issued tokens for all of the federated sites without authenticating again. This is a powerful single-sign-on scenario.

Furthermore, when you log on to SharePoint 2013 using claims-based authentication mode, the front end does not redirect you to an external IP/STS for authentication. Instead, it communicates on the back end with the internal IP/STS of SharePoint, using SOAP as the communication protocol.

If you want to realize a complete WS-Federation scenario, you need to register an external IP, together with all the information about its STS. Then you will be able to authenticate with third-party solutions, whereupon you will experience the WS-Federation passive requestor scenario concretely.

When you want to register an external IP, you can use Windows Active Directory Federation Service (AD FS) 2.0, which is available out of the box in Windows Server 2008 or higher; federate with Windows Azure ACS, which will be covered later in this chapter; or implement an IP of your own. Because this book targets developers, the next section will explain how to implement a custom IP from scratch, using Microsoft Visual Studio 2012. Nevertheless, in many cases, you may prefer using AD FS 2.0 or ACS instead of writing custom code.

Implementing an IP/STS with WIF

WIF is a framework natively provided by Microsoft in Microsoft .NET Framework 4.5. WIF supports .NET developers while developing claims-based solutions, whether they work on the service provider side or implement an IP/STS of their own. Targeting .NET 3.5 and 4.0, WIF 1.0 is still available, as well. In fact, SharePoint 2013 internally uses WIF 1.0 with some custom extension libraries to provide OAuth support. The WIF 4.5 runtime is included in the .NET 4.5 runtime, while the WIF 1.0 runtime is available as a free download from *http://www.microsoft.com/downloads/en/details.aspx?FamilyID=eb9c345f-e830-40b8-a5fe-ae7a864c4d76.*

Note If you need to develop custom solutions, download the .NET Framework 4.5 software development kit (SDK), which is included in Visual Studio 2012, and the Identity and Access Tool, which is available at *http://visualstudiogallery.msdn.microsoft.com/e21bf653-dfe1-4d81-b3d3-795cb104066e*. If you want to create custom solutions based on WIF 1.0, download the WIF 1.0 SDK, which is available at *http://www.microsoft.com/downloads/en/details.aspx?FamilyID=c148b2df-c7af-46bb-9162-2c9422208504.*

WIF 1.0 is compatible with WIF 4.5, so in this chapter you will worth with WIF 4.5 on the IP/STS side. (The WS-Federation active scenario is out of scope for this book.) In the next sections, you will learn how to use WIF 4.5 to implement an IP/STS solution, which can be used to implement a web-based WS-Federation passive requestor scenario, suitable for realizing a single-sign-on user experience shared across multiple sites, whether or not they are implemented with SharePoint. To better follow along, open the .NET solution called DevLeap.IPSTS, which is available in the companion code samples. To work with this code, you must have .NET 4.5, WIF 4.5, and the Identity and Access Tool. Remember, Visual Studio 2012 already includes WIF 4.5 as part of .NET 4.5.

Building an STS

Imagine your company maintains a shared repository of credentials that is based on the standard ASP.NET Membership Providers infrastructure for authenticating users, and you plan to use it for accessing both a SharePoint site and a classic ASP.NET site. To implement a new STS for this scenario, you first need to create a new website project of type ASP.NET Empty Web Application in Visual Studio 2012.

Important The WIF 1.0 SDK includes an STS Web Site template, but the WIF 4.5 SDK does not. Moreover, because many of the types and namespaces defined in the WIF libraries were renamed and changed between WIF 1.0 and WIF 4.5, you cannot start creating an IP/STS project with WIF 1.0 and then upgrade it to WIF 4.5.

The project template prepares a new empty website project to which you must add a few pages and code files:

- **Default.aspx** A welcome page providing some useful links to interact with the IP/STS. You will find this page in the companion sources, but it will not be discussed in this chapter.
- **Issue.aspx** The page that provides the authentication UI and that wraps the IP/STS service on the back end.
- **FederationMetadata.xml** An XML file providing all the information about the endpoint and the security configuration of the IP/STS. It is fundamental, and, for security reasons, it will be digitally signed. You can create it manually, or you can use some out-of-the-box classes of WCF and WIF to generate it automatically.

Moreover, to use the WIF 4.5 libraries in the IP/STS website project, you need to add references to the System.IdentityModel, System.IdentityModel.Selectors, and System.IdentityModel.Services assemblies.

Next, you need to configure the ASP.NET profile, membership, and role providers. This example uses the ASP.NET Profile engine to store information for custom user profiles, which will be converted into claims. In Listing 20-1, you can see an excerpt of the web.config file of the IP/STS web application. For detailed explanations of the membership and role configuration, please refer back to Chapter 19.

LISTING 20-1 An excerpt of the web.config file of the IP/STS sample web application

```
<?xml version="1.0"?>
<configuration>

  <!-- Configuration omitted for the sake of brevity -->

  <system.web>
    <compilation debug="true" targetFramework="4.5" />
    <httpRuntime targetFramework="4.5" />

    <authorization>
      <deny users="?" />
    </authorization>

    <authentication mode="Forms">
      <forms name=".DEVLEAPIPSTS"
             requireSSL="true"
             defaultUrl="~/Default.aspx"
             loginUrl="~/Issue.aspx"
             cookieless="UseDeviceProfile"
             enableCrossAppRedirects="false"
             slidingExpiration="false"
             timeout="300" />
    </authentication>

    <membership defaultProvider="FBASQLMembershipProvider">
      <providers>
        <add connectionStringName="SharePointFBA" applicationName="/"
             passwordAttemptWindow="5" enablePasswordRetrieval="false"
             enablePasswordReset="false" requiresQuestionAndAnswer="true"
             requiresUniqueEmail="true" passwordFormat="Hashed"
             name="FBASQLMembershipProvider"
             type="System.Web.Security.SqlMembershipProvider, System.Web,
Version=4.0.0.0, Culture=neutral, PublicKeyToken=b03f5f7f11d50a3a" />
      </providers>
    </membership>

    <roleManager enabled="true" defaultProvider="FBASQLRoleManager">
      <providers>
        <add connectionStringName="SharePointFBA" applicationName="/"
             name="FBASQLRoleManager"
             type="System.Web.Security.SqlRoleProvider, System.Web,
Version=4.0.0.0, Culture=neutral, PublicKeyToken=b03f5f7f11d50a3a" />
      </providers>
    </roleManager>
```

```
    <profile defaultProvider="FBASQLProfile">
      <properties>
        <add name="Name" type="String" />
        <add name="Email" type="String" />
        <add name="Gender" type="String" defaultValue="Neutral" />
        <add name="FavoriteColor" type="String" defaultValue="Yellow" />
      </properties>
      <providers>
        <add connectionStringName="SharePointFBA" applicationName="/"
             name="FBASQLProfile"
             type="System.Web.Profile.SqlProfileProvider, System.Web,
Version=4.0.0.0, Culture=neutral, PublicKeyToken=b03f5f7f11d50a3a" />
      </providers>
    </profile>

  </system.web>

  <!-- Configuration omitted for the sake of brevity -->

</configuration>
```

As shown highlighted in bold, the configuration defines a user profile made of four properties:

- ***Name*** A string representing the user's name
- ***Email*** A string representing the user's email
- ***Gender*** A string representing the user's gender
- ***Favorite Color*** A string providing the user's favorite color

Later, you will use these profile properties to populate users' claims. Moreover, in the "Creating a custom claims provider" section, you will authorize users based on their gender and favorite color.

Now consider Listing 20-2: the ASPX code defining the Issue.aspx page. From a UI perspective, this page provides only the controls for authenticating end users. Because in the current sample IP/STS we will use the out-of-the-box Membership Provider API of ASP.NET, the Issue.aspx page will simply contain an ASP.NET *Login* web control.

LISTING 20-2 The ASPX code of the Issue.aspx page

```
<%@ Page Language="C#" AutoEventWireup="true" CodeBehind="Issue.aspx.cs"
Inherits="DevLeap.IPSTS.Issue" %>

<!DOCTYPE html>
<html xmlns="http://www.w3.org/1999/xhtml">
<head runat="server">
    <title>Sample IP/STS Issue Page</title>
</head>
<body>
    <form id="form1" runat="server">
        <div>
            <asp:Login ID="loginControl" runat="server"
                OnAuthenticate="loginControl_Authenticate" />
        </div>
    </form>
</body>
</html>
```

As you can see, the core business logic of the Issue.aspx page is behind the *OnAuthenticate* event of the *Login* control, which is handled by the *loginControl_Authenticate* event handler method. By default, the *Login* control authenticates users by itself, using ASP.NET membership. Nevertheless, to implement a custom IP/STS, you will need to provide some custom code for users' authentication. Listing 20-3 implements that method.

LISTING 20-3 A code excerpt illustrating the *loginControl_Authenticate* event handler method of the *Login* control

```
protected void loginControl_Authenticate(object sender, AuthenticateEventArgs e)
{
    IIdentity identity = null;

    if (Membership.ValidateUser(loginControl.UserName, loginControl.Password)) {
        // Authentication succeeded
        identity = new GenericIdentity(loginControl.UserName);
    }
    else {
        return;
    }

    if (identity != null) {
        // Set Authentication cookie
        FormsAuthentication.SetAuthCookie(identity.Name,
            loginControl.RememberMeSet);
        // Generate and issue the security token
        ProcessRequest(identity);
    }
    else {
        return;
    }
}
```

Aside from implementing the authentication logic, the event handler simply creates a .NET identity, which is an instance of a type implementing the *IIdentity* interface, and passes it to a *ProcessRequest* method, which does the real job from the WS-Federation viewpoint. Listing 20-4 implements the *ProcessRequest* method.

LISTING 20-4 The full implementation of the *ProcessRequest* method within the Issue.aspx page

```
protected void ProcessRequest(IIdentity identity) {
    var principal = new ClaimsPrincipal(
        new ClaimsIdentity[] { (ClaimsIdentity)identity });

    FederatedPassiveSecurityTokenServiceOperations.ProcessRequest(
        this.Request,
        principal,
        DevLeapSecurityTokenServiceConfiguration.Current.
        CreateSecurityTokenService(),
        this.Response);
}
```

As the code excerpt illustrates, aside from creating an instance of the *ClaimsPrincipal* type, the *ProcessRequest* method simply invokes the *ProcessRequest* method of the *FederatedPassiveSecurityTokenServiceOperations* type, which is available out of the box in WIF 4.5. That method accepts some arguments related to the current HTTP *Request* and *Response* objects, the current user principal, and an instance of a type that inherits from the *SecurityTokenService* class, which is the real core engine of the IP/STS. The infrastructural types are defined in a dedicated class library project so that the code for the sample project can be better organized.

Note The code behind the Issue.aspx page does some other things that will not be covered within the text of this chapter. However, you will find the complete and fully functional code in the companion sample.

Listing 20-5 shows the implementation of the *DevLeapSecurityTokenServiceConfiguration* type, which is defined in the infrastructural class library and handles the creation of the custom *SecurityTokenService* instance.

LISTING 20-5 The source code of the *DevLeapSecurityTokenServiceConfiguration* class

```
public class DevLeapSecurityTokenServiceConfiguration :
SecurityTokenServiceConfiguration
{

    private static Lazy<DevLeapSecurityTokenServiceConfiguration>
    _configuration =
    new Lazy<DevLeapSecurityTokenServiceConfiguration>(delegate {
            return (new DevLeapSecurityTokenServiceConfiguration());
        }, true);

    public DevLeapSecurityTokenServiceConfiguration() :
        base(ConfigurationManager.AppSettings["IssuerUri"],
        X509Helper.RetrieveSigningCredentials()) {
        SecurityTokenService = typeof(DevLeapSecurityTokenService);
    }

    public static DevLeapSecurityTokenServiceConfiguration Current {
        get { return _configuration.Value; }
    }
}
```

The main part of the *DevLeapSecurityTokenServiceConfiguration* class is the constructor, which uses the base class constructor to define the type of the class inheriting from *SecurityTokenService* that will implement the STS business logic. In the current example, the class inheriting from *SecurityTokenService* is the *DevLeapSecurityTokenService*, shown in Listing 20-6.

LISTING 20-6 The source code of the *DevLeapSecurityTokenService* class

```
public class DevLeapSecurityTokenService : SecurityTokenService {

    /// <summary>
    /// Creates an instance of DevLeapSecurityTokenService.
    /// </summary>
    /// <param name="configuration">The SecurityTokenServiceConfiguration.
    /// </param>
    public DevLeapSecurityTokenService(SecurityTokenServiceConfiguration
configuration)
        : base(configuration) {
    }

    /// <summary>
    /// This method returns the configuration for the token issuance request.
    /// The configuration is represented by the Scope class. In our case,
    /// we are only capable of issuing a token for a single RP identity
    /// represented by the EncryptingCertificateName.
    /// </summary>
    /// <param name="principal">The caller's principal.</param>
    /// <param name="request">The incoming RST.</param>
```

```
/// <returns>The scope information to be used for
/// the token issuance.</returns>
protected override Scope GetScope(System.Security.Claims.ClaimsPrincipal
principal,
    System.IdentityModel.Protocols.WSTrust.RequestSecurityToken request) {

    // RP validation disabled for the sake of simplicity
    // ValidateAppliesTo(request.AppliesTo);

    Scope scope = new Scope(request.AppliesTo.Uri.OriginalString,
        SecurityTokenServiceConfiguration.SigningCredentials);
    scope.ReplyToAddress = scope.AppliesToAddress;
    scope.SymmetricKeyEncryptionRequired = false;
    scope.TokenEncryptionRequired = false;

    return (scope);
}

/// <summary>
/// This method returns the claims to be issued in the token.
/// </summary>
/// <param name="principal">The caller's principal.</param>
/// <param name="request">The incoming RST, to obtain additional
/// information.</param>
/// <param name="scope">The scope information corresponding to this
/// request.</param>
/// <returns>The outgoing claimsIdentity to be included in the issued
/// token.</returns>
protected override System.Security.Claims.ClaimsIdentity
    GetOutputClaimsIdentity(System.Security.Claims.ClaimsPrincipal principal,
    System.IdentityModel.Protocols.WSTrust.RequestSecurityToken request,
    Scope scope) {

    if (null == principal) {
        throw new ArgumentNullException("principal");
    }

    Claim[] targetClaims = null;
    XmlSerializer xs = new XmlSerializer(typeof(ClaimTypes));

    ProfileBase profile = ProfileBase.Create(principal.Identity.Name);
    if (profile != null) {
        using (StreamReader sr = new StreamReader(
            HttpContext.Current.Server.MapPath(
            ConfigurationManager.AppSettings["ClaimTypesFilePath"]))) {
```

```
                ClaimTypes cts = xs.Deserialize(sr) as ClaimTypes;
                targetClaims =
                    (from c in new List<ClaimTypesClaimType>(cts.ClaimType)
                        select new Claim(c.Type,
                            (String)profile.GetPropertyValue(c.Name),
                            ClaimValueTypes.String)
                    ).ToArray();
            }
        }

        ClaimsIdentity ci = new ClaimsIdentity(targetClaims);
        return (ci);
    }
}
```

The two key points of interest in the *DevLeapSecurityTokenService* class are the *GetScope* and *GetOutputClaimsIdentity* methods. The *GetScope* method defines the scope of the token issuance. In particular, it defines the X.509 certificate that will be used to sign and eventually encrypt the security token that the IP/STS will release. In the *GetScope* method, you could also validate the calling relying parties if you want to accept token requests from authorized relying parties only—and generally speaking, you should do that. Moreover, the *GetOutputClaimsIdentity* method is the core method of the STS and provides, as its result, an instance of the *ClaimsIdentity* type, which will represent the claims that will be included in the output security token. As shown in Listing 20-6, the *DevLeapSecurityTokenService* class populates the collection of claims of the current user by accessing his or her user profile and reading the list of available claims from an XML file like the one shown in Listing 20-7.

LISTING 20-7 The XML file with the full list of claims provided by the sample IP/STS

```
<?xml version="1.0" encoding="utf-8" ?>
<ClaimTypes xmlns="http://schemas.devleap.com/SampleIPSTS/ClaimTypes">
  <ClaimType Name="Email"
        Description="The Email address of the subject."
        Optional="false"
        Type="http://schemas.xmlsoap.org/ws/2005/05/identity/claims/
¬       emailaddress" />
  <ClaimType Name="Name"
        Description="The Name of the subject."
        Optional="false"
        Type="http://schemas.xmlsoap.org/ws/2005/05/identity/claims/name" />
  <ClaimType Name="Gender"
        Description="The Gender of the subject."
        Optional="true"
        Type="http://schemas.xmlsoap.org/ws/2005/05/identity/claims/gender" />
  <ClaimType Name="FavoriteColor"
        Description="The Favorite Color of the subject."
        Optional="true"
        Type="http://schemas.devleap.com/SampleIPSTS/claims/favoritecolor" />
</ClaimTypes>
```

Notice that the claims defined in Listing 20-7 correspond exactly to the user-profile properties declared in the web.config file in Listing 20-1.

Note Generating the FederationMetadata.xml file is beyond the scope of this chapter, but you will find the file in the companion code samples. To create your own FederationMetadata.xml file, you can try two freely distributed tools from Thinktecture: Federation Metadata Generator (*http://static.thinktecture.com/christianweyer/FederationMetadataGenerator_1.0.zip*) and the StarterSTS project (*http://startersts.codeplex.com/*). Be careful, however, because these tools target WIF 1.0, *not* WIF 4.5. Although they are fine for generating the FederationMetadata tool, you should not use them for creating an IP/STS. Moreover, if you are looking for a ready to go IP/STS solution you can take a look at the IdentityServer project made available by ThinkTecture at the following URL: http://thinktecture.github.io/.

With the fundamental parts of the custom IP/STS implementation in place, you're ready to consume it, first from an ASP.NET relying party and then from SharePoint 2013.

Building a relying party

To test the IP/STS, you can add a new ASP.NET website project to the current solution by clicking File | New Project in Visual Studio 2012, and choosing an ASP.NET Empty Web Application project model. Next, you need to configure identity federation using the Identity and Access Tool. Right-click the web project in Visual Studio 2012 to access the menu, then choose Identity And Access (see Figure 20-3).

Note If Identity And Access is not listed on the menu, the tool is not installed. See the instructions at the beginning of the chapter for installation help.

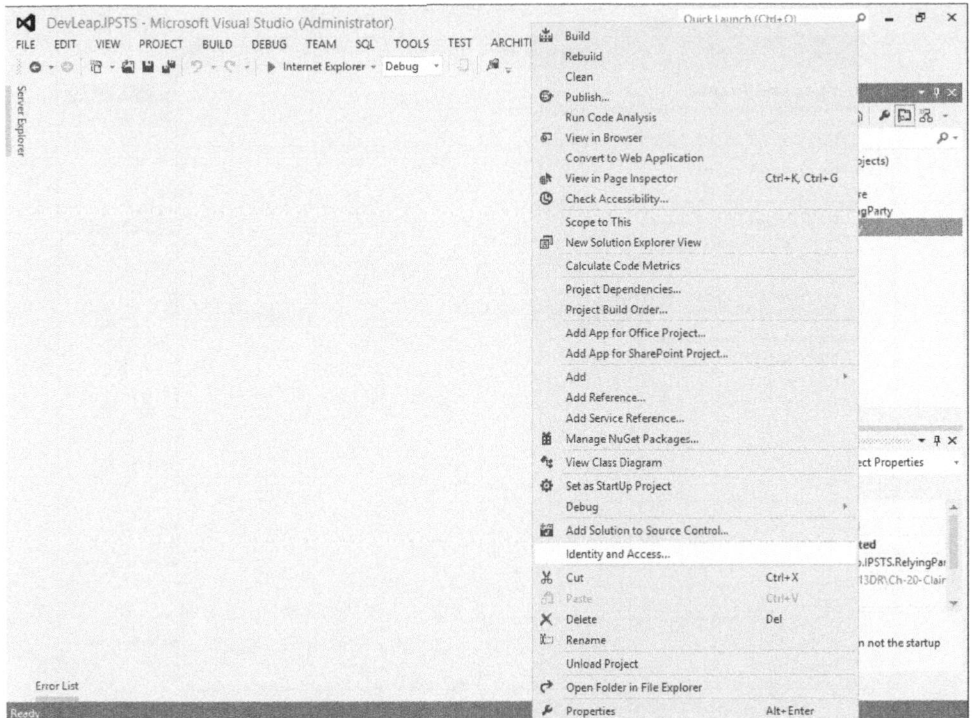

FIGURE 20-3 The menu extension to configure the Identity and Access Tool for a web project in Visual Studio 2012.

The Identity and Access Tool prompts you to select whether you want to federate your web app with a local development STS, which is provided out of the box by the Identity and Access Tool; with Windows Azure ACS; or with a business IP/STS like the one in the previous section (see Figure 20-4).

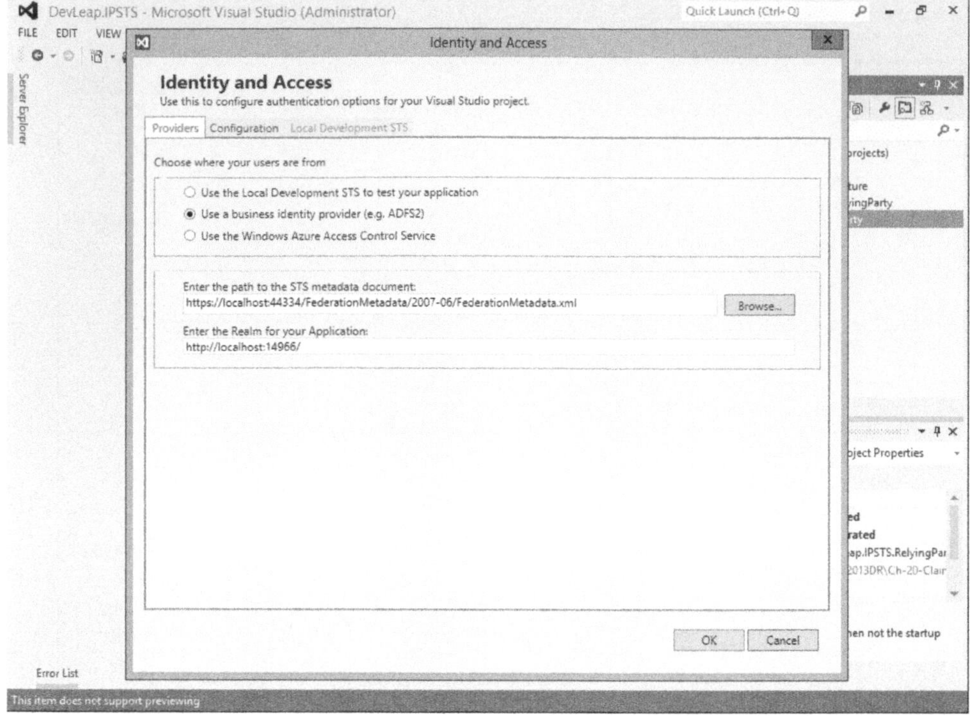

FIGURE 20-4 The UI provided by the Identity and Access Tool for federating a web application in Visual Studio 2012.

For the example, select the Use A Business Identity Provider option and provide the URL of the FederationMetadata.xml file published by the custom IP/STS. Click the OK button to configure your web application according to your choices.

More Info For further details about WIF, IP/STS, and the Identity and Access Tool, read *Programming Windows Identity Foundation*, by Vittorio Bertocci (Microsoft Press, 2010) or *A Guide to Claims-Based Identity and Access Control: Authentication and Authorization for Services and the Web*, by the Patterns & Practices team (Microsoft Press, 2013). You can also read Vittorio Bertocci's blog, at *http://www.cloudidentity.com/*, and in particular the post "A Refresh of the Identity and Access Tool for VS 2012," from March 2013.

Take a closer look at the web.config file after the Identity and Access Tool modifies it. Two new configuration sections, *system.identityModel* and *system.identityModel.services*, were defined targeting the WIF 4.5 infrastructure. The standard ASP.NET authentication method was set to *None*, because authentication events will be intercepted by an *HttpModule* class of WIF called *WSFederationAuthenticationModule*, available in the *System.IdentityModel.Services* namespace. In addition, a module corresponding to the *SessionAuthenticationModule* class was registered. This last module avoids repeating authentication against the IP/STS for each request, storing the session security token in a cookie stored securely and locally for the current web application. Listing 20-8 shows the configuration of the *system.identityModel* and *system.identityModel.services* sections of the XML configuration file.

LISTING 20-8 An excerpt of the web.config file related to the WIF 4.5 sections

```
<system.identityModel>
  <identityConfiguration>
    <audienceUris>
      <add value="http://localhost:14966/" />
    </audienceUris>
    <issuerNameRegistry type="System.IdentityModel.Tokens.
ConfigurationBasedIssuerNameRegistry, System.IdentityModel, Version=4.0.0.0,
Culture=neutral, PublicKeyToken=b77a5c561934e089">
      <trustedIssuers>
        <add thumbprint="A60699901F8483C72034EA165074392D8E4FC08C"
        name="Issue.aspx" />
      </trustedIssuers>
    </issuerNameRegistry>
  </identityConfiguration>
</system.identityModel>
<system.identityModel.services>
  <federationConfiguration>
    <cookieHandler requireSsl="false" />
    <wsFederation passiveRedirectEnabled="true"
        issuer="https://localhost:44334/Issue.aspx"
        realm="http://localhost:14966/"
        requireHttps="false" />
  </federationConfiguration>
</system.identityModel.services>
```

Highlighted in bold, the key points of this listing are:

- The list of the audience URIs, which are the URLs that represent the relying party.
- The list of trusted issuers, which are the token issuers that are trusted by the current website. Each trusted issuer is identified by the thumbprint of its certificate. It is important to update this value when moving from a development environment, based on a test certificate, to a production environment using a real certificate.
- A *wsFederation* element, which defines the configuration details of the WS-Federation protocol. For example, through this element you can enable the passive requestor profile, the URI of the token issuer, and the realm (that is, the web address) of the relying party. Remember that the realm will be evaluated by the STS to determine whether the current site (relying party) has been authorized to request token issuing or not.

Now, if you start browsing the site, you will be prompted for logging in to the IP/STS before being able to access the relying-party site. To see the real result, however, you need to add a Default.aspx page to the relying-party web project and define a bunch of code for rendering the claims. Listing 20-9 provides a code excerpt of the *Page_Load* event of the Default.aspx page.

LISTING 20-9 A code excerpt of the *Page_Load* event of the Default.aspx page of the relying-party web project

```
protected void Page_Load(object sender, EventArgs e) {
    if (this.User != null && this.User.Identity != null) {
        ClaimsIdentity ci = this.User.Identity as ClaimsIdentity;
        if (ci != null) {
            var claims = (from c in ci.Claims
                          select new { c.Type, c.Value }).ToArray();

            this.gridClaims.DataSource = claims;
            this.gridClaims.DataBind();
        }
    }
}
```

As you can see, the code simply defines a LINQ query against the collection of claims of the current *ClaimsIdentity* instance, corresponding to the currently authenticated user. The result of the LINQ query is bound to a *GridView* control defined in the ASPX markup of the Default.aspx page. Figure 20-5 shows the result after authenticating with a sample user (assuming you have properly configured users' profiles).

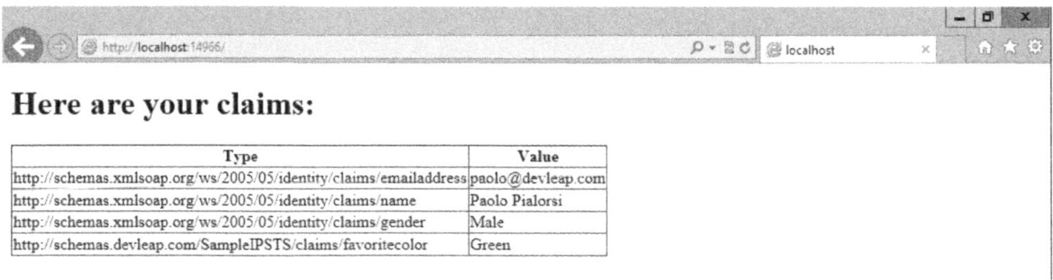

FIGURE 20-5 The output of the Default.aspx page after authentication with a sample user.

SharePoint trusted IPs

As you saw in Chapter 19, SharePoint 2013 uses WIF and the WS-Federation specification as a kind of authentication provider. Thus, you can register the example IP/STS as a trusted IP in SharePoint 2013. To do this, you must complete some configuration steps.

Trusting the IP/STS

To begin, you need to trust the IP from the perspective of SharePoint. Therefore, you need to retrieve the certificate of the IP/STS and register it in the list of trusted issuers of SharePoint. If you are consuming an STS published by a third-party IP, then you can extract the public key of the certificate from the FederationMetadata.xml file, selecting the following XPath node:

```
EntityDescriptor/RoleDescriptor/KeyDescriptor/KeyInfo/X509Data/X509Certificate
```

You can simply copy the content of that XML node into a text file and save it with a .cer file extension.

Otherwise, if you are working with an IP/STS published by the same machine on which you are running SharePoint, you can export the .cer certificate file from the local-machine certificate store. You then can import the .cer file into the private SharePoint 2013 certificate store either by using a Windows PowerShell script or the UI of the SharePoint Central Administration (SPCA). In Windows PowerShell, use the following syntax:

```
$cert = New-Object System.Security.Cryptography.X509Certificates.
X509Certificate2("IPSTSCert.cer")
New-SPTrustedRootAuthority -Name "DevLeap Sample IP/STS" -Certificate $cert
```

With this cmdlet, you can retrieve an instance of the *X509Certificate2* class by referencing the .cer file path, and then load it by invoking the *New-SPTrustedRootAuthority* cmdlet specific to SharePoint 2013. If the certificate is not trusted by the servers in your SharePoint 2013 farm—for example, if it is a custom self-created certificate—you will have to trust the whole certificate chain in the SharePoint 2013 farm. Executing the script on a single server is sufficient to trust the whole farm.

If you prefer to use the UI of SPCA, browse to the Security section, select Manage Trust, and then in the Trust Relationships ribbon group, click the New button to add a new item. You will have to provide a name and the path to the .cer file to the Establish Trust Relationship page, as shown in Figure 20-6.

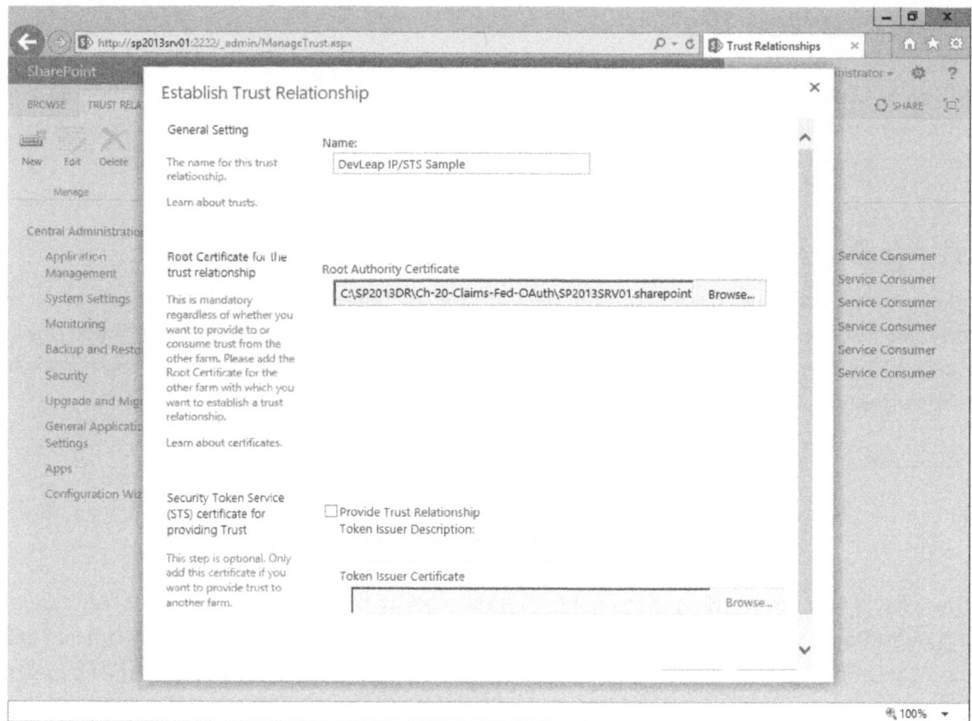

FIGURE 20-6 The Establish Trust Relationship page for registering a new trust relationship.

Registering the IP and mapping claims

Now you are ready to register the custom IP/STS in SharePoint 2013. To begin, define the claims that you would like to manage, and then map them to claims that will be available on the SharePoint side. Each time you authenticate a subject by using an external IP/STS, you have the capability to map the claims emitted by the STS in the security token to claims of the SharePoint side. For example, the custom IP/STS discussed earlier returns a claim of type *http://schemas.devleap.com/Claims/Gender*, which represents the gender of the current user from the IP/STS viewpoint. In SharePoint, you will have the opportunity to map this claim to another claim type, or you can leave it as-is. The claims-based authentication infrastructure of SharePoint will translate claims for you during user authentication.

Important The claims-mapping capability is extremely useful and important, because you could have multiple IPs registered for a single web application, and the capability to translate claims from one type to another allows SharePoint to normalize claims during authentication. You also have the capability to implement custom claim providers, inheriting from the class *SPClaimProvider*, to augment claims of a current principal during the authentication phase.

To register claims mapping, you can use a few commands in Windows PowerShell. Here are the commands for mapping the claims issued by the custom STS:

```
$map1 = New-SPClaimTypeMapping -IncomingClaimType "http://schemas.xmlsoap.org/ws/2005/05/
identity/claims/emailaddress" -IncomingClaimTypeDisplayName "Email" -SameAsIncoming

$map2 = New-SPClaimTypeMapping -IncomingClaimType "http://schemas.xmlsoap.org/ws/2005/05/
identity/claims/gender" -IncomingClaimTypeDisplayName "Gender" -SameAsIncoming

$map3 = New-SPClaimTypeMapping -IncomingClaimType "http://schemas.devleap.com/SampleIPSTS/
claims/favoritecolor" -IncomingClaimTypeDisplayName "FavoriteColor" -SameAsIncoming
```

Here, any *email*, *gender*, and *favoritecolor* claims are left as they are when they come in (see the argument *-SameAsIncoming*).

The last step for registering an external IP is to create a new entry for the IP in the list of available providers. Again, you can use a Windows PowerShell script to accomplish this:

```
$realm = "http://claims.sp2013.local/_trust/default.aspx"
$signinurl = "https://localhost:44334/Issue.aspx"
New-SPTrustedIdentityTokenIssuer -Name "DevLeap Sample IP/STS" -Description "DevLeap Sample IP/
STS" -Realm $realm -ImportTrustCertificate $cert -ClaimsMappings $map1,$map2,$map3
-SignInUrl $signinurl -IdentifierClaim $map1.InputClaimType
```

The script defines the *$realm* variable, which corresponds to the *realm* of the claims-consumer site. The value of this URL (*/_trust/default.aspx*, relative to the target SharePoint site) corresponds to a page that will be automatically added to the root folder of your SharePoint web application when you activate a trusted IP as an authentication technique. That page will be almost empty in terms of ASP. NET markup, and it will inherit its behavior from the page *TrustedProviderSignInPage*, defined in the *Microsoft.SharePoint.IdentityModel.Pages* namespace. This page will only redirect the user's browser to the IP/STS logon page.

Another variable defined in the script is the URL of the logon page of the IP/STS (*$signinurl*). Finally, the script registers a new *SPTrustedIdentityTokenIssuer* instance by invoking the cmdlet *New-SPTrustedIdentityTokenIssuer*. The arguments provided to this cmdlet in the previous example are for the name and description of the new IP, the realm of the target SharePoint site, the X.509 certificate of the IP/STS, and the sign-in URL, claims mappings, and type of the claim that will be considered as the identifier claim for the authenticated subject.

Configuring the target web application

To complete the configuration process, you need to add the new IP to the list of authentication providers for the target web application. On the SPCA page, in the Application Management section, click Manage Web Applications. A window appears that presents the list of all the available web applications. Choose the web application for which you want to enable the IP/STS as one of the authentication methods. Next, on the ribbon, click the Authentication Providers command. In the window that appears, click the Default Configuration hyperlink. The Edit Authentication configuration page opens, as shown in Figure 20-7. Here, you can select the new IP.

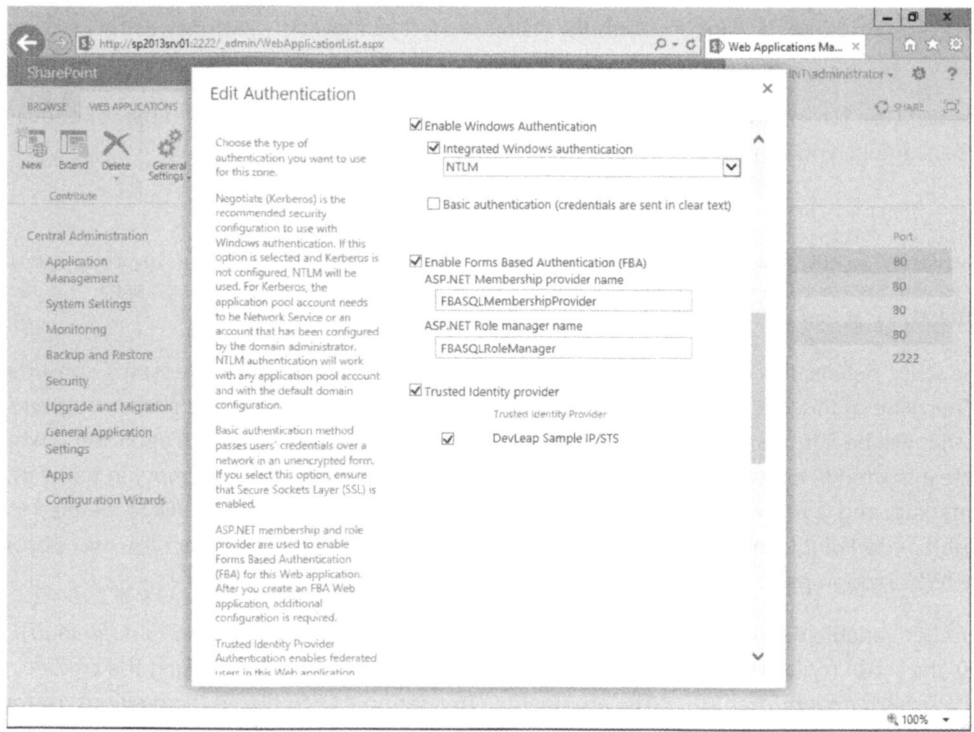

FIGURE 20-7 The Edit Authentication configuration page of SPCA.

That's it! Now you're ready to authenticate your users by using the custom IP/STS. Figure 20-8 shows the authentication options that are presented to any end user willing to authenticate.

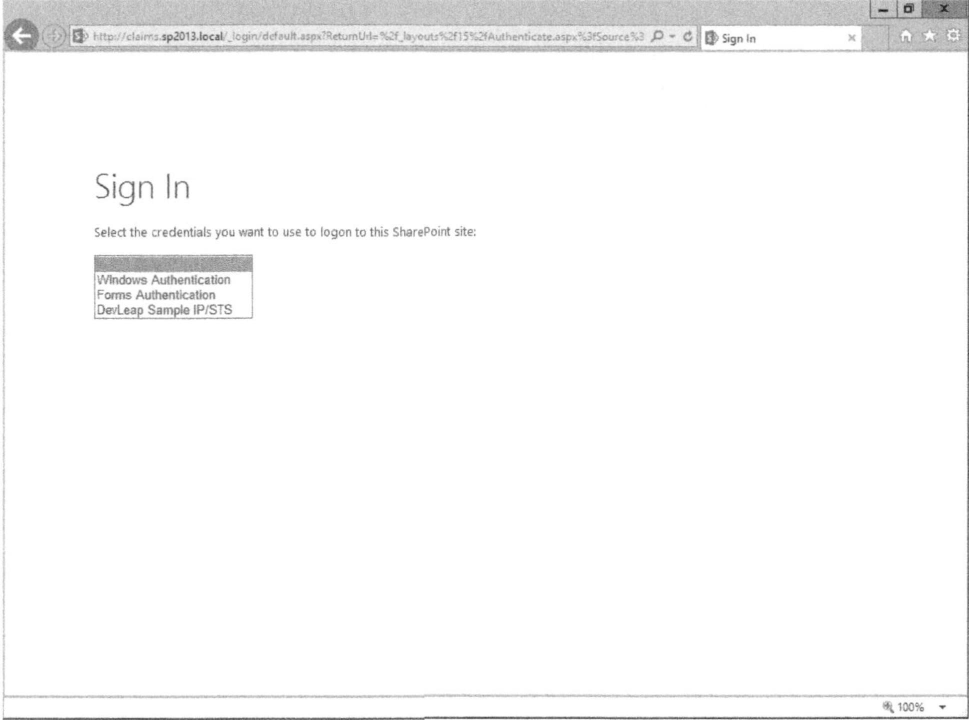

FIGURE 20-8 The authentication options displayed to the end user.

The DevLeap Sample IP/STS option will redirect the user to the logon page of the IP/STS. Of course, if you configure the IP as the unique authentication provider, your users will be redirected automatically to the IP/STS without stepping into the authentication method selection page.

Now you will also be able to configure users authenticated by the IP as specific SharePoint users and give them specific permissions. Figure 20-9 shows the Share dialog window, with a search result obtained by searching against the currently configured IP.

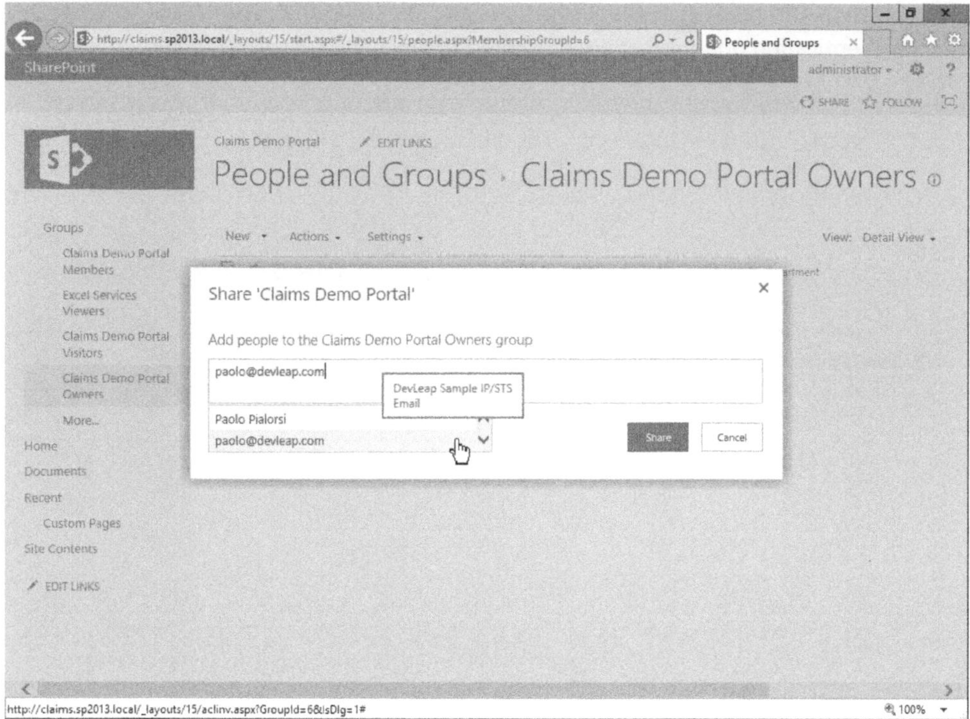

FIGURE 20-9 The Share window of SharePoint for adding people and groups.

If you try to access the sample site you defined in the "Building a relying party" section, you will be authenticated automatically and have access to the site. Thus, you are experiencing a real single-sign-on user experience.

Creating a custom claims provider

When SharePoint authenticates a user via claims-based authentication, it engages a *claim provider*, which is a class providing claims augmentation and name resolution utilities. *Claims augmentation* allows for adding some custom claims to the security token retrieved by the authentication infrastructure. *Name resolution* allows for adding capabilities to search, resolve, and provide friendly values for claims, people, and roles in the *PeoplePicker* control.

Depending on the authentication type you use, SharePoint will access one of three default claims providers:

- ***SPActiveDirectoryClaimProvider*** Used by Windows Authentication
- ***SPFormsClaimProvider*** Used by FBA
- ***SPTrustedClaimProvider*** Used by SAML-based (IP) authentication

The claims provider engaged for SAML-based tokens provides claim augmentation capabilities, but it does not provide real name-resolution functionality. In fact, when you shared your site with people and groups, as shown in Figure 20-9, you were simply using a fake model for claims and name resolution. The *PeoplePicker* control accepts any text value you provide to it and resolves it as if it is a real claim value provided by the federated IP/STS. Unfortunately, this behavior can lead to confusion for the end users. Usually, when using SAML-based authentication, you should also implement a custom claims provider to fix this standard behavior.

To better experience this issue, open SPCA and select the Manage Web Applications menu item in the Application Management menu group. Then select the web application you previously configured for using the external IP/STS, and click User Policy on the ribbon. If you add a new user policy from the resulting dialog box, and you choose to search for a specific set of users or roles while within the *PeoplePicker* control, you will see the search dialog box shown in Figure 20-10.

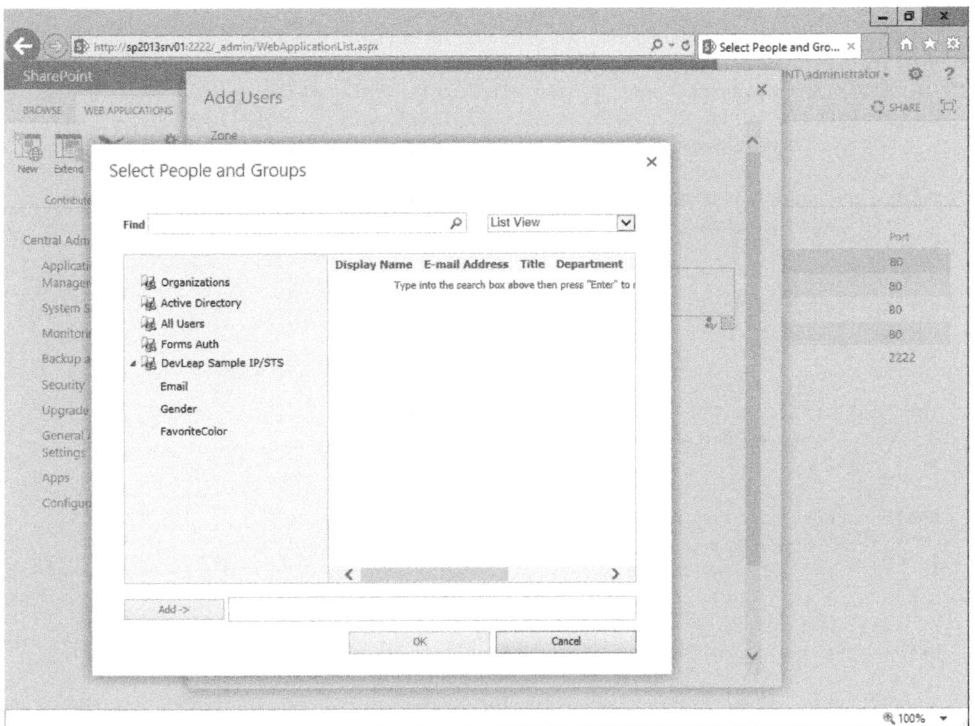

FIGURE 20-10 The Select People And Groups dialog box of a *PeoplePicker* control.

Within the Select People And Groups dialog box, you can search for people and groups, based on claims values. You will be able to write any text value, however, even if that value does not exist or is not handled by the federated IP/STS. To fix this behavior, you will need to implement a custom claims provider.

Note The sample illustrated in this chapter is based on the article "Claims Walkthrough: Writing Claims Providers for SharePoint 2010," by Steve Peschka, available on TechNet, at *http://msdn.microsoft.com/en-us/library/ff699494.aspx.*

A custom claims provider, like those available out of the box, is just a class that provides claims augmentation and name resolution capabilities. Listing 20-10 provides an excerpt of a sample claims provider class, supporting the claims provided by the custom IP/STS illustrated previously.

LISTING 20-10 An excerpt of a sample claims provider class for supporting custom claims

```
public class DevLeapClaimsProvider: SPClaimProvider {

    private static String genderClaimType =
        "http://schemas.xmlsoap.org/ws/2005/05/identity/claims/gender";
    private static String favoriteColorClaimType =
        "http://schemas.devleap.com/SampleIPSTS/claims/favoritecolor";
    private static String fidelityProgramLevelClaimType =
        "http://schemas.devleap.com/SampleIPSTS/claims/fidelityProgramLevel";

    public DevLeapClaimsProvider(String displayName)
        : base(displayName) {
    }

    public static String ProviderDisplayName {
        get { return "DevLeap Claims Provider"; }
    }

    internal static String ProviderInternalName {
        get { return "DevLeapClaimsProvider"; }
    }

    public override String Name {
        get { return ProviderInternalName; }
    }

    // Available values for the Gender claim
    private String[] genderValues = new String[] { "Male", "Female" };

    // Available values for the FavoriteColor claim
    private String[] favoriteColorValues = new String[] { "White", "Green",
    "Yellow", "Red", "Blue", "Black" };

    // Available values for the FavoriteColor claim
    private String[] fidelityProgramLevels = new String[] { "Bronze", "Silver",
        "Gold", "Platinum" };

    // Code omitted for the sake of brevity ...
}
```

The class was created in a .NET 4.5 Class Library project, which references the basic Microsoft.SharePoint.dll assembly and the Microsoft.IdentityModel.dll assembly for WIF 1.0. The basic idea of this sample claims provider is to provide predefined values for the *gender* and *favoriteColor* claims, as well as to augment the security token of authenticated users with a *fidelityProgramLevel* claim, which can assume only four values: *Bronze*, *Silver*, *Gold*, or *Platinum*.

Although the companion code provides claims augmentation and name resolution functions, the code illustrated in Listing 20-10 simply defines the basic infrastructure of the class. As you can see, the custom claims provider class inherits from the *SPClaimProvider* abstract class, which is available in the *Microsoft.SharePoint.Administration.Claims* namespace of the Microsoft.SharePoint.dll assembly. The *SPClaimProvider* base class provides many members that can be overridden, depending on the type of capabilities you want to provide through your custom claims provider. First of all, and regardless the type of claims provider you are implementing, you need to override the *Name* property to provide a name unique at the farm level for the custom claims provider.

To implement name resolution, you need to override the following abstract methods:

```
protected abstract void FillSchema(SPProviderSchema schema);

protected abstract void FillClaimTypes(List<String> claimTypes);

protected abstract void FillClaimValueTypes(List<String> claimValueTypes);

protected abstract void FillEntityTypes(List<String> entityTypes);
```

To implement claims augmentation, you must override the following members:

```
public abstract bool SupportsEntityInformation

protected abstract void FillClaimsForEntity(Uri context, SPClaim entity,
    List<SPClaim> claims);
```

Optionally, you can override members to support hierarchies, to resolve claims, or to support searching claims:

```
public abstract bool SupportsHierarchy

protected abstract void FillHierarchy(Uri context, String[] entityTypes,
    String hierarchyNodeID, int numberOfLevels, bool includeEntityData,
    SPProviderHierarchyTree hierarchy);

public abstract bool SupportsResolve

protected abstract void FillResolve(Uri context, String[] entityTypes,
    String resolveInput, List<PickerEntity> resolved);

protected abstract void FillResolve(Uri context, String[] entityTypes,
    SPClaim resolveInput, List<PickerEntity> resolved);
```

```
public abstract bool SupportsSearch

protected abstract void FillSearch(Uri context, String[] entityTypes,
    String searchPattern, String hierarchyNodeID, int maxCount,
    SPProviderHierarchyTree searchTree);
```

As you may gather from the names of the abstract properties, you need to declare your support for any specific functionality. For example, if you want to support search capabilities, you will need to override the *Boolean SupportsSearch* property, returning a value of *true*, and then you will have to override the *FillSearch* method. Listing 20-11 shows a code excerpt of the implementation of the *FillSearch* method, which is invoked by the *PeoplePicker* control when searching for a specific value.

LISTING 20-11 An excerpt of a sample claims provider class, showing the *FillSearch* custom method

```
protected override void FillSearch(Uri context, string[] entityTypes,
    string searchPattern, string hierarchyNodeID, int maxCount,
    Microsoft.SharePoint.WebControls.SPProviderHierarchyTree searchTree) {

    // Check if the picker is requesting the types we effectively return
    // Because this custom claims provider returns roles
    // simply continue in case the request is for role claims
    if (!EntityTypesContain(entityTypes, SPClaimEntityTypes.FormsRole))
        return;

    // Nodes where we will stick our matches
    Microsoft.SharePoint.WebControls.SPProviderHierarchyNode matchNode = null;

    #region Fidelity Program Levels

    // Look to see if the value that is typed in matches any of the claims values
    foreach (string level in fidelityProgramLevels) {
        if (level.ToLower().StartsWith(searchPattern.ToLower())) {
            // We have a match, create a matching entity
            PickerEntity pe = GetPickerEntity(level,
                fidelityProgramLevelClaimType, "Fidelity Program Level");

            // Add the level node where it should be displayed too
            if (!searchTree.HasChild(level)) {

                // Create the node so we can show our match in there too.
                matchNode = new
                    SPProviderHierarchyNode(
                    DevLeapClaimsProvider.ProviderInternalName,
                    level,
                    level,
                    true);
```

```
                // Add it to the tree
                searchTree.AddChild(matchNode);
            }
            else
                // Get the node for this team.
                matchNode = searchTree.Children.Where(theNode =>
                    theNode.HierarchyNodeID == level).First();

            // Add the match to our node.
            matchNode.AddEntity(pe);
        }
    }
    #endregion

    // The same is done for gender and favoriteColor claims
    // Code omitted for the sake of brevity

}
```

Now you are ready to deploy the custom claims provider implementation. To achieve this, you need to create a SharePoint farm-level solution with a custom feature and a feature receiver in it. The only goal of the farm-level solution is to copy the assembly containing the custom claims provider into the Global Assembly Cache (GAC) of the servers in the SharePoint farm.

Important Because you need a farm-level feature, you will not be able to use a custom claims provider in Office 365—all the information you are reading about custom claims providers is only suitable for an on-premises scenario.

Moreover, you will have to implement a specific kind of feature event receiver that inherits from the *SPClaimsProviderFeatureReceiver* class. You will use it to enable the claims provider on the farm by settings its *IsUsedByDefault* property to a value of *true*. By default, when you install a claims provider onto a target farm, it is configured as disabled. Listing 20-12 details the feature receiver used to deploy the custom claims provider described in this section.

LISTING 20-12 An excerpt of the feature receiver for deploying a custom claims provider

```
public class ProvisioningFeatureEventReceiver : SPClaimProviderFeatureReceiver {

    private void ExecBaseFeatureActivated(
        Microsoft.SharePoint.SPFeatureReceiverProperties properties) {
        base.FeatureActivated(properties);
    }

    public override string ClaimProviderAssembly {
        get { return typeof(DevLeapClaimsProvider).Assembly.FullName; }
    }

    public override string ClaimProviderType {
        get { return typeof(DevLeapClaimsProvider).FullName; }
    }

    public override string ClaimProviderDisplayName {
        get { return DevLeapClaimsProvider.ProviderDisplayName; }
    }

    public override string ClaimProviderDescription {
        get { return "A sample provider to augment claims and resolve " +
            "claims provided by sample IP/STS"; }
    }

    public override void FeatureActivated(SPFeatureReceiverProperties properties)
{
        ExecBaseFeatureActivated(properties);
        SPClaimProviderManager cpm = SPClaimProviderManager.Local;
        foreach (SPClaimProviderDefinition cp in cpm.ClaimProviders) {
            if (cp.ClaimProviderType == typeof(DevLeapClaimsProvider)) {
                cp.IsUsedByDefault = true;
                cpm.Update();
                break;
            }
        }
    }
}
```

After installing and deploying the solution and activating the feature, you will have to map the custom claims provider with the target web application in which you want to use the provider. To map a web application to a specific claims provider, you can use a small PowerShell script like the one Listing 20-13.

LISTING 20-13 A PowerShell script for registering a custom claims provider onto a target web application

```
Add-PSSnapin Microsoft.SharePoint.PowerShell -erroraction SilentlyContinue

$AuthNAppHostHeader = "claims.sp2013.local"
$Zone = "Default"

$cp = Get-SPClaimProvider | where-object {$_.TypeName -eq "DevLeap.IPSTS.
Providers.DevLeapClaimsProvider"}

$webApp = Get-SPWebApplication "http://$AuthNAppHostHeader"
if ($webApp.IisSettings.ContainsKey($Zone)) {
    $settings = $webApp.GetIisSettingsWithFallback($Zone)
    $providers = $settings.ClaimsProviders

    if( -not($providers.Contains($cp))) {
        $providers += $cp
        Set-SPWebApplication -Identity $webApp -Zone $Zone
            -AdditionalClaimProvider $providers
        Write-Host "Registered" $cp.DisplayName "on" $webApp.Url "in zone $Zone"
    } else {
        Write-Host $cp.DisplayName "already registered on" $webApp.Url
        "in zone $Zone"
    }
}
```

More Info For further details about how to deploy a custom claims provider, you can read the article "How to: Deploy a claims provider in SharePoint 2013," available at *http://msdn.microsoft.com/en-us/library/ee535443.aspx.*

Now you are ready to check the result. Back on the User Policy page of the web application, check the new capabilities that you will find in the Select People And Groups dialog box. Figure 20-11 illustrates the new layout of the dialog box. By searching a particular value, like the value *Gold* for the fidelity program level, you will see the result highlighted in the proper claim node.

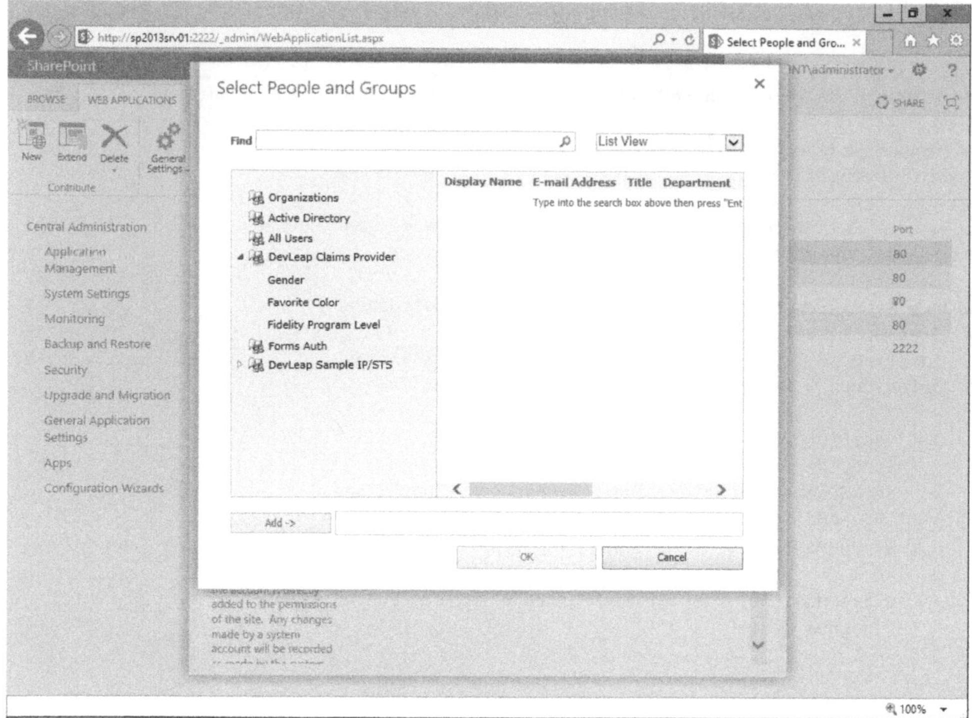

FIGURE 20-11 The Select People And Groups dialog box of a *PeoplePicker* control with the custom claims provider configured.

Consider that the sample claims provider discussed in this section augments claims, too. In fact, after installing the custom claims provider in the list of users' claims, you will find a *fidelityProgramLevel* claim. Figure 20-11 shows the presence of the new custom claim provider, as you can see in the DevLeap Claims Provider item in the hierarchy on the left side of the screen.

While in Figure 20-12 you can see the claims of the currently logged in user, in particular you can see the *gender*, *favoriteColor*, and *fidelityProgramLevel claims*.

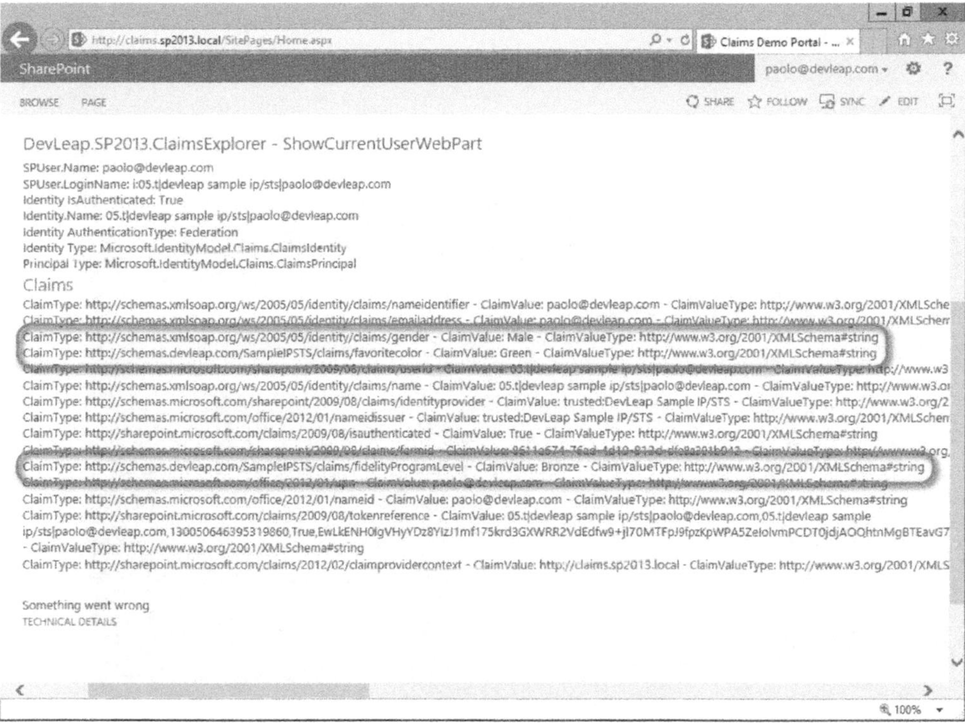

FIGURE 20-12 The list of claims related to a logged-in user, after claims augmentation.

Federating with Windows Azure ACS

So far, you have seen how to create a custom IP/STS, how to configure a SharePoint web application to use the IP/STS, and how to define a custom claims provider to provide end users with a better experience. You will probably agree, however, that the process is not overly easy, and using an out-of-the-box solution would be better than developing so much code. Luckily, Windows Azure offers ACS, an out-of-the-box IP/STS service that supports custom IPs, as well as such consolidated and well-known authentication engines as Facebook, Windows Live ID, Google, Active Directory Federation Services (AD FS) 2.0, and more. In this section, you will learn how to take advantage of Windows Azure ACS in SharePoint 2013. Before you begin, either create a Windows Azure account and a subscription, or log in to the management portal of Windows Azure, (*https://manage.windowsazure.com/*) with your existing account.

In the management portal, focus your attention on the Active Directory group of services. Here, you can create a new ACS namespace. Figure 20-13 illustrates the controls to use.

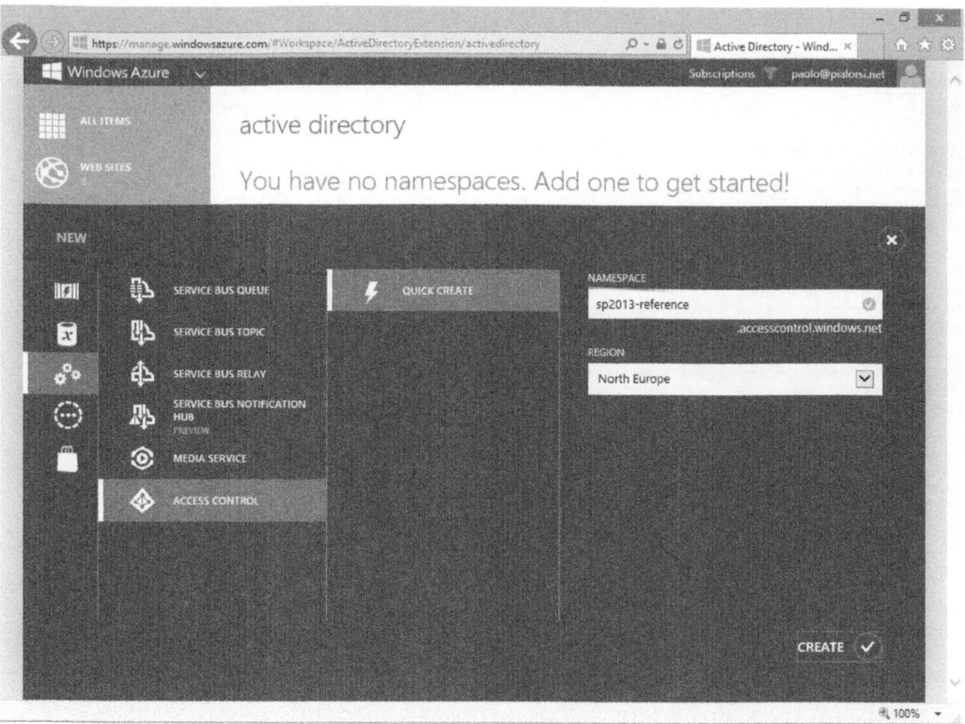

FIGURE 20-13 The UI for creating a new Windows Azure ACS namespace.

Simply provide a name for the target namespace, choosing a name unique in the Windows Azure ACS world, and a region where your service will be provisioned. Click Create, and the new service instance will be ready to work with. Select it, and click the Manage button in the lower command bar of the management portal, to manage the service. You will be presented with a dedicated web management portal like the one shown in Figure 20-14.

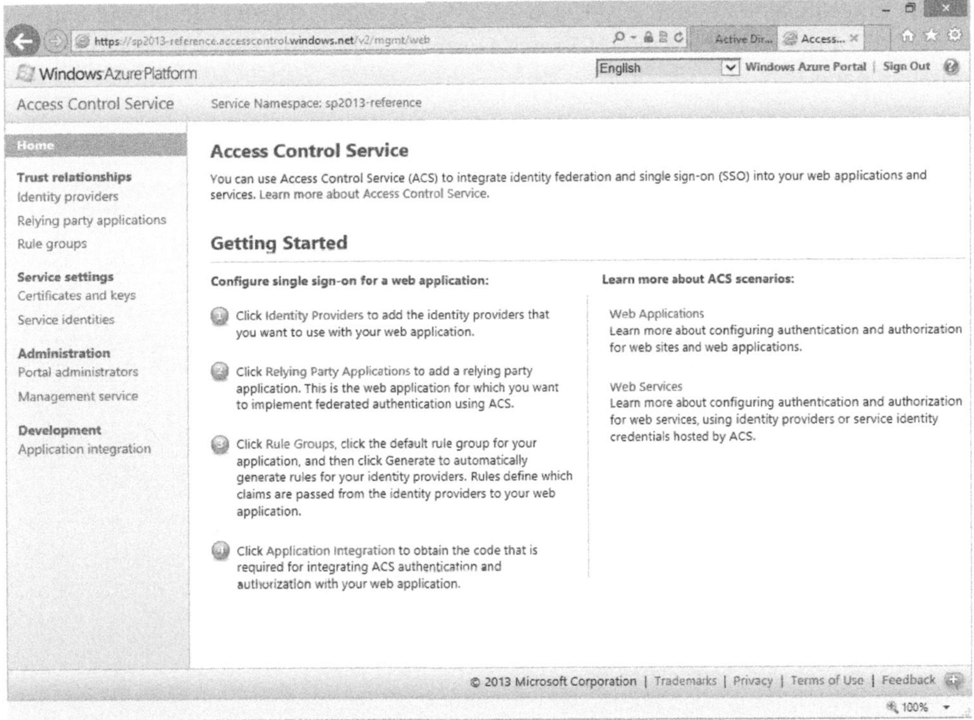

FIGURE 20-14 The home page of the web portal for managing a Windows Azure ACS instance.

The home page of the Windows Azure ACS instance management portal provides links to configure all the various aspects of the service. First, you need to choose and configure the IPs. By default, every ACS service instance is configured to authenticate users using Microsoft Account, but you can configure as many IPs as you want, as long as they fall into one of the following categories:

- **WS-Federation** Defines all the available federation services that are compliant with the WS-Federation specification. For instance, AD FS 2.0 is one possible option for this category.
- **Facebook** Allows use of Facebook as an external IP.
- **Windows Live ID** Uses the Microsoft Account IP offered by Microsoft.
- **Google** Uses Google as the IP for authenticating users.
- **Yahoo!** Uses Yahoo! as the IP for authenticating users.

Imagine that you want to provide authentication services using Facebook users' credentials or Microsoft Account. To use Facebook, first you must create and configure a Facebook app on the Facebook developer portal: log in to the Facebook developer portal (*http://developers.facebook.com*)

and choose to create a new app. You will have to configure at least the Site URL of your app, which will be the URL of the Windows Azure ACS service instance. Figure 20-15 shows the Facebook app configuration panel.

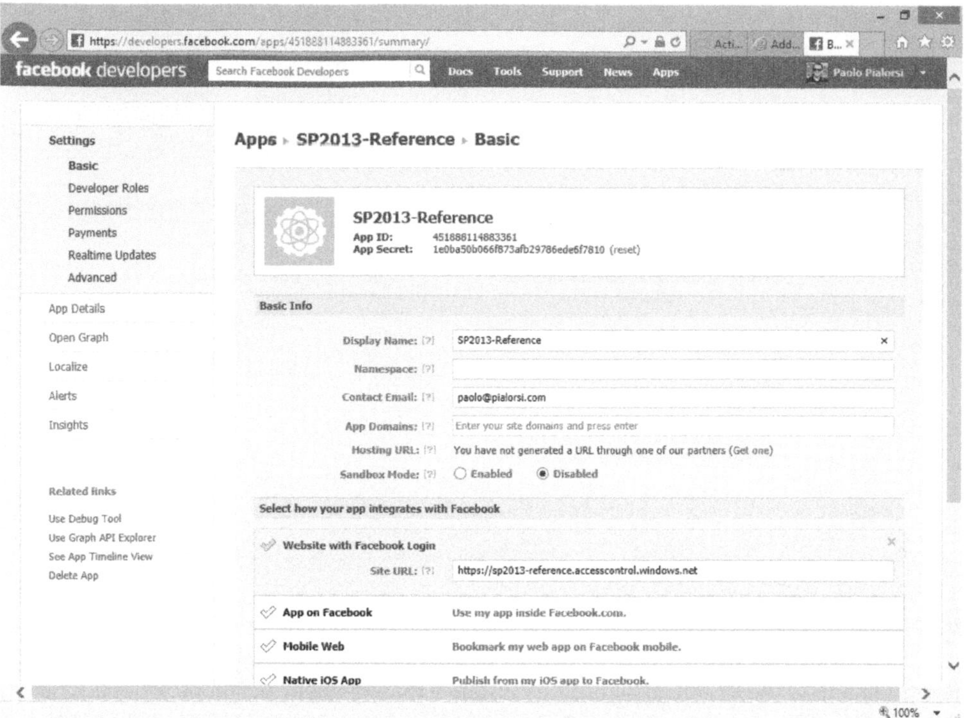

FIGURE 20-15 The page for managing the configuration of a Facebook app.

At the very top of the page, notice the app ID and the app secret for the current app. You will need these to properly configure the Windows Azure ACS integration with Facebook. Behind the scenes, ACS uses OAuth to talk with Facebook and converts the OAuth context information into claims in a security token that will be provided to SharePoint 2013. After creating the Facebook app, go back to the management site for your ACS service and click the Identity Providers menu on the left side of the home page. Choose to add a new Identity Provider and select Facebook as the type. You will be prompted with a page like the one shown in Figure 20-16.

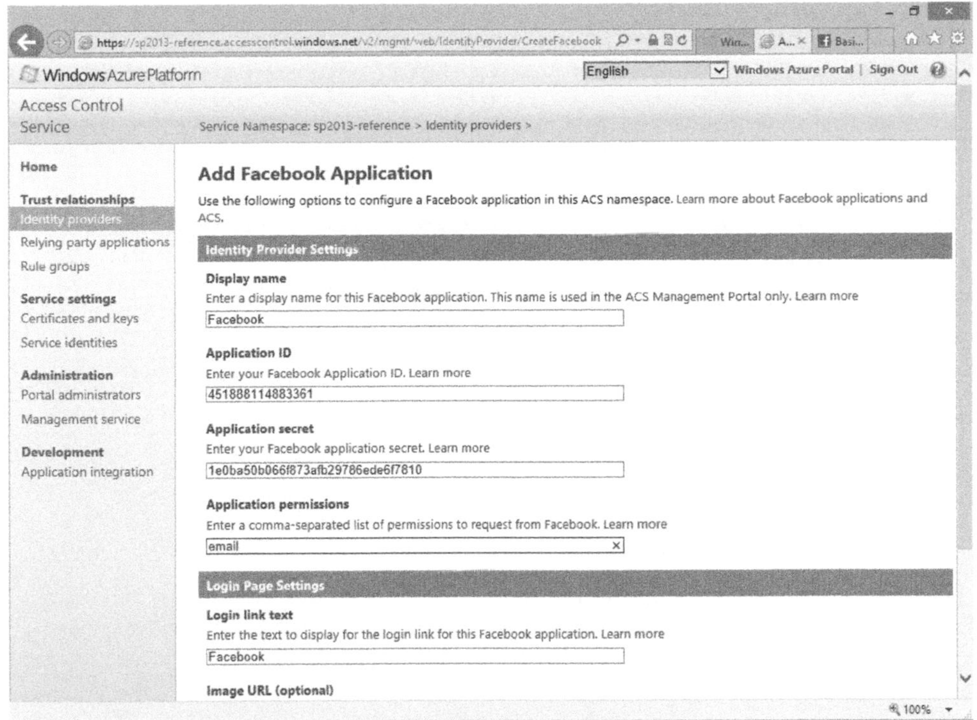

FIGURE 20-16 The page for adding a new IP based on Facebook.

On this page, you will have to configure the Application ID field with the value of the app ID taken in Facebook, and the Application Secret field with the value of the app secret taken from Facebook. Save the new IP.

The next step is to configure the relying parties. Click the Relying Party Applications menu item on the left of the ACS management portal to access the page shown in Figure 20-17. Here, you can create as many relying parties as you want. Every single relying party will participate in the unique single-sign-on experience provided by the ACS IP. For this example, simply configure a target SharePoint web application. Let's say the URL of the target SharePoint web application is *http://claims.sp2013.local*.

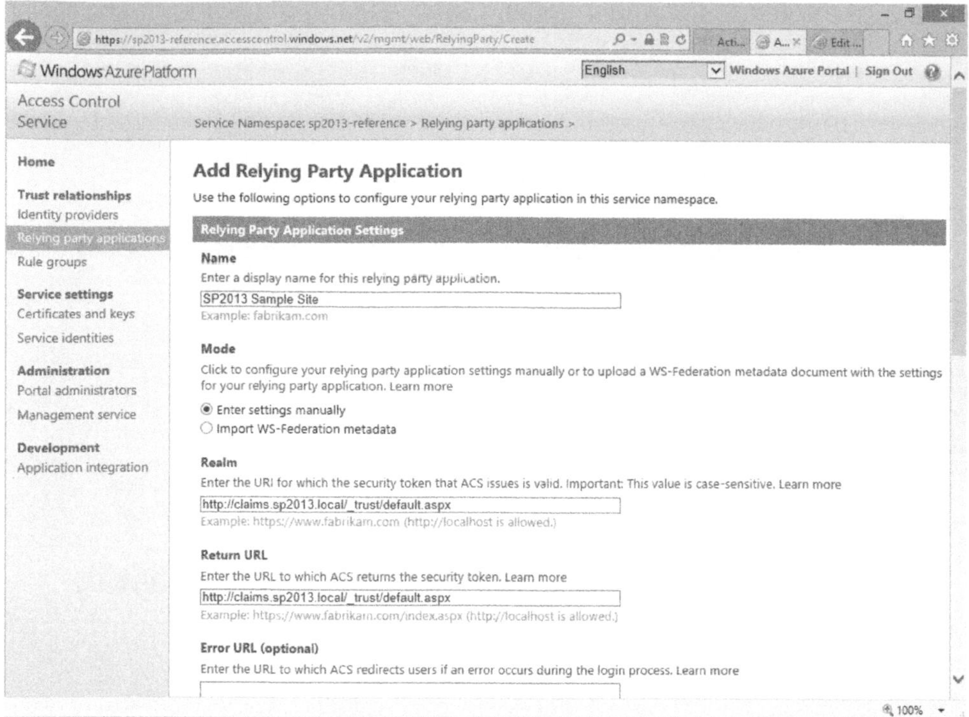

FIGURE 20-17 The page for creating a new relying party in Windows Azure ACS.

To configure a SharePoint 2013 relying party, aside from providing a name for the relying party, you must also configure the realm and the return URL targeting the */_trust/default.aspx* relative URL. Thus, for the sample web application with URL *http://claims.sp2013.local/*, you need to provide both for the realm and for the return URL the value of *http://claims.sp2013.local/_trust/default.aspx*. While configuring a new relying party, you will also have the opportunity to choose which IP will be available for each relying party. In this case, assume the default Windows Live ID and Facebook. Next, choose the format of the SAML token that will be sent back to the relying party. For SharePoint 2013, choose a SAML 1.1 token, unless you do not want to customize the out-of-the-box capabilities of SharePoint.

Figure 20-18 shows the second part of the page for creating a relying party. Notice the options for configuring the IPs, the SAML token format, and the token lifetime in seconds. The token lifetime should be larger than the corresponding value configured in SharePoint, which by default is 600 seconds. For example you can use a value of 3000 seconds or more. The available range for the token lifetime is between 0 and 86400 (1 day).

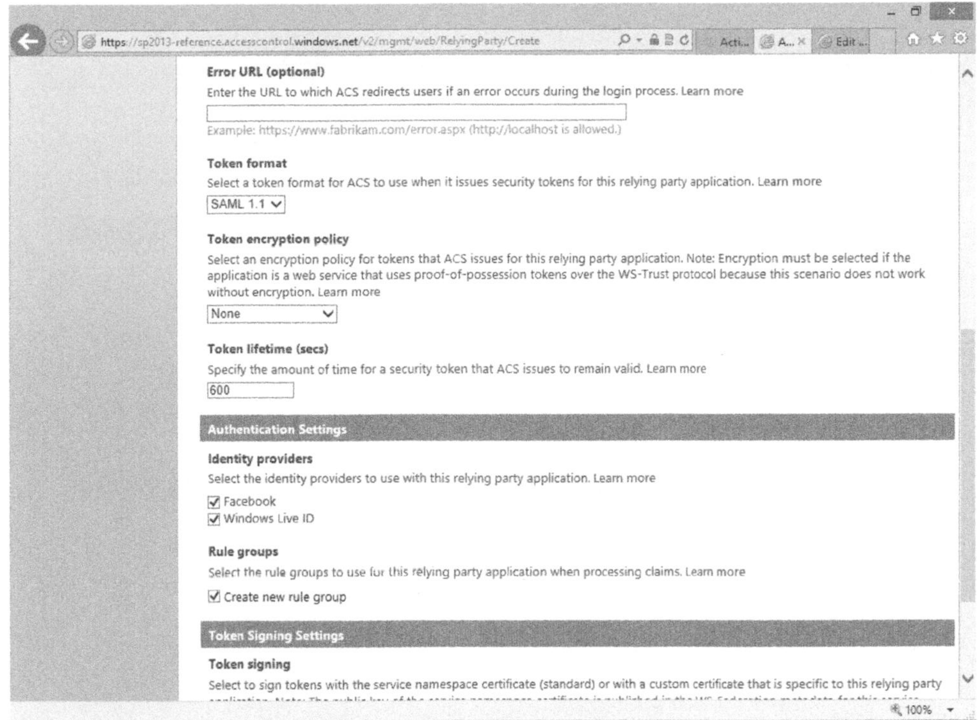
https://sp2013-reference.accesscontrol.windows.net/v2/mgmt/web/RelyingParty/Create
Error URL (optional)
Enter the URL to which ACS redirects users if an error occurs during the login process. Learn more
Example: https://www.fabrikam.com/error.aspx (http://localhost is allowed.)
Token format
Select a token format for ACS to use when it issues security tokens for this relying party application. Learn more
SAML 1.1
Token encryption policy
Select an encryption policy for tokens that ACS issues for this relying party application. Note: Encryption must be selected if the application is a web service that uses proof-of-possession tokens over the WS-Trust protocol because this scenario does not work without encryption. Learn more
None
Token lifetime (secs)
Specify the amount of time for a security token that ACS issues to remain valid. Learn more
600
Authentication Settings
Identity providers
Select the identity providers to use with this relying party application. Learn more
Facebook
Windows Live ID
Rule groups
Select the rule groups to use for this relying party application when processing claims. Learn more
Create new rule group
Token Signing Settings
Token signing
Select to sign tokens with the service namespace certificate (standard) or with a custom certificate that is specific to this relying party
100%

FIGURE 20-18 The second part of the page for creating a new relying party in Windows Azure ACS.

From the same page, you can define the rules for signing and encrypting the tokens, and you can also provide a custom X.509 certificate dedicated to a specific relying party.

After creating one or more relying parties, you need to configure how Windows Azure ACS will handle and eventually transform the claims received from the external IPs before sending the security tokens to the target relying parties. In fact, ACS can apply transformations and translations of claims before sending the security tokens to the target relying party. By default, you can create a set of automatic rules, but if necessary, you can also define simple translation rules that can read a claim and provide another claim or a fixed value as output. Creating rules is mandatory, and by default ACS has no rules defined. Click the Rule Groups menu item on the left of the management site, and then click the Generate button in the middle of the page. Figure 20-19 illustrates the page for generating rules.

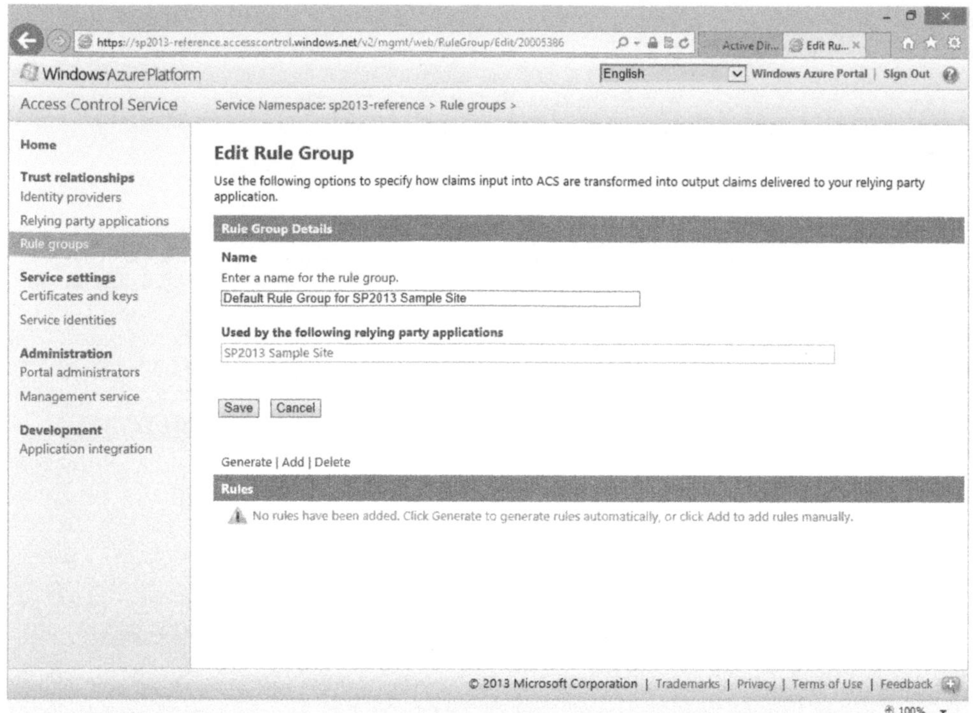

FIGURE 20-19 The page for creating rule groups in Windows Azure ACS.

So far, you have configured the Windows Azure ACS service for SharePoint integration. On the ACS management site, there are some other pages for configuring certificates, signing and encryption keys, assigning identities local to the ACS service, and defining administrators of the ACS service. To federate SharePoint 2013 with ACS, however, you don't need to bother with these. Simply click the Application Integration menu item to see the URLs that you will have to use to integrate SharePoint with ACS. Figure 20-20 shows the resulting Application Integration page.

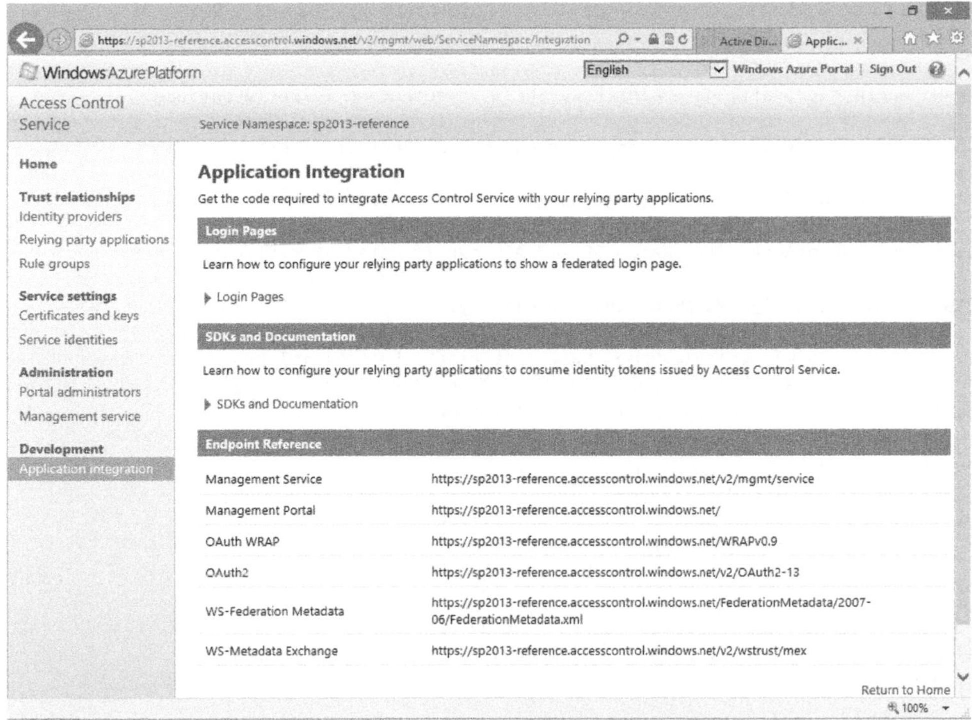

FIGURE 20-20 The Application Integration page for integrating external applications with Windows Azure ACS.

From this page, you will have to navigate with a web browser to the WS-Federation Metadata URL. There, you will find the X.509 certificate used by ACS to sign the security tokens that will be sent to SharePoint. As described previously, in the "Trusting the IP/STS" section, you will have to copy the text content of the following node:

```
EntityDescriptor/RoleDescriptor/KeyDescriptor/KeyInfo/X509Data/X509Certificate
```

Then you must save the copied text into a file with extension .cer. The last thing to do is execute some PowerShell commands to federate SharePoint 2013 with ACS. Listing 20-14 provides a sample PowerShell script for this task.

LISTING 20-14 A PowerShell script to federate Windows Azure ACS with SharePoint 2013

```
Add-PSSnapin Microsoft.SharePoint.PowerShell -erroraction SilentlyContinue

$cert = New-Object System.Security.Cryptography.X509Certificates.
X509Certificate2(
    "C:\SP2013DR\Ch-20-Claims-Fed-OAuth\ACS-Certificate.cer")

New-SPTrustedRootAuthority -Name "SP2013 ACS certificate" -Certificate $cert

$map0 = New-SPClaimTypeMapping -IncomingClaimType
    "http://schemas.xmlsoap.org/ws/2005/05/identity/claims/nameidentifier"
    -IncomingClaimTypeDisplayName "NameIdentifier" -LocalClaimType
    "http://schemas.xmlsoap.org/ws/2005/05/identity/claims/username"
$map1 = New-SPClaimTypeMapping -IncomingClaimType
    "http://schemas.microsoft.com/accesscontrolservice/2010/07/claims/
identityprovider"
    -IncomingClaimTypeDisplayName "IdentityProvider" -SameAsIncoming
$map2 = New-SPClaimTypeMapping -IncomingClaimType
    "http://schemas.xmlsoap.org/ws/2005/05/identity/claims/emailaddress"
    -IncomingClaimTypeDisplayName "Email" -SameAsIncoming

$realm = "http://claims.sp2013.local/_trust/default.aspx"
$signinurl = "https://sp2013-reference.accesscontrol.windows.net:443/v2/
wsfederation"

$ip = New-SPTrustedIdentityTokenIssuer -Name "SP2013 ACS"
    -Description "SP2013 ACS"
    -Realm $realm -ImportTrustCertificate $cert -ClaimsMappings $map0,$map1,$map2
    -SignInUrl $signinurl -IdentifierClaim $map0.InputClaimType
```

As you can see, the script is almost the same as the one used in the "Registering the IP and mapping claims" section. Now the ACS IP is ready to be used. In SPCA, edit the authentication providers of a target web application and add the new IP to the list of the trusted IPs. Figure 20-21 shows the UI with two IPs available: the custom one and the ACS IP.

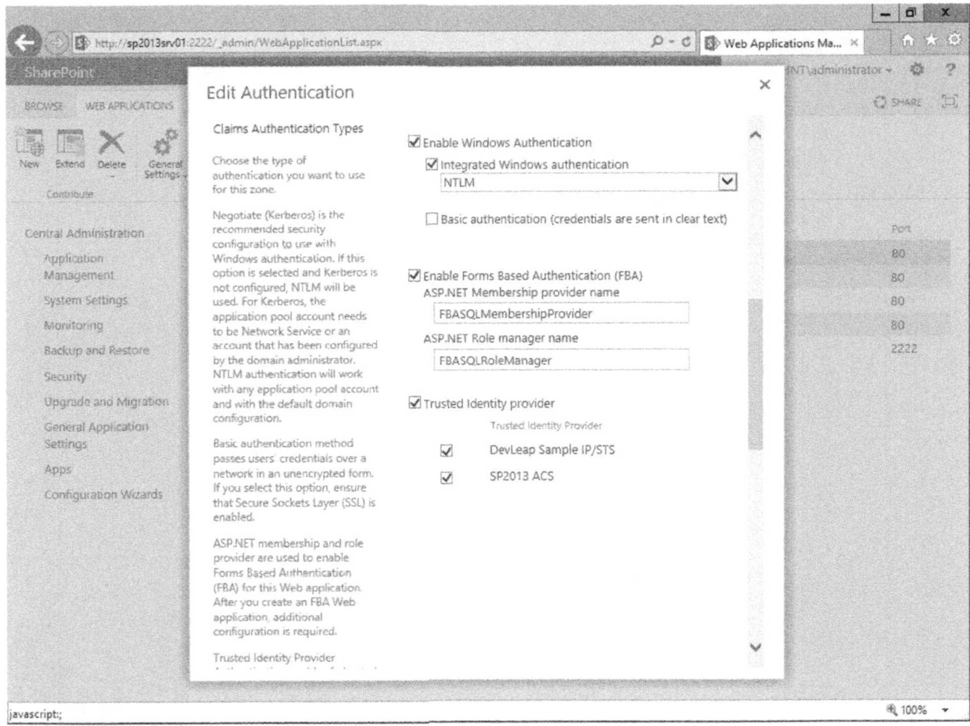

FIGURE 20-21 The page for configuring trusted IPs for a target web application.

As soon as you add the new trusted IP, you will be able to authenticate using Windows Azure ACS. Figure 20-22 shows the authentication options provided to the end users.

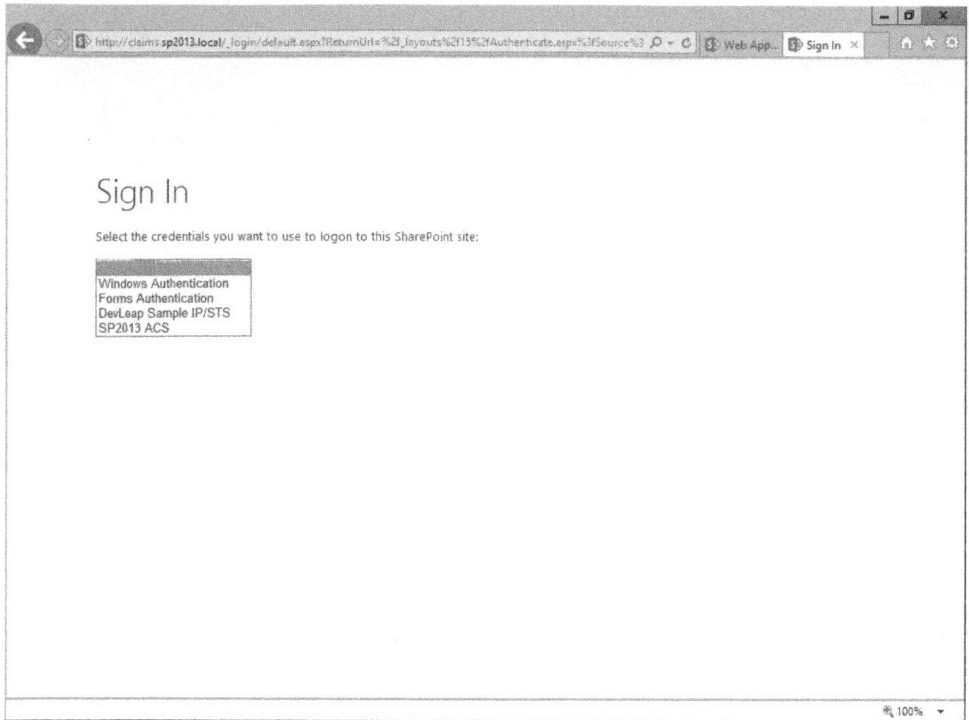

FIGURE 20-22 The page for selecting the authentication method for accessing a web application.

Figure 20-23 shows the logon page provided by Windows Azure ACS, where end users can choose to authenticate using Windows Live ID or Facebook. Be aware that the page provided by Windows Azure ACS is autogenerated with a standard and very simple template. However, you can customize this page with your own layout.

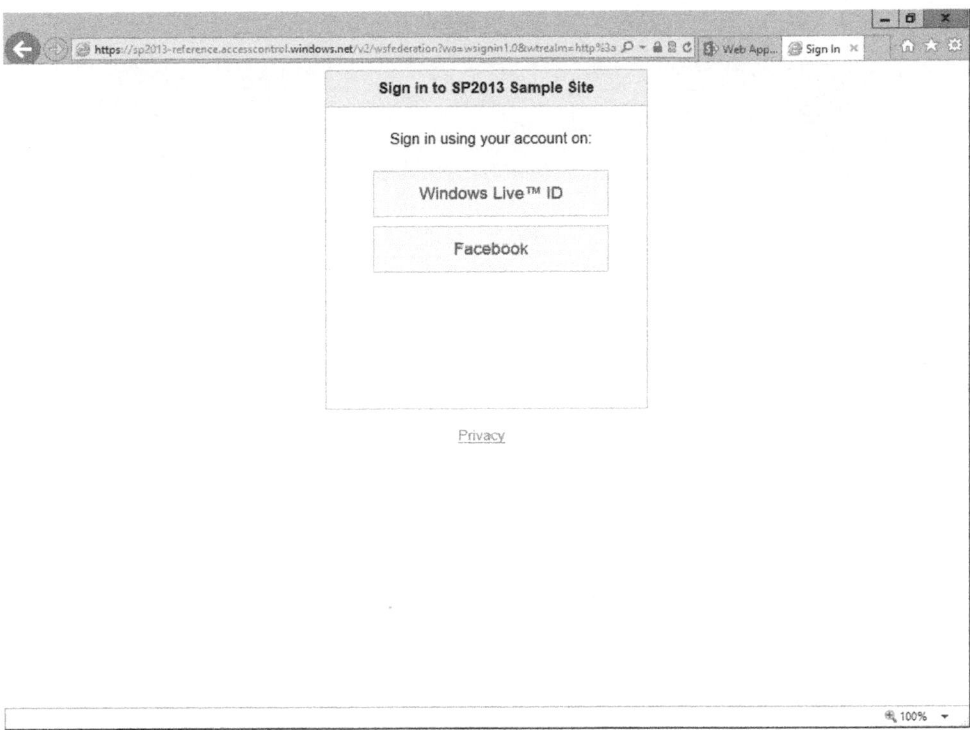

FIGURE 20-23 The logon page provided by Windows Azure ACS.

Click the Facebook button and you will be redirected to the standard Facebook login page, which will provide information about the target app that is requesting authentication. In the current example, the Facebook app name is SP2013-Reference. Figure 20-24 shows the Facebook login page.

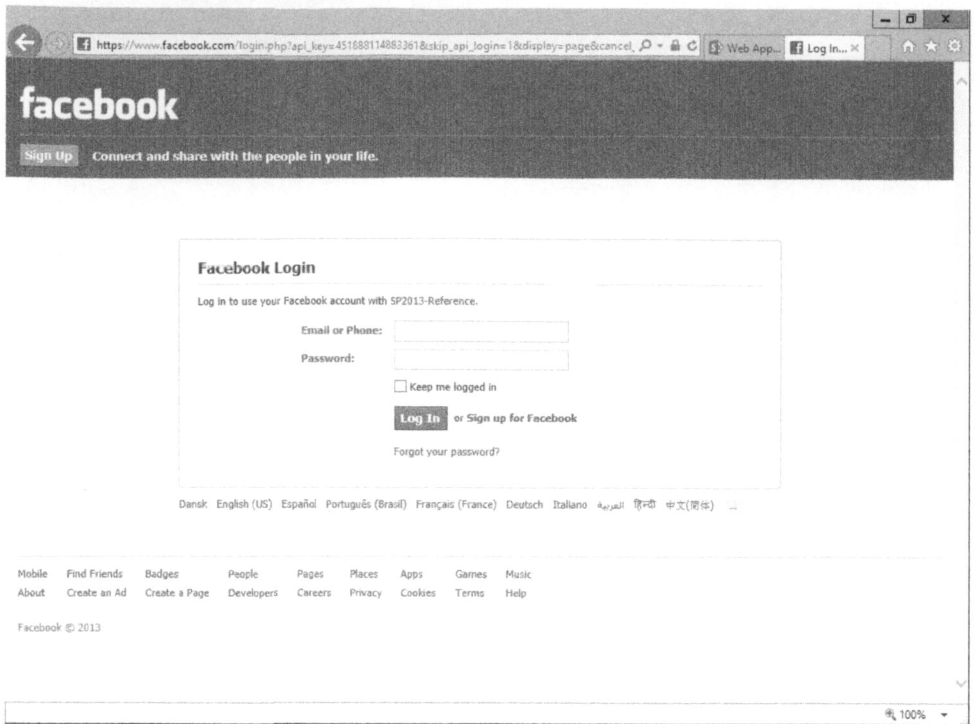

FIGURE 20-24 The login page of Facebook while authenticating through Windows Azure ACS.

After authenticating, the end users will be prompted with a request to authorize the Facebook app (which in reality will be ACS) to access some of the profile information of the currently authenticated user. The profile information and properties will be those you configured while creating the IP in ACS. Facebook will prompt this page (Figure 20-25) to each end user only the first time he or she authenticates using that Facebook app.

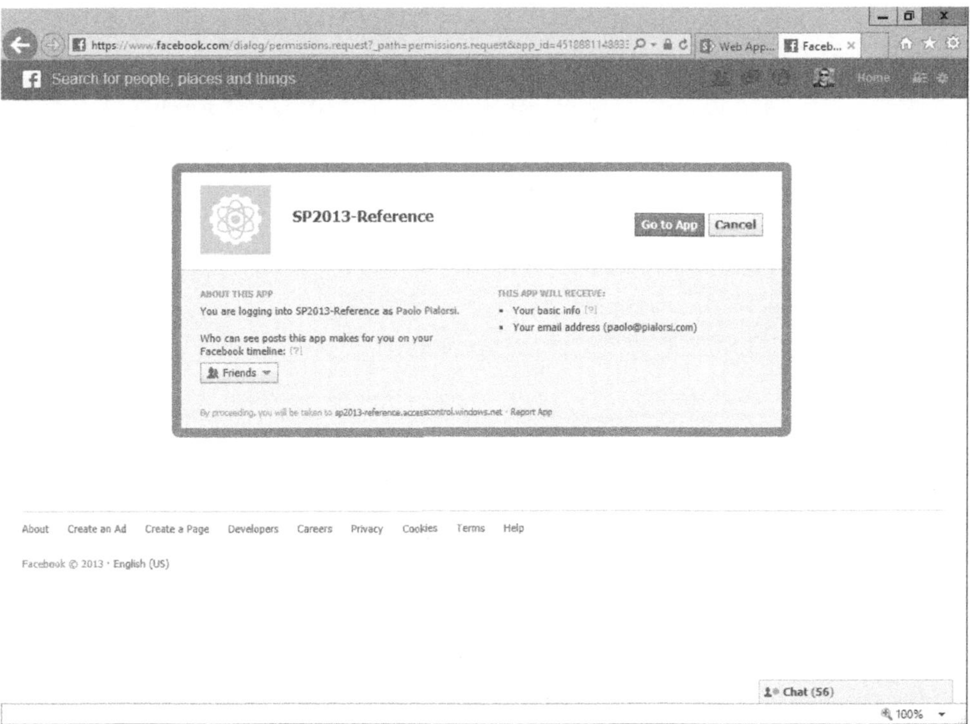

FIGURE 20-25 The page of Facebook for authorizing Windows Azure ACS to access the user's profile information.

Clicking the Go To App button redirects your end user to ACS and then to SharePoint 2013. Remember that you are using a WS-Federation passive requestor, so the user will be redirected passively back and forth between SharePoint, ACS, and the external IP.

If the user is authorized to access SharePoint, you will be able to find a rich set of claims describing his or her digital identity. Figure 20-26 shows the home page of the sample web application, which browses all the claims available in the currently logged-in user's profile. As you can see, there are claims providing information about the email, the name, and the Facebook session ID. If necessary, you will be able to read this information from the identity of the current user, which is of type *ClaimsIdentity*, and, for example, use the Facebook APIs to retrieve additional information, as long as the user provided you with authorization to do so.

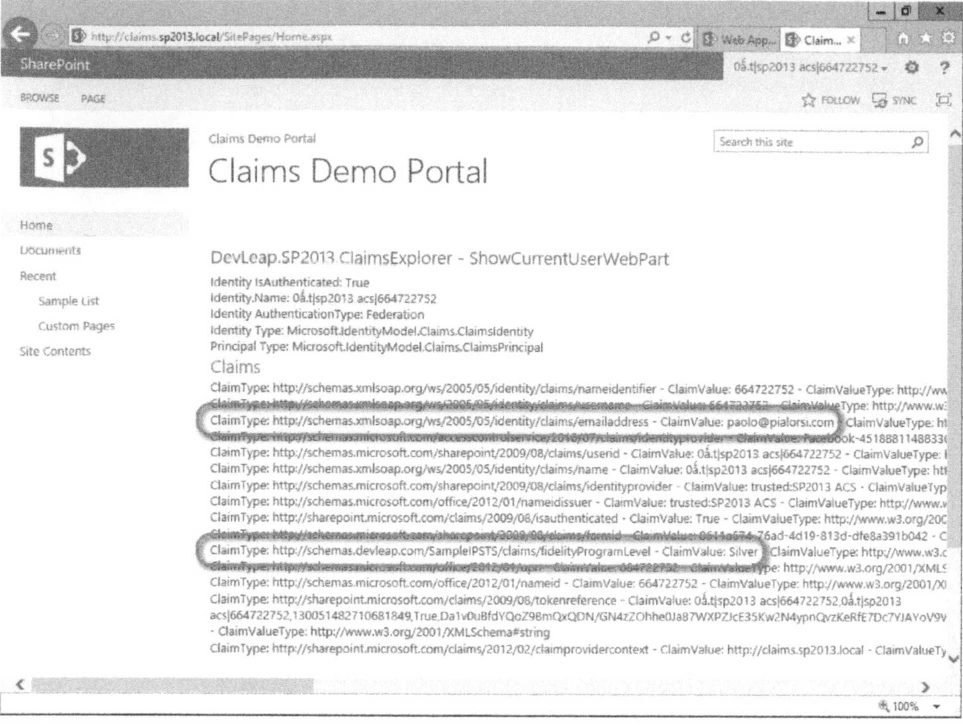

FIGURE 20-26 The home page of the sample web application after an end user has been authenticated with ACS and Facebook.

Notice that the current web application is also configured for using the custom claims provider created previously. Thus, in the list of users' claims, you will still find the Fidelity Program Level claims. This means that the custom claims provider augments the claims of an authenticated user regardless of the IP you used to authenticate him or her.

Understanding OAuth

So far, you've learned how the authentication engine of SharePoint behaves when authenticating users and roles in a claims-based world. What about SharePoint apps? As you remember from Chapter 8, "SharePoint apps," every app has a security principal of its own, called the app principal, and whenever a SharePoint app needs to consume a SharePoint site, an authentication and authorization process based on the OAuth protocol takes place.

OAuth is the protocol that defines how to manage all the phases for authenticating an app against a remote repository of data and a remote API, as well as how to authorize that app to perform exactly a well-defined set of operations. An open protocol, OAuth authenticates apps and enables secure API authorization from desktop and web applications through a standard, web-based technique.

Nowadays, every web application provides some content and features to authenticated users. Think about SkyDrive, Flickr, Facebook, LinkedIn, and similar sites. Each requires users to authenticate by providing credentials and allows authenticated users to manage their personal data. Take SkyDrive as an example. You can log into SkyDrive using your Microsoft Account; you can upload content, share content with others, and read content shared with you by someone else. Moreover, you can use a Windows Store app, running within a Windows 8 tablet PC, to read or write files stored on your SkyDrive storage. The same thing could happen using an iPhone, an iPad, or any other device capable of consuming the APIs published by SkyDrive. Furthermore, suppose you want to share your photos stored on SkyDrive with external services, such as an external photo-printing service. Usually, when you need to share your content with someone else or with an external app, you should not share your user credentials with any of the apps or users with whom you share your content. In fact, if you were to share your credentials, those users or external apps would have exactly the same rights and capabilities you would have for your own data, including the capability to delete your files, change your permissions, and even change your password. Of course, this would be too much. On the contrary, you usually authorize external users or apps to do something against your own data, keeping you as the only owner of that data and providing to the third parties only those permissions that are effectively required, usually for a limited period of time. For example, think again about the photo-printing service. You would probably allow an external photo-printing service to access your photos on SkyDrive only for reading, and perhaps for only half an hour—just enough time to download and print the photos. But how is it possible to share this content with third-party apps without sharing you user credentials, and with imposed time limits?

In SharePoint 2013, whenever a SharePoint app wants to access content related to a site or a specific user, the authentication and authorization engine works as illustrated in the schema in Figure 20-27.

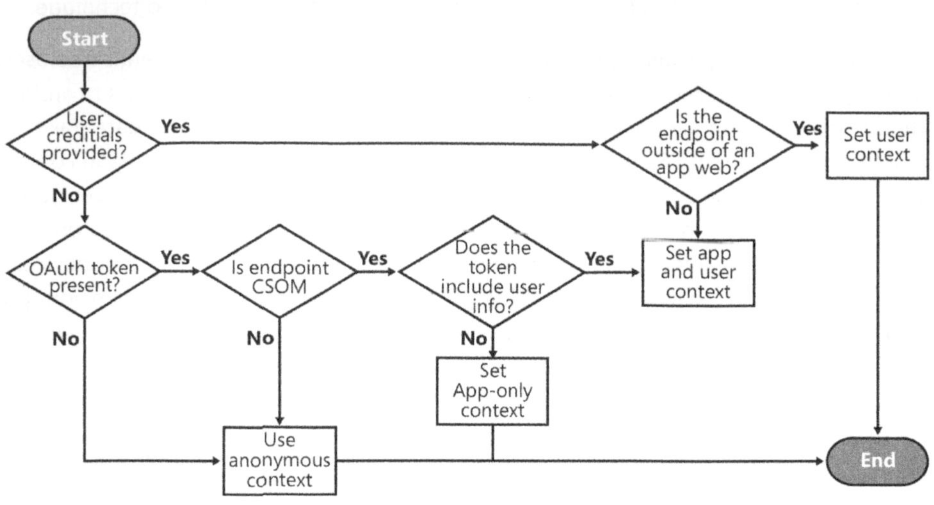

FIGURE 20-27 A functional diagram of SharePoint 2013 authentication, including OAuth.

When SharePoint 2013 begins to authenticate an incoming request, it first looks to see if the incoming request contains a SAML token with a user identity. If SharePoint finds a SAML token, it can then assume that the incoming request was initiated by an end user, not by an app. Once it finds a SAML token, SharePoint 2013 then inspects the target URL of the incoming request to see whether it references a standard SharePoint site or a child site associated with a specific app. If the incoming request targets a standard site, SharePoint 2013 handles authentication and authorization tasks as described in previous sections. If the incoming request targets an app web, SharePoint 2013 initializes the call context with both a user identity and an app identity.

When an incoming request does not contain a SAML token, SharePoint 2013 knows that a user did not initiate the request. In this scenario, the SharePoint 2013 authentication pipeline inspects the incoming request to see if it contains a security token identifying a developer or a hosted app. Once SharePoint 2013 finds a security token identifying an app, it sets up a call context with the app identity, and optionally the user identity as well.

While invoking the CSOM or the new REST APIs, SharePoint will expect and validate the security token, and will provide access to content and APIs according to the permissions provided to the target app, and to the user for which the app is acting.

Internally, the OAuth protocol uses an app ID, which uniquely identifies every app, as well as an app shared secret, which allows every app to communicate securely with the target service provider or API, being able to secure communication and authenticate against the target service provider or API as a specific app. When the service provider, which could be SharePoint 2013, authorizes the app to do something, or does not authorize the app to do something, it evaluates the authorization rules both of the app and of the current end user. If both of them have the rights for the APIs that are requested, then the result is consent; otherwise; it will be a denial.

In Chapter 8, you learned that when you create a SharePoint app, you can create an app ID or client ID and a shared secret, using the Seller Dashboard for the Office Store (if you are using Microsoft Office 365), or using some dedicated administrative pages (if the app targets an on-premises environment). In both cases, SharePoint 2013 uses OAuth in conjunction with Windows Azure ACS.

Remember, however, that SharePoint 2013 uses OAuth only for authentication and authorization of apps and for consuming the CSOM. All the other authentication and authorization techniques ignore the OAuth protocol and maintain their classic way of working.

Configuring server-to-server apps

Sometimes, while defining the security context of an app that will be used on-premises, you may not want to define an app ID and an app shared secret. Instead, you would prefer to trust an app, without relying on Windows Azure ACS, OAuth, and so on. Luckily, there is a suitable option that allows working in a high-trust, or server-to-server (S2S), configuration. This configuration involves sharing between the app and the target SharePoint farm of an X.509 certificate, which will be used to secure and authenticate the communication between SharePoint and the target app. To configure the S2S scenario, follow these steps:

1. Access the SharePoint 2013 management interface using a user account that is a member of the administrators of the target machine, as well as a user that has been configured as a shell admin for SharePoint, using the *Add-SPShellAdmin* command.
2. Verify that the User Profile service is installed and at least started on one of the application servers in the farm.
3. Verify that the App Management service is installed and started in the current farm.
4. Create or obtain the .cer file corresponding to the X.509 certificate you want to use for the high-trust configuration between SharePoint 2013 and the external app.
5. If you want to manually generate the certificate from scratch, you can use the following syntax:

   ```
   makecert.exe -r -pe -n "CN={Name}" -b {StartDate} -e {EndData} -ss my
       -sr localMachine -sky exchange
       -sp "Microsoft RSA SChannel Cryptographic Provider" -sy 12 file.cer
   ```

   where the *-r* argument instructs the tool to create a self-signed certificate. The *-pe* argument marks the private key as exportable. The *-b* and *-e* arguments define the start and end dates of validity of the target certificate. The *-ss* and *-sr* arguments specify storing the certificate in the personal store of the local machine. The *-sky* argument with a value of *exchange* instructs the tool to create a certificate with message-exchange capabilities (signature and encryption). Last, the *-sp* and *-sy* arguments declare the kind of CryptoAPI provider that will be used. If you want, you can also use IIS for creating a self-signed certificate, instead of using the *makecert* command-line tool.

6. Start the SharePoint management shell or the Windows PowerShell ISE, and import the SharePoint 2013 cmdlets.

7. Load the .cer file related to the X.509 certificate that you will use for the high-trust scenario and invoke the following cmdlet:

    ```
    $certificate = New-Object
        System.Security.Cryptography.X509Certificates.X509Certificate2(
        "{CERFilePath}")
    ```

    {CERFilePath} is the path of the .cer file related to the X.509 certificate file to use.

8. Execute the following PowerShell commands:

    ```
    $appId = "{AppID}"
    $spweb = Get-SPWeb "{AppURL}"
    $realm = Get-SPAuthenticationRealm -ServiceContext $spweb.Site
    $fullAppIdentifier = $appId + '@' + $realm
    New-SPTrustedSecurityTokenIssuer -Name "{FriendlyName}"
    -Certificate $certificate -RegisteredIssuerName $fullAppIdentifier
    ```

    The *{AppID}* argument is the lowercase ID that identifies the app to trust, and it can be read from the app creation wizard when you create a new provider-hosted app. The *{AppURL}* argument is the URL of the app on the target server. *{FriendlyName}* is a friendly name that will be used to identify the high-trust relationship.

9. Register the app within the App Management service by using the following PowerShell command:

    ```
    $appPrincipal = Register-SPAppPrincipal -NameIdentifier
        $fullAppIdentifier -Site $spweb -DisplayName "{DisplayName}"
    ```

    {DisplayName} will be the name representing the high-trust app in SPCA.

10. Configure explicit permission for the target app, using the following cmdlet:

    ```
    Set-AppPrincipalPermission -appPrincipal $appPrincipal -site $web
        -right {Level} -scope {Scope}
    ```

    The arguments *{Level}* and *{Scope}* define the permissions exactly as you saw them in Chapter 8, in the section "The Permissions tab."

After completing these steps, you will be ready to execute you SharePoint app, which will be a provider-hosted app running in an on-premises environment. Every authentication and authorization request between SharePoint 2013 and the app configured as high trust will be based on the just-defined X.509 certificate.

Summary

In this chapter, you learned about claims-based environments, WS-Federation, and how to use WIF to develop an IP/STS for a custom IP. You also saw how to register an IP/STS implemented with WIF into SharePoint for the purpose of authenticating SharePoint users through an external and trusted IP. Then you learned how to use Windows Azure ACS as an option for using an external IP/STS as a service. Lastly, the chapter discussed how SharePoint 2013 takes advantage of OAuth and S2S security while authenticating and authorizing SharePoint apps.

Index

Symbols

A

B

C

D

E

F

G

H

I

J

K

L

M

N

Q

R

S

T

U

X

Y

Z

About the Author

PAOLO PIALORSI is a consultant, trainer, and author who specializes in developing distributed application architectures and Microsoft SharePoint–based enterprise solutions. During his professional career, he has passed more than 40 Microsoft certification exams. Paolo has a great deal of experience working with SharePoint, and he is a Microsoft Certified Master (MCM) for SharePoint 2010. He is one of the content owners of the Italian version of the SharePoint & Office Conference, and he is a popular speaker at worldwide industry conferences.

He is the author of many Microsoft Press books on Microsoft .NET, Microsoft Windows 8, and SharePoint. Recent books include *Programming Microsoft LINQ in Microsoft .NET Framework 4*, *Build Windows 8 Apps with Microsoft Visual C# and Visual Basic Step by Step*, *Build Windows 8 Apps with Microsoft Visual C++ Step by Step*, and *Microsoft SharePoint 2010 Developer Reference*. He has also written three Italian-language books, on the topics of .NET, XML, and web services.

You can reach Paolo via the following:

- **The SharePoint Developer Reference blog** *http://www.sharepoint-reference.com*
- **Twitter** *@PaoloPia; http://www.twitter.com/PaoloPia*
- **LinkedIn** *http://it.linkedin.com/in/paolopialorsi/*

CPSIA information can be obtained at www.ICGtesting.com
Printed in the USA
BVOW101653110713

325068BV00006BA/2/P